Clinical Social Work Practice in Behavioral Mental Health

SECOND EDITION

Clinical Social Work Practice in Behavioral Mental Health

A Postmodern Approach to Practice with Adults

Roberta G. Sands

University of Pennsylvania

Allyn and Bacon

Boston ■ London ■ Toronto ■ Sydney ■ Tokyo ■ Singapore

Editor-in-Chief, Social Sciences: *Karen Hanson*
Series Editorial Assistant: *Alyssa Pratt*
Executive Marketing Manager: *Jackie Aaron*
Production Editor: *Christopher H. Rawlings*
Editorial-Production Service: *Omegatype Typography, Inc.*
Composition and Prepress Buyer: *Linda Cox*
Manufacturing Buyer: *Julie McNeill*
Cover Administrator: *Jenny Hart*
Electronic Composition: *Omegatype Typography, Inc.*

Library of Congress Cataloging-in-Publication Data

Sands, Roberta G.
    Clinical social work practice in behavioral mental health : a postmodern approach to
practice with adults / Roberta G. Sands.—2nd ed.
        p. cm.
    Rev. ed. of: Clinical social work practice in community mental health. 1991.
    Includes bibliographical references and index.
    ISBN 0-205-29699-8 (alk. paper)
    1. Psychiatric social work—United States.   2. Community mental health
services—United States.   3. Chronic diseases—Psychological aspects.   I. Sands, Roberta G.
Clinical social work practice in community health.   II. Title.
HV690.U6 S26   2001
362.2'2'9073—dc21
                                                                        00-029298

Printed in the United States of America

10 9 8 7 6 5 4 3 2 1   05 04 03 02 01 00

To Samuel b'ahava

CONTENTS

PREFACE

The second half of the last century saw dramatic changes in the field of mental health. Public psychiatric hospitals, which had housed over half a million individuals at their peak in 1955, released thousands of former residents to communities that were unprepared to absorb, no less treat, these individuals. The community mental health centers that had arisen nationwide were treating individuals with less severe mental health problems with psychotherapy, crisis intervention, and other modes of intervention. Meanwhile clinical researchers were developing and empirically testing a variety of promising biopsychosocial interventions. By the year 2000, numerous treatments for individuals suffering from depression, anxiety, substance abuse, and more severe disorders had been found effective. While knowledge was expanding, resources were declining. Concerns about the rising costs of health and mental health care produced today's managed mental health or behavioral health care environment.

Amidst all these changes, social workers maintained a vital presence. They have been ubiquitous in community mental health centers, emergency services, hospitals, residential programs, partial hospitalization programs, vocational rehabilitation programs, and in behavioral health carve-outs. Social workers have been providing clinical services to clients who need time-limited psychotherapy and ongoing supportive care. Members of a profession that sees itself at the interface between the person and the environment, social workers offer a critical link between the client, the mental health team, and the community.

This book is written for those who wish to gain specialized knowledge of social work practice in the field of mental health and particular knowledge about working with adults with mental health difficulties. One of the book's audiences is social work graduate students who are taking courses in or are specializing in mental health. Advanced undergraduate students who are interested in mental health or are preparing for a career in this field are another audience. A third audience is mental health practitioners. Although this book was written from a social work perspective, clinicians and students of related professions, such as nursing and rehabilitation, may benefit from reading this volume. This book does, however, assume prior foundation knowledge of human behavior and social work practice theory, microcounseling skills, and some familiarity with the *Diagnostic and Statistical Manual of Mental Disorders (DSM-IV)* (American Psychiatric Association, 1994).

This book provides both a framework for practice and a description of interventions. Guided by a biopsychosocial conceptual framework and interdisciplinary research, this book offers a way to understand clients holistically and use up-to-date knowledge to guide practice in a climate in which psychopharmacology, the *DSM-IV*, and behavioral managed care entities exert a dominating influence.

This second edition has some novel features that are especially attuned to the contemporary milieu. For one, it incorporates a postmodern perspective through which to think about practice issues (see Chapter 1). Accordingly, it highlights the social construction of categories, context, multiple meanings, subjugated voices, and the method of deconstruction. In order to accentuate the client's perspective, quotations from the consumer literature are highlighted in bold in the book. Second, the book is revised and adapted to practice in a managed care environment in which short-term, cost-effective interventions are emphasized. This edition includes *best practices,* exemplars of interventions and treatment programs that are effective and consistent with social work values. In addition, the book discusses alternative healing methods that clients may use.

Other special features to note are:

- extensive information about medication
- emphasis on empirically supported and research-informed practice
- chapters on feminist theory and practice; cultural, racial, and ethnic issues; and legal and ethical issues
- case examples of model interventions
- descriptions of practice with clients with mental health problems commonly seen in mental or behavioral health settings today
- three chapters on working with adults with severe and persistent mental illness
- questions, case studies, and suggested activities at the conclusion of the chapters

Because today's practice applies knowledge from what has already been traditionally described as *mental health* to what are now called either mental health or *behavioral health* settings, this book integrates the two terms with the designation *behavioral mental health.* The practice described in this book is with adult clients who are moderately to severely affected by mental health problems. These difficulties include depression, anxiety, severe mental illness, and substance abuse (including dual diagnoses). Consistent with today's practice environment, the locus of treatment that is emphasized is the community, but many of the interventions that are described can be used within hospitals and other institutions. Although efforts have been made to be comprehensive, certain boundaries had to be drawn. This book does not discuss interventions with persons who simply have "problems in living" or difficulties that are principally environmental. Moreover, it does not give attention to treatment of children and adolescents, persons with personality disorders and dementia, and adults with dual diagnoses of mental illness and mental retardation or developmental disability.

The book is organized as follows. It begins with an orienting chapter, in which the reader is introduced to the leading concepts, themes, and contexts that are addressed in the field of behavioral mental health and in the book. The paradigm change from community mental health to behavioral health is described, research-informed practice is discussed, and definitional issues surrounding mental health, normality, and mental illness are examined. In this introductory chapter, the postmodern perspective of this book is described and a postmodern practitioner is envisioned. The book then is divided into two parts. Part One, A Framework for Practice, contains six chapters. The first (Chapter 2) looks at the historical context of social work practice in the field of mental health. The next, the conceptual framework, describes the terms, theories, and perspectives related to the book's integrated biopsychosocial perspective. Chapter 4 describes elements of a comprehensive biopsychosocial assessment that is in keeping with the conceptual framework. Here the mental status exam, a functional assessment, and the psychosocial summary are described, and model formats are provided. Chapter 5 is concerned with the legal and ethical issues that social workers face when they try to practice within the framework of their professional values and the legal system. Ethical dilemmas pertaining to managed care are discussed here. The next two chapters address gender and culture. Chapter 6 incorporates a postmodern feminist perspective and describes and gives an example of postmodern feminist practice. Chapter 7 provides a framework for culturally competent practice with African Americans, Native Americans/Alaska Natives, Asian Americans, and Hispanics/Latinos.

Part Two, Intervention, contains six chapters. Although the primary emphasis here is on psychosocial modalities, information on psychotropic medication is provided because psychopharmacology is used so frequently in practice settings that serve clients with the problems discussed in these chapters. Chapters 8 and 9 describe best practices with persons suffering from depression and anxiety, respectively, and provide illustrative cases. Because persons with severe and persistent mental disorders constitute a population with a significant need for intervention and care, three chapters are devoted to their treatment. Chapter 10 describes definitional and theoretical issues, research findings, the philosophy of psychosocial rehabilitation, community support systems, and best practices. The next chapter, on community care, discusses case management and describes a range of community resources appropriate for persons with severe and persistent psychiatric disorders, including a few best practices. The third chapter on treatment with this population (Chapter 12) focuses on medication, social skills training, and family psychoeducation and family education. Chapter 13, which was written by Diana M. DiNitto and Deborah K. Webb, is about clinical practice with clients who abuse substances and those who have the dual diagnoses of mental illness and an addictive disorder. This chapter provides definitions of substance abuse and comorbidity, describes the continuum of educational and treatment programs, and addresses special treatment issues. All the intervention chapters refer to rapid assessment and other tools that can be used to assess client progress and outcomes.

Acknowledgments

I gratefully acknowledge the help of a number of individuals who made this revision possible. I would especially like to thank Samuel Klausner, to whom this book is dedicated, whose love and confidence in me sustained me through this project. I also want to thank Phyllis Solomon, director of the NIMH-funded Social Work Mental Health Research Center at the University of Pennsylvania School of Social Work, who offered many valuable suggestions about how to revise this book. In addition, I benefited from a seminar on mental health policy that Phyllis Solomon and Trevor Hadley organized. Several speakers at the seminar—particularly Richard Baron and Aileen Rothbard as well as the two organizers—offered insights that were incorporated in this book. Next I thank Daphne Genyk for reviewing the section of the book on managed care and Amy Zaharlick for her advice on the culture chapter. I cannot sufficiently thank the clients with whom I have worked over the years whose stories have been reconstructed into case studies that are included in this book. I also learned a great deal from mental health professionals with whom I have worked. Former colleagues at the Ohio State University in the Postmodern

Feminism Study Group (particularly Kathleen Nuccio, Laurel Richardson, Patti Lather, Linda Raphael, Amy Zaharlick, and Gisela Hinkle) are deeply appreciated for sparking my interest in postmodernism. I would also like to thank the following reviewers: Lloyd Hawes, University of South Dakota; Michael Evan Johnson, Tuskegee University; Margaret Severson, University of Kansas; and Dianna J. Simon, Loma Linda University. Finally, I gratefully acknowledge the stimulus provided by Judy Fifer of Allyn and Bacon to revise this book and the help of others at Allyn and Bacon who contributed to its publication.

1

Getting Oriented

Themes and Contexts

Social workers should base practice on recognized knowledge, including empirically based knowledge relevant to social work and social work ethics.
—National Association of Social Workers, "NASW Code of Ethics," 1996

…what we call our data are really our own constructions of other people's constructions of what they and their compatriots are up to.
—Geertz, *The Interpretation of Cultures,* 1973

With all the fluctuation that characterizes this postmodern era, one condition has remained stable: Clinical social workers continue to be major players in the field of mental health. Social workers have been and still are the most numerous full-time equivalent professionals working in outpatient psychiatric clinics, partial care facilities, and multiservice mental health settings (Witkin et al., 1998). Among members of the National Association of Social Workers, mental health is the leading field of practice, with close to 40 percent indicating that this is their primary area (Gibelman & Schervish, 1997). Mirroring practitioners, more students in master's programs that offer concentrations in fields of practice or social problems are enrolled in mental health or community mental health than any other specific area (Lennon, 1998). Likewise, more master's degree students are situated in mental health field placements than any other practicum types (Lennon, 1998).

Although social workers have maintained their prevalence, the topography of mental health practice has changed substantially. In the decade intervening between the first and second editions of this book, new managed care concepts, breakthroughs in psychopharmacology, and additional strategies of treatment with demonstrated effectiveness have entered the fray. Research and clinical experience have illuminated "best practices," although some clients have elected to use alternative healing methods. These developments have made the field more challenging for clinicians but more mystifying for social work students and practitioners new to the mental health field. This book aims to illuminate this complexity so that social workers will be better equipped for practice in the twenty-first century.

The mental health social workers who are the subject of this book are the clinicians. Clinical social workers work with and on behalf of individuals, families, and small groups to help relieve their suffering and improve their psychological and social functioning. Knowledgeable about human behavior theories, as well as a variety of modes of intervention, clinical social workers make psychosocial assessments, formulate goals, and provide psychotherapeutic interventions or treatment. Although professionals of other disciplines share some of the same knowledge and engage in similar activities, clinical social workers have a broader perspective than their colleagues in other disciplines. Social workers view clients and their problems in relation to the contexts in which these difficulties occur and intervene in the social environment as well as the psychological and interpersonal domains. They are especially committed to enhancing clients' strengths and promoting connections between clients and the community. When interpersonal and institutional barriers interfere with clients' ability to obtain resources, clinical social workers engage in social change activities to eliminate obstacles and create resources. Professionals with a mission to promote human welfare and social justice, clinical social workers are particularly concerned with the plight of oppressed populations.

This description of clinical social work encompasses what is called *direct social work practice,* a general term that applies to practice in a wide range of field settings among various populations and problem areas. The direct social work practitioner in most specialized fields draws from diverse sources of knowledge, theories, and methods. She or he works with clients and systems to prevent and solve problems, change maladaptive behaviors, resolve psychological issues, develop social networks, and use community resources. Treatment is psychological and social.

In the field of mental health, the clinician's therapeutic and prevention roles predominate and are interconnected. Mental health social workers are principally psychotherapists and case managers. As therapists, they use their knowledge of human behavior theories, differential diagnosis, and treatment modalities, as well as research findings on practice effectiveness, to produce changes or promote the psychosocial functioning of clients and to remedy their situations. An additional dimension is the promotion of *empowerment,* enhanced feelings of competence resulting from clients' self-directed activity.

Clinical social work in mental health also includes case management. Work with the severely mentally ill in particular necessitates that workers advocate on behalf of clients, link consumers with resources, monitor their treatment plans, and mediate solutions to problems. Clinical social workers functioning as case managers promote clients' use of personal and community supports; in addition, social workers provide that support themselves. (See Chapter 11 for a discussion of case management in relation to the severely mentally ill.) Whether one functions as a case manager or as a therapist, or one integrates these roles, the social worker has extensive contacts with colleagues in related disciplines, employees of other human service agencies, landlords, physicians, lawyers, and others. Through these contacts clinical social workers connect clients with community resources and work to reduce institutional barriers to mental health services.

Social work practice in mental or behavioral health takes place in a number of different settings. Among these are community mental health centers, outpatient clinics, psychiatric hospitals or units within general hospitals, psychosocial rehabilitation services, substance abuse treatment programs, emergency or crisis intervention centers, partial hospitalization programs, supported apartments, group homes, and managed behavioral care carve-outs. Although sponsors such as these specialize in clients with mental health difficulties, family service and child welfare agencies, homeless shelters, and private practices also serve clients with mental health and substance abuse issues. This book was written with the former set of treatment centers in mind, but much of what is described here applies to other settings as well.

This chapter aims to orient readers to the context of behavioral or mental health practice today and the themes that run through this book. The next section explains the paradigm shift from community mental health to behavioral health under managed care. It shows that although the terminology has changed, the behavioral health ideology incorporates and repackages ideas of the earlier community mental health and deinstitutionalization movements. The second topic that is introduced in this chapter is research-informed practice, including knowledge derived from psychiatric epidemiology, biological research, and practice-effectiveness research. This is followed by definitions that are important to understanding the field. The chapter concludes with an explanation of the postmodern perspective of this book and what it means to be a postmodern practitioner.

From Community Mental Health to Behavioral Health

The practice of clinical social work in the field of mental health is affected by the recent paradigm shift from community mental health to behavioral health. The thinking behind the former was that the community should assume responsibility for the prevention and treatment of mental health problems. This focus on the community was reinforced by the ideology of the concurrent deinstitutionalization movement—the belief that the locus of treatment should be in the community rather than the hospital. The shift to behavioral health represents a change in the structure and accountability as a consequence of managed care. The term *behavioral health* is used in current managed care environments to describe the prevention and treatment of mental health and substance abuse problems.

Community Mental Health

Community mental health is a concept, philosophy of intervention, social movement, ideology, and policy that dominated the field of mental health during the last few decades of the twentieth century. In its initial conceptualization by Gerald Caplan (1961), the community was thought to generate stress that, in turn, produced psychopathology. Public policies in keeping with the community mental health concept supported the creation and expansion of services close to consumers in their local communities.

Caplan (1964) incorporated a public health model of prevention into his philosophy. Accordingly, intervention on three levels would reduce the incidence, duration, and degree of impairment associated with mental illness.

Three Levels of Prevention.   The first level of mental health prevention, *primary prevention,* has the goal of reducing the incidence (rate of new cases) of mental disorders by addressing their causes. This level focuses on the community and the conditions within it that may be toxic. Primary prevention invites research into potential biological, environmental, and psychological causes. When this research identifies groups that are at a high risk of developing a particular problem, preventive interventions, such as education, can be directed at that sector of the population. Primary prevention focuses on providing supports, which may be physical (food, housing), psychosocial (relationships), and sociocultural (cultural values, customs, and expectations), and preventing barriers to the flow of supports, such as racism (Caplan, 1964).

The second level, *secondary prevention,* has the goals of reducing the prevalence of actual cases (old and new) in the community and shortening the duration of time in which individuals experience problems, thus preventing existing problems from getting worse. Early identification (case finding), assessment, and intervention (crisis intervention and short-term therapy) are some ways in which this level of prevention is implemented. Prompt and effective individual, family, and group psychotherapies also apply to the secondary level.

Tertiary prevention refers to reducing the rate of mental disability in the community through rehabilitation. The goal here is to restore individuals with serious psychiatric problems to as high a level of functioning as possible and to prevent complications (Langsley, 1985b). Tertiary prevention is directed at the community as well as at clients and their social networks (Caplan, 1964). On the community level, efforts are made to prevent or reduce stigma, ignorance, and other barriers to recovery through advocacy and community education. When applied to individuals with severe mental disabilities, tertiary prevention aims to thwart decompensation, homicide, and suicide.

In addition to the three levels of prevention, several principles guided the community mental health practice from the beginning. Because many of these principles are invoked in the behavioral health paradigm, the original understanding of these terms is in order.

Principles of Community Mental Health Practice.   The community mental health movement embraced a set of principles that constituted a belief system or ideology. Those that will be discussed are comprehensiveness, continuity of care, accessibility, multidisciplinary teams, and accountability. One of the foremost principles was that services should be *comprehensive* (Langsley, 1985a). This meant that communities should provide a wide range of mental health services at various levels of intensity from outreach programs to outpatient clinical services to day treatment to hospitalization. Within these services, alternatives such as psychotherapies (individual, family, and group), social skills training, and vocational rehabilitation were to be offered. The community itself was to have a diverse range of residential settings, such as halfway houses and supported housing, in which clients may live (Bachrach, 1986). Community treatment was to be responsive to all age groups (including children and older adults), available around the clock and on an emergency basis, and address special problems such as substance abuse. Services were to be flexible and adapted to the needs of the populations served (Bachrach, 1986).

A related principle was that *continuity of care* was to be assured (Langsley, 1985a). This was a way to prevent clients from falling through the cracks in the context of a service delivery system that was complex, fragmented, and bureaucratic. It meant that services should be linked—"a system of services with easy flow of patients among its component parts" (Bloom, 1984, p. 4). For example, clients leaving psychiatric facilities were to be connected to treatment services when they were discharged. The case manager made sure that linkages were made and acted on.

Community mental health services were supposed to be *accessible* to those who sought treatment (Langsley, 1985a). This meant that they were to be located near clients' residences or places of work, accessible by public transportation, and available during evenings (at least for emergencies) and weekends. To assure this, community mental health services were distributed into *catchment areas* or service units that served residents in a particular geographic area. Facilities were also to be accessible to persons with physical disabilities, and provisions were to be made for communicating with those who could not hear. Furthermore, services were to be culturally and gender sensitive.

Another principle of community mental health was that treatment providers should organize into *multidisciplinary teams* (Langsley, 1985a). Teams were comprised of psychiatrists, psychologists, community mental health nurses, social workers, recreation therapists, and counselors, among others. Some members had expertise in particular mental health domains, such as housing or vocational rehabilitation. Indigenous (paraprofessional) mental health workers, who lived in the neighborhood, also participated (Bloom, 1984). Multidisciplinary teams make it possible for the knowledge, skills, and perspectives of diverse members to contribute to a holistic understanding of the client and the provision of multidimensional treatment or rehabilitation.

A final principle was *accountability* (Langsley, 1985a).The citizen board members who governed mental health agencies were responsible not only to those who sought treatment but also to those who were well (Langsley, 1985a). Accountability also applied to consumers, who participated increasingly in the governance of community mental health agencies. As consumers recognized their potential power, they asserted themselves increasingly over time.

Although community mental health and deinstitutionalization were distinct movements within the mental health field, their ideologies converged. Community mental health practitioners assimilated some of the values toward hospitalization assumed by advocates of deinstitutionalization.

Deinstitutionalization. *Deinstitutionalization* is a philosophy, process, and ideology (Bachrach, 1976; Mechanic, 1989) that began to unfold in the United States in the late 1950s when the principal locus of treatment began to change from hospitals to the community. In 1955, the number of patients residing in state and county psychiatric hospitals peaked at 559,000. After that time, these facilities were substantially (but not completely) depopulated. By 1992, the inpatient population was down to 72,096 residents (Witkin et al., 1998), a substantial reduction. This process was facilitated by the development of medications that could be prescribed and taken in the community. Another condition that supported deinstitutionalization was a switching of costs from the state to the federal level in the 1960s, which made it possible for persons who were formerly long-term hospital residents to live in the community (Mechanic, 1989).

Although some advocates of deinstitutionalization hoped that hospitals could be entirely eliminated, the philosophy in practice revolved around the appropriate use of hospitals.

Instead of maintaining a large cadre of persons with severe mental illness in custodial care, hospitals would care for persons with acute exacerbations (flare-ups) for a brief period of time in which they would be stabilized. Short-term hospitalizations could be provided in psychiatric units of local general hospitals (rather than state facilities located some distance from clients' homes), with follow-up treatment to help them maintain their gains provided in the community.

Deinstitutionalization was supposed to involve two processes—(a) the avoidance of hospitalization and (b) the concurrent development of community services that would serve as alternatives to institutionalization (Bachrach, 1976). The first process meant that community treatment strategies, such as placement in a day treatment program, were to be pursued before considering hospitalization. This mechanism of diversion was dependent on the second process, the existence or creation of community alternatives such as crisis and emergency services, group homes, family care homes, outpatient treatment centers, vocational rehabilitation programs, and other options (for today's options, see Chapter 11). Unfortunately, many communities did not assume the responsibility of developing community alternatives and assuring their use. Many discharged patients were "dumped" on city streets without a place in which to live and without outpatient care. Another consequence of deinstitutionalization was the development of a "revolving door syndrome," with the same individuals flowing in and out of the hospitals on a regular basis. The increase in admission rates that followed deinstitutionalization suggests that brief hospitalizations were not long enough to allow recovery to take place, and/or that some clients did not receive or follow up on referrals to agencies providing aftercare. A further flaw in the implementation of this policy was that some residents of psychiatric hospitals were reinstitutionalized in nursing homes and prisons. With the passage of time it has become clear that state hospitals continue to be needed in some areas to care for persons who are poor community risks, "revolving door" patients, and those who require long-term hospitalization (Bachrach, 1996).

Deinstitutionalization evolved as a public policy during the 1960s, a period of heightened social consciousness and advocacy for the rights of marginalized populations. In the 1960s and 1970s practices such as involuntary commitment, custodial care without treatment, and coercive forms of intervention were successfully challenged in courts on constitutional grounds. (See Chapter 2 for a review of this history and Chapter 6 for a discussion of some legal issues.) But deinstitutionalization was also an ideology that was associated with certain values (Mechanic, 1989). First, hospitalization was considered an undesirable alternative that should be replaced with other methods of intervention. Second, it was considered desirable for persons with mental health difficulties to be free to live normal lives, integrated as fully as possible into the fabric of the community (cf. Wolfensberger, Nirje, Olshansky, Perske, & Roos, 1972).

Although proponents of deinstitutionalization and community mental health identified with these values, there were others who saw in the emergence of deinstitutionalization an opportunity for taxpayers to save money. Hospitalization is the most expensive form of psychiatric treatment that there is. States had been bearing a significant economic burden for long-term hospital care. When liberal thinkers depicted institutionalization as undesirable, conservatives responded by closing state hospitals. Other policies such as limiting admissions to those who were a danger to themselves and others and retaining people in the hospital over relatively short periods of time also appeared to be economically advantageous to taxpayers. Cost-mindedness continues to drive policy under managed care.

Behavioral Health under Managed Care

Managed care is a means of structuring, financing, and administering health care that aims to be cost-effective, efficient, and high in quality. It came to the fore at a time when health care costs in the United States were skyrocketing and appeared to be out of control. It has changed the face of health care and mental health practice and introduced certain terms and concepts that require explanation.

In contrast to the fee-for-service, *indemnity* model in which third-party payers, such as health insurance companies, pay for each medical visit or procedure, with managed care, physicians are paid for services at a negotiated rate. A primary care physician (PCP) coordinates services and makes decisions about the need for outside referrals and procedures. Under managed care, interventions must be preapproved, reauthorized at intervals, and evaluated in terms of outcomes.

Behavioral health services may be provided under a managed health care insurance plan. There are two main types: health maintenance organizations (HMOs) and preferred provider organizations (PPOs). HMOs are prepaid plans in which the member uses specific health providers that are part of the organization's network. These providers may be employed directly by the HMO or may be groups or individuals who contract with the HMO. In a PPO the member has the option of using the organization's preferred network or going outside the network, in which case there are additional costs. Consumers in PPOs pay a modest copayment for each visit (Jackson, 1995). One can use providers outside HMO and PPO networks in an emergency. A third type, the point of service plan (POS), which may be a separate alternative or part of an HMO or PPO, also allows consumers flexibility in using network and nonnetwork providers, with different terms applying to different sets of providers (Corcoran & Vandiver, 1996). Behavioral health care in HMOs and PPOs may be provided through a kind of carve-out arrangement, a contract with a managed behavioral health care organization (MBHO) that provides mental health and/or substance abuse services (Edmunds et al., 1997). Alternatively behavioral health may be integrated into the health care provider system. Providers of behavioral health services under any of these managed care arrangements usually agree to accept what is called a *capitated* rate. This is a specific amount per user that the provider is given for a particular time period (e.g., per month).

In 1995, about 60 percent of people living in the United States were in some kind of managed health care plan (Health Insurance Association of America, 1996). About 25 percent had other kinds of coverage. Many states have obtained waivers from the Health Care Financing Administration, making it possible for some people on Medicaid to enroll in managed care plans (McGuirk, Keller, & Croze, 1995). Similarly, Medicare beneficiaries may receive their benefits through a managed care arrangement. Full-time employees of relatively large companies provide individual (and sometimes family) coverage as a fringe benefit, with some or no cost sharing between the employer and employee. Over 16 percent of the U.S. population had no health insurance in 1998 (U.S. Department of Commerce News, 1999).

Clients in need of mental health or behavioral health sevices may or may not have health insurance. Some lose their private insurance when mental health problems make it difficult for them to maintain their jobs. For those who are insured, behavioral health benefits may be limited. The Health Maintenance Organization Act of 1973 (PL 93-222) established a minimal level of behavioral health coverage by HMOs at twenty outpatient visits and thirty days of inpatient treatment a year (Jackson, 1995). The Mental Health Parity Act of 1996, which went into effect in 1998, requires equity in insurance coverage between physical and mental health problems, but this legislation has loopholes.

The introduction of managed care into mental health and substance abuse practice has centered attention on cost-effectiveness and prevention. *Cost-effectiveness* refers to the need to assess the connection between cost and outcomes to assure the best outcome at the least cost. Expensive treatment strategies, such as hospitalization and long-term psychotherapy, are avoided if alternative, less expensive approaches are feasible, available, and sound. When more expensive treatment is authorized, it is monitored to determine whether it is working and the amount of time this level of intensity of intervention is required. In general, brief, time-limited treatment or crisis intervention is preferred. Managed care organizations do not support time- and money-consuming psychotherapy that aims to restructure the personality (Poynter, 1998). Reduction of symptomatology, restoration of functioning, and behavioral change are the primary goals (Poynter, 1998). Effectiveness is measured through the use of indicators determined by the managed care organization, an external group that conducts a utilization review, the provider, and/or the behavioral health delivery system. Although outcomes are usually measured on a system basis, individual practitioners can use instruments that measure the outcome of treatment, the extent to which goals are attained, and (in the case of clients with long-term problems) intermittent progress. (Suggestions for practitioner instruments are offered elsewhere in this volume.) Another means of assessing effectiveness is to ask consumers how they found services. Managed care organizations use client satisfaction surveys that they tailor to the needs of the particular program (Corcoran & Vandiver, 1996).

Prevention is an integral part of managed care. Managed health care plans in the private sector emphasize wellness and health promotion strategies such as giving up smoking and drinking, and stress management. Public managed care, which will be described next, uses prevention approaches such as family education, peer support groups, and psychosocial rehabilitation (Corcoran & Vandiver, 1996).

Clients on Medicaid and Medicare in most areas of the country can receive health and mental health care under a managed care arrangement. Local mental health authorities or boards, which have administrative and financial oversight of their districts, have an important role in the provision of care for these public sector clients (Hoge, Davidson, Griffith, Sledge, & Howenstine, 1994). Because managed care of public sector clients is still relatively new, its scope and functions are in the process of being defined. One group of authors identified five core functions that are needed to provide comprehensive treatment for clients who are recipients of public support. Four of these are reminiscent of community mental health ideology.

1. *Gatekeeping.* At points of entry into the system, efforts are made to admit clients the mental health authorities define as target populations, to limit admission to more expensive services by adhering to restrictive criteria, and to divert clients to alternative, less expensive forms of treatment.

2. *The community is the locus of activity.* Treatment is to be in the local community where clients, their support networks, and services are located.

3. *Provision of comprehensive services.* Local mental health authorities and service providers are to assess needs, allocate resources, and overcome barriers to access, so that the needs of the target population can be met.

4. *Continuity of care* is to be facilitated by coordinating services that are currently needed and those that will be needed over time.

5. *Maximizing economic efficiency* can be realized by consolidating funding streams, using these funds flexibly, and introducing incentives to providers to deliver efficient, effective services.

6. *Accountability* should be established at the delivery level by assigning a particular staff member, such as a case manager, as the point person. Local mental health authorities are accountable to the public for the effective operation of the mental health service delivery system. (Based on Hoge et al., 1994.)

The Committee on Quality Assurance and Accreditation Guidelines for Managed Behavioral Care, which developed a framework to guide the evaluation of behavioral health care arrangements, found that arranging *wraparound* or *enabling services* to address clients' social needs was also an important function. The committee recommended services such as social welfare, housing, vocational, and other rehabilitative services for persons with severe mental illness and chronic substance abuse problems (Edmunds et al., 1997). Another recommendation was that behavioral health programs should be responsive to racial and ethnic minorities and persons with co-occurring mental illness and substance abuse. The committee stated that efforts should be made to employ providers who are culturally competent and use innovative and alternative treatments, even if research on the effectiveness of these strategies has not as yet been conducted (Edmunds et al., 1997). Elsewhere in this book, services for persons with severe mental illness (Chapter 11), culturally sensitive practice (Chapter 7), and treatment of persons with co-occurring disorders (Chapter 13) are discussed.

Comparing Behavioral Health and Community Mental Health

As the successor to the community mental health paradigm, behavioral health embraces many of the same goals and practices as its predecessor. On the other hand, some of the tenets of community mental health and deinstitutionalization have been recast to meet the expectation of cost-effectiveness under managed care. Moreover, there are some dimensions of behavioral health under managed care that are new and will have to be learned by clinical social workers practicing in this field.

Under both paradigms the *community is the primary locus of treatment.* Even if hospitalization is needed, treatment in a psychiatric unit in a local community hospital is preferred over hospitalization in a hospital that is far from home. The definition of community, however, may be different with behavioral health. Under community mental health, clients were served by centers that were in their neighborhood (or catchment area). This is not necessarily the case under behavioral health.

Another community mental health principle maintained in behavioral health is *continuity of care.* Under community mental health, it was important that a client be followed by someone in the system as he or she moved among services, for example, from the outpatient clinic to the hospital and back to the community. One way to assure continuity of care for persons with severe and persistent mental illness was to appoint a case manager who would coordinate clients' care, act as their advocate, and make sure that they received social and other nonmedical services (see Chapter 11). Behavioral care has incorporated the concept of continuity and its previous meaning, and it also uses case managers. Some managed care organizations hire *care managers* (sometimes also called case managers, but they have a different charge) to oversee the management of services and costs (Schreter et al., 1996).

Under managed care the term *continuum of services,* which facilitates continuity of care, is also used. This refers to a range of services at varying levels of restrictiveness that should be included in a behavioral health system (Jackson, 1995). The continuum goes from outpatient therapy to long-term hospitalization with intensive outpatient care, crisis intervention, partial hospitalization, residential treatment, and acute inpatient treatment in between (Schreter, Sharfstein, & Schreter, 1997). Continuity of care is contingent on the existence of a continuum of services in the community, which is not always the case, particularly in rural areas. Where services exist, concern centers on whether systems of care are *integrated,* as many providers, treatment sites, and payers may be involved with the same client (Schreter et al., 1997). Consideration of the level of restrictiveness is reminiscent of the judicially determined requirement that persons with mental illness receive treatment in the least restrictive environment that is consistent with their need for care. Under managed care, the concern with restrictiveness is related to the need to minimize costly intensive treatments when other, less expensive modalities can remedy the same problem. Regardless of the motivation, hospitalization is an undesirable alternative under behavioral care (as it was under deinstitutionalization). Still there is recognition that hospitalization is needed at times.

Several other tenets of community mental health continue under the behavioral health paradigm, notably *prevention.* The three levels of prevention are still relevant under the new paradigm, although the extent to which each level is implemented is not clear. With respect to mental illnesses that are genetic and entail impairment in the brain, prevention involves early intervention and monitoring to limit the impact of the disease on the individual.

It continues to be important that services are *accessible* to consumers by having twenty-four-hour coverage, being nearby, posing no architectural barriers, and being responsive to diverse cultures. Attention to special populations such as the severely mentally disabled and older adults and the activity of multidisciplinary teams are also highlighted in both paradigms. Likewise both community mental health and behavioral health ideologies affirm that services should be *comprehensive* (thus, the continuum of care) and accountable. When behavioral care is administered in the private sector, however, there is accountability to business interests. In the public sphere, the needs of the community must be considered.

Implications of Behavioral Health for Clinical Social Work

Behavioral health under managed care introduces some procedures and expectations that affect social workers. In some agencies and practices, clinical social workers are extensively involved in requests for authorization and reauthorization of services. These may involve telephone calls and/or the submission of paperwork. Social workers may experience requests to justify continued work with a client as intrusive and object to an outside party's weighing of cost saving over what they consider the best interest of the client. Differences in judgment and values can raise troubling ethical issues for social workers. In addition, the introduction of administrative requirements and paperwork can complicate the client-worker relationship (Poynter, 1998). Although utilization reviews and quality assurance have been part of mental health delivery for some time, documentation requirements have increased.

At the very least, behavioral health care has made the already complicated mental health scene more complex. Interactions with clients need to be considered in the context of their behavioral health insurance, the agency, available services, and the best interest of the clients. Mental health agencies are funded by multiple sources, public and private, including sponsors of supportive services. With so many parties involved, it is a challenge for social workers to maintain a focus on clients and their empowerment.

Another consideration for clinical social workers is that the behavioral health scene has become increasingly competitive. Managed care organizations may be biased toward physicians and providers with Ph.D.s, although social workers can provide similar services at a lower rate (Jackson, 1995). The best way to overcome these biases is for social workers to be knowledgeable and competent. We turn next to some areas of research knowledge that inform competent social work practice.

Research-Informed Practice

The knowledge that informs social work practice comes from a variety of disciplines, including social work. The sources that will be highlighted in this book are psychiatric epidemiology, biology, and practice-effectiveness research. Research findings from these sources have an impact on priorities within the mental health field and the practitioner's selection of interventions. (From this point on, the terms *mental health, behavioral health,* and *behavioral mental health,* which combines the two concepts, will be used interchangeably.)

Psychiatric Epidemiology

Clinical social work practice in behavioral mental health is informed by psychiatric epidemiological research. *Epidemiology* is the study of the distribution of diseases in a population in an environmental context. A project of significance to public health, it looks at conditions that might point to the origin, cause, and distribution of pathology, such as the transmission of body fluids and acquired immunodeficiency syndrome. Epidemiological research involves the use of sophisticated methods of sampling and statistical methods of analysis.

Epidemiological research is predicated on the paradigm of "host/agent/environment" (Kellam, 1987). The host is the person with the disease; the agent is the causal factor. When epidemiology has been applied to psychopathology, research has rarely been able to identify a specific agent that causes a mental disorder. Unlike physical diseases, psychological disorders are not infectious. The causes are multiple and interactive. Epidemiological studies have found varying levels of association among a number of social, environmental, and demographic variables and the disorder.

Two terms that are widely used in epidemiological research are *incidence* and *prevalence*. Incidence refers to the number of new cases of a particular disorder that occur in a given period of time (e.g., in a year). Prevalence refers to the total number of cases (new cases and existing cases) in a population. *Point prevalence* refers to the prevalence at a particular point of time (e.g., today), *period prevalence* to a period of time longer than a day (e.g., six-month prevalence), and *lifetime prevalence* to any time in a person's life (Kaplan & Sadock, 1998). Epidemiologists also look at variables that may be associated with the incidence and prevalence of particular disorders such as age, race, gender, and socioeconomic status.

Psychiatric epidemiological research advanced tremendously during the second half of the twentieth century. Early research looked at both aggregated data of cases in treatment and large community samples, but each of these strategies had methodological problems. The focus on cases in treatment, usually in public facilities, resulted in the exclusion of people who do not seek help (for various social and cultural reasons) and those who are treated privately. Epidemiological studies of communities have the advantage of being more inclusive, but early studies were hampered by their collection of mental status data by lay interviewers and by difficulty converting findings about symptoms into diagnoses. Among the classic early investigations were Hollingshead and Redlich's (1958) study of the community and persons in treatment in the area of New Haven, Connecticut, which found a relationship between social class and diagnosis and treatment; and Srole's Midtown Manhattan Study (Srole, Langer, Michael, Kirkpatrick, & Rennie, 1962; Srole & Fischer, 1986), which found that 14 percent of the population studied were considered impaired in 1954 and 12 percent in 1974.

During the last two decades of the twentieth century, psychiatric epidemiological research benefited from the development of instruments that were capable of generating diagnostic information and could be administered by nonprofessional interviewers (Weissman, Myers, & Ross, 1986). Among these are the Diagnostic Interview Schedule (DIS) (Robins, Helzer, Croughan, & Ratcliff, 1981) and the Composite International Diagnostic Interview (CIDI) (World Health Organization, 1990).

The DIS was used in the National Institute of Mental Health (NIMH) Epidemiological Catchment Area (ECA) Program, a group of studies implemented in the late 1970s and early 1980s (Regier et al., 1984). These extensive studies took place in five urban areas—New Haven, Connecticut; Baltimore, Maryland; Durham, North Carolina; St. Louis, Missouri; and Los Angeles, California. Both institutionalized and noninstitutionalized residents of these communities were surveyed once and then again a year later, thus providing comprehensive and longitudinal data (Freedman, 1984). These studies gathered information on the prevalence of specific psychiatric disorders, associated demographic factors, and patterns of usage of physical and mental health services for mental health problems. This ambitious program of research has provided fruitful information about the distribution of mental disorders in the United States. The findings are limited, however, because the five surveys took place in urban areas with university-based psychiatric facilities; it is not clear to what extent the results apply to people who live in rural areas and other locations where mental health services are not so accessible (Kessler, Abelson, & Zhao, 1998).

The National Comorbidity Survey (NCS), also funded by NIMH, attempted to remedy this deficiency (Kessler et al., 1994). The NCS sample was more representative of the United States, but the age range was limited to persons between the ages of 15 and 54. This study used the CIDI to assess diagnoses. Whereas the DIS was compatible with the *Diagnostic and Statistical Manual (DSM-III)* (American Psychiatric Association [APA], 1980), the CIDI converted to the *DSM-III-R* (APA, 1987). Neither the National Comorbidity Survey nor the Epidemiological Catchment Area Study included personality disorders other than the antisocial type (Kessler et al., 1998).

Regardless of their limitations, both of these epidemiological studies have contributed substantially to knowledge about the distribution of the disorders that are included, as well as the use of treatment facilities. For example, the NCS produced two startling findings. For one, the twelve-month and lifetime prevalences of any CIDI disorder among persons ages 15 to 54 are 30.9 and 49.7 percent, respectively. Moreover, comorbidity (the co-occurrence of two or more disorders) was the rule rather than the exception for twelve-month and lifetime prevalences (Kessler et al., 1994). Other results of these two studies will be referred to elsewhere in this book.

Biological Research

Another avenue that informs mental health practice is biological research. With increasing evidence that many mental disorders are diseases of the brain, attention has been focused on understanding how the brain works, underlying causes of brain dysfunction, and how to use pharmacological means to overcome biochemical deficiencies. This has resulted in a vast body of research on neuroanatomy, genetics (including molecular biology), brain imaging, and psychopharmacology. For example, the Human Genome Project has been engaged in a process of deciphering the codes in human DNA that have implications for mental disorders.

During the twentieth century there was considerable dissension within the mental health field about the role of biology in the etiology of mental disorders. Freud's seminal work on the role of early life experiences in generating mental conflict directed attention to developmental, family environmental, and personality factors that contribute to mental illness (particularly neuroses). One consequence of Freud's work and that of others who focused on early life experiences was that families were blamed for engendering mental illness in their progeny. It was not until after the breakthroughs in psychopharmacology that began to occur in the middle of the century and spurred the process of deinstitutionalization mentioned earlier that the biological viewpoint became prominent. During the last decade of the twentieth century, a new generation of medications emerged that promises to enhance the quality of life of persons with mental illnesses.

With its focus on person-environment interactions, the field of social work has been reluctant to incorporate biological knowledge into its own knowledge base, even though the biopsychosocial perspective is recognized as central to understanding practice (Johnson et al., 1990; Saleebey, 1992). But increasingly, social workers in the field of mental health have been writing about the importance of biological knowledge (Johnson, 1996) and, in particular, the need for practitioners to understand the structure of the brain and psychopharmacology (Bentley & Walsh, 1996, 1998). Chapter 3 of this volume provides an introduction to some important information drawn from biology and related scientific disciplines (neurophysiology, psychopharmacology, genetics). Later chapters on intervention show how this knowledge applies to understanding and intervening with clients with different kinds of mental health problems.

In keeping with postmodernism, which will be described later in this chapter, this book views biological and psychosocial perspectives as integrally related. Although professions may carve knowledge into spheres that each of them "owns," persons are complex biopsychosocial (and spiritual) wholes whose lives are constituted and created in a web of experiences. The integrative biopsychosocial conceptualization that is used in this book is described in Chapter 3.

Practice-Effectiveness Research

An additional but equally important area of knowledge that is critical to practice is research on practice effectiveness. This refers to research carried out in practice settings by investigators in social work and other fields. These studies incorporate a wide range of research strategies. Some involve controlled studies in which participants are randomly assigned to different conditions. The experimental group receives the intervention that is being tested (e.g., short-term cognitive therapy) while the control group or groups receive some other usual type of treatment (e.g., medication) or no treatment. Some studies are longitudinal; that is, participants are followed over a period of time. These studies can assess whether the differences of various interventions last and the long-term effectiveness of certain kinds of interventions. Cross-sectional studies survey participants who represent a spectrum of the population at a particular moment in time.

Some psychiatric intervention research tests the efficacy of different medications. These studies may be *double-blind;* that is, neither the psychiatrist nor the patient knows whether the latter is receiving a real medication or a *placebo,* which is a substance that lacks any medicinal value. A certain percentage of patients will improve on the placebo, probably because they have confidence in the doctor or some other psychological reason (this is called the *placebo effect*). Some research compares interventions with drugs with psychosocial treatments and combined drug and psychosocial treatments. Some of these studies are referred to in the chapters on intervention with different populations.

Although psychiatrists and psychologists have been conducting research on mental health practice for some time, social workers are relatively new at this. During the last decade of the twentieth century, this situation was redressed by the creation of mental health research centers that would foster social work research at universities around the country. The clinical research cited in this book was conducted by psychiatrists, psychologists, sociologists, and social workers. Both qualitative and quantitative studies have been referenced. Qualitative research, such as ethnography or narrative studies, offers the reader a valuable client perspective that is often missing in experimental studies.

This book also describes some programs and interventions that are exemplars of best practices. The criteria for inclusion come from quantitative and qualitative reports of results, frequent references to them in the literature, and their congruence with social work values. Examples of best practices are introduced in Chapter 6 as well as the intervention chapters.

Before becoming conversant with research findings of epidemiological, biological, and practice-effectiveness research, it is necessary to become grounded in the basics. The next section will describe some of the definitional issues that are fundamental to understanding mental health.

Definitional Issues

Many of the terms used in the field of mental health are controversial. There is little consensus about what is meant by *normality* and *mental health. Mental illness* has been regarded as both a "myth" and a "metaphor" (Szasz, 1961). Many terms, such as *psychopathology,* derive from the field of psychiatry. Others, such as *adaptation* and *problems in living,* are particularly compatible with the orientation of social workers.

Normality, Mental Health, and Mental Illness

The terms *mental health, normality,* and *mental illness* are social constructions based on Western values. *Mental health* and *normality* suggest positive psychological functioning, whereas *mental illness* suggests dysfunctioning. Mental health and mental illness suggest a medical model, whereas normality implies a statistical one. Mental health is frequently used as a euphemism for mental illness—as illustrated by "mental health" centers that remediate "mental illness." The relatively new term, *behavioral health,* adds to the confusion.

Normality.   The terms *mental health* and *normality* have similar meanings but different connotations. On the surface, normality suggests a statistical criterion (Offer & Sabshin, 1966)—the average or mean; the most common behavior, the mode; or one or two standard deviations from the mean. Studies employing statistical measures, however, have produced surprising results. Psychiatric epidemiological studies of normal community samples have found that a substantial proportion of the population had symptoms of psychological problems. In the Midtown Manhattan Study of an urban area (Srole et al., 1962) and a study of a rural community in Nova Scotia (Leighton et al., 1963), only about 20 percent of the subjects were rated "well." The more recent National Comorbidity Survey mentioned earlier, came up with a lifetime prevalence of close to 50 percent in any disorder (Kessler et al., 1994). Accordingly, mental illness seems to be "normal."

The term *normality* also suggests adaptation to the social context (Offer & Sabshin, 1966). Normal persons accommodate to the demands of society, meet legal and social obligations, and generally fit in with the contours of society. Although such persons are not troublesome, they are not necessarily creative or self-actualized. Persons who merely adapt to situational demands generally do not have the "peak experiences" of insight, self-awareness, or integration described by Maslow (1968). Furthermore, they do not necessarily have integrity, independence, or courage. Indeed they may acquiesce to injustices, exploitation, and persecution.

Jackson (1977) described difficulties in defining normality in the paper, "The Myth of Normality." "There is no standard of psychological 'normality' or 'good health,'" he said (p. 157). The dichotomy between the normal and abnormal is false and based on the assumption that psychopathology is fixed and tangible. In fact, individuals, as well as families, vary in their potentialities, emotional expression, and behavior:

> …there is no such animal as the normal person. Instead there is a wide variance in adaptive patterns and behavioral repertoires. How a person acts varies with the culture, the subculture, the ethnic group, and the family group in which he lives. (p. 162)

In order to offset cultural biases that occur in evaluating a person in relation to conventional ideas about normality, Jackson recommended the assessment of individuals in terms of their functioning in a number of contexts and activities.

Regardless of how one defines normality, one must recognize the relation of prevailing concepts to the expectations of the culture. Cultures vary in their expression of and response to anguish, pain, and deviance. Judgments about what is good, desirable, and acceptable are culturally relative.

Mental Health.   On the simplest level, mental health is characterized by the *absence of mental illness* (Jahoda, 1958). Accordingly, mentally healthy individuals do not have psychiatric disorders, such as those described in the *DSM-IV* (American Psychiatric Association, 1994). Gross psychopathology (e.g., delusions, hallucinations) is not present or observed. Such persons do not communicate feelings of distress or present evidence of mental illness. Ordinarily they are not receiving mental health treatment.

The problem with this definition is that there is a sociocultural process that intervenes between the presence of symptoms and diagnosis. Many individuals have signs of psychiatric disorders that neither they nor others consider indicators of mental disorder. Individuals comprising the person's intimate network may view the person's behavior as a personal idiosyncrasy, a sign of divine powers, or an expression of a developmental stage. The group's ideas about what is normal may contrast with what mental health professionals consider mental illness. In order for diagnosis to take place, someone or some system will have to establish that what was previously considered normal is abnormal (Scheff, 1984).

Mental health also can be viewed as an *aspect of health*. The World Health Organization (1948) defined health as "the state of complete physical, mental and social well-being and not merely the absence of disease or infirmity." Although this definition leaves open the nature of "well-being," it does suggest that health encompasses a few areas of functioning and that all are essential. Furthermore, it links mind, body, and social life.

Mental health also represents an *optimal or ideal state*. Jahoda's (1958) concept of "positive mental health" includes attitudes toward oneself; growth, development, or self-actualization; personality integration; autonomy; environmental mastery; and perception of reality. This definition emphasizes high levels of functioning, which go beyond well-being or the absence of disease. Accordingly, individuals may seek psychotherapy to promote their growth, self-acceptance, or confidence. The qualities selected, however, reflect what this culture values—the autonomous, striving, differentiated individual. Other cultures value other qualities such as humility and willingness to sacrifice oneself.

Another criterion for mental health is *subjective* (Scott, 1970). Accordingly, the mentally healthy individual feels happy, satisfied, or self-confident. This criterion has been measured in research studies with happiness and life satisfaction scales. Subjective perceptions are, however, problematic as a standard for mental health. Persons under the influence of substances may have artificially produced feelings of satisfaction or happiness. Similarly, individuals with bipolar (manic-depressive) disorder are likely to rate themselves as extremely happy when they are manic. Furthermore, happiness and unhappiness are, to some extent, related to one's environment. Under some environmental conditions, one cannot be happy (Jahoda, 1958).

When political conditions are oppressive, mental health takes on a cast that may differ from what looks like mental health under freedom. During the time of slavery, for example, acts of defiance and subterfuge may have been signs of mental health. Similarly members of the underground in Nazi Germany and dissidents under other repressive regimes can be viewed as healthy. Among those who are oppressed by political systems, some individuals are able to transcend their situations by discovering meaning in suffering (Frankl, 1984). Meaning can be realized through defiance, contemplation, or acceptance.

In this volume mental health will be considered a state of psychosocial functioning that ranges from dysfunctional (mental illness) to functional to optimal. Optimal captures qualities of positive mental health as defined by the individual's own culture. Functional refers to the ability to take care of oneself and participate in community life purposefully and constructively. Dysfunctional describes impairment in the capacity to take care of oneself and participate in the community and includes patterns that are destructive of oneself and others.

Mental health is described as a continuum in Figure 1.1. According to this model, an individual is more or less functional with respect to different activities. A person may function at a relatively high level in some areas (manages own apartment, uses transportation), but at the dysfunctional level in others (interpersonal relationships, employment). The goal of intervention is to help the person maintain, restore, or improve psychosocial functioning in specific areas.

Mental health is a phenomenon of the individual, family, group, community, culture, and nation. What affects one of these systems affects others. On the individual level, mental health encompasses the expression and management of emotions, cognitions, behavior, and values as well as the social, occupational, and management skills needed for survival. Physical, psychological, and social dimensions are connected.

Mental Illness.   During the early 1960s, Thomas Szasz (1960, 1961) launched an attack on the usage of the concept of mental illness. To Szasz the term applied appropriately to brain (organic) or neurological diseases but not to discrepant beliefs, values, behaviors, social relationships, and the like, which were commonly viewed as symptoms of mental

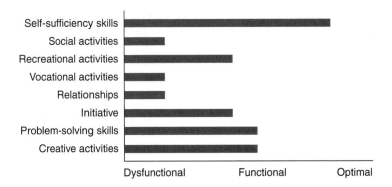

FIGURE 1.1   Description of Mental Health Functioning

disease. Many persons adjudged mentally ill hold unusual beliefs (e.g., "I am Napoleon") or violate legal norms (the criminally insane), but they do not have objective bodily illnesses. Although these individuals may be troubled, Szasz said, they are experiencing "problems in living," not mental illness. Because the term *mental illness* is applied where there is no evidence of medical pathology, Szasz said, mental illness is a "myth." Szasz was not alone in his criticism of concepts of mental illness and related social practices. Scheff (1984) described a social process in which deviant behavior gets defined as mental illness.

Behaviorists objected to the medical vocabulary, labeling, and assumption that there was an inner cause of psychological problems. They preferred to look at environmental contingencies that support the presentation of maladaptive behavior. Existential phenomenologists were critical of the use of the scientific method in the study of mental illness. According to their thinking (see, e.g., Esterson, 1970), it was not possible to be objective in assessing mental illness because such determinations are made in the course of interacting with a client. In addition, many social factors (family, environment) surrounding the client contribute to what is socially defined as mental illness.

Some of the criticism was in response to inappropriate labeling of mental illness. During the 1960s, for example, some young political activists who went south to register African American voters were incarcerated in mental hospitals for alleged paranoia (Coles, 1970). Labeling behaviors or practices that differ from those valued by mainstream society (e.g., homosexuality, substance abuse, illegal acts) as symptoms of mental illness is a means of invalidating persons who are different.

The authors of the last three editions of the *Diagnostic and Statistical Manual of Mental Disorders* (APA, 1980, 1987, 1994) have attempted to address some of the definitional problems that have been described, as well as questions that had been raised about the scientific merits of previous editions. For one, they assigned specific criteria to each psychiatric diagnosis. This should deter labeling and other inappropriate uses of psychiatric diagnoses. Second, they ran extensive field tests in an attempt to arrive at reliable diagnoses and compare alternative criteria (APA, 1980, 1994). Third, they acknowledged that the boundaries between physical and mental disorders, among different mental disorders, and between a particular mental disorder and no mental disorder are nebulous (APA, 1994). Finally, the manual authors came up with their own definition of *mental disorder,* the term which they use for *mental illness.* The definition in the *DSM-IV* (APA, 1994) is as follows:

> In *DSM-IV* each of the mental disorders is conceptualized as a clinically significant behavioral or psychological syndrome or pattern that occurs in an individual and that is associated with present distress (e.g., a painful symptom) or disability (i.e., impairment in one or more areas of functioning) or with a significantly increased risk of suffering death, pain, disability, or an important loss of freedom. In addition, this syndrome or pattern must not be merely an expectable response to a particular event, for example, the death of a loved one. Whatever its original cause, it must currently be considered a manifestation of a behavioral, psychological, or biological dysfunction in the individual. Neither deviant behavior (e.g., political, religious, or sexual) nor conflicts that are primarily between the individual and society are mental disorders unless the deviance or conflict is a symptom of a dysfunction in the person, as described above. (pp. xxi–xxii)

This definition clearly places the disorder *inside the person,* and not in social interactions. It excludes individual reactions to painful life events (e.g., bereavement) unless these events are accompanied by an inordinate degree of distress. Furthermore, it discounts unhappiness, which often prompts people to seek psychotherapy. Although the definition draws a distinction between mental disorders and moral deviance, the *DSM-IV* does not require that mental illnesses represent organic disorders. Behavioral, affective, and cognitive evidence of distress and impairment in psychosocial functioning are usually assessed through a clinical interview, not biological tests. Clinicians make judgments about whether certain behaviors, emotions, and beliefs are to be viewed as symptoms of mental disorders. Inevitably these judgments are made by referring to a vague normative model. As Wakefield (1992) asserts, the concept of mental illness lies "on the boundary between biological facts and social values" (p. 373).

Another term used to describe mental illness is *psychopathology.* This medical term refers to the scientific study of diseases of the mind and refers to their etiology (origin or cause), their nature, and the course the diseases take. This term is used in the literature interchangeably with mental disorder, mental disease, mental illness, and abnormality. This book considers knowledge of psychopathology, mental illness, and mental disorders to be linked with the values of Western culture and its naming practices. Because practitioners need to work within the social constructions of the culture in which they live, the term *mental disorder* and the definition in the *DSM-IV* will be accepted as cultural givens. With this in mind, the following criteria are indicators of mental disorders:

1. *Subjective distress.* The individual must report emotional pain, somatic distress, discomfort, lack of control, or volitions that contradict personal values.
2. *Impaired psychosocial functioning.* The individual is unable to take care of personal needs (bathing, dressing, grooming, eating) or cannot fulfill ordinary social functions (working, going to school, household management, caring for dependents, reciprocating in interpersonal relationships), or is destructive or self-destructive. Other

expressions of impaired psychosocial functioning include indirect strategies of problem solving (e.g., time-consuming rituals, approach-avoidance patterns, and passive-
aggressive behavior).

3. *Bizarre behavior.* The individual initiates actions that have no instrumental purpose
   and that substantially deviate from behavior that is functional within the individual's
   subculture (e.g., smearing the walls with feces in mainstream U.S. society).

4. *Sensory dysfunctioning.* The individual's sensory mechanisms are deficient; that is,
   the senses of vision, hearing, taste, touch, or smell do not correspond with stimuli
   emanating from the shared social environment.

5. *Disturbed thinking.* The individual has cognitions that are false, unrealistic, intrusive, or incongruent with those that are shared by the individual's subculture.

Individuals with severe mental illness are likely to meet all of these criteria. Others will
meet only a few. Clients who present concerns, symptoms, or behaviors that involve none
of these or only the first criterion probably have problems in living or display socially deviant behavior.

The polemics over what normality, mental health, and mental illness are, which have
been described, underscore how difficult it is to define and classify human experiences.
Preferences for particular terms over others seem to be rooted in differences in theoretical
orientation, which in turn are linked to ideology and power. The following discussion on
postmodernism will shed further light on definitional issues.

Postmodernism

Postmodernism is an intellectual movement that has swept across disciplines and fields of
professional practice over the last couple of decades. It is associated with the rapid changes
that have emerged—particularly mass communication, information systems, globalization,
and technology—which paradoxically have brought people closer together and farther
apart. Postmodernism challenges basic assumptions about the nature of knowledge and
thought that have characterized modern Western societies since the Enlightenment. The
concerns that are associated with this movement undermine the belief that categories are
fixed, reality is real, and knowledge is certain. Postmodernism questions the modernist
project of arriving at universal, explanatory systems of thought (including scientific ones).
Because the field of mental health is predicated on the ideas that categories of illness are
determinate, misperception of reality is symptomatic of mental illness, and mental disorders can be understood scientifically, postmodernism raises serious questions about the validity of the entire realm of mental health.

Post*modern* thought is a development of post*structuralist* thought, the latter of
which is associated with European figures such as Derrida (1978) and Foucault (1965).
Poststructualists are critical of structuralists such as Freud and Marx, who had developed
grand theories describing universal, lawful, underlying structures. Some of the philosophers associated with postmodernism are Baudrillard (1988), Lyotard (1984), and Rorty

(1979). The boundaries between poststructuralism and postmodernism are ambiguous; clearly they overlap.

Poststructuralist/postmodern thought begins with a critique of language. At question is the relationship between the sign (a written or spoken symbol, such as a word) and the signified (what the sign means). Challenging the idea that language *reflects* a pregiven true reality, poststructuralism asserts that language *constitutes* a reality that is historically and socially contingent and, thus, fluid (Weedon, 1987). Another way of describing the reality constituted in language is that it is "socially constructed" (Berger & Luckmann, 1966). As a consequence of the mutability of what is immediately perceived as real, meanings become *multiple,* unstable, and subject to diverse interpretations.

Poststructuralists are critical of *logocentrism,* the idea that there is a logical, rational, unified order that is neutral and objective (Grosz, 1989). The logocentrism, which characterizes Western, post-Enlightenment thought, is problematic because it ignores the complexity that is embedded in language (Derrida, 1976). For one, logocentrism assumes that categories that constitute knowledge are essential; that is, they are inherent. Derrida (1978) asserts that the meanings of these categories change in relation to context. Logocentrism is also problematic in its characteristic dependence on *binary categories,* terms that are defined in relation to their polar opposites. Derrida notes whenever there are binaries, there is an implicit hierarchy, with one term valued over the other (e.g., male over female, white over black). Viewing categories as binary opposites is misleading because the two terms are not entirely different or opposite. To capture the idea that the meanings of the binary terms may overlap and there may be meanings associated with one term that are not captured by the other, Derrida used the term *différence* (Grosz, 1989). Accordingly, one can have a situation of *both/and* where both meanings of terms that are commonly viewed as opposites are applicable.

Although binary terms have multiple meanings, diverse interpretations are not immediately accessible. Language is a site in which political interests struggle for dominance (Weedon, 1987). Foucault's (1975, 1980) writings highlight the ways in which those who have power are able to establish their meanings as *the* meanings and impose these on others. Postmodernists use the terms *master narratives* and *dominant discourses* to describe ideas that overshadow other coexisting narratives in the public domain. Mental illness, patriarchy, and progress are examples of master narratives.

Even though knowledge of master narratives allows one to understand the values of dominant sectors of society, it obscures the narratives of disenfranchised or "subjugated" populations, such as persons with severe mental illness or those who are poor, members of ethnic minority groups, or women. Postmodernists and poststructuralists have developed a method called *deconstruction* to uncover meanings that are not immediately apparent because they are those of persons who lack the power to directly voice their concerns. This is done by situating the text (a body of written or spoken language) in the political, social, and historical contexts in which it occurs; identifying biases and moving them to the periphery of the text; and treating marginal perspectives as if they are central. In this way subjugated voices (i.e., those of oppressed groups) can be heard. "The term 'deconstruction' has also come to mean more generally any exposure of a concept as ideological or culturally constructed rather than natural or a simple reflection of reality" (Alcoff, 1997,

p. 353 n. 24). Here our concern is with ideology, subjugated voices, and concealed power relations.

As is evident in deconstruction, postmodernism is attentive to the contexts in which knowledge is constructed and communicated. Clinicians need to be knowledgeable about local contexts—the norms of their particular agency and the managed care entities with which they interact, the functions of different professions working there, and the situations of each client with whom they work. In addition, they need to understand other contexts such as mental health policies and concepts that are used in the behavioral health field. One of the goals of this book is to communicate specialized knowledge that will help social workers interpret what is happening in their agencies and with clients who come for help.

There are many implications of postmodernism for the mental health field, some of which will be discussed here. Clearly the categories of mental disorders that are described so carefully in the *DSM-IV* (APA, 1994) are problematic. There is no "essential" schizophrenia or any other name used to designate that a person's mind is out of order. Schizophrenia, like other categories, is heterogeneous and diverse. Every person with schizophrenia is unique. Diagnoses are prototypes, not essences, with diversity among them that needs to be acknowledged. And, of course, these are categories of disorders, not people.

Furthermore, the meanings of the binary terms within the field of mental health need to be unpacked. For example, mental health and mental illness, often construed as opposites, may overlap. As suggested earlier, one may have a particular mental disorder, yet function well in particular areas of life (e.g., self-sufficiency skills, work, family relationships, friendships). In other realms, *both/and* also applies. With respect to the previous discussion of community mental health and behavioral health paradigms, at this historical moment, we have two simultaneous, overlapping systems in place—behavioral health *and* community mental health. Some individuals have behavioral health insurance that is "managed"; others have insurance coverage that is private and more covertly controlled. Some are beneficiaries of Medicare or recipients of Medicaid whose health care may or may not be managed whereas still others have no insurance. As indicated, the ideologies of community mental health and behavioral health *both* converge *and* diverge. Some mental health centers that exist today may be ideologically close to those established in the 1970s whereas other centers may be more managed. Furthermore, the ways in which funding streams are blended nowadays indicate that the public and private sectors overlap.

In this text, a number of *both/and's* are included. For one, even though this is an updated text, it does not assume that new knowledge is better than or replaces old knowledge unless this has been demonstrated. Thus, both old and new knowledge is included. Second, although the strengths perspective is a dominant narrative in social work, this book acknowledges that persons with mental health difficulties have strengths *and* vulnerabilities, both of which operate simultaneously. Third, qualitative and quantitative approaches to research and practice are viewed as valuable. Practice is an art *and* a science.

Another feature of this book that is consistent with postmodernism is the highlighting of client voices, whose constructions of meaning can become dominated by professionals. One way in which this is done is by incorporating quotations from the consumer literature in the chapters. To make these voices visible, they will be inserted in bold at the beginnings of chapters and within chapters. Some client quotations are contrasted with quotations of professionals that follow. Along the same lines, indigenous methods of healing—whether they are herbal, spiritual, communal, or ceremonial—will be discussed.

Finally, this book acknowledges uncertainty in the knowledge contained herein (cf. Pozatek, 1994). It recognizes that the world and its inhabitants exist in an unstable, evolving state in which assumptions are made and taken for granted about what is real, what is known, and what is meaningful. Thus, this book incorporates findings from medical and social science research with modernist assumptions. At the same time it recognizes that this knowledge does not apply to all people from all cultures in every context and is subject to change over time. In other words, the postmodernist perspective in this book encompasses modernism while being critical of universal tendencies within modernist scientific thinking. Furthermore, the knowledge presented herein is socially constructed from the author's and others' experiences. It represents a particular portrayal of social work in behavioral mental health that, it is hoped, will be useful to practitioners.

The Postmodern Practitioner

In keeping with the perspective of this book, a postmodern clinical social work practitioner is envisioned. Such a person will be knowledgeable about developments in the biological and social sciences, such as psychopharmacology and epidemiological research, but sensitive to contexts in which findings apply and do not apply. She or he will be familiar with best practices and research on practice effectiveness, while questioning whether these strategies will help a particular client. The postmodern practitioner will be particularly attuned to client voices, meanings, and ways in which clients heal themselves and whether his or her agency and community hear and respond to client perspectives. Such a practitioner will be familiar with the categories of disorders described in the *DSM-IV* yet understand that classifications are not essences. The postmodern practitioner will be able to manage managed care so that its benefits for clients can be realized to the fullest extent possible. Artist and scientist, the postmodern clinical social work practitioner constructs meaning to help clients construct what is meaningful to them.

To assist the development of a postmodern practitioner, the chapters in Part One establish the social, cultural, historical, legal, and theoretical contexts of practice. Where possible the text is deconstructed so that suppressed voices can be identified and heard. In Part Two, a postmodern approach is incorporated in discussions about intervention.

R E F E R E N C E S

Alcoff, L. (1997). Cultural feminism versus post-structuralism: the identity crisis in feminist theory. In L. Nicholson (Ed.), *The second wave: A reader in feminist theory* (pp. 330–355). New York: Routledge.

American Psychiatric Association. (1980). *Diagnostic and statistical manual of mental disorders (DSM-III)* (3rd ed.). Washington, DC: Author.

American Psychiatric Association. (1987). *Diagnostic and statistical manual of mental disorders (DSM-III-R)* (3rd ed., rev.). Washington, DC: Author.

American Psychiatric Association. (1994). *Diagnostic and statistical manual—Fourth edition (DSM-IV)*. Washington, DC: Author.

Bachrach, L. L. (1976). *Deinstitutionalization: An analytical review and sociological perspective* (DHEW

Publication No. ADM 76-351).Washington, DC: U.S. Government Printing Office.

Bachrach, L. L. (1986). The challenge of service planning for chronic mental patients. *Community Mental Health Journal, 22,* 170–174.

Bachrach, L. (1996). The state of the state mental hospital in 1996. *Psychiatric Services, 47*(10), 1071–1078.

Baudrillard, J. (1988). *Jean Baudrillard: Selected writings* (M. Poster, Ed.). Stanford, CA: Stanford University Press.

Bentley, K. J., & Walsh, J. (1996). *The social worker and psychotropic medication: Toward effective collaboration with mental health clients, families, and providers.* Pacific Grove, CA: Brooks/Cole.

Bentley, K. J., & Walsh, J. (1998). Advances in psychopharmacology and psychosocial aspects of medication management: A review for social workers. In J. B. W. Williams & K. Ell (Eds.), *Advances in mental health research: Implications for practice* (pp. 309–342). Washington, DC: NASW Press.

Berger, P. L., & Luckmann, T. (1966). *The social construction of reality: A treatise in the sociology of knowledge.* New York: Doubleday/Anchor.

Bloom, B. L. (1984). *Community mental health: A general introduction* (2nd ed.). Monterey, CA: Brooks/Cole.

Borus, J. F. (1988). Community psychiatry. In A. M. Nicholi (Ed.), *The new Harvard guide to psychiatry* (pp. 780–796). Cambridge, MA: Belknap Press of Harvard University Press.

Caplan, G. (1961). *An approach to community mental health.* New York: Grune & Stratton.

Caplan, G. (1964). *Principles of preventive psychiatry.* New York: Basic Books.

Caplan, R. B., in collaboration with Caplan, G. (1969). *Psychiatry and the community in nineteenth-century America.* New York: Basic Books.

Coles, R. (1970, November). A fashionable kind of slander. *The Atlantic,* 53–55.

Corcoran, K., & Vandiver, V. (1996). *Maneuvering the maze of managed care: Skills for mental health practitioners.* New York: The Free Press.

Derrida, J. (1976). *On grammatology* (G. C. Spivak, Trans.). Baltimore: Johns Hopkins University Press.

Derrida, J. (1978). *Writing and difference* (A. Bass, Trans.). Chicago: University of Chicago Press.

Edmunds, M., Frank, R., Hogan, M., McCarty, D., Robinson-Beale, R., & Weisner, C. (Eds.), (1997). *Managing managed care: Quality improvement in behavioral health* [Summary]. Washington, DC: National Academy Press.

Esterson, A. (1970). *The leaves of spring.* Middlesex, UK: Penguin Books.

Foucault, M. (1965). *Madness and civilization.* New York: Vintage Books.

Foucault, M. (1975). *Discipline and punish: The birth of the prison.* New York: Vintage Books.

Foucault, M. (1980). *Power/knowledge: Selected interviews and other writings 1972–1977* (C. Gordon, Ed.; C. Gordon, L. Marshall, J. Mepham, & K. Soper, Trans.). New York: Pantheon Books.

Frankl, V. E. (1984). *Man's search for meaning* (rev. & updated). New York: Washington Square Press.

Freedman, D. X. (1984). Psychiatric epidemiology counts. *Archives of General Psychiatry, 41,* 931–933.

Gibelman, M., & Schervish, P. H. (1997). *Who we are: A second look.* Washington, DC: National Association of Social Workers.

Grosz, R. (1989). *Sexual subversions.* Sydney, Australia: Allen & Unwin.

Health Insurance Association of America. (1996). *Sourcebook of health insurance data, 1995.* Washington, DC: Author.

Hoge, M. A., Davidson, L., Griffith, E. E. H., Sledge, W. H., & Howenstine, R. A. (1994). Defining managed care in public-sector psychiatry. *Hospital and Community Psychiatry, 45* (11), 1085–1089.

Hollingshead, A. B., & Redlich, F. L. (1958). *Social class and mental illness.* New York: Wiley.

Jackson, D. (1977). The myth of normality. In P. Watzlawick & J. H. Weakland (Eds.), *The interactional view* (pp. 157–163). New York: Norton.

Jackson, V. H. (Ed.). (1995). *Managed care resource guide for social workers in agency settings.* Washington, DC: National Association of Social Workers.

Jahoda, M. (1958). *Current concepts of positive mental health.* New York: Basic Books.

Johnson, H. C. (1996). Violence and biology. *Families in Society, 77*(1), 3–18.

Johnson, H. C., Atkins, S. P., Battle, S. F., Hernandez-Arata, L., Hesselbrock, M., Libassi, M. F., & Parish, M. S. (1990). Strengthening the "bio" in the biopsychosocial paradigm. *Journal of Social Work Education, 26*(2), 109–123.

Kaplan, H. I., & Sadock, B. J. (1998). *Synopsis of psychiatry: Behavioral sciences/Clinical psychiatry,* 8th ed. Baltimore, MD: Williams & Wilkins.

Kellam, S. G. (1987). Families and mental illness: Current interpersonal and biological approaches (Part 1). *Psychiatry, 50,* 303–307.

Kessler, R. C., Abelson, J. M., & Zhao, S. (1998). The epidemiology of mental disorders. In J. B. W. Williams & K. Ell (Eds.), *Advances in mental health research: Implications for practice* (pp. 3–24). Washington, DC: NASW Press.

Kessler, R. C., McGonagle, K. A., Zhao, S., Nelson, C. B., Hughes, M., Eshleman, S., Wittchen, H-U., & Kendler, K. S. (1994). Lifetime and 12-month prevalence of DSM-III-R psychiatric disorders in the United

States: Results from the National Comorbidity Survey. *Archives of General Psychiatry, 51,* 8–19.

Langsley, D. G. (1985a). Community psychiatry. In H. I. Kaplan & B. J. Sadock (Eds.), *Comprehensive textbook of psychiatry/IV* (4th ed., pp. 1878–1884). Baltimore, MD: Williams & Wilkins.

Langsley, D. G. (1985b). Prevention in psychiatry: Primary, secondary, and tertiary. In H. I. Kaplan & B. J. Sadock (Eds.), *Comprehensive textbook of psychiatry/IV* (4th ed., pp. 1885–1888). Baltimore, MD: Williams & Wilkins.

Leighton, D. C., Harding, J. S., Macklin, D. B., et al. (1963). *The character of danger: Stirling County study no. 3.* New York: Basic Books.

Lennon, T. M. (1998). *Statistics on social work education in the United States: 1997.* Alexandria, VA: Council on Social Work Education.

Lyotard, J.-F. (1984). *The post-modern condition: A report on knowledge.* Minneapolis, MN: University of Minnesota Press.

Maslow, A. H. (1968). *Toward a psychology of being.* New York: Van Nostrand Reinhold.

McGuirk, F. D., Keller, A. B., & Croze, C. (1995). *Blueprints for managed care: Mental healthcare concepts and structure.* U.S. Department of Health and Human Services: SAMHSA.

Mechanic, D. (1989). *Mental health and social policy* (3rd ed.). Englewood Cliffs, NJ: Prentice-Hall.

Mechanic, D. (1989). Toward the year 2000 in U.S. mental health policymaking and administration. In D. A. Rochefort (Ed.), *Handbook on mental health policy in the United States* (pp. 477–503). New York: Greenwood Press.

"Mental health center violations alleged." (1990, May). *NASW News, 35*(5), 16.

Offer, D., & Sabshin, M. (1966). *Normality: Theoretical and clinical concepts of mental health.* New York: Basic Books.

Poynter, W. L. (1998). *The textbook of behavioral managed care: From concept through management to treatment.* Bristol, PA: Brunner/Mazel.

Pozatek, E. (1994). The problem of certainty: Clinical social work in the postmodern era. *Social Work, 39*(4), 396–403.

Regier, D. A., Myers, J. K., Kramer, M., Robins, L. N., et al. (1984). The NIMH Epidemiologic Catchment Area Program: Historical context, major objectives, and study population characteristics. *Archives of General Psychiatry, 41,* 934–941.

Robins, L. N., Helzer, J. E., Croughan, J. L., & Ratcliff, K. S. (1981). National Institute of Mental Health Diagnostic Interview Schedule: Its history, characteristics and validity. *Archives of General Psychiatry, 38,* 381–389.

Rorty, R. (1979). *Philosophy and the mirror of nature.* Princeton, NJ: Princeton University Press.

Saleebey, D. (1992). Biology's challenge to social work: Embodying the person-in-environment perspective. *Social Work, 37*(2), 112–125.

Scheff, T. (1984). *Being mentally ill* (2nd ed.). New York: Aldine.

Schreter, C. et al. (1996). *Managed mental health care: What to look for, what to ask.* The Center for Mental Health Services.

Schreter, R. K., Sharfstein, S. S., & Schreter, C. A. (1997). Managing care, not dollars. In R. K. Schreter, S. S. Scharfstein, & C. A. Schreter, (Eds.), *Managing care, not dollars: The continuum of mental health services.* Washington, DC: American Psychiatric Press, Inc.

Scott, W. A. (1970). Research definitions of mental health. In H. Wechsler, L. Solomon, & B. M. Kramer (Eds.), *Social psychology and mental health* (pp. 13–27). New York: Holt, Rinehart and Winston.

Srole, L., & Fischer, A. K. (1986). The midtown Manhattan longitudinal study: Aging, generations, and genders. In M. M. Weissman, J. K. Myers, & C. E. Ross (Eds.), *Community surveys of psychiatric disorders* (pp. 77–107). New Brunswick, NJ: Rutgers University Press.

Srole, L., Langer, T. S., Michael, S. T., Kirkpatrick, P., & Rennie, T. A. C. (1962). *Mental health in the metropolis: The midtown Manhattan study.* New York: McGraw-Hill.

Szasz, T. S. (1960). The myth of mental illness. *The American Psychologist, 15,* 113–118.

Szasz, T. S. (1961). *The myth of mental illness.* New York: Delta.

U.S. Department of Commerce News (1999, October 4). Increase of 1 million uninsured people, Census Bureau says. Census Bureau, Health Insurance Coverage: 1998. http://census.gov/Press-Release/www/1999/cb99-189.html.

Wakefield, J. C. (1992). The concept of mental disorder: On the boundary between biological facts and social values. *American Psychologist, 47*(3), 373–388.

Weedon, C. (1987). *Feminist practice and poststructuralist theory.* Oxford, UK: Basil Blackwell Ltd.

Weissman, M. M., Myers, J. K., & Ross, C. E. (1986). Community studies in psychiatric epidemiology: An introduction. In M. M. Weissman, J. K. Myers, & C. E. Ross (Eds.), *Community surveys of psychiatric disorders* (pp. 1–19). New Brunswick, NJ: Rutgers University Press.

Witkin, W. J., Atay, J. E., Manderscheid, R. W., DeLozier, J., Male, A., & Gillespie, R. (1998). Highlights of organized mental health services in 1994 and major national and state trends. In R. W. Manderscheid, &

M. J. Henderson (Eds.), *Mental health, United States, 1998,* Center for Mental Health Services, DHHS Pub. No. (SMA) 99-3285 (pp. 168–204). Washington, DC: Superintendent of Documents, U.S. Government Printing Office.

Wolfensberger, W., Nirje, B., Olshansky, S., Perske, R., & Roos, P. (1972). *The principle of normalization in human services.* Toronto, Ont.: National Institute on Mental Retardation.

World Health Organization. (1948). Constitution and basic documents. Geneva, Switzerland: Author.

World Health Organization. (1990). *Composite International Diagnostic Interview (CIDI), Version 1.0.* Geneva, Switzerland: Author.

2

Historical Context

We must try to return, in history, to that zero point in the course of madness at which madness is an undifferentiated experience, a not yet divided experience of division itself.

—Foucault, *Madness and Civilization: A History of Insanity in the Age of Reason,* 1965

There must be something the matter with him
because he would not be acting as he does
unless there was
therefore he is acting as he is
because there is something the matter with him

—Laing, *Knots,* 1970

Mental illness is a social construction that locates deviant behavior in the individual. It is difficult to locate a "zero point" in history prior to a social explanation that "something is the matter with" someone. Although the Bible and the Greek philosophers described the same phenomenon, contemporary understanding is historically situated in the modern era in which scientific medicine is the dominant discourse. Prior constructions of what is now viewed as mental illness included being possessed by the devil, witchcraft, and divine punishment. In the past, persons who are today regarded as "having" a mental illness lived with their families, among vagrants, in institutions, and in communities such as Geel, Belgium, a forerunner of community mental health (Roosens, 1979).

Given that mental illness is the operative social construction within which social workers practice in behavioral health contexts, it is beneficial to understand the history of mental health treatment and social workers' part in that history. This chapter describes the history of mental health in the United States and how social work practice evolved in relation to changing sociopolitical contexts. That history is constituted by individuals, celebrated and unknown. In keeping with a postmodern perspective that moves voices at the margins to the center (hooks, 1984), the voices of consumers will be represented in bold.

Mental health treatment in the United States was influenced by concepts and intervention strategies that had evolved in Europe, including the idea handed down by the Greeks that mental illness was the consequence of an imbalance of the "humors" (body fluids) and that in order to restore harmony, procedures such as bloodletting, enemas, and emetics were required (Katz, 1985). In response to the widespread use of these strategies, as well as restraints such as chains and straitjackets, moral treatment took hold in France, England, and Italy during the Enlightenment. Under moral treatment, restraints were replaced with kindness, meaningful activity, and the promotion of patients' physical, emotional, and spiritual well-being (Dain, 1964).

Mental health practice in the United States incorporated ideas of moral treatment as well as practices from earlier times. These ideas were adapted to conditions in this country as it became transformed from an agrarian to an industrial nation.

Colonial Period

During the American colonial period, persons with serious mental difficulties were handled in a number of ways (Leiby, 1978). One alternative was to place them in private madhouses run by physicians in their homes. Because of the cost, these arrangements were open only to those whose relatives could pay. Another solution was for families to keep the individual at home. Home care, however, often meant that the relative was confined in an attic or cellar, restrained behind bars, or put in chains. A third alternative remained for those who did not have a family that was willing to be responsible. These individuals fell under the aegis of the poor laws and their treatment depended on circumstances. Some were farmed out to families who gave them various degrees of freedom. Others lived in the woods. Vagrants and individuals who were violent were likely to be put in jail (Leiby, 1978).

There were, however, a few early institutions. The Quaker-run Pennsylvania Hospital was the first to accept the mentally ill (1756). Another in Williamsburg, Virginia (founded 1773) was the first public institution for this population.

The Beginnings of Psychiatry in the United States

The U.S. physician credited with fathering psychiatry in the United States was *Benjamin Rush* (1745–1813), a signer of the Declaration of Independence. Considered a proponent of moral treatment, Rush believed that although insanity was physiological, intense intellectual activity or emotional shock ("moral" influences) could damage the brain (Caplan, 1969). The brain was considered "malleable" and, thus, experiences that promote health can alter the brain:

> The essence of moral treatment was the belief that, because of this great malleability of the brain surface, because of its susceptibility to environmental stimuli, pathological conditions could be erased or modified by corrective experience. Therefore, insanity, whether the result of direct or indirect injury or disease, or of overwrought emotions or strained intellectual faculties, would be cured in almost every case. (Caplan, 1969, p. 9)

This interpretation of moral treatment recognized the impact of the environment on psychological experiences.

Rush's ideas and practices contained many contradictions. A medical practitioner who believed that mental diseases were physiological, he did not adequately explain the linkage between environmental and organic factors (Dain, 1964). On the one hand, he believed in kindness and humane care. On the other, he used techniques such as bleeding, purges, restraining devices, and shock (Caplan, 1969). Rush's political ideas and practices contained similar contradictions. A slave owner, he was active in the abolition movement. Although he thought women should have educational opportunities, he believed that they should be subordinate (Alexander, 1986).

Nineteenth Century

Moral Treatment

During the early part of the nineteenth century, a number of other influential U.S. physicians of the mind (called *alienists* at that time) embraced moral treatment. Eschewing many of the physical methods inherited from medieval times and used by Rush, these physicians created in both private and public hospitals an environment that was intimate, caring, and beneficent. The Quaker model of moral treatment was adopted by four of the eight U.S. asylums built prior to 1824 (Dain, 1964).

Medical superintendents, who lived on the hospital grounds and shared meals and activities with residents, administered moral treatment personally. They encouraged patients to work, play, read, and, if interested, attend religious services. Hospitals that were guided by a philosophy of moral treatment

> …resembled what is now advocated by community psychiatry. Environmental factors in the causation of mental disorder were recognized and were counter-acted by manipulation of the physical and social milieu of the asylum. This was done in large measure by mobilizing staff and patients into small groups to support and control the individual strictly but without undue coercion.… There were attempts to involve other care-giving groups, such as teachers and clergymen, in the treatment of the insane. And, in spite of geographic isolation, violent dislocation of the patient from the community was avoided because the undesirability of long-term institutionalization was recognized and because the entire therapeutic program was designed to inculcate normative cultural values and modalities so that the individual could return to society better able to cope with its demands. (Caplan, 1969, pp. 37–38)

Moreover, physicians established relationships with nearby communities by educating the public about insanity, inviting the community residents to events at the hospital, and sending patients to live or work in these communities (Caplan, 1969). Many of the ideas and practices of the community mental health movement have roots in moral treatment as it was interpreted in the nineteenth-century United States (Caplan, 1969).

Although some persons with psychiatric problems were treated in benign hospitals that provided moral treatment, there were few such facilities and many were private. Other institutions that took in deviant populations did not distinguish between the mentally ill and other populations, such as the mentally retarded, epileptics, criminals, and the homeless. Consequently, many of the poor mentally disabled were confined in almshouses and prisons (Rothman, 1971).

It was in this context that *Dorothea Lynde Dix* (1802–1887) began her campaign. Dix was a schoolteacher who retired when she was in her thirties, following an emotional and physical collapse (Kreisler & Lieberman, 1986; Marshall, 1937). After returning home from a trip to Europe, where she had gone to recover her strength, she was uncertain about what to do with her life. In 1841 she was asked to teach a Sunday school class in a jail in East Cambridge, Massachusetts. Upon assuming this volunteer work, she found poor women who seemed to be suffering from mental disorders imprisoned together with criminals.

> She was shocked to see them among hardened criminals, and entirely devoid of medical and moral treatment. Upon inquiry she learned that their only crime against society was their affliction. She inspected their quarters and to her horror found them bare, cold, and unheated. She asked the jailer why there was no stove or other heat in the part of the jail reserved for the insane, and why nothing was done to make their living as comfortable as that furnished for persons who had committed actual crimes against society. The jailer tried to dismiss the matter by saying that "lunatics" did not feel the cold as others, and that a fire would be very unsafe. (Marshall, 1937, p. 61)

Subsequently, Dix visited other prisons, almshouses, and other places in which persons with mental disabilities were confined in Massachusetts and reported her findings of widespread inhumane care and neglect in a "memorial" to the state legislature. For thirty years Dix traveled from state to state, investigating conditions of the poor mentally ill and advocating for more humane care in public institutions. She traveled 60,000 miles by train, stagecoach, and riverboat, paying personal visits to over 9,000 individuals (Marshall, 1937). Dix is credited with the expansion or creation of thirty-two mental hospitals (Katz, 1985). In contrast with late twentieth-century mental health reformers, however, Dix worked for the creation of more or expanded state hospitals rather than for their reduction or elimination.

One of Dix's goals was that the federal government assume some responsibility for the care of the mentally ill. As a result of vigorous lobbying activities, Dix got Congress to introduce a bill that would have had the federal government appropriate land to the states for the benefit of the indigent mentally ill. In 1854 the bill was passed by both houses of Congress but was vetoed by President Franklin Pierce, who said that the federal government would be overstepping its powers if it were to provide for the poor in the states. An attempt to override the veto failed (Marshall, 1937). Nevertheless, Dix served as a model for future social workers to emulate.

Decline of Moral Treatment

Despite the work of Dix, the practice of moral treatment declined. Success stories told by early advocates of moral treatment were not borne out by later experience (Caplan, 1969). In the latter half of the nineteenth century, the population of public asylums grew and changed in complexion. It now included large numbers of alcoholics, violent persons, and immigrants, who reportedly did not adapt to the benign regime of moral treatment. With overcrowded conditions and a population that was difficult to manage, methods of restraint from previous eras were resurrected, and programs that primarily provided custodial care became the norm (Caplan, 1969; Rothman, 1971). Consequently, the institutions became warehouses for poor social rejects.

During this period, the ideas of Darwin and the organic viewpoint in medicine dominated thinking. The mentally ill were considered genetically defective inferior beings, who were unfit for survival. In view of their alleged deficiencies, treatment was deemed irrelevant (Williams, Bellis, & Wellington, 1980). Although some medication was dispensed, medical attention was largely given to conducting pathological research on the brains of deceased patients (Caplan, 1969).

Still some community treatment took place during the nineteenth century. Early in the century the Eastern Lunatic Asylum in Williamsburg, Virginia, sent some patients to live with families and others to work (Caplan, 1969). According to the *Social Work Year Book 1935,* family care was in use in the state of Massachusetts as early as 1885 (Pollock, 1935). The same year an outpatient mental hygiene clinic was established at the Pennsylvania Hospital, and two years later a similar clinic opened at the Boston Dispensary (French, 1940).

Reform Begins Again

During the last few decades of the nineteenth century, a movement for reform developed. One issue that provoked interest was the false commitment of individuals to mental asylums. Some of the victims of this practice were women, the most well known being *Elizabeth (E. P. W.) Packard* (1816–1897). Packard's husband was able to commit her to the state mental hospital in Jacksonville, Illinois, against her will because the law at that time did not protect the rights of married women. Packard (1865/1974) argued that she was falsely imprisoned because her religious values differed from those of her husband, a Calvinist minister:

> **This impious, Calvinistic attempt to *chain my thoughts,* by calling me "insane," for opinion's sake, and imprisoning me on this account, is a *crime* against the constitution of this free government and also a crime against civilization and human progress.** (p. 23)

After Packard succeeded in suing her husband and the superintendent of the hospital in which she had been confined, she led a national movement to promote legislation protecting individuals from commitment without a jury trial and to assure that those who are hospitalized receive humane treatment. Some states responded by authorizing committees of visitors who could investigate conditions in mental hospitals. Others gave patients the right to send uncensored letters outside the hospital (Grob, 1983; Wrench, 1985).

Another manifestation of reform was the establishment of the National Association for the Protection of the Insane and the Prevention of Insanity, which advocated better treatment and protection of the rights of patients in public asylums. A forerunner of the mental hygiene movement that was to follow early in the twentieth century, this organization was founded simultaneously with the annual meeting of the National Conference of Charities and Corrections that convened in Cleveland in 1880 and was initiated largely by social workers, psychiatrists, neurologists, and lay reformers. Unfortunately this organization died after only four years of existence (Deutsch, 1949; Grob, 1983).

Another organization that was critical of the prevailing practices in mental institutions (asylums) was the New York Society of Neurology. This group had concerns about the medical qualifications of physicians as well as the supervision, treatment, and rights of patients. Nevertheless, neither the lay reformers nor the members of the National Conference of Charities and Corrections or the Society of Neurology were able to overcome the power of the Association of Medical Superintendents of American Institutions of the Insane, members of which ran the principal psychiatric establishments and that functioned as a self-contained guild that did not listen to criticism from outside its ranks (Caplan, 1969). Its control over psychiatric institutions continued until it was challenged by stronger forces in the twentieth century.

The Reform Movement in the Early Years of the Twentieth Century

The years between the turn of the century and 1920 encompass what is known as the Progressive Era in U.S. history. This was a period of reaction to the consequences of unregulated free enterprise and industrialism—poverty, arduous working conditions, and politics corrupted by business interests. During this era of reform, printed media publicized the evils of child labor, sweatshops, prisons, and mental hospitals. This stimulated a reconsideration of the responsibility of the federal government to the people and of people to each other.

During the Progressive Era, environmental and psychological perspectives on the cause and nature of mental illness were dominant (Rothman, 1979). The social sciences looked at the impact of social class and economic conditions on individual well-being. The social work scholars Sophonisba Breckinridge and Edith Abbott (1912) incorporated a social environmental perspective in their influential book, *The Delinquent Child and the Home.* Meanwhile new psychological theories were introduced. Pioneer social workers and reformers whose thinking was consonant with the emerging social work profession assimilated these ideas.

Mental Hygiene Movement

An individual who, like Elizabeth Packard, became a social reformer following his institutionalization was *Clifford W. Beers* (1876–1943), a graduate of Yale University. Following three years of confinement in public and private mental asylums, Beers recovered and published *A Mind That Found Itself,* an autobiographical account of his experiences. Beers (1907/1923) described his suicide attempt, delusions, depression, and mania in vivid detail and reported the abusive and punitive treatment to which he had been subjected when he was hospitalized:

> **After fifteen interminable hours the strait-jacket was removed. Whereas just prior to its putting on I had been in vigorous enough condition to offer stout resistance when wantonly assaulted, now, on coming out of it, I was helpless. When my arms were re-**

leased from their constricted position, the pain was intense. Every joint had been racked. I had no control over the fingers of either hand, and could not have dressed myself had I been promised my freedom for doing so. (p. 133)

Beers's book was praised by leading figures in psychology and psychiatry of that time and was widely read. The same year that the book came out, Beers founded the Connecticut Society of Mental Hygiene and in 1909 he started the National Committee for Mental Hygiene, which later became the National Mental Health Association. Thus began the mental hygiene movement, which "has generally been seen as a turning point in psychiatric history" (Caplan, 1969, p. 179).

The mental hygiene movement, in which lay citizens and professionals participated, laid the groundwork for the later community mental health movement. Although Beers's original goal was the reform of conditions in psychiatric institutions, prevention became the mental hygiene movement's primary mission. The National Committee on Mental Hygiene collected data, studied legislation, conducted surveys of institutions, encouraged research and publications, and educated the public (Bassett, 1933). These are the kinds of activities social work planners perform.

One of the early supporters of the mental hygiene movement was the neurologist and psychiatrist, *Adolf Meyer* (1866–1950). An immigrant from Switzerland, Meyer held positions in several state hospitals before becoming director of the Phipps Psychiatric Clinic at Johns Hopkins University in Baltimore, Maryland, in 1909. Meyer's conception of mental health was holistic, encompassing the mind, the body, and the environment. He viewed individuals as social beings whose life situations influence their psychological reactions. Accordingly, Meyer required that his staff of physicians collect data on the patient's life history, family, economic circumstances, and neighborhood—a process that required visits to the patient's home, work, and community (Deutsch, 1949). Meyer envisioned the development of a comprehensive mental hygiene system in the community with psychiatric centers that are linked to state hospitals (Lubove, 1965). His ideas are compatible with the person-environment perspective in social work as well as the integrated systems perspective of the community mental health movement. Not surprisingly, his ideas were attractive to pioneer mental health social workers.

Early Social Workers in Mental Health

Julia Lathrop was a social work reformer who worked with Dr. Meyer when both were employed at the state hospital in Kankakee, Illinois. A resident of the settlement house Hull House in its early years, she was a strong advocate for the mentally ill (Costin, 1986). Upon reading the proof of Beers's *A Mind That Found Itself,* Lathrop wrote the following statement of endorsement of the author's proposed national organization:

> I have felt for some time that a national society for the study of insanity and its treatment, from the social as well as the merely medical standpoint, should be formed. I am glad to follow in the line you have indicated and to have my name appear as one of the honorary trustees. I have talked with Miss Addams and she has agreed to the use of her name and will so inform you soon by letter. (Beers, 1907/1923, p. 271)

Lathrop became a founder of the National Committee for Mental Hygiene. She later served as chief of the United States Children's Bureau.

During the first decade of the twentieth century, several social workers held positions in hospitals for the psychiatrically impaired. Adolf Meyer's wife, *Mary Potter Brooks Meyer,* appears to have been the first such worker. A volunteer recruited by her husband, she visited psychiatric patients in the wards of Manhattan State Hospital and in their homes (Deutsch, 1949; Lubove, 1965). Mary Meyer assumed this responsibility in 1904, after a need for special personnel who would make linkages with the community was recognized (Deutsch, 1949).

Elsewhere other social workers were employed in similar capacities. *Edith N. Burleigh,* who began working in the Neurological Clinic of Massachusetts General Hospital in 1905, was responsible for conducting social investigations and treatment (Southard & Jarrett, 1922). In 1906 a social worker was assigned to the psychiatric wards of Bellevue Hospital in New York City (Southard & Jarrett, 1922). The same year, the New York State Charities Aid Association hired *E. H. Horton,* a trained social worker, as an aftercare agent, who helped patients find housing, employment, and other resources in the community. Her employment was a significant moment for the aftercare movement that had been promoting assistance to discharged psychiatric patients since the 1890s (Deutsch, 1949). In 1911 Charities Aid convinced the State of New York to have Manhattan State Hospital hire an aftercare worker. Within a few years, other states (Massachusetts, Illinois, Pennsylvania, New Jersey) appointed social workers in inpatient psychiatric facilities.

The social worker who, together with Dr. E. E. Southard, coined the term *psychiatric social work* and pioneered the field's development was *Mary C. Jarrett.* Jarrett was a caseworker who in 1913 became chief of social service of the Boston Psychopathic Hospital, of which Southard was medical director. This formal psychiatric social work department was designed to be an integral part of the hospital. Southard and Jarrett described the social work function in their classic book, *The Kingdom of Evils* (1922). They stated therein that the social worker's primary responsibility was social investigation—gathering facts regarding the patient's medical and social history from the patient and others in the community—a function that was viewed as extremely helpful to the diagnostic process in certain cases. Another important social work responsibility was individual casework, through which patients and families were helped "to secure the largest measure of social well being possible" (Southard & Jarrett, 1922, p. 526). Social workers also mediated relationships among doctors, social workers outside the hospital, patients, families, and friends. The social service department assumed responsibility for research and the training of social work students. Southard and Jarrett's description of the functions of the psychiatric social worker and the social work department provided a model for others to follow.

World War I and Its Aftermath

World War I created conditions that promoted the development of social work practice in mental health. During the war, the American Red Cross organized a Home Service Bureau that looked after the families of soldiers and sailors. Trained Charity Organization Society workers, working for this bureau and providing psychosocial services to military families, departed from their earlier focus on the poor; similarly, middle-class families who did not have previous exposure to social workers became recipients of a new kind of service (Briar & Miller, 1971; Robinson, 1930).

Meanwhile many soldiers were experiencing "shell shock" or "war neurosis." In response to the emergency needs of soldiers in army hospitals and those who would be returning, Boston Psychopathic Hospital, together with the National Committee for Mental Hygiene, and Smith College, developed the first training program for psychiatric social workers at Smith College in 1918. Mary Jarrett, who was responsible for the curriculum of this eight-week summer program, later became associate director of Smith College Training School for Social Work (Clark, 1966; Deutsch, 1949). Around the same time other schools of social work—The New York School, Chicago School of Civics and Philanthropy, and Pennsylvania School of Social and Health Work—began to include psychiatric studies in their educational programs (Fink, Anderson, & Conover, 1968).

Although interest in the psychological aspects of human functioning was growing, social work of the first two decades of the twentieth century adhered primarily to economic and sociological perspectives (Robinson, 1930). The settlement house movement drew attention to the effects of poverty and environmental deprivation on human lives while the charity organization movement tried to remedy poverty through discretionary giving of alms and friendly visiting.

A key social work publication of this period was Mary Richmond's *Social Diagnosis* (1917), which outlined a way in which to collect social data from a variety of sources and examine evidence before coming to conclusions. Richmond contributed to the development of a professional (i.e., scientific) approach to casework. Although she believed that she was interested in personality, she focused primarily on the person in relation to the environment (Clarke, 1947).

Emergence of the Psychological Perspective

The 1919 National Conference of Social Work was the scene of a turning point in the history of clinical social work in mental health. Mary Jarrett presented a paper, "The Psychiatric Thread Running Through All Social Case Work," in which she argued that the psychiatric thread "constitutes the entire *warp* of the fabric of case work" (Jarrett, 1919, p. 587). In this significant presentation, Jarrett noted that half the cases cited by Mary Richmond in *Social Diagnosis* were characterized by psychiatric problems. Jarrett urged that the mastery of psychiatric knowledge be required of all social workers, not only those who specialize in psychiatric social work. Other speakers at this historic conference (Jessie Taft, Dr. Southard, Dr. Glueck) echoed Jarrett's promotion of the psychiatric perspective. In keeping with the change in the climate of ideas, Richmond's later book, *What Is Social Case Work?*, emphasized the psychological dimension more than her previous work did (Deutsch, 1949).

The state of knowledge of the mind, meanwhile, was expanding. In 1909 Freud came to the United States to give a series of lectures on psychoanalysis at Clark University in Worcester, Massachusetts. Freud was interested in neuroses, which could be treated in the community through intensive analysis of the individual. Although his views about childhood sexuality were shocking to some, his ideas about the impact of early life experiences on adult personality and his "talking cure" were stimulating.

By the 1920s psychoanalysis acquired a following among intellectuals and medical professionals (Lubove, 1965). It appealed to social workers for a number of reasons. Despite Richmond's "scientific" casework, many clients were not responding to the approach she outlined. Psychoanalysis recognized that unconscious, irrational, intrapsychic dynamics comprise forces that resist treatment. "The client had to be enlisted in the struggle against his difficulties—caseworker and client were to be allies against the enemy within" (Briar & Miller, 1971, p. 13). Freudian theory provided both a framework for understanding the personality and a means to intervene. Social workers who underwent psychoanalysis themselves recognized the benefits of understanding oneself.

In the third decade of the twentieth century, however, psychoanalysis was only one of a number of theories that were under discussion. Behavioral psychology was developed in this country by J. D. Watson (1878–1958) and E. L. Thorndike (1874–1949). A U.S. psychiatrist, William Healy (1869–1963), was concerned with the psychological problems related to juvenile delinquency. Although he acknowledged the influences of genetics, the family, and environmental conditions, Healy was interested primarily in the psychology of the individual. His focus on "mental imagery" anticipates cognitive theory:

> ...whatever influences the individual towards offense must influence first the mind of the individual. It is only because the bad companion puts dynamically significant pictures into the mind, or because the physical activity becomes a sensation with representation in psychic life, or the environmental conditions produce low mental perceptions of one's duty toward others, that there is any inclination at all toward delinquency. (Healy, 1915/1924, p. 28)

With the impetus provided by the mental hygiene movement, interest in prevention abounded during the 1920s. Not surprisingly, children—especially "delinquents"—became the population of concern. The Commonwealth Fund supported the establishment of seven child guidance clinics throughout the country, ushering in the child guidance movement. The focus on children appears to have some relation to the emphasis in Freudian psychology on the formative role of the early years of life. Moreover, the writings of Healy, which were read by social workers, emphasized early intervention.

Robinson (1930) considered the 1920s a period in which the psychological perspective became important to social work. Two schools of thought—psychiatric interpretation and behavioristic psychology—were dominant. The former was based on the psychoanalytic ideas of Freud, the latter on social behaviorism. Psychiatric interpretation at that time looked at symptoms as responses to inner needs and encouraged a search for cause-effect relationships. In contrast, behavioristic psychology looked at external factors and emphasized "habit training, conditioning and reconditioning in treatment" and saw "the interview as a stimulus–response situation where the behavior of the interviewer sets the response of the interviewee" (Robinson, 1930, pp. 83–84). Robinson was interested in interactive patterns, rather than a history of social facts, as well as the relationship between worker and client (Robinson, 1930).

According to Grinker et al. (1961), the psychiatric knowledge that practicing psychiatric social workers of that time had was primarily of the diagnostic categories developed by the psychiatrist Emil Kraepelin. Still social workers employed in psychiatric settings began to think of themselves as specialists. In 1926 they formed the American Association of Psychiatric Social Workers (French, 1940).

The trend toward specialization within social work aroused some concern that the profession would become splintered. The Milford Conference of Social Work Professionals attempted to reconcile differences in its 1929 report, *Social Case Work: Generic and*

Specific (1929/1974). This document outlined common features of all fields of social work and unique features of special fields. The psychiatric social worker was to work in hospitals and agencies that gave special consideration to personality deviations. Psychiatric social casework included participation in diagnostic activity and individual therapy.

The extent to which social workers employed in psychiatric settings actually did participate in diagnosis and treatment in the 1920s is not entirely clear. Grinker et al. (1961) identified three functions of inpatient psychiatric social workers—history taking, providing information about resources to psychiatrists and patients, making visits to homes, schools, and employers, and taking patients on special trips. In these capacities, the social worker functioned as a "handmaiden" to the psychiatrist, carrying out medical recommendations "without developing an independent relationship with patients" (Grinker et al., 1961, p. 118). In the next two decades, however, changes in the economy and in the field of social work paved the way for more professional autonomy.

The 1930s and 1940s

During the 1930s, when the country was plagued by the Great Depression, the federal government sponsored an array of services to relieve mass poverty and unemployment. Meanwhile psychiatric hospitals were becoming overcrowded (Deutsch, 1949), challenging inpatient facilities to come up with alternative ways to take care of residents. "To relieve the situation and to obviate the necessity of building new institutions, it is proposed to place patients in family care to a greater extent than has previously been attempted in this country" (Pollock, 1935, p. 274). Social workers were to arrange and supervise these community placements.

The 1930s and 1940s saw the expansion of outpatient services in public agencies and private offices, with mental health teams consisting of a psychiatrist, a psychologist, and a social worker providing the professional personnel. The *Social Work Year Book of 1935* reported that child guidance clinics had long waiting lists (Stevenson, 1935).

Meanwhile a schism between two schools of thought within the social work profession was brewing. The Diagnostic School, based in New York, was influenced by Freud's psychoanalytic theory. This school emphasized internal unconscious processes, rooted in the past, which were diagnosed and treated through social casework. The Functional or Rankian School, represented by Virginia Robinson and Jessie Taft in Pennsylvania, espoused a theory that focused on time, conscious action, the agency's function, and client responsibility. The social work programs based in these cities (the forerunners of schools at Columbia and the University of Pennsylvania) offered different theoretical perspectives and modes of practice to their students.

By the late 1930s psychiatric social workers had established themselves in Red Cross and Veterans' Administration services, public and private hospitals, child guidance clinics, mental hygiene clinics (some of these "traveling clinics"), general hospital clinics, educational institutions, mental hygiene societies and state departments of mental hygiene, public health nursing organizations, family welfare agencies, and private practice (French, 1940). Functions varied by setting. Psychiatric social workers employed by hospitals gathered social histories, worked with inpatients and their families from the time of admission to the completion of parole (period of supervision following discharge), promoted adjustment and environmental changes, and participated in programs of community education. Outpatient social workers working with adults performed similar functions, whereas child guidance social workers were principally psychotherapists. Social workers employed by mental hygiene societies engaged in community organization, program planning, and data gathering.

World War II and Its Aftermath

Experiences related to World War II raised the consciousness of the nation about mental health problems and the need for expanded services. The high rate of rejection of prospective soldiers by the Selective Service system highlighted the prevalence of mental health problems among civilians. The psychiatric difficulties experienced by inducted soldiers who had passed the psychological screening examinations demonstrated that mental health difficulties could be experienced by healthy individuals who are exposed to stress (Klerman, 1986).

During the war, psychiatric social work services became part of the complex of military medical services—hospitals, mental health clinics, convalescent centers, and the like. The introduction of psychiatric services into the Veterans' Administration facilities stimulated the growth of mental health social work (Knee & Lamson, 1971).

In 1946 The National Mental Health Act was passed, ushering in a period of federal responsibility for mental health. This significant piece of legislation authorized federal funds for training mental health professionals (including social workers), research, and the development of community-based psychiatric services. Three years later the National Institute of Mental Health (NIMH) of the Public Health Service of the Department of Health, Education, and Welfare was established, and Dr. Robert Felix became its first director. The function of NIMH was to administer programs outlined in the 1946 act and to promote mental health education and prevention.

During the 1940s and 1950s social workers in mental health settings expanded their roles. The social data that they gathered on clients' families and home environments were used to help establish the diagnosis. Social workers had increased contacts with the community because of the placement of discharged patients on parole or convalescent care with their own or foster families (Fink, Anderson, & Conover, 1968). Furthermore, the shortage of psychiatrists at this time necessitated the use of social workers as psychotherapists (Nacman, 1977).

Meanwhile, the knowledge base of social work was changing. Following the publication of Anna Freud's *The Ego and the Mechanisms of Defense* in 1946 in the United States, psychoanalysis was revised by a group of U.S. psychiatrists. The ego psychology that emerged was more palatable to social workers because it was less deterministic than Freud's psychoanalysis and more emphasis was placed on reality and conscious processes. Ego psychology was absorbed by the dominant Diagnostic School, which began to emphasize reality relationships, adaptation, coping, and mastery. Still the University of Pennsylvania continued to embrace the functional approach. Meanwhile new developments in the field of mental health, as well as national and international events, paved the way social workers would be practicing community mental health.

Changing Approaches to Mental Health Treatment: 1950–1980

The second half of the twentieth century saw dramatic changes in mental health policies and practices. In 1953 the therapeutic effects of the drug chlorpromazine on psychotic and agitated patients were reported. The symptom control this medication produced made it possible for hospitals to discharge some of their residents. Around the same time reports from England about a therapeutic community (Jones, 1953) stimulated thoughts about community alternatives to hospitalization.

During the 1950s an ideology centered around community mental health was coalescing. In Boston Erich Lindemann and Gerald Caplan developed preventive strategies such as strengthening social networks, providing mental health education, and restructuring communities (Klerman, 1986). Lindemann developed theory and practice approaches about grief as he worked with survivors of the Coconut Grove nightclub fire. Both men developed the theoretical base for crisis intervention, which has been used extensively by social workers employed in mental health agencies.

During World War II and the Korean War effective strategies to treat shell shock and related reactions were developed in the military. Wartime experience revealed that psychiatric disability related to combat could be reduced by adhering to the principles of *immediacy, proximity, centrality, expectancy,* and *simplicity* (Ursano & Holloway, 1985). Soldiers who were seen soon after they were affected and in close proximity to the combat zone had a better chance of recovering and returning to their units than those who were sent to remote hospitals. A central coordinating system (called *triage*) was used to identify those individuals with emotional problems and to give priority to those with the most urgent needs. Treatment was simple and was accompanied by a high expectation that the soldier would recover. These principles are compatible with crisis intervention theory.

In 1955 Congress passed and President Eisenhower signed the Mental Health Study Act, which authorized a national study of mental health treatment. The need for a study grew out of concern about the high numbers of patients residing in public psychiatric hospitals and the cost of their care (Klerman, 1986). The Joint Commission on Mental Illness and Mental Health that was subsequently established undertook a comprehensive study of the domain of mental health, the results of which were reported in *Action for Mental Health* (Joint Commission on Mental Illness and Mental Health, 1961). The commission's report recommended comprehensive mental health services in local communities, the continuation of state hospitals, and increased federal funding.

On February 5, 1963, President John F. Kennedy delivered an address to the 88th Congress on the issues of mental illness and mental retardation. This was a momentous occasion—the first time a U.S. president gave a special speech on these issues. Kennedy recommended a "bold new approach"—community care:

> This approach is designed, in large measure, to use Federal resources to stimulate State, local, and private action. When carried out, reliance on the cold mercy of custodial isolation will be supplanted by the open warmth of community concern and capability. Emphasis on prevention, treatment, and rehabilitation will be substituted for a desultory interest in confining patients in an institution to wither away. (Kennedy, 1963, p. 3)

In October 1963 Kennedy signed the Mental Retardation Facilities and Community Mental Health Center Construction Act.

Between 1965 and 1980 a series of federal mental health bills fostering the implementation of community mental health systems was passed (see Table 2.1). In 1965 funds were allocated for the construction and staffing of community mental health centers. The federal government outlined the kinds of services that should be included in a community mental health system—inpatient, outpatient, community education, partial hospitalization, and emergency services. Later acts identified specific services (e.g., alcohol and drugs) to

TABLE 2.1   Major Federal Mental Health Legislation: 1946–1980

Year	Act
1946	National Mental Health Act (PL 79-487): authorized the establishment of the National Institute on Mental Health
1955	National Mental Health Study Act (PL 84-182): authorized the establishment of the Joint Commission on Mental Illness and Mental Health
1963	Mental Retardation Facilities and Community Mental Health Center Construction Act (PL 88-164): outlined five community mental health services and authorized expenditures for construction only
1965	Community Mental Health Centers Construction Amendments (PL 89-105): construction and staffing Medicare Act (PL 89-97) Medicaid established in Title XIX of the Social Security Act
1967	Amendment to the community mental health center law, providing an extension of the staffing and construction funding (PL 90-31)
1968	Alcohol and Narcotic Addict Rehabilitation Amendments (PL 90-574): funding for facilities providing treatment of drug and alcohol addiction
1970	Reauthorization of community mental health center program (PL 91-211): continuing staffing grants, providing for services for children and adolescents, supporting services in poverty areas, and including consultation and education
1972	Supplemental Security Income (SSI) program established (PL 92-603)
1975	Amendments to community health center program (PL 94-63), expanding number of required services, including drug and alcohol rehabilitation and prevention and services for the severely mentally disabled
1977	Reauthorization of the community mental health center program for one year (PL 95-83)
1978	Reauthorization of the community mental health center program (PL 95-622) for two years
1980	Mental Health Systems Act (PL 96-398): gave priority to services for vulnerable populations such as persons with severe mental disabilities; increased emphasis on advocacy; authorized for four years

be offered and populations (children, older adults) that should be served. Medicare and Medicaid, as well as supplemental security income (SSI), provided sources of financial support for the mentally disabled. In 1977 the National Institute of Mental Health initiated the pilot Community Support Program (CSP) in order to stimulate states to develop support systems to sustain the severely mentally ill who were living in the community. The last progressive federal mental health act during this period was the Mental Health Systems Act of 1980, which recognized the needs of the severely mentally ill and other vulnerable, underserved populations.

Although the original intent of the report, *Action for Mental Health* (Joint Commission, 1961), was to provide community support for persons with severe mental disabilities, the programs that were implemented in the 1960s and 1970s were for a wide spectrum of populations, many of whom had less serious difficulties (Klerman, 1986). Nevertheless, *deinstitutionalization*—the movement of severely mentally disabled patients from the hospital to the community—had a momentum of its own. A paradigm shift from an emphasis on institutionalization to community treatment created a need for social workers who were knowledgeable about community resources and treatment.

Deinstitutionalization was supported by a series of judicial decisions that, in effect, reconstructed mental health policy. *Wyatt v. Stickney* (1971/1972), a case in Alabama, concluded that patients who had been involuntarily committed had a right to treatment and that adequate standards of treatment should be defined. The decision stipulated that the institution should have sufficient, qualified staff and that each patient should have an individualized treatment plan. Several cases (*Lake v. Cameron,* 1966; *Covington v. Harris,* 1969; *Dixon v. Weinberger,* 1975; *Welsch v. Likins,* 1974) affirmed that treatment should take place in the least restrictive environment that was compatible with a client's needs. These cases gave recognition to the individual's capacity for autonomy and promoted discharge planning for community alternatives to hospitalization, such as halfway houses, group homes, and family care homes. In the case of *O'Connor v. Donaldson* (1975), the Supreme Court ruled that unless an individual was dangerous (to self or others), a state hospital could not retain the person involuntarily (Budson, 1978; Levine, 1981; Perlin, 1986).

The preceding court cases supported the rights of clients. They are reflective of a shift in the national climate from an ideology of "state as parent" that looks after human needs, which was characteristic of the Progressive Era, to a civil rights orientation (Rothman, 1978). The earlier perspective was paternalistic, yet it promoted care. During the 1960s and 1970s, however, reformists held the state responsible for coercive practices and social control (Rothman, 1978). (For a discussion of legal and ethical issues, see Chapter 5.)

Meanwhile, the practices of involuntary commitment, cruel or nonexistent treatment, and inhumane methods of control became the subject of critical discourse (Cooper, 1967; Laing, 1967; Scheff, 1966; Szasz, 1970). Kesey (1962) dramatized the concerns of an emerging antipsychiatry movement in *One Flew Over the Cuckoo's Nest,* a play in which a spirited hospital patient is subjugated by the staff. Participants in the antipsychiatry movement, which included some social workers, raised questions about the use of shock treatment, lobotomies, and restraints, as well as the authority of psychiatrists. Many sought the liberation of psychiatric patients from the oppressive mental health system. This movement was concurrent with the Vietnam War, during which time some conscientious objectors performed alternative service as aides in psychiatric hospitals.

Social work responded to the social movements of the 1970s by exploring theories that are alternatives to psychoanalysis (Turner, 1974). The systems approach, which facilitates the identification of problems in the social environment, emerged as a perspective that could be adapted to social work practice (Pincus & Minahan, 1973; Siporin, 1975). With increased recognition that problems do not reside exclusively within the individual, attention was also given to family and group processes. Social workers employed in mental health settings became aware of systemic impediments to the realization of the rights of clients to treatment and discharge and advocated on behalf of mental health clients.

At the same time as social workers were broadening their understanding of social functioning and modes of intervention, graduate-level social workers who worked directly and therapeutically with clients began to call themselves clinical social workers. In 1971 the National Federation of Societies for Clinical Social Work was founded. The National Association of Social Workers and the Clinical Association worked vigorously to help pass licensing laws in the states and advocated for insurance coverage for the services of social workers. Licensure and vendorship made it possible for many social workers to engage in private practice.

Changes in Mental Health Policies: 1981–2000

During the last two decades of the twentieth century, the mental health paradigm changed again. The federal government stopped providing direct funding of community mental health programs. The block grant strategy, which will be described next, routed federal funding through the states. The development of managed care of behavioral health during this period also affected the context of practice.

In 1981, under the Reagan administration, the Omnibus Budget Reconciliation Act (PL 97-35) passed. This legislation established block grants to states, which would determine how these funds would be used. This act replaced the progressive Mental Health Systems Act and promoted a shift of responsibility from the federal government to the states. The implementation of the Omnibus Budget Reconciliation Act during the 1980s was accompanied by a decline in federal funding. During the Reagan administration, too, many psychiatric clients were threatened with the loss of their supplemental security income (SSI) when stricter criteria for disability were applied. Many of these cases were successfully appealed.

Although federal leadership in mental health faltered during the Reagan years, a couple of developments during this administration aroused attention to mental health needs. During Reagan's first term, John Hinckley attempted to kill the president and seriously injured one of his associates. Hinckley was diagnosed as a paranoid type of schizophrenic who was not receiving proper mental health treatment. Another development during this administration was Nancy Reagan's "just say no to drugs" campaign, which stimulated primary prevention of substance abuse among youth.

In the late 1980s community mental health systems faced financial constraints and increasing demands to serve the indigent seriously mentally ill and other vulnerable populations. Advocacy groups such as the National Mental Health Association, the National Alliance for the Mentally Ill, the National Depressive and Manic Depressive Association, as well as various local consumer groups, became a significant force in the field of mental health.

Since the Omnibus Budget Reconciliation Act of 1981, additional federal laws have provided direction to the implementation of services funded to the states through block grants. The State Comprehensive Mental Health Services Plan Act (PL 99-660) of 1986 required that states draw up plans that would describe the community-based system of services for individuals with severe mental illness that they would establish and implement, and come up with a target number of clients they expected to serve. The law stipulated that states had to provide case management if they were to receive federal funding. This act was reauthorized four years later under the Mental Health Amendments of 1990 (PL 101-639) (Rochefort, 1993). In 1986 the Protection and Advocacy Services Act, which offered protection to consumers, became law. A year later the Stewart B. McKinney Homeless Assistance Act (PL 100-77), which included funds for special services to the homeless with mental illness, was passed. This act was reauthorized in 1988 and 1990 (Rochefort, 1993). In 1990 the National Affordable Housing Act (PL 101-625) authorized funds for housing and services for the homeless with mental health and substance abuse problems.

In 1990 the Americans with Disabilities Act (ADA, PL 101-336) was passed. The ADA prohibited discrimination in employment, education, public accommodations, public services, and transportation against persons with mental as well as physical disabilities. The protections against discrimination in employment in the ADA were more extensive than those in the previous Rehabilitation Act of 1973, which only applied to employment in federal agencies or organizations with federal contracts of more than $2,500. The Americans with Disabilities Act of 1990 extended protection against discrimination to private employers of fifteen or more persons (Hermann, 1997). Although some conditions remain excluded from coverage, the passage of the ADA was a tremendous victory for advocates of rights of persons with mental disabilities.

During the 1980s and 1990s, managed health care became increasingly widespread as a cost-effective means to provide employees with a health care benefit. The term *behavioral health* came to describe mental health and substance abuse treatment within managed care programs or carved out through a contract with a separate entity. Still persons who were not employed by an organization that provided a health care benefit, those who were unemployed, and persons who were not beneficiaries of Medicare or recipients of Medicaid remained uncovered. During Clinton's first term he tried and failed to pass legislation that would assure universal health insurance. Meanwhile the private sector stepped up its efforts to manage physical and behavioral health care, including the care of clients receiving Medicare and Medicaid.

One law that was passed around this time was the Mental Health Parity Act of 1996 (MHPA), which went into effect in January 1998. This law called for equal coverage for physical and mental illness in annual and lifetime limits under group health insurance plans with mental health benefits in organizations serving more than fifty employees. The Mental Health Parity Act had many loopholes, including exclusion of coverage for substance abuse treatment.

Clinical social workers have been living through these policy changes and working with and around them. The twentieth century left many unsolved problems in its wake—for example, homelessness, diversion of persons with severe mental illness into the criminal justice system and nursing homes, insufficient services, and the absence of treatments that "cure." As the twenty-first century unfolds, clinical social workers face new challenges serving vulnerable populations in an environment that is dominated by managed care.

Summary and Deconstruction

This chapter described the history of mental health treatment in the United States and social work's place in this history. The chapter highlighted the role played by European practices, noted individuals, the world wars, and federal public policies, as well as ideologies. Some of the reformers who were depicted suffered themselves from mental illness (Clifford Beers) or from institutionalization for an alleged illness (Elizabeth Packard). Besides these prominent figures were persons at the margins who were hidden away in attics by their families, chained in prisons or mental hospitals, sheltered in poorhouses, or incarcerated against their will in mental hospitals. Some of those who were hospitalized were immigrants who did not speak English and people of color whose differences may have been construed as symptoms of mental illness. Little is known about the suffering of individuals such as these.

Paradigms of mental illness and its treatment have changed many times over the course of U.S. history. For example, the reformer Dix in the nineteenth century viewed hospitalization as desirable, but civil rights advocates in the 1960s and 1970s saw hospitalization as abhorrent. Although the confluence of events, such as medical discoveries, the Great Depression, and war, appeared to influence social changes, power relations and economic factors underlie the construction of these reforms.

Meanwhile the evolving social work profession has had internal debates about its theoretical frameworks, how clinical it wants to be, and to whom it is accountable—the client, the agency, or the community. It now has an additional constituency to consider, that is, managed care entities. Furthermore, there are differences of opinion about the value of scientific practice. Rather than being divisive, these debates can result in new constructions about addressing the behavioral or mental health problems of the future.

DISCUSSION QUESTIONS

1. Discuss changes over time in the role of the federal government in relation to mental health treatment. What has contributed to these changes?

2. How have changing concepts and ideas about the role of biology and the environment affected treatment of mental illness?

3. To what extent have charismatic individuals influenced the course of mental health history in the United States?

4. On the basis of the history presented in this chapter, what progress has been made in the treatment of persons with serious mental health problems?

5. Which populations were the primary beneficiaries of the community mental health movement?

6. Discuss the relationship of wars to the evolution of clinical social work practice in mental health.

7. How have changing philosophies of treatment affected the development of social work practice in mental health?

8. What challenges do clinical social workers working in behavioral mental health settings face today?

REFERENCES

Alexander, J. K. (1986). Rush, Benjamin. In W. I. Trattner (Ed.), *Biographical dictionary of social welfare in America* (pp. 644–646). New York: Greenwood Press.

Bassett, C. (1933). Mental hygiene. In F. S. Hall (Ed.), *Social work yearbook 1933* (pp. 297–301). New York: Russell Sage Foundation.

Beers, C. W. (1907/1923). *A mind that found itself: An autobiography.* Garden City, NY: Doubleday, Page.

Breckinridge, S. P., & Abbott, E. (1912). *The delinquent child and the home.* New York: Charities Publication Committee.

Briar, S., & Miller, H. (1971). *Problems and issues in social casework.* New York: Columbia University Press.

Budson, R. D. (1978). In J. Goldmeir, F. V. Mannino, & M. F. Shore (Eds.), *New directions in mental health care* (chap. 1). (DHEW Publication No. ADM 78–685). Adelphi, MD: National Institute of Mental Health.

Caplan, R. B., in collaboration with Caplan, G. (1969). *Psychiatry and the community in nineteenth-century America.* New York: Basic Books.

Clark, E. (1966). The development of psychiatric social work. *Bulletin of the Menninger Foundation, 30,* 161–173.

Clarke, H. I. (1947). *Principles and practice of social work.* New York: Appleton-Century.

Cooper, D. (1967). *Psychiatry and antipsychiatry.* London: Tavistock.

Costin, L. (1986). Lathrop, Julia Clifford. In W. I. Trattner (Ed.), *Biographical dictionary of social welfare in America* (pp. 478–481). New York: Greenwood Press.

Covington v. Harris, 419 F.2d 617 (D.C. Cir. 1969).

Dain, N. (1964). *Concepts of insanity in the United States, 1789–1865.* New Brunswick, NJ: Rutgers University Press.

Deutsch, A. (1949). *The mentally ill in America.* New York: Columbia University Press.

Dixon v. Weinberger, 405 F. Supp. 974 (D.D.C. 1975).

Fink, A. E., Anderson, C. W., & Conover, M. B. (1968). *The field of social work.* New York: Holt, Rinehart and Winston.

French, L. M. (1940). *Psychiatric social work.* New York: Commonwealth Fund.

Freud, A. (1946). *The ego and the mechanisms of defense.* Trans. by C. Baines. New York: International Universities Press.

Grinker, R. R., et al. (1961). The early years of psychiatric social work. *Social Service Review, 35,* 111–126.

Grob, C. (1983). *Mental illness and American society, 1875–1940.* Princeton, NJ: Princeton University Press.

Healy, W. (1915/1924). *The individual delinquent.* Boston: Little, Brown.

Hermann, D. H. J. (1997). *Mental health and disability law in a nutshell.* St. Paul, MN: West Publishing Co.

hooks, b. (1984). *Feminist theory: From margin to center.* Boston: South End Press.

James, J. F. (1987). Does the community mental health movement have the momentum needed to survive? *American Journal of Orthopsychiatry, 57,* 447–451.

Jarrett, M. C. (1919). The psychiatric thread running through all social casework. *Proceedings of the National Conference of Social Work,* Atlantic City, NJ.

Joint Commission on Mental Illness and Mental Health (1961). *Action for mental health.* New York: Basic Books.

Jones, M. (1953). *The therapeutic community.* New York: Basic Books.

Katz, S. E. (1985). Psychiatric hospitalization. In H. I. Kaplan & B. J. Sadock (Eds.), *Comprehensive textbook of psychiatry/IV* (pp. 1576–1582). Baltimore, MD: Williams & Wilkins.

Kennedy, J. F. (1963). Message from the President of the United States relative to mental illness and mental retardation. (88th Congress, House of Representatives Document No. 58, pp. 1–14).

Kesey, K. (1962). *One flew over the cuckoo's nest: A novel.* New York: Viking Press.

Klerman, G. L. (1986). The scope of social and community psychiatry. In G. L. Klerman, M. M. Weissman, P. S.

Appelbaum, & L. H. Roth (Eds.), *Social, epidemiologic, and legal psychiatry* (pp. 1–14). New York: Basic Books.

Knee, R. I., & Lamson, W. C. (1971). Mental health services. In R. Morris (Ed.), *Encyclopedia of social work* (16th ed., Vol. 1, pp. 802–813). New York: National Association of Social Workers.

Kreisler, J. D., & Lieberman, A. A. (1986). Dorothea Lynde Dix. In W. I. Trattner (Ed.), *Biographical dictionary of social welfare in America* (pp. 241–244). New York: Greenwood Press.

Laing, R. D. (1967). *The politics of experience.* New York: Ballantine.

Lake v. Cameron, 364 F.2d (D.C. Cir. 1966).

Leiby, J. (1978). *A history of social welfare and social work in the United States.* New York: Columbia University Press.

Levine, M. (1981). *The history and politics of community mental health.* New York: Oxford University Press.

Lubove, R. (1965). *The professional altruist: The emergence of social work as a career 1880–1930.* Cambridge, MA: Harvard University Press.

Marshall, H. (1937). *Dorothea Dix: Forgotten samaritan.* Chapel Hill, NC: University of North Carolina Press.

Nacman, M. (1977). Mental health services: Social workers. In *Encyclopedia of social work* (17th ed., Vol. 2). Washington, DC: National Association of Social Workers.

O'Connor v. Donaldson, 422 U.S. 563 (1975), 1 MDLR 336.

Packard, E. P. W. (1865/1974). *Great disclosure of spiritual wickedness!! in high places. With an appeal to the government to protect the inalienable rights of married women.* Original version published by the author in Boston. Reprinted, New York: Arno Press.

Perlin, M. L. (1986). Patients' rights. In G. L. Klerman, M. M. Weissman, P. S. Appelbaum, & L. H. Roth (Eds.), *Social, epidemiologic, and legal psychiatry* (pp. 401–422). New York: Basic Books.

Pincus, A., & Minahan, A. (1973). *Social work practice: Model and method.* Itasca, IL: R. E. Peacock.

Pollock, H. M. (1935). Mental diseases. In F. S. Hall (Ed.), *Social work year book 1935* (pp. 273–277). New York: Russell Sage Foundation.

Richmond, M. (1917). *Social diagnosis.* New York: Russell Sage Foundation.

Robinson, V. P. (1930). *A changing psychology of social case work.* Chapel Hill, NC: University of North Carolina Press.

Rochefort, D. A. (1993). *From poorhouses to homelessness.* Westport, CT: Auburn House.

Roosens, E. (1979). *Mental patients in town life: Geel, Europe's first therapeutic community.* Beverly Hills, CA: Sage Publications.

Rothman, D. J. (1971). *The discovery of the asylum. Social order and disorder in the new republic.* Boston: Little, Brown.

Rothman, D. J. (1978). The state as parent: Social policy in the Progressive Era. In W. Gaylin, I. Glasser, S. Marcus, & D. Rothman (Eds.), *Doing good: The limits of benevolence.* New York: Pantheon Books.

Rothman, D. J. (1979). *Incarceration and its alternatives in 20th century America.* Washington, DC: U.S. Department of Justice.

Scheff, T. (1966). *Being mentally ill.* Chicago: Aldine Atherton.

Siporin, M. (1975). *Introduction to social work practice.* New York: Macmillan.

Social case work: Generic and specific (1929). A Report of the Milford Conference. New York: American Association of Social Workers. Reprinted 1974 by the National Association of Social Workers, Washington, DC.

Southard, E. E., & Jarrett, M. C. (1922). *The kingdom of evils.* New York: Macmillan.

Stevenson, G. S. (1935). Psychiatric clinics for children. In F. S. Hall (Ed.), *Social work year book 1935* (pp. 350–353). New York: Russell Sage Foundation.

Szasz, T. (1970). *Ideology and insanity.* Garden City, NY: Anchor Books.

Turner, F. J. (Ed.). (1974). *Social work treatment: Interlocking theoretical approaches.* New York: Free Press.

Ursano, R. J., & Holloway, H. C. (1985). Military psychiatry. In H. I. Kaplan & B. J. Sadock (Eds.), *Comprehensive textbook of psychiatry/IV* (4th ed., pp. 1900–1909). Baltimore, MD: Williams & Wilkins.

Welsch v. Likins, 373 F. Supp. 487 (D. Minn. 1974).

Williams, D. H., Bellis, E. C., & Wellington, S. W. (1980). Deinstitutionalization and social policy: Historical perspectives and present dilemmas. *American Journal of Orthopsychiatry, 50,* 54–64.

Wrench, S. B. (1985). Packard, Elizabeth Parsons Ware. In A. Whitman (Ed.), *American Reformers* (pp. 627–628). New York: H. W. Wilson.

Wyatt v. Stickney, 325 F. Supp. 781, *aff'd,* 334 F. Supp. 1341 (M.D. Ala. 1971) and 344 F. Supp. 373 (M.D. Ala. 1972), *aff'd sub nom.*

CHAPTER

3

A Biopsychosocial Conceptual Framework

…our new knowledge has allowed us to identify structures that prove that the mind and the body are inseparable, that psyche equals soma, and vice versa.
—Hedaya, *Understanding Biological Psychiatry,* 1996

While a new medication, Risperdal, stopped the voices after almost a year's treatment, I am personally responsible for keeping the voices out of my life. Language cannot describe the daily struggles I have had to endure to stay outside of my schizophrenia and to start a new life.
—Steele, "Outside Schizophrenia," 1997

Traditional approaches to understanding human behavior have highlighted competing paradigms such as nature *versus* nurture, mind *versus* body, and biology *versus* the environment. Even the newer development of social constructionism has been described in opposition to empiricism (Atherton, 1993) and essentialism (Epstein, 1987). Another traditional strategy is to identify psychological, social, and biological factors that are thought to be determinants of human behavior. These dualistic and linear strategies to knowledge formation have limited applicability to behavioral health today.

A postmodern understanding of human behavior requires an integrated understanding of biological, psychological, and social environmental perspectives. The emphasis is on *both* the interplay among them *and* the infusion of one with the others. As the opening quotations assert, the mind and body are inseparable. Moreover, individual mindbodies are part of and connected with the social worlds that sustain or neglect them, provide them with constructions for meaning-making, and designate which responsibilities are personal and which belong to others.

The biopsychosocial conceptual framework of this book is predicated on an integrative model of health, illness, and disease (Weiner, 1984; Weiner & Fawzy, 1989). Accordingly, health refers to adaptive biopsychosocial functioning, that is, functioning that promotes, assists, and fosters the ability to live fruitfully in the social environment. Health is a positive goal that depends on biogenetic, psychological, and social factors and is maintained by

47

proper nutrition, good sanitation, stable political conditions, and an adequate standard of living (Weiner & Fawzy, 1989). Health can change as the person matures and acquires social experience over time. Disease is associated with biochemical, immunological, structural, functional, or genetic impairment, whereas illness is a psychosocial state characterized by malaise, dissatisfaction, or pain (Weiner, 1984).

In contrast with the Western biomedical model, the integrative model views illness and disease as multifaceted and complex rather than as well-defined entities that have a single physical cause (Weiner, 1984). Diseases are heterogeneous (varied) and have diverse, multiple, and complex causes and manifestations. This model is not deterministic, that is, no assumption of linear cause-effect influences is being made (Zimmerman, 1989). Thus, disease and illness are not necessarily related causally or sequentially. One can feel ill without having a disease, and one can have a disease without feeling ill (Weiner & Fawzy, 1989). Social supports can protect a person with a genetic predisposition from developing a disease, whereas poverty and other stressors can foster an outbreak or exacerbation of a disease (Weiner, 1984). Regardless of whether one is ill or has a disease, or both, one has a natural proclivity toward healing (Weiner, 1984).

This model applies to mental as well as physical health. Accordingly, psychopathology is viewed as a disturbance in biopsychosocial integration and is manifested by difficulties in adapting to the demands of the environment. The person with psychopathology will have difficulty with cognition (or cognitive processing), performing adaptive behavior, emotional expression, or perceiving the demands of the environment. The person may experience or have symptoms of distress (illness) or manifest through laboratory examinations signs of structural or genetic impairment (disease). Table 3.1 summarizes the characteristics of an integrative biopsychosocial model.

Take the case of twenty-six-year-old Daniel, who is a client at a state hospital after-care unit. This man, who has been given the diagnosis of schizophrenia, undifferentiated type, continuous, has been hospitalized six times and has lived with his parents and in three group homes. Recently he moved into an efficiency apartment where he lives alone. Daniel has no overt symptoms of psychosis, but he has flat affect, responds slowly, and appears apathetic—symptoms that are viewed as "residual" or "negative." During a recent home visit by his case manager, Daniel appeared depressed and reported that he was not eating

TABLE 3.1   Characteristics of an Integrative Biopsychosocial Model

Differentiation among health, disease, and illness	Health and growth as positive developments
Multiplicity of influences and effects	Strengths and vulnerabilities
Complex expression	Individualization
Proclivity toward healing	Client empowerment
Heterogeneity/diversity	Multiple contexts
Nonlinear causality	Construction of meaning

regularly and was sleeping a great deal. The case manager took him out for coffee at which time Daniel expressed his distress at having reached his goal of being independent but he remained lonely.

Daniel has the disease of schizophrenia. As the discussion on neuroimaging in the following section indicates, evidence of structural damage to the brain can be found in persons with schizophrenia in CT scans and other neurophysiological tests. Furthermore, Daniel feels ill (depressed) not only because he has schizophrenia, but because he is alone and is wary about his future. Daniel's disease has residual effects that interfere with his social functioning. The biological, psychological, and social aspects of his disease are interrelated.

During the last few decades of the twentieth century, evidence of a disease process and genetic explanation for substance abuse and major mental disorders accumulated. Research findings of this biological revolution enhanced understanding and paved the way for improved means of intervention. Biological knowledge does not, however, replace other sources of knowledge that contribute to understanding of a *particular client* experiencing *particular difficulties* in a *particular social context*. Individual clients express their subjective pain through cognitive, behavioral, somatic, and emotional affective symptoms as well as the ways in which they function in particular environments. Symptoms and psychosocial functioning converge in individuals who manifest socially constructed psychiatric disorders. Accordingly, clients must be *individualized* and viewed in the *multiple contexts* of their lives.

The biopsychosocial framework used in this book is consistent with the strengths perspective (Weick, Rapp, Sullivan, & Kisthardt, 1989), that is:

> All people possess a wide range of talents, abilities, capacities, skills, resources, and aspirations. No matter how little or how much may be expressed at one time, a belief in human potential is tied to the notion that people have untapped, undetermined reservoirs of mental, physical, emotional, social, and spiritual abilities that can be expressed. (p. 352)

Nevertheless, because persons with behavioral health problems have vulnerabilities that can result in decompensation, *strengths and vulnerabilities* are included in the conceptual framework.

Above all, the client is viewed as *an individual with a disorder*, not a category. Knowledge about a particular psychiatric disorder and modes of treatment are applied with the idea that the client is a person with dignity and that even the disorder is uniquely manifested in the individual. Furthermore, the client is viewed as an active participant rather than a passive recipient of services. The client has legal and ethical rights (e.g., least restrictive environment, self-determination) that should be protected (see Chapter 5) as well as the right to competent, informed, effective service. The social worker assures that the client participates in the development of the treatment plan and goal setting and that the client makes his or her own decisions to the extent possible. The clinical social worker recognizes that the client has the capacity for growth or self-transformation based on a perceived inner sense of his or her own needs (Weick, 1987). The social worker helps clients who are oppressed by sexism, racism, handicapism, homophobia, ageism, or classism in their struggles, promoting their *empowerment* (cf. Solomon, 1976).

This perspective also assumes that clients actively engage in a process of meaning-making. As humans, they have some awareness of their place in the cosmos and their relationship to themselves, others, and the material environment. Existence has a purpose that is to be discovered and realized. Individuals seek wholeness, connectedness, actualization, and growth as they and their respective cultures define these qualities. Meaning-making can be viewed as a process that is developmental (Kegan, 1982) and spiritual, as well as perceptual-cognitive (Sands, 1986). Individuals *construct meaning* from the concepts available in their environment. As Table 3.1 shows, the construction of meaning is part of the integrative biopsychosocial model.

This chapter describes ways of knowing from a variety of disciplines that are relevant to behavioral health practice. Although the biopsychosocial conceptual framework stresses integration, this chapter will discuss biological and psychosocial perspectives in separate sections. Separate treatment of these ways of knowing, as well as subtopics within each of them, is a consequence of the social construction of knowledge into areas that are developed by separate academic and professional disciplines, as well as the propensity within Western thought to break knowledge into categories. Integration across categories will be discussed in the example and deconstruction pieces at the end of the chapter.

Biological Knowing

During the last few decades of the twentieth century, major mental illnesses such as schizophrenia and bipolar disorder came to be understood as diseases of the brain. Researchers have learned much about genetics, the structure and functioning of the brain, and psychopharmacology. Because psychiatrists working in interdisciplinary behavioral health settings apply this knowledge to clients with whom social workers practice, social workers need to understand these phenomena.

Understanding the Role of Genetics

Inherited potential is believed to be involved in the etiology (cause) of a number of mental disorders. A large body of research examines genetic patterns associated with schizophrenia and mood disorders. Some studies have explored genetic components of alcoholism, anxiety disorders, and personality disorders. Traditionally researchers have undertaken family risk, twin, and adoption studies. Today the spotlight is on molecular genetics.

Family Risk.   One means of looking at genetic influences has been to study the prevalence of a particular disease in families with the disease and compare rates in genetically linked groups with the rate in the general population. Such research requires intensive investigation of the families of persons with an identified mental disorder through a standardized interview of relatives or from records. This research begins with an identified client (proband or index case) and proceeds to first-degree relatives (parents, siblings) and more distant family members (Rainer, 1985). A genetic hypothesis is supported when the prevalence of a psychiatric disorder is higher among first-degree than more distant relatives, and when the rate among relatives is higher than that of the general population. First-degree relatives of persons with bipolar disorder, for example, have a 15 to 21 percent risk of getting unipolar (major depression) or bipolar disease, whereas the risk for the general population is about 1 percent (Rainer, 1985).

Twin Studies.   Another approach has been to study *monozygotic* (identical) and *dizygotic* (fraternal) twins. Clinical cases identified as afflicted twins are the basis for investigating whether the cotwin or other family members have had a similar mental illness. A significant genetic relationship can be inferred if the relationship between monozygotic twins is higher than that between dizygotic twins, and if the rate between dizygotic twins is similar to that among siblings (Rainer, 1985). The rate of co-occurrence is called the *concordance rate.* Research studies of schizophrenia in twins have revealed a higher rate among monozygotic than dizygotic twins (Gottesman & Shields, 1972; Kendler, 1988). The rate for dizygotic twins and siblings is similar. Furthermore, research has found that the closer the biological relationship, the higher the rate.

Twin studies have been undertaken for mood and anxiety disorders, too. With respect to bipolar psychotic mood disorders, the concordance rate for same-sex dizygotic twins is 23 percent whereas the rate for monozygotic twins is 68 percent (Klerman, 1988). For anxiety disorder, the rate for dizygotic twins is 5 to 10 percent; for monozygotic it is 30 to 40 percent (Andreasen, 1984). These rates indicate that genetics is a factor in anxiety and bipolar disorders and that its role in bipolar disorder is stronger than it is in anxiety disorders.

However illuminating these findings may be, they also raise questions about the social environment. If genetic factors were the only influence, the concordance rates between monozygotic twins would be 100 percent. Clearly other factors are involved. Twins share a similar prenatal environment; within the family, however, one of a pair of twins may be treated differently from the other (Rainer, 1985). Because it is difficult to separate the contributions of social, environmental, and genetic factors in the etiology of the disease, another approach has been used—adoption studies.

Adoption Studies.   Adoption studies may take a variety of forms. Some compare adopted children whose biological mothers are afflicted with a mental disorder with a control group of adopted children with normal parents; others compare children with and without a family history of a mental disorder with children raised by afflicted foster parents. The incidence of mental disorders among the children raised in different homes and the characteristics of parents are compared.

Studies of adoptees have been undertaken largely to determine the differential roles of genetics and environment in schizophrenia. Results indicate a higher prevalence of schizophrenia and of schizophrenic spectrum disorders (related disorders such as the schizotypal personality disorder) among children of schizophrenics than among controls (Rainer, 1985). Studies using the reverse strategy, that is, first identifying adopted adults with schizophrenic spectrum disorders and then interviewing relatives, have found an excess of schizophrenia and spectrum disorders among relatives (Kendler, 1988). Furthermore, paternal half-siblings of adoptees with schizophrenia have an unusually high rate of schizophrenia diagnoses, challenging the contributions of interuterine environment and early mother-child relationship (Rainer, 1985).

Overall, the twin and adoption studies suggest that genetics and the environment affect persons with schizophrenia, with genetics exercising a stronger effect. Kendler (1988) estimates that inheritance contributes between 60 and 70 percent to the variance in liability of schizophrenia, whereas environment contributes less than 20 percent. Nevertheless, these studies have their limitations. Controlled adoption studies require random assignment of children to adoptive homes. Ethically this cannot be done. Many of the adoption studies include different disorders under schizophrenic spectrum disorders, thus affecting the comparability between studies (Rainer, 1985). Moreover, family association does not mean that there are genetic markers for schizophrenia and related disorders. Genetic information can be more clearly acquired through molecular genetic studies.

Molecular Genetic Studies.   The discovery of DNA (deoxyribonucleic acid, the substance of chromosomes) and technological developments in the field of molecular genetics have made it possible to study genetics more directly than the previously described methods. Before long the international Human Genome Project will achieve its goal of mapping the sequencing of genes of human and a few nonhuman organisms (Craddock & Owen, 1996).

Two strategies that molecular genetic researchers use are *linkage* and *association* studies. Linkage studies investigate DNA markers in families in which a number of individuals have a disease; association studies compare unrelated individuals who have the disease with controls (Craddock, 1996). These two strategies make it possible for scientists to map chromosomal regions of the disease genes and explore candidate genes within these areas (Craddock & Owen, 1996; Mowry, Nancarrow, & Levinson, 1997).

Although molecular genetics promises to identify abnormal proteins and genetic markers (Kaplan & Sadock, 1988), thus far the search for single genes responsible for specific mental disorders has produced limited results. A genetic marker for Huntington's disease has been located on chromosome 4 (Andreasen & Black, 1995), for example.

Huntington's disease is an inherited neurological disease that produces symptoms of dementia (cognitive impairment) and jerky movements in middle-age adults. Intensive genetic studies of families in Venezuela and the United States led to the identification of a specific gene for the disease on chromosome 4 (Gusella et al., 1983). This discovery led to the development of testing of at-risk individuals for the presence of the designated gene before they have children themselves. Molecular genetic research has also located mutations in genes on chromosomes 1, 14, and 21 that are associated with early onset Alzheimer's disease (Kaplan & Sadock, 1998). Although research has linked bipolar disorder and schizophrenia to several chromosomes each (Craddock, 1996), findings are inconclusive (Moldin & Gottesman, 1997).

Prominent researchers believe that for many of the major mental disorders, multiple genes that interact with each other and environmental factors are involved (Craddock, 1996; Moldin & Gottesman, 1997; Mowry, Nancarrow, & Levinson, 1997). The term *polygenetic inheritance* is used to describe a complex genetic transmission process (Mathysse & Kety, 1986). It is anticipated that aggregated genetic information on psychiatric disorders gathered through the Human Genome Project will lend itself to more definitive research (Craddock & Owen, 1996).

If abnormal genes are identified, new strategies of intervention will be necessary. These could include gene replacement therapy, new medication, and genetic counseling (Moldin & Gottesman, 1997), all of which involve the person as a psychological being. Furthermore, ethical issues around genetic testing and the social problem of genetic discrimination are likely to follow (Moldin & Gottesman, 1997).

Family History. A less complicated means of assessing genetic factors is to look at the relationship between family history of the disease and responsiveness to medication. An example is found among persons with bipolar disorder. Lithium responders are more likely than nonresponders to have family members with bipolar disorder (Mendlewicz, Fieve, & Stallone, 1973). Family history of mood disorders, alcoholism, and the development of side effects to drugs can be helpful in the diagnosis and treatment of persons with mental disorders (Rainer, 1985).

Understanding the Brain

Another direction of biological research has been on the brain. The brain is a complex system in which information is received, processed, and transmitted. Although it depends on oxygen and glucose in order to function, it cannot store either of these (Palfai & Jankiewicz, 1991). The brain is depicted as having three structures—the hindbrain, the midbrain, and the forebrain (Bentley & Walsh, 1996). From an evolutionary perspective, the *hindbrain* or "reptilian brain" is the oldest. It consists of the brain stem, the cerebellum, and pons. The *brain stem* is responsible for maintaining unconscious life support processes. Behind the brain stem is the *cerebellum,* which coordinates the body's movement and receives information from joints and muscles. The *pons* connects parts of the brain with each other, as well as the central nervous system. The *midbrain* mediates hearing, seeing, and movement. The largest section, the *forebrain,* consists of the *hypothalamus,* the *limbic system,* and *thalamus,* which regulate biological functions, emotion, and sensory information, respectively (Bentley & Walsh, 1996).

The brain has also been described structurally as consisting of two hemispheres. The *left hemisphere* is responsible for language and analytic thinking whereas the *right hemisphere* is the source of nonverbal, emotional, holistic thinking in right-handed individuals (Hedaya, 1996). A third way in which the brain structure has been viewed is in terms of its *lobes.* The four lobes, their locations, and functions are as follows:

- *frontal* (in the front; responsible for self-awareness and decision making, motivation, regulation of emotional expression and motor behavior)
- *parietal* (above the ear; responsible for coordination of sensation and motor behavior, spacial orientation, recognition of people and objects)
- *temporal* (near the temples; responsible for memory formation, emotion, language comprehension, and learning)
- *occipital* (in the rear; responsible for vision, visual perception, and visual memory). (Hedaya, 1996; Kaplan & Sadock, 1998)

An alternative way to think about the brain is in terms of anatomical (cf. structural) and functional systems, all of which interact with each other (Andreasen & Black, 1995). Among the former is the large *prefrontal system,* the part of the cerebral cortex that integrates information from different sources to facilitate decision making and planning; generates insight; and executes complex and novel behaviors (Andreasen & Black, 1995; Hedaya, 1996). These high-level cognitive activities are known as executive functions. Other anatomical systems are the *limbic,* which seems to play a role in assigning meaning to sensory information and memories (Kaplan & Sadock, 1998), and the *basal ganglia* system, which regulates motor activity and the expression of cognition and emotion (Andreasen & Black, 1995). The functional systems include memory, language, and attention, as well as the executive functions that are associated with the prefrontal system (Andreasen & Black, 1995).

The significance of these various systems emerged in research on individuals with brain impairment, such as aphasia, head injuries, and brain tumors. Associations have been made between the person's clinical presentation of self and the location of the structural damage (or lesion). In the past, the brains of persons with potential lesions could only be studied after death. Through modern technology, it is now possible to study the neurophysiology of living individuals.

Obtaining Pictures of the Brain

A number of neuroimaging techniques are now used to obtain pictures of the brain. These techniques make it possible to determine if and where there are structural abnormalities and the parts of the brain in which mental activity takes place. Brain imaging assists in the process of diagnosis, particularly in the differentiation of physiological disorders from psychiatric ones, and in research on some disorders. Some techniques, such as the CT (computerized tomographic) scan and the MRI (magnetic resonance imaging), are used to assess the *structure* of the brain. Other techniques, such as the fMRI, PET (positron emission tomography) scan, and the SPECT (single photon emission computed tomography), show brain *functioning,* that is, where brain activity is taking place (where the blood flows) while the person performs cognitive and perceptual tasks. Table 3.2 describes these techniques and their advantages and disadvantages.

An older neurophysiological technique, the electroencephalogram (EEG), also can be used to describe brain activity and is particularly helpful in identifying seizures, tumors, and head injuries (Andreasen & Black, 1995). The EEG records electrical activity in the form of wave patterns elicited from electrodes placed around the surface of the brain. Another technique, the BEAM (brain electrical activity mapping) converts signals emitted in the EEG into a map of brain activity (Andreasen, 1984; Taylor, 1987). Although these two techniques are not as sophisticated as those described in Table 3.2, they are inexpensive, accessible, noninvasive, and do not expose the individual to radiation (Andreasen & Black, 1995).

Through these technological developments, evidence of structural abnormalities among persons with schizophrenia has been accumulating. Enlargement of the lateral and third ventricles, malfunctioning of the frontal and temporal lobes of the brain and the limbic system, as well as atrophy have been associated with schizophrenia. The regions affected facilitate the reception, understanding, and organization of information from the world (Taylor, 1987). Nevertheless, these findings are not common to all persons with this

TABLE 3.2   Neuroimaging Techniques

Technique (and Type)	Description	Advantages and Disadvantages
CT Scan (computerized tomographic scan) (structural type)	Produces computerized image of the brain.	*Advantages:* readily available, convenient, takes a short time, useful in emergencies.
		Disadvantage: produces some radiation.
MRI (magnetic resonance imaging) (structural type) fMRI (Functional MRI)	Creates high-resolution images of slices of the brain; can display brain along multiple dimensions.	*Advantages:* high resolution, based on magnetism (not radiation), multidimensional.
	Shows location of brain activity while performing cognitive and perceptual tasks.	*Disadvantages:* poses risk to persons with metal in skull or who use pacemakers, threatening to persons who are claustrophobic.
PET Scan (positron emission tomography scan) (functional type)	Uses radioactive isotopes to show how and where the brain responds to stimuli and where neurotransmitters and medication bind.	*Advantages:* excellent resolution, variety of applications.
		Disadvantages: expensive, limited availability, exposure to radioactivity, technical difficulties associated with the tracers that are used.
SPECT (single photon emission computed tomography) (functional type)	Uses radioactive isotopes to show where cerebral blood flows during brain activity.	*Advantages:* tracers that are used can be stored easily.
		Disadvantages: poor resolution, risks associated with using radioactivity.

Sources: Based on Andreasen (1984); Andreasen & Black (1995); Kaplan & Sadock (1998).

disorder (Andreasen, 1984; Cohen, 1989). Furthermore, they are also found among individuals with mania and dementia (Andreasen, 1984).

Another purpose of neuroimaging is to observe the activity of neurotransmitters, which have become important in understanding the action of psychopharmacological agents used to treat mental disorders. We turn next to neurons and neurotransmitters.

Understanding Neurons and Neurotransmitters

Neurons are nerve cells that receive and transmit messages (or signals) from and to other neurons. The signals that they process within themselves are electrical, but those that they transmit are chemical (Hedaya, 1996). Figure 3.1 illustrates the various parts of the neuron and how these parts interact with other neurons. The *cell body* is its interior, which is composed of fatty material, the nucleus, and protein synthetic material. The *cell nucleus* contains the cell's DNA, the genetic material, and plays an important role in the cell's growth and activities. The cell is covered with a *cell membrane.* Jutting out from the cell body are numerous branchlike extensions called *dendrites,* which receive signals from other neurons and transmit them to the cell body. Another extension of the cell body is the *axon,* which transmits electrical signals from this neuron to others. Axons vary in length; some extend a few feet. Normally axons are covered with a fatty *myelin sheath,* which protects it, and *nodes* (or openings) that facilitate the transmission of signals. At the end of the axon are one or more *presynaptic terminals,* where *synaptic vesicles* are located. *Neurotransmitters,* chemicals produced by the neuron, are released (or fired) from these vesicles into the *synapse* where they interact and bind with dendrites from other neurons. Whatever chemical neurotransmitters are not taken by the other neuron is taken back by the initial cell by a "reuptake pump" (Hedaya, 1996).

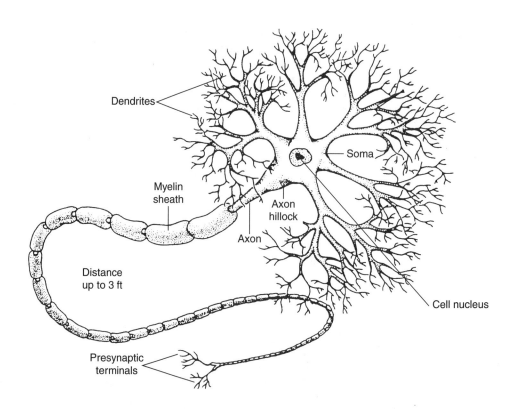

FIGURE 3.1   A Neuron and Its Parts

Source: From *Drugs and Human Behavior,* (p. 100, Figure 9.1), by T. Palfai and H. Jankiewicz, 1991, Dubuque, IA: William C. Brown Publishers. Copyright © 1991 by William C. Brown Publishers. Reprinted with permission of the McGraw-Hill Companies.

There are numerous types of neurotransmitters produced by neurons. Among those that are most relevant to the study of mental disorders are dopamine, norepinephrine, serotonin, and GABA. Dopamine seems to play a role in the production of psychoses; norepinephrine is related to mood disorders; serotonin is connected with depression, schizophrenia, and other psychoses; and GABA may be related to anxiety (Andreasen & Black, 1995). Psychopharmacological agents regulate the release of neurotransmitters by slowing, activating, blocking, and reversing the production process (Andreasen & Black, 1995; Hedaya, 1996).

Learning about Psychopharmacology

Major changes in the understanding and treatment of persons with psychiatric problems have arisen through the discovery of pharmacological agents that reduce disturbing symptoms. Advances in the development of pharmacotherapy have produced symptomatic relief for numerous psychiatric conditions and have enabled many individuals who would have been hospitalized for life to live in the community.

The discovery in the middle of the twentieth century of the effectiveness of chlorpromazine (Thorazine) in tranquilizing and reducing psychotic symptoms of schizophrenia was a major scientific breakthrough. This was followed by the development of other *neuroleptic* (antipsychotic) drugs and an increased understanding of brain functioning. Although these drugs reduced the prominence of psychotic symptoms, they did have deleterious side effects and did not address negative symptoms such as apathy. As Chapter 12 will explain, second-generation antipsychotics such as risperdal (Risperidone) and clozapine (Clozaril) have remedied some of the deficiencies of the earlier drugs.

Medications for mood disorders have also been introduced and refined. During the late 1940s Cade discovered that lithium carbonate could control manic symptoms in bipolar disorder. Although this drug was not tested in the United States until the late 1950s and 1960s (Fieve, 1975), lithium soon became a major drug prescribed for bipolar and related mood disorders. More recently other mood stabilizers (anticonvulsants and calcium channel inhibitors) have been prescribed for persons who do not respond to lithium. Additional pharmacological agents that treat depression have also been used with success. At first the older drugs, heterocyclic antidepressants and monoamine oxidase inhibitors, were routinely used, but like the older neuroleptics, they had troublesome side effects. More recently selective serotonin reuptake inhibitors (SSRIs) and atypical antidepressants have become prominent. Some of the antidepressant agents also are effective in treating anxiety. Medication used to treat depression will be discussed in Chapter 8, anxiety in Chapter 9, and schizophrenia and bipolar disorder in Chapter 12.

Although medication can treat symptoms, it does not eliminate the psychosocial problems of individuals who take the medication, clients' feelings about being dependent on drugs, or the side effects of the drugs. Medications such as neuroleptics do not cure the disease and only partially eliminate symptoms. Some prescribed drugs, especially those that treat anxiety and sleep disorders, are addictive. Some medications affect sexual potency or desire.

Although social workers do not prescribe medication, they work with clients who receive or need psychopharmacotherapy. Social workers have become increasingly aware of their need to be knowledgeable about psychotropic drugs, their expected effects, and their deleterious side effects (Bentley & Walsh, 1996; Gerhart & Brooks, 1983; Libassi, 1990; Matorin & De Chillo, 1984; Willinger, 1997). Often social workers refer clients to psychiatrists for an evaluation for medication. For those clients who are already on medication, social workers are able to observe the extent to which medications are working, client compliance, potential interactions with other substances, and other complications. Social workers should be able to recognize physical, psychological, and social side effects of drugs and work with the client and others involved in the client's care (Bentley & Walsh, 1996). As future chapters will explain, psychosocial interventions are often implemented in conjunction with medication.

Physical Health Maintenance

The biopsychosocial perspective recognizes that the human body needs protection, care, and nurturance throughout the life cycle. Protection is provided in part by a safe, sanitary living environment that is heated during cold weather. Persons without safe homes are subject to the vicissitudes of street life, where they may be physically beaten, raped, and robbed. Poor sanitary conditions in some homes are a seedbed for the development of physical disease. Homes in which physical or psychological abuse prevails are dangerous to physical safety and mental health.

Physical nurturance is fostered by eating a well-balanced diet. Eating healthy foods in moderation and regularly keeps the body going. Furthermore, eating can be a social activity that connects people with one another. Deficiencies and excesses in one's diet can lead to physical and psychiatric disorders. Persons with particular health problems, such as diabetes, must restrict their diets in certain ways. Clients on some psychotropic medications also must make changes in their diet.

Drinking is an activity that some people are able to do in moderation. Others, however, abstain because of their personal or cultural values or because they are alcoholics who cannot control their drinking. Except for persons who are on prescribed medications or are addicted to chemical substances, people do not need alcohol or drugs. (See Chapter 13 for further discussion on chemical addiction.)

Physical health maintenance is a lifelong activity that begins in infancy when parents are responsible for maintaining their offspring's health. In adulthood one is expected to be responsible for one's own physical well-being by eating properly, getting sufficient sleep, exercising, and monitoring one's own physical health. Adults prevent health problems by consulting physicians and dentists on a regular basis for checkups and when they feel sick. Persons who take care of their bodies in this way are exercising control over their physical health.

During times of stress, the body can break down. Conditions such as poverty, widowhood, and job loss are associated with diminished resistance to disease (Weiner & Fawzy, 1989). When multiple stressors converge on the same person around the same time, a person's coping resources are pushed to the limits. At such times concurrent physical and psychological symptoms may develop. Similarly, when one is physically ill, one may develop psychological symptoms that are a reaction to the illness. Here, too, the biological and psychological components are connected.

Psychological Knowing

Psychological theories provide explanations for the inner workings of the mind, that is, underlying motivations that drive human action. Because these explanations often involve biological functions (e.g., instincts) and socially valued goals (e.g., love), it is difficult to separate the psychological from the biological and social. In this section, two theories that are socially constructed as psychological will be described. Both of these theories—ego psychology and cognitive theory—provide frameworks for understanding normal and psychopathological behavior. Ego psychology was chosen because of its contributions to understanding and treating mental disorders, its emphasis on the relationship, and its concern with mastery and coping; cognitive theory was chosen for its strong record of practice effectiveness.

Understanding Ego Psychology

Ego psychology is a reconstruction of Freud's psychoanalytic theory, particularly his structural theory. Initially developed by Hartmann (1958) and his colleagues (Kris and Loewenstein), it has been enriched by the writings of Anna Freud (1946), Erikson (1950, 1959), and White (1959), as well as object relations theorists. Its departures from classical, doctrinaire psychoanalysis (especially the drive theory and psychic determinism) and its emphasis on the reciprocal relationship between the person and the environment make ego psychology particularly compatible with social work.

In psychoanalysis and ego psychology, three hypothetical structures—the ego, id, and superego—comprise the psychic system. The id represents impulses, desires, and wishes that know no boundaries; the superego encompasses the conscience and ego ideal; and the ego is responsible for perception, reality testing, and mediation. In ego psychology the ego is vested with more independence than it had in classical psychoanalysis. In psychoanalysis, the ego derives from the id and attempts to achieve the aims of the id in realistic ways. In ego psychology, both ego and id arise from an undifferentiated matrix that is present at birth; ego and id become differentiated from this matrix and develop separately and in concert with each other. The ego develops apparatuses of primary autonomy, inborn capacities for perception, intelligence, thinking, motility, and the like, which can develop outside psychic conflict. In addition, the ego develops apparatuses of secondary autonomy, defenses that are associated with conflict early in life but which are later transformed through a process change of function to interests, goals, and preferences. With the expansion and increased autonomy of ego functions in ego psychology, the ego became more than a mediator among the three parts of the psychic system and between the psyche and the external reality. The ego in ego psychology organizes, forms object relations, and promotes adaptation (Blanck & Blanck, 1974, 1979; Dixon, 1981; Hartmann, 1958).

Adaptation refers to the capacity to achieve a state of equilibrium with the environment. It includes the ability to survive, respond, make one's needs known to others, and solve problems. An active process, it depends partially on the possession of biological equipment and partially on the capacity of the environment to respond. According to Hartmann (1958), people are born with a capacity to adapt to an "average expectable environment," that is, an environment that is safe, provides food and warmth, and is reasonably nurturant. A child cannot be expected to cope with an abusive environment. Hartmann also posits that there is a reciprocal relationship between the person and the environment. Strengths and deficits in the person and the environment affect each other.

Ego psychology builds on, reinterprets, and makes modifications of Freud's drive theory. Freud postulated that there are two primary drives that motivate human behavior— libido and aggression. Blanck and Blanck (1979) assert that these drives should be distinguished from affects; that is, libido and love are not equivalent, nor are aggression and hostility. On the basis of Freud's later work, Blanck and Blanck conclude that libido refers to the drive to unite or bond with others and that aggression refers to undoing connections (and, consequently, destroying them). This interpretation permits aggression to include the separation-individuation process, which was described by Mahler, Pine, and Bergman (1975). The two drives, as revised, are complementary rather than polar opposites. Like the ego and id, they are innate capacities latent in the undifferentiated matrix. In early life, the libido is dominant, fostering the development of object relations. Soon the drive to be separate and individuated becomes dominant. But both drives coexist and function in concert with each other (Blanck & Blanck, 1979).

Building on the ideas of Hartmann and other ego psychologists, White (1959) postulated that there is a source of motivation for human behavior that does not emanate from the two drives. This source does not seem to have as its goal the one Freud proposed, the reduction of tension. White identified a motivation for competence that is exemplified in exploration, manipulating objects, and mastery—activities that are pursued for their own sake. He stated further that participation in activities such as these may, in fact, increase tension rather than reduce it. Competence motivation, which is associated with the ego, engages the person with the environment.

White came up with a new term, *effectance,* to capture the feeling of efficacy (having an impact on the environment), which comes from the exercise of competence. He suggested that independent ego energies provide fuel for effectance. The emphasis on mastery of the environment through effective activity (i.e., coping) is an important contribution to ego theory.

Ego psychology also includes a developmental perspective. It acknowledges that early life experiences, such as losses and other traumatic events, can impede healthy development. On the other hand, it recognizes Erikson's (1950, 1959) contribution that human growth is a continuous activity that occurs throughout the life span. Although his eight developmental stages are presented as polar opposites (*trust versus mistrust, autonomy versus shame and doubt, initiative versus guilt, industry versus inferiority, identity versus identity diffusion, intimacy versus isolation, generativity versus stagnation,* and *integrity versus despair*), Erikson viewed each stage on a continuum and considered all stages to exist in some form concurrently. Accordingly, his developmental stages are not problematic from a postmodern perspective.

Ego psychology has also been enriched by the contributions of neoanalytic and object relations theorists in the United States and England who are interested in childhood development. Although there is considerable diversity among individual thinkers, they share an emphasis on the development of object relations. Objects are persons, the self and others, who take on a life of their own as structures that are introjected within the psyche. The infant develops into a social human being in the context of social interactions with significant others. Through an emotionally charged interpersonal relational process, the ego incorporates representations of the self and significant others into the self. At first infants fuse with their principal caregivers. In time and with some ambivalence, they become aware of differences and they become more independent. As they develop, they form mental images (internalized representations) of themselves and others, which allow them to carry significant others and others' images of themselves with them as they become separate. Successful negotiation of early developmental stages promotes the formation of permanent, stable personality structures (Blanck & Blanck, 1986).

The cumulative contributions of ego psychologists and object relations theorists make it possible to obtain a more expansive view of the role of the ego in adaptive functioning. The ego promotes personality organization and object relations (Blanck & Blanck, 1979, 1986). It regulates internal processes, links the person with the environment, and promotes mastery. The ego helps the individual distinguish between internal and external demands, control impulses, and develop interpersonal relationships. It fosters growth throughout the life cycle through a process of bonding (libido) and separation-individuation. The defense mechanisms described by Anna Freud (1946) and others are also associated with the ego.

The Therapeutic Relationship.

The psychoanalytic school—which includes ego psychology, neoanalytic, and object relations theory, as well as feminist theory within this framework—has made a tremendous contribution to understanding the therapeutic relationship. This relationship provides a context in which a client can receive nurturance and acceptance that he or she may not have had as a child. The process of working through issues from the past that are transferred to the therapist makes it possible for clients to correct distortions in the structure of their personalities and develop more realistic relationships with others. As described in feminist theory that has emerged from the Stone Center, relationships are central to personal growth and self-realization (Jordan, 1997a). Empathetic understanding from a clinician can reduce a client's isolation and promote his or her feelings of connectedness (Jordan, 1997b). Although many managed care plans restrict the time period in which relationship issues can be worked through, the quality of the therapeutic relationship (or alliance) remains important.

Ego Psychological Treatment.

Ego psychology is implemented in the context of a therapeutic relationship in which the social worker conveys empathy, acceptance, and support. The therapist serves as an auxiliary ego to the client. Goldstein (1995) describes two types of ego psychological treatment: ego supportive and ego modifying. The ego-supportive approach aims to help the client adapt or achieve mastery over an immediate problem, crisis, or stressful situation. Intervention focuses on a current situation and engages the client's conscious thoughts and feelings. Change is directed at the person, the environment, and/or the interaction between the person and the environment. The therapist works with the existing and latent strengths of the client's ego and builds on these. Through understanding, reflecting on, and utilizing these capacities, the client comes to resolve an immediate problem and attain a sense of satisfaction in utilizing internal capacities and external supports. Ego-supportive treatment may be brief or long term.

The ego-modifying strategy emphasizes the development of insight and the resolution of intrapsychic conflict. Accordingly, past historical material is utilized and the transference that arises in the therapeutic relationship is interpreted. The client is engaged in a process of self-disclosure, uncovering, and working through recurrent maladaptive patterns. Generally ego-modifying treatment is long term and appropriate only for certain clients. Goldstein (1995) recommends this strategy primarily for clients with good ego strengths but some maladaptive patterns and says that it can be used selectively with clients with more severe pathology. For the client who has developmental deficits that interfere with object constancy, the social worker becomes an object for the client and facilitates the development of object constancy. This kind of intervention takes a great deal of skill.

Ego-supportive treatment is beneficial to persons with severe mental disorders, such as schizophrenia, who need ongoing support yet cannot tolerate intrusive therapy. Ego-modifying treatment can also be helpful to persons with borderline and narcissistic personality disorders as well as other characterological and neurotic difficulties. In this volume, however, therapeutic work with persons with personality disorders is not emphasized.

Understanding Cognitive Theory

Cognitive theory focuses on thinking, beliefs, interpretations, and images. Associated with diverse theorists, most hold that emotional reactions and maladaptive behavior are mediated by thoughts. Cognitive theory has been intellectually traced to the Greek stoic philosophers (Beck, 1985). It was introduced to psychological thought by Adler and Kelly (Chatterjee, 1984). Today a cognitive perspective is shared by social scientists and therapists concerned with information processing, stress theory, interactional processes, self-efficacy, and irrational belief systems. Many have combined cognitive theory and therapeutic procedures with behavioral approaches in cognitive-behavioral therapy (e.g., Meichenbaum, 1977).

Cognitive theories have introduced a number of concepts that provide anchors for understanding. One is the *scheme* or *schema.* Piaget (1936/1974), a cognitive developmental theorist, proposed that in the course of acting in relation to the environment, the infant develops schemes or structural units that correspond with and organize experience. As the child grows, the schemes widen, become more complex, and become encoded in symbolic forms. Cognitive theorists have used the term *scheme* to refer to the individual's units of thought or information. Accordingly, one may have a scheme for one's parents ("they care about me"), one's friends ("they do not care enough about me"), and so on. Kelly (1963) came up with a related term, *personal construct,* to describe an individual's mode of interpreting experiences and anticipating consequences.

Another term used in cognitive theory is *automatic thoughts* (Beck, 1976). These are messages one gives oneself, often in a telegraphic form, which precede an experience of emotional arousal. The messages may be instructional, interpretive, self-praising, or self-critical. Persons experiencing depression, for example, may have thoughts about their own worthlessness; those with anxiety may think about unrealistic dangers that lurk in the environment. Automatic thoughts are evident in verbal self-statements and mental images. According to Beck (1976), automatic thoughts influence subsequent emotions and behavior.

Appraisal is a kind of automatic thought in which a judgment is made about the nature of an event and its meaning. Lazarus and Folkman (1984) view appraisal as a cognitive process that intervenes between the presentation of a stimulus and the development of stress. They describe three kinds of stressful appraisals—harm/loss, threat, and challenge. In harm/loss, a loss in physical functioning, property, or personal relationship is recognized. With threat, loss or harm is anticipated, usually on the basis of something that has already happened. Challenge is associated with possible learning or growth that may occur. Appraisals such as these, together with a person's reservoir of coping mechanisms, play a part in determining whether a person will go into a crisis or effectively manage a stressful life event.

Attributions, a term from social psychology, are causal explanations of an event (Sarasan & Sarasan, 1989). Associated with one's cognitive schemes, attributions blame, assign responsibility, or give credit to oneself, other persons, nature, or other phenomena. Usually a distinction is made between internal and external attributions, that is, whether one holds oneself or outside forces responsible for one's situation (Rotter, 1966). Depressed persons tend to blame themselves for their troubles, regardless of whether or not they are responsible for the situation. In cognitive therapy, efforts are made to correct inappropriate attributions.

Two founding cognitive theorists are Albert Ellis and Aaron Beck. Ellis developed a therapy known as *rational emotive therapy* (RET). He holds that irrational beliefs (B), aroused by activating events (A), are responsible for the development of neurotic symptoms or dysfunctional behaviors (C). Beliefs that engender these consequences are generally grandiose, narcissistic, and unrealistic, such as the ideas that one must be loved by all people one considers significant; that one must be thoroughly competent; and that when one gets frustrated, the situation in which one finds oneself is awful (Ellis & Harper, 1975). These beliefs have an exaggerated quality and often use the words *should* and *must.* Irrational beliefs represent logical fallacies in which one misconstrues oneself, others, and situations.

Ellis recognizes that behaviors, beliefs, and emotions are related. By changing irrational beliefs through a course of therapy, dysfunctional emotions and behaviors dissipate and are replaced by constructive ones. Therapy consists of identifying irrational ideas, refuting them through logical argument, and replacing irrational with rational self-talk. RET is didactic and experiential. It utilizes homework assignments, role play, practice exercises, and imagery. Generally it is short term and concerned with conscious, current experiences (Ellis, 1979).

Aaron Beck's cognitive theory and therapy are similar to Ellis's. Beck (1976, 1985) believes that automatic thoughts trigger affects (anxiety, sadness, anger, affection) and behavior (flight, withdrawal, attack, approach). Characteristic of normal and psychopathological reactions, automatic thoughts can become so distorted that they result in dysfunctional responses. These thoughts are endowed with meaning that is idiosyncratic to the individual and specific to the psychopathological syndrome.

Beck (1985) identified several cognitive errors made by depressed and anxious people. One, called *selective abstraction,* is a generalization that accounts for only one aspect of a situation, while at the same time other components of the situation are ignored (e.g., "I am a bad mother because my child got a C"). This is similar to another error, *overgeneralization,* in which an inference resting on one experience is applied to all like situations ("I can't do anything right"). Another logical error is *arbitrary inference.* Here an inaccurate conclusion is drawn from a neutral experience (e.g., "Jack is avoiding me" when Jack, in fact, did not see anyone). With *personalization* one endows events with meaning related to oneself. In this case others' statements or affective responses ("mother looks perturbed") are viewed as causally related to one's own behavior ("I hurt her feelings"). Another cognitive error is *dichotomous* (or *polarized*) *thinking.* Here the individual perceives only two contrasting and extreme alternatives—a phenomenon that is often described as tunnel vision. With *magnification* or *minimization* one exaggerates the difficulty of a task or underestimates one's ability to accomplish it.

Depressed persons make cognitive errors to support negative pictures of themselves, their experiences, and the outlook for the future—three dimensions that Beck (1985) describes as the *cognitive triad.* They may, for example, generalize from a single experience (e.g., "I was turned down for a job") to prospects in the distant future ("no one will ever hire me"). They see themselves as totally worthless and attribute neutral actions on the part of others to themselves. Anxious persons err in their interpretation of signals of danger. Accordingly, they become apprehensive in situations that are objectively safe. Thoughts focus on an anticipated catastrophe, such as death, losing control, or failure.

Beck's treatment appears to give more attention to the therapeutic relationship than Ellis's. Therapist and client are viewed as partners working together to bring about cognitive restructuring. The therapist conveys warmth, acceptance, and understanding. Like the RET therapist, Beck's therapist is an intellectual guide, who leads the client in understanding the belief system that is related to the problem and in making changes in thinking and behavior.

Cognitive treatment begins with helping the client identify automatic thoughts (Beck, 1985). The client may be asked to describe a stressful situation in order to recognize the thought that precipitated it, or to keep a diary of fleeting thoughts. After the thoughts are identified, the cognitive errors embedded in the thoughts are discussed. Distortions in thinking are identified and alternative explanations are proposed. This process, *reattribution training,* opens up alternative ways of thinking (schemes) to the client. Next cognitive distortions, such as overgeneralizations, are subjected to an empirical test in the outside world (Beck, 1985). The client is given the task of testing false expectations (e.g., "no one wants to talk to me") by initiating new activities (e.g., talking to a number of people and documenting their responses). These exercises may be rehearsed in advance and are discussed after they are performed. Afterward the client's distortions are reexamined in the light of empirical findings. The client's level of stress is monitored during the course of treatment (Beck, 1985).

Cognitive therapy is used to help individuals understand and modify thoughts associated with anxiety, depression, phobias, obsessions, compulsions, mania, delusions, and other conditions (Beck, 1976, 1985) (see Table 3.3). Usually therapy is brief and focused on an immediate problem. In this volume special attention will be given to Beck's method of treating depression (see Chapter 8). Empirical findings on Beck's model of treatment of depression indicate that not only is cognitive therapy effective, it is sometimes superior to treatment with antidepressant drugs used alone (Beck, 1985).

Social Environmental Knowing

Another way of knowing considers the social environment, that is, behaviors that are stimulated by and reinforced by others, interactions with other persons, and other contextual

TABLE 3.3 **Application of Cognitive Therapies**

Concepts	Targeted Symptoms	Techniques
Schemes	Depression	Identify irrational ideas
Automatic thoughts	Anxiety	or automatic thoughts
Appraisal	Phobias	Refutation
Attributions	Obsessions	Reattribution training
Cognitive errors	Compulsions	Empirical testing
	Mania	
	Delusions	

Source: Based on Bandura (1982); Beck (1976, 1985); Ellis (1979); Lazarus and Folkman (1984).

considerations. Some social environmental ways of knowing that are relevant to mental health practice will be described next.

Understanding Behavioral Theories

Behavioral theories are concerned with environmental events or conditions that surround behaviors. These theories assume that regardless of whether behaviors are adaptive or maladaptive, they are learned. Through an understanding of scientific principles of learning, one can implement procedures that extinguish, maintain, or modify existing behaviors and foster the development of new ones.

Behavioral theories are empirically grounded. Originally based on animal research, they have been carefully applied to and researched in relation to human individuals and groups. Behavioral therapies employ rigorous scientific procedures in the assessment process, during implementation, and in evaluation. In each case, specific, observed, problematic behaviors are identified, and changes are implemented, monitored, and measured. Behavioral therapies have a strong record of practice effectiveness (Thomlison, 1986).

Within the behavioral school, there are three major approaches, each of which has contributed to an understanding of the person in relation to the environment and to therapeutic approaches. These are respondent (classical) conditioning, operant (instrumental) conditioning, and social learning theory. Although these schools emerged sequentially, in practice their boundaries have come to be blurred. As indicated, some behavioral therapies are informed by and integrated with the cognitive perspective.

Respondent Conditioning. *Respondent conditioning* was the earliest of the behavioral theories to appear. Also called classical conditioning and stimulus-response (S-R) theory, it was discovered by the Russian physiologist, Pavlov, who, in the course of his work with dogs, noticed that the dogs produced saliva automatically when they were given meat, a reaction he called an *unconditioned reflex.* But salivation also occurred in response to a bell that had been previously presented together with the meat but was later presented alone. Pavlov concluded that the bell, a neutral stimulus, acquired the capacity of the meat, a natural stimulus, to evoke the response after the two were paired together a few times. Pavlov called the meat an *unconditioned stimulus* (US) and the salivation an *unconditioned response* (UR) and determined that these were connected through a biological, reflexive process. He described the bell as a *conditioned stimulus* (CS) and the saliva produced by the bell alone a *conditioned response* (CR) and concluded that these became connected through a process of pairing or association (Chance, 1979).

Pavlov also noticed that dogs would salivate when something similar to the conditioned stimulus was presented, for example, a bell with a different tone. He called this tendency to respond to related stimuli *stimulus generalization* (Chance, 1979). Nevertheless, dogs could be taught to discriminate between similar stimuli when they were reinforced (or rewarded) for responding to some but not to other objects. Pavlov called differential conditioning *stimulus discrimination* (Chance, 1979).

In the process of experimentation, Pavlov induced dysfunctional behavior in the laboratory. Dogs that had learned to discriminate between similar stimuli (e.g., a circle and an ellipse) were asked to make finer and finer distinctions between two closely related pictures. When the dogs reached the limits of their capacity to discriminate, they became aggressive. Pavlov used the term *experimental neurosis* to characterize the dogs' behavior. It demonstrated that dysfunctional behavior is a product of frustrating environmental conditions (Chance, 1979).

Two therapeutic procedures are based on respondent conditioning. One, *extinction,* is based on Pavlov's discovery that a conditioned response could be eliminated. If the conditioned stimulus is presented repeatedly without the unconditioned stimulus, the association between conditioned and unconditioned stimuli weakens. The result is *extinction.* The principle of extinction is used to eliminate undesirable behaviors.

Another therapeutic technique that is based on principles of respondent conditioning is *systematic desensitization.* Developed by Wolpe (1982), systematic desensitization pairs an unconditioned stimulus, such as relaxation exercises, with a conditioned stimulus (e.g., a mental image of a situation about which one is phobic). A client who begins the session with relaxation exercises is presented with a hierarchy of situations, from the least anxiety provoking to the most, to imagine. The client participates in this exercise up to the point of experiencing anxiety. In subsequent sessions, the client proceeds through the hierarchy of situations, increasing tolerance along the way.

Systematic desensitization is based on the principle of *reciprocal inhibition* (Wolpe, 1982). Relaxation, an inhibiting stimulus, produces an effect that is the opposite of anxiety. By pairing relaxation with mental images of situations producing a phobia, the bond between the phobic situation and the anxiety loosens. The result is the elimination of an undesired (phobic) response. Systematic desensitization does, however, work with cognitions (mental imagery), placing it in the borderland between a behavioral and a cognitive technique (Wolpe, 1982).

Operant Conditioning.   *Operant conditioning* is a more widely held current behavioral theory. It differs from respondent conditioning in its emphasis on the *consequences* (or what follows) behavior, that is, the *reinforcement.* Also called *instrumental conditioning,* it is associated with B. F. Skinner. Skinner's theory is considered radical behaviorism because its attention to environmental contingencies minimizes the role of cognitive processes (Maddi, 1980).

According to operant conditioning, a behavior is strengthened (i.e., it is likely to recur) when it is followed by a reinforcement (Salkind, 1985). The reinforcement may be a reward or some action, consequence, or occurrence that increases the likelihood that the previous behavior will recur. *Positive reinforcements* are actions, stimuli, or consequences that follow the occurrence of a behavior, and which usually result in increased satisfaction. These may be primary (of biological importance, such as food) or secondary (of acquired value, such as a gold star). *Negative reinforcements* are consequences that allow one to escape or avoid an unpleasant situation (e.g., eliminating critical behavior following the performance of desired behavior) (Salkind, 1985). Regardless of whether the reinforcements are positive or negative, they promote the continuance of the preceding behavior.

Punishment is also used in operant conditioning (Crain, 1985). Punishment is an unpleasant or aversive consequence that results in decreasing a behavior. Punishments may be positive (add an unpleasant experience) or negative (something desired is taken away). Spanking, losing privileges, and having to pay fines are examples of punishments. Punishments (as well as reinforcements) should be tailored to the individual. Sometimes what appears to be a punishment (e.g., yelling at someone) becomes a reinforcement (increased attention).

Behavior modification based on principles of operant conditioning can be implemented successfully when several principles are observed. For one, the reinforcement should occur immediately after the behavior. Second, reinforcers that are meaningful to clients and relevant to their level of maturity should be chosen. Third, a schedule of reinforcement should be adopted. Initially a continuous schedule, in which reinforcement occurs following every desired behavior, might be adopted. This requires constant attention, but it does maintain the behavior. Later an intermittent schedule in which reinforcements are dispensed according to a fixed ratio (e.g., every sixth time), a fixed interval (e.g., every 10 seconds), or on a variable or random schedule may be desirable (Salkind, 1985). Intermittent reinforcement more closely parallels the operation of the real world.

A variety of behavior modification techniques can be used to create desirable behaviors as well as extinguish undesirable ones. *Shaping* consists of progressively reinforcing behaviors as they come closer and closer to what is desired (Crain, 1985). At first behaviors that are in the ballpark of the desired behavior are reinforced (e.g., a child's sound "mm"). Later behaviors that more closely resemble what is desired (e.g., "mum") are reinforced until the desired outcome is achieved (e.g., "mama"). Persons with phobias can eliminate fears by gradually approaching the object feared. Close approximations are reinforced.

Another technique that is used is *time-out*. A kind of negative punishment, it is implemented by removing an individual from a pleasant situation to an unpleasant one. An example of this was the removal of a client who had an annoying cough that was not medically caused from the day treatment program room to a "coughing room" in which there was no furniture or other attractive stimuli. The client's deprivation of positive reinforcement from the group through this punishment resulted in a reduction in the frequency of his coughing behavior.

A third approach is the *token economy*. Tokens are items such as chips that can be traded in for products or privileges. Many residential institutions and some community programs utilize this mechanism. Clients in programs using this procedure earn tokens for desirable behaviors but can lose them when they violate rules. This way, clients can work toward goals that they choose and learn the consequences of not abiding by rules of the program. A problem encountered by clients who have lived in residential settings utilizing a token economy arises when they move into the community. It is easier to manipulate rewards and punishments in a controlled than in a natural environment.

Behavior modification therapy is implemented after careful study. Initially extensive information about problematic behaviors is sought. Specific data about the *antecedents* (what precedes the behavior), the *behavior* itself, and the *consequences* are gathered. This includes what happens, when, where, who is involved, and how often. The client, parents, or caregiver may be asked to document the specific observable events and frequency of the behavior prior to intervention to gather *baseline data* on the initial problem. Very often charts or inventories are used to record this information. On the basis of this information, problematic behaviors are prioritized and one or more target behaviors are selected for modification. Next an individualized program is set up. The client and the worker together select and create a contract, spelling out the *contingencies* (conditions under which reinforcements and/or punishments will occur) and the reinforcements. Accordingly, the individual is able to receive reinforcements after performing certain behaviors (e.g., listen to music after maintaining a diet for a day). If the individual does not live up to the terms of the contract, punishments may be instituted (e.g., must give money to opposing political party). Homework assignments are given in response to issues raised in therapy sessions. Data and charts are kept throughout the process and for a short time following achievement of the goal (Thomlison, 1986).

Behavior modification is widely used in the field of mental health. It has been used successfully to treat individuals with addictive, fearful, sexual, and obsessive-compulsive behaviors, as well as physiological problems (Walen, Hauserman, & Lavin, 1977). It is used with groups and families, with children and older adults. Approaches with individuals with anxiety will be described in Chapter 9.

Social Learning Theory.   *Social learning theory* is a behavioral theory in which observational learning is emphasized. Associated with Rotter (1954) and Bandura (1977), it also uses principles of classical and operant conditioning. In recent years social learning theory has been giving increased attention to cognition. Because of its recognition of mental processes that mediate between behaviors that are observed and those that are performed, social learning theory may be considered a cognitive-behavioral theory.

According to social learning theory, behavior is acquired by observing other persons or events. One need not perform the behavior oneself to learn about it. Observers can learn or acquire new behaviors by watching, listening to, or reading about models. Observation encompasses the process (what models do, how they perform) and the consequences (rewards or punishments provided to the model or observer) that are perceived to occur. Inferences are made about what can be anticipated (*expectancy*) and rules that guide the model's behavior (*abstract modeling*) (Bandura, 1977). Observers develop inner symbolic representations of what they have seen and match their own behaviors with these. This way they can reproduce behaviors they have observed.

Social learning theory is guided by the principle of *reciprocal determinism* (Bandura, 1978). Accordingly there is a three-way interaction among the behavior, the external environment, and internal events (including cognition). The environment affects the individual's behavior through the mediation of cognition; the individual's behavior and cognition in turn affect the environment.

Four interrelated subprocesses promote observational learning—attention, retention, motoric reproduction, and reinforcement and motivational processes (Bandura, 1977). First of all, the model must be able to attract the *attention* of the observer. Qualities such as beauty, status, power, and emotionality seem to promote attention. Second, the observer must be able to remember and store what was observed. *Retention* is aided by two representational systems that encode what is observed. One system, imaginal, consists of pictorial representations of what is observed. The other, verbal, is comprised of words that describe what was seen. The third subprocess is *motoric reproduction,* the transformation of recalled symbolic representations into behavior. Here one matches one's performance with a mental image or verbal representation of what is to occur. Motoric reproduction requires practice, integration, and performance. In the process of performance, the individual corrects errors and makes adjustments. The fourth process is called *reinforcement and motivational processes* and encompasses incentives to reproduce observed behavior. When one recognizes that the model is rewarded rather than punished, or that the reproduction of observed behavior is rewarded, there is reason to replicate the behavior.

Behavioral change, maintenance, or control can occur through the use of reinforcements, punishment, and self-regulation. Reinforcements and punishments can be applied to the participant or observer or to oneself. Individuals can regulate their own behaviors by observing and assessing their own behaviors and cognitions and by responding and correcting their own behaviors. Through self-regulation, the self (through its cognitive faculties) takes on the function of the environment of providing rewards and punishments (Lundin, 1983). The self develops a feeling of *self-efficacy,* or competence (Bandura, 1982).

Clinical social workers can use principles of social learning theory in their practice with clients by modeling prosocial behaviors for clients with asocial or antisocial tendencies. In working with clients with phobias, social workers can convey confidence in the face of situations that clients fear. Social workers can model the desired behavior first and then have clients practice and perform what was observed. Similarly social workers can demonstrate the performance of social skills, assume the client's role in role plays, and otherwise model desirable behaviors for clients with severe mental disabilities. Social skills training with this population will be described in Chapter 12. Table 3.4 illustrates how the various behavioral therapies are applied.

Understanding Social Interactions and Transactions

However useful psychological and behavioral theories may be, they provide little insight on interactions between individuals and transactions between persons and their environment. Among the social work theories that address these interactions are the ecological perspective, family therapy theory, and small group theory.

The *ecological perspective* uses ecological concepts from biology as a metaphor with which to describe the reciprocity between persons and their environments (Germain & Gitterman, 1995). Accordingly, attention is on the goodness of the fit between an individual or group and the places in which they live out their lives (Germain & Gitterman, 1995). The ecological perspective's emphasis on health, potentiality, and competence

TABLE 3.4   **Application of Behavioral Therapies**

Types[*]	Target Symptoms	Techniques and Procedures
Respondent Operant Social learning	Maladaptive behavior of the severely mentally disabled Dysfunctional family patterns Anxiety Depression Addictions Obsessive-compulsive behavior	Extinction Systematic desensitization Reinforcement (positive and negative) Punishment Shaping Token economy Role modeling Role rehearsal Role playing

[*]Although the types listed were once discrete, today techniques and concepts from the various schools overlap.

highlights human adaptability and problems in living rather than psychopathology (Germain & Gitterman, 1987). Furthermore, it looks at stress and coping.

The ecological perspective is social in its focus on human relatedness, attachment, and person-environment transactions. Germain and Gitterman (1987), for example, view human relationships as the outcomes of interactions and regard the need for relatedness, support, and affiliation as essential to human functioning. Individual problems may be rooted in maladaptive relationships with other persons or institutions—problems that may be remedied through social environmental interventions as well as an individual approach.

More than the other perspectives, this one provides a framework for the practitioner to identify forces within and outside a client system as well as the transactions between systems that contribute to a problem and can assist in the development of a solution. Attention is drawn to the function the problem serves within each system and those forces in the person and environment that contribute to the maintenance of the problem. Furthermore, resources that can improve the fit between person and environment by fostering growth, development, and affiliation are identified. The social environment presents obstacles and provides resources for change.

The ecological perspective is applicable to all clients but is particularly germane to understanding and intervening with clients who are severely mentally disabled, many of whom are poor, socially isolated, and underserved by the human service system. In working with this population, the clinical social worker can bridge the gap between the person and the environment to create a better fit. With its emphasis on competence, mastery, and coping in the context of the natural environment, ecological theory provides a lens that can be helpful in understanding the situation of these clients and mobilizing resources and supports that are needed (Libassi, 1988).

Family therapy theories also address social interactions, particularly those among members of family units. Depending on the theoretical perspective used (e.g., transgenerational, behavioral, structural, contextual, strategic), problematic interactions are viewed as patterns acquired from previous generations, learned behaviors that are reinforced, or some other interpretation. Clinicians work with the nuclear family or household as a whole, with subunits (parents, children), and multiple generations of family members, helping them change dysfunctional patterns to more constructive modes of interaction.

Therapeutic intervention with a family aims to change structure, communication patterns, organization, and behaviors. Roles and responsibilities may be reallocated; boundaries between members and between the family and others may be redefined; feelings may be expressed, shared, and understood; and dysfunctional behaviors may be identified and changed.

The newer narrative and constructionist approaches to family therapy (see especially White & Epston, 1990) are in keeping with the postmodern perspective of this book. These approaches engage the family in a collaborative process of meaning-making. Families are encouraged to tell their stories, deconstruct them so that they hear how they have incorporated narratives of the dominant culture within these stories, and rewrite them (Diamond, 1998). Some innovative methods such as the reflecting team (Anderson, 1991) are used. Although their effectiveness has not yet been demonstrated in empirical research, they are compatible with managed care because these approaches can be implemented over a short period of time and focus on the client's goals (Kelley, 1998).

In behavioral health practice, the individual is usually identified as the "case." Nevertheless, the family may be contributing to or reinforcing maladaptive individual patterns. In such instances, the family should have some involvement in treatment. Often the problem can be appropriately defined as familial, in which case the family should be the locus of treatment. In work with families with severe mental disorders, the family needs to be educated about the nature of the family member's disorder and how to respond. In such cases family (psycho)educational approaches are used (see Chapter 12).

Groups, like families, comprise a context in which interpersonal interactions take place. A natural way for individuals to get together, groups lend themselves to therapies in which the group processes are used to help people in various ways. Groups are used widely in outpatient behavioral health settings to provide psychotherapy, support, and psychoeducation. They are also used in inpatient substance abuse and mental health residential treatment, as well in partial hospitalization programs.

Like family therapy theory, group theory has a variety of schools, each with its own perspective. Some of the therapeutic groups incorporate behavioral, psychoanalytic, and existential theories into practice. Most groups incorporate concepts from small group theory.

Groups provide a context in which clients can express their feelings, identify problematic behaviors, gain insight into their problems, and make changes. With the support of a peer group and clinical social workers, clients can talk about or nonverbally act out problems that they ordinarily would keep to themselves. The group serves as a point of reference and support for the client to achieve autonomy, self-determination, and a feeling of competence and worth. The acceptance the group provides enables the client to achieve self-acceptance.

Group intervention techniques vary according to the goals and purpose of the group and the theory that drives it. The group approach to social skills training is described in Chapter 12.

Understanding Other Dimensions of Context

The term *social environment* encompasses other areas that characterize clients' lives. Although the word *environment* sounds external, the dimensions that will be addressed next are parts of clients' inner as well as external worlds. Behavioral health practice is affected by the cultures and genders of clients and workers, and by which cultures and genders are dominant in the larger society.

Cultures are communities that have a common history, knowledge, language, values, and behavior. Their shared ways of viewing experience enter into their daily interactions among themselves and with outsiders and are transmitted through socialization processes from one generation to the next. Patterns of perceiving, experiencing, evaluating, and knowing provide persons who are socialized in a particular culture with unique ways of viewing the world. Culture is expressed in verbal and nonverbal behavior, artifacts, rituals, stories, and social organization.

Although mental health is a master narrative in today's mainstream U.S. culture, many clients do not share this perspective. Cultures vary in their definitions of emotional problems and where they place responsibility (the individual, a curse engendered in a previous generation, the gods, etc.). Moreover, cultures provide their own ways of treating emotional troubles or their equivalents and specialized personnel, such as folk healers.

Social work practitioners work with members of diverse ethnic groups whose family interaction patterns, style of communication, and behavior may be different from that of the social worker. Culture is an important dimension of understanding that should be brought into the assessment and treatment of clients. The impact of culture on the delivery of mental health services will be discussed in Chapter 7.

Gender is another dimension of self and society that inevitably enters into behavioral health practice. Some of the psychological theories that were used in the twentieth century defined normal human development and personality in terms of male behavior. New knowledge about women's ways of knowing has made it possible for men and women to live more fully on their own terms. Chapter 6 will discuss gender issues in behavioral health from a postmodern feminist perspective.

Integrating Biological, Psychological, and Social Ways of Knowing

It was stated earlier in this chapter that the division of areas of knowledge into separate disciplines has made it necessary to present biological, psychological, and social environmental perspectives as separate sections. Because the practitioner works with clients who are biopsychosocial wholes, there is a need to understand how these perspectives converge in the individual client.

One way in which these elements come into play is in the development of a psychiatric episode. Even though an individual may have a genetic predisposition for a mental disorder, he or she may not develop the disorder. During everyday life, individuals are faced with myriad events that can be construed as threatening or benign. When a person who is vulnerable to stress is surrounded by people who are patient, protective, and caring, these significant others may offer interpretations or interventions that can prevent events from being experienced as threatening. When persons like this who buffer stress are not available, life occurrences that tax the person's capacity to cope can precipitate a psychiatric episode. Accordingly, environmental stressors can arouse a latent biological phenomenon, while environmental supports can impede it. Furthermore, a psychological process (the construction of the meaning of a stressor) can be aided and averted by those who contribute to its interpretation. The role of stressors and supports in the genesis of schizophrenia will be developed further in the discussion of the stress-vulnerability-coping model in Chapter 10.

This book addresses four groups of mental disorders—severe and persistent mental illness (schizophrenia, major mood disorders, and related disorders); depression; anxiety; and substance abuse. In the chapters on intervention with persons with these disorders, the biological, psychological, and social environmental dimensions are described and applied to treatment. With an integrated understanding of how these elements converge in the individual client, social workers can implement interventions that account for the client's complexity.

Summary and Deconstruction

Clinical practice in behavioral health is informed by an integrative biopsychosocial perspective. Accordingly neither biological, nor psychological, nor social dimensions determine mental health. Instead, knowledge and theories arising from these perspectives infuse each other and are interrelated. The integrative model proposed here is nonlinear and multifaceted. It is predicated on a view of the person as an active agent who strives for empowerment and meaning. Health and mental health are viewed as positive goals. Clients' strengths and vulnerabilities are recognized and respected.

The revolution in biological knowledge during the last few decades of the twentieth century can be viewed from the perspectives of those at the margins, particularly clients, but also social workers, who are largely informed by psychological and social knowledge.

The dominance of the biological narrative has reinforced the position of psychiatrists and medicine. As a consequence, psychiatrists are "providing care" in the form of prescriptions, which clients are "receiving." This promotes a relationship of inequality in knowledge and power, which is an impediment to the goal of client empowerment. Furthermore, psychiatrists' knowledge has become "the" knowledge that has the potential of obscuring clients' self-knowledge and awareness of what they want to know.

Similarly but in a different vein, social workers' knowledge can become underestimated while biological knowledge is overvalued. Although social workers' expertise in the person-environment interaction is integral to behavioral health practice, as well as the ordinary, daily lives of clients, in an atmosphere of biological hegemony, this knowledge can be overlooked.

In this postmodern era in which information is freely available in cyberspace, the ownership of knowledge has become anachronistic. A day may arrive when clients insist on certain treatments and mental health professionals become the respondents.

Case Study

Mrs. Marilyn Holden is a well-groomed Caucasian forty-year-old woman of average height who came to the outpatient mental health center at the suggestion of the admissions director at a nursing home where her husband was recently placed following a stay in the state psychiatric hospital. Mrs. Holden had told the director that ever since she had her husband committed to the state hospital, she has felt depressed.

Mrs. Holden told the clinical social worker at the mental health center that she had her husband committed because he was "acting up" at home. He was drinking a keg of beer every three or four days, cursing loudly, and hitting her and the children (a boy and a girl who are twelve and fourteen, respectively). In the past, he has choked her, pulled out her hair, doused her with beer, and has threatened to hurt the children. When he raised a knife at their son recently, she called the police, who brought him to the state hospital. Mrs. Holden explained that her husband was given the diagnosis of Huntington's disease several years ago, but he refused to take the medication that was prescribed after he was told that he could not drink while taking the medicine. He has not worked for five years because of difficulties he had holding a job. He has been receiving Social Security and Medicare. She has been working part time.

Mrs. Holden said that she and her husband have been married twenty-two years. They met in high school and married after they were graduated. Mrs. Holden said that during the first two years of their marriage they lived with her parents, who supported them until the couple were able to obtain stable jobs and save money for housing. During that period, her parents were critical of her for marrying when she was young. Later the couple were able to buy a home, where Mrs. Holden and the children live now. Mrs. Holden expressed affection for her husband "the way he used to be" but said that he has changed. During the last few years, he has followed her around the house and has made her account for her every move. Although his sexual demands have increased, she has felt increasingly repelled. Mrs. Holden expressed feelings of guilt about "dumping him" in the state hospital and a nursing home, at the same time she admitted feeling relieved.

Mrs. Holden said that during the past few years, the children have taken "breaks" from the family by staying with her mother and friends. They have spoken of "hating" their father and fearing that they would inherit the same disease. Mrs. Holden said that she had no idea when she married him that this disease ran in his family; she learned about it only after her husband was diagnosed and she began to ask questions. Since then she learned that his mother and uncle died of the disease and that cousins have the disease today. His family does not like to talk about it.

Mrs. Holden said that when Mr. Holden was living at home, she thought about killing him with a billy club. Since he has been out of the home, however, she has thought about killing herself. She said that she felt confused about "what she owed her husband and what she owed the children" and believes that over the years she has been a "bad mother" and now she is a "bad wife." She said that she had been ignoring his abusive behavior and drinking in the past, even though these behaviors affected her and the children. She reported feeling like a failure and wished that she could feel better about herself.

Mrs. Holden said that her mother continues to provide support to her family. Her mother believes that Mrs. Holden did "the right thing" in placing him in a nursing home but did "the wrong thing" over the years in ignoring the feelings of the children. Mrs. Holden has frequent contact with her mother, a widow in poor health, whom Mrs. Holden helps with household chores and shopping. Other supports include friends and the Huntington's disease support group. There are relatives on her husband's side who are critical of her for placing him in the nursing home. Nevertheless, none of them was willing to have him stay with them. Mrs. Holden requested support from the social worker in sticking with her decision to leave her husband in the nursing home and asked for help dealing with the children. She also expressed bewilderment at how she would live her life without her husband at home.

Discussion Questions

1. Identify biological, psychological, and social issues in this case. How are they connected?
2. Identify the theories discussed in this chapter that are most applicable to this case.
3. Why is Mrs. Holden depressed?
4. What irrational ideas are affecting Mrs. Holden's feelings?
5. How has Mr. Holden's disease affected the family? (Include the extended family.)
6. What are some cognitions or narratives that enter into Mrs. Holden's thinking about herself as a woman?
7. How might Mrs. Holden become empowered?
8. What meaning did Mr. Holden have to Mrs. Holden? Why was it so difficult for her to let go?
9. What issues remain to be resolved for Mrs. Holden, for the children, and for the family? How does Mr. Holden fit into the picture?

R E F E R E N C E S

Anderson, T. (Ed.). (1991). *The reflecting team.* New York: W. W. Norton.

Andreasen, N. C. (1984). *The broken brain: The biological revolution in psychiatry.* New York: Harper & Row.

Andreasen, N. C., & Black, D. W. (1995). *Introductory textbook of psychiatry* (2nd. ed.). Washington, DC: American Psychiatric Press.

Atherton, C. R. (1993). Empiricists versus constructionists: Time for a cease-fire. *Families in Society, 74,* 617–624.

Bandura, A. (1977). *Social learning theory.* Englewood Cliffs, NJ: Prentice-Hall.

Bandura, A. (1978). The self system in reciprocal determinism. *American Psychologist, 33,* 344–358.

Bandura, A. (1982). Self-efficacy mechanism in human agency. *American Psychologist, 37,* 122–147.

Beck, A. (1976). *Cognitive therapy and the emotional disorders.* Madison, CT: International Universities Press.

Beck, A. (1985). Cognitive therapy. In H. I. Kaplan & B. J. Sadock (Eds.), *Comprehensive textbook of psychiatry/IV* (pp. 1432–1438). Baltimore, MD: Williams & Wilkins.

Bentley, K. J., & Walsh, J. (1996). *The social worker and psychotropic medication: Toward effective collaboration with mental health clients, families, and providers.* Pacific Grove, CA: Brooks/Cole.

Blanck, G., & Blanck, R. (1974). *Ego psychology: Theory and practice.* New York: Columbia University Press.

Blanck, G., & Blanck, R. (1979). *Ego psychology II: Psychoanalytic developmental psychology.* New York: Columbia University Press.

Blanck, R., & Blanck, G. (1986). *Beyond ego psychology: Developmental object relations theory.* New York: Columbia University Press.

Chance, P. (1979). *Learning and behavior.* Belmont, CA: Wadsworth.

Chatterjee, P. (1984). Cognitive theories and social work practice. *Social Service Review, 58,* 64–80.

Cohen, D. (1989). Biological basis of schizophrenia: The evidence reconsidered. *Social Work, 24,* 255–257.

Craddock, N. (1996). Psychiatric genetics. *British Journal of Psychiatry, 169,* 386–392.

Craddock, N., & Owen, M. J. (1996). Modern molecular genetic approaches to psychiatric disease. *British Medical Bulletin, 52,* 434–452.

Crain, W. C. (1985). *Theories of development: Concepts and applications* (2nd ed.). Englewood Cliffs, NJ: Prentice-Hall.

Diamond, J. (1998). Postmodern family therapy: New voices in clinical social work. In R. A. Dorfman (Ed.), *Paradigms of clinical social work* (pp. 185–224). New York: Brunner/Mazel.

Dixon, S. L. (1981). *An introduction to ego psychology and the dynamics of human behavior.* Lexington, MA: Ginn.

Ellis, A. (1979). Rational-emotive therapy as a new theory of personality and therapy. In A. Ellis & J. M. Whiteley (Eds.), *Theoretical and empirical foundations of rational emotive therapy* (pp. 1–60). Monterey, CA: Brooks/Cole.

Ellis, A., & Harper, R. A. (1975). *A new guide to rational living*. North Hollywood, CA: Wilshire Book.

Epstein, S. (1987). Gay politics, ethnic identity: The limits of social constructionism. *Socialist Review, 17*(3/4), 9–54.

Erikson, E. (1950). *Childhood and society.* New York: Norton.

Erikson, E. (1959). Identity and the life cycle. *Psychological Issues, 1,* 50–100.

Fieve, R. (1975). *Moodswing: The third revolution in psychiatry.* New York: William Morrow.

Freud, A. (1946). *The ego and mechanisms of defense.* New York: International Universities Press.

Gerhart, U. C., & Brooks, A. D. (1983). The social work practitioner and antipsychotic medications. *Social Work, 28,* 454–460.

Germain, C., & Gitterman, A. (1987). Ecological perspective. In A. Minahan et al. (Eds.), *Encyclopedia of social work* (18th ed., Vol. 1, pp. 488–499). Silver Spring, MD: National Association of Social Workers.

Germain, C. B., & Gitterman, A. (1995). Ecological perspective. In R. L. Edwards & J. G. Hopps (Eds.), *Encyclopedia of social work* (19th ed., Vol. 1, pp. 816–824). Washington, DC: NASW Press.

Goldstein, E. (1995). *Ego psychology and social work practice* (2nd ed.). New York: Free Press.

Gottesman, I. I., & Shields, J. (1972). *Schizophrenia and genetics: A twin study vantage point.* New York: Academic Press.

Gusella, J. F., Wexler, N. S., Conneally, P. M., Nayer, S. L., Anderson, M. A., et al. (1983). A polymorphic DNA marker genetically linked to Huntington's disease. *Nature, 306,* 234–238.

Hartmann, H. (1958). *Ego psychology and the problem of adaptation.* New York: International Universities Press.

Hedaya, R. J. (1996). *Understanding biological psychiatry.* New York: W. W. Norton.

Jordan, J. V. (Ed.). (1997a). *Women's growth in diversity: More writings from the Stone Center.* New York: The Guilford Press.

Jordan, J. V. (1997b). A relational perspective for understanding women's development. In J. V. Jordan (Ed.), *Women's growth in diversity: More writings from the Stone Center* (pp. 9–24). New York: The Guilford Press.

Kaplan, H. I., & Sadock, B. J. (1988). *Synopsis of psychiatry: Behavioral sciences/clinical psychiatry* (5th ed.). Baltimore, MD: Williams & Wilkins.

Kaplan, H. I., & Sadock, B. J. (1998). *Synopsis of psychiatry* (8th ed.). Baltimore, MD: Williams & Wilkins.

Kegan, R. (1982). *The evolving self: Problems and process in human development.* Cambridge, MA: Harvard University Press.

Kelley, P. (1998). Postmodern approaches: Education for a managed care environment. In G. Schamess & A. Lightburn (Eds.), *Humane managed care?* (pp. 430–441). Washington, DC: NASW Press.

Kelly, G. A. (1963). *A theory of personality.* New York: Norton.

Kendler, K. S. (1988). The genetics of schizophrenia and related disorders. In D. L. Dunner, E. S. Gershon, & J. E. Barrett (Eds.), *Relatives at risk for mental disorder* (pp. 247–263). New York: Raven Press.

Klerman, G. (1988). Depression and related disorders of mood (affective disorders). In A.M. Nicholi, Jr. (Ed.), *The new Harvard guide to psychiatry* (pp. 309–336). Cambridge, MA: Belknap Press of Harvard University Press.

Lazarus, R. S., & Folkman, S. (1984). *Stress, appraisal, and coping.* New York: Springer.

Libassi, M. F. (1988). The chronically mentally ill: A practice approach. *Social Casework, 69,* 88–96.

Libassi, M. F. (1990). *Psychopharmacology in social work education.* Rockville, MD: National Institute of Mental Health.

Lundin, R. W. (1983). Learning theories: Operant reinforcement theories and social learning theories of B. F. Skinner and Albert Bandura. In R. J. Corsini & A. J. Marsella (Eds.), *Personality theories, research and assessment* (pp. 287–330). Itasca, IL: Peacock Press.

Maddi, S. (1980). *Personality theories: A comparative analysis* (4th ed.). Homewood, IL: Dorsey Press.

Mahler, M., Pine, F., & Bergman, A. (1975) *The psychological birth of the human infant.* New York: Basic Books.

Matorin, S., & De Chillo, N. (1984). Psychopharmacology: Guidelines for social workers. *Social Casework, 65,* 579–589.

Matthysse, S., & Kety, S. S. (1986). The genetics of psychiatric disorders. In S. Arieti (Ed.), *American handbook of psychiatry* (2nd ed.): Vol. 8. *Biological psychiatry* (pp. 160–169). New York: Basic Books.

Meichenbaum, D. H. (1977). *Cognitive behavior modification: An integrative approach.* New York: Plenum Press.

Mendlewicz, J., Fieve, R. R., & Stallone, F. (1973). Relationship between the effectiveness of lithium therapy and family history. *American Journal of Psychiatry, 130,* 1011–1013.

Moldin, S. O., & Gottesman, I. I. (1997). At issue: Genes, experience, and chance in schizophrenia—Positioning for the 21st century. *Schizophrenia Bulletin, 23*(4), 547–561.

Mowry, B. J., Nancarrow, D. J., & Levinson, D. F. (1997). The molecular genetics of schizophrenia: An update. *Australian and New Zealand Journal of Psychiatry, 31*(5), 704–713.

Palfai, T., & Jankiewicz, H. (1991). *Drugs and human behavior.* Dubuque, IA: William C. Brown Publishers.

Piaget, J. (1936/1974). *The origins of intelligence in children.* Trans. by M. Cook. New York: International Universities Press.

Rainer, J. D. (1985). Genetics and psychiatry. In H. I. Kaplan & B. J. Sadock (Eds.), *Comprehensive textbook of psychiatry/IV* (4th ed. pp. 25–42). Baltimore, MD: Williams & Wilkins.

Rotter, J. (1954). *Social learning and clinical psychology.* Englewood Cliffs, NJ: Prentice-Hall.

Rotter, J. B. (1966). Generalized expectancies for internal versus external control of reinforcement. *Psychological Monographs, 80.*

Salkind, N. J. (1985). *Theories of human development* (2nd ed.). New York: Wiley.

Sands, R. G. (1986). The encounter with meaninglessness in crisis intervention. *The International Forum for Logotherapy, 9,* 102–108.

Sarasan, I. G., & Sarasan, B. R. (1989). *Abnormal psychology.* Englewood Cliffs, NJ: Prentice-Hall.

Solomon, B. (1976). *Black empowerment: Social work in minority communities.* New York: Columbia University Press.

Taylor, E. H. (1987). The biological basis of schizophrenia. *Social Work, 32,* 115–121.

Thomlison, R. J. (1986). Behavior therapy in social work practice. In F. J. Turner (Ed.), *Social work treatment: Interlocking theoretical approaches* (pp. 131–153). New York: Free Press.

Walen, S. R., Hauserman, N. M., & Lavin, P. J. (1977). *Clinical guide to behavior therapy.* Baltimore, MD: Williams & Wilkins.

Weick, A. (1987). Reconceptualizing the philosophical perspective of social work. *Social Service Review, 61,* 218–230.

Weick, A., Rapp, C., Sullivan, W. P., & Kisthardt, W. (1989). A strength perspective for social work practice. *Social Work, 34,* 350–354.

Weiner, H. (1984). An integrative model of health, illness, and disease. *Health and Social Work, 9,* 253–260.

Weiner H., & Fawzy, F. I. (1989). An integrative model of health, disease, and illness. In S. Cheron (Ed.), *Psychosomatic medicine: Theory, physiology, and practice* (Vol. 1, pp. 9–44). Madison, CT: International Universities Press.

White, M., & Epston, D. (1990). *Narrative means to therapeutic ends.* New York: W. W. Norton.

White, R. F. (1959). Motivation reconsidered: The concept of competence. *Psychological Review, 66,* 297–333.

Willinger, B. H. (1997). Psychopharmacology and clinical social work practice. In J. R. Brandell (Ed.), *Theory and practice of clinical social work.* New York: Free Press.

Wolpe, J. (1982). *The practice of behavior therapy* (3rd ed.). New York: Pergamon.

Zimmerman, J. H. (1989). Determinism, science, and social work. *Social Service Review, 63,* 52–62.

CHAPTER

4

The Biopsychosocial Assessment

The examiner closely listens to what is said and not said, structuring the exam-
ination in a way that allows broad exploration in many areas for potential ab-
normalities, as well as in-depth exploration of evident symptoms or signs.

—Trzepacz and Baker, *The Psychiatric Mental*
Status Examination, 1993

...instead of asking, "What's wrong with this individual?" we can ask, "What
are the strengths that have helped this person survive? What are her aspira-
tions, talents, and abilities? What social, emotional, and physical resources
are needed to support her growth and well-being?"

—Weick, "Building a Strengths Perspective
for Social Work," 1992

Above all else, I want my life to have meaning apart from my diagnosis.
–Dykstra, "First Person Account: How I Cope," 1997

From a postmodern perspective, a biopsychosocial assessment is a process of construction and reconstruction created from multiple perspectives. Professionals elicit the client's
narrative and observe his or her emotions, cognitions, and behavior. Although they view
the client's report as primary data, they also take into account the findings from medical
and psychiatric evaluations and information provided by family members and the staff of
social agencies. They draw from the various ways of knowing, described in Chapter 3, to
assess each unique individual (otherwise known as a case). These professional interpretations may highlight "abnormalities" and/or strengths, depending on the perspective of the
evaluator. But they are largely professional constructions in which the client's system of
meaning may or may not be addressed (Kleinman, 1988).

For many years, social workers viewed assessment from a linear perspective. Accordingly, assessment was the second of three discrete stages of intervention. During the
first stage, *study,* the practitioner gathered facts from the client, significant others, and
agencies the client may have used. This process included listening to the client's life history, as well as obtaining information about the client's significant relationships, occupa-

tion, and social environment. After sufficient data were gathered, the social worker could proceed to the second stage of *diagnosis*. At this point the clinician would arrive at an understanding of the client's personality and factors in the past and present that seemed to cause current difficulties. A diagnostic formulation that emphasized psychodynamics was made. The final stage, *treatment,* followed from the diagnosis. Specific diagnoses suggested particular treatment approaches.

In this volume the term *biopsychosocial assessment* will be used to denote a broad understanding of the client's situation, biological, psychological, and social functioning, and needs. The assessment includes but goes beyond the specific *DSM-IV* (American Psychiatric Association, 1994) diagnosis. The biopsychosocial assessment will be viewed as a process *and* a product (Hepworth & Larsen, 1982). Because understanding changes from week to week, the process is dynamic, always under revision. At a given moment the participants in the assessment process inscribe the results of their thinking in a written report, which also may be called a biopsychosocial assessment. The written assessment, however, is a snapshot, frozen in time.

In today's managed care environment, the assessment is a critical component of behavioral health care. The clinician is expected to document the client's presenting problems and symptoms and arrive at an accurate diagnosis and treatment plan. Third parties use this information to decide whether the problems that are described and the proposed treatment call for reimbursement (Corcoran & Vandiver, 1996). The assessment should also indicate the anticipated time frame for treatment, keeping in mind today's emphasis on short-term intervention. The goals and means of measuring goal attainment are further elements used by third parties. The initial assessment is revisited over time in continuation or utilization reviews.

The assessment described here will focus on the individual. Although family and group modes of intervention are prevalent in clinical practice today, case records are predominantly on individuals. This is not to say that an individual's family and social milieu are excluded. In the assessment described here, the multiple contexts of an individual's life are described.

This chapter includes the following topics: (a) components of a comprehensive interdisciplinary assessment; (b) assessing the client's psychiatric symptoms; (c) thinking about the biopsychosocial assessment; (d) writing a biopsychosocial summary; and (e) case review with an interdisciplinary treatment planning team.

Components of a Comprehensive Interdisciplinary Assessment

Ideally an assessment of a client is constructed by a team of mental health professionals, all of whom have some direct contact with the client. Such a team might include a psychiatrist, a social worker, a nurse, a physician, a psychologist, a recreation therapist, and a vocational rehabilitation specialist. A team has the resources of diverse specialties, each of which has a unique lens through which to perceive the client. The team uses the expertise of different professionals to gather and make sense of data, which are pooled and integrated. The inclusion of multiple professionals promotes a more comprehensive understanding of the client and client system.

The major components of an interdisciplinary assessment are as follows:

- Medical assessment
- Psychological testing
- Rapid assessment instruments
- Functional assessment
- Psychosocial history
- Psychiatric evaluation, mental status examination, and diagnosis

A given client's assessment may include some or all of these components or additional elements related to the agency's function. The following sections will describe each of the components listed and will indicate which discipline usually performs each task.

Medical Assessment

Behavioral health clients should initially and routinely have complete medical examinations. Physical evaluations can determine the client's overall state of health and the presence of particular medical problems. Findings from physical evaluations can inform decisions about psychiatric diagnoses, guide psychiatrists in the prescription of medications, and provide information that social workers can take into account in their work with clients.

Medical assessments usually involve an interview in which the physician asks the client to describe his or her chief complaints and medical history, after which the doctor conducts a physical examination and, in some cases, orders or runs particular tests. Psychiatrists, mental health teams, or individual practitioners who refer clients to physicians may request certain laboratory tests such as the dexamethasone suppression test (DST) for depression or a urine screening test for substance use, and in some cases, neurophysiological tests such as the CT scan (see Chapter 3). Sometimes the physician who conducts the physical examination will refer the client to specialists in other medical disciplines. This process usually results in the construction of one or more medical diagnoses or the determination that the person is healthy.

The physical examination helps mental health practitioners clarify the psychiatric diagnosis. Many medical illnesses, such as those listed in Table 4.1, as well as substance abuse, produce symptoms that resemble those associated with some psychiatric disorders. Generally, physical disorders should be ruled out, that is, determined to be nonexistent or

TABLE 4.1 Examples of Physical Disorders in Which Psychiatric Symptoms Are Presented

Huntington's disease	Nutritional deficiency disease
Multiple sclerosis	Systemic lupus erythematosus
Cardiovascular disease	Amyotrophic lateral sclerosis
Hypoglycemia	Human immunodeficiency virus (HIV) infection
Parkinson's disease	

Source: Adapted from Kaplan & Sadock (1988, 1998).

irrelevant, before psychiatric diagnoses are constructed. There are cases, however, in which a client may have one of these physical disorders (or others not listed) *and* a psychiatric disorder, so it is important to determine whether a physical disorder is present, whether the two coexist, and the extent to which they interact. The medical history and examination can also uncover the source of a medical problem; for example, a history of thyroid surgery suggests that hypothyroidism may be responsible for a client's depression (Kaplan & Sadock, 1998). In addition, certain medical conditions (including pregnancy) and age signal that some kinds of psychiatric medication are contraindicated or that the dosage should be reduced. A further advantage of a client having a medical evaluation is that this information can be inserted on Axis III of the multiaxial *DSM-IV* diagnosis.

Psychological Testing

Psychological testing may be called for under some circumstances. Such examinations help clarify the diagnosis, assess intellectual ability, and uncover unconscious material. Some psychological tests are capable of diagnosing organic brain damage. A social worker who is the first professional who sees a client should refer the client to a psychologist if clarification seems to be needed.

Psychologists have a wide repertoire of tests, which can be administered as a package. Such batteries of tests require interpretation as a whole. Among the personality tests, the one that is most commonly used in community mental health settings is the *Minnesota Multiphasic Personality Inventory,* which is usually referred to by its acronym, MMPI. This test contains over 500 questions describing emotional states, attitudes, and behaviors, such as "I have trouble making friends." Persons who take the test indicate for each statement whether it applies to them. Certain questions tap specific mental health conditions such as hypochondriasis, depression, and paranoia. Responses to some questions suggest that the respondent was lying or defensive. Results are put on a graph, in which the peaks and valleys are evident. Findings should be interpreted by a psychologist. The MMPI can be helpful in arriving at a diagnosis (Graham & Lilly, 1984).

Projective tests encourage subjects to reveal indirectly what they may find difficult to state directly. For these tests, clients are presented with ambiguous stimuli about which they are asked to talk. One well-established projective test is the *Rorschach Test,* which has subjects respond to a set of inkblots. Another is the *Thematic Apperception Test* (TAT), which contains a set of pictures about which clients are asked to develop a story. A third type of projective test is the *Sentence Completion Test* (SCT), which consists of a series of statements with blanks for the subject to complete, for example, "I am afraid of...." These tests reveal areas of conflict or anxiety.

Another test is the *Bender Gestalt* visual motor test. This test is used for adults and children primarily to detect organic dysfunction (Kaplan & Sadock, 1998) but also as a projective tool (Graham & Lilly, 1984). Here subjects are asked to reproduce certain designs, such as a circle and a square that touch.

Psychologists also administer intelligence tests to some clients who receive mental health services. Testing may be required for a vocational or rehabilitation program the client wishes to enter, or to clarify the client's potential. The best known of these tests is the *Wechsler Adult Intelligence Scale* (WAIS). There are other versions of this test for children.

Psychological testing has certain advantages. For one, the findings are empirically based. Many of the instruments used are reliable and valid. Tests provide measured scores on specific dimensions. Many psychological tests are sensitive to personality dimensions that are not revealed in face-to-face conversations and in behavior.

As valuable as psychological tests may be, they do not replace understanding the person in his or her natural environment. Testing is usually performed in a clinical environment, the demands of which differ from those of the everyday life of the client. Questions are presented in a standardized way and do not account for the diverse social, cultural, and handicapping conditions of individual clients. Tests may be biased toward norms of the white majority. Results that are distorted or reflect a transient state can become reified in a diagnosis.

Rapid Assessment Instruments

In addition to the diagnostic tests performed by psychologists, there are rapid assessment instruments that can be administered by social workers. These quickly administered tools provide information that clinicians can use to support a particular diagnosis, justify treatment, and assess progress. The client's score at the beginning of treatment can be compared with community norms and with scores of individuals whose responses fall within the clinical range. A score within the clinical range provides a justification for treatment. A client's scores at the beginning, during, and at the end of treatment can be compared to monitor and assess the client's progress and provide quality assurance information to managed care organizations (Corcoran & Vandiver, 1996). Fischer and Corcoran (1994) have compiled many of these tools in their sourcebook, *Measures for Clinical Practice.*

Most of the rapid assessment instruments in use are adapted to particular problems (e.g., poor assertiveness) or clinical states (e.g., depression). On the basis of information gathered during early sessions, the social worker determines which areas to assess and monitor during treatment. Usually it is the client who completes the instrument, but there are some that can be filled in by family members, caregivers, and the clinician. Tools relevant to the topics addressed in Part Two will be mentioned where relevant.

Functional Assessment

A further area for assessment is the extent of the client's ability to conduct his or her life independently in the community. An assessment of functioning is of particular import for those with severe mental illness who live in the community, but is also relevant for persons with mental retardation or developmental disabilities; individuals with physical impairments or handicaps; and the frail elderly. In many mental health services, the nurse is responsible for the functional assessment; but the social worker may be the one who performs this evaluation.

Among the areas that may be addressed in a functional assessment are the following:

1. Ability to communicate his or her needs to others. What language(s) does the client use (English, Spanish, sign language, gestures, none)?
2. Ability to use public transportation.
3. Ability to drive a car.
4. Ability to take care of physical needs independently—eating, bathing, grooming, dressing, use toilet unaided.

5. Ability to handle and manage money; budgeting, counting change, shopping.
6. Literacy: ability to read, reading level.
7. Physical mobility: walking, climbing stairs, transfer from wheelchair to bed.
8. Social skills: ability to interact with others, ability to initiate, develop, and maintain relationships.
9. Ability to manage a household independently—cooking, cleaning, laundry, dishes, making bed.
10. Occupational/employment skills and experience: work skills, ability to follow directions and accept supervision, ability to get to work on time.
11. Ability to assume responsibility for taking own medication consistently.
12. Sensory functions: sight, hearing, and so on.
13. Ability to protect self and others from fire.
14. Ability to protect oneself from involuntary sex, assault, and other kinds of exploitation.
15. Use of leisure time.

Scales that assess adaptive behavior skills such as the Independent Living Skills Survey (Wallace, 1986) can be used.

The functional assessment contributes to identifying the client's strengths and needs. The client's strengths and the client's, agency's, and community's resources are used to address the client's needs.

Psychosocial History

The psychosocial history is a comprehensive report on the client's current problem and symptoms, life history, and situation. It is gleaned from a number of sources—the client, significant others (family, gay/lesbian partner, friends), reports from other agencies, the case record, and so forth—provided that the client consents to the participation of others. Although the production of a written psychosocial history is frequently assigned to the clinical social worker, in some settings professionals and students of any of the mental health disciplines develop the written document.

In this volume the written psychosocial history will be referred to as a *biopsychosocial assessment*. The report will include a summary of medical findings obtained from the physician, as well as psychological and social findings. This is consistent with the biopsychosocial conceptual framework described in Chapter 3. The written assessment includes a description of the client, the presenting problem, the client's life circumstances, medical history, psychiatric history, financial/occupational information, and family/relationships. It also includes mental status information and the diagnosis. A recommended means to organize this assessment is presented later in this chapter.

Psychiatric Evaluation, Mental Status Examination, and Diagnosis

The evaluation performed by the psychiatrist can include the client's developmental, psychiatric, and social history and current symptoms. The process resembles the history taking of the social worker but reflects the medical training of the psychiatrist. The psychiatrist may explore the client's psychiatric history more closely than the social worker but pay less attention to social environmental factors. The term psychiatrists use for the psychiatric history is *anamnesis.*

In the process of explaining his or her current difficulties and history, the client reveals the symptoms. The client's reported complaints, as well as the verbal and nonverbal behavior accompanying the report, provide clues to the client's diagnosis. Further clarification of the nature of the client's psychiatric problem can be obtained by performing a *mental status examination* during the history gathering. The mental status examination is to the psychiatrist what the physical examination is to the physician. Each is a clinical means to assess the presence of *pathology* (i.e., disease) in the client and to come to an accurate diagnosis. Although psychiatrists are frequently the professionals who perform these evaluations, social workers and psychologists are also capable of conducting them. Suggested formats for reporting findings of this examination are presented in the next section of this chapter.

The psychiatric examination also includes an evaluation of the need for further medical testing and current medical needs. The psychiatrist may recommend a neurological examination, laboratory tests, or a referral for additional medical procedures. The psychiatrist has particular expertise about psychotropic medication. Some clients can benefit from psychotherapy without medication. Others require medication along with psychosocial treatment. The psychiatrist explores the client's medication history and any indications of an inclination to abuse drugs. The medication that is prescribed is related to the client's symptoms, diagnosis, and health status.

Assessing the Client's Psychiatric Symptoms

Psychiatric symptoms are human expressions of emotion and thought that have been socially constructed as indicators of mental illness. They include universal feelings such as sadness, anger, anxiety, and elation, as well as more unusual experiences such as hallucinations and delusions. Although some psychiatrists differentiate between signs (objective indicators of a psychiatric disorder) and symptoms (subjective reports by the client) (Trzepacz & Baker, 1993), from a postmodern perspective, the objective and subjective are not easily distinguished. Here we will use the term *symptoms* for both concepts. As discussed in Chapter 1, mental health professionals construct symptoms as indicators of psychopathology when the symptoms appear to be intense, long in duration, bizarre, and psychologically painful, and they interfere with psychosocial functioning.

Symptoms can be observed directly during an interview, or a client (or someone who sees the client in other contexts) may describe them. Individuals reveal their feelings in the way they present themselves to the clinician and how they respond to questions. When clients are asked to tell their story ("what brings you here today?"), they frequently share what happened, under what circumstances, how they felt, and what they thought about their experiences. For example, clients may cry while telling of a loss or express anger over someone's trying to poison them. Depending on what was said and observed, the clinician will construct symptoms out of the client's story.

Usually a client will present with more than one psychiatric symptom. The presence of a collection of symptoms that co-occur suggests one or more diagnoses. The *Diagnostic and Statistical Manual-IV* (*DSM-IV*) (American Psychiatric Association, 1994) describes those combinations of symptoms that psychiatrists and other mental health practitioners regard as indicators of specific mental disorders. The *DSM-IV* is the standard manual used in the United States for diagnosis. Managed care organizations usually require, as a condition for reimbursement, that behavioral health providers apply a *DSM-IV* diagnosis to every client. It is recommended that social workers employed in such settings become familiar with the manual, how it is used, and the major diagnostic categories. Some of them will be reviewed in the intervention chapters in Part Two of this book.

One way in which mental health professionals arrive at a diagnosis is to conduct a mental status examination as mentioned earlier. This face-to-face evaluation explores the client's complaints, symptoms, and demeanor in order to determine the nature of the difficulty, how it expresses itself, and potential diagnoses. The client is assessed in many areas to identify problematic domains and the extent of the dysfunction. The focus of the mental status examination is on *current functioning* that is evidenced during the examination.

There are various tools that are used to conduct mental status examinations. In some settings (particularly those serving older adults), practitioners use the brief Mini-Mental State Examination (Folstein, Folstein, & McHugh, 1975) to screen for cognitive and language dysfunctioning. This examination tests the individual's short-term memory, ability to perform calculations (like subtracting 7 from 100 several times), and ability to follow a series of commands. In research settings diagnostic tools such as the Structured Clinical Interview (SCID) (Spitzer et al., 1989) are used. The Structured Clinical Interview consists of questions about particular symptoms, followed by probes, which help the clinician arrive at a diagnosis. The SCID is a more lengthy, comprehensive examination than the typical mental status examination.

Although fixed formats for interviewing clients can be helpful, many practitioners gain their impressions through the history-gathering interview (psychosocial interview or *anamnesis*). At the same time the client is describing the presenting problems or complaints, the examiner is able to observe the client's affect, interpersonal behavior, mood, and so forth. As the troubling symptoms become visible, the clinician can ask questions that elicit more specific information. As the interview draws to an end, the examiner probes further into dimensions of psychosocial functioning that were either glossed over or not revealed by the client.

There are many ways to report the results of the mental status examination. Traditionally, examiners have written narrative reports that describe observed psychological functioning along multiple dimensions. Table 4.2 outlines these dimensions and provides an example of a professional mental status report on each area on "John," who was exhibiting symptoms of bipolar disorder, manic episode. As one can see in this example, John functions well in some respects but has difficulties in other respects.

In recent years it has become common for behavioral health providers to use checklists such as the one in Table 4.3. Completing forms such as this places lower demands on the examiner's time than writing narratives. Checklists, however, portray the client as a bundle of symptoms; narratives describe individual responses.

Regardless of whether clinicians write narratives or use checklists, they need to ask questions that operationalize the various dimensions of the mental status examination. One way to do this is to review instruments such as the SCID for sample questions. There are

TABLE 4.2   Areas Addressed in a Mental Status Examination (Narrative Type)

Dimension	Description	Example
General Appearance and Attitude	Appearance includes physical characteristics, mannerisms, facial expression, clothing, and grooming. Attitude refers to how the client relates to the examiner and how the client comes across.	John is tall and slender and looks young for his age (40). He was neatly dressed in khaki pants and a striped, long-sleeved shirt. He was cooperative except for a few questions that he dodged.
Behavior and Motor Activity	This includes physical activity, body movements, gestures, posture, and gait. Note the quantity and quality of activity.	John appeared restless in the waiting room but calmed down during the interview. He rubbed his hands together at times.
Speech and Language	This addresses knowledge and fluency in English and whether this or another language is primary. Determine whether loudness and speed are congruent with client's primary cultural group. Note any unusual speech patterns and how talkative the client is.	John spoke fluently, loudly, and rapidly in English, his primary language. He used puns and laughed at his own humor. At times the interviewer had to break into John's profuse talk.
Feeling, Affect, and Mood	This concerns the emotions and mood that the client verbalizes and that the clinician observes and the observed affect. Determine whether affect matches the content of the feelings (i.e., whether it is appropriate). Does the client shift quickly from one feeling state to another (lability)?	John came across primarily as happy and enthusiastic but at times he shifted into a sad state. His affect was consistent with his reported mood and was appropriate. He seemed irritated with some of the interviewer's questions.
Thought Content and Processes	This addresses the themes and preoccupations evident in the client's talk. Note unusual or unrealistic ideas. Describe the quality of the client's thinking in his or her speech.	John revealed plans to start his own travel agency but said that he lacked capital and experience in this business. He displayed flight of ideas and grandiosity.
Intelligence and Cognition	This addresses the client's general level of intelligence and intellectual functioning. Assess abstract thinking apart from education and culture. Evaluate orientation, memory, and consciousness.	John seemed to be highly intelligent and was able to interpret the saying, "A rolling stone gathers no moss" abstractly. He was oriented to time, place, and person; had no apparent impairments in immediate, recent, and long-term memory; and was alert.
Perception or Sensory Experiences	This refers to the client's ability to accurately perceive and process environmental stimuli. It explores whether the client has hallucinations, illusions, depersonalization, and/or derealization.	The client described voices telling him that he was brilliant and destined to be a millionaire. These auditory hallucinations were congruent with his grandiose mood.

Impulsivity	This refers to the ability to control aggressive, sexual, and other impulses.	The client reported that his wife was complaining about his high sexual energy. He denied having extramarital affairs. He appears to have some control over his impulses.
Judgment and Insight	This addresses the client's ability to distinguish among thoughts, feelings, and actions; to examine alternative solutions to a problem; and assume responsibility for and understand the consequences of his or her own behavior. Inquire whether the client has suicidal or homicidal ideations; and the extent to which the client acknowledges the presence of problems and his or her own role in their development.	John does not seem to have realistic ideas about how one goes about starting a business. Thus far, however, he has not borrowed or spent money toward developing a travel agency. John denied mental health problems. He said that his wife is the one who thinks he needs help. He reported having fleeting thoughts of suicide but because the thoughts disappear rapidly, he has not done anything about them. He lacked insight into his own difficulty.

Source: Adapted from Kaplan & Sadock (1988) with modifications. The example was developed by the author.

some questions that are frequently used in behavioral health settings to tap symptoms related to some of these dimensions. Here are some examples:

Orientation:	What's today's date?
	Where are you?
Hallucination:	Do you ever see things that other people do not see? (If yes) What do they look like?
	Do you ever hear things that other people do not hear? (If yes) What do they sound like? When you hear these sounds, where do they come from?
Delusion of Persecution:	Do you ever think that people are planning to hurt you in some way?
Mood:	How are you feeling today? Is this feeling typical of the way you have been feeling lately? How is your appetite? How much energy do you have?

When the client's responses to a particular question are positive, the clinician asks follow-up questions, as illustrated in some of the preceding examples.

On the basis of the information that is formulated in the mental status report, the clinician should be able to arrive at one or more diagnoses described in the *DSM-IV.* Nevertheless, this is not always possible. Despite the specificity of diagnostic categories in the manual, the same symptoms characterize a number of disorders. Rather than affix a definite category, the clinician may defer the diagnosis, pending further evaluation (including physical examinations, laboratory tests, psychological tests, interviews with significant others), or designate a provisional diagnosis and alternative categories to consider (APA, 1994).

TABLE 4.3   Mental Status Checklist

I. Appearance and Attitude
_____ appropriate dress
_____ well groomed
_____ poor hygiene
_____ poor eye contact
_____ bizarre appearance
_____ cooperative
_____ guarded

II. Behavior and Motor Activity
_____ retarded motor activity
_____ agitated motor activity
_____ tremors
_____ tics
_____ stereotyped movements

III. Characteristics of Speech
_____ English is not primary language
_____ normal speech
_____ flight of ideas
_____ speaks slowly
_____ mute
_____ thought blocking
_____ circumstantiality
_____ loose associations
_____ tangential thoughts
_____ perseveration
_____ irrelevance
_____ incoherence
_____ loud

IV. Orientation
_____ time
_____ place
_____ person
_____ reason for being here

V. Affect
_____ appropriate
_____ inappropriate
_____ flat
_____ blunted
_____ affect lability

VI. Mood/Feeling Tone
_____ normal
_____ depressed
_____ elated
_____ angry
_____ afraid
_____ optimistic
_____ pessimistic

VII. Thought Content
_____ delusions
_____ paranoid
_____ grandiose
_____ somatic
_____ ideas of reference
_____ ideas of influence
_____ obsessive and phobic ideas

VIII. Cognition
Memory
_____ long-term memory poor
_____ intermediate memory poor
_____ short-term memory poor

Attention and Concentration
_____ attention cannot be aroused
_____ attention cannot be sustained

Fund of Information/ Intelligence
_____ average
_____ below normal

IX. Perception
_____ hallucinations
_____ auditory
_____ visual
_____ other
_____ illusions

X. Insight and Judgment
_____ suicidal
_____ homicidal
_____ poor judgment
_____ denial of mental health problems

Thinking about the Biopsychosocial Assessment

The biopsychosocial assessment is constructed from the elements that have been described previously. Information from team members and others who have conducted evaluations or provided reports are assembled, examined, and discussed. This section describes the kind of information that clinical social workers think about, gather, and include in a written biopsychosocial report. In keeping with the biopsychosocial framework of this book, the report incorporates biological, psychological, and social information.

Biological Information

Biological information is obtained from the physician and the client's self-report. Social workers should also assess the client's health by inquiring about the client's nutrition, exercise, sleep, and substance use. The quality, quantity, and consistency of the client's health behaviors suggest healthy coping mechanisms or maladaptive responses. The social worker should also ask clients about their use of health care services and determine whether there are barriers (e.g., lack of health insurance) that impede service use. It is difficult to separate health from mental health. Similarly one cannot easily separate health and mental health status from the use of services, which is a social process. Because social workers' expertise is in the social domain, particular emphasis will be given here to the social dimensions of the client's life.

Social Information

The social aspects of the biopsychosocial assessment require that one understand the interpersonal relationships that are part of a person's life. This includes the family and other significant relationships. The cultures that permeate the client's life affect individual and social functioning as well.

In order to understand the social dimension of a person's life, several interrelated topics should be addressed in the assessment. Although these are discussed separately for the sake of clarity, it should be recognized that they are coexistent in the person's life. The topics to be discussed are (a) the family or household; (b) the culture or cultural group; (c) other social supports; (d) social environmental stressors and resources; and (e) tools to assess the social context.

The Family or Household.   The persons with whom a client lives or is otherwise closely connected consist of the family of origin (parents, siblings), the family of procreation (spouse, children), extended family (relatives such as grandparents, aunts, cousins), or nonrelatives (gay/lesbian or heterosexual partner, friends, residents of a group home).

In making an assessment of the family or household, one is interested in determining who is in the household, the quality of the relationships (emotionally supportive, conflictual, competitive) of the household as a whole and of component parts, the nature of the interactions (domineering, reciprocal), the strength of the bonds, and sensitive family issues. This can best be done by meeting with the family.

The problems of the behavioral health client should be looked at in relation to his or her household or family. It should be determined how the family constructs and responds to the client, and how the client constructs the family. The family's concern about the client, the members' willingness to be involved in treatment, and their resourcefulness should be assessed. Many of the dimensions described in family systems theory—boundaries (openness, permeability); communication patterns; organizational structure (roles, rules, subsystems); linkage with other systems (extended family, community); and power relations—can be assessed.

The family or household may or may not provide support to the client. The social worker should determine who is supportive in what ways, and the obstacles presented by those who are not supportive. If there are obstacles, their nature and purpose should be explored so that a strategy to overcome them can be developed.

On the other hand, the family may be burdened with the care of their relative or with crises that emerge. Family members can experience burden whether the client lives with them or separately. It is important to assess the ability of the family to provide support and care to the client. Often family caregivers themselves need support.

The Culture(s).   The individual and family may be part of an ethnic community that influences the client's identity, values, feelings of belonging, as well as individual behavior and family patterns of interaction. Cultures provide structure and meaning. For some people, however, association with a cultural group that is not valued by the larger society may be a source of conflict or ambivalence.

The clinical social worker has a responsibility to understand clients in relation to their respective culture(s). Workers who are not familiar with the client's particular ethnic group should ask questions of the client so as to encourage him or her to explain the cultural meanings. Culturally sensitive practice is discussed in Chapter 7.

The assessment should identify significant ethnic groups and describe the nature of the client's ties and identification. Cultural patterns, such as ideas about sharing private feelings, modes of decision making, valued goals, and the role of kin in their lives, should be assessed. The cultural group, with its sense of community, shared life-cycle events, and holidays is a potential resource for the client. The client's mental health problems should be viewed in terms of normative values and behaviors of the cultural group; what is psychopathological in one culture may be normal in another. The Outline for Cultural Formulation (APA, 1994), a cultural assessment tool, is reprinted in Chapter 7.

Other Social Supports.   Clients may have additional relationships that provide them with emotional support. These persons and groups provide friendship, personal help in time of need, concrete services (e.g., baby-sitting, transportation), or the like. The "supporters" may be personal friends, work associates, or neighbors. Doctors, lawyers, and ministers also provide social support, as do church or synagogue members. Barbers and beauticians, bartenders, and grocers may also be part of a client's social network.

The client may have a peer group that provides friendship at the same time it fosters a problematic behavior. Such peers may be "drinking buddies," collaborators in antisocial activity, and the like. If these groups are significant to the individual and comprise a large proportion of the client's social relationships, they may present an obstacle to treatment.

Some individuals are estranged from their families and have few friends. For whatever reason, it may be difficult for them to make or keep friends. In these cases human service workers from a number of agencies may constitute the client's social support network.

Social supports may also be in the form of organized community groups and activities. Self-help groups that focus on particular issues (e.g., alcoholism, rape, child abuse, loss of a child) provide a network of individuals who can support each other. Settlement houses, YMCAs, and Jewish Community Centers offer social programs, recreational activities, cultural events, and classes that can contribute to the well-being of clients.

Social Environmental Stressors and Resources. Clients live in environmental contexts that may provide protection from or promote stress. Financial resources and employment are assets that can buffer stress, whereas poverty and inadequate housing can exacerbate stress.

Conflict between the individual and social systems can be threatening. Legal problems over child support, debts, and driving while intoxicated involve individuals with lawyers and courts, the rules and practices of which are mystifying to those who are not familiar with the system. Defending oneself under such circumstances is costly and takes time away from employment. Trouble with the law and difficulties with other systems are taxing, making one vulnerable to physical and mental disorders.

Discrimination based on race, sex, class, age, sexual orientation, and disability is also stressful. Furthermore, holding more than one job, being a single parent, or caring for a mentally disabled person makes extra demands on a person.

Changes in one's circumstances or roles can also create stress. Accordingly, graduating, getting married, changing jobs, getting promoted, and retiring are transitions that can be anxiety provoking. Even though the client may not complain of these changes, it is expected that he or she will be making adjustments in adapting to the new circumstances.

A biopsychosocial assessment should identify the social environmental stressors in a person's life and evaluate the adequacy of supports and resources. What looks like symptoms of psychopathology may be a reaction to stressful life events or conditions.

Tools to Assess the Social Context. A number of tools can be used to assess social supports, resources, and stressors. Among these is the *ecomap* (Hartman, 1978), a drawing of social systems with which family members interact. With the ecomap, the household members are drawn in the center of a circle that is surrounded by other systems such as the behavioral health agency, extended family, the church, a child welfare agency, and so on. The ecomap portrays the quality of the relationship between individuals and these systems (e.g., conflictual, supportive). Another tool, the *genogram* (McGoldrick, Gerson, & Shellenberger, 1999), is a diagram of the family over a few generations. It is used to depict the quality of family relationships, potential "supporters," family members who generate stress, and patterns that recur within and across generations. Both the genogram and ecomap can be used productively in early interviews with clients to learn about their family and other potential social supports.

Another social assessment tool clinical social workers may find useful is the *Person-in-Environment System,* otherwise known as *PIE* (Karls & Wandrei, 1994). This is a multifactoral, problem-oriented system of classifying problems along four dimensions. The clinician identifies problems and their code numbers from the *PIE Manual* (Karls & Wandrei, 1994) and codes them along the following dimensions:

Factor I: Social Role Problems
Factor II: Environmental Problems
Factor III: Mental Health Problems
Factor IV: Physical Health Problems

Factor I describes family, other interpersonal, occupational, and special life situation roles. Each role type (e.g., family) is further classified (e.g., parent role problem) and described (ambivalence type). It is also coded with respect to severity, duration, and the quality of coping. Factor II addresses economic needs and problems with the educational, legal, health, voluntary association, and affectional support systems. The clinician records the *DSM-IV* Axis I and II diagnoses on Factor III and physical health problems on Factor IV.

The *DSM-IV* (APA, 1994) itself has axes that account for social and environmental stressors. Axis IV is the place in which clinicians list problems with a primary support group, occupational difficulties, economic problems, trouble with the legal system, and other problems that have been present in the previous year (or before that time if they are relevant). The Axis III diagnosis (health problems) is also of concern because health problems have social as well as psychological consequences. The Axis V diagnosis, Global Assessment of Functioning (GAF), is made by rating the client's psychological, social, and occupational functioning according to a scale that goes from 1 (extremely low) to 100 (superior). This scale requires that the clinician consider the overall impact of the client's psychological problems on his or her ability to enact social roles. By listing the highest GAF score in the last year as well as the current one, the clinician can estimate the client's prognosis. The Axis V diagnosis can be also used in behavioral health settings as a tool with which to monitor a client's progress.

Psychological Information

Psychological information is also an important component of the biopsychosocial assessment. This includes the client's symptoms and reported results of psychological testing, both of which have already been discussed. Some of these findings suggest areas in which the client is *vulnerable* to mental health crises. The client may also be vulnerable in the face of life changes, environmental stressors, or when someone he or she has counted on for support in the past is not available or helpful, or leaves.

The clinical social worker gives particular attention to the client's psychological *strengths*. These may be personal attributes or positive coping mechanisms. Examples of personal characteristics that can be identified and included in a biopsychosocial assessment are:

- completed an educational course of study (high school, college, technical training, business school)
- intelligent; has good analytic skills
- ability to make friends; social skills
- well groomed
- good sense of humor

- keeps appointments; is able to get places on time
- has work experience and work skills
- has a special talent (art, music, writing, storytelling)
- prepares nutritious meals
- maintains a neat apartment

Cowger (1992) organized over fifty client strengths in terms of cognition, emotion, motivation, coping, and interpersonal dimensions. Strengths are unique to the individual. Everyone has his or her own complex of strengths. Regardless of what they are, they can be brought to bear in the amelioration of problems.

Coping mechanisms are strategies individuals use to deal with ordinary, everyday problems and more challenging difficulties that come their way. In contrast with defense mechanisms, which are unconscious and automatic, coping mechanisms are conscious and deliberate. The following is a list of some coping mechanisms that some clients may use:

- seeking out information
- asking for support from others (friends or professionals)
- analyzing a problem and coming up with alternative solutions
- exercising to relieve stress
- going to a movie or reading a book
- listening to music
- thinking about the consequences if the worst-case scenario would occur
- using religious resources or praying alone
- minimizing the seriousness of the problem
- keeping a journal and reflecting on the experience

Like strengths, coping mechanisms are diverse and individualized. They help individuals manage their feelings, prevent them from becoming overwhelmed, and empower them to do something.

Writing a Biopsychosocial Summary

The preliminary biopsychosocial report pulls together, summarizes, and analyzes the findings of the initial interview(s) with the client and significant others, medical findings, reports from other agencies and professionals (if available), results of psychological and rapid assessment tests (if performed), and the findings of social assessment tools (if used). The report should be comprehensive and provide a view of the person and problem in the context of the client's life. Care should be given to present the client as an individual who is experiencing a difficulty—not as a diagnostic category.

Recommended Format

Many behavioral or mental health organizations have a preferred format for collecting and writing the summary. Often these formats reflect the purpose of the agency and its philosophy of treatment. The one presented here is broad and may not apply to the specific function of every agency. Furthermore, it is more detailed than what is generally required by managed care entities. Some of the information included here can be incorporated in summary sheets or transformed into checklists.

I. Identifying Information
   A. Demographic information: age, sex, ethnic group, current student/employment/ household roles, marital status, etc.
   B. Referral information: referral source (self or another), reason for referral.
   C. Data sources used in writing this report: interviews with identified persons (list dates and persons), examinations and tests performed, other data used.
II. Presenting Problem
   A. Detailed description of the problem, situation, and symptoms for which help is sought *as presented by the client.* Use the client's words, if possible. What precipitated the current difficulty? What feelings and thoughts have been aroused? How has the client coped so far?
   B. Who else is involved in the problem? How are they involved? How do they view the problem? How have they reacted? How have they contributed to the problem or solution?
   C. Past experiences related to current difficulty. Has something like this ever happened before? If so, how was it handled then? What were the consequences then?
   D. Other recent problems. Identify stressful life events or circumstances that have occurred in the last year, how they were managed, and what they have meant to the client.
III. Current Situation
   A. Description of family or household: who is in the household (names, ages) and relationship (natural child, stepparent, friend), quality of relationships, caregivers inside and outside the household.
   B. Social network: extended family, friends, peer groups, community affiliations.
   C. Guardianship information (if applicable).
   D. Economic situation: who is working; nature of employment; receiving public assistance, social security, SSI, or retirement income; adequacy of income; state of indebtedness. Identify economic needs, if applicable, and money management practices.
   E. Physical environment/housing: nature of living circumstances (apartment, group home or other shared living arrangement, crowded conditions, homeless); neighborhood.
   F. Significant issues, roles, or activities: student, retired, military, health problems, disabled, substance abuse, legal problems.
IV. Previous Mental Health Problems and Treatment: nature of difficulties and treatment, kind of treatment (outpatient, hospitalization), outcome of treatment; attitude toward medication and psychotherapy.
V. Background Information
   A. Family background: description of family of origin and family of procreation (if applicable).
   B. Marital/intimate relationship history.

C. Education and/or vocational training.

D. Employment history.

E. Military history (if applicable).

F. Use and abuse of alcohol or drugs, self and family.

G. Health issues: accidents, disabilities, diseases; health problems in family; nutrition; sleep; exercise, dietary restrictions.

H. Cultural background: ethnic group(s), identification and association with ethnic group. Immigration issues, if applicable. Cultural beliefs about mental health problems and their treatment.

VI. Results of Mental Status Examination and Diagnosis

VII. Analysis

A. What is the key issue or problem from your perspective? How does your perspective compare with the client's? How serious is the problem?

B. How effectively is the client functioning?

C. What factors (thoughts, behaviors, personality issues, circumstances) seem to be contributing to the problems? Are these factors within the client, in the client system, from the social environment, or from social interactions?

D. Identify the strengths, sources of meaning, coping ability, and resources that can be mobilized to help the client.

E. Identify stressors, obstacles, vulnerabilities, and needs.

F. Assess client's motivation and potential to benefit from intervention.

VIII. Recommendations/Intervention Plan

A. What course of action do you recommend? Specify:

1. Type(s) of intervention (case management; individual, family, or group therapy; environmental intervention).

2. Referral to psychiatrist for assessment for medication.

3. Referral for special program within agency (day treatment services, lithium group).

4. Referral to other agencies for services.

5. Advocacy on a particular issue.

6. Further testing.

B. What are the goals of intervention? How will you evaluate goal attainment?

C. How long do you think it will take to achieve the goals?

Name of social worker, degree, and license
Title

Section VII, analysis, will reflect the clinician's theoretical orientation. An assessment from an ego psychology perspective, for example, will assess the ego functions, developmental issues, situational stress, role performance, and environmental insufficiencies and analyze the extent to which the client's problems are related to difficulties in each of these areas (Goldstein, 1995). An assessment using cognitive theory will highlight thinking patterns that are related to current difficulties, as well as clients' perceptions of themselves, others, the environment, and their future (Beck, 1976). A behavioral assessment identifies problematic behaviors, when they occur, who is present or what happens before they occur (antecedents), and what happens afterward (consequences).

The intervention plan that is described in a preliminary form in section VIII of the outline is negotiated between the client and the social worker. Clinical social workers should offer their own perception of the client's problem and needs but should give the client the opportunity to do the same. In keeping with the values of self-determination (as well as client empowerment), the client's priorities should be reflected in the intervention plan.

Goals are evaluated in a number of ways. When they are specific enough (e.g., "Mary will leave the home one hour a day for the next week"), they can be checked off on an agency form developed for this purpose as "accomplished," "partially accomplished," or "not accomplished" after the time period passes. Alternatively, various instruments can be used to monitor goal attainment. Some practitioners assess goals that they negotiate with the client using Goal Attainment Scaling (GAS) techniques. To do this they measure achievement of each goal along an ordinal scale in a continuum of outcomes in which the worst to the most positive are described. Goal Attainment Scales are described in numerous social work texts (e.g., Sheafor, Horejsi, & Horejsi, 1994). The GAS is completed by the social worker. If the goal is to reduce the severity of symptoms, the client can complete many of the rapid assessment tools described earlier during each visit or at intervals. When goals are not accomplished, the social worker should reflect about and discuss with clients and colleagues possible reasons for this. On the one hand, it may be that the goals are not appropriate, there are barriers toward achieving them, or the client is not motivated to change. In such cases, the obstacles should be addressed and, in some cases, the goals should be changed. Alternatively, the intervention strategy may not be appropriate and should be reexamined or revised.

Many agencies have a form that staff members complete collaboratively with clients, in which the problems, needs, goals, and objectives are outlined, usually in behaviorally specific language. The items that are included are designed to conform with the requirements of the Joint Commission on the Accreditation of Health Organizations, medical assistance programs, and behavioral managed care entities. The following is a list of the kinds of items that are generally included in the intervention plan:

Description of problem areas and needs
Problem list (in priority order)
Strengths/assets
Obstacles
Goals (short term, long term)
Objectives—list objectives for each problem and indicate:
■ What is to be done (action proposed) by whom (client, staff person, etc.)
■ How objective is to be accomplished (methods)
■ Target date for achieving objective
■ Criteria for assessing accomplishment of goal and tools to be used
Review date

Goals are usually global (Jack will improve his social skills), whereas objectives are more concrete and specific (Jack will join a bowling league in the next month). Some agencies use a method of recording called *problem-oriented record keeping;* for such agencies progress notes will reflect the problems that are listed. Other agencies use a goal-oriented system, in which they record accomplishments achieving goals or objectives.

In today's managed behavioral care settings, it is very important to construct clear, behaviorally specific, measurable objectives that are linked to dealing with particular problems or symptoms. This information is needed not only during a formal intake or assessment stage but throughout the treatment or intervention process. Utilization reviews, which use this information, can occur prospectively (to show that treatment and a particular type of intervention are needed), concurrently (while treatment is taking place), and retrospectively (after treatment is completed) (Corcoran & Vandiver, 1996). Clinicians need to advance a rational case for what they want to do, what they are doing, and what they did.

Case Review with an Interdisciplinary Treatment Planning Team

Although agencies vary in their interdisciplinary practices, it is valuable to have the team participate in the assessment and treatment planning of clients. To the mental health professional, group meetings provide an opportunity to obtain perspectives of colleagues of other disciplines; to learn from group discussion and deliberation; to obtain consultation and advice from others. Furthermore, clients benefit from gaining the additional professional expertise of a team.

Some agencies follow a procedure in which all cases that have gone through an intake procedure (preliminary screening and development of the written psychosocial assessment) are discussed in an open meeting of a team of professionals. The team listens to a description of the case, deliberates over the diagnosis, and develops an initial treatment plan collaboratively. Some agencies invite the client, significant others, the case manager, and others to the meeting. At this time, cases may be assigned to another worker, to a special program, or referred to the psychiatrist or psychologist.

Many agencies also have the team conduct periodic reviews of the client's progress. The primary therapist may, for example, present a report on the client's progress in psychotherapy and in obtaining resources at periodic intervals—for example, after sixty days, ninety days, six months. In this way the diagnosis and the treatment plan can be reviewed and modified as more information is obtained and circumstances change. Moreover, the professional staff is monitoring cases corporately—thus fulfilling their responsibility to clients, the agency, and the funding sources.

Other teams meet on a daily basis to report on new developments and to come to a consensus about consistent strategies of intervention to be used in relation to particular clients. Such teams are continually revising their assessment and intervention plan to address the immediate needs of clients.

The participation of the client and significant others in the periodic reviews of the client's progress is a valuable component of this process. Treatment is not a regimen one imposes on someone. The client should be working on problems that are of personal relevance and import. Goals and objectives should reflect the client's wishes and priorities. More than paperwork required by "the system," the review provides a means to evaluate and revise the plan so that it reflects the client's voice.

Summary and Deconstruction

The biopsychosocial assessment is an open-ended, ongoing activity in clinical work with clients; it also is a written summary, frozen in time, that summarizes and analyzes information about the client that is available at the time the report is written. A number of professionals may participate in the construction of the assessment—the social worker, psychiatrist, psychologist, nurse, and other members of the agency's behavioral mental health team, and physicians who examine or conduct tests on the client. Significant others such as family members may also provide information about the client.

The key participant in the assessment process is the client. The client's story and responses to clinical interviews comprise primary data that professionals examine and analyze. Although the client clearly plays a role in the construction of the assessment, the biopsychosocial assessment is a professional activity that is biased toward categories that the professionals and their funding sources consider meaningful. Even terms such as *stressors, supports,* and *strengths* are professional constructions.

This chapter provided recommended formats for the mental status examination and the biopsychosocial summary. These are constructed from interactions with the client. However useful they are for contemporary practice, there is a need to understand the ways clients perceive themselves, others, and treatment and to work toward goals that are meaningful to them. This requires going beyond diagnosis and the other components of the biopsychosocial assessment.

D I S C U S S I O N   Q U E S T I O N S

1. Review cases in your agency, considering the following:
   a. Did the client have a physical examination or laboratory tests that facilitated the ruling out of medical conditions?
   b. Was the client's psychiatric disorder viewed in relation to the expectations of his or her cultural group?
   c. How was the diagnosis reached?
   d. Have the diagnosis and the treatment plan been reviewed periodically by a treatment-planning team?
   e. Did the client participate in the treatment-planning process? To what extent?

2. How are psychological tests used in your agency?

3. Are functional assessments performed in your agency? If not, how is information on client functioning obtained?

4. Using the suggested format, write a psychosocial summary on a case with which you are working currently. Identify the psychosocial theory or theories you are using and apply them to this case. Assess the supports and stressors that affect the client.

5. Consider the case presented for discussion at the conclusion of Chapter 3. Using sections VII and VIII of the format for a psychosocial summary suggested in the present chapter, analyze and develop a treatment plan for this case.

6. What tools and procedures would you use to assess progress on this case?

REFERENCES

American Psychiatric Association. (1994). *Diagnostic and statistical manual—Fourth edition (DSM-IV)*. Washington, DC: Author.

Beck, A. T. (1976). *Cognitive therapy and the emotional disorders*. Madison, CT: International Universities Press.

Corcoran, K., & Vandiver, V. (1996). *Maneuvering the maze of managed care: Skills for mental health practitioners*. New York: The Free Press.

Cowger, C. D. (1992). Assessment of client strengths. In D. Saleebey (Ed.), *The strengths perspective in social work practice* (pp. 139–147). New York: Longman.

Fischer, J., & Corcoran, K. (1994). *Measures for clinical practice: A sourcebook*, vols. 1 and 2. New York: The Free Press.

Folstein, M. F., Folstein, S. F., & McHugh, P. R. (1975). Mini-mental state: A practical method for coding the cognitive state of patients for the clinician. *Journal of Psychiatric Research, 12*, 189–198.

Goldstein, E. (1995). *Ego psychology and social work practice* (2nd ed.). New York: The Free Press.

Graham, J. R., & Lilly, R. S. (1984). *Psychological testing*. Englewood Cliffs, NJ: Prentice-Hall.

Hartman, A. (1978). Diagrammatic assessment of family relationships. *Social Casework, 59*, 465–476.

Hepworth, D. I., & Larsen, J. (1982). *Direct social work practice*. Homewood, IL: Dorsey Press.

Kaplan, H. I., & Sadock, B. J. (1988). *Synopsis of psychiatry* (5th ed.). Baltimore, MD: Williams & Wilkins.

Kaplan, H. I., & Sadock, B. J. (1998). *Synopsis of psychiatry: Behavioral sciences/Clinical psychiatry* (8th ed.). Baltimore, MD: Williams & Wilkins.

Karls, J. M., & Wandrei, K. E. (1994). *PIE manual: Person-in-environment system*. Washington, DC: NASW Press.

Kleinman, A. (1988). *The illness narratives: Suffering, healing, and the human condition*. New York: Basic Books.

McGoldrick, M., Gerson, R., & Shellenberger, S. (1999). *Genograms: Assessment and intervention* (2nd ed.). New York: W. W. Norton.

Sheafor, B. W., Horejsi, C. R., & Horejsi, G. A. (1994). *Techniques and guidelines for social work practice* (3rd ed.). Boston: Allyn & Bacon.

Spitzer, R. L., Williams, J. B. W., Gibbon, M., & First, M. B. (1989). *Structured clinical interview for DSM-III-R SCID*. New York: New York State Psychiatric Institute.

Trzepacz, P. T., & Baker, R. W. (1993). *The psychiatric mental status examination*. New York: Oxford University Press.

Wallace, C. J. (1986). Functional assessment in rehabilitation. *Schizophrenia Bulletin, 12*, 625–629.

CHAPTER

5

Legal and Ethical Issues

Power is everywhere; not because it embraces everything, but because it comes from everywhere.

—Foucault, *The History of Sexuality,* 1978

Are profits and caregiving compatible?

—Schamess, *"Corporate Values and Managed Mental Health Care,"* 1998

To practice as a clinical social worker in today's behavioral health care environment is to encounter laws and social practices that generate value conflicts. Values are preferred ideas or beliefs about human nature, human rights, and how social workers should intervene (Gordon, 1965; Levy, 1973, 1979). Ethics has to do with right and wrong behaviors that affect others (Levy, 1979). Because social workers are obligated to act on the basis of professional values, "as far as *professional* values are concerned, values and ethics tend to converge" (Levy, 1979, p. 2).

The core values of the social work profession are encompassed in the NASW Code of Ethics: service, social justice, dignity and worth of the person, the importance of human relationships, integrity, and competence (National Association of Social Workers [NASW], 1997). Ethical principles are based on the core values. The code affirms that the social work profession is particularly concerned with the well-being and empowerment of "people who are vulnerable, oppressed, and living in poverty" (NASW, 1997, p. 371). The code stipulates that social workers' primary responsibility is to promote the well-being and interests of clients and to respect clients' self-determination and privacy. Nevertheless, social workers are subject to laws that can supersede their loyalty to clients. In addition to clients, professional social workers are responsible to colleagues, practice settings, the social work profession, and the larger society (NASW, 1997). Thus, there are many layers of coexisting obligations and demands, any or many of which may be mobilized in a given situation.

Social work practice in mental health is affected by state and federal court decisions, laws, public policies, and regulations interpreting public policies, any of which may or may not coincide with social work values and ethics. Where they correspond, social workers can be comfortably guided by them in their clinical work. In some instances, however, professional beliefs about what is in a client's best interest may not be congruent with the law; in other instances, statutory requirements clash with fundamental professional values. In order to resolve value conflicts that may occur, social workers need to be knowledgeable about court decisions and legal principles that pertain to the balance of power between clients, who have certain rights, and the state's authority to infringe on these rights.

Similarly social workers need to understand the managed care environment and the power interests that abound and influence this environment. In the past two decades, the business sector has increasingly penetrated public and private mental health arenas creating new concepts that obfuscate the profit motive that drives its enterprises. Guided by the values of social justice and humane care, social workers need to determine whether profits and caregiving are compatible (Schamess, 1998), and if they are not, take action to rectify the situation. Considering that "power is everywhere" (Foucault, 1978, p. 93), clinical social workers in tandem with clients, agencies, and other sources, can exercise power in the interests of a humane mental health caregiving environment.

This chapter recognizes the ubiquity of power and the presence of both legal and quasi-legal authorities in and around the settings in which social workers practice. Although social work values and the legal requirements that will be discussed are more modern (i.e., based on Enlightenment ideas) than postmodern, they lend themselves to a postmodern analysis. In keeping with the postmodern perspective of this book, it is acknowledged that knowledge is local (Geertz, 1983); that is, the laws and principles that regulate practice are specific to a particular historical time and place. Supreme Court decisions and federal laws that have evolved and continue to evolve apply to the entire nation. Legislation and decisions of state and federal district courts in one's own state affect practice in these areas. Although decisions that are made in higher courts of other states are not binding elsewhere, advocates who are arguing in state and federal courts on cases involving similar issues often use these decisions as examples of appropriate decisions. State laws are sometimes consistent with decisions made in other states or with model laws created by special interest groups. Similarly, managed care entities manifest themselves differently in different localities, but there are commonalities.

This chapter addresses several topics—involuntary civil commitment, least restrictive alternative, clients' rights, confidentiality and the duty to warn, and ethical issues of behavioral managed care. It provides an overview and discusses some of the legal and ethical issues surrounding these topics and shows how power is manifested when these issues arise.

Involuntary Civil Commitment

Involuntary commitment of an individual to a psychiatric hospital or its equivalent is an exercise of power. It deprives an individual of his or her liberty, privacy, and freedom to pursue his or her own interests (Hermann, 1997). The state derives its right to commit through its historical role as parent (*parens patriae*) and through its *police power* to protect the public from danger. As parent, the state takes a benevolent interest in the welfare of vulnerable citizens, whom it tries to protect. When the state assumes the parental role, it acts in what it perceives to be the best interest of the individual. "The police power is the authority of the state to maintain peace and order and to take action to punish or confine those whose behavior threatens the persons or property of others" (Hermann, 1997, p. 146). When the state assumes police power, its focus is on the interests of the community (Brakel, Parry, & Weiner, 1985). Thus, the state is empowered to protect either the individual or the community or, at times, both.

Although states vary in their statutory requirements for involuntary civil commitment, most recognize two or three criteria that apply to the client. First, mental illness must be present. A diagnosis of a psychiatric disorder is necessary. (Some states also have statutes allowing them to commit an individual who is determined to be developmentally disabled or addicted to drugs and alcohol, provided that they meet other criteria as well [Hermann, 1997]). Second, individuals must be considered dangerous to themselves or others. This suggests suicidal or homicidal threats or acts, but some states include destructiveness toward property. The dangerousness must be related to the mental illness. The third criterion is the client's inability to provide for his or her basic needs, sometimes described as being gravely disabled. This criterion, however, usually is not the sole requirement that must be met (Brakel, Parry, & Weiner, 1985).

A postmodern analysis calls for a deconstruction of the language that is used. Accordingly, a civil commitment should be differentiated from a criminal one in which an individual is punished for a crime and, consequently, loses some of his or her civil rights. During the eighteenth and nineteenth centuries, civil commitment to psychiatric facilities was accomplished "with ease and informality. A request of a friend or relative to a member of the hospital staff for an order of admission would most often result in commitment" (Hermann, 1997, p. 142). Once committed, residents were treated as if they were prisoners with indefinite sentences. Some had difficulty getting discharged. Notwithstanding this historical legacy, the term *civil* highlights clients' rights as citizens regardless of their mental status.

As discussed in Chapter 1, the term *mental illness* is also problematic. Not surprisingly, most state civil commitment statutes are imprecise in their definitions of mental illness (Hermann, 1997). Diagnosis is used, however, even though the *DSM-IV* itself states that

> the clinical diagnosis of a DSM-IV mental disorder is not sufficient to establish the existence for legal purposes as a "mental disorder," "mental disability," "mental disease," or "mental defect." In determining whether an individual meets a specified legal standard (e.g., for competence, criminal responsibility, or disability), additional information is usually required beyond that contained in the DSM-IV diagnosis. (American Psychiatric Association, 1994, p. xxiii)

The "additional information" includes the individual's psychosocial functioning and impairments (APA, 1994) but also may pertain to dangerousness. The term *dangerousness* elicits a number of questions, particularly: What kind of danger? Based on acts performed or anticipated? Who is in danger? On what basis is dangerousness assessed? By whom? A Wisconsin case, *Lessard v. Schmidt* (1974), ruled that commitment was justified only if it is likely that a person would do "immediate harm to himself or others." Although this case called for a "recent overt act, attempt or threat to do substantial harm" (p. 1093), many other states do not have such a requirement (Hermann, 1997). Even if there is evidence of aggressive behavior from the recent past, the assessment of dangerousness is a judgment call because behavior in the future cannot be accurately predicted. In *O'Connor v. Donaldson* (1975), which went to the Supreme Court, a man who was institutionalized for years was said to be wrongfully confined because he was *not* dangerous (Brakel, Parry, & Weiner, 1985). Another Supreme Court case, *Addington v. Texas* (1979), held that the state's criteria must be based on "clear and convincing evidence," thus requiring danger-ousness to be documented. Generally psychiatrists determine whether an individual is mentally ill and make decisions around emergency admissions, but in formal hearings ju-dicial officers, a jury, an administrative board, or a psychiatric board is authorized by dif-ferent states to decide whether an individual is to be committed (Hermann, 1997).

Clinical social workers employed in emergency services, admissions departments of general and psychiatric hospitals, and outpatient mental health services participate in the process culminating in involuntary commitment to a psychiatric hospital or unit. These workers make the initial determination that a client meets criteria for hospitalization. Even though a psychiatrist is generally the practitioner who makes the decision about emergency commitment, the social worker may influence the decision and facilitate the process.

Involuntary hospitalization is a coercive procedure that, like imprisonment, confines individuals against their will. As such it is oppressive. Despite justification based on legal criteria, many clients who are committed are rational and aware of themselves and their sit-uation. Involuntary hospitalization is not synonymous with being legally incompetent, which requires additional evidence and a separate procedure. A stronger reason to partici-pate in this practice is a humanitarian wish to protect clients from harming themselves or others. In such cases, the social worker is acting "paternalistic"—"interfering with an indi-vidual's freedom for his or her own good" (Reamer, 1983, p. 254). Still, social workers who participate in commitment procedures should be aware that they are identifying with the state as *parens patriae;* that is, they are taking on a parental role in relation to an adult who may strongly object to what is transpiring.

Social workers who tend to be paternalistic may become frustrated when they find that the criteria for involuntary commitment that have been established by law make it dif-ficult to hospitalize individuals who need care. Consider this case:

> Dorothy Meadows is a sixty-five-year-old widow who has been living with her daughter and son-in-law during the last two years. Until the past month, she was attending a day treatment program at a local mental health center and taking her medication. Recently she has been fearful of "monsters" talking to her from the television, afraid to leave the house, and has been refusing to bathe.

Individuals such as Dorothy, who have psychotic symptoms, poor insight, and inadequate personal hygiene but are not a danger to themselves or others, cannot be hospitalized. Likewise, decompensated, homeless, mentally ill persons who are not taking their medica-tion may not be dangerous enough to be involuntarily committed. There is, however, a legal alternative to involuntary civil commitment to a hospital.

Involuntary outpatient commitment (IOU) is an alternative to involuntary inpatient commitment in which clients are legally committed to a community treatment center rather than to a hospital (American Bar Association, 1988). Under regulations, community resi-dence may be tied to compliance with the treatment plan, such as taking medication, par-ticipating in a partial hospitalization program, or some other requirement, with the client subject to sanctions for noncompliance (Wilk, 1997). Involuntary outpatient commitment may occur in place of hospitalization or upon discharge from a psychiatric facility. A vari-ation of IOU is *preventive commitment,* which has been instituted by some states to protect persons who look as if they might deteriorate.

Although all states have some sort of outpatient civil commitment (Fellin, 1996), the policy is controversial. On the one hand, it allows individuals who would otherwise be hospitalized to live relatively freely in the community. Furthermore, it makes it possible to treat individuals who are not likely to comply with their treatment plan. Gott (1997) noted that research has found that outpatient commitment has a positive effect on treatment outcome and that it provides an opportunity for a client to receive help. On the other hand, IOU is coercive and it puts social workers and other mental health professionals in the role of "mental health police," to say nothing of the liability it imposes on social workers whose caseloads include individuals who are considered "dangerous" (Wilk, 1997). Another approach is to assure that a client receives the least restrictive treatment that is consistent with his or her needs.

Least Restrictive Alternative

The least restrictive alternative is a legal principle that has been the basis for discharging or not hospitalizing clients with mental illness who can function in a less intrusive environment. Several court cases have affirmed that clients have a right to treatment in the least restrictive alternative (*Lake v. Cameron* [1966], *Covington v. Harris* [1969], *Wyatt v. Stickney* [1971, 1972], *Dixon v. Weinberger* [1975]). The *Wyatt* case, for example, ruled that clients in Alabama institutions for the mentally ill and mentally retarded have a right to humane treatment in conditions that introduce the least restrictions necessary to achieve the goals of treatment.

The least restrictive alternative applies to the treatment environment and the modes of intervention that are employed. Both are evaluated in relation to the treatment objectives for the individual client (Brakel, Parry, & Weiner, 1985) and eliminate the threat of dangerousness (Hermann, 1997). The *most* restrictive environment is the most confining and intrusive (Rinas & Clyne-Jackson, 1988), for example, an institution that maintains clients behind locked doors. The *least* is a community setting in which the client has little supervision. At the point of screening for admission, the client's treatment needs should be assessed in relation to alternative settings in which these needs can be met. For example, if an individual can be treated effectively in a community mental health center and partial hospitalization program while living at home, hospitalization should be avoided. Similarly clients who are hospitalized should be not be placed in constricting units, such as maximum-security wards, if this degree of restriction is not therapeutic. Clients who are transferred from less to more confining units or treatment facilities are entitled to a hearing (Brakel, Parry, & Weiner, 1985).

A 1999 Supreme Court case, *Olmstead v. L.C.,* expanded the legal basis for favoring less restrictive settings. This case, filed on behalf of two women with mental illness and mental retardation, found that maintaining individuals with disabilities isolated in state institutions when they are capable of living more independently in the community discriminated against them under Title II of the Americans with Disabilities Act of 1990 (Greenhouse, 1999). Nevertheless, this decision left open the level of services that should be available for clients to have adequate community treatment (Flynn, 1999).

The kinds of interventions employed are also encompassed under the least restrictive alternative. Those therapies that affect physical functioning (e.g., medication, shock treatment) are more intrusive than "talk" therapies; aversive treatment is more coercive than systematic desensitization; physical restraints are more confining than calm coaxing. Mental health practitioners are encouraged to use the lesser alternative that promises to help the client (Rinas & Clyne-Jackson, 1988). The client's medication also falls under the rubric of the least restrictive alternative (Brooks, 1988). Clients who object to a medication for a particular reason, such as its side effects, can be offered alternative medication that does not have these effects or a treatment strategy other than medication that is therapeutic.

Social workers are in positions in which they put the least restrictive alternative standard into effect. Whether they work in community mental health centers, behavioral health carve-outs, hospital admissions or emergency departments, residential programs, or inpatient facilities, they play an important role in determining which among a range of alternative treatment settings and services are most appropriate and beneficial and least limiting for particular clients. The social worker has a responsibility to be familiar with the particular settings, what they have to offer, the climate within each alternative, and whether there are openings at a particular time. Furthermore, they should determine the kinds of living situation and treatment that the client wants. Some clients are comfortable in settings such as personal care homes (adult foster homes) that may appear restrictive to the social worker. Clients' feelings about these important issues should be explored thoroughly. They have the right to make choices on their own behalf.

Clients' Rights

Consumers of community mental health services have the same rights as other citizens unless they are found to be incompetent. But even persons who are adjudged incompetent and have legal guardians or conservators who look out for their interests do not surrender all their rights. These guardians may have limited areas in which they make decisions on behalf of the client (e.g., money management), leaving the client with rights in other areas. "Incompetence in one area does not, per se, mean that a person is incompetent in other areas" (Zaitchik & Appelbaum, 1996, p. 455).

Many of the clients' rights that have been upheld in court cases pertain specifically to the hospitalized client. Among these are the right to treatment, the right to refuse treatment (including medication), the right to informed consent, due process, and such citizens' rights as the right to vote, the right to use the telephone, and the right to legal representation. The *Wyatt v. Stickney* (1971) Alabama case, for example, connected hospitalization with treatment; persons who are not being treated should be discharged to an appropriate setting (American Bar Association, 1984).

The client's right to refuse treatment has not as yet been addressed by the United States Supreme Court. Many states, however, make a distinction between clients' rights in emergency as opposed to nonemergency situations, denying clients their rights in the former instances. Similarly, clients who are determined to be incompetent can be given a treatment (such as medication) that they do not want. In *Rennie v. Klein* (1983), the United States Court of Appeals for the Third Circuit ruled that although involuntary patients can refuse to take antipsychotic medication in nonemergency situations, hospital staff could administer medication if they determine that patients present a danger to themselves or others (Hermann, 1997). In such cases, professional judgment (usually supported in an in-hospital procedure to establish due process) supersedes the client's wishes (Hermann, 1997).

Clients may have good reason to refuse treatment. Many medications have side effects (see Chapters 8, 9, and 12) that are difficult to tolerate. In those cases, other medications and psychotherapeutic interventions may be more suitable. Where possible, practitioners should explore the feasibility of these alternatives before the situation escalates into one in which treatment is forced. For clients who are willing to be treated but want to have a voice in how they are treated, drawing up advance directives may be appropriate.

Advance Directives

Advance directives are documents, written when an individual is competent, specifying "how decisions about treatment should be made if the person becomes incompetent" (Appelbaum, 1991, p. 983). They are used widely in health care by individuals who wish to express in advance their wishes about the use of specific, life-preserving measures (e.g., ventilators, feeding tubes). Considering that clients have varying degrees of functioning due to some mental disorders, the advance directive is a means by which clients can specify what their preferences are while they are competent in the event that they become incompetent (Appelbaum, 1991).

In mental health two types of advance directives are used. These are *instructional directives,* which are comparable to living wills, and *proxy directives,* which are something like power of attorney (Srebnik & La Fond, 1999). Instructional directives state the client's treatment preferences for mental health care during mental health crises should the individual become unable to communicate this information (Srebnik & La Fond, 1999). Among the areas of choice are types of medication and administration methods, use of restraints, preferred hospital, persons who should be notified, individuals who should be asked to assume child care, and the use of particular treatment methods (e.g., electric shock therapy) (Srebnik & La Fond, 1999). Proxy directives nominate a third party who is authorized to make decisions on behalf of the client in the event that the client becomes incompetent (Appelbaum, 1991). The proxy may be a family member or friend—someone who is trusted. An advance directive may include both instructional and proxy types. Some directives include a section signed by a psychiatrist attesting that the client is competent at the time the directive is made (Vogel-Scibilia, 1999).

Advance directives preserve clients' rights and preferences even when their functioning is compromised. Nevertheless, the instructions cannot compel a mental health provider to follow treatment methods that he or she considers undesirable, unethical, or unaffordable (Srebnik & La Fond, 1999). A further complication is that if the advance directive is written as irrevocable, it can be construed as a Ulysses contract that limits an individual's future freedom, a contract that many states are reluctant to uphold (Srebnik & La Fond, 1999).

Up until now we have been considering the rights of clients and the constraints on these rights. Next we will look at constraints and obligations that are placed on the social worker.

Confidentiality and the Duty to Warn

Confidentiality

Confidentiality is both a value and an ethical principle. Social workers are bound to maintain the privacy of communications shared by clients by not disclosing that the individual is a client and the particular information shared by the client without the client's consent, and by taking precautions to assure the security of case records. According to the Code of Ethics of the National Association of Social Workers (1997), "The social worker should respect clients' right to privacy.... Once private information is shared, standards of confidentiality apply" (p. 376).

Confidentiality should be distinguished from the closely related concept of privileged communication. Information shared in confidence with mental health professionals, lawyers, clergy, and physicians is protected from inquiry by the court ("privileged") where state laws stipulate that those particular professions have that status. In *Jaffee v. Redmond* (1996), the Supreme Court found that records and notes of licensed clinical social workers "written in the course of diagnosis and treatment are protected against involuntary disclosure by a psychotherapist-client privilege" (Gelman, Pollack, & Weiner, 1999, p. 244). Under these circumstances, the client has the right to have protected information withheld in legal proceedings. There are, however, instances in which privileged communication is disregarded. If a client signs a waiver or provides informed consent, the information can be revealed to the court or the party named in the waiver or consent form. On other occasions, such as suspected child abuse, involuntary commitment, and dangerous behavior (Rinas & Clyde-Jackson, 1988), social workers are required by law to testify.

In mental health practice, confidentiality protects a client from prejudicial community attitudes toward the mentally ill. Although social workers may regard help seeking as a strength, many uninformed people have negative attitudes toward recipients of mental health services. Some view seeking help as a moral weakness. Others assume that if one is receiving help, one is "sick" and potentially violent. Some will refuse to hire an individual with a mental health history or diagnosis. A stigma is still attached to the status of being a mental health client (Ziegenfuss, 1983).

Confidentiality is a critical feature of a therapeutic relationship. It is a way in which clients are able to feel that it is safe to share their feelings. In promising confidentiality, the social worker conveys a willingness to protect the interests of the client. Thus, confidentiality contributes to the quality of the therapeutic alliance.

Nevertheless, confidentiality is rarely "absolute" (Wilson, 1978, p. 3). Usually some information in some form is communicated inside an agency. Social workers share information about clients with colleagues and supervisors. Difficult clients may be well known by the entire staff of a mental health agency. Case records are reviewed by internal and external utilization reviewers. As discussed later in this chapter, managed care entities have access to private information that they may not adequately protect. In this day of telephone answering machines, facsimile machines, and electronic mail, special care must be taken that confidential information remains private.

There are circumstances in which the social worker is obliged to violate confidentiality. The National Association of Social Workers (1997) recognizes the limits on confidentiality in the Code of Ethics:

> The social worker should protect the confidentiality of all information obtained in the course of professional service, *except for compelling professional reasons* [emphasis added]. The general expectation that social workers will keep information confidential does not apply when disclosure is necessary to prevent serious, foreseeable, and imminent harm to a client

or other identifiable person or when laws or regulations require disclosure without a client's consent. In all instances, social workers should disclose the least amount of confidential information necessary to achieve the desired purpose; only information that is directly relevant to the purpose for which the disclosure is made should be revealed. (p. 376)

The social worker must make a judgment regarding whether the reasons are compelling and which confidences are relevant.

The Obligation to Warn

The quotation that was just cited from the most recent version of the NASW Code of Ethics incorporates discussions surrounding the *Tarasoff* cases.

Two *Tarasoff* rulings and subsequent court decisions lay out the obligations of psychotherapists to warn others of possible harm. The initial case arose under the following circumstances. Prosenjit Poddar, a graduate student who was receiving psychotherapy at the University of California Student Health Service in Berkeley, told his therapist that he intended to kill Tatiana Tarasoff, a female student who had indicated that she was not romantically interested in him. The therapist responded by (a) getting Poddar to promise that he would not act on his desires and (b) informing the campus police in order to initiate an involuntary commitment. The police investigated the matter and were assured by Poddar that nothing would happen. After Tarasoff returned from a vacation, however, Poddar killed her (Brakel, Parry, & Weiner, 1985).

On the basis of information revealed at Poddar's trial, Tarasoff's family sued two of Poddar's therapists, the University of California, and the campus police, stating that Tarasoff should have been warned that she was in danger. The state supreme court said that the therapist and police could be liable for failing to warn Tatiana. The case was later reargued before the court (in a case heard in 1976 that is referred to as *Tarasoff II*). This time the court said that the therapist could be culpable if he did not "exercise reasonable care" to protect the victim. Such steps as warning the victim or others who could warn the victim; notifying the police; or other reasonable steps were recommended (*Tarasoff v. Regents* of the University of California, 1976). The court did not have the opportunity to determine whether the therapists in this case were negligent, as an out-of-court settlement was reached. Since *Tarasoff,* rulings on a number of other cases have stipulated that the victim should be a specific and identifiable person or group of persons (Brakel, Parry, & Weiner, 1985).

Although *Tarasoff II* provided options besides warning the victim, the *Tarasoff* decisions pose a dilemma to clinical social workers. The Code of Ethics of the National Association of Social Workers provides little guidance with respect to warning victims (Weil & Sanchez, 1983). The code does specify that confidentiality can be violated only for "compelling reasons." Although clients' statements about violent intentions toward others appear to be compelling reasons, intentions are not necessarily communicated directly. A client may talk vaguely about a fear or fantasy that may or may not be acted upon. Many clients have aggressive fantasies, but most do not act on them. The social worker, however, must make a judgment about how serious the client is about carrying out such an act, whether there is a specific victim, and whether the intended victim is in danger. If the act seems likely to occur, the social worker (or other mental health professional) is obligated to warn the victim or take some other reasonable step.

The *Tarasoff* rulings put pressure on mental health workers not only to make assessments about a client's dangerousness but to *predict* whether an individual poses a threat to another. A task force of the American Psychiatric Association reported serious reservations about the ability of therapists to foresee violent behavior; mistakes can be made. Moreover, warning a victim or other appropriate parties can jeopardize the therapeutic relationship (Brakel, Parry, & Weiner, 1985). In warning another, a therapist is violating the client's trust. The resulting sense of betrayal may make it virtually impossible for the therapeutic relationship to continue.

Several channels are open to the social worker faced with such a case. First, one should get legal information about how the *Tarasoff* rulings are interpreted in one's own state. In the state of Ohio, for example, an amendment to a mental health reorganization act provides immunity to mental health workers:

> No person shall be liable for any harm that results to any other person as a result of failing to disclose any confidential information about a mental health client or failing to otherwise attempt to protect such other person from harm by such client. (Ohio S.B. 156, 1989, p. 143)

In states that do not provide immunity (and even those that do), one should consider a range of options regarding whom one should warn (the intended victim, the police, or others), as well as initiating involuntary hospitalization for the client. Consultation with another staff member, especially a psychiatrist, is desirable (Brooks, 1988). Similarly, the agency's attorney might be contacted.

Reamer (1998) suggests that the social worker should

- have evidence that the client poses a threat of violence to a third party;
- have evidence that the violent act is foreseeable—that is, sufficient evidence to suggest that the violent act is likely to occur;
- have reasonable evidence to suggest that the violent act is impending or likely to occur relatively soon; and
- be able to identify the potential victim (pp. 59–60)

before disclosing confidential information to a third party.

This section has discussed confidentiality and the duty to warn potential victims of violence. In today's managed care environment, confidentiality and other ethical issues are of paramount importance to social workers and clients. These issues are addressed next.

Ethical Issues Surrounding Behavioral Managed Care

Clinical social workers practice in an environment in which managed care entities and their behavioral health carve-outs are pervasive. Because these organizations are businesses in which the drive for profit is fundamental, their values diverge from and often conflict with core values of the social work profession. This section will revisit some of the issues addressed previously and discuss some additional issues in the context of behavioral managed care.

As discussed in Chapter 1, managed care is a means of controlling the cost of health care services, which were skyrocketing under the previously dominant fee-for-service system.

Managed care organizations review the kind, length, and location of services that are recommended by professionals and determine whether these interventions are sufficiently high in quality and cost-effective. Approval occurs prior to treatment, when clients are directed to certain providers or services (gatekeeping) (Strom-Gottfried, 1998). Monitoring of quality (utilization review) occurs prospectively, concurrently, and retrospectively (Corcoran, 1997). In behavioral health, short-term, goal-directed, time-limited interventions have been favored over long-term, continuous approaches (Corcoran, 1994). Managed care has blurred the boundaries between the public and private sectors (Paulson, 1996). Many Medicare and Medicaid recipients now have their health and mental health care managed by managed care organizations.

Managed care has been discussed and debated extensively by social workers (e.g., Corcoran & Vandiver, 1996; Schamess & Lightburn, 1998; Strom-Gottfried, 1997), who, overall, are ambivalent about its impact on the profession and clients. Although some writers assert that under the best of circumstances managed care offers social workers new employment opportunities as case managers and therapists (Paulson, 1996), others are concerned that social work values and the well-being of clients are compromised when outsiders intercede in mental health care (Schamess, 1998). This section will discuss three problematic issues—clients' rights, confidentiality, and professional autonomy.

Clients' Rights

As a profession that gives primacy to the interests of clients, social workers are concerned with clients' rights under behavioral managed care. Despite the profit orientation mentioned earlier, managed care organizations claim that clients benefit from oversight. For one, managed care groups say that they are concerned with the quality of care and protect clients from what they view as ineffective, prolonged, insight-oriented treatment. Second, the gatekeeping and monitoring of treatment can protect clients from unscrupulous providers and assure that clients are receiving the best available treatment over the least amount of time. Third, managed care entities use science-based practice guidelines and findings from outcome studies and client satisfaction surveys as bases for decisions about clients' care (Corcoran & Vandiver, 1996; Strom-Gottfried, 1998).

On the other hand, behavioral managed care organizations limit clients' choices. Depending on the particular plan, only certain mental health providers, agencies, and hospitals can be used. Clients on medication may be prescribed a drug that is less costly but has more uncomfortable side effects than more expensive medications with fewer side effects (see Chapters 8, 9, and 12 for discussions about medication). Along these lines, a client may not be told what all the options are with respect to alternative treatments, providers, and services, and the bases for decisions that are made.

In order that clients understand what is transpiring and participate in the decision-making process as much as possible, clients should be informed about the process of treatment and their choices within the process. Some managed care contracts contain nondisclosure clauses (also called gag orders) that require that the social workers conceal some aspects of the managed care group's influence with the client (Corcoran, 1997). These conflict with the social workers' obligation to provide services based on client self-determination and informed consent (NASW, 1997). Social workers should "inform clients how their delivery of services may be influenced by managed care policies and restrictions" and about the "pre-

and current authorization process," "their right to appeal a utilization decision," and "Potential invasion of their privacy by the review process" (Reamer, 1997, p. 98). In the next section, confidentiality, discussed earlier, will be revisited in the context of managed care.

Confidentiality

Behavioral managed care poses serious threats to the confidentiality of the client-worker relationship. Social workers must submit documentation to managed care companies that includes the client's name, diagnosis, and specifics about his or her treatment. The information included may be so sensitive (e.g., the person has HIV disease) that if it became known, the individual could suffer serious personal consequences (Rock & Congress, 1999). Even though the professional social worker guards the client's privacy and obtains a release from the client to share information with the behavioral managed care organization, the managed care group may not treat the client's information with the same care.

With today's technology, problems over confidentiality are heightened. Intimate details about a person's treatment may be communicated over cellular phones or answering machines, where talk may be overheard by others. Sensitive information is also transmitted by electronic mail and through attachments that may not be secure (Gelman, Pollack, & Weiner, 1999). Personal information about clients is now available on computerized information systems to which numerous individuals have access (Gelman et al., 1999). As Davidson and Davidson (1998) noted:

> With the use of managed care information systems that include telephone reviews, voice mail, faxes, cellular telephones, and highly unregulated computerized databases, there are few guarantees, if any, that sensitive information is stored securely. Rather, it appears that information, once passed from the social worker to a managed care service and logged into the medical database of a third-party insurance payer, may be as accessible as credit card information or mortgage payment records to people who know how to proceed with electronic inquiry. (p. 283)

Proposed legislation calling for universal patient identifiers on medical records that do not require a patient's consent further threaten privacy (Gelman et al., 1999).

Several authors have suggested ways in which social workers can address such threats to confidentiality. As indicated earlier, social workers should fully disclose the extent to which information that they reveal is disclosed to a managed care company (Corcoran, 1997), including the sharing of their own reports with the client. This gives the client knowledge and, for clients with financial resources, the option to pay for truly confidential treatment outside their behavioral managed care program. Consistent with the Code of Ethics, social workers should share "the least amount of confidential information necessary to achieve the desired purpose" (NASW, 1997, p. 376; Rock & Congress, 1999). Data about clients that are shared with managed care companies should be factual, concise, and specific, with interpretations clearly differentiated from facts (Gelman et al., 1999). Access to databases can be limited to individuals who have passwords, and code numbers can be used to identify particular clients described in electronic mail or case records (Gelman et al., 1999).

As stated by numerous social work scholars, there is a need for social change in dealing with confidentiality issues in relation to managed care organizations. First, social workers, provider agencies, and clients need to be educated about the threats to confidentiality posed by technology in relation to managed care and the means of protecting privacy to the extent possible (Rock & Congress, 1999). Social workers can advocate within their agencies to protect records and reports that go to managed care entities (Rock & Congress, 1999). Furthermore, they can work collaboratively with clients, agencies, and managed care organizations to promote confidentiality (Reamer, 1997). Advocacy can be on a case basis or issue basis (Sunley, 1997).

Professional Autonomy

One of the hallmarks of a profession is its ability to make decisions that affect others (Flexner, 1915). Parsons (1954) conceived of professions as having authority, within a specific sphere, that is based on technical competence. In contrast with the field of business, which is pursued egoistically for a profit, professions are "disinterested," that is, they are service oriented (Parsons, 1954). As Pellegrino (1983) stated, "To be a professional is to make a promise to help, to keep that promise, and to do so in the best interest of the patient" (p. 174). Although social work's status as a profession has been questioned (Flexner, 1915), this book takes the position that social work is a profession and it has historically participated in decision making on its own and in collaboration with individual clients, families, and members of other disciplines. In the context of managed care, autonomy encompasses the principle that the social worker can assess the client's needs and how to best address these needs (Strom-Gottfried, 1998).

Under managed care, social work's autonomy is threatened in a number of ways. Despite what a social worker recommends and believes is in the best interest of the client, a case coordinator from a managed care company can dictate how much of what kind of help the client can have. The company can overrule the social worker and recommend something else (or another provider) or terminate treatment altogether. In the event that termination is imposed by the company, a social worker is in an ethical dilemma because the Code of Ethics requires that social workers "take reasonable steps to avoid abandoning clients who are still in need of services" (NASW, 1997, p. 378). Furthermore, the social worker is subject to potentially conflicting demands on his or her autonomy—from the client and the managed care organization. Corcoran and Vandiver (1996) depict the social worker in this situation as a "double agent...who serves the best interest of the client and the pecuniary interest of the managed care organization's goals of cost containment and profit" (p. 202).

Several writers have suggested ways in which social workers can live with the behavioral managed care system without violating professional ethics. Showall (1997) suggests that social workers form collaborative, nonadversarial relationships with managed care companies and regard them as secondary clients. If these relationships do not work, the social worker may choose not to work with these companies (assuming that the social worker works as an independent practitioner). This suggests that there is a place for negotiation and persuasion in dealing with managed care companies. In the case of premature termination, Reamer (1997) recommends that social workers continue to work with the client (gratis) or make a referral elsewhere, carefully explaining the alternatives. As with confidentiality, social workers should organize colleagues and clients to promote policy changes (Reamer, 1997; Strom-Gottfried, 1998).

Summary and Deconstruction

Clinical social workers practicing in behavioral health settings today are situated among numerous sources of power—the law, clients, managed care entities, and (not to be underestimated) the power that lies within themselves to advocate for what they believe is right. Social workers have a professional obligation under the Code of Ethics to give primacy to clients—to respect their dignity and worth, their rights to self-determination and informed consent, and the confidentiality of what they revealed in the client-worker relationship. Social workers are also obligated to obey the law and at times must breach confidentiality because it is required by law. Besides these professional obligations, practitioners who work with individuals with severe mental illness must be knowledgeable about the rights of clients to live in the least restrictive environment and receive the least restrictive but most beneficial care.

Managed care organizations have entered the mental health scene as additional parties, who have the prerogative to accept or reject the recommendations of social workers and other mental health professionals. Clients are not always aware of the extent to which managed care companies can and do intrude on mental health treatment and the pressures they exert on professionals to comply with their demands. In this day of computerized databases, electronic mail, voice mail, and cellular telephones, social workers are becoming increasingly concerned that clients' confidentiality is not adequately protected.

The entrance of the private sector into the human services scene is not a comfortable development for social workers who, traditionally, have been driven by professional values rather than profits and cost-effectiveness. In today's managed care environment, these precious values are being "subjugated," leaving social workers with "guilty knowledge" about human needs and what should be done to address them (Weick, 1999). This chapter concludes with Weick's (1999) comments:

> ...guilty knowledge is dangerous knowledge. It is knowledge that sits at the edge of the dominant paradigm, insistently challenging the assumptions about the value of what we know. In social work, what we know flows from the deep wellsprings of our value perspective, overlaid by decades of rich practice experience. It is the remarkable synergy produced by our moral commitments, our social perspective, and our practice wisdom that gives social work its unique character. (p. 329)

> ....we must find the courage to speak and write in our own voice, not just among ourselves but to the world at large. (p. 332)

When social workers articulate their truths about what is ethical, they will speak up to power and attain the power to implement what they know and value.

DISCUSSSION QUESTIONS

1. Consider the rights and needs of persons with severe mental disabilities who are homeless. Are they capable of taking care of themselves? Do they recognize their need for mental health treatment? Do they have the right to live as they wish on the streets?

2. What are the obligations of the social worker with respect to a client who refuses to take prescribed medication?

3. Discuss how the rights of clients may be jeopardized by involuntary community treatment.

4. Identify several agencies in your community that provide mental health services. Assess these agencies according to their restrictiveness.

5. What are the laws, rules, and procedures used in your state with respect to involuntary commitment?

6. How is the duty to warn interpreted in your state?

7. How might a client benefit from drawing up an advance directive? How binding is an advance directive on professionals?

8. Some states have their own mental health and substance abuse bills of rights. Investigate bills of rights available in your state.

9. How do you feel about sharing particulars about a client with a case coordinator from a managed care company? Give an example of the kind of information you would provide about a hypothetical client.

10. Review the NASW Code of Ethics. Discuss how the managed care requirements are consistent and inconsistent with the code.

REFERENCES

Addington v. Texas, 441 U.S. 418, 3MDLR 164 (1979).

American Bar Association. (1984/1988). *Mental disability law primer* (3rd ed.). Chicago: Author.

American Psychiatric Association (1994). *Diagnostic and Statistical Manual of Mental Disorders* (*DSM-IV*) (4th ed.). Washington, DC: Author.

Appelbaum, P. S. (1991). Advance directives for psychiatric treatment. *Hospital and Community Psychiatry, 42*(10), 983–984.

Brakel, S. J., Parry, J., & Weiner, B. (1985). *The mentally disabled and the law* (3rd ed.). Chicago: American Bar Foundation.

Brooks, A. D. (1988). Law and the chronically mentally ill. In A. D. Brooks, K. S. Brown, L. F. Davis, P. Fellin, U. C. Gerhart, & A. B. Hatfield (Eds.), *Services for the chronically mentally ill: New approaches for mental health professionals* (Vol. 1, pp. 62–75). Washington, DC: Council on Social Work Education.

Chamberlin, J. (1978). *On our own: Patient-controlled alternatives to the mental health system.* New York: McGraw-Hill.

Corcoran, K. (1994). YES: Managed care and the marketplace. Debate 17: Is managed care good for mental health clients? In S. Kirk & S. D. Einbinder (Eds.), *Controversial issues in mental health* (pp. 240–246). Boston: Allyn and Bacon.

Corcoran, K. (1997). Managed care: Implications for social work practice. In R. L. Edwards (Ed.), *Encyclopedia of social work, 19th edition 1997 supplement* (pp. 191–200). Washington, DC: NASW Press.

Corcoran, K., & Vandiver, V. (1996). *Maneuvering the maze of managed care: Skills for mental health practitioners.* New York: The Free Press.

Covington v. Harris, 419 F.2d 617 (D.C. Cir. 1969).

Davidson, J. R., & Davidson, T. (1998). Confidentiality and managed care: Ethical and legal concerns. In G. Shaimess & A. Lightburn (Eds.), *Humane managed care?* (pp. 281–292). Washington, DC: NASW Press.

Dixon v. Weinberger, 405 F. Supp. (D.D.C. 1975).

Fellin, P. (1996). *Mental health and mental illness: Policies, programs, and services.* Itasca, IL: F. E. Peacock Publishers.

Flexner, A. (1915). Is social work a profession? In the *Proceedings of the National Conference of Charities and Correction,* 42nd annual session (pp. 576–590). Chicago: The Hildmann Printing Co.

Flynn, L. M. (1999, June 22). Supreme Court gives incremental victory to persons with mental illness in *Olmstead* decision. Press release, National Alliance for the Mentally Ill.

Foucault, M. (1978). *The history of sexuality: An introduction* (vol. 1). New York: Vintage Books.

Geertz, C. (1983). *Local knowledge.* New York: Basic Books.

Gelman, S.R., Pollack, D., Weiner, A. (1999). Confidentiality of social work records in the computer age. *Social Work, 44*(3), 243–252.

Gordon, W. E. (1965). Knowledge and value: Their distinction and relationship in clarifying social work practice. *Social Work, 10*(3), 32–39.

Gott, W. (1997). Should clinical social workers support the use of outpatient commitment to mental health treatment? Yes. In B. A. Thyer (Ed.), *Controversial issues in social work practice* (pp. 110–115, 121–123). Boston: Allyn and Bacon.

Greenhouse, L. (1999, June 23). *The New York Times,* p. A16.

Hermann, D. H. J. (1997). *Mental health and disability law in a nutshell.* St. Paul, MN: West Publishing Co.

Lake v. Cameron, 364 F.2d 657 (D.C. Cir. 1966).

Lessard v. Schmidt, 349 F. Supp. 1078 (E.D. Wis. 1972), vacated and remanded on other grounds, 414 U.S. 473 (1974), redecided, 379 F. Supp. 1376 (E.D. Wis. 1974), vacated and remanded on other grounds, 421 U.S. 957 (1975), redecided, 413 F. Supp. 1318 (E.D. Wis. 1976), LMDLR 32.

Levy, C. S. (1973). The value base of social work. *Journal of Education for Social Work, 9*(1), 34–42.

Levy, C. S. (1979). *Values and ethics for social work practice.* Washington, DC: National Association of Social Workers.

National Association of Social Workers. (1997). NASW Code of Ethics, Approved by the 1996 Delegate Assembly. In R. L. Edwards (Ed.), *Encyclopedia of social work, 19th edition 1997 supplement,* Appendix 1 (pp. 371–385). Washington, DC: NASW Press.

O'Connor v. Donaldson, 442 U.S. 563 (1975).

Ohio Department of Mental Health Reorganization Bill, S.B. 156 (1989).

Parsons, T. (1954). The professions and social structure (1939). In *Essays in sociological theory,* revised edition (pp. 34–49). New York: The Free Press.

Paulson, R. I. (1996). Swimming with the sharks or walking in the garden of Eden: Two visions of managed care and mental health practice. In P. R. Raffoul & C. A. McNeece (Eds.), *Future issues for social work practice* (pp. 85–96). Boston: Allyn and Bacon.

Pellegrino, E. D. (1983). What is a profession? *Journal of Allied Health,* 168–176.

Reamer, F. G. (1983). The concept of paternalism in social work. *Social Service Review, 57,* 254–271.

Reamer, F. G. (1997). Managing ethics under managed care. *Families in Society, 78*(1), 96–101.

Reamer, F. G. (1998). *Ethical standards in social work: A critical review of the NASW Code of Ethics.* Washington, DC: NASW Press.

Rinas, J., & Clyne-Jackson, S. (1988). *Professional conduct and legal concerns in mental health practice.* Norwalk, CT: Appleton & Lange.

Rock, B., & Congress, E. (1999). The new confidentiality for the 21st century in a managed care environment. *Social Work, 44*(3), 253–262.

Schamess, G. (1998). Corporate values and managed mental health care: Who profits and who benefits? In G. Schamess & A. Lightburn (Eds.). *Humane managed care?* (pp. 23–35). Washington, DC: NASW Press.

Schamess, G. & Lightburn A. (Eds.). (1998). *Humane managed care?* Washington, DC: NASW Press.

Showell, P. W. (1997). Best practice is always the goal. *Families in Society, 78*(1), 99.

Srebnik, D. S., & Lafond, J. Q. (1999). Advance directives for mental health treatment. *Psychiatric Services, 50*(7), 919–925.

Strom-Gottfried, K. (1997). The implications of managed care for social work education. *Journal of Social Work Education, 33*(1), 7–18.

Strom-Gottfried, K. (1998). Is "ethical managed care" an oxymoron? *Families in Society, 79*(3), 297–307.

Sunley, R. (1997). Advocacy in the new world of managed care. *Families in Society, 78*(1), 84–94.

Tarasoff v. Regents of the University of California, 551, P.2d 334 (Cal. Sup. Ct.) (Tarasoff II) (1976).

Vogel-Scibilia, S. (1999, Winter). Preparing an advance directive. *The Alliance,* NAMI Pennsylvania, pp. 5, 11.

Weick, A. (1999). Guilty knowledge. *Families in Society, 80*(4), 327–332.

Weil, M., & Sanchez, E. (1983). The impact of the *Tarasoff* decision on clinical social work practice. *Social Service Review, 57,* 112–124.

Wilk, R. (1997). Should clinical social workers support the use of outpatient commitment to mental health treatment? No. In B. A. Thyer (Ed.), *Controversial issues in social work practice* (pp. 115–121). Boston: Allyn and Bacon.

Wilson, S. (1978). *Confidentiality in social work: Issues and principles.* New York: Free Press.

Wyatt v. Stickney, 325 F. Supp. 781, aff'd, 344 F. Supp. 1341 (M.D. Ala. 1971), and 344 F. Supp. 373 (M.D. Ala. 1972), aff'd sub nom, *Wyatt v. Aderholt,* 503 F.2d 1305 (5th Cir. 1974).

Zaitchik, M. C., & Appelbaum, K. L. (1996). Legal issues: Competency, criminality and care. In S. M. Soreff (Ed.), *Handbook for the treatment of the seriously mentally ill* (pp. 447–460). Seattle: Hogrefe & Huber.

Ziegenfuss, J. T. (1983). *Patients' rights and professional practice.* New York: Van Nostrand Reinhold.

6 Postmodern Feminist Theory and Practice

And so when he speaks to me in a harsh tone, or criticizes me for something that I have done wrong or haven't done or whatever, I've tended to think to myself, "Now you're supposed to be submissive, so just ignore him." And so inside I've been building up a lot of resentment and a lot of anger.
—Jack, *Silencing the Self: Women and Depression,* 1991

As the twenty-first century unfolds, the status of women in U.S. society remains problematic. Despite a substantial increase in female participation in the civilian labor force during the last forty years of the twentieth century, the earnings of full-time women workers remain about three quarters of that of men (U.S. Census Bureau, 1997, 1999). While working predominantly in low-level jobs, women have been managing a "second shift" (Hochschild & Machung, 1989) at home. Women continue to suffer from the "feminization of poverty" (Pearce, 1979), inadequate child care, difficulty collecting child support, physical abuse, sexual harassment, and, more recently, welfare reform. Wherever they go, women are exposed to a normative structure that impedes their economic, social, and psychological well-being. Although such regulation is experienced in different ways and at varying degrees by women from different social, economic, and ethnic strata, women as a group are oppressed.

The mental health system is one of the sites in which women have been oppressed. Historically women hospitalized in asylums were subjected to barbaric psychiatric treatments and, in some cases, were sexually abused (Chesler, 1972; Geller & Harris, 1994). With most mental health clients living in the community, the concern now is whether women are receiving the appropriate kind of treatment. More women than men are treated for mental health problems, but treatment is often in the primary care sector, in which drug therapy is prominent (Rhodes & Goering, 1998). Epidemiological surveys have shown that some psychiatric disorders are more common to men and some to women (Kessler et al., 1994; Robins, Locke, & Regier, 1991) Yet gender-specific treatments are few and far between.

This chapter uses a postmodern feminist lens to discuss issues affecting women mental health clients. It describes postmodern feminism, psychological theories that construct women, gender differences in diagnosis, and postmodern feminist practice. To illustrate how women's mental health problems are related to the social context in which they emerge, the chapter discusses physical violence perpetrated against women. Furthermore, it describes one model of intervention for trauma. The chapter begins by discussing postmodern feminism in the context of other feminisms.

Postmodern Feminism in Context

During the fourth quarter of the last century, feminism emerged as a significant political and social force in the United States and other parts of the world. It began here with middle-class, white women who met in consciousness-raising groups in which they became aware that the dissatisfaction they were experiencing individually was related to existing ideologies (i.e., "the personal is political"). Through this reflective, interactional process, they came to realize that stereotypical ideas about femininity (passive, dependent, emotional), women's bodies (ideally thin), and woman's "place" (the home) were consequences of patriarchy. Men's control over economic resources, their advantaged positions in the political and occupational arenas, and their status as heads of households, as well as their physical size and strength, constrained the ability of women to achieve the freedom and opportunities they needed.

A number of women also participated in political organizations that were emerging, such as the National Organization of Women. This association, as well as many others, focused on issues such as the Equal Rights Amendment, reproductive freedom, rape, and domestic violence. Although these organizations were open to lesbians and women of color, nonheterosexual, nonwhite women tended to feel unwelcome. Furthermore, these constituencies did not have the same need to have their consciousness raised, as they were already aware of their marginal status. Still some of these women echoed Sojourner Truth's protest, "Ain't I a woman?" (hooks, 1981). The tendency of white women to speak about women as if they were all white and middle class has remained a sensitive issue among feminists today.

Feminism is not a single, monolithic theory or perspective; there are a number of feminist philosophical positions and theories. Nes and Iadicola (1989) clarified for social workers three orientations that were prominent in the 1980s—liberal, socialist, and radical. Liberal feminists seek equal opportunities and rights for women within the existing political system, whereas socialist feminists wish to change the interacting effects of sexism, racism, and class divisions in society, and radical feminists focus on patriarchy, which they wish to see overturned. Tong (1989) described several other traditions—Marxist, psychoanalytic, existentialist, and postmodern feminisms. More recently other perspectives have become prominent, including postcolonial (Mills, 1998), lesbian (Gonda, 1998), and ecofeminist (Diamond & Orenstein, 1990) theories.

Within feminist discourse, postmodern feminism has been controversial (Nicholson, 1990). Derived from poststructuralism and postmodernism in philosophy, literary theory, and the arts, postmodern feminism is critical of grand narratives (universal theories) (Lyotard, 1979) and the assumptions of objectivity, rationality, and neutrality in modern (post-Enlightenment) thought. According to postmodernism, categories that are presented as universal are social constructions (not essences) that are embedded in a particular social, cultural, or historical context and reflect power relations. Thus, when white, middle-class women talked about women and feminism in the 1970s, they were talking about women like themselves rather than those of diverse racial/ethnic groups, social classes, sexual orientations, and (inter)nationalities. Although different constituencies of women share certain problems, differences in where they are positioned in society produce multiple, diverse perspectives. Postmodern feminism recognizes and highlights this diversity (Sands & Nuccio, 1992).

Another characteristic of postmodern feminism is its critique of binary categories, which are a by-product of Western metaphysics (Grosz, 1989). European languages are structured in terms of dichotomous pairs such as male-female and black-white, in which one category is privileged and the other is devalued or considered peripheral. Moreover, these pairs are viewed as oppositional and mutually exclusive (Grosz, 1989). With respect to gender, binary categories promote the idea of opposite sexes that are very different from each other. Deconstruction is the method postmodern (and poststructural) feminists use to derail this way of thinking and reveal underlying biases.

The marriage between postmodernism and feminism has generated a number of debates among feminists (Nicholson, 1990). One of these revolved around feminist standpoint theory (Hartsock, 1997) and Black feminist standpoint thought (Collins, 1997). Whereas the former of these states that women as a collective have a unique perspective, the latter asserts that African American women have a particular slant on feminism. Hartsock (1997) incorporated what she viewed as the feminist standpoint into Marxist theory to underscore that women's position in a patriarchal society makes it possible for them to understand how ideologies obfuscate their oppression. Collins (1997) said that Black women's standpoint includes

> the presence of characteristic core themes, the diversity of Black women's experiences in encountering these core themes, the varying expressions of Black women's Afrocentric feminist consciousness regarding the core themes and their experiences with them, and the interdependence of Black women's experiences, consciousness, and actions. (p. 252)

Walker (1983) uses the term *womanist* to capture African American women's perspective. The problem with standpoint theories from the perspective of postmodern feminism is that they assume an essential female or African American female core, although Collins does allow for more within-group diversity than Hartsock does.

Another debate sparked by postmodern feminism has revolved around cultural feminism. In patriarchal societies men define their experiences, positions, and perspectives as the normal and legitimate ones and the experiences of women (and other disenfranchised groups) as "other" (de Beauvoir, 1968). As a result, women's identities are "overdetermined" by men whose constructions incorporate their own masculinist self-interests, fears, and misogyny (Alcoff, 1997). In response to this, cultural feminists have attempted to define themselves in their own terms. Cultural feminists view women as different but their constructions are positive; for example, they view "woman's passivity as her peacefulness, her sentimentality as her proclivity to nurture, her subjectiveness as her advanced self-awareness, and so forth" (Alcoff, 1997, p. 331). The problem with the cultural feminist approach is that it assumes that there is a universal female essence while it discounts the way in which the larger culture produces this and inscribes it on women's subjective identities (Alcoff, 1997).

As these examples show, postmodernism is useful as a critical tool because it points out the limitations of perspectives that essentialize characteristics that are constructed. On the other hand, postmodernism is problematic because it assumes a fluid universe in which one cannot define anyone or anything. If one cannot define *woman,* for example, how can one work for social change in the status of women (a project called identity politics)? A couple of feminist theorists have suggested ways in which to address this quandary.

Alcoff (1997) suggests that women's identity as a group can be viewed in relation to a particular political position that calls for a particular defense of womanhood. She describes how "the concept of woman as *positionality* [emphasis added] shows how women use their positional perspective as a place from which values are interpreted and constructed rather than as a locus of an already determined set of values" (p. 349). Waugh (1998) proposes that there are different postures within postmodern feminism—"strong" and "weak." The weak version at times embraces objectivity and rationalism and at other times finds the contextual, narrative, and critical approaches within postmodernism valuable. This text has adopted the weak approach in its postmodern critique and in its inclusion of findings from empirical research that purport to be objective, rational, and universal. This book assumes that one can talk about women and other categories but that such phenomena are neither singular nor fixed in time. One area in which a postmodernist critique is applicable is with respect to psychological theories.

Postmodern Feminism Meets Psychological Theories

Many of the psychological theories that have been traditionally used to guide mental health practice have constructed women as "other." Among the most problematic of these are Freud's psychoanalysis, Erikson's psychosocial theory, and Kohlberg's theory of moral development. Feminist critiques of these theories have resulted in alternative ways of thinking about women's and men's psychological development.

Specific Psychological Theories

Freud.   Much of the early feminist criticism of human behavior theories was directed at Freud. According to his psychoanalytic theory, women are "anatomically inferior" because they lack a penis. This suggests that men represent the normal way of being and women are deficient (i.e., "other"). Similarly, Freud posed that women experience penis envy—when what they really envy is man's freedom, not his penis (Chodorow, 1978). In addition, Freud believed that women were masochistic and had underdeveloped superegos.

Freud's theory focused on sexual repression. He believed that infants and children were sexual; that unresolved psychosexual issues stemming from childhood contribute to adult psychopathology—particularly neuroses. Nevertheless, trauma suffered during the early years of life could be overcome through a corrective, psychoanalytic, therapeutic relationship.

Among the women Freud theorized about was one he referred to as Anna O. This educated, intelligent woman, a patient of his friend, Josef Breuer, was later identified as

Bertha Pappenheim, one of the world's first social workers (Stewart, 1985). Freud initially believed that her hysterical symptoms and defenses were a means of protecting her from an awareness of sexually traumatic experiences that occurred during her childhood. Subsequently, Freud reinterpreted this, concluding that the sexual content represented fantasies about a parental figure. Later scholarship proposed that the "fantasies" were actual experiences of childhood sexual abuse (Masson, 1984). The attribution of real events to the imagination is a way of invalidating women's lived experiences.

Freud's genetic theory posed that there are developmental stages, which begin with infancy, that lay the foundation for later life. Of these (oral, anal, phallic, latency, genital), the phallic or oedipal stage was particularly important. During this period, boys are enamored of their mothers and develop a rivalry with their fathers, fearing that their fathers will castrate them. Boys resolve the oedipal complex by relinquishing their amorous feelings toward their mothers and identifying with their fathers. Freud hypothesized that women undergo a similar conflict in the opposite way. During the phallic stage, the female child becomes aware that she does not have a penis, blames her mother, and shifts her affection to her father (desiring to possess his penis or have his baby). She resolves the conflict by recognizing that it is hopeless to possess her father and identifies with her mother.

Feminist scholars have raised questions about Freud's interpretation of the preoedipal experiences of girls. Chodorow (1978) argues that girls' attachment to their mothers is continuous during and beyond the preoedipal and oedipal stages; that although girls form an attachment to their fathers, they do not break off from their mothers. Furthermore, girls' attachment to their mothers emphasizes relational qualities and is more prolonged and less differentiated than the mother-son relationship. Consequently, the boundaries between mothers and daughters may become blurred.

Chodorow is representative of feminist psychoanalytic thinkers in the United States and abroad who continue to find value in psychoanalytic ideas but wish to correct the misinterpretation of women in the theory. Many of these theorists identify with object relations theory, which in itself is a development of psychoanalysis. Object relations theory emphasizes the relationship between the self and others and the formation of personality patterns from the relational field (Hockmeyer, 1988). This is in contrast with classical psychoanalysis, which gives primacy to drives.

Erikson.   Erikson expanded Freud's developmental theory to encompass the entire life course. Erikson's well-known psychosocial theory poses that there are eight life stages—trust versus mistrust, initiative versus guilt, autonomy versus shame and doubt, industry versus inferiority, identity versus role diffusion, intimacy versus isolation, generativity versus stagnation, and integrity versus despair. The stages unfold in sequence according to a ground plan that Erikson called the *epigenetic principle*. In this theory, Erikson recognized the interplay of biological, psychological, social, cultural, and historical factors in the unfolding of individual lives. Erikson saw this pattern as universal.

Some of Erikson's writings have presented difficulties for feminists. On the basis of his work with children at play, Erikson concluded that boys are oriented toward performance in "outer space" whereas girls concentrate on interiority, or "inner space" (Erikson, 1968). These descriptors mirror men's and women's anatomy as well as their respective activity and passivity. This interpretation of men's and women's essences, based on observed stereotypical behavior of children, seems to contradict the sociocultural, contextual tenets of his theory. Feminists have argued with Erikson about the inner space/outer space dichotomy, which he has defended (Erikson, 1974).

A further difficulty in Erikson's theory has to do with the sequencing of his life stages for women. Erikson places the stage of identity versus role diffusion before intimacy versus isolation. Research by Douvan and Adelson (1966) found that girls address intimacy before identity issues. Furthermore, Gilligan (1982) argues that the issues of intimacy and identity are intertwined for women. Erikson's universal stages seem to be based on men's life cycle.

Kohlberg. Kohlberg was a cognitive developmental psychologist in the tradition of Piaget who developed stages of moral development. He studied children and adolescents, predominantly boys, of a range of social classes. Kohlberg came up with a sequence of developmental stages encompassing three levels—preconventional (self-serving), conventional (respecting societal norms), and postconventional (emphasizing values and principles). In his early work, there were six stages (two per level); later he relinquished the sixth stage (Crain, 1985).

Kohlberg proposed that his stages were universal, hierarchical, and sequential. One moves from the lowest level of moral development to higher stages, from the simple to the complex. Few people reach the highest stage. Each stage represents a significantly different way of thinking.

Kohlberg's stage theory was challenged by Gilligan (1982), who noticed that most of Kohlberg's subjects were boys and that when girls took the same moral development tests boys were given, girls achieved lower scores. Rather than accept the conclusion that women were morally inferior or deficient, Gilligan explained that girls do not perform as well as boys because women make moral judgments based on relational considerations rather than abstract ideas about justice. She posed that there was a (feminine) ethic of caring and responsibility that contrasted with a (masculine) ethic of justice reflected in Kohlberg's work. Criticizing Freud, Erikson, Kohlberg, and Piaget, Gilligan cited the work of several women theorists (Loevinger, Horner, Chodorow) to support her position. Gilligan pointed out that because of their fear of fusion, men have difficulty with intimacy; and conversely, because of their fear of separation, women have difficulty with autonomy. Gilligan (1982) has stimulated other thinkers to develop theory and practice that account for differences between the two ethics (or "voices") that she described in her seminal work.

Kegan. Kegan's (1982) developmental psychological theory incorporates the developmental stages of Erikson, Loevinger, Piaget, and Kohlberg while it responds to Gilligan's critique of her predecessors. Kegan proposed an evolving self that is engaged in a dynamic process of constructing and reconstructing its self and self-other relationships. The individual moves through interlocking stages (called incorporative, impulsive, imperial, interpersonal, and interindividual), always seeking a balance between the needs of the self and the desire to relate to others. Kegan's interindividual balance encompasses yearnings for both intimacy and autonomy, which he considers a lifelong conflict. He states that acknowledging both aspects of the evolving self corrects developmental theories that overemphasize autonomy and responds to feminist concerns about the importance of human attachments (Kegan, 1982). Kegan's "natural therapy" helps individuals use crises to create new meanings and, thus, achieve a new balance.

Belenky et al.   Cognitive developmental theory was also the basis for the research of Be-lenky, Clinchy, Goldberger, and Tarule (1986), whose *Women's Ways of Knowing* expanded on some of the issues that Gilligan identified. These authors conducted in-depth qualitative interviews with 135 women in high schools and colleges representing women who were ad-vantaged and disadvantaged economically and who were ethnically diverse; and 45 women who worked with clients seeking support in social agencies in their role as parents. The analysis of transcribed interviews revealed five epistemological positions that the women participating in the study took: silence (voiceless, controlled); received knowledge (accept-ing knowledge from others but not creating one's own); subjective knowledge (conceiving of knowledge privately); procedural knowledge (learning and using procedures to commu-nicate knowledge); and constructed knowledge (recognizing that all knowledge is contex-tual, seeing that one can create knowledge, and integrating subjective and objective ways of knowing). This project gave support to the notion that the metaphors of voice and silence captured women's experiences. "We found that women repeatedly used the metaphor of voice to depict their intellectual and ethical development; and that the development of the sense of voice, mind, and self were intricately intertwined" (Belenky et al., 1986, p. 18).

The Stone Center.   Gilligan's emphasis on connectedness also reverberated at the Stone Center at Wellesley College, where Miller (1986) and other feminist thinkers and thera-pists had been developing what came to be known as the relational self or self-in-relation theory (Jordan, Kaplan, Miller, Stiver, & Surrey, 1991). These authors consider "relational growth" to be "the organizing factor in women's lives" (Jordan et al., 1991, p. 1) and has some applicability to the lives of men. Stone Center writers are particularly interested in the mother-daughter relationship, the development of empathy and mutuality, and empow-erment. Like Gilligan, they are critical of developmental theorists that view autonomy as the hallmark of human development. The therapy that they espouse helps women pursue relational (as well as other) goals and develop in their connections to others.

From a postmodern perspective, the emphases on women's voice, their ways of knowing, and the relational self in these theories (all except Kegan's) are problematic be-cause they suggest that there is an essential womanness inherent in all women. They recon-struct women along feminist ideals without acknowledging differences among women. For example, some women find more meaning in their work and spiritual life than they do in relationships. Furthermore, these feminist theories give little attention to where men fit in women's theories. A more recent set of writings from the Stone Center, *Women's Growth in Diversity* (Jordan, 1997), addresses this concern by describing the self in more fluid terms and by including chapters on racial identity, lesbian relationships, and ways in which marginalized groups are shamed.

Implications for Feminist Practice

The previous discussion of psychological theories about women and the postmodern cri-tique of them demonstrate how difficult it is to arrive at a common understanding of women. The psychoanalytic paradigm, accepted by some clinicians, constructs woman as "other." Newer psychologies acknowledge the centrality of relationships in women's lives, but they have essentialized women.

There is a need for a postmodern feminist social work practice that includes feminist values and is sensitive to differences among women, among men, and between individual men and women. Some feminists have found that a narrative approach, which encourages women to tell their stories and reconstruct them during therapy, is empowering (e.g., Laird, 1989). Postmodern feminist practice also would address power discrepancies and externalize problems that mental health professionals tend to consider individually generated (White & Epston, 1990). Ideally a postmodern feminist practice would include the following characteristics:

- partnerships rather than hierarchy in the worker-client relationship
- support for the client's expression of her voice, however different from the voices of others whom she knows
- support of the client's strengths
- recognition and addressing of gender-based power dynamics in therapeutic, couple, and family relationships
- promotion of the client's self-actualization and development through relationships, work, spirituality, art, and/or other meaningful areas of life
- encouragement of clients to develop relationships of mutuality with others
- recognition and support of individual and cultural differences
- avoidance of sexist language
- acknowledgment of the economic and social issues that adversely affect women (e.g., employment discrimination, low wages, lack of child care, sexual harassment on the job, difficulties collecting child support)
- fostering of women's empowerment, particularly their self-determination, sense of personal control, and self-advocacy
- advocacy for public issues that support women's empowerment
- consideration of the social context before constructing a diagnosis of psychopathology (cf. Ault-Riche, 1986; Hare-Mustin, 1984; Land, 1995; Libow, 1986; Van Den Bergh, 1995)

Considering that the postmodern feminist approach to therapy that is outlined here is attuned to the context of women's lives, it diverges from the expectations of the mental health system, which pays a premium (literally, under behavioral managed care) for diagnoses of psychopathology. Accordingly, the postmodern feminist therapist working in an organization that emphasizes psychopathology is operating out of two models. In order to manage this discrepancy, clinical social workers need to know how the behavioral health system and epidemiological research that uses categories from the same paradigm construct women clients. Later this chapter will return to contextual issues.

The Construction of Women as Mentally Ill

Although the *DSM-IV* (American Psychiatric Association, 1994) outlines specific criteria for each diagnosis, some diagnoses are more prevalent among women whereas others are more common to men. The National Comorbidity Survey (NCS) of U.S. citizens from ages

15 to 54 identified some of these gender differences (Kessler et al., 1994). Table 6.1 presents NCS findings on the lifetime and twelve-month prevalences of some of these disorders, diagnosed according to *DSM-III-R* (APA, 1987) criteria. Looking at the disorders as groups (the "any" category), affective (mood) and anxiety disorders are more prevalent among women, whereas substance abuse/dependence is more widespread among men. Of the two "other disorders" listed, the antisocial personality disorder is more prevalent among men, whereas women have a slightly higher (but not statistically different) rate of nonaffective psychoses (Kessler et al., 1994). Among the affective disorders, major depression and dysthymia are substantially higher for women than men, whereas having a manic episode is not differentiated by gender. Women have substantially higher prevalence rates of all the anxiety disorders, whereas men have higher rates for all the substance use disorders.

Although genetic and reproductive-related factors have been proposed as explanations of women's high rate of depression, research evidence points to social factors such as life stressors, socioeconomic issues, and support by a marital partner as more relevant (Brems, 1995). Because some women conform to expected sex role behaviors (i.e., passivity and dependence), they may find themselves ill equipped to cope with feelings of anger in any way but internalization, a defense mechanism associated with depression (Brems, 1995). Another psychosocial explanation is that when women are in a subordinate position, as they often are in patriarchal relationships, they are constrained from expressing anger directly (Miller, 1991) and, thus, turn the anger inward. In her study of depressed women, Jack (1991) found that depressed, angry women will view themselves from another's perspective and silence themselves. She quotes "Susan," who reflects on her interactions with her husband as follows:

> **And so when he speaks to me in a harsh tone, or criticizes me for something that I have done wrong or haven't done or whatever, I've tended to think to myself, "Now you're supposed to be submissive, so just ignore him." And so inside I've been building up a lot of resentment and a lot of anger.** (p. 141)

It is difficult for women like Susan, who live in fear, to express their anger directly, but they do get depressed. According to the self-in-relation theory, depression in women is associated with a sense of inadequacy that develops when their need for "growth-in-relationship" is thwarted (Kaplan, 1991). Women's depression may also be related to poverty, sex discrimination in employment, caregiving activities, and physical abuse.

With respect to anxiety disorders, nonspecific biological factors have been implicated (Barlow, 1988; Barlow, Esler, & Vitali, 1998) but not proved to be present—and no more so in women than men. The high rate of anxiety disorders among women has been attributed to cultural conditions that encourage women's expression of fear but discourage men's (Barlow, 1988). Similarly, women may report fears more often than men in epidemiological studies because they know it is socially acceptable to talk about their feelings. Considering that cognitive therapies have been found effective in treating anxiety disorders, attention to the content of cognitions seems relevant. Ideas about being out of control, powerless, and in danger, which are held by individuals with anxiety disorders, are consistent with women's situation in a patriarchal society.

Men's relatively high rate of substance abuse disorder may be related to their low rates of affective and anxiety disorders. Because the sex role expectations of men thwart

TABLE 6.1   Lifetime and Twelve-Month Prevalence of UM-CIDI/*DSM-III-R* Disorders*

	Male				Female				Total			
	Lifetime		12 mo		Lifetime		12 mo		Lifetime		12 mo	
Disorders	%	SE	%	SE	%	SE	%	SE	%	SE	%	SE
Affective disorders												
Major depressive episode	12.7	0.9	7.7	0.8	21.3	0.9	12.9	0.8	17.1	0.7	10.3	0.6
Manic episode	1.6	0.3	1.4	0.3	1.7	0.3	1.3	0.3	1.6	0.3	1.3	0.2
Dysthymia	4.8	0.4	2.1	0.3	8.0	0.6	3.0	0.4	6.4	0.4	2.5	0.2
Any affective disorder	14.7	0.8	8.5	0.8	23.9	0.9	14.1	0.9	19.3	0.7	11.3	0.7
Anxiety disorders												
Panic disorder	2.0	0.3	1.3	0.3	5.0	1.4	3.2	0.4	3.5	0.3	2.3	0.3
Agoraphobia without panic disorder	3.5	0.4	1.7	0.3	7.0	0.6	3.8	0.4	5.3	0.4	2.8	0.3
Social phobia	11.1	0.8	6.6	0.4	15.5	1.0	9.1	0.7	13.3	0.7	7.9	0.4
Simple phobia	6.7	0.5	4.4	0.5	15.7	1.1	13.2	0.9	11.3	0.6	8.8	0.5
Generalized anxiety disorder	3.6	0.5	2.0	0.3	6.6	0.5	4.3	0.4	5.1	0.3	3.1	0.3
Any anxiety disorder	19.2	0.9	11.8	0.6	30.5	1.2	22.6	0.1	24.9	0.8	17.2	0.7
Substance use disorders												
Alcohol abuse without dependence	12.5	0.8	3.4	0.4	6.4	0.6	1.6	0.2	9.4	0.5	2.5	0.2
Alcohol dependence	20.1	1.0	10.7	0.9	8.2	0.7	3.7	0.4	14.1	0.7	7.2	0.5
Drug abuse without dependence	5.4	0.5	1.3	0.2	3.5	0.4	0.3	0.1	4.4	0.3	0.8	0.1
Drug dependence	9.2	0.7	3.8	0.4	5.9	0.5	1.9	0.3	7.5	0.4	2.8	0.3
Any substance abuse/dependence	35.4	1.2	16.1	0.7	17.9	1.1	6.6	0.4	26.6	1.0	11.3	0.5
Other disorders												
Antisocial personality	5.8	0.6	...	...	1.2	0.3	...	...	3.5	0.3	...	...
Nonaffective psychosis[†]	0.6	0.1	0.5	0.1	0.8	0.2	0.6	0.2	0.7	0.1	0.5	0.1
Any NCS disorder	48.7	0.2	27.7	0.9	47.3	1.5	31.2	1.3	48.0	1.1	29.5	1.0

*UM-CIDI indicates University of Michigan Composite International Diagnostic Interview; NCS, National Comorbidity Survey.

[†]Nonaffective psychosis includes schizophrenia, schizophreniform disorder, schizoaffective disorder, delusional disorder, and atypical psychosis.

Source: From "Lifetime and 12-month prevalence of DSM-III-R psychiatric disorders in the United States: Results from the National Comorbidity Survey," by R. C. Kessler, K. A. McGonagle, S. Zhao, C. B. Nelson, M. Hughes, S. Eshlman, H-U Wittchen & K. S. Kendler, 1994, *Archives of General Psychiatry, 51,* pp. 8–19, Table 2, p. 12. Copyright © 1994 by American Medical Association. Reprinted with permission.

their expression of feelings, men may cope with sadness and apprehension by drinking and/or taking drugs. Substances stimulate artificial feelings of grandiosity and confidence. To some men, the ability to handle alcohol enhances their feelings of masculinity. On the other hand, data linking alcohol-related disorders to genetic factors are stronger for men than women (Kaplan & Sadock, 1998).

The higher lifetime prevalence for men of antisocial personality disorder can also be attributed to biological and social factors. The neurotransmitter serotonin and the limbic system, as well as factors in the parental home, have been implicated in antisocial individuals (Sperry, 1995). Without definitive evidence for biological and psychological hypotheses, however, a social explanation seems more appropriate. Some of the behaviors subsumed under antisocial personality disorder are violent acts, aggressive behavior, family violence, and drug dealing. These are overt acts of aggression that, like drinking, may enhance some men's images of themselves as men. In contrast to women whose mental illness–linked behavior "has been associated more with private, self-damaging acts, where aggression is directed at the self," men's antisocial behavior is directed at others and often is labeled criminal (Pilgrim & Rogers, 1999, p. 57). Men threaten others whereas women punish themselves or fear retaliation from others.

According to Table 6.1, the lifetime prevalence of any disorder for all participants is 48 percent and the twelve-month prevalence is 29.5 percent, both of which sound high. These figures reflect comorbidity (having two or more disorders) by some of the participants. The National Comorbidity Survey found that women had higher lifetime and twelve-month rates of prevalence than men for three or more concurrent disorders (Kessler et al., 1994). This gender discrepancy, like others, may be attributed to women's willingness to report and the culture's willingness to hear about their symptoms of mental illness. The difference may also be explained by the idiosyncratic way in which diagnoses of mental illness are constructed. From a postmodern feminist perspective, the context in which problems arise is more germane to practice than the diagnosis. Problems emanating from relationships—emphasized in feminist psychological theories—may be precipitating a multiplicity of psychiatric symptoms.

Looking at the Context: Problematic Relationships

Many of the emotions and thoughts that women present and therapists construct as symptoms of mental disorders are associated with women's interpersonal relationships. If relationships are central to women's lives, disturbances in them should be agonizing. Women can run into difficulties with others in intimate and casual romantic relationships, friendships, work, and other areas of their daily lives. Most of these problems can be resolved without professional intervention. Here we will focus on a relationship issue that has serious consequences for the victim (or survivor) and society as a whole—physical abuse in intimate relationships. This situational problem can precipitate its own set of symptoms or exacerbate preexisting mental health problems.

Physical Abuse

For some time, violence perpetrated against women in the family was a hidden, private problem. Some people believed that male heads of families had the right to beat their wives. Incidents of family violence were underreported or not reported to the police at all. Research that emerged in the 1970s and 1980s revealed that the problem was pervasive in U.S. society (Straus, Gelles, & Steinmetz, 1988). Spouse abuse occurred among all social classes, all levels of education and income, in cities and rural areas, and among all ethnic groups. Today we are cognizant of physical abuse in gay and lesbian relationships as well as unmarried heterosexuals. Other family members, particularly children, are also subject to domestic violence, including sexual abuse. On the other hand, some children abuse each other or their parents, and some adults abuse their elderly parents (see, e.g., Bookin & Dunkle, 1985; Harbin & Maddin, 1979).

Here the focus is on violence (battering) perpetrated against women who are spouses or partners living together. Because women are frequently the victims of abuse, family violence has been considered a women's issue. This may be because women's advocacy groups were instrumental in the reconstruction of battering as a public rather than private problem, but as a public problem, it is one that concerns all of us. As a consequence of the activities of women's groups around the country, laws that had protected abusers have been changed and resources that protect survivors have been created. Today many communities have shelters where battered women and their children can go during a crisis and centers where they can receive emotional support, legal advice, and counseling. In some communities, police and physicians have been trained to treat victims of abuse sensitively and to call in social workers or trained volunteers who can help the women deal with the immediate situation and the complex feelings that usually follow. In addition, domestic violence hotlines have been established and campaigns advertising their existence have been implemented. Advocacy for changes in the law and the creation of more and improved community services continue to this day.

Women are vulnerable to physical abuse in their homes, where there are few adult observers. When violence takes place in private space in the context of a relationship, it is difficult for women to view the violent behavior as a problem and to see themselves as violated. Women whose batterers blame them for the violence may agree and hold themselves rather than the batterers responsible. In a similar vein, women may be confused or angry over coercive, nonconsensual sex with their partner, but they are unlikely to construct the partner's behavior as rape. The same act perpetrated outside the home by a stranger is more clearly identifiable as a crime.

Although women tend to deny the seriousness of physical abuse when it occurs in personal relationships, they do react. They are fearful for themselves and their children and worry about the future. If they are physically hurt, they may go to the hospital where a health or mental health professional might inquire whether there was abuse. Afraid to implicate their partner, some women will construct a fabricated account of what happened; most return home and continue the abusive relationship. At this point the partner may show remorse and treat the woman solicitously (Walker, 1979). Consistent with the cycle of violence, however, the partner's tension increases gradually over time (Walker, 1979). During this period, the woman avoids saying or doing anything that she thinks might precipitate a similar reaction; she walks on eggshells. Then another incident occurs. This time the woman may seek safety with a family member or a shelter for battered women. In either case, it is highly likely that she will return to the batterer. Whether her reasons for returning are based on economic dependence, emotional attachment, or fear, this pattern of leaving and returning can be frustrating to social workers trying to protect women who are at risk of being murdered.

Physical abuse involves acts of aggression perpetrated by a stronger person against a weaker one. An assertion of power, it is a prototype of sexism and misogyny. Although some women affirm that they love the person who abuses them, it is difficult to understand how feelings as disparate as love and violence can commingle. Whether the violence involves battering or rape or both, physical violence is predicated on the belief that women are not valuable in themselves; they are there to be overtaken. To the extent that violence is promoted or overlooked by others, society is implicated.

Trauma as an Alternative Construction

When violence comes to the attention of mental health professionals, however, the tendency is to construct it as the woman's individual problem. The array of emotions that battered women present as a consequence of damage inflicted on them is frequently transformed into a psychiatric diagnosis. One nonpathological construction of their emotional state is that they are traumatized, but trauma becomes pathologized with the diagnosis post-traumatic stress disorder. Many other diagnoses are also assigned to women who have been traumatized by violence, including dissociative identity disorder (multiple personality disorder) and adjustment disorders. Individuals who have been physically or sexually abused as children have a tendency to get into relationships as adults in which they reexperience trauma (Herman, 1992). Women with severe mental illnesses (see Chapters 10 to 12), who frequently have been abused as children, are particularly vulnerable to being victimized as adults (Goodman, Rosenberg, Mueser, & Drake, 1997). Trauma or a history of trauma is also associated with borderline personality disorder, suicide attempts, substance abuse, depression, psychotic symptoms, and panic disorder (Alexander & Muenzenmaier, 1998).

In her book, *Trauma and Recovery,* Judith Herman (1992), a feminist psychiatrist, has synthesized research on men traumatized by war or political captivity and women who have been sexually or physically abused. She mentioned there that because it is difficult for bystanders to acknowledge the pain of those who have been traumatized, and victims themselves are often silenced by their perpetrators and social norms that define some of their experiences as unspeakable, little sustained interest has been given to survivors of trauma. Herman noted that it took organized political movements (e.g., by Vietnam veterans and women's organizations) to draw public attention to the needs of individuals who have endured traumatic experiences.

Herman (1992) observed three themes common to individuals who are subjected to psychological trauma. The first of these is *terror,* the overwhelming fear of danger, harm, or death. Terror occurs at the time of the focal event but remains in a fragmented form afterward. Individuals with post-traumatic stress disorder experience hyperarousal (high sensitivity to signals of danger) as a means of protection against such events in the future. Although they do not think about the traumatic event constantly, frightening memories of the episode intrude on and interrupt their everyday lives. Some individuals unconsciously reenact traumatic experiences. Terror is also characterized by emotional constriction or numbing in which individuals become detached from others and from themselves. Herman described a "dialectic of trauma" in which there are swings between intrusion and constriction (Herman, 1992).

The second theme Herman (1992) identified is *disconnection,* a rupture in the relationship between the victim and others. The traumatic event impairs the individual's sense of self, which in turn undermines self-confidence and basic trust. When trust is compromised, relationships with others and faith in God are affected. The nature of the event and individuals' capacity for resilience determine the level of psychological damage (Herman, 1992). Individuals who are relatively young and have preexisting psychiatric disorders may be more vulnerable than others (Herman, 1992). In the aftermath of the traumatic event they need protection from others and a safe environment. Safety is particularly problematic for women who live with their abuser. Those who have supportive partners, family members, and friends can be helped to find a safe place in which to recuperate and people who will listen to them, accept them compassionately, and help them mourn. Public attitudes toward people in their situation and the responsiveness of the legal system to reported crimes also enter into the issue of disconnection (Herman, 1992).

Captivity is a dimension of trauma that applies to situations that occur repeatedly over time in which the perpetrator has control over the victim (Herman, 1992). The victim may be physically restrained (e.g., a prisoner of war), or she may feel imprisoned because psychological, economic, social, and legal dependencies keep her subjugated. The perpetrator exercises coercive control over the victim's mind so that she thinks the way he wants her to think. Some of the techniques used to achieve this are issuing threats (against the victim or others), outbursts of violence, arbitrary enforcement of trivial rules, supervision of the victim's physical activities (eating, sleeping, etc.), the use of intermittent rewards, and the destruction of personal attachments (creating isolation). These methods foster increased reliance on the perpetrator and ultimately total surrender of the self (Herman, 1992). According to Herman (1992), the *DSM* diagnosis of post-traumatic stress disorder does not accurately describe survivors of captivity, who, in contrast with individuals exposed to a single event, are traumatized repeatedly over time. She suggests a new category, complex post-traumatic stress disorder, for experiences such as these (see Herman, 1992, Chapter 6).

Best Practice: Herman's Recovery Model

The intervention (or recovery) program that Herman (1992) recommends is in keeping with the parameters of postmodern feminist practice described earlier. As such, this is considered a best practice and is summarized in Table 6.2. Although it is discussed here in the context of the physical abuse of women, Herman's model applies to survivors of incest, political imprisonment, and war trauma, who may be men or women. Recovery is predicated on a relationship between the therapist and client that empowers the client and promotes her connections with others. The client is in charge of her own recovery; the therapist bears witness to the abuse and fosters the process of healing. The therapist retains professional neutrality while joining with the survivor in asserting that the crime that was committed was immoral (Herman, 1992). The therapist is sensitive to and handles the survivor's transference and the therapists's own countertransference. The parameters of the therapeutic contract are discussed, including the responsibilities of each party, the expectation of honesty and openness, and mutual commitment to the survivor's recovery.

Herman (1992) describes three stages of recovery—the establishment of safety, remembrance and mourning, and reconnection with ordinary life. These follow from her

TABLE 6.2 ■ BEST PRACTICE   Herman's Model of Recovery from Trauma

Aims

- "Bear witness" to the traumatic experience and, thus, validate it.
- Provide a relationship that supports the survivor's recovery.
- Help the survivor integrate the trauma into his or her life experiences.
- Help the survivor reconnect with others.

Assessment

- Record life history, especially before the traumatic event or situation.
- Name the problem (arrive at a psychiatric diagnosis, if applicable).
- Share the name with the survivor and explain what it is.

Themes common to survivors

- Terror
- Disconnection
- Captivity (if same situation occurs repeatedly over time)

Stages of recovery

- Establishment of safety
- Remembrance and mourning
- Reconnection

Characteristics of intervention

- Supportive, empowering relationship
- Initial concern for safety issues
- Survivor controls her own recovery
- Listening to and validating the survivor's story
- Professional neutrality but not moral neutrality
- Grief work
- Connection with others

Format

- Individual therapy
- Group therapy

Time frame

- First stage can be accomplished through crisis intervention or short term therapy (six weeks to three months)
- Variability in length of second and third stages.

Source: Based on Herman (1992).

description of the characteristics of trauma summarized earlier, as well as her synthesis of the stages of treatment of hysteria, combat trauma, multiple personality disorder, and complicated post-traumatic stress disorder described by others (Herman, 1992). These stages do not necessarily progress in a linear sequence. The first, *the establishment of safety,* has several components. To begin with, the problem should be assessed and named. Giving the survivor's experiences a name—even a psychiatric diagnosis—can be liberating to a person who is overwhelmed by feelings she does not understand. Next, the survivor should be helped to regain control and restore her safety. She may feel out of control in her thinking, bodily functions, and interpersonal relationships. She can be helped with her thinking through the development of trust in the therapeutic relationship and can be assisted with behavioral strategies (e.g., relaxation exercises) and medication. If there are physical injuries, these should be given medical attention. Sufficient sleep, exercise, and a proper diet can also help her restore her bodily functions. She should be helped in finding a safe environment in which to live, a task that usually involves mobilizing support from individuals other than the perpetrator and persons who are likely to undermine her recovery. But even if the survivor continues to have contact with the perpetrator, she can be helped to develop a safety plan in the event of another episode (Herman, 1992).

During the second stage, the focus is on *remembrance and mourning,* and the survivor tells her story (Herman, 1992). Herman advises against exploring traumatic memories during the first stage, when the survivor is fragile and feels vulnerable. When ready, the client should be asked to tell the story as fully and completely as possible, including her feelings, images, and bodily sensations. The purpose of doing this is to objectify it and give it a reality that can eventually be integrated into the person's life (Herman, 1992). Relating the story takes time because there is much resistance and repression that protect painful, sometimes humiliating, memories. The process begins with a review of the survivor's life before the traumatic event or situation and the set of circumstances that preceded it. The clinician takes the role of "an open-minded, compassionate witness, not a detective" (Herman, 1992, p. 180) or investigator. It is possible that the survivor's "narrative truth" will not be consistent with the "historical truth" (Spence, 1982). The clinician follows the client's lead, exploring the survivor's everyday experiences and the memories she already has. When painful memories are revealed, sufficient time is left in the therapeutic interview for the individual to decompress from the telling.

Mourning takes place in the aftermath of telling of the story (Herman, 1992). There are many losses to mourn—the self, attachment to the perpetrator, bodily integrity, and other losses. During this period the survivor may have fantasies of retaliation against or forgiveness of the perpetrator or may wish for some kind of compensation. The relinquishment of these fantasies is part of the process of mourning and may enable the survivor to extricate herself emotionally from the perpetrator. During this period the clinician "bears witness" while holding the survivor responsible for her own recovery (Herman, 1992). Although mourning is painful, it does facilitate the return of emotional energy and involvement with others.

The third stage, *reconnection,* pertains to rebuilding the self and a personal life (Herman, 1992). At this time the survivor revisits safety issues addressed in the first stage (her body, her physical environment, etc.), but now she expends increased energy outward toward others, empowering herself in the process. One task involved in this stage is facing fear. This can be done by taking a class in self-defense, participating in a wilderness excursion, and/or confronting family members and/or the perpetrator. Another task is to come to terms with valued aspects of herself and building a new self from these. She sheds her victim identity and celebrates her survivor identity (Herman, 1992). An important task of this stage is to reconnect with others—deepening previous relationships with family members, friends, and the therapist and creating new ones. Consistent with Erikson's stage of generativity versus stagnation, she becomes concerned about the next generation, including her children, if she is a parent. At this point, some survivors become active in social causes such as the battered women's movement and may speak out publicly about their experiences. Although resolution of the trauma is never complete, the survivor who works through the issues that have been described is able to live a fulfilling life with control, confidence, satisfying relationships with others, and feelings of well-being (Herman, 1992).

Discussion

This model of intervention with survivors of trauma (men as well as women) is sensitive to the clients' loss of power in the past and, accordingly, respects their efforts to assume control over their own lives at their own pace. It works with the client where she is in the process of self-understanding and self-possession and helps her take charge of her own life. It uses a narrative approach in helping the client construct and reconstruct her past and paves the way for her to reconstruct herself in the future.

Although Herman's recovery program does not call itself postmodern, it is in keeping with this philosophical approach. It breaks form (a characteristic of postmodern architecture) in integrating what has been written about different kinds of traumas experienced by men and women in different contexts. Furthermore, it recognizes that the local context can generate psychological symptoms, even in the absence of the original event or situation stimulating the symptoms. Accordingly, women's excess of mental health symptoms may be the consequence of past and current situations in their lives that oppressed them as women. Finally, Herman's (1992) focus on recovery, healing, and survivorship is relevant to clinical social work practice with anyone who has been exposed to adverse life events.

As Herman (1992) suggests, much of the healing is done by the client in relation to others in her social network or in the community. We turn next to professional and nonprofessional alternatives to the trauma therapy that was described.

Other Ways of Healing

Clinical social work practice with women requires awareness of the status and vulnerabilities of women in contemporary U.S. society. As suggested, some of the symptoms that women present in behavioral health settings derive from their status as "other," such as poverty, underemployment, and physical abuse. Careful assessment of a woman's situation should determine whether the problem lies in the person, the situation, or interpersonal interactions. The woman may need housing, financial help, a job, or a friend rather than psychotherapy or psychopharmacology.

Traditional approaches of individual, family, and group therapy tend to be hierarchical and, thus, patriarchal. Women and other groups whose voices have been silenced need to have relationships of partnership and equality in which to heal. In particular, they need therapeutic relationships, therapies, and communities that help them to control their own lives and make their own decisions.

Several adjunct or alternative approaches to healing are suggested. One is that women form their own self-help groups, such as the consciousness-raising groups that women developed during the 1960s and 1970s. These groups, as well as some professionally led women's groups, are designed to be nonhierarchical. Feminist-oriented therapy groups encourage women to value other women (and, therefore, themselves), to be assertive, and to be androgynous. In addition, social activism in women's causes may be therapeutic.

Some particular mental health issues are best addressed in single sex groups. Traditional approaches to intervening with individuals with substance abuse tend to be male oriented; women's groups may be able to incorporate a more gender-appropriate approach (see Chapter 13). Men who batter women can benefit from all male groups in which they can safely address their own behavior. Women who have been raped or who are adult survivors of incest also feel safer sharing their feelings with same-sex groups.

Summary and Deconstruction

This chapter has focused primarily on women, particularly their status as "other" and the postmodern perspective that there is no essential womanness, for women are diverse. There are other sectors of the population for whom the same argument can be made, but they were missing from this chapter. These include, but are not limited to men, gays and lesbians, persons with visible and invisible disabilities, and the aging. In Chapter 7, racial, ethnic, and cultural minorities will be considered as "others." Here a similar argument will be made about men.

Just as there are many feminisms and many versions of womanness, so are there multiple masculinities. Many, perhaps most, men fall short of the ideal of masculinity in U.S. society that is valorized by the media and applauded by movie audiences. Some men fall short of the ideal of masculinity of their particular ethnic subculture as well. The discrepancy between the ideal and actual may propel some men to engage in aggressive acts in which they demonstrate their power over women or the society that constructs standards they find impossible to meet. Substance abuse and antisocial personality disorder—psychiatric disorders more frequent among men than women—are characterized by exaggerated expressions of masculinity and sexism.

Like women, men are diverse. There are male secretaries, ballet dancers, hair dressers, and interior decorators, as well as executives, military men, athletes, and politicians. Although men in the former group are frequently constructed as feminine or gay, they are men who live out different versions of masculinity. Like women, they are oppressed by dominant constructions of gender.

Social constructions of masculinity are evident in behavioral health settings in which, it is often observed, it is difficult to engage men in treatment. Many men seem to believe that asking for help that requires revealing of one's inner feelings and weaknesses is demasculinizing. This is so regardless of the gender of the clinician. Being a client is feminine. Unless social workers and other clinicians address men's feelings about being male clients, they are likely to meet a great deal of client resistance.

Work with men and women in the mental health field demands sensitivity to gender issues, knowledge of theories as they apply to women and men, and familiarity with alternative approaches to psychotherapy. Application of these strategies can enhance women's and men's capacities to make decisions, assert themselves, and make their own unique contribution to society.

Case Study

Ruth Manger is a thirty-five-year-old, divorced Caucasian woman who sought help from an employee assistance program for "financial problems." She explained that she held two jobs, was paying off a mortgage and several loans, and had high legal expenses. Although some of her debts were related to home repairs and car payments, Mrs. Manger attributed her financial state to her commitment to her former husband, Leo, who is in jail for murdering his girlfriend, Linda. The client believes that he was unjustifiably incarcerated, that he killed Linda in self-defense after she threatened to turn him in to the police for dealing with drugs. Mrs. Manger said that she and her husband broke up because of his relationship with Linda, but since Leo has been imprisoned, Leo has apologized for leaving her and has proclaimed his love for Ruth. Mrs. Manger has responded by visiting him daily and trying to help him receive fair treatment from the legal system.

In the process of assisting Leo in his negotiations with lawyers, Mrs. Manger became convinced that the court-appointed lawyer was neglecting him. With Leo's concurrence, they hired a private attorney. Mrs. Manger took a second mortgage of $5,000 on her house in order to pay this lawyer. When the case went to trial, Leo lost. An appeal is currently under way. In order to pay for the appeal, Mrs. Manger has borrowed money through her bank card.

Mrs. Manger reported feeling "nervous," having frequent headaches, and losing weight. She has less energy but more on her mind than she ever had. She feels overwhelmed with her financial responsibilities and, with two jobs, she has little time to spend with Patricia, her sixteen-year-old daughter. Patricia is a good student, who keeps busy with her school activities and babysitting. At times, however, Patricia complains that her mother does not seem interested in her. Mrs. Manger said that her daughter has been loyal to her, as have a few of her friends. On the other hand, her brother and sister have told her that she is "crazy" to pursue the relationship with Leo and have urged her to give him up. Mrs. Manger thinks that since the murder was publicized in the newspaper, some of her coworkers have gossiped about her. Having two jobs gives her an "escape" from the criticism of others. Nevertheless, both are low-paying jobs that provide few intrinsic rewards.

Mrs. Manger is the middle of three children. Her brother and sister have stable marriages and "no problems"; she has had two divorces. When she was a child, she was picked on by her older sister and physically abused by her father. Mrs. Manger suspected that her father was not her real father. Her parents died soon after her first marriage fifteen years ago. Mrs. Manger and her first husband were divorced after five years of marriage, when Patricia was four, following an episode in which her husband molested their daughter. The client said that her "ex" still paid a small amount of child support but he is not allowed to visit. Mrs. Manger met Leo eight years after her first divorce, after she had bought her house. She said that she was happy with Leo until he began to run around. She said that neither of them used drugs when they were together, but Leo may have sold drugs occasionally. Over the years he worked as an auto mechanic at several different garages. Sometimes he would come up with extra money about which she would not ask questions. She described Leo as a smooth-talking man who was able to charm his way through life. Mrs. Manger said that she loved Leo but wondered if, as her brother and sister said, she was "crazy."

Discussion Questions
1. How would you assess this case?
2. Why do you think Mrs. Manger has remained in this relationship?
3. In what ways are Mrs. Manger's depression and anxiety related to her situation as a woman?
4. How might the dynamics of trauma be related to her behavior?
5. What issues is this client refusing to face? Why?
6. How is patriarchy contributing to what is happening here?
7. What strengths does Mrs. Manger have? How is she using her strengths?
8. How might she be helped using a postmodern feminist approach?
9. If you were working with Mrs. Manger, how would you proceed?
10. What kinds of professional and self-help strategies does your community offer for similar women? For women who are physically abused or raped? For lesbians who have been physically abused or raped? For men who have been battered or raped? What kinds of services does your community need for diverse groups of women and men who have been traumatized?

REFERENCES

Alcoff, L. (1997). Cultural feminism versus post-structuralism: The identity crisis in feminist theory. In L. Nicholson (Ed.), *The second wave: A reader in feminist theory* (pp. 330–355). New York: Routledge.

Alexander, M. J., & Muenzenmaier, K. (1997). Trauma, addiction, and recovery. In B. L. Levin, A. K. Blanch, & A. Jennings (Eds.), *Women's mental health services: A public health perspective* (pp. 215–239). Thousand Oaks, CA: Sage.

American Psychiatric Association. (1987). *Diagnostic and statistical manual of mental disorders (DSM-III-R)* (3rd ed., rev.). Washington, DC: Author.

American Psychiatric Association (APA). (1994). *Diagnostic and statistical manual—Fourth edition (DSM-IV)*. Washington, DC: Author.

Ault-Riche, M. (1986). A feminist critique of five schools of family therapy. In M. Ault-Riche (Ed.), *Women and family therapy* (pp. 1–24). Rockville, MD: Aspen.

Ballou, M. B., & Gabalac, N. W. (1985). *A feminist position on mental health*. Springfield, IL: Charles C. Thomas.

Barlow, D. H. (1988). *Anxiety and its disorders: The nature and treatment of anxiety and panic*. New York: The Guilford Press.

Barlow, D. H., Esler, J. L., & Vitali, A. E. (1988). Psychosocial treatments for panic disorders, phobias, and generalized anxiety disorder. In P. E. Nathan & J. M. Gorman (Eds.), *A guide to treatments that work* (pp. 288–318). New York: Oxford University Press.

de Beauvoir, S. (1968). *The second sex*. New York: Modern Library.

Belenky, M. F., Clinchy, B. M., Goldberger, N. R., & Tarule, J. M. (1986). *Women's ways of knowing: The development of self, voice, and mind*. New York: Basic Books.

Bookin, D., & Dunkle, R. E. (1985). Elder abuse: Issues for the practitioner. *Social Casework, 66*, 3–12.

Brems, C. (1995). Women and depression: A comprehensive analysis. In E. E. Beckham & W. R. Leber (Eds.), *Handbook of depression* (2nd ed., pp. 539–566). New York: The Guilford Press.

Chesler, P. (1972). *Women and madness*. Garden City, NY: Doubleday.

Chodorow, N. (1978). *The reproduction of mothering: Psychoanalysis and the sociology of gender*. Berkeley, CA: University of California Press.

Collins, P. H. (1997). Defining Black feminist thought. In L. Nicholson (Ed.), *The second wave: A reader in feminist theory* (pp. 241–259). New York: Routledge.

Crain, W. C. (1985). *Theories of development: Concepts and application* (2nd ed.). Englewood Cliffs, NJ: Prentice-Hall.

Diamond, I., & Orenstein, G. F. (Eds.). (1990). *Reweaving the world: The emergence of ecofeminism*. San Francisco: Sierra Club Books.

Douvan, E., & Adelson, J. (1966). *The adolescent experience*. New York: Wiley.

Erikson, E. H. (1951). *Childhood and society*. New York: Norton.

Erikson, E. H. (1968). *Identity: Youth and crisis*. New York: Norton.

Erikson, E. H. (1974). One more time the inner space: Letter to a former student. In J. Strouse (Ed.), *Women and analysis* (pp. 320–340). New York: Grossman.

Erikson, E. H. (1980). *Identity and the life cycle*. New York: Norton.

Erikson, E. H. (1982). *The life cycle completed.* New York: Norton.

Geller, J. L., & Harris, M. (1994). *Women of the asylum.* New York: Anchor Books/Doubleday.

Gilligan, C. (1982). *In a different voice.* Cambridge, MA: Harvard University Press.

Gonda, C. (1998). Lesbian theory. In S. Jackson & J. Jones (Eds.), *Contemporary feminist theories* (pp. 113–130). New York: New York University Press.

Goodman, L. A., Rosenberg, S. D., Mueser, K. T., & Drake, R. E. (1997). Physical and sexual assault history in women with serious mental illness: Prevalence, correlates, treatment, and future directions. *Schizophrenia Bulletin, 23*(4), 685–696.

Grosz, E. (1989). *Sexual subversions.* Boston: Allen & Unwin.

Harbin, H. T., & Madden, D. J. (1979). Battered parents: A new syndrome. *American Journal of Psychiatry, 136,* 1288–1291.

Hare-Mustin, R. T. (1984). A feminist approach to family therapy. In P. P. Rieker & E. H. Carmen (Eds.), *The gender gap in psychotherapy: Social realities and psychological processes.* New York: Plenum Press.

Hartsock, N. C. M. (1997). The feminist standpoint: Developing the ground for a specifically feminist historical materialism. In L. Nicholson (Ed.), *The second wave: A reader in feminist theory* (pp. 216–240). New York: Routledge.

Herman, J. L. (1992). *Trauma and recovery.* New York: Basic Books.

Hochschild, A., & Machung, A. (1989). *The second shift.* New York: Viking.

Hockmeyer, A. (1988). Object relations theory and feminism: Strange bedfellows. *Frontiers, 10,* 20–28.

hooks, b. (1981). *Ain't I a woman.* Boston: South End Press.

Jack, D. C. (1991). *Silencing the self: Women and depression.* Cambridge, MA: Harvard University Press.

Jordan, J. V. (Ed.). (1997). *Women's growth in diversity: More writings from the Stone Center.* New York: The Guilford Press.

Jordan, J. V., Kaplan, A. G., Miller, J. B., Stiver, I. P., & Surrey, J. L. (1991). *Women's growth in connection: Writings from the Stone Center.* New York: The Guilford Press.

Kaplan, A. G. (1991). The "self-in-relation": Implications for depression in women. In Jordan et al. (1991), *Women's growth in connection: Writings from the Stone Center* (pp. 206–222). New York: The Guilford Press.

Kaplan, H. I., & Sadock, B. J. (1998). *Synopsis of psychiatry* (8th ed.). Baltimore, MD: Williams & Wilkins.

Kegan, R. (1982). *The evolving self: Problem and process in human development.* Cambridge, MA: Harvard University Press.

Kessler, R. C., McGonagle, K. A., Zhao, S., Nelson, C. B., Hughes, M., Eshleman, S., Wittchen, H-U, & Kendler, K. S. (1994). Lifetime and 12-month prevalence of DSM-III-R psychiatric disorders in the United States: Results from the National Comorbidity Survey. *Archives of General Psychiatry, 51,* 8–19.

Laird, J. (1989). Women and stories: Restorying women's self-constructions. In M. McGoldrick, C. Anderson, & F. Walsh (Eds.), *Women in families: A framework for family therapy* (pp. 427–450). New York: W. W. Norton.

Land, H. (1995). Feminist clinical social work in the 21st century. In N. Van Den Bergh (Ed.), *Feminist practice in the 21st century* (pp. 3–19). Washington, DC: NASW Press.

Libow, J. (1986). Training family therapists as feminists. In M. Ault-Riche (Ed.), *Women and family therapy.* Rockville, MD: Aspen.

Lyotard, J-F. (1979). *The postmodern condition: A report on knowledge.* Minneapolis, MN: University of Minnesota Press.

Masson, P. (1984, February). Freud and the seduction theory. *The Atlantic Monthly,* 33–60.

Miller, J. B. (1986). *Toward a new psychology of women* (2nd ed.). Boston: Beacon Press.

Miller, J. B. (1991). The construction of anger in women and men. In Jordan et al. (Eds.), *Women's growth in connection: Writings from the Stone Center* (pp. 181–196). New York: The Guilford Press.

Mills, S. (1998). Post-colonial feminist theory. In S. Jackson & J. Jones (Eds.), *Contemporary feminist theories* (pp. 98–112). New York: New York University Press.

Nes, J. A., & Iadicola, P. (1989). Toward a definition of feminist social work: A comparison of liberal, radical, and socialist models. *Social Work, 34,* 12–21.

Nicholson, L. J. (Ed.). (1990). *Feminism/postmodernism.* New York: Routledge.

Pearce, D. (1979). The feminization of poverty: Women, work, and welfare. *Urban and Social Change Review, 2,* 28–36.

Pilgrim, D., & Rogers, A. (1999). *A sociology of mental health and illness* (2nd ed.). Buckingham, UK and Philadelphia, PA: Open University Press.

Rhodes, A., & Goering, P. (1998). Gender differences in the use of outpatient mental health services. In B. Lubotsky Levin, A. K. Blanch, & A. Jennings (Eds.), *Women's mental health services* (pp. 19–33). Thousand Oaks, CA: Sage.

Robins, L. N., Locke, B. Z., & Regier, D. A. (1991). An overview of psychiatric disorders in America. In L. N. Robins & D. A. Regier (Eds.), *Psychiatric disorders in America* (pp. 328–366). New York: The Free Press.

Sands, R. G., & Nuccio, K. (1992). Postmodern feminist theory and social work. *Social Work, 37*(6), 489–502.

Spence, D. P. (1982). *Narrative truth and historical truth: Meaning and interpretation in psychoanalysis.* New York: W. W. Norton.

Sperry, L. (1995). *Handbook of diagnosis and treatment of the DSM-IV personality disorders.* New York: Brunner/Mazel.

Stewart, R. L. (1985). Psychoanalysis and psychoanalytic psychotherapy. In H. I. Kaplan & B. J. Sadock (Eds.), *Comprehensive textbook of psychiatry/IV* (4th ed., pp. 1331–1365). Baltimore, MD: Williams & Wilkins.

Straus, M. A., Gelles, R. J., & Steinmetz, S. K. (1988). *Behind closed doors: Violence in the American family.* Newbury Park: Sage.

Tong, R. (1989). *Feminist thought: A comprehensive introduction.* Boulder, CO: Westview Press.

U.S. Bureau of the Census. (1997). *Statistical abstract of the United States: 1997* (117th ed.). Washington, DC: U.S. Government Printing Office.

U.S. Bureau of the Census. (1999). Table A, Income 1997. www.census.gov/hhes/income/income97/in97sum.html.

Van Den Bergh, N. (1995). Feminist social work practice: Where have we been…Where are we going? In N. Van Den Bergh (Ed.), *Feminist practice in the 21st century* (pp. xi–xxxix). Washington, DC: NASW Press.

Walker, A. (1983). *In search of our mother's gardens.* New York: Harcourt.

Walker, L. (1979). *The battered woman.* New York: Harper and Row.

Waugh, P. (1998). Postmodernism and feminism. In S. Jackson & J. Jones (Eds.), *Contemporary feminist theories* (pp. 177–193). New York: New York University Press.

White, M., & Epston, D. (1990). *Narrative means to therapeutic ends.* New York: W. W. Norton.

7 Racial, Ethnic, and Cultural Issues

To engage these issues…takes psychiatric research out of the laboratory and to the social margins, to clinicians who are struggling under adverse conditions to care for homeless men and women who are mentally ill, to providers caring for persons suffering both from mental illness and the effects of use of alcohol or addictive drugs, to American Indian patients in emergency rooms of rural hospitals, to poor Latino or African American men and women in crowded urban clinics, to recent arrivals to our country suffering the traumatic effects of state violence who live in continuing terror that they will be deported, to clinicians attempting to provide care for a broad range of disadvantaged Americans within the constraints of for-profit managed care organizations.

—Good, "Culture and *DSM-IV:* Diagnosis, Knowledge, and Power," 1996

The United States is a multicultural society in which the historically dominant white majority has regarded nonwhite as "other." In the field of mental health, "others" located at the "social margins" (Good, 1996, p. 130) are subject to having their emotions and behaviors overinterpreted or underinterpreted as symptoms of psychopathology (Lopez, 1989). The resulting diagnostic errors and oversights have alerted mental health and other human service professionals to the need to be culturally competent and ethnically sensitive (Devore & Schlesinger, 1996; Green, 1995; Juliá, 1996; McGoldrick, Giordano, & Pearce, 1996). According to the Code of Ethics of NASW (National Association of Social Workers, 1997), cultural competence is integral to ethical social work practice. The postmodern clinical social work practitioner is knowledgeable about different cultures and sensitive to racial and ethnic issues immanent in behavioral health practice. To begin with, this requires an understanding of terminology.

Definitions

Race, ethnicity, and *culture* are social constructions that are intermixed with the distribution of economic resources, social status, and political power in U.S. society. All refer to ascribed differences that have various meanings, depending on whether one is an insider or outsider to the group designated. When deconstructed, each of these terms has multiple layers of meaning, and each term overlaps the others.

The term *race* refers to a population in which inherent biological traits are passed on from one generation to the next (Goldsby, 1977). Skin color is one of many traits that are genetically transmitted. The biological use of the term *race,* however, is problematic. Because of migrations and sexual relations across groups, few traits are distinctive to a particular race, for example, the same blood-group types prevail across populations. Similarly, all the racial groups are comprised of individuals of many hues. Race is a construction of difference that uses scientific discourse to legitimize the superiority of one group over others (Pilgrim & Rogers, 1999). It has persisted as a category because it helps maintain the "norm of between-group disparity" (Helms & Cook, 1999, p. 16). *Racism* is intolerance directed against a group based on constructed racial differences. It is expressed in institutional arrangements, the opportunity structure, and interpersonal behavior.

The term *ethnicity* makes it possible for one to avoid the biological fallacy associated with race. Ethnicity refers to the history, culture, and national origin that form a basis for group identity, beliefs, customs, and political organization. Ethnic groups are bound by a common heritage, language, beliefs, and interactional patterns that infuse their family and intragroup contacts. There are numerous white ethnic groups such as the Irish, Italians, Greeks, Amish, and Jews (who are also a religious group). Knowledge of the particular ethnic groups (tribes or clans) from which many African Americans originated has been lost, overshadowed by the slave experience that followed their exportation. The socially constructed Hispanic group of people of Latin American or Spanish origins is comprised of a variety of ethnic, racial, and national groups, some of which are of non–Spanish Caribbean and South American ancestry (Castex, 1994).

Culture refers to a common body of knowledge, values, symbols, ways of perceiving, and behaviors that are learned and passed on to others. A particular way of knowing, evaluating, and perceiving may be referred to as a specific culture (e.g., Navaho). Although much of cultural knowledge is out of awareness, it is transmitted through a number of communication systems (Hall, 1959). Ethnicity is related to culture, but ethnicity is also the basis for identity and political action (i.e., identity politics). Some ethnics view themselves in relation to their group's history, religion, folkways, and values. Others, however, find meaning in joining with their people to pursue political goals. Accordingly ethnicity may be behavioral (cultural) or ideological (political) (Harwood, 1981).

Multiculturalism and *cultural diversity* are also used to describe cultural, ethnic, and racial differences. These terms encompass numerous types of differences (e.g., sexual orientation, gender, age, disability) representing a variety of aspects of human diversity. Because these terms dilute the significance of race, they tend to be disempowering to racial and ethnic groups (Helms & Cook, 1999). Hopps (1982, 1987) identified a similar problem with broad application of *ethnicity* and *minority*. Whereas the term *minority* once suggested that a group was small in size, it now is used to indicate that the group lacks power. This is the only term among those discussed so far that speaks to the disadvantaged political and economic position of the groups to which it refers.

Certain ethnic minority groups—African Americans, Hispanics/Latinos, Native Americans, and Asian Americans—have been subjected to discriminatory practices that have interfered with their ability to survive and succeed in the larger society. These groups have histories of being subjugated and exploited, resulting in high vulnerability to poverty, infant mortality, malnutrition, and unemployment. Because of their color or ethnicity, they have been branded as outsiders and systematically excluded from the mainstream. The obstacles they have faced in meeting the demands of living in a hostile environment generate stress and tax their coping resources. As Table 7.1 illustrates, disproportionate numbers of racial and ethnic minority groups are classified as living at the poverty level. The per capita income of people of Hispanic origin is about half that of white non-Hispanics. Native Americans and Alaskan Natives, who were not listed in this table because data for the same year were not available, also have a high level of poverty. In 1990, 31.2 percent of them were living at the poverty level (U.S. Bureau of the Census, 1997).

Although race (or color) is a salient category in the United States, it does not have the same meaning in other societies. During a trip to Cuba in the 1960s, Alice Walker (1983) found differences between African Americans and Black Cubans in their perceptions of themselves:

> Watching young black Cubans is exhilarating but, frankly, I also felt bereft. Unlike black Americans, who have never felt at ease with being Americans, black Cubans raised in the revolution take no special pride in being black. They take pride in being Cuban. Nor do they appear able to feel, viscerally, what racism is. The more we insisted on calling ourselves *black* Americans and spoke of *black* culture, the more confused and distant they grew. (pp. 210–211)

Just as race and class interact in ways that exacerbate oppression in the United States, so does gender interact with race and class. As a consequence, women of color "are in multiple jeopardy, facing as they do the combined forces of racism, sexism, and, in many cases, poverty" (Hopps, 1982, p. 4). The feminization of poverty among single women and their children is especially pronounced among black and Hispanic mother-headed families (Sands & Nuccio, 1989).

TABLE 7.1 Poverty Status among Different Populations

Group	Number Poor (in millions)	% Poor	Per Capita Income
African Americans	9.7	26.5	$12,351
Hispanic origin*	8.3	27.1	$10,773
Asian and Pacific Islanders**	1.5	14.0	$18,226
White, non-Hispanics	24.4	11.0	$21,905
All racial/ethnic groups	35.6	13.3	$19,241

*May be of any race and includes many distinct groups that differ in national origin, time of immigration, and socioeconomic characteristics.

**Includes many distinct groups that differ in culture, time of immigration, and socioeconomic characteristics.

Source: U.S. Bureau of the Census (1999a).

This chapter is concerned with cultural issues that affect the practice of clinical social work in community mental health. Here the terms *cultural* and *ethnic* groups, as well as *ethnic minority,* will be used interchangeably to refer to racial minorities.

The four socially constructed groups that will be emphasized are the African Americans, Asian Americans/Pacific Islanders, Native Americans/Alaskan Natives, and Hispanics/Latinos. These are the groups that the white majority has been regarding as "other." Although these groups are often characterized as nonwhite racial groups or people of color, some individuals within these categories self-identify as Caucasian. Other individuals, who are of mixed backgrounds, identify with one group or see themselves as biracial or multiethnic. To understand the disadvantaged position of the four groups, a common thread that enters into each of their histories is described next.

History of Oppression

The United States was founded and developed through a series of acts of aggression that were directed at minorities of color. The first settlers, the Native Americans and Alaska Natives, are thought to have emigrated from Asia by crossing the Alaskan land bridge some 20,000 years ago (Kitano, 1985). At the time Columbus came to America, some 1,000 tribes and millions of people were scattered across the continent (Blanchard, 1987). Others lived throughout Central and South America. These indigenous populations presented a formidable barrier to European conquerors, who thought that they had "discovered" a new land. The Europeans dealt with the Native Americans by engaging in warfare with them, trading goods, entering into treaties with them, and depriving them of sources of their livelihood. In the process, a large proportion of Native Americans were killed whereas others fell prey to deception and diseases and were introduced to alcohol.

After the United States was founded, public policies that undermined Native American cultures were implemented. These included the displacement of Native Americans from their land, the creation of reservations, sending Native American children away to American-style boarding schools, and land redistribution (Kitano, 1985). Today there are over 500 tribes (Lewis, 1995) and 2.4 million persons (U.S. Bureau of the Census, 1999b). The status of Native American tribes as nations within a nation has created jurisdictional confusion over land, civil rights, and child placement for a number of generations (Johnson, 1982). The loss of land, tribal unity, and cultural identity has had a long-range impact on those Native Americans who have survived.

The European conquerors began settlements in the New World in the sixteenth century. The French, English, Dutch, and Swedish settled in the eastern and northern sections of what is now the United States. The Spanish conquered Mexico and subsequently penetrated the natives' land, culture, and language, and married indigenous Indian women. In keeping with the pattern of expansion that was normative among Europeans at that time, the Spaniards moved into what is now the southwestern part of the United States. Later the new American nationals perpetuated this practice in the doctrine of manifest destiny.

The European settlers imported Africans to serve as slaves to the colonists. Considered property, the Africans were sold for use as plantation laborers and "bred" for their progeny. Plantation owners further subjugated the African women by raping them. The forced immigration, exploitation, and separation of Africans from the same African societies resulted in the destruction of indigenous African cultures. Restrictions against marriage and the sale of African American family members undermined the establishment of stable African American families.

Although the Civil War was fought primarily to preserve the Union, conflict over the spread of slavery into newly acquired territories was one of the issues that divided the North and the South before the Civil War. The war did, nevertheless, result in the abolition of slavery and the granting of the rights of citizenship and the right to vote to African Americans. In the years that followed the Civil War, public policies, such as poll taxes and grandfather clauses, as well as illegal and malevolent activities, such as lynchings, impeded African Americans from participation in American life. The Supreme Court case *Plessy v. Ferguson* of 1896 endorsed segregation in establishing the principle of separate but equal education for African Americans and whites. Even after this decision was overturned in *Brown v. the Board of Education of Topeka, Kansas* in 1954 and subsequent legislation outlawed segregated housing and employment discrimination, racism and poverty have kept African Americans oppressed (Kitano, 1985).

During the midnineteenth century Asian immigrants (primarily single Chinese men) entered the country on the West Coast for reasons similar to those of the white immigrants from Europe who were arriving—to improve their economic lot (Kitano, 1987). They worked as miners, railroad workers, domestic servants, and as laborers in manufacturing industries. Few started families here because of the shortage of Chinese women and the enactment of antimiscegenation laws. Because they accepted low wages, their presence aroused the rancor of whites (the "yellow peril") who were competing for the same jobs (Kitano, 1985). Discrimination against the Chinese was expressed in the passage of Chinese Exclusion Acts in 1882 and 1902 and the later Immigration Act of 1924.

From 1890 to 1924, however, Japanese were allowed to immigrate to Hawaii and the United States with their families (Kitano, 1985). Although they and their children became acculturated, they, too, suffered from discrimination. During World War II, racism directed at the Japanese reached hysterical proportions, culminating in the placement of Japanese Americans in internment camps. Other Asian populations that have come to the United States are the Filipinos, Koreans, Pacific Islanders, and Southeast Asians, whose immigration was facilitated by the Immigration Act of 1965 and subsequent public policies. The Southeast Asians were refugees from Vietnam, Laos, and Cambodia who sought asylum during the wars and political changes that ravaged their lands (Kitano, 1987).

The United States acquired Texas and the southwestern territories from Mexico during the Mexican American War, which ended in 1848, and through the Gadsden Purchase of 1853. (Mexico gained its independence from Spain in 1821.) At the time, the land was occupied by a diverse population of persons of Spanish or Mexican descent, Native Americans, and mestizos (mixed people of Indian and Spanish origins). Although the Mexicans had been granted rights of citizenship through the treaty that had been signed, in the ensuing years, Anglo Americans took over the land and secured dominance by controlling the economic, political, and educational institutions (Gibson, 1987). Nevertheless, immigrants from Mexico continued to flow into the Southwest and other parts of the United States where they were able to work. In addition, undocumented (illegal) aliens penetrated the Mexican-American borders and worked as cheap farm laborers. Other Hispanic groups, such as Puerto Ricans and Cubans, migrated in search of economic opportunities and political asylum.

Throughout U.S. history, African Americans, Native Americans and Alaska Natives, Asians, Pacific Islanders, and Hispanics have faced economic exploitation and poverty. African Americans were required to work as slaves; other minority groups were used as cheap labor. Ethnic minorities of color continue to be overrepresented among the poor. Their life expectancy is lower and infant mortality rates are higher than whites'. Segregated from the mainstream, their children have had an inferior or culturally insensitive education, in which the values of the dominant culture have been imposed as normative. Inadequate education perpetuates their exclusion from vocational and educational avenues of advancement. Minorities of color continue to have unmet basic needs for economic support, housing, and health care.

Multiple Contexts

Postmodern social work practice with oppressed minorities recognizes the multiple contexts that characterize the lives of these populations. Chestang (1976) identified two systems—the nurturing system and the sustaining system—that provide emotional support and economic livelihood to African Americans. The nurturing system consists of family and friends in the ethnic community who provide warmth and support and facilitate expressiveness; the sustaining system represents the material, political, and social provisions of the external society. The ethnic minority group member lives within, negotiates with, and needs both systems. Nevertheless, the perceptions, demands, and attitudes of the two systems may conflict. Although ethnic minorities tend to want to adapt to life amidst the dominant culture, they are asked to identify with the larger culture's racism (Norton, 1978). In order to function effectively in both worlds, ethnic minorities develop strategies that permit them to cope with conflicting environments. Social work educators have recommended that students and practitioners recognize and understand the "dual perspectives" of ethnic minority clients (Norton, 1978) and foster group pride and empowerment (Solomon, 1976).

Social scientists of the past obfuscated the position of oppressed minorities in relation to the "American dream." The idea that the United States was a melting pot into which all ethnic groups can mix was relevant and appealing to poor, white ethnic European immigrants, who were better able to accommodate to the similar U.S. culture than racial minorities with very different cultures (de Anda, 1984). White immigrants were more likely to be served by mainstream social welfare agencies than minorities of color (Lum, 1986), whereas minorities of color faced structural barriers, such as Jim Crow laws and employment discrimination, that stood in the way of their assimilation.

During the 1960s, the melting pot theory lost credibility. This was a period in which ethnic minority groups became a significant political force that forged the civil rights movement. Their political activities, as well as increasing evidence that people of color remained poor, were misconstrued, leading to the development of the cultural deficit model, which described poor, ethnic minorities as culturally deprived (de Anda, 1984). During this period of the War on Poverty, educational and social programs to address these "deficits" were developed. The cultural deficit model was later discredited because it evaluated diverse cultures from the perspective of middle-class norms (de Anda, 1984).

Another model that was introduced emphasized cultural differences among diverse populations (de Anda, 1984). This model, however, went overboard in emphasizing the separateness of each cultural group. Instead de Anda (1984) recommends the bicultural socialization model, which, like the dual perspective, recognizes that there are differences as well as areas of overlap between cultures. Ethnic minority clients may need help maintaining their own identity while functioning in mainstream society. Social workers can assist them by finding or acting as mediators, translators, and role models; helping them develop their problem-solving skills; and advocating for changes in the majority culture (de Anda, 1984).

Although theories of ethnicity describe two contexts, ethnic minority clients function in a multiplicity of situations that may or may not be congruent with the majority/minority polarity. Ethnic minorities may, for example, have contact with other ethnic groups. In cities with large ethnic populations, Puerto Ricans, African Americans, Chinese, and other ethnic groups have cross-cultural contact in the local community. Regardless of clients' own ethnic group, they encounter professionals such as doctors, teachers, and social workers who represent a range of cultural backgrounds. Everyday life experiences may entail a series of encounters with individuals, groups, and institutions that are diversely constituted.

Ethnicity and Mental Health Help Seeking

The public sponsorship of most mental health services makes it possible for consumers to represent a spectrum of ethnic groups. Clients of diverse cultural groups perceive and interpret their problems through a lens that is refracted according to the belief systems of their respective cultures. Cultural definitions and categories influence the labeling of behaviors or emotional states as problematic and the kinds of responses that are considered appropriate. Accordingly, the individual will seek help within his or her own primary culture and/or in the institutionalized system of mental health care.

Medical sociologists use a number of terms that are helpful in understanding help seeking among ethnic minority groups. Among these are *sick role, health behavior,* and *illness behavior.* The sick role was described by Parsons (1964) as a legitimized social status in which sick persons have the right to be free of blame and to abdicate their usual responsibilities at the same time they have the obligation to desire to get well and to cooperate with treatment. Health behavior refers to activities of presumably healthy persons to prevent disease or detect it prior to the development of symptoms, whereas illness behavior refers to activities of persons who feel ill to determine the state of their health and find an appropriate remedy (Kasl & Cobb, 1966). A semiannual dental checkup is an example of health behavior; a medical appointment for a cold is illustrative of illness behavior.

Sociocultural variables influence the assumption of the sick role and the practice of health and illness behaviors. In order to legitimately engage in sick role behavior, one's culture must recognize that the person is sick and sanction appropriate rights and obligations. This requires the perception of the symptoms as meaningful and the view that release from social obligations is appropriate. If the culture does not have a category that corresponds to the symptoms, it is unlikely that the person will be considered sick. Similarly health behavior is culturally relative. Although preventive dentistry and regular pediatric care may be normative among middle-class U.S. citizens, these practices are not congruent with ideas of other cultures. Illness behaviors are activities that follow from the perception that one is ill. These responses, however, may be dictated by one's culture. Accordingly, one may seek a shaman, ingest herbs, or go to the doctor.

In medical anthropology a distinction is made between *disease* and *illness. "Disease* refers to a malfunctioning of biological and/or psychological processes, while the term *illness* refers to the psychosocial experience and meaning of perceived illness" (Kleinman, 1980, p. 72). With illness the social and cultural patterns of perceiving, thinking, responding, and coping come into play. Most medical practitioners in the United States adhere to a disease (biomedical) model. The model is realized through an impersonal technological system in which the person is viewed as an object that houses the disease. Frequently this results in the treatment of the disease and the neglect of the person, and a divergence between the technological "voice of medicine" and the psychosocial "voice of the lifeworld" (cf. Mishler, 1984). For example, a medical practitioner in the United States may define an *ataque* as a psychogenic seizure, whereas a Puerto Rican layperson may define the same event as a spell that was instigated by spirits. The distinction between illness and disease that is described here is incorporated in the conceptual framework of this book (see Chapter 3). This chapter turns next to the actions of individuals who perceive that they are ill.

Illness Behavior

When applied to mental health, illness behavior refers to the use of formal mental health services. Research on the illness behavior of diverse ethnic and racial groups has found that different ethnic groups use different types of services, but in keeping with the postmodern perspective of this book these differences are not consistent across studies.

An analysis of the use of mental health services in a six-month period from the Yale Epidemiologic Catchment Area Project found that Caucasians, as well as women, the more educated, persons between ages 25 and 64, and the unmarried were most likely to use services (Leaf et al., 1985). A report from a similar study in St. Louis found that among individuals with major depression, whites were more likely than African Americans to consult with a mental health professional (Sussman, Robins, & Earls, 1987). Other studies, however, have revealed that African Americans frequently confer with mental health professionals. Broman (1987) found that blacks were more likely than whites to seek help from mental health professionals (e.g., psychiatrists or psychologists at mental health centers) and other sources (e.g., teachers, lawyers, and social workers in agencies, emergency room staff), and whites were more likely to seek assistance from members of the clergy and medical professionals. Furthermore, African Americans were more likely than Caucasians to seek mental health professional help for economic and physical health problems. A later study by the same research group on data on African Americans found that many users of social service agencies received help from social workers and that they were satisfied with the help they got (Taylor, Neighbors, & Broman, 1989).

A study of the use of public mental health services in San Francisco and Santa Clara counties in California found differences among groups in the use of particular types of services (Hu, Snowden, Jerrel, & Nguyen, 1991). In comparison with whites, African Americans were more likely to use emergency services whereas Asian Americans and Hispanics/Latinos were less likely to do so. With respect to inpatient care, Asian Americans were less likely than whites to use this service, but neither Hispanics nor African Americans differed from whites. Hispanics were more likely but Asian Americans and African Americans were less likely than whites to use case management services. The pattern was different with regard to individual outpatient services in which Asians and Hispanics were more likely than whites to use services and African Americans were less likely. Among these groups, Asian Americans were the only group that used more individual outpatient services than whites. Some of these findings were confirmed in other studies. Snowden and Holschuh (1992) also found that African Americans were more likely to use emergency care than whites. Others have concluded that Asian Americans underutilize mental health services (Matsuoka, Breaux, & Ryujin, 1997). Snowden and Cheung (1990) noted that although Asian Americans/Pacific Islanders were less likely than whites to be admitted to county and state inpatient mental health services, they remained longer. On the other hand, African Americans and Native Americans were more likely than whites to be admitted to inpatient facilities (Snowden & Cheung, 1990).

The findings that have been reported indicate that some ethnic minorities are not using certain mental health services at the rate that whites are using them. This does not mean however, that ethnic minorities are not doing anything about their emotional problems. They may be seeking support from close kin, friends, or spiritual leaders in their ethnic community. Furthermore, they may be consulting individuals in their culture who are designated as healers, or they may be consuming special foods or herbs that are indigenous remedies for psychological distress. Caldwell (1996) found that when African American women perceive that their problems are severe and they have many symptoms of distress, they will use a combination of informal and professional help. Taylor, Neighbors, and Broman (1989) note that informal helpers often link African Americans to the formal delivery system. When ethnic minorities do not use the formal system, however, it may be because the practices of mainstream agencies are not attuned to cultural differences.

Misdiagnosis

Because most social workers are white and many clients are from other racial or ethnic groups, white professionals unfamiliar with diverse cultures may misinterpret what they observe (Davis & Proctor, 1989) and construct inappropriate diagnoses. This can also occur when the professional is a member of one ethnic minority group and the client is of another group or groups. Symptoms of mental illness appear differently in individuals from different cultures and have different meanings (Kleinman, 1988).

Without knowledge of other cultures, the practitioner is likely to rely on stereotypical ideas, which can result in misdiagnosis. Clients of diverse cultures may present symptoms in ways that are consistent with their cultures but incongruent with the categories of mental illness that are described in the *DSM-IV*. Because of differences in world views and behaviors, the client and the clinician may interpret the same symptoms differently.

Over the years, the symptoms of African Americans have been misinterpreted, resulting in overdiagnosis of schizophrenia and underdiagnosis of mood disorders. Cross-cultural studies have shown a widespread practice in U.S. psychiatry of assigning the diagnosis of schizophrenia when affective (mood) disorders, especially bipolar disorder, were appropriate (World Health Organization, 1975). Although both schizophrenia and affective disorders have associated psychotic symptoms, U.S. psychiatrists have interpreted these symptoms as manifestations of schizophrenia, especially when clients were African American (Jones & Gray, 1986).

Misdiagnosis is partially attributable to a misinterpretation of African Americans' presentations of themselves in clinical settings. Some symptoms, such as paranoia and flat affect, are adaptive strategies adopted by African Americans to survive in an alien culture. Grier and Cobbs (1968) speak of a "'healthy' cultural paranoia" that is essential for adaptive functioning:

> For a black man survival in America depends in large measure on the development of a "healthy" cultural paranoia. He must maintain a high degree of suspicion toward the motives of every white man and at the same time never allow this suspicion to impair his grasp of reality. (p. 135)

However adaptive paranoia may be, it is often regarded as a symptom of paranoid schizophrenia or paranoid personality disorder, which are also overdiagnosed among African Americans (Steinberg et al., 1977). Similarly, controlled emotional expression in response to a white therapist who is not trusted may be misinterpreted as blunted or flat affect, which are symptoms of schizophrenia (Jones & Gray, 1986).

Misdiagnosis of African Americans may result in overlooking mood and related disorders. Allen (1986) reports a high incidence of post-traumatic stress disorder (PTSD) among black veterans of the Vietnam War. In the process of talking about the trauma of war in psychotherapy, African American veterans have revealed that they are haunted by memories of genocide against a Third World people, racism in the military, and postwar racism. Allen believes that depression underlies PTSD. Furthermore, symptoms of PTSD may be masked by substance abuse, psychophysiological complaints, and disorganized behavior.

Diagnostic problems have been reported for other ethnic minority groups. Escobar (1987) discusses the prevalent presentation of somatic complaints by Hispanics. These symptoms accompany depressive and schizophrenic disorders but rarely are of sufficient scope to indicate a *DSM* diagnosis of somatization disorder. Chinese Americans also present somatic complaints (Lim & Lin, 1996).

One way to assess whether one group is being misdiagnosed (overdiagnosed or underdiagnosed) is to compare the rate of clinical diagnosis of specific disorders for different ethnic groups with their rate in the general population. Epidemiological studies, which survey symptoms of *DSM* disorders, have identified some intergroup differences in the prevalence of specific disorders, but there is inconsistency in the findings across studies. The Epidemiological Catchment Area (ECA) Study found that a significantly higher proportion of black men ages 45 to 64 and 65 and older than white men and a higher proportion of black women between ages 45 and 64 than white women had ever experienced a psychiatric disorder (Robins, Locke, & Regier, 1991). The difference between black and white older men may have been due to their response to a test for cognitive impairment, which penalized individuals who were educationally disadvantaged (Robins et al., 1991). The ECA also found that African Americans have a relatively high lifetime prevalence of simple phobia and agoraphobia (Eaton, Dryman, & Weissman, 1991) and Hispanics have high rates of alcohol use disorders (Helzer, Burnam, & McEvoy, 1991).

The National Comorbidity Survey, however, had some new and different findings. In comparison with whites, African Americans in the NCS had lower prevalences of mood and substance use disorders and lifetime comorbidity (Kessler et al., 1994). In contrast with the ECA results, there were no differences between blacks and whites in prevalences of anxiety disorders (Kessler et al., 1994). A new finding in the NCS was that Hispanics had higher rates of current mood disorders and active comorbidity than non-Hispanic whites (Kessler et al., 1994).

An analysis by the Substance Abuse and Mental Health Services Administration (SAMHSA, 1996) of mental health data on the National Household Survey on Drug Abuse also found between-group differences on certain disorders. Generalized anxiety disorder was more frequent among whites and Hispanics than African Americans. Panic attacks were higher among whites and blacks than Hispanics, except for the group aged 26 to 34 in which the rate for Hispanics was between the other two groups. A further finding of this study was that whites between ages 26 to 34 and 35 to 49 were more likely to have an episode of major depression than the other two groups (SAMHSA, 1996).

A surprising finding of a more culturally sensitive epidemiological survey of urban and rural Mexicans living in California was that immigrants had half the total *DSM* disorders of those who were born in the United States (Vega et al. 1998). The rates of the native born were close to the rates for Hispanics in the NCS, with substance abuse and anxiety disorders particularly prominent (Vega et al., 1998). This study defies popular wisdom that migration adversely affects mental health (Escobar, 1998). However informative, this and other studies provide little information on the prevalences of different disorders among other groups of Hispanics/Latinos as well as Asian Americans/Pacific Islanders and Native Americans (Snowden & Cheung, 1990). Without more complete data on the distribution of psychiatric disorders among ethnic groups, it is difficult to determine whether some groups are being overdiagnosed or underdiagnosed with a particular disorder.

Cultural Dimensions of the *DSM-IV* Diagnosis and Treatment

Culture in the *DSM-IV*

In contrast with previous diagnostic manuals, the *DSM-IV* (American Psychiatric Association, 1994) has given some consideration to the impact of culture on the expression of psychopathology. The introduction to the *DSM-IV* advises clinicians not to use norms from their own culture to evaluate behaviors, experiences, or beliefs that come from another culture. Many of the chapters on groups of disorders have a section on specific culture features to describe cultural variations that one might see. An appendix (I) includes an outline for cultural formulation and a glossary of culture-bound syndromes. Unfortunately, the outline for cultural formulation, as well as additional culturally distinctive categories, was not given the prominence that the National Task Force on Culture and Psychiatric Diagnosis, which developed it, had wanted (Good, 1996; Lewis-Fernández, 1996). This outline is reproduced as Table 7.2. It is recommended that social workers use it for cultural assessments of clients from diverse cultures.

TABLE 7.2   Outline for Cultural Formulation

The following outline for cultural formulation is meant to supplement the multiaxial diagnostic assessment and to address difficulties that may be encountered in applying DSM-IV criteria in a multicultural environment. The cultural formulation provides a systematic review of the individual's cultural background, the role of the cultural context in the expression and evaluation of symptoms and dysfunction, and the effect that cultural differences may have on the relationship between the individual and the clinician.

As indicated in the introduction to the manual (see p. xxiv), it is important that the clinician take into account the individual's ethnic and cultural context in the evaluation of each of the DSM-RV axes. In addition, the cultural formulation suggested below provides an opportunity to describe systematically the individual's cultural and social reference group and ways in which the cultural context is relevant to clinical care. The clinician may provide a narrative summary for each of the following categories:

Cultural identity of the individual.   Note the individual's ethnic or cultural reference groups. For immigrants and ethnic minorities, note separately the degree of involvement with both the culture of origin and the host culture (where applicable). Also note language abilities, use, and preference (including multilingualism).

Cultural explanations of the individual's illness.   The following may be identified: the predominant idioms of distress through which symptoms or the need for social support are communicated (e.g., "nerves," possessing spirits, somatic complaints, inexplicable misfortune), the meaning and perceived severity of the individual's symptoms in relation to norms of the cultural reference group, any local illness category used by the individual's family and community to identify the condition (see "Glossary of Culture-Bound Syndromes" below), the perceived causes or explanatory models that the individual and the reference group use to explain the illness, and current preferences for and past experiences with professional and popular sources of care.

Cultural factors related to psychosocial environment and levels of functioning.   Note culturally relevant interpretations of social stressors, available social supports, and levels of functioning and disability. This would include stresses in the local social environment and the role of religion and kin networks in providing emotional, instrumental, and informational support.

Cultural elements of the relationship between the individual and the clinician.   Indicate differences in culture and social status between the individual and the clinician and problems that these differences may cause in diagnosis and treatment (e.g., difficulty in communicating in the individual's first language, in eliciting symptoms or understanding their cultural significance, in negotiating an appropriate relationship or level of intimacy, in determining whether a behavior is normative or pathological).

Overall cultural assessment for diagnosis and care.   The formulation concludes with a discussion of how cultural considerations specifically influence comprehensive diagnosis and care.

Culture-Specific Syndromes

In this book attention is being given to culture-bound syndromes, which are specific to certain cultures. With the continuous migration of refugees from around the world, such syndromes appear in U.S. mental health practice. Examples of culture-specific syndromes are described in the sections on individual cultural groups that follow.

Culturally Sanctioned Healers

Just as cultures have specific syndromes, there are also certain persons among them who are sanctioned to treat identified conditions. Although mainstream U.S. society has assigned this role to psychiatrists, psychologists, and social workers, some ethnic groups have indigenous healers who treat ailments in ways that are congruent with the beliefs and norms of the culture. Folk healers, or *shamen,* are the equivalents of therapists. They are described by Mexican Americans as *curanderos* and by Puerto Ricans as *espiritismos* or spiritists. Native Americans, Asians, and Haitians are also known to have their own healers. Shamen may prescribe herbs, a special diet, exercise, or a healing ritual. Some of the beliefs, values, and healing practices that are associated with specific ethnic groups will be described in the next section.

Clinical Social Work Practice with Specific Ethnic Groups

Social work practice with persons of diverse ethnic minority groups is guided by knowledge of the specific culture, the degree of clients' identification with their culture of origin, and their assimilation into the dominant U.S. culture. The specific group is influenced by its history of oppression, its social constitution, the local ecology, and economic factors. Those ethnic minority clients who live principally among their own people in isolated villages have less contact (and possibly less conflict) than those who are thrust into a competitive urban environment. Those who live in ethnic enclaves within larger multicultural communities experience the push and pull of different world views on a regular basis. New immigrants deal with the loss of their homeland as well as adaptation to a new culture.

This section will provide descriptive information and suggested strategies for social work practice with individuals of African American, Asian American/Pacific Island, Latino/Hispanic, and Native American ethnicity. The danger in presenting this material is that it will create or affirm stereotypes. In reading this section, the reader is advised to keep in mind that there is as much diversity within cultures as between cultures; and to recognize that although persons who are socialized in a particular culture generally have knowledge of the beliefs and practices of their group, individuals do not uniformly accept these beliefs or engage in these practices. In no way are the values and behaviors that are described here to be viewed as inherent, universal, "essential" characteristics of everyone associated with the group.

Furthermore, cultural ways are viewed as resources which can aid clients in their resolution of mental health problems. Accordingly, indigenous definitions and categories (what is called the *emic* perspective), which ethnic minority clients bring to the social worker–client relationships, are the ways in which the clients and their cultures view their problems. Indigenous categories encompass the illness rather than the disease. As such they are an important source of meaning to the particular culture. Concepts of mental health and constructs of illness that are specific to a culture are just as valid as Western disease constructs. The clinical social worker starts from the client's perspective, helping the client work through the problem in culturally congruent terms.

Social workers who identify with the dominant culture may have certain biases that interfere with their work with ethnic minority clients; For example, the European American values of individualism, independence, competitiveness, and achievement are different from the values of sharing, modesty, and intergenerational connectedness that are held by some ethnic minority groups. Similarly certain interpersonal behaviors that are valued by the dominant culture (e.g., assertiveness, eye contact, informality) are considered improper among persons of other cultures, whereas other behaviors (e.g., silence, deference) may be preferred by some ethnic minority groups. Expectations that clients verbalize their feelings, admit their weaknesses, and confront persons who arouse their anger are based on European American therapeutic models. In order to work with ethnically different clients, social workers must control their biases and accept clients on their own terms.

Because of potential differences between clinicians and clients, two approaches to behavioral health service delivery have been recommended: "(i) increasing cultural competence of mental health staff by training existing personnel or hiring ethnic minorities; and (ii) the need for culturally sensitive programs" (Takeuchi, Uehara, & Maraba, 1999, p. 555). Ethnic minority service centers with clinicians who speak the same language and share the same culture or mainstream centers with minority, bilingual clinicians on the staff are particularly ethnic sensitive. Programs such as these, however, are few and far between. An alternative strategy is to hire interpreters. The choice of an interpreter, however, should be culturally congruent and consistent with the client's preferences. Because of the personal nature of therapeutic conversations, interpreters who are young or of a different sex may not be appropriate. In any case, mental health staff need to be knowledgeable about characteristics of different ethnic groups, keeping in mind within-group diversity and the degree to which the clinician and client identify with their own group (Helms & Cook, 1999).

African Americans

With close to 35 million persons, representing 12.8 percent of the general population, African Americans are the largest of the ethnic minority groups in the United States (U.S. Bureau of the Census, 1999b). Although some came voluntarily as immigrants from the Caribbean and South America, most are the descendants of Africans who were forcibly captured and brought to North America, where they were sold as slaves. The Africans came from a number of west African ethnic communities. Their dispersion throughout the southern colonies interfered with the perpetuation of their native cultures. In recent years, new voluntary immigrants from Africa have arrived (Kamya, 1997).

Black experience of life in the United States has been marked by domination, exploitation, and economic hardship. From the time the first Africans came here, they were regarded as chattel, whose value came from their usefulness in the white-dominated U.S. economy. The master-subject relationship that was established early in the United States' history relegated African Americans to a subhuman status in which their worth, rights, and dignity were denied (Bosmajian, 1974). Even after laws were changed to include African Americans as citizens with rights, inequality has been maintained through institutional racism.

Institutional racism directed at African Americans is reflected in census data. As Table 7.1 showed, 26.5 percent of African Americans are poor (U.S. Bureau of the Census, 1999a). The median income for black households in 1997 was $25,050; per capita income was $12,351 (U.S. Bureau of the Census, 1999a), representing an increase from the previous year. Close to 40 percent of African American families headed by women (which is the most prevalent family structure) were poor in 1997, a proportion that is a decline from the previous year (U.S. Bureau of the Census, 1999c).

Despite the high rate of poverty among African Americans, many are educated and employed as professionals and skilled laborers. Although a majority live in the South (U.S. Bureau of the Census, 1988c), many have migrated to the North and to the West Coast and live primarily in urban centers (Hines & Boyd-Franklin, 1982). As a whole, African Americans are a heterogeneous population whose social problems are a function of the interaction of class, gender, and race.

Cultural Values and Norms.   African American cultural values and norms derive from three sources—residues of African culture, values of the mainstream United States, and responses and adaptations to the victim system that arose from oppression, poverty, and racism (Pinderhughes, 1982). Variation among individuals reflects these diverse sources of identification, as well as differences in social class, education, urban/rural environment, region of the country, and individual differences.

Nobles (1976) describes the African world view as one that values cooperation, collective responsibility, and interdependence and is expressed psychobehaviorally in sameness, groupness, and commonality. Similarly, the Afrocentric paradigm focuses on collective identity, spirituality, and an affective approach to knowing (Schiele, 1996). African values and behaviors stand in sharp contrast with European values of competition, individuality, and difference. African values are expressed in strong kinship bonds (Hill, 1971; Leigh & Green, 1982) and an emphasis on religion and spirituality (Boyd-Franklin, 1989).

Although Boyd-Franklin (1989) affirms that "there is no such thing as *the* Black family" (p. 6), she and others (e.g., Leigh & Green, 1982) describe several patterns that characterize many African American families. For one, families extend beyond nuclear arrangements to include informally adopted children, friends ("aunts" and "uncles"), and distant and closely related biological kin. Children may be raised by grandparents or in multigenerational households. The paternal relatives of a child in a mother-headed, single-parent family may be an important component of the family kinship system. Kinship networks are cooperative and interdependent.

Some writers describe the flexible family roles that are apparent in many African American families (Boyd-Franklin, 1989; Hill, 1971). The employment of both black women and black men has resulted in sex roles that tend to be egalitarian and family organization that is cooperative (Leigh & Green, 1982). During times of crisis, the extended kinship system can be mobilized to assume absentee roles (Hines & Boyd-Franklin, 1982).

Children are socialized to be assertive and independent and are valued for themselves rather than for their ability to manipulate the physical world (Leigh & Green, 1982).

Religion or spirituality is frequently cited as a source of strength among African Americans (Boyd-Franklin, 1989; Hines & Boyd-Franklin, 1982; Hill, 1971; Leigh & Green, 1982; McAdoo, 1987). Rooted in the African experience and oppression during slavery, religion and religious institutions provide structures for meaning, emotional expression, affiliation, and political organization. The church is a place in which African Americans can feel at home, reach out for spiritual support, express deep feelings, and receive acceptance. A source of meaning beyond the material world, religion is a counterforce that provides hope for change. Although most of the organized religions with which African Americans are affiliated are Christian, some are Muslim. Despite the importance of the church in Black history and Black life, some African Americans are not religious (Solomon, 1976).

African American culture is also influenced by the victim system that has developed around them. Pinderhughes (1982) describes this as "a circular feedback process" in which negative feedback "threatens self-esteem" and "reinforces problematic responses in communities, families, and individuals" (p. 109). Barriers to achievement by African Americans lead to poverty, low wages, and "glass ceilings" which have turned a minority of blacks to the underground economy for support (Hines & Boyd-Franklin, 1996). Financial strain adversely affects the ability of the family to foster individual development and work cooperatively with others to improve the community. Limited in resources, communities deteriorate and become a negative influence. This results in increased powerlessness (Pinderhughes, 1982; Solomon, 1976).

Indigenous Concepts of Health, Mental Health, and Mental Illness.   African American concepts of mental health and mental illness are influenced by those of the dominant white culture and by religious beliefs. As U.S. citizens, African Americans have been socialized to accept mainstream biomedical concepts (Jackson, 1981) and to use mainstream health and mental health services. For some, however, religion provides a primary system of meaning for human experiences. Some African Americans explain their psychological symptoms in religious or folk terms and view using the formal treatment system negatively (Hines & Boyd-Franklin, 1996).

Culture-Specific Syndromes.   One of the culture-specific syndromes that is seen in African Americans and persons of Caribbean background is called *falling out*. It is characterized by sudden collapse, paralysis, and inability to speak or see. Hearing remains unimpaired and eyes are open during these episodes (Jackson, 1981). Another is *rootwork,* which attributes maladies to evil forces (APA, 1994).

Illness Behavior.   African Americans use supports within the nurturing and sustaining systems to assist them with mental health problems (Chestang, 1976). Historical and ongoing oppression create distrust of mainstream services; thus, during times of crisis, they are likely to turn to friends, family, neighbors, and religious resources for help (Hines & Boyd-Franklin, 1996). African Americans who do use mainstream mental health services may hesitate to be open with clinicians. Past experience with the public assistance, child welfare, and court systems has taught blacks to be wary (Boyd-Franklin, 1989). Accordingly, their resistance may be viewed as a strength (Boyd-Franklin, 1989; Grier & Cobbs, 1968). It is not realistic or prudent to trust members of the ruling class of oppressors unless they prove themselves to be trustworthy.

Some research indicates that African Americans have fewer sessions of psychotherapy than whites and that they leave treatment prematurely (Cole & Pilisuk, 1976; Sue, 1977). Thus, quality as well as quantity of contact needs to be improved. If the clinician is not African American, he or she should acknowledge this difference and explore potential racial barriers early in their work together (Hines and Boyd-Franklin, 1996).

Implications for Treatment.   Mental health problems experienced by African Americans must be seen in the context of their socioeconomic status and the suffering they have endured as people of color in a predominantly white society. Although the cultural values and adaptations to the macro system that African Americans have made are sources of strength, they vary from patterns of white Americans of European extraction who usually have dominant roles in mental health institutions. Unless clinicians of other ethnicities come to understand and appreciate the differences and strengths of African Americans, they are likely to rely on inappropriate values and stereotypes in their treatment of Blacks.

The heterogeneity among African Americans and the complex families and modes of mutual assistance and self-help within Black communities call for a systems approach to assessment and treatment. The family system and the diverse sources of support within the nurturing and sustaining systems should be identified. Clients should be helped to build supports and to eliminate obstacles to their individual and collective betterment. In order to counteract the effects of discrimination, clinical practice with African Americans should be empowering (Solomon, 1976). Clients should be helped to use their own inner resources as well as community resources to attain goals of their own choosing that are consistent with their values. They should be assisted to be instrumental in developing and effecting solutions to identified problems. Furthermore, African Americans should be encouraged to organize politically to attain solutions to collective problems.

Native Americans/Alaska Natives

Native Americans and Alaska Natives were the indigenous people occupying the land that the European explorers thought they had discovered. They represent over 500 tribes (Lewis, 1995), each of which has developed in its own way. Among their population of 2.4 million persons, approximately a quarter retain their own language (Red Horse, 1988; U.S. Bureau of the Census, 1999b). Close to 50 percent are concentrated in California, Arizona, New Mexico, and Oklahoma, and a majority live in or near urban centers (Red Horse, 1988). In 1990 23 percent lived on reservations, in historic areas, in Alaska Native villages, and on tribal trust lands (U.S. Bureau of the Census, 1997b). The Eskimos and Aleuts of Alaska are more likely to live in their native homelands than in urban centers (Red Horse, 1988).

Regardless of where they live, Native Americans have contact with nonnatives to varying degrees. Some have been educated in white-dominated boarding schools, whereas others have been educated in multicultural schools that are closer to home. Those who live in cities and participate in the labor force have many opportunities for cross-cultural contact.

Differing patterns of assimilation have resulted in diverse Indian family styles. Red Horse (1988) describes the *traditional* type as one in which the native language is preferred, the extended kinship system organizes community life, the land is revered, and the native religion is practiced. *Neotraditional* families are similar to the traditional ones, except that they may have adopted another religion, such as Christianity, and some prefer Spanish. *Transitional* families retain native values, language, and extended kinship ties in their intimate lives but adopt the customs and language of outsiders in their contacts with the wider community. If they live in an urban area, they try to bridge the gap by making frequent trips to their homeland. The fourth type that Red Horse describes is *bicultural*. These families prefer English, live in nuclear units, and convert to other religions. Nevertheless, the adults may know their native language and religion and have an awareness of the sacredness of the land. The *acculturated* families are assimilated with the dominant culture; they associate primarily with nonnatives and retain few Indian values. A revival of traditional values, traditions, and language and criticism of the U.S. institutional system characterize the *panrenaissance* families.

Disproportionate numbers of Native Americans have low incomes and suffer from poverty. In 1989 the median family income among Native Americans and Alaska Natives was $19,900 (U.S. Bureau of the Census, 1997a). At that time the poverty rate for Native Americans was 31.2 percent, for individual Native Americans and 27.2 for Native American families (U.S. Bureau of the Census, 1997a). Similarly, life expectancy and education of Native Americans are relatively low and unemployment is high. Conditions associated with poverty—deficient housing, malnutrition, disease, and infant mortality—are prevalent. Over 25 percent of the families are headed by women without a spouse present (U.S. Bureau of the Census, 1997a). Accidents and alcoholism are leading causes of death (Carpenter, 1980; Kunitz & Levy, 1981).

Cultural Values and Norms.   Although the diversity among Native American tribes or nations makes it difficult to arrive at a set of values that applies to all groups, efforts that have been made reveal consistencies. Among these are *holism, harmony,* and *community.* In contrast with normative Caucasian Americans who perceive person and environment as separate entities, Native Americans enculturated in their own traditions find unity and continuity among natural, supernatural, and human phenomena (Anderson & Ellis, 1988; Kunitz & Levy, 1981; Lewis, 1985; Nofz, 1988). Indians feel connected to their families, peers, and forebears and the land, which is held sacred (Nofz, 1988; Red Horse, 1988). Their sense of attuneness or harmony with the natural world affects their sense of time. The Pueblos Indians schedule events when the time feels right; Navajos are oriented to the here and now; and the Hopi conceive of time in terms of the growth patterns of animals and food (Hall, 1959). Apparently Native Americans do not focus on the future in the same way that others living in the United States do.

Native Americans tend to value the welfare of the group over individual achievement. They are obligated to share their resources with their families and clans (Nofz, 1988). Because of these values, Native American children are in the untenable position in public schools that emphasize individuality and competition (Anderson & Ellis, 1988). Native Americans avoid conflict or confrontation. They value privacy and do not like it when outsiders interfere with their lives (Lewis & Keung Ho, 1975; Trimble, Manson,

Dinges, & Medicine, 1984). Unfortunately, behavior that is in keeping with their culture is frequently perceived by outsiders as passivity, shyness, and lack of ambition (Anderson & Ellis, 1988). On the other hand, they view the efforts of therapists to elicit personal experiences, thoughts, and feelings as intrusive or inappropriate (Lewis & Keung Ho, 1975; Trimble et al., 1984). Native Americans value listening; silence is a form of communication (Sutton & Broken Nose, 1996).

Native Americans have extended families of biological and nonkin relatives who socialize the young into the culture (Red Horse, 1980b). With the movement of the Native American population to cities, many families are separated from each other geographically. Yet they do form communities within cities and return to their childhood homes for special ceremonies (Red Horse, 1980b). Although the Native American population tends to be young, the elders occupy a position of respect in the community (Red Horse, 1980a). Grandparents are particularly important (Sutton & Broken Nose, 1996).

Indigenous Concepts of Health, Mental Health, and Mental Illness.   Native American cultures do not distinguish between health and mental health. Consistent with their holistic view of the person and the environment, Native Americans view disturbances in their mental health in relation to other aspects of their lives as well as the cosmos (Trimble et al., 1984). The Navajo Indians see physical and mental illness as manifestations of disharmony in nature that may represent the intrusion of supernatural forces or some other external cause. The disharmony could be caused by a breach of a taboo, an intrusion of spirits, witchcraft, or an etiological agent, such as an animal or the wind (Kunitz & Levy, 1981). Ghosts, spirits of the dead, and witchcraft are capable of interfering with the living.

Culture-Specific Syndromes.   Trimble et al. (1984) describe a number of psychiatric syndromes specific to Native Americans. One of these, *pibloktoq,* or arctic hysteria, is a dissociative episode followed by seizures (American Psychiatric Association, 1994). This syndrome is common among female Alaskan Eskimos. Another, characterized by fainting and preoccupation with death, is called *soul loss.* Here the soul, which enters the body at birth and leaves at death, appears to be departing the body (Kunitz & Levy, 1981). On the other hand, *spirit intrusion* is a form of possession by ghosts, evil spirits, or demons that is manifested by symptoms of agitated depression, somatization, and hallucinations. Native Americans may experience a range of behavioral and somatic symptoms as a result of *taboo breaking.* When they violate taboos against forms of sexual expression (e.g., incest), murder, and other forbidden behaviors, they may become afflicted with what outsiders consider mental illness (Trimble et al., 1984). An additional syndrome, *Hi-Wa itch,* is characterized by insomnia, anorexia, depression, and suicide. It is experienced by Mohave American Indians in response to an undesired separation from someone who is loved (Kaplan & Sadock, 1988).

Illness Behavior.   Illness behavior is consistent with the degree of assimilation of the Indian family. Accordingly, one would expect individuals from traditional and neotraditional families to make use of herbal remedies and participate in ritual healing ceremonies; transitional families to utilize indigenous and mainstream methods; but bicultural and acculturated families to rely principally on U.S. institutional care (Red Horse, 1988).

Among the Native Americans there are persons and groups who serve as healers. They may be shamen, medicine persons, traditional healers, or clergy (for converts to Christianity), who provide culturally congruent forms of help. Some healers provide herbal remedies; others engage afflicted persons in healing ceremonies. At times a Caucasian American clinician will make a referral to a native healer. In the following case, an Indian doctor diagnosed and successfully treated a young woman with "soul loss sickness" by calling upon his own gifts to find and retrieve her lost soul:

> … he also stated that his spirit power had advised that the patient should become a spirit dancer for her own future protection, or else ancestral spirits would again take hold of her soul and cause her serious ills. Drumming started and while the patient appeared to re-enter the trance state in which she had been put initially under the effect of continuous rhythmic chanting and drumming, the *Indian Doctor* made gestures as if capturing the lost soul from the air, holding it in his closed hands. He then transferred the soul back to its owner by rubbing it on the patient's chest and sides. (Jilek & Jilek-Aall, 1981, p. 22)

Implications for Treatment. Mental health treatment of Native Americans within the mainstream mental health system should be consistent with the values and behaviors of the Indian's particular tribe and his or her degree of assimilation with mainstream U.S. culture. Some writers believe that Native Americans view family therapy as interference, whereas group treatment that is focused and task-centered is in keeping with the peer group orientation of Native Americans (Lewis & Keung Ho, 1975; Nofz, 1988). Nevertheless, other writers have been able to implement culturally sensitive family treatment with middle-class Native Americans (Attneave, 1982).

In treating Native Americans who have problems with alcohol, special attention should be given to the cultural component of drinking. For Native Americans drinking tends to be a peer group phenomenon that is associated with comradeship and solidarity rather than an individual means of escape (Anderson & Ellis, 1988). For some, drinking may be a way of overcoming shyness or their marginal social status (Anderson & Ellis, 1988; Nofz, 1988). Alcohol treatment in groups can use the peer group to promote cohesion without use of alcohol as a catalyst. Similarly, the cultural context of another social problem, suicide, should also be recognized (Davenport & Davenport, 1987). The clinician should inquire about the characteristics of the client's tribe and his or her preferred language and determine with which culture(s) the client identifies (Sutton & Broken Nose, 1996).

Asian Americans/Pacific Islanders

Asian and Pacific Island Americans are a growing population that consists of persons who have cultural roots in East Asia (Japan, China, Korea), Southeast Asia (Indonesia, Vietnam, Cambodia, Laos, Thailand, the Philippines, Burma), and the Pacific Islands (Guam, Samoa, Hawaii, and Tonga). Although the discussion here does not pertain to them, individuals from South Asia (Pakistan, India, Sri Lanka) are also considered Asian Americans (Kuramato, Morales, Munoz, Murase, 1983). The Chinese, Filipinos, and Japanese are the most populous Asian Americans (U.S. Bureau of the Census, 1997c).

Asian American populations have immigrated to the United States in waves at different historical moments. Elderly Asian Americans who came here from the old country and newer immigrants tend to adhere to traditional values and folkways, whereas those whose families have lived in the United States for a few generations tend to be more acculturated (Ishisaka & Takagi, 1982). In delivering ethnic sensitive mental health services, clinicians should consider generational and cultural differences, as well as the circumstances around immigration.

Asian Americans have been given the dubious compliment of "model minority" (Kim, 1973). Behaviors such as diligence and the willingness to make sacrifices, as well as relatively high educational levels and median incomes and low utilization of mental health resources have been viewed as indicators of successful adaptation (Crystal, 1989; Sue, Sue, & Sue, 1981). These findings belie problems with racism, the struggle for survival, and the stress that characterize the lives of Asian Americans and present obstacles to mental health resource utilization. Furthermore, the image of success has aroused the animosity of other minorities and has rendered Asian Americans ineligible for some affirmative action programs (Crystal, 1989).

Reports of relatively high incomes of Asian Americans obscure a number of factors that contribute to the appearance of success (Crystal, 1989). For one, they are underemployed in relation to their education. Many Asian American immigrants who have been professionally trained and certified in their countries of origin have not been able to acquire licenses in the United States. Instead they take jobs that are not commensurate with their skills. Second, their incomes appear high because of the prevalence of two wage earners in the same family. Third, aging Asian Americans and Pacific Islanders have an unusually high rate of poverty (Crystal, 1989). Fourth, some Asian Americans, especially those from Southeast Asia, are poor (Lee, 1996). As Table 7.1 showed, the poverty rate of Asian Americans/Pacific Islanders is 13.3 percent and the per capita income is below that of whites.

Cultural Values and Norms.   Although there is much diversity among Asian American and Pacific Island American cultures of origin, several values and cultural norms are common. Some of these are derived from the eastern religions of Confucianism, Buddhism, and Taoism. The interrelated values that will be emphasized here are family continuity, filial piety, avoidance of shame, and self-control.

The family is a pivotal source of values for Asian and Pacific Island Americans. Among those of East Asian origin, the family links individuals with their ancient forebears on the paternal side and insures the perpetuation of the family's good name (Shon & Ja, 1982). In keeping with these goals, families tend to be hierarchical, male dominated, and highly structured (Shon & Ja, 1982; Sue & Sue, 1988). Children are obligated to exhibit filial piety, that is, they are to be deferential, obedient, and loyal to their families (Ho, 1981). Grandparents and parents are afforded a great deal of respect and authority. Above all, family members must avoid shaming the family, the welfare of which supersedes the pursuit of individual goals (Ishisaka & Takagi, 1982). Asian Americans and Pacific Islanders are sensitive to appearances; if personal problems or behaviors that are discrepant with family and community expectations come to be known to others, the Asian American feels shame and loses face (Ho, 1981). Perpetrators of such behaviors not only disgrace themselves; they dishonor the family.

Among Asian Americans from Laos or Thailand, sex roles are more egalitarian. In Thailand there was greater sex role differentiation among the urban upper class than the rural people (Moore, 1974). Among the Laotians, traditional sex roles are observed in the family, yet women exert a great deal of influence in financial decisions and elicit deference (LeBarr & Suddard, 1960).

Asian Americans value self-control and emotional restraint (Ho, 1981; Sue & Sue, 1988). Families expect members to control their emotions and avoid antisocial behavior. Asians who subscribe to these values regard them as a sign of maturity (Ishisaka & Takagi, 1982). Indeed restraint may be viewed as a resource, in that it promotes qualities of self-discipline, patience, and diligence, which are instrumental in achieving success in American society. It is not, however, consonant with prevailing models of mental health treatment that require emotional expression.

Indigenous Concepts of Health, Mental Health, and Mental Illness.   Traditional Asian medicine embraces a holistic concept of health, mental health, and treatment (Marsella & Higginbotham, 1984). Mind, body, and spirit are thought to be a unity rather than separate systems. Health is equated with harmony or balance (Gould-Martin & Ngin, 1981). Traditional Chinese conceive of illness (mental or physical) as a dysharmony between two life forces, *yin* and *yang* (Kleinman, 1980). Life forces, such as the wind, can disrupt the balance by entering the body during periods of vulnerability (Gould-Martin & Ngin, 1981). Indigenous healing methods aim to restore internal harmony as well as the unity between the person and the environment, which is as extensive as the Cosmos.

Cultures of Asia and the Pacific have developed three explanations of the origins of behavioral dysfunction (Ishisaka & Takagi, 1982). The *social explanation* places responsibility on untoward circumstances, such as a death, marital conflict, or job loss. The position of victimization rather than individual responsibility is highlighted—evoking sympathetic responses, advice, and release from ordinary responsibilities from others. The second explanation, *moral,* arises when a person has violated values that the community regards as sacred. For the most part, these involve forsaking family obligations and prescribed modes of conduct. Community elders, priests, and family members intervene in response to these transgressions. The third explanation is *organic.* Asian cultures accept physical or somatic explanations and symptoms as part of life. Asian Americans have an easier time accepting somatic explanations than Western theories that blame the individual or family for dysfunctional behaviors (Ishisaka & Takagi, 1982).

Asians attach a great deal of stigma to mental illness, which invokes thoughts about family curses, witchcraft, and other supernatural forces (Marsella & Higginbotham, 1984). In order to avoid shame, Asians limit their concept of mental illness to the most severe psychotic problems (Kleinman, 1980). Symptoms that would be considered expressions of nonpsychotic mental health problems in Western cultures tend to be treated by health professionals or indigenous healers (Kleinman, 1980).

Culture-Specific Syndromes.   A number of syndromes of dysfunction that are prevalent among groups of Asian origins have been described in the literature. Among these are the following.

Amok is an outburst of aggression that is particularly prevalent among Southeast Asian (especially Malaysian) men. It begins with a period of brooding and can eventuate in an act of homicide. Later the amoker experiences exhaustion and amnesia and may kill himself. The expression, *running amok,* derives from this syndrome (Favazza, 1985; Kaplan & Sadock, 1988; Westermeyer, 1985).

Koro is an attack of anxiety associated with sexual organs. Men develop an intense fear that their penis is shrinking and receding into the stomach and that the result will be death. Women have similar fears centering on their breasts and labia. Koro is seen primarily in Asia, but has been reported in the West (Favazza, 1985; Westermeyer, 1985).

Latah is a startle response that is precipitated by a mild but sudden stimulus. The individual obeys and imitates the speech of others, regardless of the consequences. A syndrome of women of Southeast Asia, it has also been identified among the Bantu of Africa, the Ainu of Japan, and Malaysians (Favazza, 1985; Kaplan & Sadock, 1988; Westermeyer, 1985).

Illness Behavior.   Although low rates of utilization of mental health services have been reported in the literature, such findings should not be interpreted to mean that mental health problems are not prevalent or that Asian Americans do not need help (Crystal, 1989). Illness behavior is partially a function of the historical segregation and exclusion of Asian Americans from the mainstream, which made it necessary for ethnic communities to rely on each other and on indigenous resources to manage mental health problems. Moreover, cultural attitudes emphasize the primacy of families and extended networks as care givers of members with mental health problems. The cultural values of "saving face" and avoiding shame promote the maintenance of secrecy over problems to which stigma is attached (Crystal, 1989).

Asian American communities have their own healers, herbalists, physicians, and fortune tellers who provide culturally relevant help. Some Asian Americans treat themselves at home with herbs, which can be purchased in ethnic neighborhood herb shops (Gould-Martin & Ngin, 1981). Other home treatments include special foods, tonics, and patent medicines (Kleinman, 1980). Asian Americans may contact indigenous or Western-style physicians, as well as sacred healers, before they are willing to see a psychiatrist (Kleinman, 1980). Some engage in exercises such as *tai chi* and *chi gong* (Lee, 1996).

Implications for Treatment.   Mental health treatment of Asian Americans and Pacific Islanders should be in keeping with their cultural values and concepts of mental illness. The clinician should be an authority figure who respects the roles and relationships in the client's family. Demands that the client express emotions and direct anger at family members are inappropriate. On the other hand, therapy that emphasizes self-control, will power, and avoidance of disturbing thoughts may be helpful (Lee, 1982). The clinician should be aware that psychological problems are a source of stigma and may be expressed somatically. Furthermore, clinicians should recognize that Asian Americans may interact with others in ways that are in accord with cultural norms of proper behavior when, for example, they avoid eye contact (Toupin, 1981). Asian Americans have responsibilities to their families that continue throughout their lives. Rather than viewing intergenerational dependence as a problem, it should be viewed as a culturally congruent obligation (Lee, 1982) and as a strength.

Many Asian American communities have developed their own mutual assistance organizations that address the social, economic, and cultural needs of the community. These self-help organizations have arisen from needs that are not met by the larger community.

Social work clinicians who work with Asian Americans should become familiar with the particular organizations that are available in the communities in which their Asian American and Pacific Islander clients live and link clients with these organizations when the client needs are consistent with the services offered by these organizations.

The diversity among Asian Americans and Pacific Islanders calls for knowledge specific to each group. Particular attention should be given to the circumstances around immigration, identification with the original culture, and the extent of assimilation and integration into mainstream U.S. culture. Asian Americans/Pacific Islanders commonly present problems over acculturation, domestic violence, and war trauma and symptoms of somatization, dissociation, anxiety, and depression, but presenting issues differ among specific groups (Lee, 1996).

Hispanics/Latinos

The term *Hispanic* was constructed by the federal government to describe people from South America, Central America, North America, and the Caribbean, and others whose origins are Spanish (Castex, 1994). Several additional terms describe persons of Mexican background—Mexicans, Mexican Americans, and Chicanos. Some Hispanics prefer to be called *Latino* (masculine) or *Latina* (feminine). Considering that all these terms are constructions that have certain biases, here the terms *Hispanic* and *Latino* are used interchangeably. Although many Hispanics/Latinos speak Spanish as their primary language, substantial numbers are bilingual or predominantly English speaking; some speak other languages. Hispanics are multi-hued—black, brown, red, yellow, white, and various mixtures—and multiethnic. They are also heterogeneous in their lifestyles, cultural identification, politics, social class, education, and occupations.

According to 1999 estimates, there are 31.4 million Hispanics of any race, comprising 11.5 percent of the United States' population (U.S. Bureau of the Census, 1999b). These figures are probably an underestimate because of an unknown number of undocumented immigrants who enter the United States illegally. Hispanics are the second most populous and the fastest growing ethnic minority group in the United States. It is projected that by the middle of the twenty-first century, they will constitute close to 25 percent of the entire population (U.S. Bureau of the Census, 1998). Although their fertility rate is high, as Table 7.1 showed, so is their poverty rate. In 1997 close to 40 percent of Hispanic Americans were foreign born, having come largely from Mexico, Cuba, the Dominican Republic, and El Salvador; among Latinos in the United States, close to two-thirds are of Mexican origin (U.S. Bureau of the Census, 1998). Although Hispanics live throughout the country, they are concentrated in New Mexico, California, Texas, Arizona, Nevada, Florida, Colorado, and New York (U.S. Bureau of the Census, 1998).

Cultural Values and Norms.   Latinos have certain values that permeate their cultures. Primary among these is *respeto* (respect), which is accorded to one's parents, grandparents, elders, oneself, and others (Galan, 1985). Individuals are accorded respect on the basis of their inner qualities rather than their possessions—a form of individualism called *personalism* (Bernal, 1982; Garcia-Preto, 1982). Nevertheless, they do value hierarchy, especially within the family. Families tend to be patriarchal with traditional sex role expectations. Men are expected to be strong, hardworking, and dominant; women, passive, virtuous, and self-sacrificing (Garcia-Preto, 1982; Galan, 1985). The terms *machismo* and *marianismo* capture respective male and female sex role ideals. Financial pressures have made it necessary for women to participate in the labor market.

Hispanic families include biological and unrelated persons, who provide companionship and support to each other. Children have unrelated godparents who function as substitute parents and advisers to the family. Families tend to be large, cohesive, and interdependent. The strong emotional bonds within the family and three-generational families (Falicov, 1982) suggest that intergenerational enmeshment is normative.

Indigenous Concepts of Health, Mental Health, and Mental Illness and Their Causation.   Most of the Hispanic cultural groups do not distinguish between health and mental health (Delgado, 1977; Schreiber & Homiak, 1981). Like the Native Americans and Alaska Natives, they have a holistic view of the mind and body. When disorders that would be viewed as "psychiatric" in mainstream U.S. culture are viewed as folk illnesses, they are treated by folk healers or with folk remedies and/or by physicians or mental health professionals. Whichever sources are used, attention to the person as a whole, rather than a specific system, is in order (de la Rosa, 1988).

Mexican Americans have a concept of illness and disease that is sometimes called the *hot/cold theory* (Schreiber & Homiac, 1981). Rooted in the early Greek balance of humors theory, it views illness (mental or physical) as a state of disequilibrium caused by excessive exposure to heat or cold. Various internal and external objects, as well as emotional experiences, are classified as either hot or cold. For example, water and certain foods are considered cold; the sun and herbal teas are classified as hot. Treatment consists of neutralizing the excessive condition by drawing it off or consuming its opposite.

Among Puerto Ricans, *spiritism* is a prevalent belief. This is based partially on the Roman Catholic idea of a duality between material and spiritual worlds. One form of spiritism, *santeria,* is Nigerian in origin (Berthold, 1989). Adherents of spiritism believe that disembodied spirits of divine or deceased beings attach themselves to individuals at the time they are born and continue to influence their lives (Berthold, 1989; de la Rosa, 1988; Harwood, 1981b). Good spirits, such as one's guardian angel, help and protect individuals and influence their reaching higher goals. On the other hand, bad spirits can instigate problems either on their own or at the request of a living person who recruits them to engage in sorcery. The workings of malevolent spirits can result in physical or mental ailments (Harwood, 1981b).

Culture-Specific Syndromes.   Some syndromes are reported with excess among Hispanics. Puerto Ricans are susceptible to *ataques,* sometimes referred to as the *ataques de nervios* (nervous attacks). These are seizures that usually occur following emotionally disturbing events, but they may be unpredictable and idiosyncratic (Harwood, 1981b). Their core feature is the feeling of being out of control (Guarnaccio, Rivera, Franco, & Neighbors, 1996). *Ataques* are more common among persons of lower socioeconomic classes and among women and are culturally sanctioned under trying circumstances, such as at a death (Harwood, 1981b). Another syndrome that occurs with frequency among Hispanics is *susto,* or fright. Similar to anxiety disorders, it is characterized by such symptoms as diarrhea, loss of appetite, weight loss, restlessness, and vertigo. Like *ataques, susto* develops at times of stress (Schreiber & Homiac, 1981).

Illness Behavior.   Hispanics have a number of natural support systems available to them to help with health and mental health problems—the family system, the church, merchants' and social clubs, and folk healers (Delgado & Humm-Delgado, 1982). The family system provides emotional support, baby-sitting services, and home remedies (over-the-counter drugs, herbs, etc.) to persons with health or mental health problems. Another supportive system is the church, the Roman Catholic church being the most prominent. Although the historical link of the Roman Catholic church with the external power structure has created ambivalence toward religion among Hispanics, for some the church provides a source of meaning, consolation, and support (Gibson, 1985). Merchants' and social clubs are organizations that provide information, supplies, and social contacts that are culturally congruent. One type is a botanical shop (*botanica*), which sells herbs and objects needed in healing ceremonies, gives advice about illnesses, and makes referrals to folk healers. Another establishment is the *bodega* (grocery store), which not only sells native food but also makes referrals (Delgado & Humm-Delgado, 1982).

The fourth system consists of folk healers, which have different names and functions for different Hispanic groups. Puerto Rican Americans go to spiritists for help with anxiety or somatic symptoms that have no organic cause (Delgado, 1978). Spiritists may recommend that clients participate in a healing ceremony that is attended by family members, mediums (persons who have the power to communicate with spirits), and others with infirmities. During the ceremony, candles are lit, prayers are read, the cause is discovered, and a spiritual cleansing is enacted. Spiritism, however, is not the only form of folk healing. Those Puerto Ricans and Cubans who practice *santeria* engage in its healing ceremony. Another type of folk healer is the herbalist, who recommends herbs in keeping with the hot/cold theory. A third type of healer found in Hispanic communities is the *curandero,* who views illness as the result of alienation from the Roman Catholic church. The *curandero's* treatment aims to bring the individual closer to the church and its teachings (Delgado & Humm-Delgado, 1982).

Implications for Treatment.   Latino clients make their own decisions, in consultation with significant others, with respect to the use of indigenous and/or mainstream mental health services. Because of a tendency to focus on somatic complaints, some Hispanics may use the health care system when the mental health care system may seem to be more appropriate. Those who do use the mental health care system should be provided with culturally congruent treatment. Delgado (1988) finds commonalities between folk healing and psychodrama that make it feasible to incorporate aspects of spiritism into group work treatment. He recommends that group leaders be authoritative, that the membership be diverse, and that activities rather than only verbal expression be emphasized. Similarly, Berthold (1989) sees parallels between spiritist healing and psychoanalytic treatment. The invocation of invisible spirits and causes in spiritism is not unlike the mobilization of unconscious forces and the ego in psychoanalysis. Both systems "work the cause" and restore individual functioning.

Summary and Deconstruction

This chapter described the historical context, concepts, and motifs relevant to understanding and working with clients from diverse racial, ethnic, and cultural groups. It discussed sociological and anthropological concepts and examined illness behavior and misdiagnosis of ethnic minorities. The chapter focused particularly on African Americans, Native Americans/Alaska Natives, Asian/Pacific Islanders, and Hispanics/Latinos—who are constructed as "other" in the United States. Although each group is itself multicultural, some general characteristics of each group were described. Postmodern clinicians use this knowledge as a resource but avoid essentializing individuals and groups.

Cultural information can contribute to ethnic sensitivity and cultural competence, but this is not enough. Clinical social workers need to reflect on the norms and values of their own ethnicities and their attitudes toward their own group and people who are different. Although most social workers are Caucasian, few contemplate their white racial identity and what it means to have privileges based on an accident of birth. Those social workers who are African American, Native American, Asian, or Latino may also be of mixed racial and ethnic background, including Caucasian. They have feelings about any of these categories and, in many cases, being partially white. Although this chapter did not directly address other differences (e.g., religion, social class, gender, sexual orientation, and disability), these, too, enter into cross-cultural behavioral health practice. Regardless of one's cultural background, one identifies with varying degrees of positive and negative feeling with one's own group(s).

Helms and Cook (1999) describe a process of maturation of ego statuses that people of color (including clinicians) experience. It begins with negative identification with one's own group (conformity), and proceeds with dissonance (ambivalence), immersion (idealization of one's own group), and emersion (euphoria over being with people of one's own group). It moves to internalization (positive identification with one's own group), and integrated awareness (valuing one's collective identity and those of other oppressed groups). The authors describe a similar but reverse process in which whites undo their racial stereotypes and white privilege and become autonomous (nonracist and humanistic) (Helms & Cook, 1999). With knowledge and self-awareness, one is ready to engage in clinical social work practice with people of diverse cultures.

D I S C U S S I O N   Q U E S T I O N S

1. Define and differentiate race, ethnicity, minority group, and culture.

2. Discuss whether the following groups are cultures: gay men, lesbians, the physically disabled (persons who are blind, deaf, in wheelchairs, etc.), persons with chronic mental illness, battered women, and recovering alcoholics.

3. Explain the impact of historical oppression on minorities of color.

4. Why do you think it is common among some ethnic minority groups to present psychological problems in terms of somatic complaints?

5. What is the responsibility of the clinical social worker whose ethnicity is different from that of a client with respect to relationship building, assessment, and treatment?

6. Consider the cultural issues in the following cases:
   a. A Native American man referred to Alcoholics Anonymous refuses to discuss his problems with the heterogeneously constituted group.
   b. An African American woman informed a white intake worker that she comes from a "black middle-class family." A white American does not ordinarily say, "I come from a white middle-class family," although he or she might report a "middle-class" background. Why do you suppose the African American woman described her family background in the way she did?
   c. A woman of Puerto Rican ethnicity came to the mental health clinic with her mother. When the social worker indicated that only the daughter was to be interviewed, the daughter and mother were visibly shaken.
   d. An older Chinese American man who appeared to be socially withdrawn said very little about his problem to the white, youthful female clinician, even though a Chinese (female) interpreter was provided.

7. In what ways do European American values conflict with the values of other cultural groups?

8. Explain how race, gender, and social class interact with one another with respect to mental health.

9. What is meant by bicultural socialization? What are the implications of this phenomenon for clinical practice?

10. What are culture-specific syndromes? Explain their implications for assessment and treatment.

11. In what ways might clinical social workers and indigenous healers work together?

12. How do you explain the low utilization of some mental health services by some groups and the higher use by other groups?

Suggested Activity

Ethnographic interviewing is a means of getting to know persons of diverse cultural backgrounds, which is used by anthropologists and researchers of other disciplines who have a cultural perspective. Such an approach facilitates understanding of the emic (indigenous) perspective. After reading about ethnographic interviewing in the following sources, conduct an ethnographic interview with a client of a culture that is different from your own. Then write a narrative report following the Outline on Cultural Formulation (see Table 7.2).

1. Green, J. W. (1995). Language and crosscultural social work. In J. W. Green (Ed.), *Cultural awareness in the human services* (pp. 130–154). Boston, MA: Allyn & Bacon.

2. Spradley, J. P. (1979). *The ethnographic interview.* New York: Holt, Rinehart and Winston.

REFERENCES

Allen, I. M. (1986). Posttraumatic stress disorder among Black Vietnam veterans. *Hospital and Community Psychiatry, 37,* 55–61.

American Psychiatric Association (APA) (1994). *Diagnostic and Statistical Manual of Mental Disorders,* (4th ed.). (*DSM-IV*). Washington, DC: Author.

de Anda, D. (1984). Bicultural socialization: Factors affecting the minority experience. *Social Work, 29,* 101–107.

Anderson, M. J., & Ellis, R. (1988). On the reservation. In N. A. Vacc, J. Wittmer, & S. B. DeVaney, (Eds.), *Experiencing and counseling multicultural and diverse populations* (2nd ed., pp. 107–126). Muncie, IN: Accelerated Development.

Attneave, C. (1982). American Indians and Alaska Native families: Emigrants in their own homeland. In M. McGoldrick, J. K. Pearce, & J. Giordano (Eds.), *Ethnicity and family therapy* (pp. 55–83). New York: Guilford Press.

Bernal, G. (1982). Cuban families. In M. McGoldrick, J. K. Pearce, & J. Giordano (Eds.), *Ethnicity and family therapy* (pp. 187–207). New York: Guilford Press.

Berthold, S. M. (1989). Spiritism as a form of psychotherapy: Implications for social work practice. *Social Casework, 70,* 502–509.

Blanchard, E. L. (1987). American Indians and Alaskan Natives. In A. Minahan (Ed.), *Encyclopedia of social work* (Vol. 1, pp. 141–150). Silver Spring, MD: National Association of Social Workers.

Bosmajian, H. (1974). *The language of oppression.* Washington, DC: Public Affairs Press.

Boyd-Franklin, N. (1989). *Black families in therapy: A multisystems approach.* New York: The Guilford Press.

Broman, C. L. (1987). Race differences in professional help seeking. *American Journal of Community Psychology, 15,* 473–489.

Brown v. Board of Education of Topeka, Kansas, 348 US 8861 (1954).

Cafferty, P. S. J., & Chestang, L. (Eds.). (1976). *The diverse society: Implications for social policy.* Washington, DC: National Association of Social Workers.

Caldwell, C. H. (1996). Predisposing, enabling, and need factors related to patterns of help-seeking among African American women. In H. W. Neighbors & J. S. Jackson (Eds.), *Mental health in Black America* (pp. 146–160). Thousand Oaks, CA: Sage Publications.

Carpenter, E. M. (1980). Social services, policies, and issues. *Social Casework, 61,* 455–461.

Castex, G. M. (1994). Providing services to Hispanic/Latino populations: Profiles in diversity. *Social Work, 39,* 288–296.

Chestang, L. (1976). Environmental influences on social functioning: The Black experience. In P. S. J. Cafferty, & L. Chestang, (Eds.), *The diverse society: Implications for social policy* (pp. 59–74). Washington, DC: National Association of Social Workers.

Cole, J., & Pilisuk, M. (1976). Differences in the provision of mental health services by race. *American Journal of Orthopsychiatry, 46,* 510–525.

Crystal, D. (1989). Asian Americans and the myth of the model minority. *Social Casework, 70,* 405–413.

Davenport, J. A., & Davenport, J., III. (1987). Native American suicide: A Durkheimian analysis. *Social Casework, 68,* 533–539.

Davis, L. E., & Proctor, E. K. (1989). *Race, gender and class.* Englewood Cliffs, NJ: Prentice-Hall.

Delgado, M. (1977). Puerto Rican spiritualism and the social work profession. *Social Casework, 8,* 451–458.

Delgado, M. (1978). Folk medicine in Puerto Rican culture. *International Social Work, 21,* 46–54.

Delgado, M. (1988). Groups in Puerto Rican spiritism: Implications for clinicians. In C. Jacobs & D. D. Bowles (Eds.), *Ethnicity and race: Critical concepts in social work* (pp. 34–47). Silver Spring, MD: National Association of Social Workers.

Delgado, M., & Humm-Delgado, D. (1982). Natural support systems: Source of strength in Hispanic communities. *Social Work, 27,* 83–89.

Devore, W., & Schlesinger, E. G. (1996). *Ethnic-sensitive social work practice* (4th ed.). Boston: Allyn and Bacon.

Eaton, W. W., Dryman, A., & Weissman, M. M. (1991). Panic and phobia. In L. N. Robins & D. A. Regier (Eds.), *Psychiatric disorders in America: The epidemiologic catchment area study* (pp. 155–179). New York: The Free Press.

Escobar, J. I. (1987). Cross-cultural aspects of the somatization trait. *Hospital and Community Psychiatry, 38,* 174–180.

Escobar, J. I. (1998). Immigration and mental health: Why are immigrants better off? *Archives of General Psychiatry, 55,* 781–782.

Estrada, L. F. (1987). Hispanics. In A. Minahan (Ed.), *Encyclopedia of social work* (Vol. 1, pp. 732–739). Silver Spring, MD: National Association of Social Workers.

Falicov, C. J. (1982). Mexican families. In M. McGoldrick, J. K. Pearce, & J. Giordano (Eds.), *Ethnicity and family therapy,* (pp. 134–163). New York: Guilford Press.

Favazza, A. R. (1985). Contributions of the sociocultural sciences: Anthropology and psychiatry. In H. I. Kaplan & B. J. Sadock (Eds.), *Comprehensive textbook of psychiatry* (4th ed., pp. 247–265). Baltimore, MD: Williams & Wilkins.

Galan, F. J. (1985). Traditional values about family behavior: The case of the Chicano client. *Social Thought, 11*(3), 14–22.

Garcia-Preto, N. (1982). Puerto Rican families. In M. McGoldrick, J. K. Pearce, & J. Giordano (Eds.), *Ethnicity and family therapy* (pp. 164–186). New York: Guilford Press.

Gibson, G. (1985). Chicanos and their support systems in interaction with social institutions. In M. Bloom

(Ed.), Life span development (2nd ed., pp. 464–479). New York: Macmillan.

Gibson, G. (1987). Mexican Americans. In A. Minahan (Ed.), *Encyclopedia of social work* (Vol. 2, pp. 135–148). Silver Spring, MD: National Association of Social Workers.

Goldsby, R. A. (1977). *Race and races* (2nd ed.). New York: Macmillan.

Good, B. J. (1996). Culture and DSM-IV: Diagnosis, knowledge and power. *Culture, Medicine and Psychiatry, 20,* 127–132.

Gould-Martin, K., & Ngin, C. (1981). Chinese Americans. In A. Harwood (Ed.), *Ethnicity and medical care* (pp. 130–171). Cambridge, MA: Harvard University Press.

Greeley, A. M. (1976). Why study ethnicity? In P. S. J. Cafferty & L. Chestang (Eds.), *The diverse society: Implications for social policy* (pp. 3–12). Washington, DC: National Association of Social Workers.

Green, J. W. (1995). *Cultural awareness in the human services,* (2nd ed.). Boston: Allyn and Bacon.

Grier, W. H., & Cobbs, P. M. (1968). *Black rage.* New York: Bantam Books.

Guarnaccia, P. J., Rivera, M., Franco, F., & Neighbors, C. (1996). The experiences of *ataques de nervios:* Towards an anthropology of emotions in Puerto Rico. *Culture, Medicine and Psychiatry, 20,* 343–367.

Hall, E. T. (1959). *The silent language.* New York: Anchor Books.

Harwood, A. (Ed.). (1981a). *Ethnicity and medical care.* Cambridge, MA: Harvard University Press.

Harwood, A. (1981b). Mainland Puerto Ricans. In A. Harwood (Ed.), *Ethnicity and medical care* (pp. 397–481). Cambridge, MA: Harvard University Press.

Helms, J. E., & Cook, D. A. (1999). *Using race and culture in counseling and psychotherapy: Theory and process.* Boston: Allyn and Bacon.

Helzer, J. E., Burnam, A., & McEvoy, L. T. (1991). Alcohol use and dependence. In L. N. Robins & D. A. Regier (Eds.), *Psychiatric disorders in America: The epidemiologic catchment area study* (pp. 81–115). New York: The Free Press.

Hill, R. B. (1971). *The strengths of Black families.* New York: National Urban League.

Hines, P. M., & Boyd-Franklin, N. (1982). Black families. In M. McGoldrick, J. K. Pearce, & J. Giordano (Eds.), *Ethnicity and family therapy* (pp. 84–107). New York: Guilford Press.

Hines, P. M., & Boyd-Franklin, N. (1996). African American families. In M. McGoldrick, J. Giordano, & J. K. Pearce (Eds.), *Ethnicity and family therapy* (2nd ed., pp. 66–84). New York: The Guilford Press.

Hirayama, H., & Cetingok, M. (1988). Empowerment: A social work approach for Asian immigrants. *Social Casework, 69,* 41–47.

Ho, M. K. (1981). Social work with Asian Americans. In R. H. Dana (Ed.), *Human services for cultural minorities* (pp. 307–316). Baltimore, MD: University Park Press. Originally published in *Social Casework, 57,* 195–201.

Hopps, J. (1982). Oppression based on color. *Social Work, 27,* 3–5.

Hopps, J. G. (1987). Minorities of color. In A. Minahan (Ed.), *Encyclopedia of social work,* 18th edition, vol. 2, (pp. 161–171). Silver Spring, MD: NASW.

Hu, T., Snowden, L. R., Jerrell, J. M., & Nguyen, T. D. (1991). Ethnic populations in public mental health: Services choice and level of use. *American Journal of Public Health, 81,* 1429–1434.

Ishisaka, H. A., & Takagi, C. Y. (1982). Social work with Asian- and Pacific-Americans. In J. W. Green (Ed.), *Cultural awareness in the human services* (pp. 122–156). Englewood Cliffs, NJ: Prentice-Hall.

Jackson, J. J. (1981). Urban Black Americans. In A. Harwood (Ed.), Ethnicity and medical care (pp. 37–129). Cambridge, MA: Harvard University Press.

Javier, R. A. (1989). Linguistic considerations in the treatment of bilinguals. *Psychoanalytic Psychology, 6,* 87–96.

Jilek, W., & Jilek-Aall, L. (1981). The psychiatrist and shaman colleague: Cross-cultural collaboration with traditional Amerindian therapists. In R. H. Dana (Ed.), *Human services for cultural minorities* (pp. 15–26). Baltimore, MD: University Park Press. Originally published in *Journal of Operational Psychiatry* (1978), *9*(2), 32–39.

Johnson, B. B. (1982). American Indian jurisdiction as a policy issue. *Social Work, 27,* 31–37.

Jones, B. E., & Gray, B. A. (1986). Problems in diagnosing schizophrenia and affective disorders among Blacks. *Hospital and Community Psychiatry, 37,* 61–65.

Juliá, M. (1996). *Multicultural awareness in the health care professions.* Boston: Allyn and Bacon.

Kamya, H. A. (1997). African immigrants in the United States: The challenge for research and practice. *Social Work, 42,* 154–165.

Kaplan, H. I., & Sadock, B. J. (1988). *Synopsis of psychiatry* (5th ed., chap. 5.6). Baltimore, MD: Williams & Wilkins.

Kasl, S. V., & Cobb, S. (1966). Health behavior, illness behavior, and sick role. *Archives of Environmental Health, 12,* 246–266.

Kessler, R. C., McGonagle, K. A., Zhao, S., Nelson, C. B., Hughes, M., Eshleman, S., Wittchen, H-U., & Kendler, K. S. (1994). Lifetime and 12-month prevalence of DSM-III-R psychiatric disorders in the United States: Results from the National Comorbidity Survey. *Archives of General Psychiatry, 51,* 8–19.

Kim, B-L. C. (1973). Asian Americans: No model minority. *Social Work, 18,* 44–53.

Kitano, H. H. L. (1985). *Race relations* (3rd ed.). Engle-wood Cliffs, NJ: Prentice-Hall.

Kitano, H. H. L. (1987). Asian Americans. In A. Minahan (Ed.), *Encyclopedia of social work* (Vol. 1, pp. 156–171). Silver Spring, MD: National Association of Social Workers.

Kleinman, A. (1980). *Patients and healers in the context of culture.* Berkeley, CA: University of California Press.

Kleinman, A. (1988). *The illness narrative: Suffering, healing, and the human condition.* New York: Basic Books.

Kunitz, S. J., & Levy, J. E. (1981). Navajos. In A. Harwood (Ed.), *Ethnicity and medical care* (pp. 337–396). Cambridge, MA: Harvard University Press.

Kuramoto, F. H., Morales, R. F., Munoz, F. U., & Murase, K. (1983). Education for social work practice in Asian and Pacific American communities. In J. C. Chunn II, P. J. Dunston, & F. Ross-Sheriff (Eds.), *Mental health and people of color* (pp. 127–155). Washington, DC: Howard University Press.

Lawson, W. B. (1986). Racial and ethnic factors in psychiatric research. *Hospital and Community Psychiatry, 37,* 50–54.

Leaf, P. J., Livingston, M. M., Tischler, G. L., Weissman, M. M., Holzer, C. E. 3d, & Myers, J. K. (1985). Contact with health professionals for the treatment of psychiatric and emotional problems. *Medical Care, 23,* 1322–1337.

LeBar, F. M., & Suddard, A. (1960). *Laos: Its people, its society, its culture.* New Haven, CT: HRAF Press.

Lee, E. (1982). A social systems approach to assessment and treatment for Chinese American families. In M. McGoldrick, J. K. Pearce, & J. Giordano (Eds.), *Ethnicity and family therapy* (pp. 527–551). New York: Guilford Press.

Lee, E. (1996). Asian American families: An overview. In M. McGoldrick, J. Giordano, & J. K. Pearce (Eds.), *Ethnicity and family therapy,* (2nd ed., pp. 227–248). New York: The Guilford Press.

Leigh, J. W., & Green, J. W. (1982). The structure of the Black community: The knowledge base for social services. In J. W. Green (Ed.), *Cultural awareness in the human services* (pp. 94–121). Englewood Cliffs, NJ: Prentice-Hall.

Lewis, R. (1985). Cultural perspectives on treatment modalities with Native Americans. In M. Bloom (Ed.), *Life span development* (2nd ed., pp. 458–464). New York: Macmillan.

Lewis, R. G. (1995). American Indians. In R. L. Edwards (Ed.), *Encyclopedia of social work* (19th ed., pp. 216–225). Washington, DC: NASW Press.

Lewis, R. G., & Keung Ho, M. (1975). Social work with Native Americans. *Social Work, 20,* 375–382.

Lewis-Fernández, R. (1996). Cultural formulation of psychiatric diagnosis. *Culture, Medicine and Psychiatry, 20,* 133–144.

Lim, R. F., & Lin, K. M. (1996). Cultural formulation of psychiatric diagnosis. Case No. 03. Psychosis following Qi-Gong in a Chinese immigrant. *Culture, Medicine and Psychiatry, 20,* 369–378.

Lopez, S. R. (1989). Patient variable biases in clinical judgment: Conceptual overview and methodological considerations. *Psychological Bulletin, 106,* 184–203.

Lum, D. (1986). Social work practice and people of color. *A process-stage approach.* Monterey, CA: Brooks/Cole.

Marsella, A. J., & Higginbotham, H. N. (1984). Traditional Asian medicine: Applications to psychiatric services in developing nations. In P. B. Pedersen, N. Sartorius, & A. J. Marsella (Eds.), *Mental health services: The cross-cultural context* (pp. 175–197). Beverly Hills, CA: Sage Publications.

Matsuoka, J., Breaux, C., & Ryujin, D. H. (1997). National utilization of mental health services by Asian Americans/Pacific Islanders. *Journal of Community Psychology, 25,* 141–145.

McAdoo, H. P. (1987). Blacks. In A. Minahan (Ed.), *Encyclopedia of social work* (18th ed., Vol. 1, pp. 194–206). Silver Spring, MD: National Association of Social Workers.

McGoldrick, M., Giordano, J., & Pearce, J. K. (1996). *Ethnicity and family therapy,* 2nd ed. New York: The Guilford Press.

Mishler, E. G. (1984). *The discourse of medicine: Dialectics of medical interviews.* Norwood, NJ: Ablex.

Moore, F. J. (1974). *Thailand: Its people, its society, its culture.* New Haven, CT: HRAF Press.

National Association of Social Workers (NASW). (1997). NASW Code of Ethics. Approved by the 1996 NASW Delegate Assembly. In R. L. Edwards (Ed.), *Encyclopedia of social work,* (19th ed.) 1997 supplement (pp. 371–385). Author: NASW Press.

Nobles, W. W. (1976). Black people in white insanity: An issue for Black community mental health. *The Journal of Afro-American Issues, 4,* 21–27.

Nofz, M. P. (1988). Alcohol abuse and culturally marginal American Indians. *Social Casework, 69,* 67–73.

Norton, D. G. (Ed.). (1978). *The dual perspective: Inclusion of ethnic minority content in the social work curriculum.* New York: Council on Social Work Education.

Oliver, M. (1983). *Social work with disabled people.* London: Macmillan.

Parsons, T. (1964). *The social system.* New York: Free Press.

Pilgrim, D., & Rogers, A. (1999). *A sociology of mental health and illness* (2nd ed.). Buckingham, UK and Philadelphia, PA: Open University Press.

Pinderhughes, E. (1982). Afro-American families and the victim system. In M. McGoldrick, J. K. Pearce, & J. Giordano (Eds.), *Ethnicity and family therapy* (pp. 108–122). New York: Guilford Press.

Plessy v. Ferguson, 163 US, 537 (1896).

Red Horse, J. G. (1980a). American Indian elders: Unifiers of Indian families. *Social Casework, 61,* 490–493.

Red Horse, J. G. (1980b). Family structure and value orientation in American Indians. *Social Casework, 61,* 462–467.

Red Horse, J. G. (1988). Cultural evolution of American Indian families. In C. Jacobs & D. D. Bowles (Eds.), *Ethnicity and race: Critical concepts in social work* (pp. 86–102). Silver Spring, MD: National Association of Social Workers.

Robins, L. N., Locke, B. Z., & Regier, D. A. (1991). An overview of psychiatric disorders in America. In L. N. Robins & D. A. Regier (Eds.), *Psychiatric disorders in America: The epidemiologic catchment area study* (pp. 328–366). New York: The Free Press.

de la Rosa, M. (1988). Puerto Rican spiritualism: A key dimension for effective social casework practice with Puerto Ricans. *International Social Work, 31,* 273–283.

Sands, R. G., & Nuccio, K. (1989). Mother-headed single parent families: A feminist perspective. *Affilia, 4,* 25–41.

Schiele, J. H. (1996). Afrocentricity: An emerging paradigm in social work practice. *Social Work, 41,* 284–294.

Schreiber, J. M., & Homiak, J. P. (1981). Mexican Americans. In A. Harwood (Ed.), *Ethnicity and medical care* (pp. 264–336). Cambridge, MA: Harvard University Press.

Shon, S. P., & Ja, D. Y. (1982). Asian families. In M. McGoldrick, J. K. Pearce, & J. Giordano (Eds.), *Ethnicity and family therapy* (pp. 208–228). New York: Guilford Press.

Snowden, L. R., & Cheung, F. K. (1990). Use of inpatient mental health services by members of ethnic minority groups. *American Psychologist, 45,* 347–355.

Snowden, L. R., & Holschuh, J. (1992). Ethnic differences in emergency psychiatric care and hospitalization in a program for the severely mentally ill. *Community Mental Health Journal, 28,* 281–291.

Solomon, B. (1976). *Black empowerment: Social work in oppressed communities.* New York: Columbia University Press.

Steinberg, M. D., Pardes, H., Bjork, D., & Sporty, D. (1977). Demographic and clinical characteristics of Black psychiatric patients in a private general hospital. *Hospital and Community Psychiatry, 28,* 128–132.

Substance Abuse and Mental Health Services Administration. (1996). Mental health estimates from the 1994 National Household Survey on Drug Abuse. Rockville, MD: Author.

Sue, D. M., & Sue, D. (1988). Asian-Americans. In N. A. Vacc, J. Wittmer, & S. B. DeVaney (Eds.), *Experiencing and counseling multicultural and diverse populations* (2nd ed., pp. 239–262). Muncie, IN: Accelerated Development.

Sue, S. (1977). Community mental health services to minority groups. *American Psychologist, 32,* 616–624.

Sue, S., Sue, D. W., & Sue, D. W. (1981). Asian Americans as a minority group. In R. H. Dana (Ed.), *Human services for cultural minorities* (pp. 287–294). Baltimore, MD: University Park Press. Originally published in *American Psychologist* (1975), 30, 906–910.

Sussman, L., Robins, L., & Earls, F. (1987). Treatment-seeking for depression by black and white Americans. *Social Science and Medicine, 3,* 187–196.

Sutton, C. T., & Broken Nose, M. A. (1996). American Indian families: An overview. In M. McGoldrick, J. Giordano, & J. K. Pearce (Eds.), *Ethnicity and family therapy* (2nd ed., pp. 31–44). New York: The Guilford Press.

Takeuchi, D. T., Euhara, E., & Maramba, G. (1999). Cultural diversity and mental health treatment. In A. V. Horwitz & T. L. Scheid (Eds.), *A handbook for the study of mental health: Social contexts, theories, and systems* (pp. 550–565). Cambridge, UK: Cambridge University Press.

Taylor, R. J., Neighbors, H. W., & Broman, C. L. (1989). Evaluation by Black Americans of the social service encounter during a serious personal problem. *Social Work, 34,* 205–211.

Toupin, E. S. W. A. (1981). Counseling Asians: Psychotherapy in the context of racism and Asian-American history. In R. H. Dana (Ed.), *Human services for cultural minorities* (pp. 295–306). Baltimore, MD: University Park Press. Originally published in *The American Journal of Orthopsychiatry* (1980), 50, 76–86.

Trimble, J. E., Manson, S. M., Dinges, N. G., & Medicine, B. (1984). American Indian concepts of mental health: Reflections and directions. In P. B. Pedersen, N. Sartorius, & A. J. Marsella (Eds.), *Mental health services: The cross-cultural context* (pp. 199–220). Beverly Hills, CA: Sage Publications.

U.S. Bureau of the Census. (1988a). *The Hispanic population in the United States: March 1988. Advance report.* (Current Population Reports, Series P-20, No. 431). Washington, DC: U.S. Government Printing Office.

U.S. Bureau of the Census. (1988b). *Money income and poverty status in the United States: 1987.* Advance data from the March 1988 current population survey. (Current Population Reports, Series P-60, No. 161). Washington, DC: U.S. Government Printing Office.

U.S. Bureau of the Census. (1988c). *The Black population in the United States: March 1988.* (Current Population Reports, Series P-20, No. 442). Washington, DC: U.S. Government Printing Office.

U.S. Bureau of the Census. (1989a). *Household and family characteristics: March 1986.* (Current Population Reports, Series P-20, No. 419, Table F). Washington, DC: U.S. Government Printing Office.

U.S. Bureau of the Census. (1989b). *Poverty in the United States: 1987.* (Current Population Reports, Series P-60, No. 163, Table 1). Washington, DC: U.S. Government Printing Office.

U.S. Bureau of the Census. (1997a). *Statistical abstract of the United States: 1997* (117th ed.). Washington, DC, 1997, Table No. 52. Based on U.S. Bureau of the Census, *1990 Census of Population, Characteristics of American Indians by Tribe and Language,* 1990 CP-3-7.

U.S. Bureau of the Census. (1997b). *Statistical abstract of the United States: 1997* (117th ed.). Washington, DC, 1997, Table No. 51. Based on U.S. Bureau of the Census, *1990 Census of Population Characteristics, American Indian and Alaska Native Areas* (SP-1-1A).

U.S. Bureau of the Census. (1997c). *Statistical abstract of the United States: 1997* (117th ed.). Washington, DC, 1997, Table No. 30. Based on U.S. Bureau of the Census, *1990 Census of Population, General Population Characteristics, United States* (CP-1-1).

U.S. Bureau of the Census. (1998). *Press release: Hispanic Heritage Month.* Obtained from http://www.census.gov/Press-Release/cb98-ff.11.html.

U.S. Bureau of the Census (1999a). *Money income in the United States: 1997 and Poverty in the United States: 1997.* March 1998 supplement to the Current Population Survey (CPS). Obtained from http://www.census.gov/hhes/poverty/poverty 97/pov97hi.html.

U.S. Bureau of the Census. (1999b). *Resident population estimates of the United States by sex, race, and Hispanic origin: April 1, 1990 to July 1, 1999.* Population Estimates Program, Population Division, Washington, DC Obtained from http://www.census.gov/population/estimates/nation/intfile3-1.txt.

U.S. Bureau of the Census. (1999c). *Number of African Americans in poverty declines while income rises, Census Bureau reports* (press release). Obtained from http://www.census.gov/Press-Release/cb98-176.html.

Vega, W. A., Kolody, B., Aguilar-Gaxiola, S., Alderete, E., Catalano, R., & Caraveo-Anduaga, J. (1998). Lifetime prevalence of DSM-III-R psychiatric disorders among urban and rural Mexican-Americans in California. *Archives of General Psychiatry, 55,* 771–778.

Walker, A. (1983). My father's country is the poor. *In search of our mother's gardens* (pp. 199–222). New York: Harcourt Brace Janovich.

Westermeyer, J. (1985). Psychiatric diagnosis across cultural boundaries. *American Journal of Psychiatry, 142,* 798—805.

World Health Organization. (1975). *Schizophrenia: A multinational study.* Geneva, Switzerland: World Health Organization Press.

8 Clinical Practice with Depressed Clients

How do I go forward with all of this emptiness? I'm sick to the deepest part of my soul of trying to find inner peace. There has got to be another way, but I'll be damned if I can find it. Help.

—Long-Tims, "Still Searching," 1996

Depression is more prevalent, causes more suffering, and has a more devastating impact on individual functioning and societal welfare than the public, policymakers, and even many health professionals realize.

—Wells, Sturm, Sherbourne, & Meredith, *Caring for Depression,* 1996

Depression is a heterogeneous mood disorder that affects 6 to 20 percent of the population during their lifetimes (Kessler, Abelson, & Zhao, 1998; Regier et al., 1988). It is characterized by sadness, irritability, lack of energy or interest in life, slowed movements, pessimism, feelings of worthlessness, guilt, morbid thinking, and changes in patterns of eating and sleeping. The prevailing feeling is pain that does not seem to go away. Unbearable pain can result in suicide attempts or actualities.

Depression as a mental disorder should be distinguished from the "blues" and "down days," which are ordinary experiences that are associated with everyday disappointments, losses, and changes that are a part of life. Usually these feelings follow an event or interaction that is inconsistent with one's expectations or hopes. Feelings like these fade on their own or are relieved when one comes to terms with the situation or takes assertive action. Depressed feelings are constructed as manifestations of a mental disorder when they are experienced with great intensity, when they have a prolonged course, when they interfere with psychosocial functioning, and when they cluster with other symptoms.

A postmodern perspective on depression draws attention to the complexity of the disorder and the variability of its expression. As Table 8.1 shows, depressive symptoms occur on multiple domains. Furthermore, there are many kinds of depression and each individual puts his or her own unique inscription on it. Social scientists and clinicians, however, have found that classifying the disorders helps in the development and implementation of effective interventions. A careful reading of classifications of depression in the *DSM-IV* (American Psychiatric Association, 1994) makes manifest the many versions of depression.

TABLE 8.1 **Symptoms of Depression**

Type of Symptom	Description
Biological	Decreased or increased appetite, changes in sleeping patterns (hypersomonia, insomnia, early morning wakening), decreased libido, diminished energy
Cognitive	Worthlessness, hopelessness, self-depreciation, self-blame, guilt, pessimism, incompetence, deprivation, expectation of failure or punishment
Affective (mood)	Sadness, dejection, downcast, suffering, disinterest, irritable
Behavior	Slowed or diminished activity, withdrawal from usual activities, excessive sleeping, crying, passivity, decreased interpersonal/social behavior

The diagnoses in the *DSM-IV* (APA, 1994) that include marked symptoms of depression are mood disorder due to a general medical condition, substance-induced mood disorder, bipolar I disorder, bipolar II disorder, cyclothymic disorder, major depressive disorder, schizoaffective disorder (depressive type), dysthymic disorder, and adjustment disorder with depressed mood—to say nothing of the not otherwise specified (NOS) versions of these disorders, and bereavement. In addition, there are diagnoses of depression in the appendix of the *DSM-IV* that are sometimes incorporated in the NOS category—minor depressive disorder, premenstrual dysphoric disorder, recurrent brief depressive disorder, and mixed anxiety-depressive disorder. Two of the diagnoses (mood disorder due to a general medical condition and substance-induced mood disorder) are based on etiology; some are based on history of a manic, mixed, or hypomanic episode (e.g., bipolar I and II and cyclothymic disorders); and others are based on chronicity (dysthymic and cyclothymic disorders) (APA, 1994). Within many of the mood disorders are specifiers (denoted by "x" digits) that describe the severity, chronicity, onset, special features, and other characteristics of the most recent (e.g., severe with psychotic depression, postpartum onset, and atypical features) and recurrent episodes (e.g., seasonal pattern) (APA, 1994).

The *DSM-IV* distinguishes between *unipolar* disorders, which are characterized by low moods, and *bipolar* disorders, which generally have highs and lows. This chapter will focus on the treatment of two unipolar illnesses—major depressive disorder without psychotic features and dysthymic disorder—in which neither is complicated by substance abuse. The psychotherapeutic treatments that will be described are for depressions that are in the mild to moderate range of severity. Individuals with severe or recurrent major depressive disorders may benefit from the interventions for persons with serious mental illness that are described in Chapters 11 and 12. Because the two depressive disorders that are the focus of this chapter have a high rate of comorbidity with other psychiatric disorders (Kessler et al., 1998), their treatment plan should take the other disorders into consideration. Those with concurrent substance abuse disorders may respond to some of the interventions described in Chapter 13. We will now proceed to describe major depressive and dysthymic disorders. Next biological aspects, social dimensions, and psychosocial theories will be explained. A discussion of medication issues, interpersonal therapy, cognitive therapy, and alternative ways of healing will follow.

Description of Major Depressive Disorder and Dysthymia

The *DSM-IV* describes a *major depressive disorder* as a mood disorder in which there has been at least one two-week episode of illness in which there occurred either a depressed mood or loss of interest in life. The symptoms must represent a change from previous functioning and are not the consequence of a general medical condition, alcohol, or drugs (prescribed or street drugs). According to the *DSM-IV*, five or more of the following symptoms must be present in an adult during a depressive episode:*

1. depressed mood most of the day, nearly every day, as indicated by either subjective report or observation made by others
2. markedly diminished interest or pleasure in all, or almost all, activities most of the day, nearly every day
3. significant weight loss when not dieting or weight gain
4. insomnia or hypersomnia nearly every day
5. psychomotor agitation or retardation nearly every day
6. fatigue or loss of energy nearly every day
7. feelings of worthlessness or excessive or inappropriate guilt nearly every day
8. diminished ability to think or concentrate, or indecisiveness, nearly every day
9. recurrent thoughts of death, recurrent suicidal ideation without a specific plan, or a suicide attempt or a specific plan for committing suicide.

If the individual meets the criteria of a mixed episode (symptoms of manic and depressive episodes) or the person has these symptoms as a result of a recent loss (bereavement), the episode is not considered a major depressive one. Individuals may have single or recurrent episodes of major depressive disorder (APA, 1994). As indicated, major depressive disorders may be accompanied by psychotic features. If there are psychotic symptoms, the clinician needs to determine whether one of the major psychotic disorders (schizophrenia, schizophreniform disorder, schizoaffective disorder, delusional disorder, psychotic disorder NOS) is more appropriate (APA, 1994).

Dysthymic disorder is a depressive mood disorder that persists for at least two years (APA, 1994). It is less severe than major depressive disorder but it is pervasive. According to the *DSM-IV*, two or more of the following symptoms must be present while depressed:†

1. poor appetite or overeating
2. insomnia or hypersomnia

---

*List is reprinted with permission from the Diagnostic and Statistical Manual of Mental Disorders, Fourth Edition, p. 327. Copyright © 1994 American Psychiatric Association.

†List is reprinted with permission from the Diagnostic and Statistical Manual of Mental Disorders, Fourth Edition, p. 349. Copyright © 1994 American Psychiatric Association.

3. low energy or fatigue
4. low self-esteem
5. poor concentration or difficulty making decisions
6. feelings of hopelessness.

As with major depressive disorder, other diagnoses should be considered before dysthymic disorder—particularly substance abuse, a general medical condition, schizophrenia, manic episodes, and others. Dysthymic disorder may have an early (before age 21) or late (age 21 or older) onset (APA, 1994).

Although diagnostic criteria for major depressive and dysthymic disorder appear to distinguish them, their features do overlap. Some say that major depressive disorder is characterized by more *vegetative symptoms* (e.g., early morning awakening, loss of sex drive, loss of appetite) than dysthymic disorder (Clayton, 1998). When an episode of major depression is superimposed on dysthymic disorder, the term *double depression* is used. In such cases, an individual may recover from one of the disorders, both, or neither (Clayton, 1998).

Multiple Dimensions

Biological Aspects

Evidence of a biological basis for depression comes from genetic and psychopharmacological research. Studies of genetic factors have found a higher percentage of depression among relatives of persons with depression than in the general population (Klerman, 1988). Studies of twins have revealed that identical twins have a rate of concordance for major mood disorders that is two to five times the rate for fraternal twins (McGuffin & Katz, 1989). The limited number of adoption studies have yielded inconclusive results relevant to unipolar illness (DeRubeis, Young, & Dahlsgaard, 1998).

Research on the effects of antidepressants on animal models and humans suggests that two neurotransmitters, serotonin and norepinephrine, are associated with mood disorders (Kaplan & Sadock, 1998). Other neurotransmitters may also be involved. Brain neuroimaging research has not come up with a consistent profile for unipolar depression (Kaplan & Sadock, 1998). It is likely that biological, psychological, and social dimensions are intertwined.

Epidemiological and Social Factors

Most large-scale epidemiological studies of groups at risk of depression have found that the lifetime prevalence for women is approximately twice that of men (Boyd & Weissman, 1986; Regier et al., 1988), although in the more recent National Comorbidity Survey the proportion was a little lower (Kessler et al., 1998). The higher rate for women can be explained by hormonal differences, learned helplessness (to be explained later), and childbirth (when the onset is postpartum) (Kaplan & Sadock, 1998) as well as patriarchal relationships, which silence women (Jack, 1991). It may be that the rates for men and women are comparable, but men manifest depression in their higher rate of substance abuse and trouble with the law (Weissman & Klerman, 1977). Depression increases with age up to age 65 after which it decreases (Regier et al., 1993; Weissman & Myers, 1978). The Epidemiological Catchment Area Study found no significant differences by ethnic or racial group (Regier et al., 1993).

The risk factors most plausibly causally related to major depressive disorder across epidemiological studies are being female, prior depression, being divorced or separated, poor general health, major adverse life events, and low socioeconomic status (Kaelber, Moul, & Farmer, 1995). The factors that most plausibly protect people from major depression are being employed, extended education, financial stability and prosperity, and effective health care delivery systems (Kaelber et al., 1995).

Psychological Aspects

Various psychological theories provide explanations for the development of depression. According to *psychoanalytic theory,* depression has reverberations in the oral stage of human development (Hirschfeld & Goodwin, 1988). Persons who have had conflictual experiences during this period (e.g., through the death of a parent or dysfunctional patterns of communication) may be fixated in this stage. As adults, such individuals continue to be dependent on others to meet needs that were not sufficiently satisfied during the first couple of years of life. Later experiences of loss or perceived loss threaten their ego integrity. On the other hand, persons who have not been orally deprived may regress to the oral stage in response to a loss. Regardless of whether fixation or regression is involved, the depressed individual suffers from the loss of an introjected object (Freud, 1917). During uncomplicated bereavement (mourning), the depressed person grieves, reliving past experiences and letting go of the lost object "bit by bit" to free energy for the development of new relationships. If the loss is complicated (melancholia), the individual will have ambivalent and angry feelings toward the internalized object and, thus, toward the self. If suicidal, the individual will want to obliterate the self/object. The melancholic person has a more difficult time breaking loose of the lost object than the mourner (Freud, 1917).

Attachment theory has also been used to explain reactions to object loss. Based on observations of mothers and infants, as well as ethological research, Bowlby (1969) posed that there is a human instinct to adapt to one's environment, which is expressed initially in attachment to maternal figures and later in relationships with others. Attachment behavior is expressed in efforts to be in close proximity to a specific object; closeness arouses feelings of security whereas separation arouses anxiety. During the developmental process, young people relinquish their attachment to parents as principal love objects and form relationships with peers (Weiss, 1982). In adulthood, love relationships based on attachment provide a source of meaning as well as security and comfort (Marris, 1982). Loss is a disruption of the attachment process that is accompanied by longing, protest, and a search for the lost object. Grief work entails the relinquishment of the lost object and the restoration of meaning (Marris, 1982).

Another explanation uses the concept of *learned helplessness.* Based on Seligman's (1975) experimental work with dogs, which became passive after experiencing exposure to shock under conditions from which there was no escape, the theory poses that helplessness (and the accompanying belief that one lacks control over one's environment) is learned. When opportunities to escape are presented to someone who has been exposed to harsh, unpredictable demands, the response is passivity. Learned helplessness explains the behavior of abused spouses who are paralyzed in their situations. It is also an analogue to depression.

Beck's *cognitive theory* of depression is another contemporary theory. Depressed persons have cognitions that represent misinterpretations of their experiences and depressogenic assumptions (Beck, Rush, Shaw, & Emery, 1979). The cognitions are represented in a "cognitive triad"—a view of oneself as defective or inadequate, a tendency to interpret experiences negatively, and a dim view of the future—and in cognitive structures (schemas) that categorize experiences. The depressed person uses inappropriate schemas based on faulty assumptions to interpret life events. In cognitive therapy these distorted beliefs are examined, challenged, and replaced by more accurate ones (Beck et al., 1979). (See Chapter 3, Understanding Cognitive Theory.)

According to *behavioral (learning) theory,* depression is a motivational deficit, which is associated with a lack of social skills and a low level of self-generated activities that produce positive reinforcements (Rosenhan & Seligman, 1984). Without sufficient reinforcements, individuals do not feel motivated to act. Instead they become passive and feel depressed. Behavioral therapy aims to enhance social skills, increase the activity level, increase reinforcement, and promote assertiveness.

The theories relevant to this chapter are cognitive (or cognitive-behavioral) and interpersonal. Cognitive and behavioral theories were introduced previously in Chapter 3. Interpersonal theory will be explained within the presentation on interpersonal therapy after the following review of medications used to treat depression.

Medication

Clinical social workers work with clients who may need or are already receiving medication. In order to understand and monitor clients' medications and make proper referrals, knowledge is helpful. Because of the many different drugs that are now available to treat depression and their diverse side effects, it is important to have some understanding of these medications and their characteristics.

Antidepressant Medication

Antidepressant medication is used to treat the emotional pain and biological symptoms of depression. Medication is not required for everyone who is depressed. Among those who need this intervention, different individuals benefit from different medications. Some of the same drugs used to relieve depression also help anxiety disorders (see Chapter 9) and depression associated with schizophrenia and schizoaffective disorder (see Chapter 12). Similarly, some medications used to treat other disorders (e.g., antipsychotics, mood stabilizers, and antianxiety agents) are used to supplement or augment the effects of antidepressants—a strategy known as *polypharmacy.* The medications that will be described here treat primarily moderate to severe unipolar depression—particularly major depression, dysthymia, and "double depression."

Moderate to severe unipolar depression can be treated effectively with tricyclics and tetracyclics, selective serotonin reuptake inhibitors (SSRIs), alternative antidepressants, and monoamine oxidose inhibitors (MAOIs). Individual clients respond differently to different medications but some individuals do not respond to any (Rickels, 1999). Each of these drugs takes three to five weeks to effect a therapeutic response (Nemeroff & Schatzberg, 1998). Table 8.2 provides a sketch of these groups with the generic and trade names of specific drugs and their adverse side effects.

Tricyclic Antidepressants (TCAs).   TCAs are a group of drugs that have a similar chemical structure and effect on the neurotransmitter amines. The first of these compounds that was developed is imipramine (Tofranil). Others include amitriptyline (Elavil), trimipramine (Surmontil), doxepin (Sinequan), desipramine (Norpramin), nortriptyline (Aventyl), and protriptyline (Vivactil). Clomipramine, which is used to treat obsessive compulsive disorder, is in this group of antidepressants. *Tetracyclic antidepressants* (e.g., maprotiline and amoxapine) have a chemical structure that is similar to that of TCAs. Both affect serotonin and norepinephrine levels by interfering with their reuptake at the presynaptic nerve ending (Andreasen & Black, 1995; Kaplan & Sadock, 1998).

Although there is little difference in effectiveness among the tricyclics and tetracyclics, they have different associated side effects. Amitriptyline, doxepin, and trimipramine are the most sedating; desipramine and proptriptyline are the least sedating (Kaplan & Sadock, 1998). The sedating effect, however, may be desirable because it improves sleep. The tricyclics vary, too, in associated *anticholinergic effects,* that is, symptoms such as dry mouth, retention of urine, constipation, and blurred vision. The most anticholinergic are imipramine, amitryptyline, trimipramine, and doxepin; the least anticholinergic is desipramine (Kaplan & Sadock, 1998). TCAs also produce *orthostatic* (or postural) *hypotension,* that is, a lowering of blood pressure when one changes one's position, which can be a problem for older adults, who may fall and fracture themselves as a consequence. Other side effects are listed in Table 8.2. A major risk is overdosing.

Selective Serotonin Reuptake Inhibitors (SSRIs).   Although tricyclics used to be the standard medication for major depression, SSRIs have become the drugs of choice (Kaplan & Sadock, 1998). They are recommended because they are at least as effective as tricyclics but are safer and have less disturbing side effects. They produce fewer anticholinergic effects, less sedation, and little weight gain or orthostatic hypotension. There are, however, adverse side effects for SSRIs as well, but some of these can be reduced by decreasing the dosage (Nemeroff & Schatzberg, 1998). Furthermore, there is a debate about whether SSRIs are as effective as other drugs in the treatment of severe depression (Cowen, 1998).

Alternative Antidepressants.   In recent years, a number of additional antidepressant drugs have been introduced. Venlafaxine is a selective serotonin and noradrenaline reuptake inhibitor (SSNRI) that has the advantage of not producing anticholinergic and sedating effects (Cowen, 1998). Furthermore, it appears to be particularly effective with individuals with severe depression and those who do not respond to some of the other medications (Nemeroff & Schatzberg, 1998). Bupropion does not produce orthostatic hypotension,

TABLE 8.2 Antidepressant Drugs

Group/Generic Name	Trade Name	Side Effects[1]
Tricyclics (TCAs) and tetracyclics		Sedation, anticholinergic effects, seizures, orthostatic hypotension, sexual dysfunction, weight gain, amenorrhea, cardiovascular effects, overdose. Sudden withdrawal can cause anxiety.
imipramine	Tofranil	
amitriptyline	Elavil, Endep	
trimipramine	Surmontil	
doxepin	Sinequan, Adapin	
desipramine	Norpramin	
nortriptyline	Aventyl, Pamelor	
protriptyline	Vivactil	
(clomipramine)[2]	(Anafranil)	
maprotiline	Ludiomil	
amoxapine	Asendin	
mirtazapine	Remeron	
Selective serotonin reuptake inhibitors (SSRIs)		Nausea, diarrhea, constipation, appetite loss, headache, insomnia, dizziness, sweating, sexual difficulties, low sodium state.
fluoxetine	Prozac	
(fluvoxamine)	(Luvox)	
paroxetine	Paxil	
sertraline	Zoloft	
citalopram	Celexa	
Alternative antidepressants		Similar to SSRIs. Headache, insomnia, nausea. Sedation, orthostatic hypotension. Headache, dry mouth, somnolence.
venlafaxine	Effexor	
bupropion	Wellbutrin	
trazodine	Desyrel	
nefazodone	Serzone	
Monoamine oxidase inhibitors (MAOIs)		Eating certain foods can produce a tyramine-induced hypertensive crisis. Adverse interactions with other drugs. Orthostatic hypotension, edema, weight gain, insomnia, sexual dysfunction, blurred vision, sweating, dry mouth, overdose.
isocarboxazid	Marplan	
phenelzine	Nardil	
tranylcypromine	Parnate	

[1]Except for the alternative antidepressants in which a sample of side effects was listed for each antidepressant, the side effects listed apply to each group in general.

[2]Items in parentheses are antidepressants recommended to treat obsessive compulsive disorder.

Sources: Based on Cowen (1998), Kaplan & Sadock (1998), Nemeroff & Schatzberg (1998).

anticholinergic effects, cardiovascular effects, sedation, or sexual dysfunction (Nemeroff & Schatzberg, 1998).

Trazodine and nefazodone are structurally related to each other. Trazodine has fewer side effects than TCAs, has less severe cardiac effects, and is less likely to produce sexual dysfunction than SSRIs (Cowen, 1998). On the other hand, it has the disadvantages of orthostatic hypotension, excessive sedation, nausea, and dizziness (Cowen, 1998; Nemeroff & Schatzberg, 1998).

Monoamine Oxidase Inhibitors (MAOIs).   Although effective in treating depression, MAOIs pose risks and have troubling side effects. Persons who take MAOIs are advised to avoid certain foods and beverages (e.g., aged cheese, smoked food, chocolate, wine, beer, fava beans) that are high in tyramine content. Consumption of these products can precipitate a hypertensive crisis (sweating, dizziness, high blood pressure) that is life-threatening. Early indicators of an impending crisis are headaches, nausea, and vomiting. MAOIs have additional adverse effects such as orthostatic hypotension, weight gain, edema, and sexual dysfunction that need to be monitored (Kaplan & Sadock, 1998).

Antidepressants and Women.   Even though a disproportionate number of women suffer from depression, their unique needs have not been taken into account in the development of antidepressant drugs. Women have special concerns about weight gain, amenorrhea, and medication during pregnancy. Social workers whose clients are on medication can encourage clients to discuss their concerns over these issues with psychiatrists and inquire about alternative medications. Although research is scant, it appears that taking tricyclics toward the end of pregnancy can cause anticholinergic side effects in the mother and child (Miller, 1996). More research has been conducted on the effects of women taking fluoxetine. Studies show that taking this medication after the first trimester is associated with no increase in malformations in the newborns (Miller, 1996).

Antidepressants and Older Adults.   Although depression is a serious problem among older adults, most participants in controlled clinical drug studies are younger (NIH Consensus Development Conference, 1991). Many of the antidepressants that have been described pose risks to older adults. The tricyclics have cardiac effects, produce orthostatic hypotension, and have anticholergic effects (especially constipation), which can interfere with the health of older adults. Prescription of too large a dosage or self-administered overdoses can be lethal. Some of the newer drugs may be advantageous to older adults. It may take older adults a longer time than younger adults to respond to an antidepressant (NIH Consensus Development Conference, 1991).

Regardless of the clients' gender, age, health status, or other characteristics, they need to know about alternative drugs and other treatments that are available. As the next section will explain, psychosocial interventions have an excellent record of efficacy.

Research on Medication and Psychotherapy

During the 1980s, the National Institute of Mental Health undertook and completed the Collaborative Research Study of the Treatment of Depression (Holden, 1986). Subjects consisted of 239 outpatients who were randomly assigned to treatment with (a) the tricyclic, imipramine hydrochloride, plus clinical management, (b) cognitive therapy, (c) interpersonal therapy, or (d) a clinically managed placebo. This study was undertaken in research centers in Pittsburgh, Washington, DC, and Oklahoma City. In the sixteen-week period of treatment, all four treatments resulted in reduced depression and improved functioning (Elkin et al., 1989). Among the four interventions, imipramine plus clinical management was the most effective, the clinically managed placebo was the least, and the psychotherapies were in between but closer to clinically managed imipramine. When participants were classified in terms of the severity of the depression, active medication or interpersonal therapy was favored for the severely depressed, but there was no difference in effectiveness among the four treatments for the less severely depressed (Elkin et al., 1989). Although imipramine produced rapid initial improvement, by sixteen weeks cognitive and interpersonal therapies produced comparable effects (Holden, 1986). The equivalence of psychotherapeutic and psychopharmacological treatments indicates that clients who are unable to take or who do not respond to antidepressant medication, as well as those who do not believe in using pharmaceutical products, have a safe and effective alternative.

Although many kinds of psychotherapies are used to treat depression, with and without pharmacotherapy, two "best practices" will be explained and illustrated next. Interpersonal and cognitive therapies have been chosen because of the research evidence of their effectiveness and their compatibility with the managed care expectations that interventions be short term. Still, it is recognized that many practitioners use psychodynamic approaches. Before considering one of these or other psychotherapies, the clinician should, of course, make a thorough assessment of the client's mental status and situation. Often depression is related to a stressful life situation that can be remedied through crisis intervention and the mobilization of environmental supports. Furthermore, the client should be screened for substance abuse, which can complicate treatment (see Chapter 13). A thorough physical examination is advised to determine whether a medical condition is causing the depression. Clients who are suicidal should be evaluated for hospitalization.

Best Practice: Interpersonal Therapy

The first "best practice" to be discussed, interpersonal therapy (IPT), was developed by clinicians and researchers associated with the New Haven–Boston Collaborative Depression Project (Weissman & Klerman, 1989). It has been tested on nonbipolar depressed persons, using comparison groups treated with medication, alternative therapies, and placebos. Its effectiveness alone or in combination with medication has been substantiated (Weissman & Klerman, 1989).

Interpersonal therapy recognizes that depression develops in an interpersonal and social context (Klerman, Weissman, Rounsaville, & Chevron, 1984). Theoretically interpersonal therapy is rooted in the psychobiological thinking of Adolf Meyer (see Chapter 2) and the interpersonal theory of Harry Stack Sullivan. Meyer viewed psychiatric disorders as the outcome of attempts to adapt to the environment; Sullivan was interested in the interactions *between* people (Weissman & Klerman, 1989). The team responsible for the development of interpersonal therapy also acknowledge the contributions of other theorists (e.g., Frieda Fromm-Reichmann and Silvano Arieti) who looked at the social and interpersonal dimensions of depression.

This therapy recognizes that depression derives from many sources and has diverse forms of expression. A number of causes—genetics, environmental stress, personality characteristics, and early life experiences—"combine in complex ways to produce the etiology and pathogenesis of depression" (Klerman et al., 1984, p. 38). Similarly, depression may be manifested differently in different clients. The proponents of this therapy use the medical model when they define depression as an illness and allow clients to assume the sick role (Klerman et al., 1984). Although medication may be used, the focus of psychotherapy is social.

Interpersonal therapy is a brief, focused, present-oriented, time-limited form of treatment (Kierman et al., 1984). The weekly psychotherapy usually lasts twelve to sixteen weeks, during which time one or two problems related to an individual's current interpersonal relationships and life situation are addressed. No attempts are made to alter the personality structure or promote insight into intrapsychic conflicts, defenses, and the transference. Primarily an individual therapy, significant others can be involved as needed. Early life experiences, dysfunctional behaviors, and distorted cognitions are viewed in relation to current interpersonal relationships rather than as problems in themselves (Klerman et al., 1984).

The Therapeutic Relationship

The relationship between the clinician and the client in interpersonal therapy is developed along the lines established by Rogerian therapy; that is, the therapist is warm and nonjudgmental and communicates unconditional positive regard (Klerman et al., 1984). A positive transference is left alone; discord between the client and the clinician is compared with problematic interpersonal relationships in the client's life. In interpersonal therapy the clinician is more active than in ego psychological treatment. Nevertheless, the client is responsible for making changes. The clinician assumes the role of client advocate and provides support, reassurance, and optimism to promote the client's efforts to change (Klerman et al., 1984).

The Intervention Process

Interpersonal therapy is implemented over three phases, each of which encompasses specific activities. At all times work is directed at achieving the goals of interpersonal therapy—reduction of depressed symptoms and improvement of interpersonal functioning. The content of these phases that will be summarized hereafter is adapted from Kierman et al.'s *Interpersonal Psychotherapy of Depression* (1984).

During the *initial phase* of one to three sessions, the client describes the symptoms and the interpersonal context of his or her life, a diagnosis is made, and a treatment contract is developed. Before a diagnosis is made, a client is referred to a physician to discern whether a medical condition is producing the depression. Meanwhile the clinician gathers information about the client's history, symptoms, and current functioning. The team that developed interpersonal therapy recommends the use of the Hamilton Rating Scale for Depression to guide the review of symptoms with the client. This scale includes questions that probe for a depressed mood, feelings of guilt, insomnia, suicidal ideations, somatic anxiety, psychomotor retardation, sexual symptoms, weight loss, and the like. If the symptoms are consistent with a diagnosis of depression (and a medical condition is ruled out), the clinician links the symptoms with a diagnostic label and informs the client that he or she is depressed.

The clinician then proceeds to educate the client about depression. This includes the nature of depression, its course, and means of treatment. Facts about its prevalence in the general population, distribution among men and women, and the effectiveness of treatment should be explained. The clinician should convey optimism about prospects for recovery. At this point, the client is given permission to adopt the sick role, which allows the client to be excused from some social role obligations while seeking treatment. Next the client may be referred to a psychiatrist for an evaluation for medication.

During the initial phase, information is gathered and an assessment is made of the interpersonal context of the client's life. The clinician can start by asking the client to explain what was happening in his or her life when the symptoms began. The client is asked to identify and describe relationships with significant persons (family members, friends, coworkers), recent life events (infidelity, laid off from a job), and contexts (home, work) that constitute the contours of the person's life. The clinician encourages the client to talk about conflictual interpersonal relationships and interactions and about expectations of each party in a relationship. The client is asked to identify positive and negative aspects of relationships and how these relationships might change. Although the emphasis is on current relationships and life situations, the client may also talk about important past relationships.

Discussions about the interpersonal context should facilitate the identification of major problem areas. The developers of interpersonal therapy identified four issues that predominate in clients with depression. These are grief, interpersonal disputes, role transitions, and interpersonal deficits. The clinician and the client try to arrive at a mutual decision about one or two primary issues that will become the focus of treatment. In order to do this, the clinician promotes the client's awareness of the relationship between symptoms of depression and interpersonal issues.

The initial phase concludes with the clinician providing an oral summary of the problem, an explanation of the concepts of interpersonal therapy, and the development of a treatment contract. First the clinician communicates an assessment of the major problems and how they are related to the interpersonal context of the client's life. For example, Tom Smith, a thirty-five-year-old, recently separated man, was told:

> You seem to be depressed about being apart from your wife and children. You are living alone now, and you seem to be feeling lonely. It is clear that you do not want to lose your family and you are hoping that your wife will change her mind. Your wife, however, is acting as if she wants a divorce. You seem to be confused about what to do—try to win her back or come to terms with a divorce.

Some clients may have difficulty grasping the relationship between their mood and the interpersonal context of their lives. Instead they may blame themselves for their problems. These clients need to be told that life is made up of people and that the way relationships go affects feelings. Similarly, the lack of significant relationships can interfere with one's happiness. As one clinician put it:

Relationships are complicated; they cause problems. On the other hand, not having relationships is also difficult.

The explanation of concepts of interpersonal therapy includes practical aspects (short-term, weekly one-hour sessions, fees, rules about cancellation and missed appointments) and expectations. The client is given the responsibility to use the sessions to review relationships and bring up current issues and feelings, including feelings about the therapeutic relationship.

The treatment contract consists of an oral agreement on the major problems and on two or three goals to be reached during therapy. These goals should be related to the problems and should be realistic and achievable within the short time span of treatment. For example, the thirty-five-year-old man described earlier had problems in all four areas (grief, interpersonal disputes, role transitions, interpersonal deficits). The contract, however, was to work on limited goals:

1. Understand the circumstances and disputes that led up to the separation (interpersonal dispute).
2. Determine whether the disputes between his wife and him can be repaired (interpersonal dispute).
3. If the marriage cannot be repaired, grieve over the loss of previous roles (husband, live-in father) and come to terms with and assume new roles (single man, visiting father) (role transition).

During the *intermediate phase* the problem areas and related goals are addressed, and at the same time attention is paid to the client's depressive symptoms. Efforts are made to engage the client in treatment and to prevent its disruption. During therapy, the client is encouraged to understand the relationship between symptoms and interpersonal problems. As Table 8.3 indicates, the intervention goals and strategy during the intermediate phase are related to the problem area.

If the issue is grief, the client is helped to mourn by reviewing life with the lost person up to and following the loss, exploring feelings, and establishing new relationships. When role transition is the problem, the client is encouraged to discuss the advantages and disadvantages of the previous and new roles, mourn the loss of the old role through the expression of feelings, and develop a positive attitude, supports, and skills that are consistent with the new role. As for interpersonal disputes, the history, stage of dispute, and discrepant role expectations are discussed and actions are taken to reconcile or resolve the problem. If the client has interpersonal deficits, the goals are to reduce social isolation and develop new relationships through a review of past relationships, identification of repetitive interpersonal patterns, and a discussion of parallels between the interaction with the therapist and relationships in the client's personal life. For Tom Smith, the intermediate phase went as follows:

Mr. Smith explained, tearfully, that he and his wife were happy during the first ten years of their marriage, although there had been hard times. Last year, when he became unemployed, his wife took a job at a local warehouse, her

TABLE 8.3   Implementation of Interpersonal Therapy During the Intermediate Phase

Problem	Goals	Strategies
1. Grief (over a death)	1. Facilitate mourning process. 2. Help the patient reestablish interest and relationships to substitute for what has been.	1. Review depressive symptoms. 2. Relate onset of symptoms to death of significant other. 3. Reconstruct the patient's relationship with the deceased. 4. Describe the sequence of events and consequences of events just prior to, during, and after the death. 5. Explore associated feelings (negative as well as positive). 6. Consider ways of becoming involved with others.
2. Role transitions (change from one situation and associated role to another)	1. Mourn and accept the loss of old role. 2. Help the patient to regard the new role as more positive. 3. Restore self-esteem by developing a sense of mastery regarding demands of new roles.	1. Review depressive symptoms. 2. Relate depressive symptoms to difficulty in coping with some recent life change. 3. Review positive and negative aspects of old and new roles. 4. Explore feelings about what is lost. 5. Explore feelings about the change itself. 6. Explore opportunities in the new role. 7. Realistically evaluate what is lost. 8. Encourage appropriate release of affect. 9. Encourage development of a social support system and of new skills called in a new role.
3. Interpersonal disputes (conflicts)	1. Identify dispute. 2. Choose plan of action. 3. Modify expectations or faulty communication patterns to bring about a satisfactory resolution.	1. Review depressive symptoms. 2. Relate symptoms' onset to overt or covert dispute with a significant other with whom patient is currently involved. 3. Determine stage of the dispute (renegotiation, impasse, dissolution). 4. Understand how nonreciprocal role expectations relate to dispute (issues, different expectations and values, options, likelihood of finding alternatives, resources). 5. Are there parallels in other relationships (benefits, assumptions)? 6. How is the dispute perpetuated?
4. Interpersonal deficits	1. Reduce the patient's social isolation. 2. Encourage formation of new relationships.	1. Review depressive symptoms. 2. Relate depressive symptoms to problems of social isolation or unfulfillment. 3. Review past significant relationships including their negative and positive aspects. 4. Explore repetitive patterns in relationships. 5. Discuss patient's positive and negative feelings about therapist and seek parallels in other relationships.

first job. Although she claimed that she loved her job, Mr. Smith thought that she "changed for the worse" since working. She went out drinking after work with her new friends (while he babysat) and lost interest in housework. Meanwhile Mr. Smith had trouble finding a new job. Finally he located a well-paying job as a truck driver. When he told his wife that she no longer had to work, she refused to quit her job. In the past few months, they were increasingly distant. Their sex life was minimal and they hardly saw each other (he worked days and she worked nights). Mr. Smith said that he wants his old Cindy back, but the new Cindy does not seem to want him. He suspected that she was having an affair.

In the course of therapy during the intermediate phase, Mr. Smith recognized that his wife had changed over the years from a dependent "girl" to a woman who wanted more independence. He, however, wanted their relationship to stay the same. He also recognized that his wife was not satisfied with his unsteady pattern of working and wanted security. He expressed willingness to change himself by changing his expectations of the relationship.

Nevertheless, Mr. Smith's efforts to meet with his wife to discuss his willingness to change were unsuccessful. Mrs. Smith blocked his calls with an answering machine and did not return his messages. When he picked up the children for visits, a relative or friend greeted him at the door. His letters were not answered, except for a brief note advising him that all communications should be handled through her attorney. Mr. Smith heard rumors that she was going out with her boss. Finally Mr. Smith was served with divorce papers.

The accumulation of circumstances led Mr. Smith and the clinician to believe that it was not possible to resolve the interpersonal dispute between Tom and Cindy Smith; that divorce was inevitable. At this point he began to grieve the loss of Cindy and his role as husband and live-in father. Mr. Smith cried during therapy sessions and reported early morning wakening, loss of appetite, and feelings of depersonalization. He was referred to a psychiatrist for an evaluation for medication, which was prescribed. Meanwhile Mr. Smith shared his feelings about not having a wife and not sharing a home with her and the children; he had a difficult time being alone. He reported having great love for his wife, even though she did not seem to love him. He said that having a wife and family to go home to gave him a purpose for living and people to work for. Further exploration of his feelings, however, led to his expression of anger and anguish. He felt that he had been a devoted husband who was "dumped" when someone more affluent came along. He felt rejected sexually (and as a man) and longed for his wife's affection.

Nevertheless, Mr. Smith continued to work as a truck driver. Toward the end of the intermediate stage, he and the clinician discussed ways he could be a visiting father. He came up with such ideas as taking the children camping, on picnics, and to the zoo. He also (working through a lawyer) negotiated a visitation plan that included dinner a couple of evenings a week and overnight visits on weekends. In addition, Mr. Smith considered other ways to fill up his empty evenings, such as visiting his father and siblings (who had been making efforts to reach out to him), becoming involved in a local church, and joining Parents without Partners. Mr. Smith said that he did not feel ready to go out with other women at this time. Although he still reported sadness over the loss of his wife and the family as he knew it, he recognized that it was possible to build a new life in the future.

Early in the *termination phase* (last three or four sessions) the client is told that therapy will be ending shortly. The client is given the opportunity to express feelings about termination and about the therapist. The clinician helps the client grieve over the impending loss while at the same time assuring the client that he or she is capable of coping independently, The remaining time is used to evaluate the gains made in treatment and to prepare for the future. At times issues of loss that were present during treatment are replayed:

> Upon hearing that he had only four sessions left, Mr. Smith expressed sadness and feelings of hopelessness. At this point, the clinician reviewed with him the issues of loss that he has been facing and difficulties he has been having in being alone. Mr. Smith expressed gratitude to the therapist for being there and tried to convince her to extend the sessions beyond the twelve that had been agreed upon. The therapist noted that there were parallels in his wanting the therapy to last and his unwillingness to accept the impending divorce from his wife. Mr. Smith described himself as a "needy guy who doesn't see the handwriting on the wall." When asked how he felt about termination, the client expressed feelings of rejection. After a couple of sessions, however, he recognized that the therapy was supposed to be twelve weeks and that he had benefited from it. Mr. Smith said that although he felt bad about the divorce and about termination, he felt challenged at having a chance to rebuild his life as a single man. He reported joining a support group for single adults at a nearby church and increased contacts with his children, father, and siblings. Hopeful for a better future, he no longer was depressed.

Methods of Interpersonal Therapy

In interpersonal therapy, the clinician uses a number of methods.

Exploration.   This method elicits information about the client's problems and symptoms through directive and nondirective questioning and responses. Nondirective techniques include open-ended questions, nonverbal or minimal communication ("uh huh"), encouraging the client to continue to talk, inviting the client to expand on ideas that are presented, and the use of silence as an encourager. Directive techniques include asking questions related to specific symptoms and interpersonal relationships.

Encouragement of Affect.   This method promotes the expression and experience of painful emotions. The clinician elicits the client's feelings ("how did you feel about that?") and responds by accepting the client's pain. This is especially useful in work with clients who have difficulty identifying and expressing their feelings. For clients who are overwhelmed with affect, the client should be helped to control feelings.

Communication Analysis.   This method analyzes communication breakdown, especially in problems involving interpersonal disputes. The clinician asks the client to describe in detail specific incidents of faulty communication. Together they identify ambiguous messages, false assumptions, and indirect methods of response. Alternative interpretations and responses are suggested.

Clarification.   The clinician attempts to get the client to rethink a previous statement and, thus, arrive at a deeper understanding of what has been said. This can be achieved by paraphrasing a client's message, asking the client to rephrase his or her own words, examining the implications of what a client has said, or drawing attention to unusual beliefs and inconsistencies between messages.

Behavior Change Techniques.   These techniques encourage behavior changes that are discussed or modeled during therapy to be enacted in the client's interpersonal behavior in everyday life. These are implemented through directive techniques, such as limited setting, giving suggestions or advice, providing information or education, modeling, and provision of direct assistance; decision analysis; and role playing. Therapeutic efforts to assist the client in the resolution of problems are predicated on the client's willingness to assume responsibility for his or her own actions. Accordingly, directive techniques are used cautiously in such a way to preserve the client's autonomy. With decision analysis the client examines alternative solutions to a problem and probable consequences of each option. The clinician offers ideas about solutions and helps the client think through the alternatives, but the client makes decisions. With role playing, the clinician plays the role of a person in the client's life with whom the client is having a problematic relationship. This technique is used so that the clinician can assess the nature of the problem and the client can learn more constructive communication strategies.

Use of the Therapeutic Relationship.   Although interpersonal therapy does not emphasize the development of a transference, the client is encouraged from the beginning to share positive and negative feelings about the clinician and the therapeutic process. Moreover, if the client interacts with the clinician in distorted ways, the clinician will discuss these patterns with the client. Distortions in the client-therapist relationship are of diagnostic value; they suggest ways in which the client interacts with others. The clinician's acceptance of the clients' feelings about the clinician provides an opportunity to correct distortions and deal with sensitive issues in relationships.

In the case that was described in this chapter, several of these techniques were used. Exploratory techniques were used in the initial and intermediate phases to determine what was going on in Mr. Smith's life, who his significant others were, and whether repair of the marital dispute was possible. When Mr. Smith provided this information in a distorted way ("she's changed for the worse"), clarification techniques were used to determine what and who had changed and why. When the client realized that there was no hope of reconciliation, he began to grieve. The clinician encouraged him to express feelings, which were primarily sadness, loneliness, anger, anguish, and longing. Mr. Smith also felt the loss of his wife as a sex partner and felt that his masculinity had been challenged by a competitor. Mr. Smith was encouraged to change his behavior through a discussion of options that were available to him as he made the transition to the roles of visiting father and single adult. The therapeutic relationship was used in the end to help Mr. Smith deal with the separations in his life.

Interpersonal therapy encompasses perspectives and strategies employed by clinical social workers. First, it gives the social field the primary focus of attention, which is consistent with the person-in-situation perspective used in social work. Second, it focuses on relationships, which are critical in working with depressed women. Third, it includes stages of intervention and techniques that are widely used in the field. Research studies have found that not only is interpersonal psychotherapy is efficacious with adults who are acutely depressed but it is also efficacious with depressed geriatric and HIV-positive clients (Markowitz & Weissman, 1995).

Interpersonal therapy is particularly compatible with the biopsychosocial conceptual framework of this book. For one, it recognizes that depression has a biological base. Where appropriate, clients are offered the opportunity to take medication and assume the sick role. Second, it recognizes the social environmental context in which human problems arise and psychological problems that contribute to becoming frozen in social roles. Interpersonal therapy recognizes that there are multiple forces that influence the development and creation of problems. Its emphasis on the social context differs from the emphasis on cognition that is evident in the approach that will be discussed next.

Best Practice: Cognitive or Cognitive-Behavioral Therapy

The second best practice, cognitive therapy, was developed by Aaron Beck and his associates (Beck, 1976; Beck, Rush, Shaw, & Emery, 1979) but its roots go back to Plato (Karasu, 1990). The therapy is predicated on the idea that automatic thoughts and images (cognitions) precipitate depression and other symptoms of emotional disturbance. Automatic thoughts are "specific subvocations or self-statements that occur automatically and without conscious effort" (Sarcot & Beck, 1995, p. 333). Treatment is directed at changing distorted, maladaptive, inaccurate cognitions to more adaptive ones. Sometimes called cognitive-behavioral therapy, the treatment uses behavioral as well as cognitive strategies. Table 8.4 compares the cognitive and interpersonal approaches.

Although cognitive therapy does not preclude biological or developmental explanations or the use of medication (Beck, 1976), it is concerned principally with the thought patterns or schemas that underlie depression. A life experience, such as a loss, can activate latent schemas (e.g., attitudes about loss) that developed earlier in life. A person with unipolar depression is likely to interpret later life events in ways that emphasize the negative aspects, ignore the context, and reflect poorly on the individual. Selectively attending to those elements of the situation that coincide with "depressogenic" schemas, the individual

TABLE 8.4 **Major Features of Two Best Practices for Treating Depression Psychotherapeutically**

Feature	Cognitive Approach	Interpersonal Approach
Major theorists	Plato, Adler, Beck, Rush	Meyer, Sullivan, Klerman, Weissman
Concepts of pathology and etiology	Distorted thinking: dysphoria due to learned negative views of self, others, and the world	Impaired interpersonal relations: absent or unsatisfactory significant social bonds
Major goals and mechanisms of change	To provide symptomatic relief through alteration of target thoughts; to identify self-destructive cognitions; to modify specific erroneous assumptions; to promote self-control over thinking patterns	To provide symptomatic relief through solution of current interpersonal problems; to reduce stress involving family or work; to improve interpersonal communication skills
Primary techniques and practices	Behavioral/cognitive; recording and monitoring cognitions; correcting distorted themes with logic and experimental testing; providing alternative thought content; homework	Communicative/environmental: clarifying and managing maladaptive relationships and learning new ones through communication and social skills training; providing information on illness
Therapist role/ therapeutic relationship	Educator/shaper: positive relationship instead of transference; collaborative empiricism as basis for joint scientific (logical) task	Explorer/prescriber: positive relationship/transference without interpretation; active therapist role for influence and advocacy

Source: From "Toward a Clinical Model of Psychotherapy for Depression, I: Systematic Comparison of Three Psychotherapies," by T. B. Karasu, 1990, *American Journal of Psychiatry, 147*(2), p. 141. Copyright © 1990 by the American Psychiatric Association. Reprinted by permission.

construes the situation in a partial way, without considering the whole (Beck et al., 1979). The following are examples of maladaptive explanations of a brief exchange between two coworkers at the coffee pot one morning:

> *Conversation:*
> AL: Hi Bob. How ya' doing?
> BOB: Pretty good. How are you?
> AL: OK. Gotta go. (Rushes off)

> *Bob's maladaptive explanations of Al's rushing off:*
> Al doesn't like me.
> Al doesn't like me anymore.
> I wonder what I did wrong.

An accurate assessment of this situation reveals that Al greeted Bob with warmth and friendliness. Yet Bob viewed the interaction as a reflection of Al's negative feelings toward him. Alternative explanations for Al's behavior are: (a) Al had an appointment or a meeting; (b) Al needed to prepare for a busy day of work; and (c) Al went to the coffee pot for coffee, not to socialize. Essentially Al's reasons had nothing to do with Bob. The negative interpretation was a reflection of Bob's schemas.

Persons who are depressed are prone to make inaccurate interpretations of their experiences. Automatic negative thoughts intervene between life events and emotional responses, creating a negative bias. Depressed persons view life events that would ordinarily be viewed as undesirable, disappointing, or neutral as catastrophes. Convinced that their perception of reality is the same as reality (Beck, 1976), they feel pain associated with their own biased interpretations. Soon they become preoccupied with themes of rejection, inadequacy, and failure and blame themselves for unfortuitous experiences. As the depression deepens, the depressive themes predominate and reality testing becomes impaired (Beck, 1985).

The Therapeutic Relationship

Beck's cognitive therapy is implemented through a collaborative relationship between the clinician and the client. The therapist fosters those conditions that facilitate the development of a relationship and which are described in Rogerian therapy—warmth, genuineness, accurate empathy (Beck et al., 1979). Much attention is given to developing rapport and building trust. Although cognitive therapy emphasizes cognitions, emotions are important as well. The client is given the opportunity to express feelings and the clinician accepts the feelings the client shares.

Although the relationship is a partnership, the roles of clinician and client are different. The cognitive therapist may be viewed as a teacher, the client as a learner. The clinician explains cognitive theory to the client, provides structure to the sessions, asks questions of the client, and assigns homework. Before proceeding with the therapeutic work, the clinician explains that they will be working together to develop hypotheses and test them out (Hirschfeld & Shea, 1985). The clinician assumes an active role in identifying problems, in focusing on specific issues, and in the implementation of cognitive and behavioral techniques (Beck, 1985). The client is expected to describe feelings, cognitions, and behaviors, to work at revising inaccurate thoughts, and to carry out assigned activities and homework.

The Nature of Cognitive Therapy

Like interpersonal therapy, cognitive therapy is brief, present oriented, and focused. The time period varies from ten to twenty-five weeks (Jarrett & Rush, 1989). After termination, some clients continue in 4 or 5 "booster" sessions (Sacco & Beck, 1995). Although cognitive therapy can be implemented in couple and group formats (Jarrett & Rush, 1989), the individual approach will be described here.

Cognitive therapy employs the scientific method that is used in research. Throughout the process, information is gathered, hypotheses are tested, and logical conclusions are drawn. The clinician and the client examine thoughts and interpretations and create and evaluate experiments clients perform in their daily lives that test hypotheses. The client is encouraged to discard ideas that are illogical and do not reflect observed reality.

Hypotheses and experiments provide insight into underlying depressogenic assumptions and rules (Beck et al., 1979), which also can be tested. Beck identified several "silent assumptions" (Sacco & Beck, 1995, p. 339) that are related to depression:

1. In order to be happy, I have to be successful in whatever I undertake.
2. To be happy, I must be accepted by all people at all times.
3. If I'm not on top, I'm a flop.
4. It's wonderful to be popular, famous, wealthy; it's terrible to be unpopular, mediocre.
5. If I make a mistake, it means that I am inept.
6. My value as a person depends on what others think of me.
7. I can't live without love. If my spouse (sweetheart, parent, child) doesn't love me, I'm worthless.
8. If somebody disagrees with me, it means he doesn't like me.
9. If I don't take advantage of every opportunity to advance myself, I will regret it later. (Beck, 1976, pp. 255–256)

The goals of cognitive therapy are to promote relief of depressive symptoms and to prevent a recurrence (Beck et al., 1979). Subjectively, the client should have enhanced feelings of satisfaction and well-being. These goals are achieved by teaching the client to:

(a) Learn to identify and modify his faulty thinking and dysfunctional behavior and (b) recognize and change the cognitive patterns leading to dysfunctional ideation and behavior. (Beck et al., 1979, p. 75)

The Process of Cognitive Therapy

Beck and his associates describe a process in which the strategies and methods vary over time. Prior to admission to treatment, they perform a preliminary evaluation of potential clients. The evaluation includes a history of the current difficulty, past history, a mental status examination, and a battery of tests. Among the tests that are used are the Schedule of Affective Disorders and Schizophrenia, the Hamilton Scale for Depression, the Hopelessness Scale, the Scale for Suicide Intentionality, the Minnesota Multiphasic Personality Inventory, the Spielberger State-Trait Anxiety Scale, and the Beck Depression Inventory (Beck et al., 1979).

The First Interview.   During the first interview, attention is initially given to establishing rapport, inquiring about the client's expectations of therapy, and eliciting attitudes toward the self, the clinician, and therapy. On the basis of information that was gathered during the preliminary evaluation and observations about the client's mental status that are made in this session, the clinician identifies complaints ("I do not see any reason to go on") and transforms them into target symptoms (suicidal thoughts) or problems (difficulty completing school work) (Beck et al., 1979). When more than one symptom or problem is identified, potential targets are prioritized on the basis of the distress they arouse in the client and their amenability to treatment. The clinician and the client come to a negotiated agreement about the symptom or problem that will be focal.

The clinician devotes considerable time during the first session to educating the client about cognitive therapy. The cognitive theory of depression and intervention techniques (see next section) should be explained. Particular attention is given to the client's responsibility to perform homework assignments between sessions. Beck and associates give the client a booklet, *Coping with Depression* (Beck & Greenberg, 1974) to read. They inquire about the client's activity level, and ask the client to keep a record of the activities that he or she performs between this session and the next. Before this interview concludes, the client's feelings about the interview are elicited (Beck et al., 1979).

The Second Interview.   During the second interview, the client is again encouraged to share feelings about the first session, but is also invited to raise questions about the reading material or the process. The clinician answers the client's questions and responds to questions. In addition, the homework assignment on activities is reviewed. If the client appears to be having difficulty getting motivated to be active, the clinician and the client together develop a schedule of activities to be performed by the client. The client is given the homework assignment of rating each activity performed with respect to degree of mastery and pleasure (Beck et al., 1979).

Sometime during the first few interviews, the clinician presents the client with a "case formulaion" that serves as a framework for the therapeutic process (Sacco & Beck, 1995, p. 333). Throughout therapy, sessions are structured. They begin with the clinician and the client developing an agenda of what they wish to accomplish during the session (Beck et al., 1979). This usually includes the client's summary of experiences since the last session and a review of the homework assignment. Issues and concerns pertaining to the previous session can also be raised. The client and the clinician together identify problems and negotiate about which ones will be addressed in the session. The client chooses among strategies suggested by the clinician (e.g., role playing, refuting automatic thoughts, etc.) for looking at targeted problems in the session. Sessions also include an elicitation of the client's feelings, summary statements by the clinician, and a description of the next homework assignment (Beck et al., 1979).

In each session the client is asked about depressive symptoms and about events that have occurred since the previous meeting. The clinician responds to the reported experiences by inquiring about the client's feelings, thinking, and behavior. During these discussions the client reveals distorted thinking that is associated with life events. The clinician begins to point out the relationship between the client's negative cognitions and depression (Beck et al., 1979).

Middle Phase.   During the middle phase of intervention, attention is given to automatic thoughts that are associated with disturbing feelings (sadness, anxiety, and lack of interest in life). Clients may be asked to perform homework assignments in which they record the circumstances related to these feelings, that is, the precipitating event and cognitions. During the sessions, clients are questioned about aspects of the situations they describe (orally or in assignments) that they may have excluded. This is because persons who are depressed frequently construct their experiences narrowly, omitting dimensions that do not conform with their negative schemas. The clinician challenges the client's distorted thinking and presents alternative explanations based on a comprehensive consideration of evidence. In addition, the clinician elicits (during the sessions and in homework assignments) rational alternative explanations from clients. Other techniques are used to help clients identify dysfunctional cognitions and restructure them. Clients are given further information about the relationship between their feelings and depressogenic assumptions. At times, clients are asked to test out their assumptions in assigned activities to be performed between sessions.

Concluding Sessions.   As therapy draws to a close, the client is given more responsibility for initiation of the agenda, homework assignments, and setting goals. Cognitive and behavioral techniques are used to anticipate and practice rational strategies of interpreting experiences. During the last few sessions, the client is prepared for termination and for retaining the benefits of thinking constructively in the future. Client and clinician discuss issues the client is likely to face in the future and strategies with which to handle them.

Methods of Cognitive Therapy

Cognitive therapy employs an array of cognitive and behavioral methods and procedures, some of which are used throughout therapy and others that vary in relation to the severity of the depression and the stage of therapy.

Behavioral Methods.   If the client is severely depressed, behavioral strategies are used early in the process. Clients who are so depressed that they cannot get out of bed, for example, are helped to become more active through the use of *activity schedules* and *graded task assignments* (Beck et al., 1979). At first the clinician has the client write up a schedule of daily activities. If the client does not appear to be sufficiently active, the clinician and the client develop a schedule of hourly activities that expand upon the client's usual repertoire. New and more demanding activities are added gradually over time (graded task assignments). Clients are also asked to keep a record of activities that are accomplished and to grade them on a scale from 0 to 5 according to the degree of pleasure (P) and sense of mastery (M) that are experienced (Beck, 1979, 1985).

Other behavioral techniques complement cognitive strategies (Beck, 1979). *Role playing,* with the clinician and the client taking the roles of parties described by the client, makes visible the difficulties a client is having in a social interaction. Identified problems are often related to automatic thoughts. In addition, *cognitive rehearsal* helps clients prepare mentally for the performance of tasks the client anticipates will be difficult. With this technique, the client is asked to imagine performing a task, step by step. In walking through the situation, the client identifies obstacles and thinking patterns that impede accomplishment of the task. The cognitive rehearsal is repeated until the obstacles are overcome in the imagination. Then the client is asked to perform the task in real life. In addition, *diversion* techniques are used. The client is encouraged to become distracted from painful emotions by engaging in other activities, focusing on environmental stimuli, and imagining pleasant scenes.

Cognitive Methods.   Although cognitive techniques are implemented throughout therapy, the nature of these techniques varies over time. In the beginning, the clinician uses a didactic approach to explain what automatic thoughts are and how they affect emotions and behavior (Beck et al., 1979). Then the client is helped to *identify automatic thoughts* in his or her daily life. The client may be given a homework assignment to keep a record of events and associated negative cognitions and emotions that occur between sessions. This assignment, as well as specific examples that the client offers during sessions, can be used as a basis for a *discussion of cognitive errors*. The client and the clinician together look at the facts and the client's interpretation of the event and *generate alternative explanations.* Such a logical examination can result in *distancing* oneself from one's experience (becoming more objective) and in shifting responsibility from the client to another source (*reattribution*). The client can learn how to modify negative cognitions through a homework assignment in which automatic thoughts and alternative explanations are listed, or through a process of questioning and presenting modified interpretations during the session (Beck, 1985; Beck et al., 1979).

During the course of therapy, *hypotheses* that underlie a client's behavior are identified and *tested empirically.* For example, Mrs. Dell, who was depressed and slightly overweight, spent little time outside her home. She explained that she only shops for groceries early in the morning because later in the day, when the store is crowded, people stare at her large body. The hypothesis the clinician formulated was, "Because you are depressed, you expect other people to view you in a negative way." This woman was asked to shop at various times and keep track of the number of people who stared at her each time she shopped. She discovered that whatever time she went, very few people stared at her.

Case Example

Maxine Brown is a 45-year-old married woman who entered therapy saying that she was so far down and could not get up. She reported a loss of appetite, sleeping excessively, and a lack of energy. Mrs. Brown said that she was having difficulty getting motivated to take care of all the people who needed her and felt like a failure as a wife and stepmother. The client related that she has been married to Mr. Brown for a year and that everything was "perfect" until Mr. Brown's sixteen-year-old son Todd moved in with them 4 months ago. Todd leaves his dirty clothes scattered throughout the house, uses foul language, and expects Mrs. Brown to pick up after him. Mrs. Brown said that instead of feeling love for Todd, she resents him.

Mrs. Brown said that she could hardly manage her responsibilities before Todd moved in. She has a part-time job as a bookkeeper, is principal caregiver for a sick uncle who lives alone in an apartment Mrs. Brown cleans, and has homemaking responsibilities. Mrs. Brown explained that Mr. Brown takes care of the lawn and home repair but considers housework "woman's work." Although the client usually keeps up with the housework, since Todd moved in with them, she has let the laundry and cleaning accumulate. She has been going to work regularly, but she does not work as quickly as she used to.

When asked how Todd came to live with them, Mrs. Brown said that his mother arranged this with Mr. Brown several months ago. Apparently Todd's mother was planning to remarry and the relationship between Todd and her gentleman friend was not good. When asked if she was involved in the decision to take Todd, she said that her husband did not ask her; he acted as if they had no choice. When asked how she felt about not being asked, Mrs. Brown said she felt slighted. She said that she would have agreed to take Todd if she were asked, because Mr. Brown had an obligation to his son, but she would have liked to have been part of the decision. Mrs. Brown said that she has a great deal of resentment built up inside because after she struggled for fifteen years as a single parent, her own children are independent and she was looking forward to married life as a couple without parental responsibilities. She wondered if she was a selfish person.

During the preliminary evaluation and the first interview, the clinician established that Mrs. Brown had a diagnosis of major depressive disorder, single episode. The client reported that there were previous times in her life when she felt depressed, but she has always been able to "snap out of it." According to the Beck Depression Inventory, Mrs. Brown was mildly to moderately depressed. She showed strengths in continued functioning at home and at work.

In the first session, the client and the clinician (a social worker) identified several problems and target symptoms. They agreed that she had problems communicating her feelings to her husband, difficulty setting limits with her stepson, and problems managing her responsibilities. Target symptoms were sadness, lack of motivation, anger, and lack of interest in eating. She had vague suicidal thoughts but no intention to kill herself. The client and the social worker agreed that Mrs. Brown's difficulty getting motivated to perform her responsibilities and the anger that Mrs. Brown felt but did not express would be the target symptoms initially. The client was asked to bring an hourly schedule of her daily activities to the next session.

At the beginning of the next session, the clinician and Mrs. Brown developed an agenda for this meeting. They would review the client's homework, discuss events of the past week, and explore the target symptoms they had discussed last time. When Mrs. Brown handed the schedule to the social worker, she mentioned that she did not feel that she accomplished very much during the past week. Nevertheless, the clinician observed that Mrs. Brown's schedule was packed. The client spent most of her time cooking, cleaning, taking care of others, or at work; and she spent little time resting or engaging in recreational activities. When asked what else she thinks she should have accomplished, Mrs. Brown said that she did not clean her uncle's kitchen, did the laundry only twice a week, and did not clean her stepson's room, although it was a mess. This led into a discussion of events in her life during the last week. Mrs. Brown said that she felt better after the last interview and that since then she has become more aware of her anger. She said that she resents cleaning up after her stepson; therefore, she puts off the task of cleaning his room. She also has resentment toward her husband for agreeing to have his son come and toward Mr. Brown's former wife for sending him here. Mrs. Brown said that she feels tired as well as resentful. The social worker then asked the client to explain her expectations of herself in relation to Todd. Mrs. Brown said that she expects herself to feel love toward Todd and to care about him as she cared about her own children. She believes that she has an obligation to take on the responsibility of mothering him without resenting it. She views this as something she owes her husband, who is the principal wage earner. The social worker asked Mrs. Brown if she thought she could force herself to feel love if she did not feel this emotion. Mrs. Brown supposed that she could not, but blamed herself for not being able to love Todd. She said that she wished that she were not so angry at Todd; that maybe she could feel love if she did not feel anger. The social worker questioned Mrs. Brown's reasoning about feeling love.

SOCIAL WORKER: What makes you think you must love Todd?

MRS. BROWN: If I'm his stepmother, I should love him.

SOCIAL WORKER: You can be a stepmother to him without feeling love.

MRS. BROWN: How can I? If I didn't love him, I'd be a cruel stepmother.

> **SOCIAL WORKER:**   It sounds as if you believe that you need to love him in order to treat him well—that if you didn't love him, you'd be cruel.
>
> **MRS. BROWN:**   I'm not cruel and I don't hate him; but I don't especially like him either. I think I could like him better if he would cooperate.

The social worker and the client then discussed Mrs. Brown's resentment of Todd's lack of cooperation further. This led into the following discussion:

> **SOCIAL WORKER:** Can you be more specific and tell me what you are angry at Todd about?
>
> **MRS. BROWN:**   He doesn't seem to be in the least concerned about me and all the work he has created for me. He doesn't make his bed or clean his room. He doesn't bring his dishes to the table. He doesn't do the laundry. My girls took care of their own rooms and they used to help me with the dishes, Todd doesn't do anything.
>
> **SOCIAL WORKER:**   It sounds as if you believe he has responsibilities around the house and he isn't doing his part.
>
> **MRS. BROWN:**   Yes.
>
> **SOCIAL WORKER:**   I wonder if you have communicated this to him.
>
> **MRS. BROWN:**   I never had to tell my girls; they just knew. I keep waiting for Todd to volunteer to do something but he seems to expect to be waited on. He should know he has responsibilities.
>
> **SOCIAL WORKER:**   It looks as if he does not know. He can't read your mind. Now that he's living with you, it's up to you to tell him what the rules are.
>
> **MRS. BROWN:**   You mean I should tell him what I want him to do around the house?
>
> **SOCIAL WORKER:**   Yes, tell him what you expect of him. Regardless of how you feel about him, you have the right to have expectations of him.

The homework that was assigned after this session had two parts. The first assignment was for Mrs. Brown to communicate her expectations of Todd to both her husband and Todd. It was important for Mrs. Brown to explain to her husband that she could not assume responsibilities that should be Todd's. In addition, Mrs. Brown was to continue to record her activities, but was to rate them in terms of the pleasure she received. Meanwhile she was encouraged to do more activities that she enjoyed.

Next time Mrs. Brown reported satisfaction in how the conversation with Todd went. She told him that he was responsible for cleaning his room, setting the table, and washing the dishes. He complained but said he would go along with what she wanted. She said that her husband questioned her decision to have Todd set the table and wash the dishes, but when she told her husband that Todd's lack of cooperation was contributing to her depression, he supported her. Mrs. Brown rated all her activities in the low end of the scale in pleasure, except for an hour a day she took to watch TV, which she rated 3 (on a scale that went from 0 to 5).

During the next few sessions, Mrs. Brown reported feeling satisfied that Todd was cooperating. Nevertheless, she still felt depressed. The social worker identified some of the client's beliefs that seemed to be problematic for her. Mrs. Brown believed that she had to be a perfect housekeeper and that she had to take care of whatever was asked of her by family members. Her depressogenic assumption was "in order to be happy, I have to be successful in whatever I undertake" (Beck, 1976, p. 255). During one session, the following conversation took place:

> **SOCIAL WORKER:**   What do you think would happen if you did not do all of the chores you usually do next week?

MRS. BROWN: I would feel like a failure.

SOCIAL WORKER: What do you think would happen to the work you did not complete?

MRS. BROWN: I would probably get it done the following week.

SOCIAL WORKER: So it is possible that you can do fewer things than you usually do?

MRS. BROWN: I could do less. But whatever I do get done does not seem to be enough.

SOCIAL WORKER: How can you tell what's "enough"?

MRS. BROWN: When I'm exhausted, I know I've done enough. I usually work until I am exhausted.

SOCIAL WORKER: What do you think would happen if you stopped working on chores before you reached the exhaustion point?

MRS. BROWN: I don't know; I've never done that.

SOCIAL WORKER: Perhaps we can work this into your homework assignment for this week.

MRS. BROWN: I'd be willing to try that.

With this and other homework assignments, Mrs. Brown recognized that she did not have to work as hard as she was working; that she could accomplish smaller amounts of work at a given time, yet leave time to engage in activities that are pleasurable. With her stepson doing his share, she had more positive feelings toward him. As she approached termination, she began to think of ways in which she could obtain help from a homemaker home health aide for her uncle. During the last few sessions, she discussed her reluctance to share her feelings about Todd's coming to live with them when her husband first brought up the topic. She recognized that she had the distorted belief that she was not allowed to express her feelings when they deviated from what she thought were her husband's expectations. Mrs. Brown expressed confidence that she could improve her relationship with her husband as well as her own sense of well-being by breaking this unstated rule. In the last interview, Mrs. Brown reported that she and her husband had a discussion about chores around the house and that they agreed to distribute the household tasks more equitably and to go out to eat once a week. She said that she has learned to pace herself better and was no longer depressed.

As this case illustrates, cognitive therapy can be used to help depressed individuals who have distorted ideas to change their thinking and behavior. A short-term therapy with a record of effectiveness, it can promote relief from painful emotions and dysfunctional ways of thinking about oneself, others, and the future. A therapy that is guided by scientific reasoning, it promotes logical thinking, which can be useful in problem solving. Such an approach is appealing to clinicians who value intellectual processing and to clients who are capable of learning to examine their beliefs.

Instruments Used to Assess and Monitor Depression

A number of psychometric tools and rapid assessment instruments are used to assist in the diagnosis of depression and to monitor treatment. Some of these lend themselves to evaluations of outcomes. The following instruments are suggested. Those preceded by an asterisk are included in Fischer and Corcoran's (1994) *Measures for Clinical Practice: A*

Sourcebook. References are given in parentheses for instruments found elsewhere. Unless indicated, these are completed by the client.

> Beck Depression Inventory (Beck, Ward, Mendelson, Mock, & Erbaugh, 1961)
> *Brief Depression Rating Scale (completed by clinician)
> Hamilton Rating Scale for Depression (completed by clinician) (Hamilton, 1960)
> *Inventory to Diagnose Depression
> *Zung Self-Rating Scale for Depression

Other Ways of Healing

The two major interventions that were described in this chapter are professionally directed and have been found effective in clinical research trials. But from a client's perspective, other remedies may be more immediately satisfying and helpful. Individuals who are depressed may seek alternatives that do not have the sanction of professionals but hold promise and seem to work for others.

Currently there are a number of herbal remedies that consumers use to treat depression that can be purchased without a prescription at health food stores or from Web sites. The most well known of these is St. John's wort or *hypercium perforatum.* Researchers at the National Institute of Mental Health are studying this herb to assess its effectiveness and side effects. The problem with using an unregulated substance such as this is that there is variation in purity, content, and strength among the various brands on the market and it is not clear how much of which brand an individual should take. Furthermore, these drugs may have side effects and/or interact with prescribed medications. A writer for the newsletter, *NAMI Advocate,* urged consumers and their families "to keep track of the research in this area" and "Definitely talk to your doctor before changing your treatment regimen or trying any new intervention" (Lee, 1998–1999, p. 26).

Other alternative ways of treating depression are exercise, light therapy (for seasonal affective disorder), and fish oils (Lee, 1998–1999). Furthermore, individuals may develop their own ways of coping with depression such as listening to music, talking to friends, reading, playing solitaire, or gardening. Support groups such as those sponsored by the National Depressive and Manic Depressive Association are available in some communities.

Summary and Deconstruction

This chapter began by distinguishing between ordinary mood changes and depressions that are socially constructed as psychopathological. It then reviewed the varied symptoms and complex classification of depressions. Clearly there is no "essential" depression; there are *depressions.* Depressions are heterogeneous, as are the individuals who experience them. For the clinician, however, knowledge of the types of depression can inform their implementation of interventions.

This chapter described two psychotherapies that exemplify best practices in the treatment of mild to moderate depression. These are both short term, so they are compatible with requirements under managed care arrangements. Both are focused, present oriented, and structured. Interpersonal therapy includes education about depression and focuses on one or two issues. Cognitive (or cognitive-behavioral) therapy attends principally to distorted ideas that are associated with depression. Medication may be used concurrently with either of these psychotherapies.

Medication is commonly prescribed by psychiatrists and physicians to provide symptomatic relief of depression. This chapter reviewed the various types that are currently available—SSRIs, trycyclics and tetracyclics, MAOIs, and alternative antidepressants. Individuals differ in their response to different drugs and some individuals do not respond to any. Although the newer drugs appear to have fewer side effects, questions still remain about the appropriateness of these drugs for pregnant and lactating women and older adults.

Depression has been attributed to biological, psychological, and social factors that interpenetrate each other. Women are particularly prone to depression, perhaps because they have learned to be helpless, have difficulty with separations, and have responded to patriarchal behavior by silencing their own voices (Jack, 1991). In this respect, changes in power relations between men and women would contribute to the reduction in the rate of depression among women. Likewise, there is a need to attend to the behaviors of some men and women that mask their depressions. These include substance abuse, criminal behavior, child abuse, social withdrawal, eating problems, underachievement, and even overachievement. Social workers need to be attuned to the possibility that depression is the underlying motif of these behaviors. Finally one needs to attend to clients' ways of healing themselves.

Case Study

Katie is a nineteen-year-old single woman who was referred to the outpatient department of a community hospital after a medical examination revealed that most of her physical symptoms did not have a physical cause. The symptoms she complained about were weight loss, headaches, menstrual irregularity, and low energy. The physician referred her to a clinical social worker in the hospital. Katie subsequently told the social worker that she felt confused and sad; she did not know what to do with her life.

At the time of her first interview, Katie was living with Max, who worked as a long-haul truck driver. She said that he was ten years older than she and had a seven-year-old son from a previous marriage who lived with his mother. Katie met Max at the restaurant where she works as a waitress. Since moving in with Max six months ago, the symptoms have become more and more evident. When asked to talk further about the circumstances surrounding her moving in with Max, Katie said that "In moving in with Max, I lost my parents." When asked to explain, she said that her parents considered her "loose" and have cut off communication with her. Katie does, however, keep in close contact with her brother and sister, who live together in an apartment in town. Her siblings tell her about her parents and what her parents say about Katie.

Katie said that even though she loves Max, moving in with him has not been as wonderful as she had anticipated. For one thing, he is out of town a great deal, so she is alone in their apartment much of the time. Because she is living with him, she does not feel comfortable running around with her old crowd. Last week, however, she did go out with one of the men with whom she works. It started out as a casual invitation on Richard's part that they go out for a drink, but she ended up sleeping with him. Even though Max was out of town, she did not spend the whole night with Richard. The next morning she felt terrible qualms of guilt. Nevertheless, she has not been able to get Richard out of her mind. She sees Richard every day at work and they continue to be friends. Nevertheless, Katie feels that she is "over my head in handling life."

When asked further about her family of origin, she said that she was an "abused child:' She said that her father used to "kick me around while my mother stood and watched." She said that her brother and sister were also abused, but she was the only one who used to fight back with her father, even though she was small. She said that her brother and sister have managed to forgive her parents, but she cannot. Still it bothered her that they do not want to communicate with her.

Katie said that even though she and Max have two incomes, they are struggling financially. Max has to pay child support. She does not earn very much. When asked what her goals for herself were, she said that she always wanted to make something of her life, but she feels trapped. She said that a high school diploma doesn't get you very far, but she can't afford to go to college. She would like to get married some day but she does not feel mature enough to do so in the near future. She has thoughts about getting into work involving animals, which she loves, but does not know how to start. Her immediate goal, she said, was to feel "unconfused."

Discussion Questions

1. Which of the approaches to treatment for persons with depression seems more suitable to this case—cognitive therapy or interpersonal therapy? Why?
2. Develop a plan for intervention in this case using one of these approaches. Which issues do you think should be addressed first?
3. Do you think Katie is a good candidate for pharmacotherapy? Why or why not?
4. To what extent are Katie's problems psychological? Social environmental? Biological?
5. Depression is particularly prevalent among women. How are women's issues involved in this case?

REFERENCES

American Psychiatric Association (1994). *Diagnostic and Statistical Manual of Mental Disorders* (4th ed.). (*DSM-IV*). Washington, DC: Author.

Andreasen, N. C., & Black, D. W. (1995). *Introductory textbook of psychiatry* (2nd ed.). Washington, DC: American Psychiatric Press.

Beck, A. T. (1976). *Cognitive therapy and the emotional disorders.* Madison, CT: International Universities Press.

Beck, A. T. (1985). Cognitive therapy. In H. I. Kaplan & B. J. Sadock (Eds.), *Comprehensive textbook of psychiatry/IV* (pp. 1432–1443). Baltimore, MD: Williams & Wilkins.

Beck, A. T., & Greenberg, R. L. (1974). *Coping with depression.* New York: Institute for Rational Living.

Beck, A. T., Rush, A. J., Shaw, B. F., & Emery, G. (1979). *Cognitive therapy of depression.* New York: Guilford Press.

Beck, A. T., Ward, C. H., Mendelson, M., Mock, J., & Erbaugh, J. (1961). An inventory for measuring depression. *Archives of General Psychiatry, 4,* 561–571.

Bowlby, J. (1969). *Attachment.* New York: Basic Books.

Boyd, J. H., & Weissman, M. M. (1986). Epidemiology of major affective disorders. In G. L. Klerman, M. M. Weissman, P. S. Appelbaum, & L. H. Roth (Eds.), *Social, epidemiologic, and legal psychiatry* (pp. 153–168). New York: Basic Books.

Clark, D. C. (1995). Epidemiology, assessment, and management of suicide in depressed patients. In E. E. Backham & W. R. Leber (Eds.), *Handbook of depression* (2nd ed., pp. 526–538). New York: The Guilford Press.

Clayton, P. J. (1998). Depression subtyping: Treatment implications. *Journal of Clinical Psychiatry, 59* Suppl. 16, 5–12.

Cowen, P. J. (1998). Psychopharmacology. In A. S. Bellack & M. Hersen (Eds.), *Comprehensive clinical psychology* (vol. 6). "Adults: Clinical formulation and treatment," ed. by P. Salkovskis (pp. 136–161). Amsterdam: Elsevier Science.

DeRubeis, R. J., Young, P. R., & Dahlsgaard, K. K. (1998). Affective disorders. In A. S. Bellack & M. Hersen (Eds.), *Comprehensive Clinical Psychology,* Vol. 6. Amsterdam: Elsevier.

Elkin, I., Shea, T., Watkins, J. T., Imber, S. D., et al. (1989). National Institute of Mental Health treatment of depression collaborative research program. *Archives of General Psychiatry, 46,* 971–983.

Fischer, J., & Corcoran, K. (1994). *Measures for clinical practice: A sourcebook* (vols. 1 and 2). New York: The Free Press.

Freud, S. (1917). Mourning and melancholia. In J. Strachey (Ed.), *The standard edition of the complete psychological works of Sigmund Freud* (Vol. 14, pp. 243–258). London: Hogarth Press and Institute of Psychoanalysis.

Hamilton, M. (1960). A rating scale for depression. *Journal of Neurological and Neurosurgical Psychiatry, 23,* 56–62.

Hirschfeld, R. M. A., & Goodwin, F. K. (1988). Mood disorders. In J. A. Talbott, R. E. Hales, & S. C. Yudofsky (Eds.), *Textbook of psychiatry* (pp. 403–441). Washington, DC: American Psychiatric Press.

Hirschfeld, R. M. A., & Shea, M. T. (1985). Affective disorders: Psychosocial treatment. In H. I. Kaplan & B. J. Sadock (Eds.), *Comprehensive textbook of psychiatry/IV* (pp. 811–821). Baltimore, MD: Williams & Wilkins.

Holden, C. (1986). Depression research advances, treatment lags. *Science, 233,* 723–726.

Jack, D. C. (1991). Silencing the self: Women and depression. Cambridge, MA: Harvard University Press.

Jarrett, R. B., & Rush, A. J. (1989). Cognitive-behavioral psychotherapy for depression. In American Psychiatric Association, *Treatments of psychiatric disorders: A task force report of the American Psychiatric Association* (Vol. 3, pp. 1834–1846). Washington, DC: American Psychiatric Association.

Kaelber, C. T., Moul, D. E., & Farmer, M. E. (1995). Epidemiology of depression. In E. E. Backham & W. R. Leber (Eds.), *Handbook of depression* (2nd ed., pp. 3–35). New York: The Guilford Press.

Kaplan, H. I., & Sadock, B. J. (1988). *Synopsis of psychiatry* (5th ed.). Baltimore, MD: Williams & Wilkins.

Kaplan, H. I., & Sadock, B. J. (1998). *Synopsis of psychiatry* (8th ed.). Baltimore, MD: Williams & Wilkins.

Karasu, T. B. (1990). Toward a clinical model of psychotherapy for depression, I: systematic comparison of three psychotherapies. *American Journal of Psychiatry, 147*(2), 133–147.

Kessler, R. C., Abelson, J. M., & Zhao, S. (1998). The epidemiology of mental disorders. In J. W. Williams & K. Ell (Eds.), *Advances in mental health research: Implications for practice* (pp. 3–24). Washington, DC: NASW Press.

Klerman, G. L., (1988). Depression and related disorders of mood (affective disorders). In A. M. Nicholi, Jr., *The new Harvard guide to psychiatry* (pp. 309–336). Cambridge, MA: Belknap Press of Harvard University Press.

Klerman, G. L., Weissman, M. M., Rounsaville, B. J., & Chevron, E. S. (1984). *Interpersonal psychotherapy of depression.* New York: Basic Books.

Lee, L. L. (1998–1999). Alternative medicine goes mainstream—What does it mean for you? *NAMI Advocate, 20*(3), 25–26.

Markowitz, J. C., & Weissman, M. M. (1995). Interpersonal psychotherapy. In E. E. Backham & W. R. Leber (Eds.), *Handbook of depression* (2nd ed., pp. 376–390). New York: The Guilford Press.

Marris, P. (1982). Attachment and society. In C. M. Parkes & J. Stevenson-Hinde (Eds.), *The place of attachment in human behavior* (pp. 185–201). New York: Basic Books.

McGuffin, P., & Katz, R. (1989). The genetics of depression and manic-depressive disorder. *British Journal of Psychiatry, 155,* 294–304.

Miller, L. J. (1996). Psychopharmacology during pregnancy. *Primary Care Update Ob/Gyn, 3*(3), 79–86.

Nemeroff, C. B., & Schatzberg, A. F. (1998). Pharmacological treatment of unipolar depression. In P. E. Nathan & J. M. Gorman (Eds.), *A guide to treatments that work* (pp. 212–225). New York: Oxford University Press.

NIH Consensus Development Conference. (1991). *Diagnosis and treatment of depression in late life* (vol. 9, no. 3).

Regier, D. A., Boyd, J. H., Burke, J. D., Rae, D. S., et al. (1988). One-month prevalence of mental disorders in the United States. *Archives of General Psychiatry, 45,* 977–986.

Regier, D. A., Farmer, M. E., Rae, D. S., Myers, J. K., Kramer, M., Robins, L. N., George, L. K., Karno, M., & Locke, B. Z. (1993). One-month prevalence of mental disorders in the United States and sociodemographic characteristics: The Epidemiologic Catchment Area study. *Acta Psychiatrica Scandinavica, 88,* 35–47.

Rickels, K. (1999, October). Psychopharmacology for social workers: Lecture and handout. University of Pennsylvania School of Social Work.

Rosenhan, D. L., & Seligman, M. E. P. (1984). *Abnormal psychology.* New York: Norton.

Sacco, W. P., & Beck, A. T. (1995). Cognitive theory and therapy. In E. E. Backham & W. R. Leber (Eds.), *Handbook of depression* (2nd ed., pp. 329–351). New York: The Guilford Press.

Seligman, M. (1975). *Helplessness: On depression, development, and death.* New York: W. H. Freeman.

Weiss, R. S. (1982). Attachment in adult life. In C. M. Parkes & J. Stevenson-Hinde (Eds.), *The place of attachment in human behavior* (pp. 171–184). New York: Basic Books.

Weissman, M., & Klerman, G. L. (1977). Sex differences and the epidemiology of depression. *Archives of General Psychiatry, 34,* 98–111.

Weissman, M., & Klerman, G. L. (1989). Interpersonal psychotherapy. In American Psychiatric Association, *Treatments of psychiatric disorders: A task force report of the American Psychiatric Association* (Vol. 3, pp. 1863–1884). Washington, DC: American Psychiatric Association.

Weissman, M. M., & Myers, J. K. (1978). Affective disorders in a U.S. urban community: The use of Research Diagnostic Criteria in a community survey. *Archives of General Psychiatry, 35,* 1304–1311.

9 Clinical Practice with Clients with Anxiety Disorders

For me, agoraphobia is an emotional/anxiety disorder (challenge) that limits my ability to go out and do things. It also limits my ability to have people in my home, as I am also considerably socially phobic. Some phobics experience panic attacks and I am one of them. For sure, this challenge does not affect everyone the same way or to the same degree. It also varies in its ability to limit me. As it is stress-related it often increases in intensity in direct correlation to the amount of stress in my life.

—Ellen, http://msw-ent.com/aphobia/index.htm

…In my view, anxiety is a diffuse cognitive-affective structure consisting of a negative feedback cycle characterized to varying degrees by components of high negative affect; a sense of both internal and external events proceeding in an unpredictable, uncontrollable fashion; and maladaptive shifts in attention.

—Barlow, *Anxiety and Its Disorders,* 1988

Anxiety is a state of tension and apprehension that is an uncomfortable but ordinary human response to a threat or danger. Experienced viscerally as well as psychologically, it is a concomitant of thinking, feeling, and behavior. In the face of unknown, unfamiliar situations, anxiety can provide a warning of danger that can help an individual mobilize resources to meet the threat. When one confronts larger questions about the meaning of the cosmos, the purpose of existence, and one's own mortality, one is likely to experience existential anxiety.

Anxiety becomes constructed as a disorder when the emotion is experienced with great frequency and intensity, when it interferes with psychosocial functioning, and when the response is out of proportion to the stimulus (Kaplan & Sadock, 1998). Although persons who suffer from anxiety disorders usually are not psychotic and can form relationships and function in social roles, many are unable to work or participate in community life without overwhelming discomfort. As the quotations that open this chapter suggest, clients and professionals construct these experiences differently.

This chapter is about anxiety disorders and clinical interventions that are used to treat some of them. According to the National Comorbidity Survey (NCS), over a twelve-month period, the prevalence of any anxiety disorder was about 17 percent, and over a lifetime it was close to 25 percent (Kessler, et al., 1994). Among the groups of disorders, the lifetime rates were highest for substance abuse/dependence disorders and next for anxiety disorders (Kessler et al., 1994). The earlier NIMH Epidemiological Catchment Area Study, which covered a wider age range of participants, came up with a similar ranking (Regier, et al., 1988). Both epidemiological studies found that anxiety disorders were more prevalent among women than men. The NCS also found that the odds of having an anxiety disorder are greater for individuals with low income and education (Kessler et al., 1994).

A postmodern perspective on anxiety disorders emphasizes its heterogeneity. There are many types of anxiety disorders and differences among individuals with each type. Some symptoms such as panic attacks and agoraphobia can occur in different kinds of anxiety disorders (American Psychiatric Association, 1994). Some individuals have more than one anxiety disorder or both an anxiety disorder and another psychiatric disorder. As Table 9.1 shows, anxiety disorders are characterized by a variety of concurrent biological, cognitive, emotional, and behavioral symptoms. The next section provides an overview of the various types of anxiety disorders.

Types of Anxiety Disorders

The *DSM-IV* describes several categories of anxiety disorders and the specific criteria necessary for their diagnosis. The major categories are as follows.

Panic disorder (PD) is characterized by unexpected panic attacks—periods of heightened emotion that are frightening and uncomfortable—and anticipatory anxiety about their recurrence (APA, 1994). According to the *DSM-IV,* at least four of a list of thir-

TABLE 9.1 Symptoms of Anxiety

Type of Symptom	Description
Biological	Perspiration, heart palpitations, dyspnea, fainting, nausea, muscular tension, shakiness, flushing, gastrointestinal disturbances, insomnia, dizziness
Cognitive	Worry, apprehension, anticipation of danger or doom; thoughts about contamination, going crazy, or dying; irrational fears; preoccupied by and ruminating about repetitive themes; thoughts of embarrassment, humiliation
Emotional	Keyed up, fearful, on edge, irritable, terrified, "nervous"
Behavioral	Hypervigilant, jumpy, tremors, pacing, avoidance behavior

teen somatic and cognitive symptoms must be present to consider episodes of anxiety as panic attacks. Among these symptoms are heart palpitations, sweating, trembling, sensations of shortness of breath, fear of losing control, chest pain, or chills (APA, 1994). The combination of physical symptoms and the cognition of impending death lead some sufferers to emergency rooms believing that they are having a heart attack.

Although for some individuals panic disorder is a discrete experience, for others panic occurs hand in hand with agoraphobia. The frequency of the convergence of these two conditions led two authorities to hypothesize that the emergence of spontaneous panic is a conditioning event that is a precursor to the development of agoraphobia (Klein & Gorman, 1987). Subsequently the person's agoraphobia revolves around the fear of having another panic attack. In an analysis of data from the Epidemiologic Catchment Area Study, panic disorder coexisting with agoraphobia was found in about one-third of the cases of panic disorder (Markowitz, Weissman, Ouellette, Lish, & Klerman, 1989). According to the NCS, the odds of having both agoraphobia and panic disorder are close to 12:1 (Kessler, 1997). The *DSM-IV* (American Psychiatric Association, 1994) accounts for their co-occurrence with the category *panic disorder with agoraphobia.*

Agoraphobia is a fear and avoidance reaction to being in a place or situation from which there is no perceived way of getting help (APA, 1994). Like any phobia, it is an irrational fear of a situation or object confrontation, which results in overwhelming anxiety. In order to prevent anticipated anxiety, persons with agoraphobia avoid the situation that is associated with the reaction. Those who also have panic attacks may fear having a panic attack in the designated situation. The *DSM-IV* describes *agoraphobia without a history of panic disorder* (APA, 1994).

Individuals with agoraphobia cope with their situation in a variety of ways. Some stay home all the time, a strategy that is incapacitating and further reinforces the fear of leaving the house. Others go out but limit their activities. These individuals may go to public places in the company of others or endure the discomforting anxiety in order to accomplish needed activities. Agoraphobics who go out alone will go out of their way to avoid the situations that disturb them; for example, a person afraid to drive on highways will use side streets. Others cope by using chemical substances.

Two other types of anxiety disorders are *social phobia* and *specific phobia. Social phobia* is an irrational fear of being in a situation in which one is expected to perform or may be observed by others. The person with a social phobia is especially sensitive to anticipated ridicule, embarrassment, or humiliation. Examples of situations that are problematic to persons with this disorder are speaking in public, eating in a restaurant, and using public lavatories. *Specific phobias* are associated with particular objects or situations. Simple and specific phobias may have co-occurring panic attacks.

Another anxiety disorder is called *generalized anxiety disorder* (GAD). This is a pervasive, chronic condition rather than one that occurs in spurts like panic disorder. Individuals with GAD worry excessively about situations or circumstances that are not, on the surface, threatening. Irrational thinking is accompanied by numerous symptoms of anxiety.

An additional type of anxiety disorder is the *obsessive-compulsive disorder* (OCD), a disabling condition that intrudes on thinking and behavior. Obsessions are persistent, irrational, ego-dystonic thoughts, impulses, or images, usually of an unpleasant nature, that take over the consciousness of a person with this disorder. They usually convey thoughts about contamination, sex, or aggression and are accompanied by self-doubt. Compulsions are irrational, stereotyped, ritualistic behaviors, which are attempts to counteract the obsessions. Examples include constant handwashing, cleaning, and checking. Compulsions are time consuming and repetitive; thus, they interfere with the accomplishment of more constructive activities. Acting out compulsions brings release but little pleasure, whereas resisting compulsions arouses anxiety. According to the *DSM-IV,* either obsessions or compulsions are required for a diagnosis of obsessive-compulsive disorder (APA, 1994). The two may, however, co-occur.

Post-traumatic stress disorder (PTSD) is an anxiety reaction to an event that threatens the life or bodily integrity of oneself or someone with whom one is closely associated. The individual may experience the event directly or witness or hear about it. The person with post-traumatic stress disorder will relive the event (cognitively and emotionally), have nightmares or flashbacks, act as if the event were recurring, or experience distress in the face of stimuli that are reminders of the event. Like PTSD, an *acute stress disorder* is a reaction to a traumatic event, but the duration is between two days and one month.

In addition to these disorders, the *DSM-IV* describes *anxiety disorder due to a medical condition* and a *substance-induced anxiety disorder.* Some medical conditions that produce symptoms of anxiety are hypoglycemia, congestive heart failure, chronic obstructive pulmonary disease, and encephalitis (APA, 1994). Likewise alcohol, cocaine, caffeine, and other substances can precipitate anxiety (APA, 1994). A medical evaluation should assess whether a medical condition or chemical substance is etiologically involved.

Explanatory Theories

Although the various types of anxiety disorders that have been described have much in common, there are many differences among them. Furthermore, there are different scientific traditions associated with each of them. Rather than discussing the scientific findings that are associated with each type, this section will provide an overview of the kinds of theories that come into play and examples of explanations pertaining to particular anxiety disorders. In keeping with the postmodern perspective of this book, biological, social, and psychological explanations are intertwined. For a given individual with a particular disorder, different strands among each of the following aspects may be relevant.

Biological Aspects

Genetic studies suggest but do not prove that anxiety disorders are inherited. With respect to panic disorders, twin studies have revealed a higher concordance rate between monozygotic than dizygotic twins (Torgersen, 1983). Furthermore, first-degree relatives of persons with panic disorder have a high risk of having the same disorder (Weissman, 1988). General anxiety disorder and obsessive compulsive symptoms are also common among first-degree relatives of individuals with these particular disorders (Andreasen & Black, 1995). Nevertheless, specific genetic markers for anxiety disorders have not been identified. Trends among first-degree relatives can be explained by social learning.

Brain imaging studies suggest that there are abnormalities in the structure and function of the brains of some individuals with anxiety disorders (Kaplan & Sadock, 1998). Further evidence that anxiety disorders are brain diseases comes from the medications that are effective in reducing symptoms. These medications suggest that the neurotransmitters norepinephrine, serotonin, and GABA play a role in the generation of anxiety disorders (Kaplan & Sadock, 1998). The section on medication in this chapter will describe the medications that are currently used to treat anxiety disorders. Another line of research links hyperventilation with panic, but the evidence is not strong enough to establish a causal relationship (Salkovskis, 1998).

Social Dimensions

Stressful life events seem to play a role in precipitating panic attacks, although prospective research is needed because most studies have elicited information about life events from clients who were in the throes of their disorders (Barlow, 1988). The social dimension seems pertinent when there is agoraphobia along with panic symptoms because individuals with agoraphobia avoid situations based on their meaning in a social context. Post-traumatic and acute stress disorders are, by definition, caused by social stressors such as war, rape, and assault. The high rate of anxiety disorders among women may be a consequence of living in a patriarchal society in which women are vulnerable to threats from the outside world and experience conflicts over remaining dependent versus becoming autonomous (Kaschak, 1992).

According to an analysis of data from the Epidemiological Catchment Area Study of a community sample (Markowitz, et al., 1989), participants who met diagnostic criteria for panic disorder (of whom 70 percent were female and 75 percent were white) scored relatively poorly on several measures of quality of life. These included subjective ratings of physical and emotional health, substance abuse, suicide attempts, impaired social and marital functioning, financial dependence, and use of treatment facilities. The findings on persons with panic disorder were comparable with those on persons with major depression but distinct from persons with neither panic nor major depression. The unusually high rate of suicidal ideations and suicide attempts among persons with panic disorder was confirmed in another analysis of the same data (Weissman, Klerman, Markowitz, & Ouellette, 1989).

Psychological Theories

A number of psychological theories explain the etiology and expression of anxiety. Many of these theories are specific to particular kinds of anxiety disorders (e.g., phobias, obsessive-compulsive disorder). To reduce the complexity and specificity of these theories, general statements will be made about each theory.

Psychoanalysis.   Freud viewed anxiety as both normal and a potential source of neurotic development (Brenner, 1955). Normal anxiety provides a signal to the organism so that it can protect itself from harm. Pathological anxiety is associated with id instincts that cannot be held in check by the ego defenses. Because the anxiety has nowhere to go and must be expressed, it takes the form of neurotic symptoms. Anxiety neuroses (cf. generalized anxiety disorder), phobic neuroses (cf. agoraphobia and other phobic disorders), and obsessive-compulsive neurosis (cf. obsessive-compulsive disorder) represent channels for the expression of unacceptable id impulses.

Freud and later ego psychology theorists attributed the development of neuroses to failure to resolve early developmental issues. Phobias, for example, are associated with conflict in the oedipal stage, particularly castration anxiety, whereas obsessive-compulsive neurosis is traceable to conflicts during the anal stage. Phobias and panic attacks have also been attributed to difficulty mastering the task of separation-individuation (Hollander, Liebowitz, & Gorman, 1988).

Existential Theory.   Existential theory explains anxiety as a fact of life. Anxiety arises when one recognizes the beauty, wonder, and tragedy of life. Camus's (1991) image of Sisyphus pushing a boulder uphill only to see it fall down after it reaches the top captures the absurdity of life's struggles when one knows that death is inevitable. Existential theory explains Freud's normal anxiety but not the severe symptoms one sees in some of the anxiety disorders.

Behavioral Theory.   According to learning theory, anxiety is a response (a behavior) that is learned in association with a painful situation. Afterward the conditioned response to this situation generalizes to other situations. This maladaptive behavior can become further reinforced by the behavior of significant others, who condone it or provide support, which then provides the person with maladaptive behavior with what are called *secondary gains,* which perpetuate the anxious response. Although this pattern appears to be insidious, it can be reversed by altering the contingencies. Behavioral methods of therapy such as systematic desensitization and in vivo exposure have been very successful in the treatment of anxiety disorders.

Cognitive Theory.   Cognitive theory poses that anxiety is a normal emotion that is needed for survival. A person with an anxiety disorder feels anxious upon misperceiving a situation as dangerous. Interestingly, such a person ignores environmental cues indicating that the same situation is safe (Beck, 1985). In the face of perceived threat, the autonomic nervous system becomes activated, motoric activity ensues (fight, flight, faint, or freeze), and faulty cognitions and problematic emotions are triggered. Accordingly a situation that is inherently neutral is "catastrophied." Cognitive therapy techniques such as imagery and cognitive restructuring can be helpful in the treatment of persons with anxiety disorders.

Recent conceptualizations of anxiety disorders are biopsychosocial, with treatments aimed at the biological symptoms, cognitions, and behaviors. The psychological interventions that will be described later in this chapter are based on cognitive and behavioral theories. Before turning to them, however, medications that are used to treat anxiety disorders will be discussed.

Medication Used to Treat Anxiety Disorders

Over the years a number of drugs have been tried and used to treat anxiety disorders. Although these medications do not cure the disorders, they do relieve distressing symptoms, making it possible for clinicians to treat problems with psychotherapy. The drugs that have been used have varying cost-benefit ratios, which clients need to weigh before agreeing to pharmacotherapy. Major drugs that have been reported to be effective in the treatment of anxiety disorders will be discussed in the following section. Table 9.2 lists the drugs by type and indicates their respective trade names.

Tricyclic Antidepressants

During the past three decades, antidepressant medications have been used to treat anxiety. The drug that has been tested the most is *imipramine* (Tofranil), a tricyclic. This drug has been shown to be effective in treating panic disorder and anticipatory anxiety associated with agoraphobia (Mavissakalian & Perel, 1989; Zitrin, Klein, Woerner, & Ross, 1983). Research indicates that it takes a high dose to treat agoraphobia but a moderate dose to treat the panic disorder (Mavissakalian & Perel, 1989). Furthermore, imipramine helps reduce nightmares, flashbacks, panic attacks, and mood disturbances in persons with post-traumatic stress disorder (Horowitz, 1989). Other tricyclic antidepressants that are used to treat panic disorder and agoraphobia as well as post-traumatic stress disorder are Elavil, Norpramin, Pamelor, and Sinequan. These drugs have the advantage of reducing anxiety while at the same time they do not pose a threat of dependence. The disadvantages of tricyclics and their

TABLE 9.2   Medications Used to Treat Anxiety Disorders

Group/Examples	Trade Name
Tricyclic antidepressants	
imipramine	Tofranil
amitriptyline	Elavil
desipramine	Norpramin
nortriptyline	Pamelor
doxepin	Sinequan
clomipramine	Anafranil
Monoamine oxidase inhibitors (MAOIs)	
phenelzine	Nardil
Selective serotonin reuptake inhibitors (SSRIs)	
fluoxetine	Prozac
fluvoxamine	Luvox
paroxetine	Paxil
sertraline	Zoloft
Benodiazepines	
clonazepamn	Klonopin
lorazepam	Ativa
alprazolam	Xanex
diazepam	Valium
Buspirone	BuSpar

side effects (sedation, postural hypotension, anticholinergic effects, etc.), were described in chapter 8.

Clomipramine (Anafranil) is a tricyclic that is used principally in the treatment of obsessive-compulsive disorder. Although clomipramine does not eliminate obsessions and compulsions entirely, it does reduce preoccupation with obsessions and ritualistic behavior (Insel & Zohar, 1987). Like other tricyclics, clomipramine takes several weeks to produce changes; when the medication is withdrawn, the disorder reasserts itself (Zohar, Foa, & Insel, 1989).

Monoamine Oxidase Inhibitors

Another antidepressant medication that is used to treat anxiety disorders is the MAOI, particularly *phenelzine* (Nardil). Like imipramine, it treats panic and phobic anxiety. Moreover, the MAOI is effective in the treatment of social phobias and atypical depression with panic attacks (Liebowitz, 1989), as well as posttraumatic stress disorders with panic attacks (Horowitz, 1989). However therapeutic, the MAOI requires restriction of certain foods and drink (e.g., smoked food, aged cheeses) and medications (e.g., antihistamines) (see Chapter 8). In addition, certain side effects are associated with this group of drugs (e.g., hypotension, sexual difficulties). For these reasons, other medications are preferred for the treatment of panic and agoraphobia.

Selective Serotonin Reuptake Inhibitors (SSRIs)

Another group of antidepressants that has proved to be effective in treating anxiety disorders is the selective serotonin reuptake inhibitors, discussed in Chapter 8. SSRIs have been found effective in treating panic disorder and social phobia (Roy-Byrne & Cowley, 1998), obsessive-compulsive disorder (Rauch & Jenike, 1998), and post-traumatic stress disorder (Yehuda, Marshall, & Giller, 1998). One of the more recently approved SSRIs for obsessive-compulsive disorder is fluvoxamine (Luvox). SSRIs have the advantage of a low profile of adverse side effects. They are, however, costly; less expensive generic versions have not, as yet, appeared on the market.

Benzodiazepines

Benzodiazepines are anxiolytics (antianxiety agents) that have historically been used to treat anxiety. Among the drugs in this group are *chlordiazepoxide* (Librium), *diazepam* (Valium), *clorazepate* (Tranxene), *oxazepam* (Serax), *alprazolam* (Xanax), and *lorazepam* (Ativan). Some of these drugs (e.g., Serax and Ativan) have a short half-life, that is, they are eliminated from the blood rapidly. Others have an intermediate half-life (e.g., Xanax), and others have a long half-life (Valium, Tranxene, Librium) (Salzman, 1989). The two short-half-life drugs, Serax and Ativan, which do not have active metabolites, and long-acting benzodiazepines with active metabolites that are prescribed in small doses and over increased intervals, are recommended for older adults (Rickels & Schweizer, 1987).

All these drugs have a calming effect. Furthermore, they produce sedation, promote sleep, and have some muscle relaxant and anticonvulsive effects (Rickels & Schweizei, 1987). The sedative effects may or may not be desired. Sedation causes drowsiness and slows reactions, which can interfere with the operation of machinery. This effect is compounded if the client uses alcohol or takes antihistamines (Rickels & Schweizer, 1987). A serious problem with these drugs is that, over time, they are addictive. Upon withdrawal, uncomfortable and disturbing experiences occur (cf. Gordon, 1979). Persons successfully treated for panic attacks, for example, can, upon withdrawal, experience *rebound panics,* recurrences that are more intense than those that were experienced previously. For these reasons, short-term use with minimal therapeutic doses (Salzman, 1989) and slow withdrawal (Barlow, 1988) are recommended.

Because the onset of the effects of benzodiazepines is rapid (especially Valium and Tranxene), these drugs are amenable to use for symptomatic relief of acute anxiety reactions (Rickels & Schweizer, 1987), such as those seen in an emergency room. Moreover, they have been found to be effective in the treatment of generalized anxiety disorder, posttraumatic stress disorder, and panic disorder (Horowitz, 1989; Noyes, Chaudry, & Domingo, 1986; Rickels & Schweizer, 1987).

Alprazolam (Xanax) has been particularly effective in the treatment of panic disorders and associated phobic anxiety. This drug appears to be less sedating than the other benzodiazepines. In addition, it has antidepressant effects on recipients, regardless of whether or not they have a secondary depression (Lesser et al., 1988). Research emanating from the Cross-National Collaborative Panic Study on approximately 500 subjects found that those who took alprazolam had a significantly higher rate of improvement in panic attacks, phobic fears, avoidance behavior, anxiety, and social disability than the control group on placebos (Ballenger et al., 1988). Improvement was evident after one week. Nevertheless, side effects that were treatment related were identified in another report by this research group (Noyes et al., 1988). These include fatigue, sedation, ataxia, amnesia, and slurred speech. These authors reported that the dropout rate among those who received the active drug was substantially lower (16 percent) than that of those who received the placebo (50 percent), a finding that suggests high acceptance of alprazolam.

Buspirone

Buspirone (BuSpar) is an antianxiety agent that is the equivalent of diazepam (valium) that does not share many of the latter's drawbacks. Buspirone does not cause sedation, engender abuse or physical dependence, or act as an anticonvulsant (Eison & Temple, 1986). Accordingly, arousal, attention, and the capacity to act and react are preserved. Another advantage of buspirone is that it does not interact synergistically with alcohol (Eison & Temple, 1986); thus, it may be useful for persons with a history of substance abuse (Salzman, 1989). Nevertheless, buspirone does not act as quickly as the diazepam. Moreover, in some cases, lack of sedation may be viewed as a drawback. Buspirone seems to be useful in the treatment of generalized anxiety disorder and in the relief of symptoms of hostility and anger (Rickels & Schweizer, 1987).

Application

The aforementioned drugs are the major medications used to treat anxiety disorders. New drugs continue to be tested and introduced all the time. Moreover, some of the antidepressants that were discussed in Chapter 8 and the neuroleptic and antimanic drugs that will be addressed in Chapter 12 are sometimes used together with some of the medications that were reviewed here. Table 9.3 lists specific anxiety disorders with drugs that have been shown to be effective in research studies.

These drugs provide symptomatic relief to those individuals who are willing to take them and who respond positively to them. Many clients who are given full information about the effects and risks associated with these medications will, however, refuse consent. Antidepressants have side effects that many individuals find disturbing. Benzodiazepines can be addicting if taken over a long period of time and are not appropriate for persons with a history of substance abuse. Older adults are more sensitive to drugs and may have medical problems that complicate or preclude psychopharmacology (Banazak, 1997). Regardless of whether or not clients receive medication, they can benefit from psychotherapy. Therapy can modify thoughts, emotions, and behaviors that medication does not touch. The forms of psychotherapy that have been most successful provide help in behaving and thinking more adaptively. Other forms of treatment promote insight into the problem that underlies the anxiety and provide an opportunity for the client to release disturbing emotions.

Research on Medication and Psychotherapy

The relative effects of medication and psychotherapy in the treatment of anxiety have not been subjected to studies as extensive as those with respect to depression. Such research is complicated by competing theoretical and practice paradigms (and, thus, vested interests) of psychiatrists and psychologists. Psychiatrists tend to have a biological orientation; psychologists tend to favor behaviorism (Klerman, 1988).

Some research looks at the relative merits of behavioral treatment and pharmacotherapy in the treatment of panic disorder and agoraphobia. Particular attention has been given to testing Klein and Gorman's (1987) model of panic and agoraphobic development. As mentioned, these researchers posed that panic precedes and conditions the development of agoraphobia. Furthermore, they suggested that imipramine is able to treat the panic attacks but not avoidant behavior or anticipatory anxiety. One group of psychiatrists found in a

TABLE 9.3   Medication Used for Specific Anxiety Disorders

Disorder	Medications
Panic disorder with and without agoraphobia	SSRIs, TCAs, MAOIs, benzodiazepines
Social phobia	MAOIs, SSRIs
Specific phobias	Do not appear to be responsive to drugs
Generalized anxiety disorder	Benzodiazepines, buspirone, TCAs
Obsessive-compulsive disorder	TCA (Clomipramine), SSRIs
Post-traumatic stress disorder	TCAs, MAOIs, benzodiazepines

Sources: Based on Cowen (1998), Rauch & Jenike (1998), Roy-Byrnet Cowley (1998), Yehuda, Marshall & Giller, Jr. (1998).

controlled study that there was significant improvement among all subjects given encouragement and instructions to practice in vivo exposure (to be explained in the next section) on their own, with those on imipramine rating higher clinically, depending on the dose of imipramine they had (Mavissakalian & Michelson, 1986). In another analysis, however, it was found that subjects who were not told to practice exposure benefited in relation to both phobic and panic symptoms. Here, too, a relation between medication dosage and the target symptoms was found (Mavissakalian & Perel, 1989). In another study in which behavior therapy with and without imipramine was compared with supportive therapy with imipramine, no differences were found among the various treatments (Klein, Zitrin, Woerner, & Ross, 1983). On the basis of these studies it appears that *medication and exposure* (as well as support), separately or together, can effectively treat panic and anticipatory anxiety.

Barlow (1988) postulates that tricyclic medication reduces anxiety rather than being specifically a treatment for panic. With somatic effects of anxiety lessened, behavioral treatments are able to be more effective. Nevertheless, he notes that because of the side effects of tricyclics (dry mouth, constipation, agitation), the dropout rates for participants in research studies are relatively high. He remarks further that one of the side effects, agitation, resembles the anxiety symptoms that are the presenting concern.

One way to bypass problems associated with medication is to pursue a course of psychotherapy first. Fortunately there are a number of treatment approaches with demonstrated effectiveness. If these strategies do not work, medication can be explored. In the next section, cognitive and behavioral approaches to the treatment of anxiety disorders will be described.

Cognitive-Behavioral Treatment of Anxiety Disorders

In today's managed care environment, short-term, measurable, and effective treatment modalities are advantageous. Cognitive-behavioral treatment can extinguish (or reduce the intensity of) disturbing symptoms of anxiety over a short period of time. Some of the methods that are used to treat anxiety disorders will be described next. The first three are used principally with persons with phobias and obsessive-compulsive disorder.

Systematic Desensitization

Systematic desensitization was developed by Joseph Wolpe and described in *Psychotherapy by Reciprocal Inhibition,* which was published in 1958. His ideas are developed further in a subsequent book (Wolpe, 1982). Wolpe applied his method of psychotherapy to adults with a spectrum of phobic conditions. His approach is predicated on the principle of reciprocal inhibition; that is, one can weaken neurotic anxiety by countering it with a competing stimulus. The strategy employed is to use a stronger stimulus to inhibit a weak form of the neurotic anxiety. Wolpe recommended as the stronger stimulus deep muscle relaxation, which produces a physical effect that is the opposite of anxiety. Relaxation diminishes the impact of anxiety-provoking scenes the client is later asked to imagine.

Systematic desensitization is carried out in four steps (Wolpe, 1982). First, the client is introduced to the Subjective Anxiety Scale. The clinician asks the client to give his or her worst experience of anxiety a rating of 100 and the state of absolute calmness a score of 0. In addition, the client is asked to rate his or her current state somewhere in between 0 and 100. Wolpe describes these ratings as *suds* (subjective units of distress).

Next the client begins training in deep muscle relaxation. Wolpe's exercises are based on those developed by Jacobson (1938), but Wolpe's are taught to the client in a period of six weeks, whereas Jacobson's took fifty or more sessions. The client is taught to contract and relax specific parts of the body, from head to toe, in incremental steps over time. The client is told, for example, to contract the fists, to feel the tension in the fist, hand, and forearm, and then to release the contracted fist and relax. (An abbreviated program of progressive relaxation of this kind is described by McKay, Davis, & Fanning, 1981.) In addition, the client is expected to practice relaxation ten to fifteen minutes twice a day at home (Wolpe, 1982).

During the third stage, the clinician, with the help of the client, constructs a hierarchy of anxiety-producing events (Wolpe, 1982). A tentative list of items to include derives from the social history, results of instruments administered to the client prior to treatment, and discussion between the client and the clinician. Items are grouped together by theme (a) to determine which are relevant to treatment (e.g., items suggesting agoraphobia, acrophobia, and claustrophobia are relevant; objective fears about getting pregnant are irrelevant) and (b) to develop separate hierarchies, each related to a different theme. The client is asked to give a suds rating to each item listed under each theme and to give a rationale for these ratings. From this information the clinician constructs a hierarchy of discrete, evenly spaced items for each theme (Wolpe, 1982). The following is an example of such a series, with suds scores listed in parentheses:

1. Being home alone, watching TV (10)
2. Walking down the block with my spouse (20)
3. Walking down the block alone (30)
4. Taking the bus with my spouse (40)
5. Taking the bus alone (50)
6. Going to the grocery store early in the morning (60)
7. Going to the grocery store on Friday afternoon (70)
8. Going to a shopping mall (any time) (80)
9. Going downtown during the week (90)
10. Going to the state fair on opening day (100)

Next comes the implementation of the desensitization procedure (Wolpe, 1982). This can be initiated in the third or fourth session, following relaxation training. After the client comes to a deep state of relaxation and eyes are closed, the clinician inquires how relaxed the client is. If the client says 0, the clinician offers a control scene, such as having the client imagine a pleasant, calm, sunny, summer day. If this does not produce anxiety, the clinician begins with the lowest-ranking scene from one of the lists of hierarchies and has the client imagine it. The client signals that the scene is being contemplated by raising a finger. After five to seven seconds, the clinician asks the client to stop and to provide a suds rating. Sometimes presentation of the same scene twice results in a lower rating the second time. Relaxation is implemented in between scenes, with the intervals between scenes being ten to thirty seconds. Subsequent sessions begin with items that have low ratings but are above 0 (Wolpe, 1982).

Flooding and Implosive Therapy

Flooding is a behavioral treatment technique that was introduced after systematic desensitization. Like its predecessor, flooding requires that the client imagine anxiety-provoking scenes. In flooding, however, the client does not get into a relaxed state prior to implementation of the procedure. Treatment consists of the clinician describing in great detail a scene that is highly anxiety provoking for the client. *Implosive therapy* is similar to flooding in its use of graphic images of disturbing scenes to extinguish anxiety. With implosive therapy the clinician adds themes based on psychoanalytic insights into the client's early experiences to the scenes described during flooding, resulting in a more intense experience than that in flooding.

In Vivo Exposure

The principle that explains the effectiveness of systematic desensitization, flooding, and implosive therapy is that *exposure to what one fears reduces anxiety.* The methods that have been described thus far rely on cognitive processes (imagination) to extinguish anxiety. More recently it has been recognized that in vivo (real-life) exposure is more readily translated into behaviors related to the client's life. In vivo exposure can be used to treat phobias (agoraphobia, social phobia, simple phobias) and obsessive-compulsive disorders.

In vivo exposure may be *prolonged* or *graduated* (O'Brien & Barlow, 1984). With prolonged exposure, the client faces the feared situation in an intense form (high on the hierarchy) early in treatment and for long periods of time. As such, prolonged exposure is akin to flooding. With graduated exposure, the client is exposed to situations that arouse little anxiety first. The client progresses over time to more threatening situations. Graduated exposure bears some resemblance to systematic desensitization but is carried out in a natural context.

The distinction between prolonged and graduated exposure highlights the significance of the dimensions of duration and intensity in relation to in vivo exposure. Research comparing these dimensions is equivocal. Some research suggests that sessions of two hours or more are more effective than shorter sessions (e.g., Stern & Marks, 1973). Nevertheless, clients who have been treated with prolonged in vivo exposure were more likely to drop out of treatment than those who were treated on a graduated basis (Barlow, 1988). Furthermore, prolonged exposure has the disadvantage of adversely affecting the interpersonal system (Barlow, 1988).

In vivo exposure can be implemented with various degrees of participation by the clinician. At one end of the continuum, the clinician directs and implements treatment from an office (e.g., exposing the client to snakelike objects and snakes in the office). Another approach is for the clinician to accompany the client to places in which the client will be exposed to disturbing stimuli (e.g., walking outside, around the clinic building). In the treatment of agoraphobia, some clinicians will accompany and provide support to small groups of clients taken to shopping malls for several hours at a time (Barlow, 1988). An alternative is for the clinician to set up a program of activities for the client to carry out independently in the community between sessions. In some cases, the clinician will promote the implementation of such a program by making home visits and involving a spouse or partner of the client (Mathews, Gelder, & Johnston, 1981). At the far end of the continuum is in vivo exposure that is carried out autonomously by clients through self-help manuals (e.g., Weakes, 1968, 1972) or client-run self-help groups.

Response Prevention

This is a method of blocking the performance of rituals by persons with obsessive-compulsive disorder. As it is described by Turner and Beidel (1988), response prevention is a means to prevent reinforcement (and, thus, continuation) of anxiety reduction through repeated, ritualistic behavior. Accordingly, the client is deterred from carrying out a compulsion. In doing so, professional staff do not use physical force; instead they intervene by distracting, redirecting, or coaxing a client not to perform the ritual. Furthermore, they do not block the client from culturally normative activities, such as showering once a day or washing hands after handling dirt. Turner and Beidel (1988) use a combination of flooding (exposure to the feared stimulus) and response prevention in their treatment program for persons with obsessive-compulsive disorder.

Thought Stopping

This is a means of interrupting the occurrence of intrusive or irrational thoughts. It is used to treat persons with generalized anxiety disorder and obsessive-compulsive disorder. It is implemented as follows. First, the client is asked to discuss and give an example of a situation in which the unwanted thoughts are present (Mahoney, 1974). Then the clinician has the client imagine being in that situation again and having these thoughts (Rimm & Masters, 1974). After the client indicates the presence of such thoughts, the clinician shouts, "Stop!" Startled, the client stops focusing on the previous thought. Exposed to this method of conditioning repeatedly, clients learn to recognize and subvocalize "stop" to themselves, thus interrupting their own thoughts. Because this method has weak empirical support (Mahoney, 1974; Turner & Beidel, 1988), it tends to be used as an adjunctive rather than as a principal treatment method.

Cognitive Restructuring

With cognitive restructuring anxiety-producing thoughts are identified, challenged, and replaced with more accurate thoughts. At first the client is helped to recognize irrational automatic thoughts that accompany anxiety. This is facilitated by the assignment of homework in which experiences of anxiety are recorded and described (what happened, what the client was thinking, how the client was feeling). During therapy, the clinician challenges the rationality of the client's thoughts. For example, a client who left a party soon after arriving, when she experienced anxiety, noted that she saw someone she had gone out with previously and whom she liked but who never asked her out again. She believed that if they were to have a face-to-face encounter at the party it would be "awful." The clinician had the client explore the many possibilities their encounter might have brought (including his asking her out again) and explained the difference between possible and probable outcomes (cf. Ellis, 1962). This client was encouraged to develop alternative ways of thinking and responding that she might have had to the occasion (e.g., people who date are bound to meet people they have dated in the past; even though she was uncomfortable seeing this man, she could still enjoy the party; one way to reduce her anxiety would have been to talk to him right away "to get it over with"; even if he does not want to talk to her, she is a worthwhile human being who has a right to be at the party and enjoy herself). Cognitive methods of treating anxiety disorders are discussed in depth by Beck, Emery, and Greenberg (1985).

Stress Inoculation Training

Stress inoculation training is a form of cognitive-behavioral therapy that helps clients develop skills in coping with stress (Meichenbaum, 1985). It engages clients as collaborators in the collection of data from their everyday experiences that arouse stress and in the selection of strategies to cope with stress. Clients learn to identify maladaptive thoughts, solve problems, regulate emotional responses, and implement coping skills. Stress inoculation can be used with a wide spectrum of populations in clinical and community settings. It incorporates many of the cognitive and behavioral techniques that were described previously (relaxation training, graded exposure, identifying automatic thoughts, modeling), as well as problem solving. Stress inoculation training can be implemented with individuals, couples, and groups.

The preceding section reviewed a variety of cognitive and behavioral methods that are used to intervene with individuals with different kinds of anxiety disorders. Many of these methods go back to the 1950s. In recent years, systematic treatment procedures for particular kinds of anxiety disorders have been developed. Several of them use or adapt several of the methods that were discussed; for example, stress inoculation training is used in treatment of post-traumatic stress disorder (Calhoun & Resick, 1993). Social skills training, which is used with adults with severe mental illness, is also helpful in the treatment of social phobia (Barlow, Esler, & Vitali, 1998). The next section will summarize one of these treatment protocols as an example of a best practice for treating panic disorder with and without agoraphobia.

Best Practice: Cognitive-Behavioral Treatment for Panic Disorder and Panic Disorder with Agoraphobia

The cognitive-behavioral treatment for panic disorder (PD) and panic disorder with agoraphobia (PDA) that is described here (Craske & Barlow, 1993) is predicated on a biopsychosocial perspective. Barlow (1988) proposed a biopsychosocial process in which the inborn alarm system that is ordinarily activated under stress becomes susceptible to responding to "false alarms" that become conditioned responses. Panic disorder is "a learned fearfulness of certain bodily sensations associated with panic attacks," and agoraphobia is "a behavioral response to the anticipation of such bodily sensations or their crescendo into a full-blown panic attack" (Craske & Barlow, 1993, p. 1). According to the cognitive hypothesis (Beck et al., 1985), panic attacks first arise from tension from life problems that leave the individual with feelings of helplessness. When bodily or mental sensations associated with tension recur, the individual interprets them as signs of imminent catastrophes that threaten his or her life or well-being. The misinterpretation generates increased anxiety and sensations that can result in a panic attack (Salkovskis, 1998) and worry about the recurrence of such an attack (Barlow, 1988). Individuals with a family history of panic disorder may be more physiologically vulnerable to reacting to internal stimuli in this way (Craske & Barlow, 1993).

Craske and Barlow's model is built on an understanding of anxiety, panic, agoraphobia, and several related concepts. Immediate anxiety is understood as *fight-flight response* to perceived danger; it is the organism's attempt to protect itself and prepare for action. In the face of a threat the autonomic nervous system becomes activated. This system has two subsystems—*sympathetic* and *parasympathetic* nervous systems. The sympathetic system, which prepares the body for action, triggers heart and blood flow, increases breathing, and stimulates sweating. The parasympathetic system protects the body by restoring it to its normal state. Persons with panic attacks fear the bodily sensations that occur when there is a fight-flight response. These sensations may be the outcome of stress, overbreathing (*hyperventilation*), hypervigilance to normal bodily changes, or interoceptive conditioning. *Interoceptive conditioning* is a form of conditioning in which panic responses are stimulated by subtle bodily sensations that occur out of awareness of the individual (Craske & Barlow, 1993). Such sensations can become conditioned by association with normal activities that produce anxiety, for example, exercise or drinking coffee (Craske & Barlow, 1993). When individuals cannot identify a cause for their panicky feelings, they devise an explanation ("I'm dying," "I'm going crazy") or blame themselves (Craske & Barlow, 1993). Agoraphobia is a flight response to bodily states that precipitate panic attacks. (For a more detailed explanation of this process in the form of a handout that can be distributed to clients, see Craske and Barlow, 1993.)

The cognitive-behavioral therapy for PD/PDA aims to educate clients about their symptoms, correct misinterpretations of bodily symptoms, provide breathing retraining, and implement exposure exercises. Table 9.4 summarizes the major elements of this intervention. Note that the treatment can be implemented in an outpatient or inpatient facility or in the client's natural environment. This is a short-term intervention, compatible with the call for brief therapy by managed care entities. The authors report that 80 to 100 percent of clients are free of panic attacks by the end of treatment and that most of them maintain these gains for at least two years (Craske & Barlow, 1993).

Assessment

Before implementing such an intervention, a thorough assessment is required. The clinician conducts an in-depth interview with the client in which a history is taken of the presenting symptoms over time, and information is gathered about other life circumstances

---

TABLE 9.4 ■ BEST PRACTICE Cognitive-Behavioral Treatment for Panic Disorder and Panic Disorder with Agoraphobia

---

Aims

- Provide information about anxiety, panic attacks, hyperventilation
- Change misinterpretations of bodily symptoms
- Provide breathing retraining; modify cognitions
- Provide repeated exposure to frightening internal cues and external situations

Settings

- Clinic
- Natural environment
- Inpatient facility

Assessment

- In-depth interviews
- Screening instruments
- Medical evaluation
- Client self-report information on panic attacks
- Behavioral approach tests

Treatment Components

- Education about anxiety, panic, cognitions, and the various treatment strategies
- Cognitive restructuring
- Breathing retraining
- Applied relaxation
- Interoceptive exposure
- Situational exposure

Number of sessions

- 10–15

Format

- Individual sessions
- Involvement of significant other toward end of treatment

Source: Based on Craske & Barlow (1993).

that may be relevant. Craske and Barlow use the Anxiety Disorders Interview Schedule—Revised (DiNardo & Barlow, 1988) to clarify the diagnosis. In addition, they ask the client to provide information on the panic attacks and to have a medical evaluation to rule out medical conditions. The clinician administers some behavioral approach tests on activities the client identifies as difficult and rates the client's anxiety at intervals. Self-report inventories are used for treatment planning and to assess changes during therapy (see, e.g., the Anxiety Sensitivity Index, Reiss, Peterson, Gursky, & McNally, 1986).

Treatment Components

The following treatment strategies are used to reduce panic and agoraphobic symptoms.

Cognitive restructuring is used to identify inaccurate and irrational ideas that the client associates with the symptoms. These cognitions may be unproven hypotheses that explain their feelings. As with Beck's cognitive therapy for depression, these cognitions are challenged (particularly overestimating the danger and catastrophizing) and tested in between-session homework assignments. Accurate cognitions replace the inaccurate ones. Cognitive restructuring is integrated into the other treatment components.

Breathing retraining is instituted to address hyperventilating, described by 50 to 60 percent of clients who are treated for panic disorder (Craske & Barlow, 1993). At first clients are asked to breath rapidly and deeply (i.e., to reproduce hyperventilation) for a minute and a half while standing. Then they are asked to what extent symptoms like these occur when they are anxious. Clients are provided didactic information about hyperventilation (described as overtaxing the body) and are retrained to breathe through their diaphragm rather than chest muscles and to control their breathing by keeping a count of the number of times they inhale and thinking, "relax," while they exhale.

Applied relaxation is training in progressive muscle relaxation. It is used to counteract muscular tension that occurs during panic attacks (Craske & Barlow, 1993). Clients are trained to contract and relax various parts of the body, one part at a time.

Interoceptive exposure aims to weaken the link between bodily cues and panic reactions by inducing feared experiences in such a way that the fear response does not occur (Craske & Barlow, 1983). Procedures such as running in place, breathing through a narrow straw, and shaking one's head from side to side are used to induce paniclike sensations. Clients are exposed to these experiences gradually and increasingly to acclimate them to biological sensations that had previously produced fear.

Situational exposure is something like the in vivo exposure that was described earlier. To deal with agoraphobia that is associated with some panic disorders, the client is exposed gradually and repeatedly to feared external situations such as malls or subways. Situational exposure weakens the link between context-related cues and anxiety and panic reactions (Craske & Barlow, 1993).

Intervention Sequence

Treatment is generally provided on an individual basis, with the option of incorporating a significant other, especially during the last few sessions. Although Craske and Barlow (1993) describe fifteen sessions, they indicate that panic symptoms can be controlled in ten. Telch et al. (1993) reported a significantly high level of effectiveness of a similar intervention using an eight-week group format.

Sessions 1 and 2.   During these introductory sessions, the client's education about anxiety and panic attacks begins, and the purpose and nature of treatment are explained. The physiology of anxiety and panic is described and the concepts of hypervigilance and interoceptive conditioning are introduced. The client is asked to describe the situations in which he or she experiences panic attacks. In addition, the expectations that the client is responsible for monitoring his or her own progress and for practicing assigned homework activities are conveyed. The client is asked to keep a record of his or her daily moods, the intensity of the client's anxiety, and the particular symptoms the client experience.

Sessions 3–5. In session 3 the client is asked to hyperventilate and then breathe slowly until the symptoms diminish. Hyperventilation and breathing control are then explained. Breathing control exercises begin in session 3 and continue in the next two sessions. The client is asked to practice diaphragmatic breathing for ten minutes twice a day as homework. The relationship between breathing control and cognitions is introduced in session 3 with cognitive restructuring occurring in the next two sessions. In session 4 it is suggested that the client overestimates the consequences of panic; in session 5 cognitive structuring is extended to catastrophizing. Homework assignments for sessions 4 and 5 are to monitor the client's own overestimating and catastrophizing and to continue breathing exercises.

Sessions 6–9. After reviewing cognitive restructuring principles conveyed in the previous sessions, the focus moves to interoceptive exposure. Initially the concept of interoceptive conditioning is revisited, and a rationale for interoceptive exposure is given. Avoidance (characteristic of agoraphobia) is explained as a consequence of bodily sensations that are viewed as frightening. The clinician then introduces some interoceptive exposure exercises to assess the client's response, measured on a scale from 0 to 8. Examples of exercises are running in place, holding one's breath, spinning in a swivel chair, and breathing through a narrow straw. The results of these exercises are used to establish a hierarchy of activities for future practicing. In the seventh session, the client integrates breathing control and cognitive restructuring with interoceptive exposure. The exercises performed in the previous level are redone starting with those that had a low rating. When the client signals feeling an uncomfortable bodily sensation, he or she is asked to remain with the feeling another thirty seconds. The clinician helps the client, too, with cognitions that impede a more prolonged exposure ("What would happen if you ran in place another thirty seconds?"). After doing these during clinical sessions and as homework for a couple of weeks, interoceptive exposure is extended to naturalistic tasks that the client avoids because they stimulate bodily sensations (session 9). Examples of these are running up steps, drinking coffee, engaging in strenuous physical exercise, and driving with the windows closed. The client rates his or her anxiety reactions and lists them in hierarchical order. Cognitions associated with these experiences are elicited and restructured. The client is asked to select two items from his or her list to practice three times each.

Sessions 10–11. During the tenth session, the homework assignment is reviewed and situational exposure is discussed. With the latter, the focus is on situations that are associated with agoraphobia, that is, situations the client avoids out of fear of anxiety and panic. Situational exposure is explained as a means to obtain control over feared events or situations and is distinguished from interoceptive exposure, which emphasizes bodily sensations. If appropriate, a significant other can be brought into treatment in session 11 at which time the procedures and their rationale are explained to that person. During this session, the significant other is asked to explain how the client's disorder has affected their life together, and strategies are developed to engage this person's help as a coach. The client, significant other, and clinician then develop a hierarchy of activities that comes out of the client's daily life to which to apply situational exposure. The couple choose one activity among these to practice three times during the next week.

Sessions 12–15.   The last few sessions, held with the client and significant other, involve the review of practice assignments and cognitions associated with carrying these out, exploring and addressing difficulties, and planning new assignments. Interoceptive exposure is integrated with situational exposure by having the client monitor his or her bodily sensations while engaging in situational exposure. The last few sessions are held on a biweekly basis.

Evaluation

Panic disorder and panic disorder with agoraphobia are frightening and disabling conditions that interfere with social functioning and the quality of one's life. The preceding treatment protocol offers an effective remedy to this condition. It may be implemented in an office or hospital setting, in a client's residence, or another natural setting. The intervention may be the only treatment, or it may be used in tandem with prescribed medication (Craske & Barlow, 1993).

This clinical procedure requires that the clinician be knowledgeable about cognitive therapy, the dynamics of panic and agoraphobia, and the specific procedures summarized earlier. It is recommended that anyone who wishes to use this protocol with clients should read further about cognitive therapy and the Craske and Barlow (1993) approach, and practice the specific procedures under supervision.

The cognitive-behavioral intervention that has been highlighted here focuses primarily on the symptoms and, to a lesser extent, on the personality of the individual who is suffering. Some of the clients with whom social workers work have complicated personalities and situations that can be better addressed with an approach that integrates ego psychology with cognitive-behavioral therapy. The following section presents an example of an individual with panic symptoms who was treated by a social worker who used an integrative approach.

Case Example: Integrated Methods

Harold Rogers is a twenty-two-year-old, single man who complained of stress when he was first seen at an outpatient service of a community hospital. He reported having difficulties sleeping, weight loss, poor appetite, and recurrent episodes of heart palpitations, chest pains, difficulty breathing, and dizziness. These experiences were occurring at least once a week in the past month in a variety of contexts—when he was alone in the car on his way to work, at work, and when he was home alone. With these disturbing symptoms, he wondered whether he was "going crazy." Upon awakening in the morning, he had thoughts of staying home from work, but he went to work anyway.

Mr. Rogers was unable to provide much information about his family background during the first interview because he experienced heart palpitations when he was asked. He did say that during the last year his parents "threw him out of the house" and "forced" him to support himself. They said he was a "bum" who sat around the house during the day, went out at night, and did not work. The client coped by at first moving in with his sister for a couple of months and getting a job and later moving in with his woman friend. He also mentioned that two months ago he had a benign tumor removed from his back. Several months ago, he added, two close friends died—one of cancer, the other in a car accident. Mr. Rogers said that when he developed the tumor, he thought that he might have cancer, too. The client said that he thinks about death a great deal and is afraid to be alone.

Mr. Rogers is a high school graduate who was working on a construction crew, building houses. The few "attacks" he has had at work occurred when he was on the roof. He reported feeling dissatisfied that this was a "lowly job" with no future. Some day he would like to have his own business as a photographer. He has thought about looking for another job but has not made any efforts to do so. He said that he has had little contact with his parents since they threw him out; he does see his older brother and sisters and has a number of friends. He reported having a good relationship with the woman he was living with (Margaret Tyler); nevertheless, she does occasionally put pressure on him to make a commitment and he does not want to get married. He also mentioned that Margaret has made his life comfortable: she cooks, cleans, and picks up after him.

Preliminary Assessment

This twenty-two-year-old, employed, single man developed panic attacks during a year of many stressful life events. Not only did he experience a "forced" separation from his parents; he took a job that he perceived as "lowly," he lost two close friends, and he had a medical condition that turned out to be benign. In addition, the woman he is living with, who provides much comfort, wants more of a commitment than he is willing to give. Thrust into a world that is uncertain, demanding, and insecure, he feels anxious. He appears to desire to escape from his current situation (by not going to work or fantasizing about another job) and has anxiety about being alone, but he has not developed an overt phobia. The theme of loss and separation predominates, with unresolved issues surrounding his separation from his parents. He seems to have some dependent traits and does not seem to reciprocate in relationships. His strengths include his working, living independently, ability to maintain relationships, and the willingness to ask for help. His symptoms of anxiety are compounded with mild depression. His *DSM-IV* diagnosis is as follows:

Axis I:	300.01	Panic disorder without agoraphobia (moderate)
Axis II:	799.90	Diagnosis deferred
Axis III:	Benign tumor removed	
Axis IV:	Psychosocial and environmental problems: forced emancipation, changes in living situation, new job, deaths of two friends, medical problem	
Axis V:	GAF = 60 (current)	
	GAF = 75 (highest level past year)	

Treatment Plan

In order to treat the panic disorder, two strategies will be pursued. For one, the client will be taught relaxation exercises in the office and will be assigned homework to practice these daily. Second, the client will be scheduled to see the staff psychiatrist. In view of his panic and concomitant mild depression, the use of an SSRI will be discussed with the doctor. Although the primary diagnosis is panic disorder without agoraphobia, he is at risk of developing agoraphobia or a specific phobia (fear of heights). To prevent this from occurring, the clinician will advise the client "not to give in to the urge to avoid going out." In addition, activities involving his going out with his woman friend to pursue his hobby (photography) will be assigned.

Development of the Case over Time

Mr. Rogers was seen weekly for three months. Initially treatment centered on his symptoms. During his consultation with the psychiatrist, it was learned that he drank beer occasionally (but not excessively) and was not eager to take medication that precluded these activities. The client, social worker, and psychiatrist agreed that medication was not necessary at this time, and they would pursue other strategies first. The social worker strongly encouraged Mr. Rogers to continue to face his fears by going to work and getting out. He practiced the relaxation exercises at home and at work. As planned, he and Margaret took expeditions in which he took photographs.

Meanwhile, the client became better able to talk about his past and his family situation. He revealed that when he was six, his father died of a heart attack at home. Soon afterward the client refused to go to school. He said that his mother took him to a child guidance center for treatment; eventually he returned to school. Mr. Rogers said that he has always been close to his mother and feels protective of her. Three years ago, however, she married a man who seemed to resent him, the only child at home. Mr. Rogers expressed anger toward the stepfather, who, he thought, convinced his mother to throw him out of the house. When asked whether he would like to return to them, he said no, he thought it was time that he was on his own. Mr. Rogers said, however, that he did miss his mother. When asked about his not seeing her, he said that he supposed that he was angry at her, too. The client spent a number of sessions expressing feelings toward his father who died when he was six, his stepfather, and his mother. He said that after his father died, he had a fear of losing his mother, even though he realized that she was in good health. As the youngest child, he had his mother's attention much of the time and he enjoyed that. In therapy, his belief that he was "entitled" to being taken care of indefinitely by his mother was challenged as irrational and childish, and cognitions supporting his parents' right to live as they want and his responsibility to support himself were substituted. At this point the client began to become aware of his reluctance to leave the nest and be on his own. This was followed by the expression of feelings of guilt about having been inconsiderate of his mother (as well as awareness that he may be taking advantage of Margaret). When asked what he thought he might do with his feelings, he said that he would like to reestablish a relationship with his mother as an independent adult. A couple of sessions were spent planning how he might initiate contact with her and rehearsing his visit with her. The client saw his mother alone at her home on one occasion, when he apologized for his past behavior and expressed the desire to be part of the family again. She accepted his feelings and invited him to bring Margaret with him to dinner the following week.

As these separation issues were worked through, the symptoms of anxiety and depression waned and the panic attacks disappeared. Still the client expressed dissatisfaction with his job and ambivalence toward Margaret. The client continued to pursue his hobby as a photographer and planned to sell some of his photographs to a publisher. When it was suggested that he and Margaret be seen together, he said that he did not want her to get involved in his personal problems. Termination was precipitated by his taking a job in a photography shop in a distant city. He said that the job paid less than his current job, but it was a "white-collar job."

In this case a combination of methods was used. At first attention was given to the distressful symptoms. Relaxation exercises were implemented in the office and assigned for practice at home. In addition, the client was encouraged to continue to face stressful situations (in vivo exposure) and to go out on photography excursions that were in keeping with his interests. When the client was ready, ego-modifying treatment in which he reflected on patterns that arose in the past was used. It was learned that separation anxiety was a long-standing issue with him; that he had a school phobia following his father's death when he was a child. The client was given the opportunity to express feelings about his loss of his father as a child and his loss of his mother's complete attention when she remarried. He expressed anger at his mother and stepfather; yet he had the desire to reconcile with them. Cognitive therapy was used to help him recognize that his feelings of entitlement were irrational and inappropriate for him at this point in his life. The client was encouraged to reconnect with his mother and stepfather and was helped to do so through behavior rehearsal of his first meeting with his mother. Soon afterward, he was able to separate from his woman friend and simultaneously pursue a job that was in tune with his life goals.

Although the specific cognitive-behavioral treatment procedure for panic disorder described earlier or the integrated approach described here work, some clients are not receptive to either strategy, or they participate in therapy while using alternative means of coping with anxiety. The following section reviews some of these.

Instruments Used to Assess and Monitor Anxiety

The following instruments are useful in assessing and monitoring anxiety and measuring outcomes. Those found in Fischer and Corcoran's (1994) *Measures for Clinical Practice* are denoted with an asterisk; other sources are indicated in parentheses. All are completed by the client unless otherwise indicated.

Hamilton Anxiety Rating Scale (Hamilton, 1959)

Yale-Brown Obsessive-Compulsive Scale (administered by clinician) (Goodman et al., 1989)

*Zung's Self-Rating Anxiety Scale

*Social Avoidance and Distress Scale

Other Ways of Healing

Anxiety is a universal feeling that is not likely to be defined as a disorder unless it seriously interferes with everyday functioning and is identified as problematic by a professional. Through a social process of help seeking and finding, diffuse and uncomfortable feelings become reconstructed as symptoms of an anxiety disorder. Regardless of whether individuals experiencing these feelings seek professional help, many of them discover a number of ways of healing on their own.

One means of helping oneself heal, which was borrowed from Eastern religions, is meditation. Some individuals find that meditation clears their minds, relaxes their bodies, and reduces their stress. One version of this, transcendental meditation (TM), is practiced as follows:

> You begin by sitting in a comfortable position and silently repeating a word or sound over and over again. If a thought other than the meditative word comes to mind, you repeat the word or sound again. It has been said that the level of rest achieved by TM is deeper than sleep. (Phalen, 1998, p. 107)

Meditation may be a component of a lifestyle that includes eating a well-balanced diet (that may be low in fat content, macrobiotic, or vegetarian), getting ample sleep, practicing yoga, and exercising. By controlling these aspects of one's life and finding inner peace, one can become empowered to take charge of one's life.

Another means of healing oneself is through religion and spirituality. Religion offers a framework in which one's experiences can make sense; religious organizations offer support for this framework, a sense of community, and opportunities to pray. Whether one finds solace in group or individual prayer, or through one's own individual form of spirituality, one may find comfort, peace, and tranquility this way.

The previous chapter mentioned herbal treatment in relation to depression. There are also herbs that are reputed to treat anxiety. Two publications that describe these treatments are Foster and Tyler's (1999) *Tyler's Honest Herbal: A Sensible Guide to the Use of Herbs and Related Products* and Robbers and Tyler's (1999) *Tyler's Herbs of Choice: The Therapeutic Use of Phytomedicinals.* Again, one should be cautious about these remedies, dosage, and how they may interact with prescribed drugs.

There are a number of organizations that provide information and help to individuals with anxiety disorders and their families. Among the national organizations are the Anxiety Disorders Association of America, the National Center for PTSD, the Obsessive Compulsive Foundation, and the National Alliance for the Mentally Ill (which includes panic disorder and obsessive-compulsive disorders among the major disorders they support). There are myriad support groups for individuals with anxiety disorders and their families in local communities. In addition, there are many self-help books and tapes (as well as Web pages) that provide information about coping with anxiety.

Summary and Deconstruction

Although *anxiety* is an ordinary response to perceived danger and to consciousness of the mysteries of the cosmos, *anxiety disorders* are extraordinary. Individuals whose inner tension is constructed as disordered experience the tension that others experience but to a heightened degree. In some respects, they live more intensely, but in other respects they suffer a great deal and are debilitated.

Anxiety disorders are heterogeneous and complex. All the anxiety disorders described in the *DSM-IV* are characterized by a set of biological, cognitive, emotional, and behavioral symptoms, many of which occur across types. With some anxiety disorders, individuals avoid certain kinds of situations (e.g., social phobias); with other disorders, they feel compelled to act in certain ways (obsessive-compulsive disorder). With some disorders the anxiety is concentrated and erupts (panic disorder); with other disorders, the anxiety is diffuse (generalized anxiety disorder). Individuals with anxiety disorders experience the same symptoms differently.

This chapter reviewed biological, psychological, and social explanations of anxiety disorders. Genetic explanations are not definitive. The numerous psychological theories attest to the heterogeneity of the disorders and individual differences; some explanations may fit more with some individuals' experience than others. The association of anxiety disorder with gender and socioeconomic class (income, education) raises questions about the role of stress in the generation of anxiety disorders.

This chapter described a model program of cognitive-behavioral treatment of individuals with panic disorder with agoraphobia. However effective the program is, it is not appropriate for all clients and does not address some of the psychosocial issues that may be pertinent. Some clinical social workers combine and integrate different methods in their work with clients. A case example illustrated how ego psychology can be used together with exposure and cognitive restructuring.

Individuals with anxiety also design their own treatments from the options they discover on their own or in their own communities. Among these are meditation, yoga, exercise, herbal remedies, and living a healthy lifestyle. In addition, some clients and members of their families participate in support groups, read self-help books, and find "answers" on Web pages. Clinical social workers need to be cognizant that individuals' ways of coping include these methods as well as (or instead of) going to professionals.

Case Study

Cynthia Brown is a medium-tall, 30-year-old, married woman who reported that she weighed 160 pounds. She has an attractive face and dresses in such a way that she looks lighter than her stated weight. She said that her problems are of her own making: because she is ashamed of being overweight, she isolates herself. She stays home most of the time and avoids opportunities to go out. She has difficulty getting herself mobilized to go to the grocery store, usually waiting until they are out of food and she must go. The client expressed concern that she will be seen at the grocery store. Whenever her husband suggests that they go out together or with another couple, she finds a reason for them not to go out.

Mrs. Brown said that even though it looks as if she "prefers" to be at home, she does not do much when she is home. She feels as if she spends all her time serving others—even the dog—but is not doing anything for herself. She and her husband, Jason, have a three-year-old daughter, Amy; her husband has a son, age 12, from a previous marriage, who lives with them. Mrs. Brown believes that her husband gives more attention to his son than to their daughter. To compensate, she devotes herself to Amy. Even though Mrs. Brown has allowed Amy to go to a nearby nursery school, she worries about her the whole time Amy is in school. She is afraid that "something will happen to Amy."

Mrs. Brown said that she and Jason met at the time Jason was separated from his first wife. At that time Cynthia was thin and worked as a model. Jason told her that his first wife had a weight problem; that her weight contributed to their divorce. Mrs. Brown has some concern that her husband will reject her. She said that she knows her refusal to go out has been getting on his nerves, too. She mentioned that when they first met, her husband used to worry that other men would want her. Now she worries that her husband will be attracted to other women.

The social worker remarked that Mrs. Brown has described a number of problems—fears about leaving the house, worries about her daughter, a weight problem, and marital difficulties—and asked her what she wanted to work on. The client said that if she could get over her anxiety about leaving the house, she thinks that the other problems will resolve themselves.

Discussion Questions
1. What kind of anxiety disorder does Mrs. Brown seem to have?
2. What kinds of intervention would you use? Whom would you involve in her treatment?
3. Identify Mrs. Brown's irrational ideas. How would you help her change these?
4. Do you think medication is appropriate for this client? Why or why not?
5. How are women's issues involved in this case?

REFERENCES

American Psychiatric Association (1994). *Diagnostic and statistical manual of mental disorders (DSM-IV)* (4th ed.). Washington, DC: Author.

Andreasen, N. C., & Black, D. W. (1995). *Introductory textbook of psychiatry* (2nd ed.). Washington, DC: American Psychiatric Press.

Ballenger, J. C., Burrows, G. D., DuPont, R. L., Lesser, I. M., et al. (1988). Alprazolam in panic disorder and agoraphobia: Results from a multicenter trial. I. Efficacy in short-term treatment. *Archives of General Psychiatry, 45,* 413–422.

Banazak, D. A. (1997). Anxiety disorders in elderly patients. *The Journal of the American Board of Family Practice, 10*(4), 280–289.

Barlow, D. H. (1988). *Anxiety and its disorders.* New York: Guilford Press.

Barlow, D. H., Esler, J. L., & Vitali, A. E. (1998). Psychosocial treatments for panic disorders, phobias, and generalized anxiety disorder. In P. E. Nathan & J. M. Gorman (Eds.), *A guide to treatments that work* (pp. 288–318). New York: Oxford University Press.

Beck, A. (1985). Cognitive therapy. In H. I. Kaplan & B. J. Sadock (Eds.), *Comprehensive textbook of psychiatry/IV* (pp. 1432–1438). Baltimore, MD: Williams & Wilkins.

Beck, A. T., & Emery, G., with Greenberg, R. L. (1985). *Anxiety disorders and phobias: A cognitive perspective.* New York: Basic Books.

Brenner, C. (1955). *An elementary textbook of psychoanalysis.* New York: Doubleday Anchor.

Calhoun, K. S., & Resick, P. A. (1993). Post-traumatic stress disorder. In D. Barlow (Ed.), *Clinical handbook of psychological disorders: A step-by-step treatment manual* (2nd ed., pp. 48–98). New York: The Guilford Press.

Camus, A. (1991). *The myth of Sisyphus and other essays.* Trans. by J. O'Brien. New York: Vintage Books.

Cowen, P. J. (1998). Psychopharmacology. In A. S. Bellack & M. Hersen (Eds.), *Comprehensive clinical psychology,* vol. 6, "Adults: Clinical Formulation and Treatment," ed. by P. Salkovskis (pp. 136–161). Amsterdam: Elsevier Science.

Craske, M. G., & Barlow, D. H. (1993). Panic disorder and agoraphobia. In D. Barlow (Ed.), *Clinical handbook of psychological disorders: A step-by-step treatment manual* (2nd ed., pp. 1–47). New York: The Guilford Press.

DiNardo, P., & Barlow, D. H. (1988). *Anxiety Disorders Interview Schedule—Revised (ADIS-R).* Albany, NY: Graywind Publications.

Eison, M. S., & Temple, D. L. (1986). Buspirone: Review of its pharmacology and current perspectives on its mechanism of action. *The American Journal of Medicine, 80* (suppl 3B), 1–9.

Ellis, A. (1962). *Reason and emotion in psychotherapy.* New York: Lyle Stuart.

Fischer, J., & Corcoran, K. (1994). *Measures for clinical practice: A sourcebook* (vols. 1 and 2). New York: The Free Press.

Foster, S., & Tyler, V. E. (1999). *Tyler's honest herbal: A sensible guide to the use of herbs and related products* (4th ed.). New York: Haworth Herbal Press.

Goodman, W. K., Price, L. H., Rasmussen, S. A., et al. (1989). The Yale-Brown Obsessive-Compulsive Scale, I: Development, use, and reliability. *Archives of General Psychiatry, 46,* 1006–1011.

Gordon, B. (1979). *I'm dancing as fast as I can.* New York: Harper & Row.

Hamilton, M. (1959). The assessment of anxiety states by rating. *British Journal of Medical Psychology, 32,* 50–55.

Hollander, E., Liebowitz, M. R., & Gorman, J. M. (1988). Anxiety disorders. In J. A. Talbott, R. E. Hales, & S. Yudofsky (Eds.), *Textbook of psychiatry* (pp. 391–443). Washington, DC: American Psychiatric Press.

Horowitz, M. J. (1989). Posttraumatic stress disorder. In American Psychiatric Association, *Treatments of psychiatric disorders: A task force report of the American Psychiatric Association* (Vol. 3, pp. 2065–2082). Washington, DC: American Psychiatric Association.

Insel, T. R., & Zohar, J. (1987). Psychopharmacologic approaches to obsessive-compulsive disorder. In H. Y. Meltzer (Ed.), *Psychopharmacology: The third generation* (pp. 1205–1210). New York: Raven Press.

Jacobson, E. (1938). *Progressive relaxation.* Chicago, IL: University of Chicago Press.

Kaschak, E. (1992). *Engendered lives: A new psychology of women's experience.* New York: Basic Books.

Kaplan, H. I., & Sadock, B. J. (1998). *Synopsis of psychiatry* (8th ed.). Baltimore, MD: Williams & Wilkins.

Kessler, R. C. (1997). The prevalence of psychiatric comorbidity. In S. Wetzler & W. C. Sanderson (Eds.), *Treatment strategies for patients with psychiatric comorbidity.* New York: John Wiley & Sons, Inc.

Kessler, R. C., McGonagle, K. A., Zhao, S., Nelson, C. B., Hughes, M., Eshleman, S., Wittchen, H-U., & Kendler, K. S. (1994). Lifetime and 12-month prevalence of DSM-III-R psychiatric disorders in the United States: Results from the National Comorbidity Survey. *Archives of General Psychiatry, 51,* 8–10.

Klein, D. F., & Gorman, J. M. (1987). A model of panic and agoraphobic development. *Acta Psychiatrie Scandinavia, 76* (suppl. 335), 87–95.

Klein, D. F., Zitrin, C. M., Woerner, M. G., & Ross, D. C. (1983). Treatment of phobias. II. Behavior therapy and psychotherapy: Are there any specific ingredients? *Archives of General Psychiatry, 40,* 139–145.

Klerman, G. L. (1988). Overview of the cross-national collaborative panic study. *Archives of General Psychiatry, 45,* 407–412.

Lesser, I. M., Rubin, R. T., Pecknold, J. C., Rifkin, A., et al. (1988). Secondary depression in panic disorder and agoraphobia. I. Frequency, severity, and response to treatment. *Archives of General Psychiatry, 45,* 437–450.

Liebowitz, M. R. (1989). Antidepressants in panic disorders. *British Journal of Psychiatry, 155* (suppl. 6), 46–52.

Mahoney, M. J. (1974). *Cognition and behavior modification.* Cambridge, MA: Ballinger.

Markowitz, J. S., Weissman, M. M., Ouellette, R., Lish, J. D., & Klerman, G. L. (1989). Quality of life in panic disorder. *Archives of General Psychiatry, 46,* 984–992.

Mathews, A. M., Gelder, M. G., & Johnston, D. W. (1981). *Agoraphobia: Nature and treatment.* New York: Guilford Press.

Mavissakalian, M., & Michelson, L. (1986). Agoraphobia: Relative and combined effectiveness of therapist-assisted in vivo exposure and imipramine. *Journal of Clinical Psychiatry, 143,* 1106–1112.

Mavissakalian, M. R., & Perel, J. M. (1989). Imipramine dose–response relationship in panic disorder with agoraphobia. *Archives of General Psychiatry, 46,* 127–131.

Meichenbaum, D. (1985). *Stress inoculation training.* New York: Pergamon.

Noyes, R., Chaudry, D. R., & Domingo, D. V. (1986). Pharmacologic treatment of phobic disorders. *The Journal of Clinical Psychiatry, 47,* 445–451.

O'Brien, G. T., & Barlow, D. H. (1984). Agoraphobia. In S. M. Turner (Ed.), *Behavioral theories and treatment of anxiety* (pp. 143–185). New York: Plenum Press.

Phalen, K. F. (1998). *Integrative medicine: Achieving wellness through the best of Eastern and Western medical practices.* Boston: Journey Editions.

Rauch, S. L., & Jenike, M. A. (1998). Pharmacological treatment of obsessive compulsive disorder. In P. E. Nathan & J. M. Gorman (Eds.), *A guide to treatments that work* (pp. 358–376). New York: Oxford University Press.

Regier, D. A., Boyd, J. H., Burke, J. D., Rae, D. S., et al. (1988). One-month prevalence of mental disorders in the United States. *Archives of General Psychiatry, 45,* 977–986.

Reiss, S., Peterson, R., Gursky, D., & McNally, R. (1986). Anxiety sensitivity, anxiety frequency, and the prediction of fearfulness. *Behaviour Research and Therapy, 24,* 1–8.

Rickels, K., & Schweizer, E. E. (1987). Current pharmacotherapy of anxiety and panic. In H. Y. Meltzer (Ed.), *Psychopharmacology: The third generation of progress* (pp. 1193–1203). New York: Raven Press.

Rimm, D. C., & Masters, J. C. (1974). *Behavior therapy: Techniques and empirical findings.* New York: Academic Press.

Robbers, J. E. & Tyler, V. E. (1999) *Tyler's herbs of choice: The therapeutic use of phytomedicinals.* Haworth Herbal Press.

Robins, L. N., Helzer, J. E., Weissman, M. M., Orvaschel, H., et al. (1984). Lifetime prevalence of specific psychiatric disorders in three sites. *Archives of General Psychiatry, 41,* 949–958.

Roy-Byrne, P. P., & Cowley, D. S. (1998). Pharmacological treatment of panic, generalized anxiety, and phobic disorders. In P. E. Nathan & J. M. Gorman (Eds.), *A guide to treatments that work* (pp. 319–338). New York: Oxford University Press.

Salkovskis, P. M. (1998). Panic disorder and agoraphobia. In A. J. Bellack & M. Hersen (Eds.), *Comprehensive clinical psychology* (Vol. 6, pp. 399–437). Amsterdam: Elsevier Science.

Salzman, C. (1989). Treatment with antianxiety agents. In American Psychiatric Association, *Treatments of psychiatric disorders: A task force report of the American Psychiatric Association* (Vol. 3, pp. 2036–2052). Washington, DC: American Psychiatric Association.

Stern, R., & Marks, I. (1973). Brief and prolonged flooding: A comparison in agoraphobic patients. *Archives of General Psychiatry, 28,* 270–276.

Telch, M. J., Lucas, J. A., Schmidt, N. B., Hanna, H. H., Jaimez, T. S., & Lucas, R. A. (1993). Group cognitive-behavioral treatment of panic disorder. *Behaviour Research and Therapy, 31,* 279–287.

Torgersen, S. (1983). Genetic factors in anxiety disorders. *Archives of General Psychiatry, 40,* 1085–1089.

Turner, S. M., & Beidel, D. C. (1988). *Treating obsessive-compulsive disorder.* New York: Pergamon.

Weakes, C. (1968). *Hope and help for your nerves.* New York: Hawthorne.

Weakes, C. (1972). *Peace from nervous suffering.* New York: Hawthorne.

Weissman, M. M. (1988). The epidemiology of panic disorder and agoraphobia. In *Review of Psychiatry* (Vol. 7). Washington, DC: American Psychiatric Press.

Weissman, M. M., Klerman, G. L., Markowitz, J. S., & Ouellette, R. (1989). Suicidal ideation and suicide attempts in panic disorder and attacks. *The New England Journal of Medicine, 18*(321), 1209–1214.

Wolpe, J. (1958). *Psychotherapy by reciprocal inhibition.* Stanford, CA: Stanford University Press.

Wolpe, J. (1982). *The practice of behavior therapy.* (3rd ed.). New York: Pergamon.

Yehuda, R., Marshall, R., & Giller, E. L., Jr. (1998). Psychopharmacological treatment of post-traumatic stress disorder. In P. E. Nathan & J. M. Gorman (Eds.), *A guide to treatments that work* (pp. 377–397). New York: Oxford University Press.

Zitrin, C. M., Klein, D. F., Woerner, M. G., & Ross, D. C. (1983). Treatment of phobias. I. Comparison of imipramine hydrochloride and placebo. *Archives of General Psychiatry, 40,* 125–138.

Zohar, J., Foa, E. B., & Insel, T. R. (1989). Behavior therapy and pharmacotherapy. In American Psychiatric Association, *Treatments of psychiatric disorders: A task force report of the American Psychiatric Association* (Vol. 3, pp. 2095–2111). Washington, DC: American Psychiatric Association.

CHAPTER

10 Intervention with Persons with Severe Mental Illness: Theories, Concepts, and Philosophies

Nineteen years ago I was diagnosed with major depression by a general practitioner who, after an examination and listening to my complaints, stunned me when he remarked that he didn't think he could help.

Seeing my distress and confusion, my physician reassured me with a weak but convincing grin, "You're not terminally ill, but I think you could benefit from an antidepressant and counseling." Oh, I would live. But, a psychiatrist? An antidepressant? "So I'll live, but I'll be insane?" Again the grin and some vague reassurance. I called to make an appointment, though.

Unfortunately, the intervening nineteen years have been marked with recurrent episodes, each one worse and longer than the one preceding it. There have been stretches when I felt better. Right now, I'm in a serious downturn.

—Lewis, *"Lewis v. Kmart:* A Fight for What's Right," *NAMI Advocate,* 1998

...after 25 years of practice, research, and listening to consumers and their families, I am more convinced than ever that recovery from severe mental illness is possible for many more people than was previously believed. I believe that much of the chronicity in severe mental illness is due to the way the mental health system and society treat mental illness and not the nature of the illness itself.

—Anthony, "A Revolution in Vision," 1992

Harold Lewis is a mental health consumer who, despite a history of severe mental illness, held increasingly responsible jobs during the ten years he worked at a discount department store. When he became disabled with major depression, he fought the company in court over his right, under the Americans with Disabilities Act, to receive long-term disability insurance for a mental as well as a physical disorder. Although he was "in a serious downturn" at the time he wrote the article from which the opening excerpt was taken, he was

231

hopeful that "someday I will again be able to generate income to contribute to my family" (Lewis, 1998, p. 11).

During an earlier era in the history of mental health, Harold Lewis would have been labeled chronically mentally ill and, perhaps, placed in a psychiatric facility for an indefinitely long period of time. The *chronic* label originated in medical practice to differentiate between acute and chronic illness. An illness is described as *acute* when there is a flare-up of symptoms that are expected to abate following treatment. In contrast, an illness is viewed as *chronic* when it is prolonged, persistent, and in some cases progressive. Now we recognize that the term *chronic mental illness,* is pejorative (Bachrach, 1988; Jimenez, 1988). The word *chronic* suggests that a psychiatric condition is permanent, irremediable, and hopeless, and engenders stigma.

Today we use the terms *severe mental illness, serious mental illness,* and *severe and persistent mental illness* rather than *chronic*. Sometimes we substitute the term *disability* for *illness*. Furthermore, we use *person first* language, for example, "a person with schizophrenia," "an adult with a severe and persistent psychiatric disorder," and the like (Estroff, 1987). As one consumer explained:

> **Just as in America the descendants of African slaves have struggled to raise their consciousness and pride by, among other things, changing the way they refer to themselves as a group...so too are we undergoing a similar process of self definition. We now feel it is pejorative to refer to us as "the mentally ill" or "schizophrenics," "bi-polars, "multiples," etc. We are *people* who have been labeled with mental illness, *people* who have been labeled with schizophrenia, *people* with dissociative disorders, etc. We want our personhood to be recognized before our psychiatric diagnosis.** (Deegan, 1997, p. 12)

As suggested, power and empowerment issues underlie the discourse about terminology. This discussion is only one example of the complex linguistic terrain faced by postmodern practitioners working with clients with severe mental illness and the systems serving them. We turn next to additional definitional issues.

Definitional Issues

One way researchers and policy analysts construct serious mental illness is to consider the 3 Ds—diagnosis, disability, and duration (Bachrach, 1988; Goldman, 1984). The *diagnoses* that are usually included under this rubric are psychotic disorders, such as schizophrenia and schizoaffective disorder, and major mood disorders, such as major depression and bipolar disorder. Multiple diagnoses (both on Axis I or distributed on Axes I and II) are also possible. The other diagnoses may include other conditions such as mental retardation and substance abuse disorders that coexist with (and often complicate) severe psychiatric disorders.

Diagnosis alone is not a satisfactory criterion because some of the disorders that were mentioned have benign outcomes. The second criterion, *disability,* refers to impairment in emotional and behavioral functioning. Individuals whose psychiatric condition renders them unable to perform such activities as employment, housework, home maintenance, mobility, child care, and self-care (personal hygiene, grooming) are said to be mentally disabled. Psychiatric disability also interferes with the ability to engage in recreational and other activities that contribute to the quality of life (Gruenberg, 1982). Receipt of Supplemental Security Income (SSI) is one way of operationalizing disability (Goldman, 1984). Functional assessments of abilities look at basic living skills, social activity, and adaptive behavior (see Chapter 4). Psychiatric disabilities are remedied in programs of rehabilitation (Bachrach, 1986).

The third criterion is *duration*. This refers to the length of time that the individual has had the diagnosis or has been functionally impaired. Although some would determine duration by looking at the length of hospitalization, such a measure is no longer adequate (Bachrach, 1988). In contrast with patterns of the past, today the emphasis is on short-term hospitalization during crises or exacerbations and long-term treatment in the community. Another reason why long-term hospitalization is an inadequate criterion is that some psychiatric conditions are characterized by recurrent episodes of acute illness rather than a continuous course (Goldman, 1984). A history of hospitalizations regardless of the length of stay (e.g., two hospitalizations in the last year), a single hospitalization of a prescribed time period (e.g., ninety days long), an accumulation of days over years (e.g., forty days in the last three years), and long-term treatment in an outpatient facility (e.g., two years) are other ways of addressing duration.

During the 1980s there was broad agreement on the relevance of the 3 Ds but dissension on "the relevant diagnostic categories, the nature and degree of disability, the length of illness, and the relative importance of each" (Schinnar, Rothbard, Kanter, & Jung, 1990, p. 1602). An NIMH task force that met in 1990 divided this population into four groups that could well be viewed as a deconstruction of the category of severe and persistent mental illness. The dimensions included:

- severe and persistent disability
- severe but not persistent disability
- persistent but not severe disability
- moderate disabilities that are not persistent (Rothbard et al., 1996)

Severity is a characteristic of the disorder (e.g., major depression, schizophreniform disorder) and the consequences (cannot work or care for a household), but if the disorder is limited to a single episode or a limited period of time and the consequences are also circumscribed, the disability is considered severe but not persistent. If, on the other hand, the disability persists (e.g., general anxiety disorder, dysthymic disorder) but does not have severe consequences (can hold a job but not advance), it is consistent with the third dimension. Other disorders may produce moderate disabilities (e.g., acute stress disorder) that with treatment are not persistent.

Legislation enacted in the last two decades of the twentieth century made it obligatory for the states to develop specific criteria for defining serious or severe mental illness. Under the Comprehensive Mental Health Services Plan Act (PL 99-660, 1986), which required that states develop plans for the implementation of community mental health services, states had to report target numbers of clients with serious mental illness who would be served. In order to do this, they had to operationalize the concept of serious mental illness. Subsequently, the federal government established guidelines to help states in this process. The ADAMHA Reorganization Act (PL 102-321, 1992), which separated the federal agencies involved in research from those concerned with services, also established a block grant for community mental health services. Funds were allocated for adults with serious mental illness (SMI) and children with serious emotional disturbance (SED). This legislation required that the service-oriented Substance Abuse and Mental Health Services Administration (SAMHSA) develop a federal definition of severe mental illness (as well as serious emotional disturbance) that could guide states in their implementation of the block grants. The following criteria were subsequently established:

- Age 18 and over,
- Who currently or at any time during the past year,
- Have had a diagnosable mental, behavioral, or emotional disorder of sufficient duration to meet diagnostic criteria specified within DSM-III-R,
- That has resulted in functional impairment which substantially interferes with or limits one or more major life activities. (SAMHSA, 1993, p. 29425)

The third criterion applies to successors to the *DSM-III-R,* but, according to the *Federal Register,* excludes diagnoses of substance use disorders, developmental disorders, and *V*-codes, unless they co-occur with one of the included mental health disorders. Moreover, it includes the diagnosis of Alzheimer's disease. Furthermore, "All these [included] disorders have episodic, recurrent, or persistent features; however, they vary in terms of severity and disabling effects" (SAMHSA, 1993, p. 29425). The federal definition excluded as a separate criterion one of the 3 Ds—duration—because this was subsumed under the diagnoses. It did, however, include disability, described as functional impairment:

> Functional impairment is defined as difficulties that substantially interfere with or limit role functioning in one or more major life activities including basic daily living skills (e.g., eating, bathing, dressing); instrumental living skills (e.g., maintaining a household, managing money, getting around the community, taking prescribed medication); and functioning in social, family, and vocational/educational contexts. Adults who would have met functional impairment criteria during the referenced year without the benefit of treatment or other support services are considered to have serious mental illnesses. (SAMHSA, 1993, p. 29425)

State definitions that were to be developed after the publication of the federal criteria were expected to be consistent with the federal one, but they could vary. A study comparing the prevalence of severe and persistent mental illness in a clinical sample from West Philadelphia using the definitions established by ten states found a great deal of difference among them. The prevalence varied from 38 percent (using Hawaii's definition) to 72 percent (using Ohio's) (Rothbard et al., 1996). The diverse definitions reflect differences among the states and their respective political constituencies in their willingness to commit resources to a wide spectrum of individuals. However political, criteria for who is included and excluded ultimately affect consumers.

Most states target psychotic disorders, such as schizophrenia and schizoaffective disorder, but they also target severe mood disorders, such as bipolar and major depressive disorders, which sometimes have psychotic features. Rarer psychotic disorders such as delusional disorder and shared psychotic disorder may also meet state criteria. Some states include borderline and other personality disorders when there is evidence of poor global functioning. Organic psychoses and neuroses and general mental disorders are sometimes included as well (Rothbard, n.d.). Table 10.1 describes the *DSM-IV* diagnostic categories that guided the development of this chapter and the two that follow.

When one views these diagnostic categories from a postmodern perspective, however, one understands these categories are not essences but rather are ways in which psychiatry has constructed its domain of practice. There is much heterogeneity within categories and crossover between categories. Needless to say, the postmodern clinician's concern is with individuals, not categories.

With respect to disability, some of the criteria states use to operationalize this concept are as follows (Rothbard, n.d.):

- Impaired activities of daily living and basic needs.
- Limited and impaired performance in employment.
- Impaired functioning in non-work activities (e.g., leisure, homemaking).
- Reliance on psychosocial, drug, or other clinical supports.

TABLE 10.1 Severe Psychiatric Disorders

Diagnostic Category	Description
Schizophrenia	Disturbance in cognitive and emotional functioning, including perception, language and communication, affect, speech, volition, and organized behavior. Characterized by prominent delusions or hallucinations and marked occupational or social dysfunctioning. Symptoms must be present at least six months, including one month in which the symptoms are active.
Schizoaffective Disorder	Disturbance in mood (depression, mania, or mixture of the two) with concurrent symptoms of schizophrenia.
Bipolar I Disorder	Disturbance in mood in which there is a history of or current manic symptoms such as grandiosity, flight of ideas, and pressured speech. It is usually also characterized by symptoms of major depression. Symptoms must be present at least one week for single episodes. Should cause marked impairment in social or occupational functioning. May have psychotic features. Chronicity of two years applies to depressive episode only.
Bipolar II Disorder	Disturbance of mood in which there are one or more episodes of major depression accompanied by hypomanic (low end of "high") symptoms.
Major Depressive Disorder	Disturbance in mood characterized by at least two weeks of marked dysphoria, insomnia, loss of interest in life, lack of pleasure, and other symptoms result in impairment in social and occupational functioning. Described as chronic when it persists for two years.

Source: Adapted from American Psychiatric Association (1994).

- Social behavior demanding intervention by mental health system or courts.
- Level of Functioning or Global Assessment of Functioning scores at admission.
- Meets eligibility criteria for SSI or SSDI.
- No current but prior disability.

Usually two or more of these criteria need to be met (Rothbard, n.d.).

There is also variability in the use of duration as a state criterion. Some states have no duration criteria whereas others consider the length of the illness and treatment (e.g., two years or more), the length of hospitalization (e.g., ninety days or more within a three-year period), the number of hospitalizations, the use of residential or partial hospitalization services, and/or the use of outpatient services (Rothbard, n.d.).

However diverse the definitions may be, epidemiologists have strived to estimate the prevalence of severe mental illness in the United States. Combining data from the National Comorbidity Survey and the Baltimore Epidemiologic Catchment Area Study, Kessler et al. (1996) estimated that 4.8 million adults had *severe and persistent* mental illness and another 5.6 million had *serious* (but not persistent) mental illness in 1990. In a later report that accounted for individuals living in homeless shelters, nursing homes, hospitals, correction facilities, and elsewhere, as well as those living in households in the community, Kessler et al. (1998) estimated that there are 12.2 million adults with severe mental illness in the United States.

Clinical social work practice with persons with severe mental illness is guided by theories, concepts, research findings, and practice philosophies that emerged in the last thirty years of the twentieth century. Although many of these developments arose from research on schizophrenia, the findings are applicable to other serious disorders. In addition to presenting this information, this chapter discusses psychosocial rehabilitation, community support systems, and strategies that are considered best practices for intervention with adults with severe psychiatric disabilities. Chapter 11 will provide information on community care, including case management and the range of community services in which psychosocial rehabilitation and community support take place. Chapter 12 will describe specific treatment strategies, such as psychopharmacology, social skill training, and family education.

Theoretical Issues

Scientific research supports the assumption that the major psychiatric disorders—schizophrenia, bipolar disorder, and some major depressions—are brain diseases. As discussed in Chapter 3, genetic studies, neurophysiological findings, and responsiveness to medication provide evidence for this assumption. Genetic studies of twins, one of whom was identified as having schizophrenia, have revealed higher rates of concordance between monozygotic than between dizygotic twins (Kendler, 1988). Studies of adoptees with schizophrenic spectrum disorders found an unusually high prevalence of schizophrenia and the spectrum disorders among natural relatives (Kendler, 1988). Similar results have been realized with respect to the genetics of unipolar depression and bipolar disorder (McGuffin & Katz, 1989). Furthermore, neurophysiological studies of the brain using sophisticated laboratory equipment have identified structural abnormalities among persons with schizophrenia, mania, and dementia (Andreasen, 1984; Andreasen et al., 1990; Taylor, 1987). The effectiveness of medication for schizophrenia, bipolar disorder, and major depression also supports the role of science.

Recognition of a biogenetic etiology represents a marked departure from the past, when psychoanalytic and family communication theories about the development of serious psychiatric disorders predominated. With respect to schizophrenia, psychoanalysis espoused the concept of the schizophrenogenic mother (Fromm-Reichmann, 1948), which not only drew attention to deficient parenting but blamed the mother. Similarly, attention to dysfunctional interaction patterns in families with a schizophrenic member engendered to such concepts as marital skew and marital schism (Lidz, Cornelison, Fleck, & Terry, 1957) and the double bind (Bateson, Jackson, Haley, & Weakland, 1956). These theories promoted a view of the family as pathological, to be blamed or treated. The same theories depicted families of persons with bipolar disorder as using the child, who later became afflicted with what was then called manic-depressive illness, to lift the family from its marginal social status (Cohen et al., 1954). Unipolar depression was attributed to parental rejection, devaluation, and early loss of a parent (Freedman, Kaplan, & Sadock, 1972). These theories have aroused considerable anguish and guilt in parents. With families assuming a significant role as caregivers today, enlightened clinicians now view families as resources and partners (Lefley & Wasow, 1994).

Stress-Diathesis Model

An alternative approach focuses on the individual with the disorder in relation to his or her internal and external processes. The *stress-diathesis* model—also described as the *vulnerability, stress-vulnerability-coping-competence,* or *stress-vulnerability-protective* model (Liberman, 1982, 1988a, 1988b; MacKain, Liberman, & Corrigan, 1994; Zubin & Spring, 1977)—evolved from research on schizophrenia. *Diathesis* refers to a biological predisposition (e.g., a family history of the same disorder) that makes one sensitive to stress. According to this model, schizophrenia arises in an individual with biologically based vulnerability, a low threshold for tolerating stress, and inadequate coping strategies. In the face of a biological, psychological, or socioenvironmental stressor, the predisposed individual has an episode or exacerbation of schizophrenia (Falloon & Liberman, 1983; Land, 1986). Empirical research shows that stress also affects the course of serious mood disorders (Hammen, 1995).

Relapse into illness seems to be related to several peripheral aspects of the stressful life experience. For one, the episode is related to the individual's perception of the dangerousness of the demand in relation to his or her ability to respond effectively (Zubin & Spring, 1977). Furthermore, the individual's capacity and efforts to cope with the demand are relevant. In the face of an overwhelming stressor, these capacities can break down. The ensuing debilitation may be temporary, but in the eventuality of a schizophrenic episode, it is more persistent (Zubin & Spring, 1977). Persons who have a history of relatively high premorbid (prior to psychosis) functioning tend to adapt better to stress than those without such a history; if there is a breakdown, they are more likely to achieve a higher level of functioning than those with a poor premorbid history (Liberman, 1982).

Socioenvironmental supports can provide a buffer against stress (Pilisuk, 1982). These consist of family, friends, neighbors, and members of a religious community. Unfortunately, many persons with severe psychiatric disabilities have small social networks comprised predominantly of kin and do not reciprocate with persons who offer support, friendship, and love to them (Sullivan & Poertner, 1989; Tolsdorf, 1976). Often professionals and social programs fill the gap in clients' natural support systems and become part of or the entire support system. Nevertheless, family members and interested friends of clients can be educated to implement strategies that can lower the level of stress experienced by clients.

Figure 10.1 is a visual representation of the stress-diathesis model. *Stressors* may be environmental or internal (biochemical, intrapsychic) events or processes that are perceived negatively and arouse anxiety and challenge the coping capacities of the vulnerable individual. *Competencies and supports* offer structure, strategies, confidence, and encouragement that can mitigate stress. When stressors and supports are in balance in a vulnerable individual, social functioning can be maintained.

A related concept, the *stimulus window* (Pepper & Ryglewicz, 1986), has to do with the level of sensory stimulation one can tolerate and the range in which one can function effectively. Although a certain amount of stimulation is desirable, too much (overstimulation) or too little (understimulation) can result in the development of psychiatric symptoms. The size of the window (range of tolerable stimulation) is related to one's mental health. A person with a healthy personality can tolerate a wide range of stimulation and extremes in quality and quantity. Many persons with schizophrenia have difficulty managing sensory stimuli and function best within a limited range. They may confuse internal and external stimuli and overreact to intense emotions. Persons with mood disorders and severe personality disorders have difficulty regulating emotions and managing stress, respectively. Drug and alcohol constitute chemical stressors that can have a negative impact on an organism that is naturally sensitive to stimulation.

FIGURE 10.1   The Stress-Diathesis/Stress-Vulnerability-Coping-Competence (Protective) Model

Vulnerabilities

Family history of severe mental disorder, genetic factors, early onset, low premorbid functioning, and/or abnormal neurological activity, which adversely affect cognition and set the stage for a high reactivity to stress

Stressors (–) [Factors that heighten the risk]	Competencies and Supports (+) [Protective factors]
Life events that are perceived as threatening or demanding	Social skills
Unstable living situation	Supportive family and friends
Interpersonal conflict or criticism	Medication use; use of other mental
("expressed emotion")	health services
Medical problem	Vocational skills
Chemical substance abuse	Coping skills

The range of stimuli that can enter an individual's stimulus window is biologically based. Individual vulnerability and the specific disorder may affect the range. Nevertheless, the upper and lower limits and flexibility to function within a range can be extended through treatment. This should be done over a long period of time and with care not to contribute to sensory overload of the client (Pepper & Ryglewicz, 1986).

A similar model explaining the same phenomenon with respect to schizophrenia is the *attention-arousal* model (Anderson, Reiss, & Hogarty, 1986). Accordingly, the person with schizophrenia has a "core psychological deficit" (Anderson, Hogarty, & Reiss, 1980) in the ability to select, sort, filter, and evaluate stimuli. This deficiency results in diffuse responses and hyperarousal to stimuli, regardless of their relevance to a situation. The individual is affected by both internal and external stimuli (information), which make a demand for information processing. When the demands increase, the organism becomes distracted, inattentive, and aroused. The person with schizophrenia responds to these stimuli by maintaining a narrow focus of attention, missing the full picture. This produces a state of disintegration and sensory malfunctioning. In a state of high arousal, an individual can perceive and behave in dysfunctional ways (e.g., hallucinations, aggressive behavior). Medication can modify the internal conditions associated with arousal and attention deficits, thus reducing vulnerability; intervention with families can reduce excessive external stimulation. Like the stimulus window concept, the attention-arousal model assumes that some, but not excessive, stimulation is desirable. Accordingly, social interaction that is low-keyed and nonintrusive facilitates psychosocial functioning, whereas intensive and demanding interaction can be deleterious.

The models introduced in this section do more than describe the biological vulnerabilities of persons with severe mental illness; they suggest avenues for intervention that can be incorporated into social work practice. Clinical social workers can, for example, help clients with severe mental illness develop and use supports, enhance their coping skills, and change conditions in their living environments that are stressful. Furthermore, social workers can help clients take care of themselves by obtaining medical care, taking their medication as prescribed, and avoiding chemical substances. More will be said about the application of these models in Chapters 11 and 12. For now, we will look at one stressor that has been the subject of a great deal of research and controversy—expressed emotion.

Expressed Emotion

During the 1950s and 1960s Brown and his associates in England conducted a series of studies on persons with schizophrenia who were discharged from the hospital to family and nonfamily settings (Brown, 1959; Brown, Carstairs, & Topping, 1958). When they determined that those male patients who lived with parents or wives had a higher rate of readmission to the hospital than those who lived with other relatives or in a community lodging, the researchers delved more deeply into the families' interactions.

The authors explored the emotional climate more thoroughly in a subsequent study of 128 men ages 20 to 49 who had been hospitalized at least one month and were discharged from eight hospitals in London (Brown, Monck, Carstairs, & Wing, 1962). All had confirmed diagnoses of schizophrenia. Those with relatives to whom they would be discharged ($N = 101$) were interviewed on three occasions—before discharge, two weeks after discharge, and at readmission or at the end of the year. During an at-home interview of the patient and at least a key relative (usually female), researchers rated the behavior of the relative toward the patient on emotion expressed, hostility, and dominant behavior that was directed toward the patient, as well as the patient's emotion expressed and hostility toward the key relative.

A substantially large percentage of the total subjects were rehospitalized (41 percent) or clinically deteriorated (64 percent) within the year; 52 percent were considered worse. The rate of decline among those who lived in lodgings was comparable with that of those who lived with parents or wives. Those who lived with siblings showed the lowest level of deterioration.

The percentages of decline of those from homes rated high on emotional involvement were significantly greater than of those from homes that were low on the same quality (76 versus 28 percent deteriorated; 56 versus 21 percent were rehospitalized; $p < .001$). Furthermore, those patients from homes with high emotional involvement by a key relative and whose mental state at the time of discharge was rated moderate or severe were vulnerable to intense contact with the relative with whom they resided. Among those who had high contact with relatives (operationalized as more than thirty-five hours per week of face-to-face interaction), 96 percent deteriorated; among those with low contact, the percentage was 50 ($p < .01$).

On the basis of these results it appeared that high emotional involvement by relatives is consistent with high levels of deterioration. Among those who lived in highly emotional homes, high contact with the patient was particularly toxic. Nevertheless, those who lived in lodgings, apart from relatives, did not fare well. Apparently, some low-intensity contact is helpful; extensive, but highly emotional contact has a deleterious effect.

Brown, Birley, & Wing (1972) replicated this study ten years later, using more sophisticated scales, which had been developed in the interim. This time the sample ($N = 101$) included women and used patients born in the United Kingdom and living in the Camberwell section of London, as well as a sample from Bexley Hospital. The new scales of family interaction patterns included the number of critical comments, hostility, dissatisfaction, warmth, emotional overinvolvement, and an overall index of expressed emotion (EE) that was derived from these variables. Two kinds of relapse were measured—change from normal or nonschizophrenic to schizophrenia; and marked exacerbation of persistent symptoms of schizophrenia.

Once again the authors found a significant relationship between high EE in the relatives and the patient's deterioration. Among the respondents from high EE homes, 58 percent relapsed; among those from low-EE homes, only 16 percent relapsed. This study also found differences in the relapse rates of men and women. The relapse rate of men was twice that of women. Moreover, married subjects had a lower rate (26 percent) than unmarried (42 percent). Regardless of marital status, the relapse rate was higher for men than for women. The women in this study, however, were older and more likely to be married than the men.

A further refinement in this study was its examination of the effects of taking antipsychotic drugs and emotional expressiveness on relapse. Although two-thirds of the subjects took medication during the study period or until relapse, drug maintenance itself was not significantly related (but was close) to outcome. Among those who took their medication and lived in high-EE homes, the relapse rate was 46 percent, whereas those in high-EE homes who did *not* take medication relapsed at a rate of 66 percent. Of those in low-EE homes, the rate was only 15 percent for those who were not on medication and 14 percent for those who were.

This line of research continued to flourish in the 1970s (e.g., Brown, et al., 1972; Vaughan & Leff, 1976) and 1980s (e.g., Leff & Vaughan, 1985; Vaughan, Snyder, Jones, Freeman, & Falloon, 1984). It has been applied to other psychiatric and medical disorders and studied in the United States, India, Germany, and Australia (e.g., Koenigsberg & Handley, 1986; Kottgen et al., 1984; Parker, Johnston, & Hayward, 1988), with some findings consistent with those found in England and some divergent. Most of this research is initiated at the time a person is hospitalized, when the Camberwell Family Interview is administered (Hooley & Hiller, 1998). The patient and relatives are followed up over time to determine the outcome. A meta-analysis of twenty-seven outcome studies of the relationship between expressed emotion and family environment among persons with schizophrenia, schizoaffective disorder, mood disorder, and eating disorder confirmed that high EE in the family is associated with high relapse rates (Butzlaff & Hooley, 1998).

Research on EE has been stimulating to researchers and practitioners but troubling to families of persons with schizophrenia and other serious disorders. Researchers have found in the family environment a construct (EE) that is consistent with hypotheses based on biological research that this population is vulnerable to stress and has difficulty processing complex information (cf. stress-diathesis and attention-arousal models). When high EE is identified, practitioners can work with families to modulate emotional intensity in their relationships. On the other hand, families find in this research a revival of parent blaming that emanated from psychoanalytic and family interaction theories. Furthermore, many questions remain about the scientific validity of this construct, its stability over time, and whether EE precipitates or is a consequence of the client's behavior (Lefley, 1992).

Research on expressed emotion alerts the clinician to potential interpersonal stressors that can result in rehospitalization. Some psychoeducational programs are designed to help families reduce criticism, hostility, and overinvolvement on the part of the family (e.g., Anderson et al., 1986). The focus on intervention with families with high EE should not, however, divert the clinician from the needs of *all* families with a relative with severe mental illness for support and education. Furthermore, attention needs to be drawn to *interactional intensity (II)* (Pepper & Ryglewicz, 1987) that can emanate from intense mental health treatment programs, in-depth psychotherapy, and other invasive strategies (cf. Oliver & Kuipers, 1996).

Accordingly, treatment programs and helping relationships should be supportive but not too demanding for those clients who are especially sensitive to emotional intensity. Vulnerable clients cannot tolerate programs in which the expectations to achieve goals are too high or therapeutic relationships are intrusive.

Although expressed emotion and interactional intensity are stressors, as mentioned earlier and depicted in Figure 10.1, the other side of the equation is comprised of compentencies and supports. Supports are incorporated in the philosophy of psychosocial (or psychiatric) rehabilitation, to which we turn next.

Philosophy of Psychosocial/Psychiatric Rehabilitation

Rehabilitation is a philosophy of care for persons with disabilities. *Psychiatric* rehabilitation was stimulated by medical programs for the physically disabled (Anthony, Cohen, & Cohen, 1984; Anthony & Liberman, 1986) and adapted to the needs of persons with severe mental illness. As such, psychiatric rehabilitation has had a medical orientation. *Psychosocial* rehabilitation grew out of the consumer-run Fountain House (see Chapter 11), which emphasized consumer empowerment and peer group support. In recent years, these parallel movements and philosophies have converged. Here the terms *psychosocial* and *psychiatric rehabilitation* are used interchangeably.

According to one of the numerous definitions in the field, "psychosocial rehabilitation is a therapeutic approach to the care of mentally ill individuals that encourages each patient to develop his or her fullest capacities through learning procedures and environmental supports" (Bachrach, 1992, p. 1456). For the clinical social worker, this means working with the client and community resources to promote the client's physical, psychiatric, and social functioning to the extent possible. Anthony and Liberman (1986) recommend that helping professionals provide "the least amount of support necessary" (p. 542), so that clients will be helped to become as self-sufficient as they can.

As Table 10.2 shows, psychiatric rehabilitation arises in the context of four stages (Anthony & Liberman, 1986; Liberman, 1988b). The first, *pathology,* involves abnormalities in the biological system, such as a lesion. Pathology can produce *impairment,* an abnormality or loss of anatomical, psychological, or physiological function or structure, which is manifested in symptoms such as hallucinations. Impairment can result in *disability,* inability, or limitation in the ability to carry out activities or perform roles in the expected manner and range, such as deficient interpersonal skills. The last stage, *handicap,* results from either an impairment or a disability. A handicap is a disadvantage that interferes with the fulfillment of a role that is culturally normative for the individual. Handicaps are exacerbated by public attitudes or stigma. Unemployment and homelessness may be consequences of a handicap.

Psychiatric rehabilitation is directed at overcoming, remedying, or compensating for disabilities and handicaps. Programs of intervention target the individual, family, group, and the social environment. Individual, group, family, or milieu therapy can be utilized to teach individuals skills in activities in daily living (self-care, transportation, laundry), interpersonal behaviors, employment, and problem solving through skills training based on social learning theory (Anthony & Liberman, 1986). Family psychoeducation promotes the social functioning of the client by addressing stress in the family (Anderson et al., 1986). Psychosocial rehabilitation clubs, such as Fountain House in New York, provide a group setting through which persons with persistent mental health problems gain work experiences, socialize with others, and obtain better housing. Environmental approaches mobilize and provide support from the natural helping network and the formal (agency) system. The result is a community support system that is adapted to the individual client. Case managers foster the development of environmental supports, while providing support themselves.

Anthony et al. (1984) describe several principles that guide psychiatric rehabilitation. First and foremost is a focus "on improving the psychiatrically disabled person's capabilities and competence" (p. 139). The emphasis is on developing responses to the environment that

TABLE 10.2 Stages in the Rehabilitation of Chronic Mental Patients, with Examples of the Elements in Each Stage

Stage	Pathology	Impairment	Disability	Handicap
Definition	Lesions or abnormalities in the central nervous system caused by agents or processes responsible for the etiology and maintenance of the biobehavioral disorder	Any loss or abnormality of *psychological, physiological or anatomical structure or function* (resulting from underlying pathology)	Any restriction or lack (resulting from an impairment) of *ability to perform an activity* in the manner or within the range considered normal for a human being	A disadvantage for a given individual (resulting from an impairment or a disability) that limits or prevents the *fulfillment of a role* that normal (*depending on age, sex, social, cultural factors*) for that individual
Example	Brain tumors or infections etiologically linked to psychotic symptoms	Positive and negative symptoms of schizophrenia (delusions, anhedonia)	Deficient social skills	Unemployment, homelessness
Interventions	Laboratory and radiographic tests	Syndromal diagnosis, pharmacotherapy, hospitalization	Functional assessment, skills training, social support	National and state vocational rehabilitation policies; community support programs

Source: From "Psychiatric Rehabilitation," by R. P. Liberman (Ed., Special issue), 1986, *Schizophrenia Bulletin, 12*(4).

promote health; symptom reduction is not sufficient. This principle is consistent with the integrated biopsychosocial conceptual framework of this book. It is accomplished by efforts to increase coping (problem-solving) skills and acquire skills in daily living, learning, and pursuing a vocation.

The second principle is that "the benefit of psychiatric rehabilitation for the clients is behavioral improvement in their environments of need" (p. 140). Efforts are to be directed at achieving a tangible, measurable outcome that can be achieved in the client's relevant environments (e.g., residential, community, employment). Simply providing services is not adequate (Farkas, Cohen, & Nemec, 1988). The idea is to improve the individual's instrumental skills (rather than to promote insight) and the person-environment fit. Although this principle seems to suggest a behavioral theoretical perspective, the third principle is that "psychiatric rehabilitation is atheoretical and eclectic in the use of a variety of therapeutic constructs" (Anthony et al., 1984, p. 141).

Even though problem solving and social skills are included under the umbrella of rehabilitation, "a central focus is on improving vocational outcome for the psychiatrically disabled" (p. 141). Some clients will be able to secure jobs in the competitive market, whereas others will hold part-time, protected, or transitional employment. Some clients will work as volunteers or manage their own homes. Work is a primary value of the larger community. The ability to hold a job enhances the individual's self-esteem and independence. Furthermore, it promotes normalization and integration. Vocational rehabilitation can be enhanced through education, training, and the modeling of work skills. Associated skills such as attendance, taking directions, and handling interpersonal conflict are also developed. Vocational rehabilitation programs provide training and practice in supervised and low-stress transitional employment settings and in natural settings. Through vocational rehabilitation a client can develop skills incrementally over time.

Psychiatric rehabilitation can be implemented best when the clinical practitioner conveys an attitude of hope (Anthony et al., 1984). Such an attitude is particularly important in work with the seriously mentally ill who, historically, have been abandoned as hopeless. As indicated previously, many persons with severe mental disabilities have recovered or improved over time. Although the media give attention to the failures of deinstitutionalization, many live successfully in the community (Sands, 1984).

Furthermore, rehabilitation requires management of dependence that is consistent with the client's needs. When a client is released from a hospital following a psychotic episode, increased dependence on family and service providers is to be expected. Dependence on others is lessened over time as the client becomes more confident and competent. "The deliberate increase in client dependency can lead to an eventual increase in the client's independent functioning" (Anthony et al., 1984, p. 142). Accordingly, some dependence is expected and even fostered after discharge from a psychiatric hospital, but over time increasing independence is encouraged.

Client participation in the rehabilitation process (Anthony et al., 1984) is essential to the success of the program. The client should participate in goal setting and make decisions about living arrangements, social activities, and treatment that are compatible with personal values and experiences. Rather than being an object on whom rehabilitation is imposed, the client should be a partner of the treatment team. This way, the client will be emotionally invested in his or her own rehabilitation. Unfortunately, many agencies do not recognize the importance of client participation, as reflected by the absence of this element in mission statements and in formal assessment procedures (Farkas et al., 1988).

According to Anthony et al. (1984), two kinds of interventions are fundamental to rehabilitation. These are client skills development and environmental resource development. Often illnesses such as schizophrenia and bipolar disorder first appear in adolescence or young adulthood, by which time the individual has not sufficiently developed any vocational, social, and living skills that are needed to function relatively independently in the community. Schizophrenia is also associated with deficits in cognitive functioning. Regardless of the mental disorder, skills that facilitate social functioning can be taught or enhanced through programmatic interventions. Environmental resources that are related to client needs can also be developed.

Psychosocial and psychiatric rehabilitation highlights the *recovery* process in which individuals learn to live with their illnesses. According to Anthony (1992), "Recovery from mental illness is not the same as cure. It means gaining control over one's life if not one's illness. It means living a useful, satisfying life even though symptoms may reoccur" (p. 18). As one consumer said, it **"means that I try to stay in the driver's seat of my life. I don't let my illness run me"** (Deegan, 1997, p. 21). Furthermore, psychosocial rehabilitation emphasizes clients' strengths or competencies (Bachrach, 1992). With its emphasis on client empowerment, hope, and abilities, psychosocial rehabilitation is compatible with the ideals of the social work profession.

In practice, psychosocial/psychiatric rehabilitation is operationalized through a wide range of programs but especially those involving employment. The programs include, but are not limited to, supported housing, case management, consumer drop-in programs, supported employment, social skills training, family intervention, and psychiatric and substance abuse treatment (Mueser, Drake, & Bond, 1997). These and other services and interventions are components of community support systems, which are discussed next.

Community Support Programs and Systems

Community support programs (CSPs) and community support systems (CSSs) refer to a pilot program (CSP) developed by the National Institute of Mental Health and the concept (CSS) that underlies this initiative (Turner & Ten Hoor, 1978). The purpose was to plan for and develop demonstration projects of comprehensive, coordinated services for adults with severe and persistent psychiatric disabilities for whom semiskilled and skilled nursing home care was inappropriate. Since 1977 the program has been implemented in every state (Torrey, 1988a).

The concept of community support system is constructed as a network of caring persons or services to help the vulnerable, severely, and persistently mentally ill to develop their potential and meet their needs without being excluded or isolated from the community (Turner & Ten Hoor, 1978). In order to meet the needs of individuals with different sociodemographic characteristics, disabilities, and levels of functioning, a broad range of support services is needed (Solomon, 1999).

Community support programs have been realized on the state level through block grants. They include an array of housing alternatives, mental health treatment facilities, financial resources, and advocacy services that enhance the capacities of communities to meet the needs of persons with severe mental illness who live in the community. Components that are missing in a community are identified, planned for, and funded.

As the CSP title and the CSS concept suggest, the community is constructed as a network of resources that can contribute to the well-being of clients. Both concepts incorporate the philosophy of psychosocial rehabilitation and embrace services congruent with this philosophy. Furthermore, programs are oriented toward the needs of clients and their families. The "Guiding Principles for Community Support Systems" suggested by the National Institute of Mental Health (1982; U.S. Department of Health and Human Services, 1980) are also consistent with the values of the social work profession.

Among the social work values that are incorporated into the guiding principles are *personal dignity, self-determination, individualization, nondiscrimination,* and *confidentiality.* Personal dignity refers to the respect that is given to clients. Respect is communicated by providing community services in such a way that clients' privacy, rights as citizens, and self-respect are honored. Self-determination is the client's right to make informed decisions. This is fostered with policies and practices in which clients establish their own goals, participate in planning meetings, choose their own residences, and maintain the greatest possible control over their lives. Clinical social workers promote individualization by tailoring services to the unique needs and preferences of the client as these change over time. Individualized services are to be available without discrimination to whoever needs them, regardless of the consumer's race or ethnic group, age, sex, sexual orientation, disability, or other characteristic. Furthermore, services are to be culturally sensitive and relevant. Finally, practitioners are to protect client records and keep information revealed in the course of professional contacts confidential (DHHS, 1980; NIMH, 1982).

The philosophy of community support is consistent with the legal principle that persons with severe mental illness live and receive treatment in the *least restrictive alternative* setting. They should live in settings and receive services in locations in which their freedom and autonomy are protected to the greatest degree possible; at the same time their safety and quality of mental health care should not be compromised. Wherever feasible, treatment should be in *natural settings* (NIMH, 1982) rather than in residences and programs that segregate clients from the community. Local communities that offer a continuum of residential placements, rehabilitation services, and treatment facilities provide options for a client to progress from a more restrictive residence (e.g., group home) to a less restricted one (e.g., own apartment) and from supported employment to full employment. Sometimes more restrictive alternatives such as hospitalization can be avoided if less restrictive alternatives such as crisis intervention services and mobile treatment teams are available in the community.

A related principle incorporated in the community support concept is to engage *natural support systems* in the lives of clients (DHHS, 1980; NIMH, 1982). Natural supports are families, friends, neighbors, clergy, hairdressers, storekeepers, and other community persons who have been or are connected with the client in a meaningful way. They are the client's first line of defense against stress; as such they constitute a tremendous resource that clients can be helped to utilize. Nevertheless, natural supports, such as family members, can become burdened with the demands of supporting someone they love. In such cases, the families need to be supported.

A further belief is that treatment should be of *indefinite duration* (NIMH, 1982). As mentioned earlier, severe mental illness is defined partly by duration. Although research by Harding, Brooks, Ashikaga, Strauss, and Breier (1987) indicates that some clients do recover from serious mental illness, others need long-term follow-up and treatment. Because the course is unpredictable, community supports need to be in place to meet needs as they arise.

An additional CSP value is *consumer empowerment* (Stroul, 1993). This includes encouraging the client to participate in *mutual and self-help groups* (NIMH, 1982). In these groups, clients exercise their own skills in problem solving and give and receive support from others. Formal and informal consumer self-help groups can help clients develop natural supports and become interdependent.

> **Self-help is a way in which people become empowered, begin to think of themselves as competent individuals, and present themselves in new ways to the world. Self-help, by its very nature, combats stigma, because the negative images of mental patients as needy and helpless ultimately must give way to the reality of clients managing their own programs and taking on increased responsibility for their own lives.** (Chamberlin, Rogers, & Sneed, 1989, p. 102)

The following is a summary of the principles that guide the CSS philosophy:

1. Services should be consumer centered.
2. Services should empower clients.
3. Services should be racially and culturally appropriate.
4. Services should be flexible.
5. Services should focus on strengths.
6. Services should be normalized and should incorporate natural supports.
7. Services should meet special needs (i.e., needs of clients of different age groups with additional other disabilities or who are homeless or placed inappropriately in the criminal justice system).
8. Service systems should be accountable.
9. Services should be coordinated. (Stroul, 1993, pp. 47–48)

Although CSS and psychosocial rehabilitation philosophies developed decades ago, they remain pertinent. They have informed the development of programs and interventions that have proved to be effective. Conceptualizations of best practices with this population draw from research on such programs and interventions.

Best Practices

Clinical social workers practicing with clients with severe mental illness work with the clients themselves and clients' family members in a community context using knowledge from intervention outcome studies as well as wisdom acquired through experience. In the following two chapters several psychosocial interventions that are supported by research will be described and exemplary programs will be highlighted.

The selections made were informed by reports on clinical outcomes and consensus treatment guidelines. In recent years, psychiatrists have been publishing consensus reports in which they recommend particular interventions at particular stages (e.g., first acute episode, continuing and maintenance treatment, etc.) for clients with particular diagnoses (e.g., schizophrenia, major depression, bipolar disorder). Written largely by psychiatrists, the reports put medication in the center and psychosocial interventions at the periphery. Table 10.3 contains the recommendations on psychosocial interventions included in one of these reports, the Schizophrenia Patient Outcomes Research Team (PORT) Treatment Recommendations (Lehman, Steinwachs et al., 1998), which were based on outcome studies summarized elsewhere (Lehman, Thompson, Dixon, & Scott, 1995). Other consensus reports on schizophrenia can be found in the *Supplement to the American Journal of Psychiatry* (American Psychiatric Association, 1997) and *The Journal of Clinical Psychiatry* (Frances, Doeherty, & Kahn, 1996). Guidelines on the treatment of major depression were published in the *Journal of Clinical Psychiatry* (vol. 59, Supplement 20, 1998); and depression in bipolar disorder in the same journal (vol. 59, Supplement 4, 1998). Successor reports are expected to be published in future years.

The psychosocial recommendations in these reports converge around several recommendations:

- case management (particularly assertive case management) in which community resources are mobilized to support the rehabilitation of the individual
- family support and interventions (family education, family psychoeducation, family consultation)
- supported employment and housing
- social skills training
- Reality-oriented (noninvasive) individual and group therapy

The next two chapters will explain such interventions and additional services. In keeping with its postmodern perspective, this book takes the perspective that *both* psychosocial *and* psychopharmacological interventions are important and should be integrated. Because this is book is for clinical social workers, however, psychosocial interventions will be emphasized.

Instruments Used to Assess and Monitor Severe Mental Illness

With severe mental illness, concern lies with psychosocial functioning as well as symptoms. The following is a list of instruments that can be used to assess and monitor psychosocial functioning and psychotic symptoms. As in the previous chapters, those instruments included in Fischer and Corcoran's (1994) collection are denoted with an asterisk.

*Auditory Hallucinations Questionnaire
*Scale for the Assessment of Negative Symptoms (administered by the clinician)
*Scale for the Assessment of Positive Symptoms (administered by the clinician)
*Cognitive Slippage Scale
Brief Symptom Inventory (Derogatis, 1975)
Quality of Life Interview (Lehman, 1988)

TABLE 10.3 ■ BEST PRACTICE   Recommendations from the PORT Study

Psychological Treatments

22. Individual and group psychotherapies adhering to a psychodynamic model (defined as therapies that use interpretation of unconscious material and focus on transference and regression) should *not* be used in the treatment of persons with schizophrenia.

23. Individual and group therapies employing well-specified combinations of support, education, and behavioral and cognitive skills training approaches designed to address the specific deficits of persons with schizophrenia should be offered over time to improve functioning and enhance other targeted problems, such as medication noncompliance.

Family Treatments.

24. Patients who have ongoing contact with their families should be offered a family psychosocial intervention that spans at least nine months and provides a combination of education about the illness, family support, crisis intervention, and problem-solving skills training. Such interventions should also be offered to non-family caregivers.

25. Family interventions should not be restricted to patients whose families are identified as having high levels of "expressed emotion" (criticism, hostility, overinvolvement).

26. Family therapies based on the premise that family dysfunction is the etiology of the patient's schizophrenic disorder should *not* be used.

Vocational Rehabilitation.

27. Persons with schizophrenia who have *any* of the following characteristics should be offered vocational services. The person (a) identifies competitive employment as a personal goal, (b) has a history of prior competitive employment, (c) has a minimal history of psychiatric hospitalization, and (d) is judged on the basis of a formal vocational assessment to have good work skills.

28. The range of vocational services available in a service system for persons with schizophrenia living in the community who meet the criteria defined in Recommendation 27 should include (a) prevocational training, (b) transitional employment, (c) supported employment, and (d) vocational counseling and education services (job clubs, rehabilitation, counseling, postemployment services).

Service Systems.

29. Systems of care serving persons with schizophrenia who are high service users should include assertive case management (ACM) and assertive community treatment (ACT) programs.

30. Assertive community treatment programs should be targeted to individuals at high risk for repeated rehospitalizations or who have been difficult to retain in active treatment with more traditional types of services.

Source: Based on Lehman, Steinwachs, and the co-investigators of the PORT Project (1998).

Summary and Deconstruction

This chapter began with an individual describing the pain he experienced in the years after he was given the diagnosis of severe depression. In another era, he may have been given an additional label of *chronic mental illness,* a pejorative term that connotes incurability and intractability and evokes attitudes of hopelessness. Today we describe the illness as *severe, serious,* and *persistent,* but even these terms are problematic because a disorder may be severe and not persistent, or serious but not severe. Although all three terms are not essences and do not apply to every individual, they do qualify individuals for services. Because of the variety of treatments available, persons formerly regarded as hopeless can now have fulfilling lives.

Three criteria have been used to determine whether individuals' mental health difficulties are serious, severe, and/or persistent. These are diagnosis, disability, and duration. The diagnoses of schizophrenia, schizoaffective disorder, bipolar disorder, and major depression often have a long course. Some states include additional disorders in their definitions. Disability refers to impairment in social role functioning in such capacities as self-care, homemaking, and employment. Duration can be applied to the length of hospitalization, the number of hospital admissions, or the equivalent supportive care provided by community mental health services. Even with these criteria, many individuals fall between the cracks.

Clinical social work practice with persons with severe mental illness is informed by a number of theories and concepts. The stress-diathesis theory describes the impact of stress and supports on a person with a biological vulnerability. Variations on this emphasize coping, competence, and protective factors. The concept of stimulus window also describes this process. The attention-arousal model explains that when persons with schizophrenia become aroused by internal and external stimuli, they become distracted and find it difficult to process the information. Expressed emotion (EE) in the family or community is an external stimulus that can create difficulty for the client. Families construe the term *EE* as family-blaming, particularly when one considers that families are assuming a major burden of care for their relative.

The terms *psychosocial* and *psychiatric rehabilitation* have different historical roots, but today they have converged. They refer to the promotion of physical, psychiatric, and social functioning to the extent possible for the individual. They aim to promote functioning with the *least* amount of support from professionals that is necessary. This suggests that clinical social workers motivated to intervene need to consider *not acting* before acting—or better still, consider how they can facilitate clients' acting on their own behalf (i.e., empowerment).

Psychosocial rehabilitation depends on the presence of community support programs. The National Institute of Mental Health initiated the development of community support programs and systems of care for persons who are living in the community. Supports consist of networks of persons, programs, and residences that promote clients' functioning and integration in community life. Questions can still be raised about whether such supports exist in particular communities and, if so, whether they are connected in some kind of network.

Among the programs that support clients are specific psychosocial interventions associated with positive outcomes that are recommended in the PORT study and other consensus reports. Although these studies put psychopharmacological interventions in the center and psychosocial ones at the periphery, all these interventions are important. The next two chapters will highlight some of these strategies.

DISCUSSION QUESTIONS

1. What is meant by the term *chronic mental illness?* Why is this term problematic? What alternative terms would you use instead? Do you think the alternative terms are less pejorative?

2. What are the implications of biogenetic explanations of the etiology of severe mental disorders for work with individuals? Work with families?

3. What roles do stress and support play in the course of severe mental disorders?

4. Explain (a) the stress-diathesis model, (b) the concept of the stimulus window, and (c) the attention-arousal model. How are these models related?

5. Explain how coping, competence, and protective factors fit in with the preceding models.

6. How has research on expressed emotion contributed to understanding of the role of the family in relation to schizophrenia? How, if at all, do findings about the family environment in these studies differ from the way in which families have been depicted in the past in psychological theories (e.g., double bind, schizophrenogenic mother)?

7. What is psychosocial rehabilitation? How does it apply to work with persons with severe mental disorders?

8. What are community support programs? How are they implemented in your community?

9. What kinds of attitudes and values are relevant to working with adults with severe mental illness?

10. What is the PORT study? What interventions other than medication does it recommend?

REFERENCES

American Psychiatric Association (1994). *Diagnostic and statistical manual of mental disorders (DSM-IV).* (4th ed.). Washington, DC: Author.

American Psychiatric Association (April 1997 Supplement). Practice guideline for treatment of patients with schizophrenia. *American Journal of Psychiatry, 154*(4), Supplement.

Anderson, C. M., Hogarty, G. E., & Reiss, D. J. (1980). Family treatment of adult schizophrenic patients: A psycho-educational approach. *Schizophrenia Bulletin, 6,* 490–505.

Anderson, C. M., Reiss, D. J., & Hogarty, G. E. (1986). *Schizophrenia and the family: A practitioner's guide to psychoeducation and management.* New York: Guilford Press.

Andreasen, N. C. (1984). *The broken brain: The biological revolution in psychiatry.* New York: Harper & Row.

Andreasen, N. C., Ehrhardt, I. C., Swayze, V. W. II, Alliger, R. J., et al. (1990). Magnetic resonance imaging of the brain of schizophrenia. *Archives of General Psychiatry, 47,* 35–44.

Anthony, W. A. (1992). A revolution in vision. *Innovations & Research, 1,* 17–19.

Anthony, W. A., Cohen, M. R., & Cohen, B. F. (1984). Psychiatric rehabilitation. In J. A. Talbott (Ed.), *The chronic mental patient: Five years later* (pp. 137–157). Orlando, FL: Grune & Stratton.

Anthony, W. A., & Liberman, R. P. (1986). The practice of psychiatric rehabilitation: Historical, conceptual, and research base. *Schizophrenia Bulletin, 12,* 542–559.

Bachrach, L. L. (1982). Young adult chronic patients: An analytical review of the literature. *Hospital and Community Psychiatry, 33,* 189–197.

Bachrach, L. L. (1986). Dimensions of disability in the chronic mentally ill. *Hospital and Community Psychiatry, 37,* 981–982.

Bachrach, L. L. (1988). Defining chronic mental illness: A concept paper. *Hospital and Community Psychiatry, 39,* 383–388.

Bachrach, L. L. (1992). Psychosocial rehabilitation and psychiatry in the care of long-term patients. *American Journal of Psychiatry, 149,* 1455–1463.

Bateson, G., Jackson, D., Haley, J., & Weakland, J. (1956). Toward a theory of schizophrenia. *Behavioral Science, 1,* 251–264.

Brown, G. W. (1959). Experiences of discharged chronic schizophrenic mental hospital patients in various types of living groups. *Milbank Memorial Fund Quarterly, 37,* 105–131.

Brown, G. W., Birley, J. L. T., & Wing, J. K. (1972). Influence of family life on the course of schizophrenic disorders: A replication. *British Journal of Psychiatry, 121,* 241–258.

Brown, G. W., Carstairs, G. M., & Topping, G. (1958). Post hospital adjustment of chronic mental patients. *Lancet, 2,* 685–689.

Brown, G. W., Monck, E. M., Carstairs, G. M., & Wing, J. K. (1962). Influence of family life on the course of schizophrenic illness. *British Journal of Preventive and Social Medicine, 16,* 55–68.

Butzlaff, R. L., & Hooley, J. M. (1998). Expressed emotion and psychiatric relapse: A meta-analysis. *Archives of General Psychiatry, 55,* 547–552.

Chamberlin, J., Rogers, J. A., & Sneed, C. S. (1989). Consumers, families, and consumer support systems. *Psychosocial Rehabilitation Journal, 12*(3), 93–106.

Cohen, M. B., et al. (1954). An intensive study of twelve cases of manic-depressive psychosis. *Psychiatry, 17,* 103–137.

Deegan, P. E. (1997). Recovery and empowerment for people with psychiatric disabilities. *Social Work in Health Care, 25*(3), 11–24.

Derogatis, L. R. (1975). *Brief symptom inventory.* Baltimore: Clinical Psychometric Research.

Estroff, S. E. (1987). No more young adult chronic patients. *Hospital and Community Psychiatry, 38,* 5.

Falloon, I. R. H., & Liberman, R. P. (1983). Interactions between drug and psychosocial therapy in schizophrenia. *Schizophrenia Bulletin, 9,* 543–554.

Farkas, M. D., Cohen, M. R., & Nemec, P. B. (1988). Psychiatric rehabilitation programs: Putting concepts into practice? *Community Mental Health Journal, 24,* 7–21.

Fischer, J., & Corcoran, K. (1994). *Measures for clinical practice: A sourcebook* (vols. 1 and 2). New York: The Free Press.

Frances, A., Doerherty, J. P., & Kahn, D. A. (1996). The expert consensus guideline series: Treatment of schizophrenia. *The Journal of Clinical Psychiatry, 57,* Supplement 12B.

Freedman, A. M., Kaplan, H. I., & Sadock, B. J. (1972). *Modern synopsis of comprehensive textbook of psychiatry.* Baltimore, MD: Williams & Wilkins.

Fromm-Reichmann, F. (1948). Notes on the development of treatment of schizophrenia by psychoanalytic psychotherapy. *Psychiatry, 11,* 263–273.

Goldman, H. H. (1984). Epidemiology. In J. A. Talbott (Ed.), *The chronic mental patient: Five years later* (pp. 15–31). Orlando, FL: Grune & Stratton.

Goldman, H. H. (1998). Deinstitutionalization and community social welfare policy as mental health policy. *Harvard Review of Psychiatry, 6,* 219–222.

Gruenberg, E. M. (1982). Social breakdown in young adults: Keeping crises from becoming chronic. In B. Pepper & H. Ryglewicz (Eds.), *The young adult chronic patient* (pp. 43–50). San Francisco: Jossey-Bass.

Hammen, C. L. (1995). Stress and the course of unipolar and bipolar disorders. In C. M. Mazure (Ed.), *Does stress cause psychiatric illness?* Washington, DC: American Psychiatric Press.

Harding, C. M., Brooks, G. W, Ashikaga, T., Strauss, J. S., & Breier, A. (1987). The Vermont longitudinal study of persons with severe mental illness, I: Methodology, study sample, and overall status 32 years later. *American Journal of Psychiatry, 144,* 718–726.

Harding, C. M., Zubin, J., & Strauss, J. S. (1987). Chronicity in schizophrenia: Fact, partial fact, or artifact. *Hospital and Community Psychiatry, 38,* 477–486.

Hooley, J. M., & Hiller, J. B. (1998). Expressed emotion and the pathogenesis of relapse in schizophrenia. In M. F. Lenzenweger & R. H. Dworkin (Eds.), *Origins and development of schizophrenia: Advances in experimental psychopathology* (pp. 477–468). Washington, DC: American Psychological Association.

Kendler, K. S. (1988). The genetics of schizophrenia and related disorders. In D. L. Dunner, E. S. Gerson, & J. E. Barrett (Eds.), *Relatives at risk for mental disorder* (pp. 247–263). New York: Raven Press.

Kessler, R. C., Berglund, P. A., Zha, S., Leaf, P. J., et al. (1996). The 12-month prevalence and correlates of serious mental illness (SMI). In R. W. Manderscheid & M. A. Sonnenschein (Eds.), *Mental health, United States, 1996* (pp. 59–70). DDHS Pub. No. (SMA)96–3098. Washington, DC: Superintendent of Documents, U.S. Government Printing Office.

Kessler, R. C., Berglund, P. A., Walters, E. E., Leaf, P. J., et al. (1998). A methodology for estimating the 12-

month prevalence of serious mental illness. In R. W. Manderscheid & M. J. Henderson (Eds.), *Mental health, United States, 1998* (pp. 99–109). DDHS Pub. No. (SMA)99-3285. Washington, DC: Superintendent of Documents, U.S. Government Printing Office.

King, D. J., & Cooper, S. J. (1989). Viruses, immunity and mental disorder. *British Journal of Psychiatry, 151,* 1–7.

Koenigsberg, H. W., & Handley, R. (1986). Expressed emotion: From predictive index to clinical construct. *American Journal of Psychiatry, 143,* 1361–1373.

Kottgen, C., Sonnichsen, I., Mollenhauer, K., et al. (1984). Families' high expressed emotion and relapses in young schizophrenic patients: Results of the Hamburg–Camberwell family intervention study II. *International Journal of Family Psychiatry, 5,* 71–82.

Jimenez, M. A. (1988). Chronicity in mental disorders: Evolution of a concept. *Social Casework, 69,* 627–633.

Land, H. M.(1986). Life stress and ecological status: predictors of symptoms in schizophrenic veterans. *Health and Social Work, 11,* 254–264.

Leff, J., & Vaughn, C. (1985). *Expressed emotion in families: Its significance for mental illness.* New York: Guilford Press.

Lefley, H. P. (1992). Expressed emotion: Conceptual, clinical, and social policy issues. *Hospital and Community Psychiatry, 43,* 591–598.

Lefley, H. P., & Wasow, M. (Eds.). (1994). *Helping families cope with mental illness.* Switzerland and United States: Harwood Academic Publishers.

Lehman, A. (1988). A quality of life interview for the chronically mentally ill. *Evaluation and Program Planning, 11,* 51–62.

Lehman, A. F., Steinwachs, D. M., and the coinvestigators of the PORT Project. (1998). At issue: Translating research into practice: The schizophrenia patient outcomes research team (PORT) treatment recommendations. *Schizophrenia Bulletin, 24*(1), 1–10.

Lehman, A. F., Thompson, J. W., Dixon, L. B., & Scott, J. E. (Eds.). (1995). Schizophrenia: Treatment outcomes research. *Schizophrenia Bulletin, 21*(4), 561–701.

Lewis, H. R. (1998, October/November). Lewis v. Kmart: a fight for what's right. *NAMI Advocate,* vol. 20, no. 2, pp. 10–11.

Liberman, R. P. (1988a). Introduction. In R. P. Liberman (Ed.), *Psychiatric rehabilitation of chronic mental patients* (pp. xvii–xxii). Washington, DC: American Psychiatric Press.

Liberman, R. P. (1988b). Coping with chronic mental disorders: A framework for hope. In R. P. Liberman (Ed.), *Psychiatric rehabilitation of chronic mental*

patients (pp. 1–28). Washington, DC: American Psychiatric Press.

Liberman, R. P. (1982). Social factors in the etiology of schizophrenic disorders. In L. Grinspoon (Ed.), *Psychiatry: 1982 Annual Review* (Vol. 1, pp. 97–112). Washington, DC: American Psychiatric Press.

Lidz, T., Cornelison, A. R., Fleck, S., & Terry, D. (1957). The intrafamilial environment of schizophrenic patients. II. Marital schism and marital skew. *American Journal of Psychiatry, 114,* 241–248.

MacKain, S. J., Liberman, R. P., & Corrigan, P. W. (1994). Can coping and competence override stress and vulnerability in schizophrenia? In R. P. Liberman & J. Yager (Eds.), *Stress in psychiatric disorders* (pp. 53–82). New York: Springer.

McGuffin, P., & Katz, R. (1989). The genetics of depression and manic-depression disorder. *British Journal of Psychiatry, 155,* 294–304.

Mueser, K. T., Drake, R. E., & Bond, G. R. (1997). Recent advances in psychiatric rehabilitation for patients with severe mental illness. *Harvard Review of Psychiatry, 5,* 123–137.

National Institute of Mental Health. (1982). *A network for caring: The Community Support Program of the National Institute of Mental Health* (Proceedings of four national conferences 1978–1979). (app. A). Washington, DC: U.S. Department of Health and Human Services.

Oliver, N., & Kuipers, E. (1996). Stress and its relationship to expressed emotion in community mental health workers. *International Journal of Social Psychiatry, 42,* 150–159.

Parker, G., Johnston, P., & Hayward, L. (1988). *Archives of General Psychiatry, 45,* 806–813.

Pepper, B., & Ryglewicz, H. (1986, October). The stimulus window: Stress and stimulation as aspects of everyday experience. *TIE Lines, 3*(3), 1–5.

Pepper, B., & Ryglewicz, H. (1987). Is there expressed emotion away from home? "Interactional intensity" ("II") in the treatment program. *TIE Lines, 4*(1), 1–3.

Pilisuk, M. (1982). Delivery of social support: The social inoculation. *American Journal of Orthopsychiatry, 52,* 20–31.

Rothbard, A. B. (n.d.) State Definitions of Persons with Chronic Mental Illness. Unpublished table.

Rothbard, A. B., Schinnar, A. P., & Goldman, H. (1996). The pursuit of a definition for severe and persistent mental illness. In S. M. Soreff (Ed.), *Handbook for the treatment of the seriously mentally ill* (pp. 9–26). Seattle: Hogrefe & Huber.

Ryglewicz, H. (1984). An agenda for family intervention: Issues, models, and practice. In B. Pepper & H. Ryglewicz (Eds.), *Advances in treating the young adult chronic patient* (pp. 81–90). San Francisco: Jossey-Bass.

Sands, R. G. (1984). Correlates of success and lack of success in deinstitutionalization. *Community Mental Health Journal, 20,* 223–235.

Schinnar, A. P., Rothbard, A. B., Kanter, R., & Jung, Y. S. (1990). An empirical literature review of definitions of severe and persistent mental illness. *American Journal of Psychiatry, 147,* 1602–1608.

Solomon, P. (1999). Evolution of service innovations for adults with severe mental illness. In D. E. Biegel & A. Blum (Eds.), *Innovations in practice and service delivery across the lifespan* (pp. 147–168). New York: Oxford University Press.

Stein, L. I., & Test, M. A. (1982). Community treatment of the young adult patient. In B. Pepper & H. Reviewing (Eds.), *The young adult chronic patient* (pp. 57–67). San Francisco: Jossey-Bass.

Stroul, B. A. (1993). Rehabilitation in community support systems. In R. W. Flexer & P. L. Solomon (Eds.), *Psychiatric rehabilitation in practice* (pp. 45–61). Boston: Andover Medical Publishers.

Substance Abuse and Mental Health Services Administration (SAMHSA). (1993, May 20). *Federal Register,* vol. 58, no. 96, pp. 29422–29425.

Sullivan, W. P., & Poertner, J. (1989). Social support and life stress: A mental health consumers' perspective. *Community Mental Health Journal, 25,* 21–32.

Taylor, E. H. (1987). The biological basis of schizophrenia. *Social Work, 32,* 115–121.

Tolsdorf, C. C. (1976). Social networks, support and coping: An exploratory study. *Family Process, 15,* 407–417.

Torrey, E. F. (1988a). *Surviving schizophrenia: A family manual* (rev. ed.). New York: Harper & Row.

Turner, J. C., & Ten Honor, W. J. (1978). The NIMH Community Support Program: Pilot approach to a needed social reform. *Schizophrenia Bulletin, 4,* 319–344.

U.S. Department of Health and Human Services. (1981). *Toward a national plan for the chronically mentally ill: Report to the secretary* (1980, December). Washington, DC: Author.

Vaughn, C. E., & Leff, J. P. (1976). The influence of family and social factors on the course of psychiatric illness. *British Journal of Psychiatry, 129,* 125–137.

Vaughn, C. E., Snaker, K. S., Jones, S., Freehand, W. B., & Falloon, I. R. H. (1984). Family factors in schizophrenic relapse. *Archives of General Psychiatry, 41,* 1169–1177.

Zubin, J., & Spring, B. (1977). Vulnerability—A new view of schizophrenia. *Journal of Abnormal Psychology, 86,* 103–126.

11

Community Care of Persons with Severe Mental Illness

Case Management and Community Resources

...over the years I have learned all different kinds of ways to help myself. Sometimes I use medications, therapy, self help and mutual support groups, friends, my relationship with God, my work, exercise, spending time in nature—all these things help me remain whole and healthy even though I have a disability.

—Deegan, "Recovery and Empowerment for People with Psychiatric Disabilities," 1997

The development of additional mental health services at the community level had both positive and negative consequences. On the positive side, some services became available for persons with less severe mental illness who had never been institutionalized. On the negative side, the multiplicity of services and the growing complexity of the mental health system made it difficult for persons with severe mental illness to successfully negotiate and access necessary services (Mechanic, 1991).

—Mueser, Bond, Drake, & Resnick, "Recent Advances in Psychiatric Rehabilitation for Patients with Severe Mental Illness," 1998

The previous chapter discussed the conceptual and philosophical bases for the care of persons considered severely mentally disabled. Under today's model of care, most of these individuals live in the community where they receive varying amounts of help from physical and behavioral health, residential, vocational, financial, and other services. This chapter describes case management, an approach often used by clinical social workers who work with this population. Because this role is enacted in the context of the community, this chapter will discuss the kinds of resources that social workers can activate to help clients who want to use them. These services are not available in every community whereas other resources not mentioned here are found in some locations. The goal here is to present a range of services and resources that are potentially beneficial.

As the opening quotations suggest, the perspectives of consumers and clients may be disparate. Clients are likely to view resources in terms of their individual needs, aspirations, feelings, and goals. Professionals tend to think that clients *should* and *would* use mental health services if they were made accessible. This chapter will emphasize the professional perspective, keeping in mind that social workers are responsible for bridging the gap between themselves and their clients. To move in this direction, we will start with a narrative of a young man who became a client.

Case Scenario

Larry Leeds is a twenty-year-old, single man who lives with his parents in a small southern town that is 100 miles from a metropolitan area. His father owns and runs a corner grocery store; his mother works as a bank teller. Larry is the oldest of three children, all boys. The family is active in the local church.

Larry was a shy child who performed well in school until his junior year in high school, when his grades declined and he became argumentative at home. Concerned about his "attitude," his mother discussed the problem with their family doctor, who recommended that the parents take Larry to the area's community mental health center for an evaluation. The staff there concluded that Larry was struggling with adolescent autonomy issues and referred him to their adolescent therapy group. Larry attended the weekly group for three months, during which time his attitude at home did not change but his grades improved. Larry became friendly with a couple of young men in the group who introduced him to marijuana.

Early his senior year, Larry became more belligerent at home and cut classes at school. He accused his father of being the devil and his mother of being a devil worshiper. He told his parents that he had special powers to ward off the devil and that they should keep out of his way. One day, while cleaning Larry's room, Mrs. Leeds discovered knives and guns hidden in a closet. She called her husband and then the family physician, who again referred her to the mental health center. Angry that the center minimized his problems the year before, Mrs. Leeds wondered if a stronger approach was necessary. She and her husband decided to take Larry to the nearest hospital, where he was admitted to the acute psychiatric unit with a diagnosis of schizophreniform disorder.

Larry was hospitalized for a month and discharged with medication (Haldol). The family was told that it was suspected that he was using street drugs, which were exacerbating his psychotic symptoms. Larry was advised to avoid friends who use drugs, to take his medication as prescribed, and to return to high school. He was referred to a private psychiatrist thirty miles away for follow-up. Larry complied with this plan and completed high school.

The following year Larry attended a community college and lived at home. About halfway through the first semester, he had an argument with his academic counselor in which Larry accused his counselor of having a pact with the devil. After Larry struck the counselor, the police were called. Larry was taken to the psychiatric unit of the community hospital, where he was admitted for the second time.

This time Larry was given the diagnosis of schizophrenic disorder, paranoid type (provisional). The diagnosis was considered provisional because the extent of Larry's drug use was unknown. The psychiatrists told the parents that the drugs bring out the paranoid symptoms. Nevertheless, the doctors said that a diagnosis of schizophrenia was probable and told the parents that this is a serious and disabling illness. Again Larry was discharged on medication, which the parents were advised to administer. This time Larry was referred to the local community mental health center for follow-up.

Larry was assigned to both a psychiatrist and a therapist at the center. He was told that the sessions would be confidential and that no one would be provided with information about him without his consent. The therapist recommended that he participate in the day treatment program that was run by the center, but Larry refused. Larry said that he wanted to return to school and live on his own. The therapist tried to work with him to help him adapt his goals to his illness. After a while Larry stopped therapy and refused to take medication. Within three months he was rehospitalized. This time the diagnosis of schizophrenia, paranoid type was confirmed.

Larry's experience is not unusual. Like many young persons with severe mental illness and their families, neither he nor his parents were aware of the seriousness of his illness until there was a crisis. Then they responded by using the personal, familial, and community resources that were available. Because the onset of his symptoms was concurrent with his passage through adolescence and his use of street drugs, it was unclear what the nature of Larry's difficulty was.

Severe mental disorders are complex in their diagnosis, treatment, and aftercare needs. The specific illnesses and their expression are heterogeneous, requiring intervention approaches that are tailored to the individual client. Before deinstitutionalization, persons with serious mental illness were treated in hospitals, which provided a range of services under one roof. Today diverse, multiple, yet individualized services need to be available in the community.

Some communities, like the one in which Larry lived, have few resources. Yet, within a radius of 100 miles, other services are available. Elsewhere there are so many resources that it requires a systems expert, such as a case manager, to identify the appropriate resources and link the client with them. Intervention with persons with serious mental illness entails the coordination of mental health services, as well as vocational, housing, and entitlement programs. Furthermore, other human needs, such as health care, socialization, transportation, recreation, artistic expression, and spiritual development, are to be addressed. The needs of families also should be met.

This chapter describes multifaceted community treatment approaches to clients with severe and persistent mental disorders. Not all such clients are young or have the diagnosis of schizophrenia, like Larry; some have less serious diagnoses, yet are functionally disabled. Others have mental disorders that have periodic peaks, such as recurrent major depression and bipolar disorder. This chapter begins with the critical function of case management and proceeds with a discussion of the community services that are potential supports to clients. Among the variety of social and rehabilitative programs that are described, a few best practices will be highlighted.

Case Management and Community Care

Case management is the practice of coordinating services for clients. It is a response to the complexity of the human service delivery system referred to in one of the quotations that opened this chapter (Mueser et al., 1998), as well as the multiple needs of clients with severe mental illness who live in the community. Case management is practiced in a number of human service fields (e.g., aging, mental retardation/developmental disabilities, health care, child welfare) and is not associated with a particular profession—or, in some sites, with being a professional at all. Yet social workers are particularly well equipped to fulfill this role and do so in many mental health settings.

Case management is accomplished through the establishment of one pivotal relationship (or, in some cases, a relationship with a team). The case manager helps the client obtain and use community resources that will facilitate his or her well-being. In the field of mental health the goals of case management are preventative (avoid decompensation, suicide, and rehospitalization) and rehabilitative (promote psychosocial functioning at the highest level possible).

The agency auspices of case managers vary. The case manager may, for example, work out of an outpatient department of a psychiatric hospital or unit; a community mental health center; a psychosocial rehabilitation program; or an adult protective service agency that serves the vulnerable aged, the physically disabled, and the severely mentally ill. Under managed care, mechanisms for providing case management for persons with severe mental illness are evolving. Clients who have private insurance may find that their primary care physician, a nurse, or a social worker is coordinating their mental health care (McClelland, 1996). Companies that have behavioral health carve-outs will refer clients to separate agencies that may offer case management services. In some areas of the country, the city or county contracts with existing community mental health services to provide case management to clients in the public sector (McClelland, 1996).

Functions of Case Management

The five basic functions of case management are assessment, planning, linkage, monitoring, and advocacy. *Assessment* is a comprehensive evaluation of the client's needs based on the client's history, diagnosis, strengths, resources, and difficulties. It requires the compilation of information from various sources (psychiatric hospital or unit, mental health center, physician, psychosocial rehabilitation services previously used) as well as the client and client system. The assessment of a person with severe mental illness should be thorough, as treatment is holistic. It is recommended that case managers gather information about the client's situation and needs in the following domains:

- housing
- physical health status and care (including use of health care services, diet, sleep, and exercise)

- mental status, diagnosis, and needs for mental health services (medication, psychosocial rehabilitation, etc.)
- sources of economic support and ability to manage own money
- primary sources of emotional support (family, friends, service providers) and the quality of these relationships
- parental status (children cared for by client or someone else)
- personal hygiene and grooming
- socialization, recreation, and leisure time activities
- vocational and employment status
- substance use and abuse
- involvement with criminal justice system and current status
- means of transportation, their accessibility, and the client's ability to use these means
- spiritual/religious orientation and needs

The case manager examines the client's situation in these areas and determines where needs are already met and where there are gaps. On the basis of the assessment, a *service plan* that is tailored to the individual client is developed. In keeping with the principles of the community support system and social work values, the client should be an active participant in the development of the plan. In cases in which families are involved in the support of a client, and clients consent to their participation, inclusion of the family is valuable (Intagliata, Willer, & Egri, 1986). Ideally the plan is also developed collaboratively with representatives of the agencies that are included in the plan. The needs, services, and means of implementation should be spelled out in specific behavioral terms.

Case managers also assure that the client is *linked* with the appropriate community support services. In order to be able to do so, case managers should be knowledgeable about the existing resources, eligibility requirements, and how to access these sources of support. In working with the chronically mentally ill, simply making a referral is not sufficient; means should be developed to facilitate the client's use of services. This may necessitate modeling for the client how to take the bus, mobilizing family members or volunteers to provide services, arranging community transportation services, or the case manager's escorting the client to the service.

The fourth function is *monitoring*. The case worker oversees the case to make sure that the client is following through with the plan. If some aspect of the plan is not implemented, the case manager determines which obstacles might be interfering and tries to remedy these. If the client is carrying out the plan but the plan is not working, it may be that some aspect of the plan should be changed.

Another component of case management is *advocacy*. In fulfillment of this role, case managers act on behalf of clients to assure that clients' rights are protected and that they obtain services for which they are eligible. If clients are denied services or are mistreated in the community, case managers pursue informal and formal strategies to overcome obstacles to receiving services.

These basic five functions emphasize the administrative role of the case manager. They are particularly compatible with the generalist skills taught in social work bachelor's programs and in the first year of social work master's programs. When several direct service functions are added, the advanced skills of the clinical social worker become a tremendous asset.

One of these additional functions is helping the client with *problem solving.* Living in the community, clients with serious mental disorders encounter everyday problems with which they have difficulty. The case manager works collaboratively with the client or client system by identifying the problem and breaking it down to manageable proportions, generating alternative solutions, and promoting decision making and actions that seem to represent the best choices under the circumstances. The need for problem-solving activity arises in the process of monitoring the client over time. The problems may be personal, interpersonal, environmental, or a combination.

A related direct service function is *crisis intervention* (Intagliata et al., 1986). Crises are eruptions of stress in reaction to problems that cannot be managed using a person's usual coping mechanisms. Persons with chronic mental disabilities are highly vulnerable to stress, which can emanate from within or from outside. Internal stressors are related to the disorder, which may have an exacerbation on its own or be the result of a client's going off the prescribed medication. External stressors such as poverty, eviction, interpersonal difficulties, problems on the job, and expressed emotion in the family—singly or in combination—can also arouse stress. Clients with severe psychiatric disorders may respond to stress in extreme ways; for example, they may threaten suicide, engage in violent behavior, or develop delusions or hallucinations (Flax, 1982). The case manager can provide support to the individual client, mobilize support from the family, intervene with persons who may be contributing to the problem, or call on community resources that can be used to resolve the crisis. This may require that the case manager make home visits, accompany the client to a psychiatric emergency service, or contact others in the community. In some cases, hospitalization is necessary. When a crisis occurs, the case manager may spend large blocks of time over a couple of days with a single client.

Consider the following crisis soon after Larry's third hospitalization, after which he was assigned a case manager.

April 4: John Martin, case manager, received a telephone call from Larry's mother, requesting that he meet with Larry. The case manager made a home visit, where he spent a couple of hours with Larry and additional time with Larry and his parents together.

Larry told the case manager that he would like to have spending money, but his parents "won't let me apply for financial aid." (John recalled that during his first meeting with Larry, John told Larry about SSI.) Larry said that when he asks his parents for money, he feels like a child.

John figured out how much money Larry would receive with SSI, considering that he was living at home, and told Larry about Medicaid, for which he was also entitled. They discussed his right to receive benefits, but Larry was troubled by the prospect of going against his parents' wishes. John identified the following issues for Larry to consider: (a) Larry's respect for his parents' feelings and his fear of their disapproval; (b) his parents' coverage for him under their medical insurance at least until he is twenty-one years old; (c) the amount of SSI he would receive versus his ability to earn the equivalent amount by doing chores for his parents, his grandparents, and neighbors.

During the family session, the case manager gave Mr. and Mrs. Leeds the opportunity to share their feelings about "not accepting welfare" and being responsible for Larry at least until he is twenty-one years old. John described the SSI program as an entitlement to which Mr. and Mrs. Leeds, as taxpayers, have contributed. Larry shared his feelings about being financially dependent on them and not having any spending money. He articulated his desire to live on his own and hold a job some day. At the conclusion of the session, the family agreed to the following:

1. Out of respect for his parents, Larry would not apply for SSI until he was almost twenty-one years old.
2. Larry's parents will pay him for performing three hours of yardwork weekly.
3. Larry will seek out similar jobs working for his grandparents and neighbors.
4. His parents will make efforts not to treat him like a child.
5. The case manager will work with Larry to make plans for services that will help him become more self-sufficient in the future, such as living in a halfway house.

Implicit in the functions that have been described is that the case manager provides a *supportive relationship.* Although the establishment of a warm, working relationship is central to all of social work practice, it is particularly important in working with persons with severe mental disabilities, who may be fearful, suspicious, or hostile. These reactions may be a consequence of an illness that impairs their ability to establish relationships (Kantor, 1988) and/or a response to a new person. It is critical for the case manager to help the client overcome his or her apprehensions and form a therapeutic working alliance (Harris & Bachrach, 1988). The case manager can achieve this by conveying positive regard, attentiveness, consistency, and friendliness; by doing things together with the client; and responding promptly to help the client with major and minor problems.

Another direct service function of the case manager is *working with the family* (Intagliata et al., 1986; Lamb, 1980). Many seriously and severely mentally ill persons live with their parents, spouses, siblings, or equivalent significant others. Even if the client lives apart from the family, emotional ties remain. The family can be a partner in the development and implementation of the service plan. Family members are able to provide information about the client, identify signs of relapse, provide transportation, monitor the client's response to treatment, and assist with everyday problems. Moreover, the family can advocate for an individual member and for the corporate needs of clients. Despite the contributions families make, they are frequently excluded from consideration.

Clinical social workers who are case managers call on their generalist skills in assessment, brokerage, case planning, and advocacy and on their clinical skills in the assessment of mental health problems and their treatment. Clinical social workers are trained to select interventions that are compatible with clients' needs, to use community resources, and to advocate for the vulnerable. We turn next to some models social workers can use to work with clients with severe mental illness as case managers or members of a community treatment team.

Models of Community Care/Case Management

During the last two decades of the twentieth century, numerous models of community care and case management for persons with severe mental illness were discussed and compared in the literature (see, e.g., Chamberlain & Rapp, 1991; Mueser et al., 1998; Solomon, 1992). As with other categories depicted in this book, community care and case management models are not unique essences; they overlap and interpenetrate each other. Among these are the broker, rehabilitation, strengths, clinical, and assertive/intensive case management models. As the following discussion will show, these prototypes have some differences in philosophy, the depth of relationship with the client, and the client–case manager ratio. It is likely, however, that in the context of work with a particular individual in a particular situation, case managers operating from different models would act similarly.

The *broker* (or expanded broker or generalist) *model* is the simplest, most basic approach. Here the case manager links the client with community resources and coordinates different service providers (Mueser et al., 1998). The broker usually works from an office and has a relatively high caseload (Solomon & Meyerson, 1997). Although the effectiveness research on this approach is inconclusive (e.g., Franklin, Solovitz, Mason, Clemons, & Miller, 1987), the broker model continues to be implemented widely.

The *rehabilitation model* "adds the functions of psychiatric rehabilitation to the functions of the broker case management model" (Anthony, Forbess, & Cohen, 1993, p. 99). Person centered, it helps clients increase their functioning in the environments that they choose. Case management that incorporates this model involves the use of a functional assessment, teaching of skills, and the establishment of an overall rehabilitation goal (Anthony et al., 1993).

A third approach is the *strengths model,* which emphasizes the client's positive attributes and the community's resources. It is guided by the following six principles:

1. The focus is on individual strengths rather than pathology.
2. The community is viewed as an oasis of resources.
3. Interventions are based on client self-determination.
4. The case manager–client relationship is primary and essential.
5. Aggressive outreach is the preferred mode of intervention.
6. People suffering from major mental illness can continue to learn, grow, and change. (Rapp, 1998, pp. 45–54)

This model is implemented through a collaborative relationship, an assessment of strengths, planning, resource acquisition, ongoing modification of the plan, and gradual disengagement (Rapp, 1998).

A fourth model, *clinical case management,* posits that the case manager is a psychotherapist, who provides a relationship that encourages the client to change internally and grow (Roach, 1993). This is a development of Lamb's (1980) earlier conceptualization of the therapist–case manager, who is the client's primary therapist as well as a broker who links clients with resources. As a therapist, the clinical case manager helps clients interpret events accurately, teaches skills, and serves as a role model. This approach requires that the case manager be knowledgeable about object relations theory and have good clinical skills and training (Roach, 1993).

The fifth model is called *assertive case management,* which is an adaptation of assertive community treatment (ACT), to be discussed shortly, to case management. With assertive case management, case managers work with common cases in teams, have small caseloads, and reach out aggressively to clients to help them cope with community living.

Usually there is emergency, round-the-clock coverage. With *intensive case management,* the case managers generally have individual caseloads; otherwise this approach is similar to the assertive model (Mueser et al., 1998). We turn next to the assertive community treatment model.

Assertive Community Treatment

Assertive community treatment (ACT) is a model of service delivery that spawned some of the case management models that have been discussed. As a program of direct service, the ACT program should be differentiated from the case management that grew out of it. During the 1970s, Leonard Stein (professor of psychiatry) and Mary Ann Test (professor of social work) of the University of Wisconsin developed a program in Dane County, Wisconsin, that was an alternative to hospitalization. "It was a comprehensive array of services that essentially transferred all the functions of the hospital to the community" (Solomon, 1999, p. 151). As it evolved, it changed its name from Training in Community Living (TCL) to Program of Assertive Community Treatment (PACT) to Mobile Community Treatment (MCT) Program. These programs provided comprehensive, continuous care to clients with severe mental illness.

The Assertive Community Treatment (ACT) program, modeled on its predecessors, was adopted wholly or partially by groups in other communities in the United States, England, and Australia. Most of the outcome research on these programs produced positive results, especially in their reduction of the use of hospitals (Stein & Santos, 1998). Philosophically ACT is compatible with the community support system principles (Stein & Santos, 1998). The authors of the PORT Study (Lehman, Steinwachs et al., 1998) and the Schizophrenia Consensus Report on treatment of schizophrenia (Frances, Doeherty, & Kahn, 1996) recommended the ACT (or PACT) program. The National Alliance for the Mentally Ill has published a manual to help communities develop such a program (Allness & Knoedler, 1998). In its Practice Guidelines for Treatment of Patients with Schizophrenia, the American Psychiatric Association recommends this approach for persons with schizophrenia "who are marginally functioning and/or poorly compliant with treatment" (American Psychiatric Association, 1997, p. 29). Accordingly, ACT is not a panacea for all clients. Table 11.1 outlines the major features of the ACT program. This will now be described as one of this book's examples of a best practice.

The assertive community treatment model has a multidisciplinary team functioning corporately as case managers.

> There are no individual caseloads. Every worker sees every member, on an informal rotating basis. As a result, workers can be deployed with maximum efficiency when several members are in crisis simultaneously or when our numbers have been depleted by illness or vacations. (Witheridge & Dincin, 1985, p. 71)

Teams have the advantage of providing continuous care for the client by anyone on the team. Furthermore, working in a group can generate creativity and energy and prevent burnout (Test, 1979).

Case management teams meet on a frequent basis, at which times clients are discussed, intervention strategies developed, and tasks distributed among the group. Clients are

---

TABLE 11.1 ■ BEST PRACTICE   The ACT Program

The desired outcomes of the ACT program are to:
- reduce the use of hospitalization
- increase quality and stability of community living
- normalize activities of daily living (e.g., employment)

The specific goals are to help clients:
- maintain good physical health
- achieve a reduction in psychotic symptoms
- maintain normalized housing
- minimize involvement in the criminal justice and law enforcement systems
- acquire and maintain a job
- maintain a substance-free lifestyle
- meet additional individualized goals

The key features of the ACT program are as follows:
- a multidisciplinary team that shares responsibility for the same group of clients
- individually tailored treatment programs
- direct provision of services
- delivery of services in the client's natural environment (home, neighborhood, place of work)
- support in daily living skills
- assertive outreach and follow-up
- crisis intervention, problem solving, helping clients cope
- teaching clients skills in the environments in which they are to use them
- low client-staff ratio
- 24-hour availability
- no time limits on the service

Sources: Based on Stein & Santos (1998), Stein & Test (1980, 1985), Test (1979).

---

seen often and regularly in the field. The Mobile Community Treatment Program in Wisconsin, designed specifically for difficult-to-treat, predominantly young clients, had two shifts of staff, who met daily between shifts and weekly as a total staff to give status reports on clients and coordinate their efforts (Stein & Diamond, 1985; Stein & Test, 1982).

The assertive community treatment model recognizes that clients with serious mental disorders have three disabling conditions that interfere with their social functioning (Stein & Test, 1985). These are strong dependence needs, a limited range of problem-solving or instrumental skills, and the capacity to develop psychiatric symptoms in the face of stress. These characteristics interfere with community living and create vulnerability to rehospitalization. On the other hand, the model recognizes that each client has strengths that are the basis for effective functioning. In order to promote a client's functioning and prevent stress, the team assertively reaches out to clients to engage them and to keep them engaged in programs. Clients who do not show up for appointments are sought out so that obstacles to their participation can be overcome.

With assertive community treatment, clients are also helped to become more independent. For some this entails separation from parents by living apart from them. At the same time supports are provided for the client, structured visiting with parents is arranged, and the community is prepared to receive new residents (Training in Community Living, 1983). In other cases, separation is not pursued. "Whether we separate patients from their families or not, we continue to work closely with families" (Stein & Test, 1984, p. 66).

One of the unique features of this model is its fostering the development of coping skills in familiar surroundings in the community. Accordingly, case managers reach out to clients in their homes and local communities. They may meet clients over coffee in the client's neighborhood, at a psychosocial rehabilitation program, or at the client's residence. The emphasis is on *in vivo* (real-life) assistance with ordinary activities in the same context in which they will be used. The team member models a skill (e.g., how to use a washing machine) where the skill is needed (e.g., the neighborhood laundromat) and teaches the skill to the client. This approach differs from a program-based strategy in which the client is expected to learn a skill in one setting and apply it to another. *In vivo* assistance is consistent with the observation that many persons with severe and persistent mental illnesses have difficulties transferring learning from one situation to another (Stein & Test, 1984).

The ACT is a service model that goes well beyond what is usually incorporated in case management programs. Stein (1992) notes that communities often expect individual case managers to do the work of a multidisciplinary team and serve as "glue" to fix a "fragmented nonsystem of public mental health care" (p. 173). He recommends that communities establish "continuous care teams" comprised of psychiatrists, psychologists, social workers, nurses, rehabilitation workers, and psychiatric technicians who specialize in difficult-to-treat clients, and that the staff-client ratio not be greater than 1:10. These teams should be available seven days a week. More stable clients should also be cared for by teams, but these can have a more limited membership, a client-staff ratio of 50:1, and be available only on weekdays. Clients followed by continuous care teams who achieve stability can be transferred to the less intensive teams.

A study of case management programs that incorporated either the treatment (cf. ACT) or broker model in five demonstration sites of the Robert Wood Johnson Program on Chronic Mental Illness found that case managers operating under both models were doing a great deal of direct service (Ridgely, Morrissey, Paulson, Goldman, & Calloway, 1996). Treatment-oriented programs, however, did provide more medication supervision, counseling, and psychotherapy. Both were engaged in a great deal of advocacy and outreach and assisted clients with skills in daily living and psychosocial services. Again it appears that case managers were more responsive to the needs of clients than the requirements of a particular model.

Assumptions Underlying Case Management/ Community Care Practice

Case management/community care with persons with severe mental illness is based on assumptions that are consistent with social work values, the philosophy of rehabilitation, CSS principles, and case management models. These are as follows:

1. Persons with severe and persistent mental illness have the capacity to live in the community with supports.
2. Such persons have strengths that can be developed and enhanced.

3. Severe mental illness creates vulnerability to stress, dependence, and poverty that are exemplified in frequent crises.

4. Persons with serious mental illnesses have the capacity to grow, change, learn, and improve their psychological and social functioning.

5. For many persons with severe mental illnesses, learning is most effective when it takes place in the environment in which it is to be used; learning takes place gradually and in incremental steps.

6. Like other citizens, persons with severe mental illness have civil rights and obligations. They have the right to freedom of speech, mobility, and autonomy so long as they do not interfere with the rights of others and do not violate the law.

7. Persons with severe and persistent mental illness have the right to participate in service planning and to make informed decisions on their own behalf.

8. Families are potential partners in the rehabilitation and planning process, provided that clients consent to their help.

9. The community has a responsibility to integrate persons with serious mental illness into the community and to develop a continuum of services to meet their needs.

10. Treatment of clients should be the least intrusive but most therapeutic and should take place in the least restrictive environment that is consistent with clients' needs.

11. The community has a responsibility to provide services to this population for a long and indefinite time period. (Suggested by Ohio Department of Mental Health, 1987.)

These assumptions recognize that severe mental illness has an unpredictable course. Because many individuals recover or make substantial gains in their functioning, their potential for growth should be recognized and incorporated into treatment planning and implementation. In being optimistic about clients' capacity to learn and develop, the case manager recognizes and works with each client's strengths and capacities. Nevertheless, the vulnerabilities to stress and dependence also should be considered, so that when a crisis occurs, the case manager is ready to engage the client in problem solving to prevent the situation and the client from deteriorating.

The responsibility for the rehabilitation of persons with severe mental illness is shared among the client, the family, the case manager, mental health services, other social service agencies, and the community as a whole. Clients are responsible for taking care of themselves and obeying the law. The community has a responsibility to respect the clients' rights, to accept them as citizens, and to respond to their needs. The case manager is in a critical position of mediating between the client and the community, yet representing the client's interests.

In keeping with these assumptions, the following strategies are recommended:

1. Reach out assertively to clients in their natural environments on a regular and consistent basis and at times of crisis.

2. Recognize clients' dependence, yet support their drive to be more autonomous.

3. Teach skills in the environments in which they are needed incrementally, supporting clients as they master each step.

4. Help clients obtain services and living situations that are consistent with their needs for support and autonomy. Decisions on housing should be guided by the clients' wishes and their capacity to cope with the new environment.

5. Encourage clients to use community resources. Especially support their use of mainstream facilities such as libraries, movies, parks, and schools, and their participation in the competitive job market.
6. Work with community representatives to help them understand and integrate persons with severe mental illness into the community.
7. Advocate for clients on the individual and community levels. This includes promoting the development of additional services that meet gaps in the existing mental health service delivery system and fostering work opportunities.
8. Help clients avoid hospitalization by addressing incipient problems at an early stage, intervening at times of crisis, referring clients to services that are alternatives to hospitalization.
9. Conduct the case management role in keeping with social work values, psychosocial rehabilitation goals, and CSS principles. Be especially attentive to clients' rights to individualization, dignity, self-determination, and the least restrictive alternative; the principles of normalization, integration, and continuity of care; and clients' civil rights.
10. Assist clients in the development of a natural support system within the community.
11. Develop constructive, collaborative relationships with families of persons with serious mental disorders. (Suggested by Ohio Department of Mental Health, 1987.)

Community Support Services and Resources

Persons with severe and disabling mental disorders can benefit from a variety of community services. The particular package of services that is appropriate for each client is related to the client's assessed psychosocial needs, the client's wishes, his or her financial condition, and the resources available in the community in which the client lives. At times, the social worker will develop new services (e.g., initiate a program for the developmentally disabled and psychiatrically impaired through cooperative programming). The kinds of community services that will be discussed here are inpatient and outpatient treatment services, housing, crisis services, partial hospitalization, vocational rehabilitation, consumer programs, health care, entitlements, and other supports.

Inpatient Treatment Services

Although current philosophy emphasizes treatment in the community, hospitalization is often needed on an emergency or intermittent basis for persons who are a danger to themselves or others and/or cannot take care of themselves. It is prompted by acute episodes and is sometimes used to regulate a client's medication. For a small number of clients, long-term hospitalization—or a structured, closed community treatment program that is the equivalent of hospitalization—is their most appropriate alternative. With managed care, however, obtaining admission to the limited number of available beds can be problematic (MHASP, 1996).

Inpatient care may be provided in local community hospitals, whether they are public, private, or university hospitals, or in Veterans' Administration hospitals, or by the military. These hospitals usually have psychiatric units in which they treat persons who are admitted. Each hospital has its own admissions procedures. In addition, some state psychiatric facilities continue to operate. Some state hospitals continue to care for clients on a long-term basis and have forensic units in which they treat persons who are criminally committed. Hospitals vary, too, in the treatment they provide. Some offer primarily medication whereas others have structural therapeutic treatment programs. Managed care entities are consulted about admission and length of stay.

Outpatient Treatment Services

For a person with a disabling mental illness, outpatient behavioral mental health treatment is a necessity. Persons with severe and persistent mental disorders require a comprehensive sustained program of care that deemphasizes traditional verbal psychotherapeutic approaches but is nonetheless therapeutic.

Clients who have been hospitalized should be linked with an outpatient mental health service prior to discharge. Joint planning before discharge between hospital social workers and the community providers is helpful (Altman, 1982). Those who have never been hospitalized may be assisted by a case manager or other mental health professional to secure these services. Outpatient services are provided in a variety of settings, depending on the community and its range of services. Community mental health centers are one source; many of them provide not only psychiatric supervision but also outpatient therapy, partial hospitalization (day treatment), emergency services, and programs particularly targeted to the seriously mentally ill. Some communities have freestanding outpatient clinics in which medication is supervised and case management is provided. Other areas have traveling outpatient teams. Still others have clinics that are associated with public hospitals, university hospitals, Veterans' Administration (VA) hospitals, ethnic-centered services, private practices, and behavioral health carve-outs.

Many persons with severe mental illness are on medication. Medication requirements within the hospital and the community are different. Moreover, the need for medication changes over time. Many psychotropic drugs have disturbing and dangerous side effects that need to be monitored. Psychopharmacology will be given special attention in Chapter 12.

Although most clients can benefit from some support, psychotherapeutic treatment should be offered on a selective basis only for those clients who are able to handle some intimacy. Structured approaches such as task-centered casework (Epstein, 1988) can help clients solve immediate problems. A calm, nonjudgmental approach on the part of the clinician is desirable.

An alternative to psychotherapy is participation in social skills training, especially in groups. With such training, clients can learn how to handle interpersonal problems and master effective social and vocational skills at the same time as they receive support from their peers. Social skills training will be described in Chapter 12.

For clients who are living with or are close to relatives, intervention with the family is helpful. One promising means of working with families is family education. This approach and others will also be discussed in the next chapter.

Although the provision of medication is sometimes equated with treatment, intervention with the severely mentally ill encompasses the broad domain of adaptive living in the community. The relationship with the case manager, together with appropriate housing, psychosocial rehabilitation services, and natural supports, can help sustain the client in the community.

Housing

The housing arrangements of persons with severe and persistent mental disorders are diverse. The kind of housing chosen and the neighborhood in which the housing is located are important to the client's well-being. Living accommodations are more or less clean, private, warm, and conveniently located. Similarly, neighborhoods are more or less tolerant, accessible, and safe.

The trend today is for clients to choose where they live and that arrangements be long term rather than transitional (Carling, 1993). This approach, *supported housing,* is rehabilitative in that clients gain skills in selecting, obtaining, and maintaining the kind of housing they want (Carling, 1993). It may include rent subsidies and intensive case management (Ridgway & Rapp, 1997). Client choice is limited, however, by an affordable housing market that is declining and discrimination against persons with mental illness and other conditions (substance abuse, mental retardation) and situations (single mothers with children, history of incarceration) (cf. Carling, 1993). Some housing arrangements are short term because a client's hospitalization or eviction interrupts a stable situation.

The Department of Housing and Urban Development (HUD) provides some housing assistance to low-income individuals and families who meet eligibility criteria (the "Section 8" program). Possible alternative housing arrangements are described next:

Living with One's Own Family. Many clients live with family members such as their parents, grandparents, sibling, spouse, children, or a romantic partner. These natural environments have the advantage of providing continuity with a previous pattern and a potentially caring environment. Some young adults live with their parents because they need supervision and are not self-sufficient.

However advantageous it may be for clients to live at home, the needs of families should be considered. Families become burdened with the care of a mentally ill member. Unless they are educated about mental illness and have sufficient supports of their own, it is likely that the time will come when they will not be able to continue to care for their ill relative.

Consider the following case:

> When fifty-year-old Molly first returned home to her husband after she was hospitalized for the sixth time, she slept all day and paced the floors at night. They shopped for food together, but her husband Ray did all the cooking and cleaning. Ray accepted his wife's condition because he was accustomed to it. When she began to accuse him incessantly of poisoning her food and going out with other women, however, Ray became angry. He was further disturbed by her refusal to bathe. A hardworking, long-suffering man, Ray reached the limits of his tolerance. In desperation he asked the case manager/social worker what other housing alternatives were possible for Molly.

Before deciding on an alternative placement in the community, other arrangements can be explored. Other family members or a community service might provide *respite care,* a temporary place in which the client can stay while the primary caregiver rests or goes on vacation. Respite care is an underdeveloped but highly needed community re-source (Zirul, Lieberman, & Rapp, 1989). Some communities provide nursing-home beds, board-and-care placements, or alternative residences for this purpose. Such programs can result in a reduction in subsequent hospital days for participating clients (Geiser, Hoche, & King, 1988). In this case, Molly was placed temporarily in a family care home, where her behavior and medication were closely monitored and a personal hygiene behavioral pro-gram was instituted. Meanwhile Ray had time to think through his needs and obligations with the help of a clinical social worker.

Family Care Homes.   Family care or adult foster homes are some of the oldest existing forms of community care for psychiatric clients. In the ideal home there are one to four cli-ents who are integrated into a family setting and encouraged to develop habits of personal care and social skills. The caretaker, who is paid for services on a per-client basis, provides the client with bed and board and assures that the client receives physical and mental health care. The caretaker administers medication, takes the client to a mental health center for appointments, and gets the client ready for social rehabilitation programs.

Family care homes vary in size, atmosphere, and the autonomy available to clients. In some homes, the clients occupy a separate floor or wing from the family, thus comprising their own group. In other homes, the clients interact daily with children or grandchildren of the caregiver and participate in family activities such as meal preparation and gardening.

Family care homes are administered by Veterans' Administration hospitals, state hospitals, mental health agencies, or the private sector. Usually they are linked to the mental health delivery system in some way. Frequently social workers, nurses, and/or other mental health workers meet with clients and caretakers at the family care homes. During such visits, changing conditions of individual clients and the household can be observed and monitored. Family care homes are subject to state licensing laws.

Boarding Homes.   Boarding, or board-and-care, homes are relatively large establish-ments, usually run for profit by nonprofessional proprietors. They, too, require licenses or certification, depending on the state. These facilities provide meals and shelter and admin-ister medication. They offer less intimate contact and supervision than family care homes; ordinarily clients are free to leave the facility and wander about in the community. Gener-ally residents share rooms with other residents.

Payment for board-and-care homes comes from public transfer programs such as Supplementary Security Income and Social Security. Most of the monthly allotment goes to the proprietor, but a small allowance is for the client. Because the margin of profit in such facilities is small, proprietors may be tempted to economize on food or deprive clients of their spending money. "Residents of these homes are highly vulnerable to being abused, neglected, and exploited" (Blake, 1987).

Many boarding homes do not provide opportunities for socialization, rehabilitation, and social skills development. They are linked with the mental health system to the extent that the mental health worker or proprietor fosters the connection. In a survey of boarding homes in Essex County, New Jersey, Blake (1987) found that medication was not ade-quately reviewed, and only 7 percent of the residents were participating in mental health services in the community. Large board-and-care homes have been criticized because they have come to resemble the back wards they are supposed to replace (Lamb & Goertzl, 1971). Residents may be left to vegetate, retreat, and hallucinate.

Group Homes.   These therapeutic residences help clients improve their skills in socialization and daily living. They provide a congregate living situation, structure, support, and on-site supervision. Group homes generally have rules that clients must honor if they want to stay. Although in the past group homes were primarily transitional facilities, today there are long-term group homes that do not "push" residents to move on (Carling, 1993).

Transitional Residences.   These facilities, which also have on-site supervision, are available on a temporary basis. While living in these residences, clients may be required to enroll in a partial hospitalization, vocational rehabilitation program, or hold a job while they receive psychiatric treatment. Staff members foster clients' development of skills in daily living so that with these supports clients can move to an autonomous living situation in the future.

Structured Rehabilitative Services.   Many communities offer a range of residential programs that are designed to be rehabilitative. The Philadelphia County Office of Mental Health/Mental Retardation, for example, operates *long-term structured residential programs* for sixteen to twenty clients who do not need hospitalization but do require treatment and rehabilitation in a secure environment (Mental Health Association of Southeastern Pennsylvania, 1996). Another structured residential program is called *residential inpatient nonhospital treatment,* which provides several months of intensive residential treatment to clients with dual diagnoses (MHASP, 1996).

Supported Apartments.   These are autonomous living units, usually operated under the sponsorship of a hospital, agency, or social rehabilitation service. Certain apartments within an existing apartment complex are designated for client use, or certain buildings or blocks of apartments are used. The agency may own the housing units or lease the apartments or homes for the clients. In other cases, the agency's role is primarily consultative.

Clients residing in supported apartments usually share units with each other. Matches may be facilitated by mental health workers or preselected by clients. Because sharing an apartment brings individuals into close contact, care should be taken to ensure that apartment mates are compatible. Furthermore, clients should have skills in food preparation, house cleaning, cooking, and doing laundry. It is desirable that they be able to manage their own money and use public transportation.

Some communities have *specialized supported apartments* for clients with special needs. These apartments may serve parents with children, clients with dual diagnoses (mental illness and substance abuse or mental retardation/developmental disabilities), or individuals who had been incarcerated.

Nursing Homes.   These facilities provide nursing and medical care as well as housing to individuals who need twenty-four-hour supervision. Generally there are different levels of care, for example, skilled and intermediate. Although age is generally not a requirement for admission, these facilities may not welcome young clients with severe mental illness nor are they necessarily equipped to treat them (Carling, 1993). Nevertheless, they do provide a protective environment for older, fragile clients.

Domiciliary Care Homes.   "Dom care" homes are for persons determined to be disabled because of a physical or mental illness or frailties of old age who do not require hospitalization or nursing home care. Individuals who live in these homes usually require some supervision or assistance in performing activities of daily living.

Single-Room Occupancy Hotels.   Some clients live in single rooms in hotels, a housing situation that has been given the acronym of SRO. These rooms are occupied primarily by poor people, usually welfare recipients. The single rooms may or may not have cooking facilities. Clients may have to use hot plates for preparing meals. Bathrooms are frequently shared. Conditions in these hotels are notoriously poor: they are unclean, cold, poorly maintained, and unsafe. Prostitution and drug dealing are rampant. Nevertheless, they are an improvement over the streets.

Other Community Residences.   The varied U.S. communities in urban and rural areas have other kinds of facilities that are used for or adaptable to persons with severe mental illnesses. Many YMCAs and YWCAs, for example, have single rooms that are amenable to the severely mentally ill because they are quiet and private. These rooms may be available in a crisis or on a long-term basis. Some communities convert hotels and motels into residences for this population.

Some clients live in housing that is public or subsidized by the government. Apartments for the elderly and disabled, many of which have medical and social service personnel on the staff, can provide comfortable living quarters for the mentally disabled. It is incumbent on the social worker/case manager to identify such alternatives in the community.

Independent Living.   Some clients are able to live in the community on their own or with a roommate. These clients are sufficiently independent to assume their own leases, manage payment of the rent, keep the apartment reasonably clean, and prepare meals without a mental health professional supervising the arrangement. Persons who live independently still may be linked with the mental health delivery system. They may be attending a clinic and/or participating in a vocational rehabilitation program.

Shelters for the Homeless.   Homelessness is a social problem that is connected with unemployment, gentrification of urban areas, substance abuse, and family conflict, as well as mental health and other social policies. Substantial numbers of the homeless suffer from severe mental illness. Homelessness among the mentally ill may be the outcome of inadequate discharge planning, noncompliance with a service plan on the part of clients, or eviction, among other factors. With little money, food, or social support—and poor coping skills—the seriously mentally ill are forced to fend for themselves. The "bag ladies" and "shopping-cart men" who are mentally ill are familiar sights in urban areas. They eat others' leftovers and collect possessions from garbage cans. It is no wonder that many of them are physically sick and that they are robbed, raped, and otherwise exploited.

Some individuals with severe mental illness are able to make their way from the streets to shelters for the homeless. Publicly run shelters accommodate large numbers of persons in open areas that provide little privacy or protection from theft or harassment. Shelters provide beds for a limited population, making it desirable for potential users to arrive early. Although they usually are not open during the daytime, some shelters offer social services or make referrals to appropriate mental health agencies and residences.

Some cities have alternative facilities that serve the same purpose as shelters for the homeless. Private organizations, often under religious auspices, run smaller, more personal facilities. Clients using these services may be allowed to stay longer than one night and may be helped to receive entitlements, obtain medication, and secure employment. Sometimes these facilities run their own programs of vocational rehabilitation (e.g., Goodwill Industries). Some alternative shelters have accommodations for families.

Jails. Another unfortunate housing alternative is the jail. Persons with mental illnesses end up in the criminal justice system when they are charged with stealing or violent behavior. These behaviors may be strategies for survival, maneuvers to get themselves rehospitalized, or manifestations of their mental disorders. When the behaviors are perceived as crimes rather than symptoms of disease, they are managed by the criminal justice system. The consequence is the criminalization of the mentally ill (Abramson, 1972). Nevertheless, some individuals are treated for mental illness while incarcerated and receive case management services when they are released.

Crisis Services

Persons with serious mental disabilities are sensitive to stress and subject to exacerbations of their psychiatric illnesses. In keeping with the requirement that treatment be the least restrictive, communities have developed a number of resources that are used to contain crises and avoid hospitalization. Among these are emergency services, crisis residences, and day hospitalization. At times, however, hospitalization is the most therapeutic alternative.

Emergency services are outpatient psychiatric units that are associated with general hospitals or mental health clinics. They treat persons who walk in or are brought in for treatment of acute psychiatric symptoms as well as stress-related reactions. Persons with severe psychiatric disorders may be escorted by family members, case managers, or the police. Police respond to a variety of situations but particularly to those in which clients are out of control or threaten violence.

Because emergency services do not operate on an appointment basis and, thus, may have an unpredictably full schedule, some units use a triage system in which all cases are screened briefly as soon as possible to determine which cases should be seen first and which require the services of a psychiatrist. Such systems are useful because many persons who use emergency services are not in crisis. Some users do not know of other community resources that can meet their needs more appropriately. Others' cultural styles make it more comfortable for them to ask for help for psychosocial needs from emergency services than from other community services. Persons with borderline personalities and young adults with severe psychiatric disabilities are thought to overuse emergency services.

Clients whose needs are perceived as urgent present acute psychotic symptoms, suicidal or homicidal behaviors, or aggression. Those who are brought in by the police tend to capture the immediate attention of staff. Case managers who accompany clients who are less visibly affected but in pain need to be assertive in requesting attention.

Emergency treatment varies according to the client's diagnosis and needs. Those with acute or extreme symptoms are screened to determine whether they meet the state's criteria for hospitalization. Those with acute psychotic symptoms are often given medication. Persons with anxiety, depression, confusion, and somatic symptoms that are related to stressful life events are helped through crisis intervention strategies.

Crisis intervention is a means of helping people under acute stress to restore their psychosocial functioning to the precrisis level at the very least. The emergency service worker must work very quickly to assess the seriousness of the problem and provide treatment. The worker does this by establishing rapport, asking the client about the precipitating event (the "last straw" that preceded the request for help) and hazardous conditions that created vulnerability to a crisis, and giving the client an opportunity to express painful emotions. In the course of hearing about the problem and the client's feelings, the emergency service worker makes an assessment and, in collaboration with the client, develops strategies to help the client solve the immediate problem. By connecting the client's symptoms with the causes of the problem and formulating a plan to address immediate issues, the worker helps the client restore cognitive functioning (Dixon, 1987).

Some emergency service workers intervene aggressively at times with violent or excited clients, placing them in lock-up rooms or putting them into restraints. Such measures, used for a limited amount of time and in conjunction with other means to help the client gain control (talking quietly and calmly to the client, medication), can be effective. Nevertheless, these emergency interventions do present ethical dilemmas for social workers because they deprive clients of self-determination and their dignity. Under all circumstances clinicians should first consider the least restrictive intervention.

Crisis residences provide temporary housing for persons with acute psychiatric problems. Alternatives to hospitalization, rather than shelters, they promote the remission of psychiatric symptoms, stabilization, and resolution of the problem that led to the acute state. The primary means of treatment are medication and crisis counseling. The goal is to restore the client to a previous level of functioning and to return the client to a suitable living arrangement in the community. Crisis residences have diverse admission criteria and limitations on the length of stay.

Crisis residential care may be provided in a separate facility (such as a crisis house) or in units within a community complex of residential facilities (such as purchased shelter in boarding houses or hotels). A study in which these two forms of crisis housing were compared found that although both were effective in preventing rehospitalization and promoting stabilization, there was more staff burnout associated with the crisis house and more substance abuse with purchased housing (Bond et al., 1989).

Acute partial hospitalization is a kind of nonresidential care that is either a community-based alternative to complete hospitalization or a means of "stepping down" from hospitalization to community care. It may be run administratively by a hospital or an outpatient mental health center. Clients participate in an intense therapeutic program but return to their usual living quarters at night. These programs are usually time limited.

Partial Hospitalization

Partial hospitalization or day treatment provides structure, support, and activities that are found in total hospitals, and at the same time it enables the client to live in the community. Rosie (1987) describes three types of programs: (a) day hospitals, which provide diagnostic and intervention services for persons with acute symptoms; (b) day treatment programs, which are used on a limited-time, goal-directed basis for clients whose acute symptoms are remitting, such as persons who are making the transition from the hospital to the community; and (c) day care centers, which focus on the maintenance or rehabilitation of severe psychiatric and psychogeriatric clients. Although these variations are not present or differentiated in every community, they do describe the kinds of programs that can meet the needs of persons with serious and persistent psychiatric disabilities.

Partial hospitalization programs may occupy their own buildings, or may be situated in wings of hospitals or within behavioral health programs. A minimum of a large community room and an office are needed. Self-contained programs located in houses with comfortable living rooms, dining areas, kitchens, laundry facilities, showers, and group therapy rooms provide a naturalistic environment in which rehabilitation can take place. Such settings lend themselves to the teaching of skills in food preparation, laundry, housecleaning, and personal grooming. With sufficient space, clients can have some, but not constant, social interaction with others.

In some programs daily activities are planned cooperatively among clients and staff. They may begin with community meetings in which the daily, weekly, or monthly activities are discussed and responsibilities are allocated. Groups make decisions about who is to do what (e.g., shop for lunch, find out about baseball tickets), when, and how. The outcome is a schedule of planned activities. An example of a day in one program is described in Table 11.2.

The therapeutic possibilities of partial hospitalization programs are manifold. Some incorporate psychodrama, poetry therapy, yoga, medication compliance groups, and social skills training, as well as formal presentations by outside experts (e.g., a nutritionist) into their program. Others conduct individual, group, and family therapy routinely or to those who can benefit from it. Programs that are under the aegis of managed behavioral care organizations tend to be tightly structured around therapy with limited time for informal socialization.

Training in activities required for daily living are incorporated in partial hospitalization programs. Clients' functioning levels should be assessed individually; the kinds of training developed should be consistent with the level of skill, comprehension, and disability of subgroups of clients. Furthermore, the topics should be relevant to the client's developmental stage and lifestyle. Some areas that can be addressed in activities training are living within a budget, using public transportation, meal preparation, shopping for clothes, housecleaning, dating, and personal grooming. Clients who are parents may benefit from sessions on child care. Clients who already have some of these skills can assist the staff in communicating and demonstrating these skills. Clients should have the opportunity to perform the skills after they are taught or modeled. For a fuller discussion of social skills training, see Chapter 12.

Regardless of the specific program components, partial hospitalization provides opportunities for socialization for persons who are likely to withdraw from others when they

TABLE 11.2   Schedule of Activities for February 1

Time	Activity
8:30 A.M.	Arrive; informal socializing over decaffeinated coffee. Card playing and checkers.
9:00 A.M.	Community meeting in living room. Schedule for February is discussed, including Valentine's Day dance. Reminder about Dr. Jones's clinic later in day; revision of list of who needs to see doctor. Discussion of headlines in the day's news.
9:30 A.M.	Stretching, yoga, and relaxation exercises.
10:15 A.M.	Occupational therapy. Group discussion, organizing, and beginning making of decorations for the Valentine's Day dance.
11:30 A.M.	Lunch preparation group leaves to prepare lunch; rest clean up.
12:00 noon	Lunch and cleanup after lunch.
1:00 P.M.	Walk to library; tour by librarian on arrival.
2:00 P.M.	Ms. Nancy Smith, home economist, will talk about budgeting one's money.
3:00 P.M.	Dr. Jones will conduct medication clinic for those due for checkup. Others have free time or time to meet with social worker.
4:00 P.M.	Leave for day.
7:00 P.M.	Psychoeducational group for families (Session 3).

are left on their own. They give participants a place to go and a means to broaden their activities, skills, and interests. In the course of the significant amount of time that is spent in these programs, staff are able to observe and monitor clients' adaptation to the community and prevent incipient problems.

Vocational Rehabilitation and Supported Employment Programs

Because work is a central life experience that can promote self-esteem, increase income, provide structure, and offer social opportunities (Baron, 1995), working is a goal of the psychosocial rehabilitation of clients with severe mental illness. Nevertheless, only 15 or 20 percent of clients are competitively employed at a given time (Anthony & Blanch, 1987). There are a number of barriers to employment, including policies around the use of Medicaid dollars, discrimination in hiring, personal discouragement, and a paucity of rehabilitation programs (Baron, 1999). Nevertheless, traditional and newer strategies of vocational rehabilitation and supported employment are available in some communities.

Vocational rehabilitation is a comprehensive program of "work therapy" that encompasses "work evaluation, training, guidance, and placement" (Jacobs, 1988, p. 247). It is also an important component of psychosocial rehabilitation. Clients can not only be helped to develop skills related to a particular line of employment; they can also be helped to use transportation to get to a job, arrive at a job on time, get along with others, and take orders from supervisors. Furthermore, they can be trained in ways to look for a job, develop a résumé, and handle an interview. Once they have found a suitable job, they can be helped to keep it (Bellack & Mueser, 1986).

Vocational rehabilitation follows from an assessment of a person's work skills (Jacobs, 1988). This is based on the individual's prior education and work history, observed behavior, and reports from previous employers, the client, or the client's family. The federal Office of Vocational Rehabilitation has local affiliates that provide testing, counseling, training, and placement of persons with physical, developmental, and psychiatric disabilities who qualify. In some cases this agency will pay for clients' college education or vocational training and for medical care required for rehabilitation.

Sheltered Workshops.   A traditional approach to vocational rehabilitation is the sheltered workshop, which employs persons with severe and persistent psychiatric and other difficulties. Here clients can participate in low-pressure, noncompetitive work settings and learn vocational skills. Generally the workdays are shorter than the usual eight hours; in some cases, clients may work only a few days. Sheltered workshops or their sponsoring organizations develop contractual relationships with industries for such tasks such as cutting, sorting, and bagging items for retail sale. Clients are assigned particular jobs and paid at a rate below the minimum wage that is related to the speed and efficiency with which the client performs the task. For example, if a client bags twenty items in an hour, whereas an "expert" (staff member) can bag forty, the client is paid half of minimum wage.

Clients are trained to perform a variety of tasks and are encouraged to improve their performance. They are able to demonstrate progress and receive increased pay for performing more and more complicated tasks at a faster rate. Furthermore, clients benefit from the experience of getting to work on time, handling interpersonal relationships on the job, and using their time productively. For some clients, working in a sheltered workshop is a step toward competitive employment. Others maintain their workshop jobs for years.

Sheltered workshops are segregated from the mainstream. Clients may be working side by side with persons with other disabilities, such as mental retardation and cerebral palsy, who are also stigmatized. Because integration and normalization are central to the philosophy of psychosocial rehabilitation, alternative strategies are often preferred.

The Clubhouse Model of Vocational Rehabilitation and Supported Employment. Fountain House, a social club founded in New York in 1948 by former psychiatric patients, is a member-run program of psychosocial rehabilitation in which work is central to its mission (Propst, 1988). The New York program has expanded tremendously since its inception and has spawned similar programs elsewhere. Today there are 340 Fountain House–based programs throughout the world that are linked through the International Center for Clubhouse Development (Macias, Jackson, Schroeder, & Wang, 1999). Three vocational programs that are typical of most clubhouses will be discussed here.

The clubhouses are organized around a *work-ordered day,* in which club members work along side staff in "work units" (Macias et al., 1999) and perform tasks that need to get accomplished. These include typing, answering telephones, running the cafeteria and coffee shop, giving tours, housecleaning, operating the duplicating machine, and data entry. Because the program is voluntary and members feel wanted and needed, motivation tends to be high. In the process of participating, members become aware of their abilities, learn new skills, and gain confidence (Propst, 1988).

Through the *Transitional Employment Program* (TEP), members are able to hold regular entry-level jobs in the community on a temporary, part-time basis. Employment placements are in business firms in the New York metropolitan area that enter a contractual agreement in which Fountain House guarantees that the work will be done but retains flexibility in splitting the job between members. If a member is unable to go to work one day, the person with whom he or she shares the job can substitute. If neither is able to work, a staff member works in their place. Members are paid the going rate for that job (minimum wage or above) for the number of hours they work. They spend the part of the day in which they are not at the TEP job at Fountain House (Propst, 1988). A survey of 120 facilities operating TEPs across the country revealed that as of August 31, 1988, there were 708 employers who provided 1,421 job opportunities that generated $5,533,735 in taxable income (Fountain House, 1988).

The third vocational option, *independent employment,* provides support for full-time, independent employment. This most recent program is available to those who aspire to and feel capable of holding a competitive job. Fountain House has an independent employment unit that offers counseling, advice, workshops, and placement services to members looking for jobs and evening and weekend supports to those who are already employed (Propst, 1988).

Supported Employment.   Some of the strategies adopted by Fountain House and other clubhouses are described as supported employment (SE). According to federal guidelines, SE has these characteristics:

- Clients work as regular employees in regular work sites for regular wages.
- Clients receive supportive services on an ongoing basis to help them maintain their jobs.
- Services are targeted for the most disabled clients (The State Supported Employment Services Program, 1987).

The trend in supported employment is to place people on the job and then train them, for example, by initially providing them with a job coach. When job placements are based on clients' preferences, job satisfaction and tenure increase (Becker, Drake, Farabaugh, & Bond, 1996). Research on programs that help clients obtain and maintain jobs in the competitive market shows that program participants have a considerably higher rate of competitive employment than controls (58 percent versus 21 percent) (Mueser et al., 1997).

One model of supportive employment that looks promising is the *Individual Placement and Support (IPS) Model,* developed by Robert Drake and his colleagues at the New Hampshire–Dartmouth Psychiatric Research Center. It integrates supported employment with either mental health or case management teams. Outcome studies on this program have produced promising results (Drake & Becker, 1996). One consumer who obtained and maintained a job through this program described the outcome for herself in this way:

> **Work helps my mental illness. I don't go up as high or down as low now. My therapist said that my symptoms are much more in control when I'm working. Work gives me a**

reason to be more in control.... A job gives you structure in your life. It's a definite positive even if you're as afraid as I was. (Bailey, 1998, pp. 9, 10)

More details on this best practice are provided in Table 11.3.

Job Clubs.   Another empowering approach to work is participating in a job club. This is a program supported by rehabilitation staff, which places the responsibility for finding a job on clients (Jacobs, 1988). The clients devote full-time to the program, which teaches job-seeking skills and provides resources (telephones, counselors, secretarial support, job leads, etc.) to help clients locate a job (Jacobs, 1988).

Supported Education

Adults with serious mental illness who wish to pursue postsecondary studies may be eligible for participation in programs of supported education. This aspect of psychosocial

---

TABLE 11.3 ■ BEST PRACTICE   The Individual Placement and Support Model (ISP)

Principles
- Rehabilitation is an integral component of mental health treatment.
- The goal is competitive employment in work settings that are integrated into the economy of the community (not prevocational or sheltered work).
- Direct employment (rather than obtaining a job after preemployment training).
- Vocational rehabilitation services are continuous and are based in work in real employment in the community.
- The mental health team provides time-unlimited supports.
- Consumers' choices and preferences are the bases for services.

Relevant staff
- Mental health (or case management) team.
- Employment specialists (supervised by a vocational supervisor who also has a caseload).

Optimal caseloads of employment specialists: 20–25 clients

Client eligibility: based on client interest

Features of model
- Quickly engage with clients in task of finding a job.
- Client takes lead in job finding but employment specialist also participates.
- Match job with client's interests, skills, and deficits.
- "Place-train" (training occurs on the job).
- Continuous and comprehensive assessment.
- Follow-along support to the client and (with client permission) to employer.
- Coaching either on site or off site, depending on client's wishes.
- Work of employment specialist is integrated with that of the clinical team.

Sources: Based on Bond (1998), Drake (1998), Drake & Becker (1996).

rehabilitation provides supports to help participants consider and pursue advanced education and take advantage of resources within a college or community college environment
(Moxley, Mowbray, & Strauch Brown, 1993). The varied programs that exist are located at
educational institutions or at clubhouses, psychiatric hospitals, and mental health centers
(Unger, 1997). Psychosocial rehabilitation strategies such as skill development, environmental support, goal development, and client choice are used (Moxley et al., 1993). Research has found that a variety of methods of supported education are associated with
subsequent enrollment in college or vocational training at six-month and twelve-month
follow-up periods (Mowbray, Collins, & Bybee, 1999).

Citizen Advocacy Groups

There are a few citizen advocacy groups whose constituencies include the general public,
professionals, client consumers, and family members. One of the oldest such groups is the
National Mental Health Association and its local branches. These organizations provide
information on mental health topics, offer educational and support groups to consumers
and families, and lobby for improved mental health legislation (Lefley, 1996). Another advocacy organization is the *Judge David L. Bazelton Center for Mental Health Law,* which
is concerned with the civil liberties of persons with mental illness as well as their rights to
housing, income support, and health care (Lefley, 1996). State Protection and Advocacy (P
& A) Centers are legal services mandated by the federal Protection and Advocacy for Individuals with Mental Illness (PAIMI) Act to protect the rights of clients with disabilities
through lawsuits and advocacy activity (Lefley, 1996).

Clubhouses, Drop-In Centers, and Consumer-Run Organizations

Clubhouses.   Consumers have developed and operated many of their own activities and
programs. Among the first such program was Fountain House, mentioned in the earlier discussion of vocational rehabilitation programs. Clubhouse participants are called "members," not clients, who belong to a community that values them:

> All members are made to feel, on a daily basis, that their presence is expected, that someone
> actually anticipates their coming to the program each morning and that their coming makes
> a difference to someone, indeed to everyone, in the program. At the door each morning
> every member is greeted by staff and members of the house, and in all ways each member
> is made to feel welcome in coming to the clubhouse.
>   All program elements are constructed in such a way as to ensure that each member
> feels wanted as a contributor to the program. Each program is intentionally set up so that it
> will not work without the cooperation of the members; indeed, the entire program would
> collapse if members did not contribute. Every function of the program is shared by the
> members working side by side with staff; staff never ask members to carry out functions
> which they do not also perform themselves. (Beard, Propst, & Malamud, 1982, p. 47)

Clubhouses modeled along the lines of Fountain House are member-run programs of
psychosocial rehabilitation. Besides the vocational programs that were described earlier,

there are evening and weekend social programs (Beard et al., 1982). During evenings, weekends, and holidays, when most working people have time off, members have opportunities to socialize with each other, attend drama performances, and celebrate holidays together.

Drop-In Centers.   Another resource that is run by consumers is the drop-in center. Like clubhouses, these are places in which clients can feel at home, socialize, and give each other support. Centers vary in their administrative structure, focus, and times at which they are open. Usually there are paid staff as well as a core group of consumer volunteers who assure that the programs run smoothly (Kaufmann, Ward-Colasante, & Farmer, 1993).

Other Consumer-Run Programs.   A variety of other consumer-run services have emerged, and it is anticipated, others will follow. Some of the demonstration projects funded by the community support program initiative of NIMH were on programs involving live-in companions, housing assistance, and a program to link inpatients to community supports (Brown & Parrish, 1995). In their research, Solomon and Draine (1995) found that case management delivered by consumers was comparable with case management provided by nonconsumers in terms of specific outcomes.

Consumer Organizations.   Consumers and their families have also developed self-help and advocacy organizations to help them deal with the stigma of mental illness, the effects of the disease, and deficiencies in the mental health service delivery system. As persons who have "been there," they know what it is like to be mistreated or to have needs, wants, and rights that are not recognized by service providers. Groups that call themselves "consumers" see themselves as citizens who have the right to receive, evaluate, choose, and refuse services. Those who use terms such as *ex-patient, former psychiatric inmate,* or *former mental health consumer* highlight, by both acknowledging and rejecting their status, the stigma associated with having a history of hospitalization and using mental health services. Similarly, the term "survivor" draws attention to positive and negative aspects simultaneously.

Client consumers help each other solve problems individually and take actions collectively. They may give advice to other consumers about particular mental health services, psychiatrists, or social workers; work for the creation of new resources; disseminate information about medication; or lobby for a desired bill. Some of these groups are unique to a locality or state; others are part of a national network. Professionals may be allowed to join but not to vote. Increasingly, government entities are supporting consumer organizations.

One of the most influential of the family consumer groups is the National Alliance for the Mentally Ill (NAMI) and its state and local affiliates. NAMI represents the interests of families of persons with severe psychiatric problems. On the local level, the group educates members and the public about mental illness, provides information about resources, promotes the development of better mental health services, and the like. Nationally NAMI advocates for research and programmatic support for clients. NAMI members are sensitive to and reject the historical trend of holding parents responsible for the development of mental illness in their children. NAMI views mental illness as a brain disease and engages in advocacy and supports research on biological treatments and biopsychosocial services. Clients and professionals can join NAMI.

Social worker case managers have a number of responsibilities in relation to consumer groups. First, they should become knowledgeable about the groups in their own community and inform clients and families about their existence, what they do, and the potential benefits (e.g., information, social contacts, empowerment, a source of meaning). Second, social workers should get to know members of consumer groups and listen to their grievances. Some of their complaints can be addressed through mediation, advocacy, and brokerage. Third, social workers might want to join some of these groups.

Health Care

Compared with the general population, individuals with serious mental illness have a shorter life span and more medical problems (Bazemore, 1996). The early deaths are due to natural causes (e.g., heart disease, infection) and unnatural causes (e.g., trauma, suicide) (Bazemore, 1996). The medical problems may be the consequences of poor health care. Because of difficulties in cognitive processing, distortions in self-awareness, and mistrust of outsiders, some persons with mental illness may not identify health problems or be unwilling to discuss them with others.

Many individuals with serious mental illnesses receive or are able to qualify for either Medicare or Medicaid; some have private insurance or are eligible for Veterans' Administration benefits. Many states have contracted with managed care entities to administer health and behavioral health services to public sector clients. Veterans may be treated in Veterans' Administration facilities. Public and private sources of insurance cover the costs of visits to physicians, medication, and hospitalization, but, especially under managed care, they have their limits. Advocacy for those who do not qualify for medical services or are refused care may be effective.

Health care management should be part of the client's individual service plan. The client should be helped to maintain a balanced diet, live in a clean environment, and identify symptoms of health problems. The client should be linked with a doctor, clinic, or hospital in which ongoing and emergency health care are available. The client's teeth, eyes, ears, and feet may need the attention of specialists.

Women clients of childbearing age can use the services of a family planning clinic or an understanding gynecologist. They should be provided with information about birth control, sexuality, and childbearing. The impact of birth control pills on their physical and mental health, as well as the interaction between psychotropic medication and pregnancy and lactation (Mogul, 1985), should be discussed. Furthermore, women should be helped to protect themselves from situations that make them vulnerable to sexual exploitation.

Schwab, Drake, and Burghardt (1988) recommend that in dealing with health care providers, the case manager act as a "culture broker." As such, the case manager should gain an understanding of the client's mental functioning; of how the client perceives his or her body, symptoms, and the medical care system; and of the constellation of the client's social system, so that communication with a physician who does not understand the client's social world can be facilitated. Furthermore, barriers to receiving health care should be identified. Using personal observations and knowledge obtained from the client's medical and psychiatric records, the case manager can bridge the gap between the client's culture and the medical system, interpreting one to the other.

Entitlements

Serious and persistent mental illness entitles persons to a range of public benefits for which they must apply. Each entitlement has its own set of requirements and stipulations. The case manager should be familiar with the programs for which an individual may qualify, eligibility requirements, and the application procedures. The case manager should work closely with the client in applying for benefits.

If clients are not working or if they are underemployed, they may be eligible for some form of financial assistance. One can qualify for Social Security disability insurance on the basis of one's own work history and mental or physical impairment; or because one is a widow or a disabled child of a person with a work history. Those who qualify for Social Security are also eligible for Medicare. If the Social Security allotment is not sufficient or if the applicants turn out to be ineligible, they can apply for Supplemental Security Income (SSI) and Medicaid. To qualify as "permanently and totally disabled" under Social Security or SSI, medical documentation must be provided. Other possible sources of financial assistance are Transitional Aid to Needy Families (TANF) for parents and their children, Veterans' Administration disability pensions, and local public welfare programs. Persons who have work histories might be eligible for disability or retirement insurance that was a fringe benefit where they worked, or unemployment compensation, if their job was terminated.

Another entitlement is food stamps. Those who are eligible for other forms of public assistance may also be eligible for food stamps. Some clients may qualify for food stamps only, or for stamps on an emergency basis only. Food stamps can be used instead of money at grocery stores. Certain restrictions apply; for example, they cannot be used to pay for cigarettes or alcohol.

With the burgeoning population of homeless, many soup kitchens and pantries have come into existence. Food kitchens provide one or two free meals a day; food pantries supply applicants with canned goods, cheese, and other food items. Often these establishments are housed in churches or community centers. Shelters for the homeless also provide users with free meals.

Clients in poor financial straits might also receive help from religious organizations that have funds for the poor. The case manager may have to make several telephone calls and personal visits to receive this kind of help. Emergency help may also be available from the city, from generous individuals, and from families of clients.

Supports for Clients Who Are Parents

Although women with severe mental illness have a fertility rate that is at least equivalent to that of the general population (Saugstad, 1989), their needs as parents have been sorely neglected. Parenting is work and, thus, can be incorporated in a program of rehabilitation if a client needs help in this area (Nicholson & Blanch, 1994).

A few intervention programs have served mothers and their children. Among these are mother-baby units in hospitals; home care programs incorporating home visits; and intensive, community-based rehabilitation of parents and children (Oyserman, Mowbray, & Zemencuk, 1994). There are a limited number of supported residential programs for mothers and children (e.g., Sands, 1995); residential treatment programs for substance abusing mothers (including those with a mental health diagnosis) are more common. In Table 11.4, The Mothers' Project, which is a program that integrates case management with services to the mother and child and is offered by Thresholds' psychosocial rehabilitation program in Chicago, is presented as another best practice.

TABLE 11.4 ■ BEST PRACTICE   The Mothers' Project at Thresholds

Principles
- Children are better off if they are cared for by their own families.
- Children need to have advocates.

Major features
- Holistic case management treats the family as a whole while it focuses on the mother-child dyad.
- Comprehensive services are home based, agency based, and community based.
- Importance of mental illness and its effect on the family are emphasized.
- Ongoing assessment includes outreach to mothers in their homes where staff help mothers with child care routines and teach mothers ways to foster children's cognitive development.

Psychosocial program
- Comprehensive individual program builds on participants' strengths.
- Opportunities and support in employment, housing, education, physical health, and social development are offered.
- Focus is on improving parenting while child(ren) are preschool age.
- Group programs promote knowledge development, social interaction, and self-esteem.

Case management services
- Brokerage of services is offered for family and child, including entitlements, money management, medical services, counseling, etc.
- On-site psychiatric services are offered.

Therapeutic nursery
- An enriched program of child care is offered for children from newborn to age 5.
- Child is encouraged to use language functionally, master cognitive processes, and develop firm sense of self.
- Teachers model child care skills while mothers work in the nursery as assistants one-half morning a week.
- Emotional support of mothers is given.

Family support services
- Education and support of fathers/husbands are emphasized.
- Weekly group for parents of mothers is offered.

Substance abuse treatment (if needed)

Source: Based on Zeitz (1995).

Support Networks

Most of the community resources that have been described comprise a *formal* network of supports that can be mobilized to help an individual client adapt to community life. Mental health services, programs of entitlement, and housing units are needed components of the formal system. Such services tend to be impersonal, however. Embedded in these services, however, are personal relationships that can emerge naturally and serve as more intimate helping resources.

Natural or informal supports are persons and groups that evolve over time and through everyday interactions. These are made up primarily of people who care—one's family, however one defines it, friends, neighbors, people with whom one prays, and co-workers. They also might include hairdressers, storekeepers, bartenders, landlords, and others with whom one interacts informally. The persons one meets in support groups and community programs can become part of the natural system of supports.

Research on the social networks of persons with severe mental health problems has found that this population tends to have small, dense networks that are comprised primarily of kin and that the networks contain few clusters (groups of people who interact with each other) and lack reciprocity (Cutler, 1984). Considering that persons with schizophrenia and some of the other severe disorders withdraw from social relationships and are threatened by emotional intensity, their narrow social world is not surprising.

One of the responsibilities of the case manager is to help the client build and expand supportive social networks. Interpersonal relationships are important because they serve as a buffer against stress and involve the individual in meaningful participation in the community. The case manager can help the client develop social networks by increasing opportunities for relationships to develop. This can result from linking the client with social and recreational groups, encouraging the client to reconnect with persons who were meaningful to him or her in the past and to maintain those current social contacts who might become friends, promoting the client's use of psychosocial rehabilitation services, creating socialization groups, and supporting the client's participation in the world of work.

The family is an important social support for some clients. Among family, the potential to care, give, and help is great and should be engaged. Nevertheless, one should also take care to modulate a client's dependence on them and encourage other relationships as well. Some communities have volunteer programs, such as Compeer, in which community people provide peer support and friendship to persons with severe mental disabilities. For clients who do not have kin, or do not have relatives who live nearby who are supportive, friends and service providers become the equivalent of a family.

Ethnic-Specific Behavioral Mental Health Centers

Clients who identify with a particular ethnic community that operates its own mental health services may feel more comfortable receiving help from their own group. Some of the larger cities have mental health or multiservice centers for different ethnic minority groups that are sensitive to the language and culture-specific needs of members of their constituencies. Staff members who speak the same language as the client and are familiar with the client's culture work there. Supports for other communities—for example, the deaf, gays and lesbians, and persons with AIDs—are also available in some behavioral health centers as well as nearby communities.

Summary and Deconstruction

This chapter has described models of community care and case management of individuals constructed as severely mentally ill. Case management is an administrative mechanism that uses an individual or team to monitor clients' community treatment. Although assertive community treatment (ACT) began as a model of treatment, it has been absorbed into case management that does not provide treatment itself but links clients with treatment services. This transformation of direct treatment into case management needs to be scrutinized so that clients will obtain sufficient services and care.

There are numerous models of case management that have been touted, but in practice it is likely that they operate similarly. Generally case managers perform assessments, monitor clients' progress, develop individually tailored service plans, and link clients with services. Regardless of the model, case managers engage in some direct work with clients and link clients with services. Some models require that case managers be more actively engaged in outreach, rehabilitation, and treatment than others. Clinical case managers provide psychotherapy along with the other tasks.

Case management is particularly needed in communities in which there are many resources but little coordination. Clients and families may not be aware of the services that exist and their rights to use them. Some communities, however, have few resources or have resources that are not sensitive to the needs of the community's ethnic/racial groups. It is not enough to have services; services must be adapted to clients' needs.

This chapter described a variety of resources that are available in some communities. These include a range of housing/residential services, inpatient and outpatient treatment facilities, supported education, crisis services, partial hospitalization, and vocational rehabilitation. In addition, clients need health care, as they are at risk of developing medical problems, and are entitled to some financial resources. Nevertheless, clinical social workers can err in *providing* too many services to service *recipients*. There is a need for client-centeredness while one "manages cases." Clients have developed and control many of their own organizations and services. These organizations provide opportunities for persons with severe mental illness to become empowered.

Case Study

Estrella and Juan Martinez, both twenty-five and Mexican Americans, live in a barrio in California. The couple met five years ago in a state psychiatric hospital, where they were both hospitalized with schizophrenia. After they were discharged, they set up housekeeping together for a while and married after Estrella became pregnant with their daughter, Lucia. Lucia is now four and Estrella is pregnant. Although neither Estrella nor Juan works regularly, they have income from SSI as well as food stamps and Medicaid. (Occasionally Juan is able to earn money doing odd jobs.) They have close ties with Juan's family in the barrio but do not socialize with anyone other than kin.

The Martinezes have had a bilingual Mexican American case manager who has helped them obtain aftercare services in a culturally sensitive mental health center. Furthermore, this case manager has acted as culture broker in arranging Estrella's prenatal care and Lucia's entry into a Headstart program. Two months ago, this case manager was promoted and replaced by a new case manager who does not speak Spanish and knows very little about the Martinezes' culture and about the needs of persons with schizophrenia. Around the same time, Juan's parents moved away and Estrella had a miscarriage. These stressors put the Martinezes at risk of decompensating.

How should the case manager intervene in this case to promote support and buffer stress in a culturally sensitive way? What community services might be helpful?

DISCUSSION QUESTIONS

1. Identify problems in the mental health delivery system that impeded the diagnosis and treatment of Larry Leeds. How might such problems be prevented?

2. What is case management? Discuss the basic functions of the case manager.

3. What additional skills does the professional social worker offer in the performance of case management?

4. Discuss the importance of the client-worker relationship in case management with persons with severe and persistent mental disorders. How intense should such a relationship be?

5. Compare the models of case management that were described in this chapter. How are they alike? How do they differ? How do they compare with assertive community treatment (ACT).

6. Consider the mental health delivery system in your community. What kinds of services are provided in relation to the categories described in this chapter? What needs are met? Identify gaps in services in your community.

7. What opportunities are available in your community for paid employment for persons with severe psychiatric disorders?

8. Why is it important to assess the physical health needs of persons with severe mental disabilities? What are some special health needs of women?

9. How can the clinical social worker/case manager help clients develop social supports?

10. Identify consumer organizations in your community. What are the concerns of each group? How do these groups relate to each other and to mental health providers?

REFERENCES

Abramson, M. F. (1972). The criminalization of mentally disordered behavior. *Hospital and Community Psychiatry, 23,* 101–105.

Allness, D. J. & Knoedler, W. H. (1998). *The PACT model of community-based treatment for persons with severe and persistent mental illnesses: A manual for PACT start-up.* Arlington, VA: National Alliance for the Mentally Ill.

Altman, H. (1982). Collaborative discharge planning for the deinstitutionalized. *Social Work, 27,* 422–427.

American Psychiatric Association. (1997). Practice guideline for treatment of patients with schizophrenia. *American Journal of Psychiatry, 154*(4), Supplement.

Anthony, W. A., & Blanch, A. (1987). Supported employment for persons who are psychiatrically disabled: An historical and conceptual perspective. *Psychosocial Rehabilitation Journal, 11,* 5–23.

Anthony, W. A., Forbess, R., & Cohen, M. R. (1993). Rehabilitation-oriented case management. In M. Harris & H. C. Bergman (Eds.), *Case management for mentally ill patients: Theory and practice* (pp. 99–118). Langhorne, PA: Harwood Academic Publishers.

Bailey, J. (1998). I'm just an ordinary person. *Psychiatric Rehabilitation Journal, 22*(1), 8–10.

Baron, R. C. (1995, Spring). Establishing employment services as a priority for persons with long-term mental illness. *American Rehabilitation,* 32–35.

Baron, R. C. (1999). The impact of behavioral managed care on employment programming for persons with serious mental illness. *International Journal of Mental Health, 27,* 41–72.

Bazemore, P. H. (1996). Medical problems of the seriously and persistently mentally ill. In S. M. Soreff (Ed.), *Handbook for the treatment of the seriously mentally ill* (pp. 45–66). Seattle, WA: Hogrefe & Huber Publishers.

Beard, J. H., Propst, R. N., & Malamud, T. J. (1982). The Fountain House model of psychiatric rehabilitation. *Psychosocial Rehabilitation, 5*(l), 47–53.

Becker, D. R., Drake, R. E., Farabaugh, A., & Bond, G. R. (1996). Job preferences of clients with severe psychiatric disorders participating in supported employment programs. *Psychiatric Services, 47,* 1223–1226.

Bellack, A. S., & Mueser, K. T. (1986). A comprehensive treatment program for schizophrenia and chronic mental illness. *Community Mental Health Journal, 22,* 175–189.

Blake, R. (1987). Boarding home residents: New underclass in the mental health system. *Health and Social Work, 12,* 85–90.

Bond, G. R. (1998). Principles of the individual placement and support model: Empirical support. *Psychiatric Rehabilitation Journal, 22*(1), 11–23.

Bond, G. R., et al. (1989). A comparison of two crisis housing alternatives to psychiatric hospitalization. *Hospital and Community Psychiatry, 40,* 177–183.

Brown, N. B., & Parrish, J. (1995). CSP: Champion of self-help. *Journal of the California Alliance for the Mentally Ill, 6*(3), 6–7.

Carling, P. J. (1993). Supports and rehabilitation for housing and community living. In R. W. Flexer & P. L. Solomon, *Psychiatric rehabilitation in practice* (pp. 99–118). Boston: Andover Medical Publishers.

Chamberlain, R., & Rapp, C. A. (1991). A decade of case management: A methodological review of outcome research. *Community Mental Health Journal, 27,* 171–188.

Cutler, D. (1984). Networks. In J. A. Talbott (Ed.). *The chronic mental patient: Five years later* (pp. 253–266). Orlando, FL: Grune & Stratton.

Deegan, P. E. (1997). Recovery and empowerment for people with psychiatric disabilities. *Social Work in Health Care, 25*(3), 11–24.

Dixon, S. L. (1987). *Working with people in crisis* (2nd ed.). Columbus, OH: Merrill.

Drake, R. E. (1998). A brief history of the Individual Placement and Support model. *Psychiatric Rehabilitation Journal, 22,* 3–7.

Drake, R. E., & Becker, D. R. (1996). The Individual Placement and Support model of supported employment. *Psychiatic Services, 47,* 473–475.

Epstein, L. (1988). *Helping people: The task-centered approach.* Columbus, OH: Merrill.

Flax, J. W. (1982). Crisis intervention with the young adult patient. In B. Pepper & H. Ryglewicz (Eds.), *The young adult chronic patient* (pp. 69–75). San Francisco: Jossey-Bass.

Fountain House. (1988). *Transitional employment.* (Survey Memorandum No. 290, pp. 718–721). New York: Fountain House.

Frances, A., Doerherty, J. P., & Kahn, D. A. (1996). The expert consensus guideline series: Treatment of schizophrenia. *The Journal of Clinical Psychiatry, 57,* Supplement 12B.

Franklin, J., Solovitz, B., Mason, M., Clemons, J., & Miller, G. (1987). An evaluation of case management. *American Journal of Public Health, 77,* 674–678.

Geiser, R., Hoche, L., & King, J. (1988). Respite care for mentally ill patients and their families. *Hospital and Community Psychiatry, 39,* 291–295.

Harris, M., & Bachrach, L. L. (1988). A treatment-planning grid for clinical case management. In M. Harris & L. L. Bachrach (Eds.), *Clinical case management, New Directions for Mental Health Services,* no. 40 (pp. 29–38). San Francisco: Jossey-Bass.

Intagliata, J., Willer, B., & Egri, C. (1986). Role of the family in case management of the mentally ill. *Schizophrenia Bulletin, 12,* 699–708.

Jacobs, H. E. (1988). Vocational rehabilitation. In R. P. Liberman (Ed.), *Psychiatric rehabilitation of chronic mental patients* (pp. 245–284). Washington, DC: American Psychiatric Press.

Kantor, J. (1988). Clinical issues in the case management relationship. In M. Harris & L. L. Bachrach (Eds.), *Clinical case management, New Directions for Mental Health Services,* no. 40 (pp. 15–27). San Francisco: Jossey-Bass.

Kaufmann, C. L., Ward-Colasante, C., & Farmer, J. (1993). Development and evaluation of drop-in centers operated by mental health consumers. *Hospital and Community Psychiatry, 44,* 675–678.

Lamb, H. R. (1980). Therapist–case managers: More than brokers of services. *Hospital and Community Psychiatry, 31,* 762–764.

Lamb, H. R., & Goertzl, V. (1971). Discharged mental patients—are they really in the community? *Archives of General Psychiatry, 24,* 29–34.

Lefley, H. P. (1996). The effects of advocacy movements on caregivers. In H. P. Lefley (Ed.), *Family caregiving in mental illness* (pp. 167–184). Thousand Oaks, CA: Sage.

Lehman, A. F., Steinwachs, D. M., and the coinvestigators of the PORT Project. (1998). At issue: Translating research into practice: The schizophrenia patient outcomes research team (PORT) treatment recommendations. *Schizophrenia Bulletin, 24*(1), 1–10.

Macias, C., Jackson, R., Schroeder, C., & Wang, Q. (1999). Brief report: What is a clubhouse? Report on the ICCD survey of USA clubhouses. *Community Mental Health Journal, 35*(2), 181–190.

McClelland, R. W. (1996). Managed care. In C. D. Austin & R. W. McClelland (Eds.), *Perspectives on case management practice* (pp. 203–218). Milwaukee, WI: Families International, Inc.

Mental Health Association of Southeastern Pennsylvania. (1996). *Philadelphia mental health guide.* Philadelphia: Author.

Mogul, K. M. (1985). Psychological considerations in the use of psychotropic drugs with women patients. *Hospital and Community Psychiatry, 36,* 1080–1085.

Mowbray, C. T., Collins, M., & Bybee, D. (1999). Supported education for individuals with psychiatric disabilities: Long-term outcomes from an experimental study. *Social Work Research, 23,* 89–100.

Moxley, D. P., Mowbray, C. T., & Strauch Brown, K. (1993). Supported education. In R. W. Flexer & P. L. Solomon, *Psychiatric rehabilitation in practice* (pp. 137–153). Boston: Andover Medical Publishers.

Mueser, K. T., Bond, G. R., Drake, R. E., & Resnick, S. G. (1998). Models of community care for severe mental illness: A review of research on case management. *Schizophrenia Bulletin, 24,* 37–74.

Mueser, K. T., Drake, R. E., & Bond, G. R. (1997). Recent advances in psychiatric rehabilitation for patients with severe mental illness. *Harvard Review of Psychiatry, 5,* 123–137.

Nicholson, J., & Blanch, A. (1994). Rehabilitation for parenting roles for people with serious mental illness. *Psychosocial Rehabilitation Journal, 18,* 109–119.

Ohio Department of Mental Health. (1987, August). *Case management training part 1: The delivery of case management in an integrated mental health system.* Columbus, OH.

Oyserman, D., Mowbray, C. T., & Zemencuk, J. K. (1994). Resources and supports for mothers with severe mental illness. *Health and Social Work, 19*(2), 132–142.

Propst, R. N. (1988). The clubhouse model and the world of work. *TIE Lines, 5*(2), 1–2.

Rapp, C. A. (1998). The strengths model: Case management with people suffering from severe and persistent mental illness. New York: Oxford University Press.

Ridgely, M. S., Morrissey, J. P., Paulson, R. I., Goldman, H. H., & Calloway, M. O. (1996). Characteristics and activities of case managers in the RWJ Foundation program on chronic mental illness. *Psychiatric Services, 47,* 737–743.

Ridgway, P., & Rapp, C. A. (1997). The active ingredients of effective supported housing: A research synthesis. Lawrence, KS: The University of Kansas School of Social Welfare. Mimeo.

Roach, J. (1993). Clinical case management with severely mentally ill adults. In M. Harris & H. C. Bergman (Eds.), *Case management for mentally ill patients: Theory and practice* (pp. 17–40). Langhorne, PA: Harwood Academic Publishers.

Rosie, J. S. (1987). Partial hospitalization: A review of recent literature. *Hospital and Community Psychiatry, 38,* 1291–1299.

Sands, R. G. (1984). Correlates of success and lack of success of deinstitutionalization. *Community Mental Health Journal, 20,* 223–235.

Sands, R. G. (1995). The parenting experience of low-income single women with serious mental disorders. *Families in Society, 76*(2), 86–96.

Saugstad, L. F. (1989). Social class, marriage, and fertility in schizophrenia. *Schizophrenia Bulletin, 15,* 9–43.

Schwab, B., Drake, R. E., & Burghardt, E. M. (1988). Health care of the chronically mentally ill: The culture broker model. *Community Mental Health Journal, 24,* 174–184.

Solomon, P. (1992). The efficacy of case management services for severely mentally disabled clients. *Community Mental Health Journal, 28,* 163–180.

Solomon, P. (1999). The evolution of service innovations for adults with severe mental illness. In D. E. Biegel & A. Blum (Eds.), *Innovations in practice and service delivery with adults: The evolution of service innovations for adults with severe mental illness* (pp. 147–168). New York: Oxford University Press.

Solomon, P., & Draine, J. (1995). The efficacy of a consumer case management team: 2-year outcomes of a randomized trial. *Journal of Mental Health Administration, 22,* 135–146.

Solomon, P., & Meyerson, A. T. (1997). Social stabilization: Achieving satisfactory community adaptation for the disabled mentally ill. In A. Tasman, J. Kay, & J. Lieberman (Eds.), *Psychiatry* (Vol. 2, pp. 1727–1750). Philadelphia: W. B. Saunders.

Stein, L. (1992). Perspective: On the abolishment of the case manager. *Health Affairs,* 172–177.

Stein, L. I., & Diamond, R. J. (1985). A program for difficult-to-treat patients. In L. I. Stein & M. A. Test (Eds.), *New directions for mental health services: The training in community living model. A decade of experience* (no. 26, pp. 29–39). San Francisco: Jossey-Bass.

Stein, L. I. & Santos, A. B. (1998). *Assertive community treatment of persons with severe mental illness.* New York: W. W. Norton & Co.

Stein, L. I., & Test, M. A. (1982). Community treatment of the young adult patient. In B. Pepper & H. Ryglewicz (Eds.), *New directions for mental health services: The young adult chronic patient* (no. 14, pp. 57–67). San Francisco: Jossey-Bass.

Stein, L. I., & Test, M. A. (Eds.). (1985). *New directions for mental health services: The training in community living model. A decade of experience* (no. 26). San Francisco: Jossey-Bass.

Test, M. A. (1979). Continuity of care in community treatment. In L. I. Stein (Ed.), *New directions for mental health services: Community support systems for the long-term patient* (no. 2, pp. 15–23). San Francisco: Jossey-Bass.

The State Supported Employment Services Program. (1987, August 14). *Federal Register,* 30546–30552.

Training in community living. (1983). *Practice Digest, 6* 4–6.

Unger, K. V. (1997). Supported education: An idea whose time has come, II. *The Journal of the California Alliance for the Mentally Ill, 8*(2), 5–7.

Witheridge, T. F., & Dincin, J. (1985). The Bridge: An assertive outreach program in an urban setting. In L. I. Stein & M. A. Test (Eds.), *The training in community living model: A decade of experience* (pp. 65–76). San Francisco: Jossey-Bass.

Zeitz, M. A. (1995). The mothers' project: A clinical case management system. *Psychosocial Rehabilitation Journal, 19*(1), 55–62.

Zirul, D. W, Lieberman, A. A., & Rapp, C. A. (1989). Respite care for the chronically mentally ill: Focus for the 1990s. *Community Mental Health Journal, 25,* 171–184.

12 Intervening with Individuals Affected by Severe Mental Illness

Medication, Social Skills Training, and Family Education

One of the wonderful things is that I can hear the birds and the wind when I'm outside. All the voices in my head are gone completely. I'm more aware each day of what's going on around me.

—Schleimer, "What I Know Now," 1997

What I have learned most about in my journey is the continuing desperation of patients and families struggling with the cruelest diseases that afflict mankind. Their stories tear at my heart because I've been there, I've felt some of what they've felt (and some that they haven't), and I will not forget the pain.

—North, "From Schiz to Shrink," 1989

In addition to the general approaches described in Chapter 11—case management and the use of community supports—there are a number of other modes of intervention that suppress symptoms, enhance social functioning, and promote the mastery of stress. This chapter describes three professionally constructed interventions—medication, social skills training, and family education—that help clients and their families cope with the impact of severe mental illness on their lives. In addition, some ways of healing that are constructed by clients will be discussed. Consistent with this book's postmodern perspective and the quotations that open this chapter, the practitioner maintains a central focus on clients' pain, their strengths and vulnerabilities, and their potential to recover.

This chapter begins with an overview on medication for persons with serious mental illness. Although social workers do not prescribe medication, they work in environments in which psychopharmacology is a fundamental strategy of intervention. Because clinical social workers observe clients over time, they are positioned to assess the impact of the medication on clients' functioning and intervene with clients' psychiatrists when there is a need for a change in clients' medication regimens. They cannot make these judgments without knowledge about medication.

Medication

During the last half of the twentieth century, medication increasingly became the standard (but not only) mode of treatment for persons with severe mental disorders. The first generation of medications addressed overt, disabling symptoms but left in its wake refractory cases, residual symptoms, and troubling side effects. The second generation promises to deal with some of the weaknesses of the first.

Psychotropic drugs are ordinarily used both to treat acute symptoms and to maintain the functioning of clients whose symptoms are not conspicuous or are in remission. They are prescribed by psychiatrists who supervise the client's use of medication over time. Nurses frequently administer and monitor medication under the direction of the psychiatrist. As case managers and therapists of clients, as well as consultants to psychiatrists and nurses, clinical social workers observe clients' attitudes toward ingesting drugs, compliance or noncompliance with the medication regimen, side effects, and signs of concomitant substance use, and decide whether and how to intervene when there is a problem involving medication.

Psychiatric assessments of the medication needs of clients take into consideration a client's physical health, individual and family health/mental health history, medication history, allergic reactions, age, sex, height, and weight, as well as findings from the mental status examination and diagnosis. Results of preliminary and intermittent physical examinations and laboratory tests guide the psychiatrist in the selection of appropriate drugs and in the monitoring of side effects. The psychiatrist should order tests that are related to the effects of particular drugs (e.g., liver function tests, complete blood count, electrocardiogram). Research findings, clinical experience, and the drug responses of the individual client also enter into decisions about which drugs to prescribe. The dosage is adjusted over time when the client's reactions to drugs can be observed not only by the psychiatrist but also by the client and those who interact with the client on a regular basis.

Medication ameliorates clients' symptoms, which are an expression of the clients' subjective states, reactions to environmental stressors, and mental disorders. Specific gestalts of symptoms that persist over time suggest diagnoses, such as those described in the *DSM-IV* (American Psychiatric Association, 1994). In turn, the symptoms and diagnosis suggest particular drugs or drug groups. Those medications that are used to treat persistent psychotic and bipolar symptoms are described here. (Medication for depression and anxiety was already discussed in Chapters 8 and 9.) The groups of medications considered are antipsychotic and mood stabilizing agents. Table 12.1 describes the medication groupings, targeted symptoms, and diagnoses. Note that there is an overlap in the use of drugs across diagnostic groups. In recent years, the use of more than one drug at a time (*polypharmacy*) has become common (Torrey, 1988). In using a couple of drugs, the major diagnosis, major symptoms, and ancillary symptoms can be addressed simultaneously.

TABLE 12.1 Medication Groupings, Target Symptoms, and Diagnoses

Medication Group	Targeted Symptoms	*DSM-IV* Diagnoses

Antipsychotic agents	**Positive Symptoms**
	Hallucinations
	Delusions
	Bizarre behavior
	Formal thought disorder
	
	Negative Symptoms
	Flat affect
	Apathy
	Social withdrawal
	Poverty of speech
	
	Behavior
	Mania
	Severe agitation
	Aggression
	Disorganized behavior
		Schizophrenia
		Schizophreniform disorder
		Schizoaffective disorder
		Mood disorders with psychotic
		  symptoms
		Delusional disorder
		Dementia of the Alzheimer's type
		  with psychotic symptoms
		Drug-induced psychoses

Mood stabilizing agents	Mania (euphoria, hyperactivity,
	  pressured speech, grandiosity,
	  flight of ideas, distractibility)
	Mood fluctuations
	Aggressive behavior
		Bipolar disorder (all types
		  and subtypes)
		Schizoaffective disorder
		Cyclothymic disorder
		Schizophrenia with mood component
		  (as adjunctive medication)

Sources: Based on American Psychiatric Association (1994); Kaplan & Sadock (1998).

Antipsychotic Medication

The group of drugs that are employed to treat psychoses are known as antipsychotics or neuroleptics. Although psychotic symptoms are the primary target of these drugs, some also have a sedating effect. Antipsychotics are used to treat schizophrenia (all subtypes), schizoaffective disorder, schizophreniform disorder, delusional disorder (with inconclusive success), bipolar and major depressive mood disorders that have associated psychotic symptoms, and other disorders. They are used on a short-term basis to manage acute episodes and for long-term treatment of severe mental disorders (Baldessarini & Cole, 1988). These drugs are capable of controlling (but not entirely eliminating) distracting hallucinations, cognitive disorganization, and agitation. Today both conventional and atypical antipsychotics are prescribed.

Conventional Antipsychotics.   First-generation, conventional antipsychotic agents are used to treat schizophrenia and other disorders with psychotic symptoms. They are most successful in the management of *positive* (or florid) *symptoms,* which are overt expressions of unusual sensory experiences (hallucinations), disturbed thinking, and/or bizarre behavior. Conventional antipsychotics are less effective with *negative* (or deficit) *symptoms*— flat affect, poverty of speech, apathy, asociality, and/or impairment in attentionality (Andreasen, 1985). They also create some disturbing side effects.

The first of these drugs to be discovered was chlorpromazine (Thorazine). Other phenothiazenes (the name of the group of drugs of which this is an exemplar) include thioridazine (Mellaril), trifluoperazine (Stelazine), and fluphenazine (Prolixin). Some of the other conventional medications that are used are listed in Table 12.2.

These medications can also be distinguished by their *potency.* A high-potency drug is one in which a low dosage is sufficient to address target symptoms. The standard dosages of high-potency drugs such as Haldol and Prolixin, (6–12 mg/day for maintenance therapy) are equivalent to standard dosages of low-potency drugs such as Thorazine and Mellaril (300–600 mg/day for maintenance therapy) (Lehman et al., 1998). In other words, a low dosage of a high-potency drug is the equivalent of a high dosage of a low-potency drug. Although these drugs are similar if prescribed in equivalent dosages, they differ in associated side effects (Kaplan & Sadock, 1988; Wittlin, 1988).

Among the side effects of some of the first-generation drugs are sedation and extrapyramidal symptoms. *Sedation* is a calming response, produced especially by the low-potency antipsychotics. Sedation helps control agitation, aggressiveness, mania, and irritability, an effect that, in some cases, is desired. On the other hand, sedation induces sleep,

TABLE 12.2   Antipsychotic Medication

Group/Generic Names	Trade Names
Conventional Antipsychotics	
chlorpromazine	Thorazine
thioridazine	Mellaril
trifluoperazine	Stelazine
fluphenazine	Prolixin, Permitil
moban	Molindone
serentil	Mesoridazine
thiothixene	Navane
haloperidol	Haldol
trilafon	Perphenazine
Atypical Antipsychotics	
clozapine	Clozaril/Leponex
risperidone	Risperdal
olanzapine	Zyprexa
quetiapine	Seroquel
sertindole	Serlect
ziprasidone	Zeldox

Sources: Based on Kaplan & Sadock (1998); NAMI (1997).

lowers awareness, and limits responsiveness—which can interfere with performance of everyday activities, work, and the operation of machinery. *Extrapyramidal symptoms* (EPSs) are disturbances in motor activity that are associated with blockage of dopamine receptors (Wittlin, 1988). Among the various symptoms are dystonias, parkinsonian symptoms, akathisia, akinesia, and tardive dyskinesia. Other side effects of these drugs are anticholinergic effects, postural hypotension, neuroleptic malignant syndrome (NMS), and sexual and reproductive difficulties. Some of the adverse side effects are described in Table 12.3.

The prevention and treatment of side effects present a formidable challenge to psychiatrists. Prevention of tardive dyskinesia is facilitated by the use of low doses of antipsychotic drugs. Another strategy is to withdraw the neuroleptic—although this can result in a temporary worsening of symptoms (Baldessarini & Cole, 1988; Matorin & De Chillo, 1984; Reid,

TABLE 12.3   Disturbing Side Effects of Conventional Antipsychotic Drugs

Side Effect	Description
Dystonias	Muscular spasms of the throat, neck, eyes, jaws, tongue, back, or whole body. These are seen frequently during the first few days of treatment, especially in young men.
Parkinsonian symptoms	Characterized by rigidity, shuffling gait, muscle stiffness, stooped posture, drooling, and a regular, coarse tremor.
Akathisia	Muscular discomfort, manifested by motor restlessness. The client is unable to sit still and appears agitated.
Akinesia	Reduced motor activity, listlessness, low spontaneity, apathy.
Tardive dyskinesia	Involuntary movements, primarily of the face, tongue, mouth, and neck, but also of the extremities. These symptoms appear after prolonged use of neuroleptics.
Anticholinergic symptoms	Symptoms include dry mouth, blurry vision, urine retention, and constipation. Nausea and vomiting are other possible symptoms.
Postural hypotension	A lowering of blood pressure related to changes in one's position. It is manifested by fatigue, loss of balance, fainting, and falling.
Neuroleptic malignant syndrome	A side effect of antipsychotic medication that is life threatening. Characterized by fever, akinesia, rigidity, delirium, dystonia, and abnormal behavior. On the surface, it looks like an acute form of schizophrenia.
Sexual and reproductive disturbances	These include difficulties having erections and ejaculating, low libido, breast enlargement, galactorrhea, and menstrual irregularities or amenorrhea. Together with such additional side effects as weight gain and skin disturbances, these symptoms can be especially disturbing to sexually active clients.

Sources: Based on Baldessarini & Cole (1988); Cohen (1988); Kaplan & Sadock (1988); Rifkin & Siris (1987); Wittlin (1988).

1989; Wittlin, 1988). Sometimes antianxiety agents such as benzodiazepines are used to ease the effects of withdrawal (Simpson, Pi, & Sramek, 1986). Antiparkinsonian agents such as Cogentin, Akineton, Benadryl, and Artane, which are used to manage extrapyramidal symptoms, are not effective with tardive dyskinesia and akathisia. Furthermore, antiparkinsonian agents, antipsychotics, and antidepressants contribute to the development of anticholinergic symptoms. Medical management of anticholinergic effects includes changing the drug or lowering the dosage. Clients are counseled to treat these symptoms by rinsing their mouths and taking laxatives (Kaplan & Sadock, 1988). Postural hypotension is associated with the use of high dosages of low-potency antipsychotics and is especially common during the initial few days of treatment. It is managed by monitoring the blood pressure and counseling clients to rise slowly and prevent injuries (Kaplan & Sadock, 1988).

Conventional antipsychotic drugs can also produce cardiac effects, jaundice, photosensitivity, blood disorders, visual problems, and allergic reactions (Baldessarini & Cole, 1988; Kaplan & Sadock, 1988). As a rule, the less potent drugs have fewer extrapyramidal side effects but are associated with more anticholinergic reactions and more postural hypotension, and are more sedating, whereas the more potent drugs produce more extrapyramidal symptoms but are less sedating and produce fewer anticholinergic effects (Baldessarini & Cole, 1988; Kaplan & Sadock, 1988; Wittlin, 1988).

Atypical Antipsychotics.   Psychopharmacological research has produced a second generation of drugs that is referred to as "atypical antipsychotics." These drugs address some of the deficiencies of the first-generation, conventional medications. The newer drugs treat the negative as well as the positive symptoms of schizophrenia and have fewer side effects than their predecessors. Research on atypical agents has been so rapid that it is anticipated that even newer drugs will be added to the list in Table 12.2 in the next few years. According to expert opinion, the atypical antipsychotics are recommended for many clinical situations as the first-line treatment for schizophrenia (Expert Consensus Panels, 1999).

One of the first of the atypical antipsychotics approved in the United States was clozapine. This medication is used largely for individuals who do not respond to conventional antipsychotic medications. It does not produce the extrapyramidal symptoms that are associated with the conventional medications, and it appears to suppress tardive dyskinesia while a client is taking this medication (Kaplan & Sadock, 1998). Furthermore, it seems to moderate negative as well as positive symptoms. On the other hand, clozapine poses the risk of agranulocytosis, which lowers the white blood cells, and can cause seizures. To prevent agranulocystosis, blood levels are monitored weekly during the first eighteen weeks of treatment and every two weeks thereafter (Cowen, 1998).

One atypical antipsychotic that does not pose this risk and has a low incidence of EPS when the dosage is low is risperidone. Risperidone does, however, have a few side effects, including sexual dysfunction in men, weight gain, postural hypotension, and mild sedation (Marder, 1997). Some of the other medications listed in Table 12.2 have similar advantages and disadvantages. Like clozapine and risperidone, olanzapine, quetiapine, sertindole, and ziprasidone treat both positive and negative symptoms and pose a low risk of EPS (NAMI, 1997). Quetiapine is associated with a low incidence of sexual dysfunction and female reproductive difficulties (Arvanitis, 1997).

Antipsychotic drugs are administered orally or intramuscularly. Oral administration is respectful of clients' dignity, autonomy, and right to self-determination. Intramuscular "depot" preparations are long-acting solutions that are given to clients who do not comply with the prescribed medical treatment. Haloperidol (Haldol) and fluphenazine (Prolixin) can be administered intramuscularly. Depot preparations may be associated with increased side effects such as tardive dyskinesia and dystonia (Kaplan & Sadock, 1988).

A history of episodes of schizophrenia suggests that the client should remain on a maintenance dose of antipsychotic medication indefinitely. Many psychiatrists, however, lower the dosage over time for the client who is stable. When the client is under stress, an increase may be advised (Kaplan & Sadock, 1988). Because schizophrenia is a heterogeneous illness with diverse outcomes, alternative strategies have been used. Some persons with long-term schizophrenia are medicated on an intermittent basis (Kane & Lieberman, 1987). These individuals are closely monitored by clinicians and families. Upon recognition of the return of symptoms, the medication regimen is restored. This strategy allows clients to have periods in which they are not subjected to the adverse side effects described. An older strategy is to provide periodic "drug holidays" in which medication is eliminated for a weekend or so. Although research studies indicate that these are associated with increased risk of tardive dyskinesia (Simpson, Pi, & Sramek, 1986), this strategy may boost the morale of clients who have been on antipsychotic medication for long periods of time. Nevertheless, drug withdrawal may convince some clients that they do not need medication at all, leaving them at risk of the return of psychotic symptoms.

Research on the effectiveness of antipsychotic medication points to its ability to reduce acute psychotic symptoms (Rifkin & Siris, 1987) and prevent relapse and rehospitalization for clients on maintenance schedules (Kane & Lieberman, 1987). Nevertheless, the side effects (especially of the first-generation drugs) and the long-term maintenance regimen that is usually recommended raise questions about the cost-benefit ratio of medication (Gerhart & Brooks, 1983). Some clients may prefer to live with the risk of rehospitalization to the discomfort of side effects of medication.

Impact on Women. Additional questions remain about the impact of antipsychotic medication on adult women. In the past, many research studies on drugs excluded women of childbearing age, the rationale being that women's cyclic hormonal changes constitute a confounding variable (Mogul, 1985). Nevertheless, it is important for women to know whether and how antipsychotics interact with their menstrual cycle, pregnancy, and lactation. Research on the effects of antipsychotic drugs ingested during pregnancy on the fetus is inconclusive. If medication is withheld, the mother's psychotic symptoms may interfere with her taking care of herself and her baby (Miller, 1991). Some psychiatrists recommend withholding medication during the first trimester (Miller, 1991) and dissuade women from breast feeding if they are taking certain medications (Kaplan & Sadock, 1998).

Impact on Older Adults. Older adults taking antipsychotic medication also require special attention. Because tardive dyskinesia is associated with long-term consumption of first-generation antipsychotics, older clients are at high risk, if they are not already afflicted with the condition. They are especially at risk of falling as a result of postural hypotonia, a side effect of some antipsychotics. Furthermore, older clients may have other medical problems that complicate the process of psychiatric diagnosis because some physical diseases generate psychotic symptoms. Moreover, older adults' physical health status (e.g., the presence of a cardiac problem) and other medications they are taking may preclude the use of certain antipsychotics. With older adults care should be taken about drug interactions and dosage. Generally they benefit from a lower dose of medication than younger clients.

Mood Stabilizing Agents

Mood stabilizing agents are used to treat bipolar disorder and other disorders with manic or hypomanic symptoms. They are also used as an adjunctive medication for other mental disorders. Table 12.4 presents the three drugs that have been shown to be effective in the treatment of acute mania and, to some extent, for the depressive phase and in maintenance treatment (Keck & McElroy, 1998). For a long time, lithium was the standard treatment, but now two anticonvulsant drugs, carbamazepine and valproate or divalproex, are also used as first-line treatments of bipolar I disorder (Kaplan & Sadock, 1998).

Lithium is used to treat bipolar disorder I in the acute phase and prophylactically to prevent the recurrence of manic and depressive episodes. For a diagnosis of bipolar I, the *DSM-IV* (APA, 1994) requires a history of a manic episode. Sometimes lithium is used together with an antipsychotic agent during acute episodes in which there are psychotic symptoms. Its rate of effectiveness is reported to be between 50 and 80 percent (Cowen, 1998; Kaplan & Sadock, 1998). Lithium has been used with some success in the treatment of schizoaffective disorder, cyclothymic disorder, and bipolar II. Bipolar II disorder is characterized by a history of hypomania (low end of mania) and at least one episode of major depression (APA, 1994). Some psychiatrists also use lithium as a supplement to antipsychotic and antidepressant medications (Kaplan & Sadock, 1998).

Lithium is prescribed initially after a physical examination and laboratory tests. It is problematic for pregnant women, persons with renal and cardiovascular disease, and individuals on low-salt diets (Dixson, 1981). Maintenance on lithium requires regular monitor-

TABLE 12.4   Mood Stabilizers

Group/Generic Names	Trade Names
Lithium	
lithium carbonate	Eskalith
	Lithobid (slow-release tablets)
	Lithotabs
	Lithonate
	Lithane
lithium citrate	Cibalith-S (syrup)
Anticonvulsants	
carbamazepine	Tegretol
valproate/valproic acid	Depakene
or divalproex	Depakote

Source: Based on Kaplan & Sadock (1998).

ing of lithium levels and periodic laboratory tests. The purpose of checking lithium blood levels is to ensure that the client is receiving a therapeutic dose and is avoiding toxicity. The margin between the therapeutic and toxic is slim. The lithium level that is usually therapeutic for the client in an acute state is higher than the level needed for maintenance (Kaplan & Sadock, 1988). For maintenance the client has blood work monitored regularly and at decreasing frequencies (from every two weeks upon discharge to every two months after six months). Lithium carbonate is ingested at prescribed intervals on a daily basis.

Lithium produces some side effects and symptoms of toxicity. The side effects include tremors of the hand, thirst, increased urine output, weight gain, cardiovascular changes, and acne (Cowen, 1998). Among the symptoms of toxicity are dry mouth, severe episodes of diarrhea, vomiting, tremors, confusion, coma, poor coordination, slurred speech, and seizures (Cowen, 1998; Kaplan & Sadock, 1998). As disturbing as these adverse effects may be, most of these symptoms are not visible to others; thus, they do not interfere with normalization or integration. Clients with bipolar disorder who are treated with lithium generally remain alert, attentive, and in touch with their environment (Sands, 1985). Nevertheless, care should be taken to prevent toxicity. Clients should be counseled to report their side effects immediately; social workers and other mental health professionals should observe bipolar clients' physical and mental states so that psychiatric intervention can be mobilized quickly if needed.

Although lithium is helpful to those individuals who respond to it, some individuals do not respond to it, have disabling side effects, or cannot take it because of concurrent health issues. Among those who tend not to respond are the "rapid cyclers," who experience several episodes of mania or depression in a year's time, and persons with bipolar disorder, mixed (Prien & Gelenberg, 1989). Currently there a couple of other drugs that can be used.

Anticonvulsants.   Two anticonvulsive drugs that have empirical support as being effective in treating manic episodes are carbamazepine and valproic acid (Keck & McElroy, 1998). These drugs have been used alone or together with lithium. Carbamazepine seems to be comparable to lithium in its effect on acute mania and as a prophylaxis for depressive and manic episodes of bipolar I disorder (Cowen, 1998; Kaplan & Sadock, 1998). But like lithium, carbamazepine has adverse effects and can produce toxicity. Among the adverse side effects are sedation, dizziness, clumsiness, a skin rash, and gastrointestinal distress (Kaplan & Sadock, 1998). There is a slight risk of agranulocytosis, and it can cause a disturbance in cardiac conduction in individuals with preexisting heart problems (Cowen, 1998). Periodic liver function tests and regular blood counts are mandatory when this medication is used (NAMI, 1999).

Valproate or valproic acid (also formulated as divalproex) is another mood stabilizer, effective in the treatment of acute mania associated with bipolar I disorder. There are some data indicating that valproate is effective with rapid-cycling bipolar I disorder, mixed or dysphoric mania, and mania due to a medical condition (Kaplan & Sadock, 1998). Likewise there is some evidence that this medication has prophylactic effects in clients who do not respond to the other two drugs that were discussed and that it is more effective preventing manic and mixed episodes that depressive ones (Cowen, 1998). The side effects of this medication include tremor, sedation, drowsiness, transient hair loss, and weight gain (Cowen, 1998; Kaplan & Sadock, 1998).

Impact on Women and Older Adults.   Women with bipolar illness risk becoming pregnant during a manic phase, which is characterized by hypersexuality and poor judgment (Miller, 1996). Lithium, carbamazepine, and valproate use during pregnancy pose risks to the mother and the unborn child (Baldessarini & Cole, 1988; Miller, 1991, 1996). Likewise, these drugs reach a nursing infant (Kaplan & Sadock, 1998). One of the side effects of valproate is amenorrhea (Cowen, 1998). Older adults who are vulnerable to renal complications are not good candidates for lithium (Prien, 1987).

Adjunctive Medications.   The three mood stabilizers that were discussed have been used with each other (two at a time). Another practice is to incorporate antipsychotic and antidepressant drugs in the treatment of bipolar disorder. As mentioned earlier, antipsychotics are frequently used to treat acute mania. They work more quickly than lithium, which takes a week to ten days to be effective. Antipsychotics are sometimes used on a long-term basis for individuals who have recurrent episodes of mania that are not controlled with lithium. Antidepressants are used together with a mood stabilizer to treat clients with bipolar depression (Frances, Kahn, Carpenter, Docherty, & Donovan, 1998), but this is done cautiously because antidepressants can precipitate mania, hypomania, and rapid cycling (Prien, 1987). We turn next to the implications of knowledge about the medications that have been discussed for social work practice.

Implications for Clinical Social Work Practice

This review of medications that are frequently prescribed for persons with psychotic and mood-fluctuating disorders provides a knowledge base for social work. Social workers should become aware of changes in the medication that have been ordered by psychiatrists, alterations in the client's behavior prior to and following medication changes, and contingencies that enter into the client's compliance with a medication regimen. Factors such as clients' attitudes toward taking medication, undesirable side effects, and the use of alcohol, street drugs, caffeine, and tobacco should be explored.

   As part of the mental health team, social workers have a role in monitoring clients' compliance with the treatment plan, including intake of prescribed drugs. As social workers with professional values of client self-determination, self-actualization, and human dignity, clinical social workers must balance their commitment to what is good for the clients with a concern for clients' rights.

   Taking medication is a responsibility that principally belongs to the client and secondarily to significant others such as parents, spouses, friends, and operators of community residences. The psychiatrist, mental health nurse, psychologist, social worker, and other team members intervene to identify and remove obstacles and promote compliance.

   One obstacle to compliance may lie in the client's feelings about taking medication. Medication may be perceived symbolically as a crutch or a reminder that he or she has a serious disorder. This feeling may be particularly acute among persons with severe mental disorders, whose psychiatric illness seems interminable. Dependence on medication may reinforce feelings of helplessness and hopelessness; interfere with self-esteem and autonomy; and contradict sociocultural values about independence, self-sufficiency, and competence.

   Some clients may have thoughts related to their psychiatric difficulty that affect their medical compliance. For example, Mike, a young man with an obsessive compulsive personality disorder as well as schizophrenia, would not take his medication on days in which he overslept. In exploring the reasons for his noncompliance, the clinical social worker discovered that the directions on the medication bottle said, "Take twice daily at 8 A.M. and 8 P.M.," and that Mike concluded, "If I've slept late, I've blown it." In this case the social worker had the psychiatrist change the written instructions to "twice daily" and counsel the client about taking two tablets daily.

Clinical social workers can help clients by encouraging them to talk about their feelings about medication, so they can sort out the realistic and the unrealistic. Such was the case with Susan:

> Susan, a twenty-five-year-old musician, had the diagnosis of bipolar disorder for three years. She had her first manic episode during her senior year of college, which resulted in her taking a leave of absence. Later she returned to college and completed her degree.
>
> Susan expressed a number of concerns about lithium. For one, she felt that it interfered with her creativity. During manic episodes, she would stay awake into the night, composing music. She felt less creative on lithium. In addition, Susan found it embarrassing to come to the clinic, where she sat with clients who talked to themselves and exhibited bizarre movements.
>
> In talking with Susan, the social worker learned that Susan was frightened of the other clients and afraid that she would develop movements like theirs. When the side effects of schizophrenia were differentiated from those of lithium, Susan felt relieved. Only then did she admit that the music she composed when she was manic was not very good (she tape recorded it once so she could listen to it later). In subsequent discussions Susan recognized that her risk for recurrent episodes was high (three members of her family had the same disorder), and that lithium could protect her from interruptions in her career.

Clients also have subjective responses to the side effects of drugs. They may feel uncomfortable with the anticholinergic effects and self-conscious about obvious extrapyramidal symptoms. Weight gain, skin eruptions, and sexual dysfunctioning may prompt some clients to take themselves off the medication. A social worker who listens attentively and probes for feelings may be able to join with the client in an effort to effect a change in the medication. This approach recognizes the client's feelings while at the same time it offers the client alternatives to noncompliance. Options include a change in dosage, introduction of antiparkinsonian medications, a change in drugs, or the use of an adjunctive medication. Social workers can encourage clients to request medication changes and arrange appointments for that purpose. Not unusually, social workers sit in on appointments with psychiatrists. So long as it is acceptable to clients, the social worker can raise issues with the psychiatrist that clients may be reluctant to raise themselves. The social worker who is aware of alternative drugs, side effects, and drug holidays can advocate for these options, if appropriate.

Medication management is another issue that may arise in the process of working with a client. Many clients take their own medications as prescribed. Others are given medication by a family member, boarding home operator, or nurse. Medication may be in the forms of capsules, tablets, or liquid, or it may be administered intramuscularly. Clients who are given medication by others may feel controlled, dependent, or childlike.

With respect to clients' rights, self-administration is the most desirable alternative. Clients who have a history of noncompliance or abuse of medication, however, may not be given that option. Social workers can work with clients and client systems to promote the maximum self-determination feasible with respect to medication and develop with clients goals that reflect their wish for more control. Tools such as calendars, daily checklists, and charts can be developed. A tool that can help in the management of medication that also gives clients control is "My Portable Medication Record," a booklet that clients can take with them when they go to different treatment settings. It provides places for the client's medical insurance information, pharmacy, emergency instructions, the doctor's name, health issues, and hospitalizations, as well as documentation of the history of medications used and their effectiveness (Conn & Edwards, 1999). In addition, clients can be encouraged to keep medication in a place that is visible and to take the medication at the same time every day. Nevertheless, some clients do forget:

> When Sol had his own apartment, he would forget to take his medication some days. Other days he would consume alcohol concurrently with prescribed medication. One day the combination caused him to sleep for two days. Sol agreed with the mental health team that it would be better if the medication were dispensed at the day treatment center; and to go to Alcoholics Anonymous. He said that when he gets his alcohol problem under control, he would like to take his medication on his own.

Sometimes social workers obtain information about clients that indicates that they are not complying with their treatment plan. The use of alcohol and street drugs, the sale of prescribed medication, hoarding of medication, and borrowing from or lending medication to others can result in adverse physical reactions and suicide. Concerns about these behaviors should be discussed directly and honestly with both the client and the psychiatrist. Mental health teams are an appropriate forum for the social worker to discuss ethical as well as treatment issues—and for the team to develop a common strategy.

In working with a client who is on psychotropic medication, a social worker is working with a *person,* not a set of symptoms or a diagnosis. Attitudes toward taking medication and self-defeating behaviors are psychosocial expressions of the client's adaptation. Other approaches—social skills training, family psychoeducation, and the selective use of psychotherapy—can address these issues more fully. Because social skills training has a great deal of empirical support, it is presented as a best practice.

Best Practice: Social Skills Training

Severe psychiatric illness can interfere with the ability to process information, solve problems, and respond in a socially appropriate way to external demands. The resulting impairments in social skills limit the clients' ability to communicate their needs, engage in everyday social interactions, and develop relationships that have the potential of enhancing the quality of their lives. Although medication can reduce symptoms, it cannot compensate for deficiencies in social skills. One psychosocial rehabilitative intervention that aims to remedy these difficulties is social skills training.

Social skills training is a form of behavior therapy that has been used to treat a range of psychological and interpersonal problems in inpatient, outpatient, and community settings (Bedell, 1994). It has been applied to the psychosocial rehabilitation of persons with serious and persistent mental health problems to help them cope more effectively with social living. It is implemented on an individual, family, or group basis in hospitals, behavioral health agencies, within programs such as partial hospitalization, and in clients' natural environments. Some clients who can benefit from social skills training have limited skills in self-care; for example, they are not able to dress themselves. Others are relatively self-sufficient but have difficulties conducting a conversation, finding a job, or making friends. Research has found that it is particularly effective in reducing symptoms and improving assertiveness and interpersonal skills among inpatients (Dilk & Bond, 1996) and that there is a positive trend that it helps improve the social functioning of outpatients (Mueser, Drake, & Bond, 1997). Social skills training is highly effective when combined with medication and family psychoeducation, but this effect lessens over time (Hogarty et al., 1991). The cognitive-behavioral model that has been the subject of the most effectiveness research is discussed here. The illustrative scenario of a group intervention is in keeping with the trend of giving increased attention to cognition and emotion (Bedell, 1994).

The conceptual basis for social skills training lies in social learning and cognitive theories (see Chapter 3). Principles of information processing and learning are incorporated in the theoretical model and its application. Accordingly to the theory guiding social skills training (Liberman et al., 1986), individuals develop social schemata (explanatory structures) that account for experience and enable them to interact with the social environment. The development of these schemata depends on (a) psychobiological functioning of memory, attention, affect, perception, and concept formation and (b) higher-order cognitive processes such as taking the perspective of another, regulating one's own behavior, and inference making. If any of these functions are deficient—which often is the case among persons with serious mental illnesses—interpersonal problem solving and coping will be adversely affected.

The ability to solve problems is an outcome of the operation of social schemata and depends on the functioning of receiving, processing, and sending skills (Liberman et al., 1986). *Receiving skills* facilitate that the content and feelings associated with messages from others be understood and interpreted accurately. Accordingly, the individual takes in verbal and nonverbal information and makes sense of it. *Processing skills* refer to the way in which decisions are made about how to respond to a message. The individual thinks through alternative ways of reacting, possible effects of each option, and makes a selection that will achieve desired outcomes. With *sending skills* one is able to transmit information in a way that the desired goal is accomplished. This requires that the content be communicated verbally and nonverbally and that pacing and timing be modulated to the social demands of the situation. When individuals are able to cope by mobilizing interpersonal problem solving to achieve personal goals, they are attaining social competence (Liberman et al., 1986).

Social skills training of persons with serious and persistent psychiatric problems is directed at (a) improving attention span and higher-order thinking; (b) enhancing receiving, processing, and sending skills; and (c) modifying the environment to support the use of improved social skills (Liberman et al., 1986). The first approach, especially the improvement of attentional skills, is usually used with clients whose psychotic symptoms severely interfere with their psychosocial functioning. Many of these lower-functioning clients are patients in

psychiatric hospitals. Here the second and third approaches, applicable in psychosocial rehabilitation settings in the community, will be explained and integrated. These approaches emphasize the development of social, vocational, and independent living skills.

Prior to implementing social skills training, the clinician makes a comprehensive assessment of the client's overall functioning (see Chapter 4), including an evaluation of the
client's social interaction skills and deficiencies. Interviews with family members, significant others, and operators of family care and boarding homes can reveal important information about the client's social performance in context (Liberman, DeRisi, & Mueser,
1989). The outline for a functional assessment that was described in Chapter 4 should
assist in the process of identifying strengths and areas in which training can be helpful.
Standardized instruments such as the Rathus Assertiveness Schedule (RAS; Rathus, 1973),
the Social Interaction Schedule (SIS; Liberman et al., app. E), and the Wallace Functional
Assessment Scale (Wallace, 1986) are useful in their identification of specific needs and in
their ability to evaluate progress over time.

During the assessment process those skills that need development should be identified. From these, specific skills are selected as goals. In keeping with the principle of self-
determination, the choice of training goals should be negotiated with the client. This way,
behaviors which the client is motivated to change are targeted. Other criteria for selecting
goals are that they revolve around specific, high-frequency, and constructive behaviors and
those which are functional, attainable, and likely to occur in the near future (Liberman et al.,
1989).

The skills that are enhanced or developed in social skills training are diverse and
depend on the needs of individual clients. They can be broken down to microcomponents
(e.g., maintaining eye contact) or into larger bodies of skills (e.g., taking the bus to the
sheltered workshop). Examples of the kinds of client competencies that can be promoted in
social skills training are as follows:

- explaining side effects of medication to the psychiatrist
- suggesting to an acquaintance that they go out for coffee together
- learning how to wash and dry clothes at a laundromat
- asking a family member for a loan
- carrying on a conversation with a person of the other sex
- looking for a job

The specific skills that are to be developed in training sessions may derive from clients'
needs identified in the assessment process; or they may be generic skills needed by many
clients, such as money management and home finding, programs for which the Clinical
Research Center at UCLA-Camarilla, California has developed packaged modules.

Liberman, DeRisi, and Mueser (1989) state that clients who cannot pay attention or
follow directions for at least fifteen minutes are not appropriate for social skills training.
Most likely these clients have uncontrolled, intrusive psychiatric symptoms such as incoherence, hallucinations, mania, and memory difficulties that interfere with their concentration.
In order to assess clients' ability to attend and remember, the authors suggest an evaluation
of clients' responses to questions about their name, birthdate, and the current date; their
ability to speak in simple sentences; their ability to understand others' talk and to listen to
others without interrupting them for three to five minutes; and their ability to follow a se-

quence of three directives (e.g., "go to the door, knock on the door, and return to your seat"). Furthermore, they recommend that candidates for skills training be able to interact with others without distracting behaviors (e.g., acting, out, talking to oneself, pacing) and articulate motivation to improve their expression of emotions. The assessment of clients' ability to participate in social skills training may involve observing their interactions in social programs, such as partial hospitalization, or trying them out in a training session.

Social skills training uses a series of role playing of problematic situations to teach participants more effective interactional skills. The major techniques utilized are behavioral rehearsal, modeling, reinforcement, shaping, and prompting (Liberman, 1988). *Behavioral rehearsal* is the practice of social skills through simulations or role plays. First clients may be asked to perform the skill as they have been doing it in the past. After they come to recognize their difficulties and alternative approaches are suggested, clients practice more effective ways of accomplishing the skill. *Modeling* refers to the performance of the desired skill by role models and subsequent learning through imitation by observers of the models, that is, clients who are having difficulty with a particular skill. In group social skills training, other clients and the clinician demonstrate effective skill performance, which becomes a model for clients. When a client is able to imitate the performance of models, approval or *reinforcement* is provided by the clinician and others present (family or group members). Reinforcement is also given following clients' successively close approximations of performance of the desired skill, a process known as *shaping.* An additional technique used in social skills training is *prompting,* or coaching. Here the clinician or trainer provides cues that will remind the client of the requirements of the situation and the skills necessary to meet these demands. The trainer may, for example, advise the client to maintain eye contact and maintain a modulated voice during a role play of a social interaction.

One of the pitfalls of social skills training is that clients sometimes have difficulties applying skills learned in training sessions to real-life situations (Liberman et al., 1986; Wallace et al., 1980). Persons with severe and persistent mental disabilities have varying abilities to generalize from one situation to another—at least with respect to complex skills. In order to promote generalization, several procedures are incorporated into the training. One is the use of *homework assignments*—exercises that the client is expected to perform outside the skills training session. These require that the client replicate the skill learned in training in the community, where prompting generally does not occur. Some writers recommend that clients be given index cards on which the week's assignment is written and that clients bring back evidence of having carried out the assignment, for example, the signature of a service provider the client was supposed to contact (Liberman, 1988). Another way to promote generalization is to carry out social skills training in the community contexts in which the skill is needed. An additional means to promote generalization is to have clients *overlearn* and practice the skills that are taught. To assure learning, the skill is modeled and practiced beyond clients' demonstration that they are able to perform the skill effectively. In addition to these approaches, families, significant others, and caregivers are asked to provide prompts and reinforcements when clients practice skills at home or in other natural environments (Liberman et al., 1986).

The group provides a format in which social skills can be modeled by participants as well as the group leaders or trainers, who may be clinical social workers. The group offers clients in need of social skills development sustained relationships from session to session and a sense of belonging. Sharing one's deficiencies as well as skills in a group facilitates a feeling of being accepted at the same time it promotes growth in incremental steps. Although the group may engender a moderate amount of stress, such stress closely replicates the stress in participants' everyday life experiences (Liberman et al., 1989). The group that will provide an illustration of social skills training consists of five clients and a clinical social worker/trainer. (For larger groups two group leaders are helpful.) The group members and their goals are as follows:

> Florence is a thirty-year-old, divorced woman diagnosed with bipolar I disorder, most recent episode depressed, mild. Although she worked in the past in sales, she has not been employed since she was able to obtain Social Security disability insurance three years ago. Florence has been stable on lithium for three-and-a-half years. Currently she is experiencing problems with her boyfriend Jack, who she believes is taking advantage of her by living with her and not paying the rent. Her immediate goal is to tell him how she feels and get him to either contribute or leave. Her long-term goals are to work as a volunteer first and later to obtain a "real" job.

> Joseph is a twenty-eight-year-old, single man who lives with his brother and sister-in-law. Around the time he developed schizophrenia, paranoid type, he became active in a charismatic religious church, which continues to be an important resource for him. Nevertheless, Joseph does not confine his religious enthusiasm to himself and other members of his church. Wherever he goes (including the waiting room of the mental health center), he preaches to people around him. Joseph does recognize that his preaching interferes with his relationships with others. His short-term goal is to engage in social conversational behavior in place of preaching when talking to persons who are not members of his church. Eventually, he would like to get a job and live independently.

> Sally, a thirty-five-year-old, married woman and mother of a three-year-old child, has been given the diagnosis of schizoaffective disorder. Currently she is home taking care of her daughter most of the time and is feeling depressed. Her husband is a truck driver, who is out of town during the week. Sally would like to have more social contacts but is afraid to initiate them. Her short-term goals are to make friends with whom she can socialize at least once a week and to tell her husband how she feels about his being out of town so much. Her long-term goal is to improve her relationship with her husband.

> Michael is a twenty-two-year-old man with both recurrent major depression and an obsessive compulsive personality disorder. He lives with his parents in a rural area. After Michael was discharged from the hospital, he began to have conflicts with his parents over his "interminable" use of the shower. Furthermore, his parents are disturbed by his sleeping late and his playing loud music. Michael's immediate goal is "to keep my parents from hassling me." His longer-term goal is to move into a group home.

Richard, thirty-five years old and married, is having difficulties taking instructions from his supervisor at the sheltered workshop. His wife, parents, and case manager are strongly supporting his continuing with the workshop job. Richard has the diagnosis of schizophrenia, chronic undifferentiated type, and a history of five hospitalizations. He is afraid that he cannot handle the pressure of the workshop. His goal is to stay on at the workshop for six months and then find a part-time job in the community. His immediate goal is to be able to listen to his supervisor better.

A group of these clients has been meeting weekly for three weeks in ninety-minute sessions with the clinical social worker Matt Hughes. The group members have begun to feel comfortable with each other and with Matt. The setting is a psychosocial rehabilitation center serving formerly hospitalized adults who live in the community. The center is housed in a store on a side street of a city in the Southwest. The social skills training group meets in a room in back of the store. In the front, other consumers play pool, socialize, and meet informally with mental health workers.

Matt began the formal group session after the participants were settled in their chairs in a circle and seemed to be finished chatting informally with each other. By this time, the social worker had greeted each of the clients individually and had gotten the impression from his conversation with Michael that the problems between Michael and his family were acute. Matt thought that Michael would need a great deal of attention today. Nevertheless, he asked all group members to give a brief report on how things went during the past week and about progress in performing their homework assignments. The clients took their turns, giving the following reports:

FLORENCE: I finally got up enough nerve to talk to Jack about paying the rent. I told him that he wasn't being fair to me and I needed his help.

MATT: Good for you, Florence!

FLORENCE: Well, it was hard. I was nervous the whole time—with good reason. Jack said that he couldn't pay the rent. He said he owed money to his sister and had to pay her back. He said that after he paid her, he would pitch in on the rent.

MATT: When will that be?

FLORENCE: He said six months. Meanwhile he promised to contribute to the groceries and pay the electric bill.

MATT: How do you feel about that?

FLORENCE: That will at least help some. I'm still not completely satisfied, but at least that's something.

MATT: I'm glad you talked to Jack about this. This was your goal and you accomplished that.

FLORENCE: I'm glad, too. But I wish I could have insisted that the rent comes first—before his debt to his sister.

MATT: Would you like to work on communicating this to Jack as your next goal?

FLORENCE: Yes, but I want to see if he really does pay for the groceries and electric bill first.

MATT: Okay. Joseph?

JOSEPH: When I went bowling with Tony and Marie Saturday, I didn't talk to anyone about religion.

MATT: Terrific!

JOSEPH: It was hard. There were a lot of people around that I wanted to preach to.

MATT: Good for you for holding back.

JOSEPH: But I didn't talk to anyone but Tony and Marie (brother and sister-in-law).

MATT: That can be your goal for next time—to talk to someone else and to talk about something other than religion.

JOSEPH: Maybe.

MATT: Sally?

SALLY: Florence didn't tell you, but she and I went out for lunch together last Wednesday. Mom babysat. I really enjoyed getting out of the house and doing something with a friend.

FLORENCE: We had a real nice afternoon. And Sally helped me get up the nerve to talk to Jack.

MATT: Sounds like it was good for both of you.

SALLY: We're planning to do it again next week.

MATT: Good for you! I'm very glad you were able to do that, Sally.

SALLY: It was easier than I thought. I just asked Florence after group last time and she said yes. Then I had to ask Mom when she could babysit and I called Florence on the phone.

MATT: You had to talk to Florence and your mother to do this, and you were able to arrange it.

SALLY: Yes. Next I want to talk to my husband about my feelings.

MATT: You can work on that next. Richard?

RICHARD: I've been trying not to get rattled when Mr. Peters (from the sheltered workshop) corrects me. I realize that that's his job, but he gets on my nerves. From the last session, I learned to listen to what he's trying to say. When I tried to listen better this week, I realized that one of the things that bothers me so much about him is his gruff voice.

MATT: What about his gruff voice bothers you, Richard?

RICHARD: I don't know. He just scares me and then I can't listen.

MATT: It sounds as if you've learned a lot in the last week. Good for you for making progress, Richard! How about you, Michael?

MICHAEL: I had a big fight with my parents yesterday.

MATT: Would you tell us about it?

MICHAEL: I was taking a shower Saturday morning and my mother knocked on the bathroom door. I ignored her because she's always doing that. When I came out, she and my father started screaming at me. They told me I'm wasting water and they can't afford to pay for all that water. I told them that water don't cost nothing and I needed to get clean. Then my parents showed me the water bill—it was

$50—and asked me to either work or leave. I started crying and ran to my room. Then they started knocking on the door to my room, which I locked. I wouldn't open the door. Then my Dad knocked the door down and made me sit down with them in the living room.

MATT: What happened next?

MICHAEL: They told me that something's gotta change or I've got to leave. They said that they can't tolerate my long showers, my sleeping late, and the radio. They said I'm a good-for-nothing bum.

JOSEPH: My brother tells me the same thing.

MICHAEL: They don't realize that I can't help it. I'd like to work. I'd like to live on my own. I'm on the waiting list for the group home and nothing's happening.

MATT: Your goal is to keep your parents from hassling you. What would you like to work on to get them to stop—at least long enough to get you into the group home?

MICHAEL: I'd be willing to cut down on my time in the shower. But I want to make sure I get clean.

MATT: Does anyone in the group have any ideas about how Michael can do this?

FLORENCE: You can bring an alarm clock into the bathroom and set the alarm.

MATT: Good suggestion. How long does it take the rest of you to shower?

JOSEPH: It takes me ten minutes.

FLORENCE: About the same.

RICHARD: Ten minutes for me, too, when I do shower. I hate to shower.

SALLY: It takes me half an hour, but I take baths, not showers.

MATT: You might use up less water in a bath than a shower.

MICHAEL: I prefer showers. And I do lose track of the time. But I do worry about getting clean.

SALLY: You might try XXX soap—it gets you clean—and it's not expensive.

MATT: Good idea, Sally! The group's come up with some good ideas, Michael. Will any of these be helpful to you?

MICHAEL: Yes, I like the idea of using an alarm clock and using XXX soap. But I don't know how to talk to my parents about this. They're about ready to kick me out and I don't want to be out on the street.

MATT: Maybe the group can help.

At this point the group format switches from an introductory phase of reporting goal accomplishments to work on a specific issue with a particular client. By this time, all of the participants have gotten engaged and have been reinforced by the clinician. Some of the group members have given suggestions and other indicators of support to others. The following segment demonstrates how a "dry run" role play of a discussion between Michael and his parents about showering is set up and enacted.

MATT: In order to get a better idea about how you and your parents communicate about your showering, we want you (Michael) and a volunteer mother and father to have a discussion the way it usually goes. Michael, you can play yourself. I would like your opinion on who in the group do you think could best play your parents.

MICHAEL: Florence can play my mother—but you've gotta talk loud and act bossy, Florence. Joseph can play my father. My father doesn't talk about religion, but he's always telling me what's right and what's wrong the way you do, Joseph.

JOSEPH: Okay, I'll do it.

MATT: You told us what happened in your shower and then your room. Let's start this role play in the living room with the three of you sitting down to talk. (Waits for Michael, Joseph, and Florence to be seated.) Suppose you get the discussion started, Joseph, with you as Michael's father.

JOSEPH: (To Michael) I've had it with you, son. You're costing us an arm and a leg and all you do is eat, sleep, and take showers.

MICHAEL: I do more than that. I mow the grass every week—and you know that.

JOSEPH: That doesn't come close to paying for the water you use. And that loud music!

MICHAEL: At least I don't have to listen to you and Mom.

FLORENCE: I can't stand seeing you sleep to 2 o'clock in the afternoon. By the time you have showered and dressed, it's almost supper time. My day's almost over and you're just waking up. And then you start with that music.

MICHAEL: I don't have to listen to this (starts to walk away).

JOSEPH: You're going to have to—or we'll throw you out.

MICHAEL: But you don't listen to my side.

At this point, Matt stops the role play and asks Michael if this was typical of what happens at home. Michael said that it was in the sense that the "discussions" usually go nowhere and he ends up wanting to leave and they end up threatening to kick him out. Matt then asks the group if they could give Michael some positive feedback on how he acted in the role play. Group members comment on his good eye contact, his clear voice, and his willingness to listen until he got angry. Matt then asks Michael how he thinks his parents were feeling. Michael admitted that they were probably frustrated because he did not listen and talked back to them. Matt then proceeds to set up the next phase as follows:

MATT: Michael, what would you like to go better in a discussion like we just role played?

MICHAEL: I wish they wouldn't yell and call me names. When they threaten to kick me out, I get scared—even though they've never carried it out. I wish I would be able to tolerate their yelling at me more—instead of wanting to leave or escaping.

MATT: Does anyone in the group have any ideas about what Michael can do better?

RICHARD: You can tell them your good points—like you want to help and you plan to move out.

MATT: Good. Anyone else?

SALLY: Try to make a deal with them—like you will take a shorter shower if they would buy you a clock and some soap.

> JOSEPH: You can agree to the shower if they would leave you alone about the other things—the radio and sleeping late.
>
> MATT: These are very good suggestions. Now suppose we do the role play over with Richard playing you.

The group now moves into the next phase in which the role play is reenacted with a model, Richard, playing Michael. The other actors remain the same. Matt directs Richard to begin the discussion with taking an attitude that shows Michael's parents that he would really like to work things out with them.

> RICHARD: (Speaking softly) I'm sorry I spent so much time in the shower. I want to be clean but I lose track of the time.
>
> FLORENCE: When you stay in the shower so long, we worry about the water bills.
>
> RICHARD: I know. I wish I could stop myself. Really, I could use your help.
>
> FLORENCE: How?
>
> RICHARD: If you can get me better soap and an alarm clock, I think I could stop myself.
>
> JOSEPH: I have an old wind-up alarm clock in the garage. You can have that, son.
>
> FLORENCE: And I can pick up that soap—if that will help.
>
> RICHARD: It would, I think it would. I really would like to work things out with you. You know, I'm on the list for the group home. But until they call me, I'd like to stay here.
>
> JOSEPH: What about the radio?

At this point Matt cut the discussion. He said he'd rather they tackle one problem at a time. Matt asked Michael what he thought about the role play. Michael said it was very different from the way things usually go at home—that he never admits that he is wrong to his parents and never asks for their help. Michael remarked that Richard did a good job playing him and that he wished he could act like that. Matt suggested that he try acting the way Richard did in the next enactment of the role play.

> MATT: When you play yourself, Michael, be sure to keep up the eye contact the way you did before. Keep your voice down, the way Richard did, and start out by telling your parents that you want to change but need their help.
>
> MICHAEL: Okay…um…Mom and Dad, I want to apologize about using up so much water with the shower. I'm just thinking about myself and not you. I really want to work things out with you.
>
> JOSEPH: We accept your apology. But we want you to change.
>
> MICHAEL: I want to change, too…but I need your help.
>
> FLORENCE: How can we help you, Michael? We would like to help.
>
> MICHAEL: I think it would help if I had a timer in the bathroom. I can set the alarm for, say, ten minutes—and you won't have to knock on the door.
>
> JOSEPH: That's easy. I have an old alarm clock in the garage.

> **MICHAEL:**   One more thing—I would like to use XXX soap. It works better. I worry about getting clean enough. I hope it's not too expensive.
>
> **FLORENCE:**   We can buy that for you if you would take less time with the shower. I am very happy that you are willing to do that, Michael.
>
> **MICHAEL:**   I realize that there are other things that bother you about me—but could we just start with this? I'm hoping to get into the group home soon, but meanwhile I do want to get along with you.
>
> **MATT:**   Cut. Very good, Michael.

At this point the group gave Michael positive feedback. They pointed out that he was reasonable rather than argumentative; that he was willing to compromise; and that he showed his parents that he could understand how they feel. Michael said that it was hard for him to admit to his parents that he was wrong and even harder to ask them to help him. Joseph said that when he played the father in the last round he felt good about Michael, whereas the first time, he felt angry. This led into a group discussion about maintaining positive communication by being honest, direct, and admitting weaknesses.

After the completion of this role play, Matt gave Michael the homework assignment of conducting a conversation like this one with his parents. Michael thought it would be more difficult in real life, but he said he would try. When asked what was hard about it, Michael said he was in the habit of seeing things as either his way or his parents' way. He said that things didn't get heated in the role play the way they do at home—that he wanted to learn how to negotiate better. This led into another role play situation involving another client.

The preceding scenario featuring Michael's problems is exemplary of the kind of interactions that occur in social skills training groups. While the focus here was on one client, the group proceeds to develop role plays and homework assignments for all the group members. Through the medium of the role play, participants learn to interact with each other, appreciate others' perspectives, and respond appropriately. Although problem solving is not the primary purpose of this group, they do learn new ways to approach problems, too. Through skills training a group's members learn to give to each other—which is central to relationship building. In addition, they learn to listen to and benefit from each other's suggestions.

Michael's difficulties could also have been handled in an individual or family session. In an individual session, the clinician plays the client or others, switching between roles. The client learns through the clinician's example and through prompts. In family-centered social skills training, the participants initially enact their usual roles. The clinician then has family members discuss feelings that underlie their interactions and gives feedback on how family members come across. In reenacting the scene, the clinician can assume the role of the client or of other family members and provide coaching to whoever needs it. Role playing of family problems in the context of the family has the advantage of being closer to real-life experience than role playing in a group. We turn next to other interventions with the family.

Intervening with the Family

Families play a key role in the care of their mentally ill relatives. Once blamed for causing psychiatric problems in their children, parents often are the principal providers of physical, emotional, and financial support to their adult children. When one deconstructs the term *family,* one sees that besides parents, grandparents, siblings, spouses or relational partners, children, unrelated kin, and close friends must be included. For persons with severe mental illness who are estranged from their families or have loose ties, case managers and operators of residential services, and other clients may be their family. Small children are often overlooked in discussions about families of the severely mentally ill but they, too, are affected by the vagaries of their mentally ill parent's illness, whether they live with the parent, another relative, or foster parents.

Family members who are caregivers for their relative may provide care in their own home, or they may maintain contact with their relative on a regular basis and/or in an emergency. As members of the client's system of care who are subject to feeling overwhelmed, their own needs for support and education are often overlooked.

Impact of Serious Mental Illness on the Family

The assumption of responsibility for a relative with serious psychiatric disorders takes its toll on families' lives (Gubman & Tessler, 1987). The afflicted relative may act argumentative, withdrawn, unmotivated, aggressive, noisy, bizarre, demanding, threatening, or uncooperative. These and other idiosyncratic behaviors disrupt the family system, which is called upon to adapt to the client's ways. Older siblings are able to cope with this situation through emancipation, and employed fathers have large blocks of time away from the family. Women in particular experience the burden of care (Thurer, 1983). The term *family burden* captures the strain families experience in coping with their ill relative's behaviors, the gap between his or her needs and the services that are available, and the ups and downs of the illness (Riesser & Schorske, 1994; Wasow, 1994).

The family's emotional reactions are a reflection of everyday stresses, social isolation, and grief. Family members have daily encounters in which the family's own needs are ignored. Unable to interpret unusual behaviors they observe, they feel bewildered or frightened. Some families protect their family member and themselves from having to explain the situation to friends by isolating themselves from others. Families grieve for the life for which they had hoped and dreamed for their disabled member, who may have shown promise as a child (Hatfield, 1987a). Moreover, they grieve over the loss of time they may have anticipated having during middle and older adulthood when one is usually relieved of child care responsibilities. Plans to travel, enjoy being a grandparent, and pursue recreational interests are supplanted by day-to-day supervision of a family member whose actions are unpredictable.

Responses of families to caring for a mentally disabled member change over time (Terkelsen, 1987). Before the onset of a psychotic episode, the family may ignore or minimize dysfunctional behavior, viewing it as a stage or temporary condition. Then something happens or someone points out that the individual has a serious problem. At first family members are reluctant to believe that anything is wrong, but evidence accrues and eventually there is a crisis that calls for the intervention of the mental health delivery system. At this time the family faces its member's status as a person with a serious mental disorder. A painful realization, this sets the family on a course in which they seek to understand causes and look for appropriate treatment resources. Families go through periods in which they are hopeful, but the ups and downs of the family member's illness leave them with worry and doubt. They mourn the family member they once knew and develop strategies to help their relative at the same time they garner support for themselves.

Frequently families lack information about mental disorders, medication, behavioral management strategies, and community services. Even if they know the diagnosis, they do not know what the diagnosis means and they do not understand the long-term implications (Gantt, Goldstein, & Pinsky, 1989). In addition, they may experience frustration in their contacts with the mental health system. They may find themselves assuming the role of case manager in a system that lacks resources and excludes them from the treatment process (Francell, Conn, & Gray, 1988). The families' most frequent complaint about professionals is, "They don't understand us" (Hatfield, 1987b).

In response to their frustrations, some family members have joined organizations that both provide mutual support and advocate for the interests of families and their mentally disabled relatives. Local affiliates of the National Alliance for the Mentally Ill (NAMI) are one avenue through which families of persons with serious and persistent mental disorders can act politically to make their needs, wants, and recommendations heard.

Clinical social workers can help relieve families of some of their burdens by listening to their voices and addressing their concerns. Families are intrinsically involved in the care of identified clients and are a major source of support. Social workers can "tune in" to the situation of families and assess how families and clients affect each other. To address their needs and help clients, a variety of family educational interventions have been developed.

Family Psychoeducation and Family Education

Family psychoeducation was initially developed primarily to help treat the individuals with the psychiatric disorder and only secondarily to assist family members (Solomon, 1996). Early psychoeducational interventions aimed to reduce expressed emotion in the family (see Chapter 10) and to promote medication compliance in order to prevent the client from relapsing. Family psychoeducational programs offered information about the relative's illness and used psychotherapeutic approaches to foster better communication and coping in the family. Recent conceptualizations of *family education* give primacy to the family's needs for support and relief from the burden of caregiving (Solomon, 1996).

Family Psychoeducation.   As with case management, numerous models of family psychoeducation emerged in the last two decades of the twentieth century. Most of these were developed in research programs investigating treatment of individuals with schizophrenia whose families had high expressed emotion. As such, they required a minimum of nine months and could call for two years of involvement (Solomon, 1996). All of these first-generation models, which were implemented in tandem with a regimen of medication for the client, have been found more effective in reducing clients' relapse rate than medication alone (Goldstein & Miklowitz, 1995; Dixon & Lehman, 1995). Because most of them focused on families with high expressed emotion or stress (Goldstein & Miklowitz, 1995), however, questions remained about their applicability to other families, as well as diagnoses other than schizophrenia. Table 12.5 summarizes the major features of the prominent first-generation programs.

Second-generation psychoeducational studies have been trying to clarify which components of the family treatments contribute to the client's remaining out of the hospital (Goldstein & Miklowitz, 1995). Among these are those of McFarlane (1990, 1994) and his

TABLE 12.5 First-Generation Family Psychoeducational Programs

Developers	Type	Major Features
Goldstein & Kopeikin (1981)	Crisis-oriented family therapy	■ Outpatient crisis treatment over six sessions following the family member's discharge from the hospital. ■ Teaches strategies of avoiding and coping with stress. ■ Teaches families how to anticipate and plan for stressful situations.
Falloon et al. (1981)	Behavioral family therapy	■ Assessment of each family member's functioning, and strengths and deficits of the family unit. ■ Education about the illness and its treatment. ■ Training family in communication and problem-solving skills in the family's home. ■ Specific behavioral strategies to resolve particular problems.
Leff et al. (1982)	Social intervention	■ Two-session educational program about the mental illness. ■ Multifamily support group. ■ In-home family treatment that includes the client.
Hogarty et al. (1986)	Psychoeducational family management	■ Therapeutic alliance with family. ■ One-day survival skills workshop for relatives that provides information and management suggestions and fosters the development of a support network among families. ■ Biweekly structured family sessions in which tasks are developed, implemented, and evaluated, with the goal of reintegrating the client into family and social roles. ■ Clients join family sessions when they are functioning adequately. They are helped with social and vocational rehabilitation.
Tarrier et al. (1988)	Behavioral-enactive and symbolic family models	■ Behavioral-enactive: role playing, behavioral rehearsal, guided practice, and goal setting. ■ Symbolic: coping skills are taught through discussion and instruction.

Sources: In addition to the sources indicated in the table, see also Dixon & Lehman (1995); Falloon (1990); Goldstein & Miklowitz (1995); and Hogarty, Reiss, & Anderson (1990).

associates (McFarlane et al., 1995) whose 1995 study compared psychoeducational multi-family group with single-family groups therapy and multifamily groups without psycho-education. McFarlane et al. (1995) built their approach on the work of Falloon et al. (1981) and Anderson, Reiss, and Hogarty (1986). Although McFarlane et al. (1995) found multi-family superior to single-family psychoeducation, other researchers (Leff et al., 1990) found no differences between the two approaches.

Analyses of the results of the studies mentioned and others have found that a variety of approaches to family intervention improves the outcome for clients (Mueser et al., 1997; Scott & Dixon, 1995). Lam (1991) identified the following components as valuable:

- connecting with the family and taking a positive approach
- providing structure and stability
- looking at what is happening in the here-and-now
- using family concepts
- working on cognitive restructuring
- taking a behavioral approach
- improving communication

Because the model developed by Anderson and her associates (Anderson, Hogarty, & Reiss, 1980, 1981; Anderson et al., 1986; Hogarty et al., 1986) meets most of these criteria, and it incorporates many social work practice concepts and strategies, we will give specific attention to this best practice.

Best Practice: Psychoeducational Family Management. The Anderson model is both client and family centered. It fosters the adaptation of the client to community life by engaging the family in efforts to reduce stress and promote medication compliance. It attempts to assuage the family's anxiety and guilt by providing members with information and helping them to cope. Efforts are directed at fostering a family environment that is stable and predictable—one in which communication is clear, boundaries are specified, and emotional expressiveness (criticism and over involvement) is minimal. The Anderson model is task centered and proceeds in incremental steps that are consistent with the client's pace of recovery. Both family therapy and educational principles are used.

This psychoeducational program proceeds in four overlapping phases—connection, survival skills workshop, reentry and application, and maintenance. During Phase I, which begins during a client's hospitalization for an acute psychotic episode, the goal is to develop a working alliance with the family, decrease guilt, and reduce stress. This is accomplished by assuming a nonjudgmental and empathetic attitude, eliciting and acknowledging the family's feelings and experiences, and acting as an ombudsman for the family. Initially the clinician meets with the family, without the mentally ill relative present, once or twice a week. When the client's psychotic symptoms recede, he or she is able to join the family sessions.

Parents who are familiar with theories that hold them responsible for mental illness in their offspring are especially vulnerable to guilt feelings. In order to offset such feelings, the clinician is respectful and avoids blaming the family. In contrast with the patient-centered approach that characterizes many hospitals, here the family's experiences in caring for their relative and with previous mental health programs are discussed. The clinician keeps the family informed about its member's progress in treatment and, in working with the treatment team, acts as a representative of the family. The family's emotional involvement is mobilized and reframed as "concern"; the family's helplessness is channeled into commitment to perform tasks that will promote the rehabilitation of its member.

Phase I concludes with the development of a treatment contract and the establishment of rules for family therapy. The contract that is negotiated identifies goals that pertain to issues that have come to the surface during this phase and are relevant to the client's recovery. Goals should be specific, realistic, and attainable. Accordingly long-range goals such as independent living are discouraged initially. The rules that Anderson and others have found useful are:

1. The family will meet regularly with the clinician (every two or three weeks) for at least a year.
2. No family member may speak for another family member.
3. No one may lose physical or emotional control during family sessions.
4. Changes will take place in incremental, separate steps.

Phase II consists of a multifamily survival skills workshop. This is offered early in the process of treatment in a single day. The major component of the workshop is the communication of factual, up-to-date information about schizophrenia and its treatment, but the multiple-family format promotes sharing and the development of a support network among participants. The information that is provided in these workshops covers the following themes:

- What is schizophrenia
- The biological genesis of schizophrenia
- The experience of schizophrenia
- The course of schizophrenia
- Prognosis
- Treatment modalities
- Pharmacotherapy and side effects
- The impact of stress on the course of schizophrenia
- Family strategies to reduce stress
- Effective communication in the family
- Avoiding social isolation
- Community resources

Other themes consistent with evolving knowledge about schizophrenia and related disorders can also be introduced. Generally the workshop is conducted by an interdisciplinary team of professionals with expertise in the topics under discussion. The participation of families of recovering clients or representatives of family advocacy groups who are supportive of the program can enhance the credibility of the psychoeducational approach.

During the workshop, families are introduced to strategies they can use to modulate stress (i.e., emotional expressiveness) in the family environment. Among these are establishing realistic expectations, structuring, setting limits, distancing, and time-out. The families are told that excessive sleep and low motivation are common following a psychotic episode; that clients can be expected to be more active over time. Having a family structure with a regular routine, rules, and reasonable expectations promotes stability and predictability. Expectations should be concrete and specific (e.g., wash the dishes every night). The family should identify behaviors they will tolerate (e.g., wearing mismatched clothes) and those they will not accept (e.g., physical abuse) and communicate to the family member with schizophrenia the limits of their tolerance. To avoid intense emotional involvement, boundary making through distancing is encouraged. Accordingly, the family accepts some withdrawal on the part of the client, avoids criticism and conflict, and develops outside interests, activities, and supports of their own. The needs of all family members are acknowledged and differentially supported. Should conflict emerge in the family, the client and/or the family member involved in the conflict withdraws from the scene (taking time-out) to his or her room or elsewhere.

During the workshop, special attention is given to communication with the client. Because persons with schizophrenia have difficulty processing information, family members are urged to keep their requests clear and simple. Multiple levels of communication and complicated messages are to be avoided. In the same vein, family members are encouraged to use "I messages" (e.g., "I don't like that") rather than indirect messages in which the person responsible, the feeling component, and the desired effect are camouflaged. Family are discouraged from reading each other's minds and engaging in discussions on abstract themes in the presence of the client. They are encouraged to focus on and reinforce positive behaviors on the part of their family member.

Although the survival skills workshop is one of several components of the Anderson model of family psychoeducation, workshops can be programs in their own right. Furthermore, they can be oriented to families of clients with disorders besides schizophrenia. Brennan (1995), for example, conducted a short-term psychoeducational multifamily group for clients with bipolar disorder and their families. It met in two-hour blocks over a period of fourteen weeks in a psychiatric center. Social workers, nurses, and case managers shared the leadership responsibility. The sessions were educational but also encouraged the development of bonds among participants.

Phase III, reentry, begins when the client leaves the hospital. Family sessions that include the client are arranged on a schedule that is consistent with the family's and client's needs—usually every two or three weeks. Crisis telephone calls and emergency sessions are accommodated. The sessions are structured around current issues and homework assignments that are allocated for work between sessions. A problem-solving, task-centered approach is used.

During this phase, which can last six months or longer, the family implements the skills that were introduced during the survival skills workshop. Accordingly, the family develops and articulates rules, sets limits, and reinforces intergenerational and interpersonal boundaries. Parents are encouraged to engage in social activities as a couple and to seek support from extended family and friends. The clinician supports the family's efforts to communicate effectively and to avoid and reduce conflict. Solutions to problems that inevitably emerge are negotiated in a calm, reasonable way.

Tasks assigned to the client increase and become more complex over time. This is in keeping with the gradual process of recovery and increasing energy level. At first the focus is on integrating the client into the family. Later participation in community activities (social rehabilitation programs, work) are supported, one step at a time. The client who is stable can work toward increasing autonomy and eventually independent living.

The kinds of issues that come up in family sessions include medication compliance, participation in household activities, and early warning signs of relapse. The family is helped to identify changes in behavior that signal the emergence of prodromal (preliminary) signs of schizophrenia. Following an exploration of possible sources of these changes—noncompliance with medication, the need for a medication change, stress—appropriate remedies are pursued.

Phase IV, continued treatment or disengagement, is oriented toward consolidating and maintaining the goals achieved and resumption of normalized living. Anderson and others present this phase to families as optional. Families may elect to terminate, to have periodic maintenance sessions, to continue to work on previous goals, and/or to develop a new contract in which other problems are addressed. Some families have the need for continued support with ongoing intrafamilial problems. Others foresee difficulties surrounding a family member's emancipation. During this phase, when the family may be dealing with latent family issues, the intervention is not unlike the family therapy that is practiced with other client populations.

McFarlane (1990) enhanced the psychoeducational family management model by making special efforts to reduce families' social isolation and feelings of stigma. He and his colleagues did this by encouraging families to expand their social networks and by becoming a social support group. They resocialized participating families to give and receive support from each other, reinforced interfamily assistance, and used the group process to create cross-parenting linkages and cross-family conversations.

Family Education.   However effective family psychoeducational programs have been, family members have tended to view their fundamental assumption (expressed emotion) as family-blaming (Solomon, 1996). In recent years, family education has become decoupled from family psychoeducation. There are two primary models of family education—the workshop and family consultation. *Educational workshops*, organized by both professionals and family consumers, provide a format in which family members can learn about the various psychiatric disorders, medication, and community resources and are encouraged to develop coping skills, including mutual support. These programs generally extend over a period of eight to twelve weeks. They are open to families interested in participating. Rather than having a single focus on helping families manage expressed emotion, they emphasize family strengths and resilience (Marsh et al., 1997). *Family consultation* consists of a one-to-one relationship between a consultant and a family unit or family member. The consultant, who may be a professional or family member, provides advice, guidance, and support on an as-needed basis (Solomon, 1996).

The T.E.C. Family Center, a special program of the Mental Health Association of Southeastern Pennsylvania that is funded by the City of Philadelphia Office of Mental Health/Mental Retardation, offers multifamily workshops and in-person and telephone consultation to family members of adults with severe mental illness who live in the Philadelphia area. T.E.C. is an acronym for training, education, and consultation. The center originally offered a generic, ten-week family workshop, some of which has been incorporated into the NAMI Family-to-Family Program that will be described later. T.E.C. now offers workshops on specific illnesses such as schizophrenia, mood disorders, and border-line personality disorder.

During the past few years, T.E.C. has been running separate educational workshops for spouses and partners. The spouse workshops arose because of high attrition rates of partners from workshops designed by and for parents and siblings (Mannion, Mueser, & Solomon, 1994). The curriculum was developed from a series of focus groups with spouses and partners. The Spouse Coping Skills Workshops are cofacilitated by a professional and spouse peer consultant. They take place in community settings. When T.E.C. initially instituted this workshop, two-hour sessions were held weekly over a period of twelve consecutive weeks, but more recently it has been redesigned to take place over eight weeks, with family consultation offered as an adjunct. After the workshop is over, participants are encouraged to join a specialized spouse support group or one of the many family support groups that are offered throughout the city and suburban areas. A pilot study of the twelve-week intervention indicated that spouses who completed the workshop had increased knowledge of the illness and coping strategies, reduced personal distress, and reduced negative attitudes toward their ill partner (Mannion et al., 1994).

A model syllabus of T.E.C.'s Spouse Coping Skills Workshop is presented in Table 12.6 as an example of a best practice. As noted, each session has an information topic and a coping topic. The specific topics listed are modified somewhat from one spouse workshop to the next to reflect the needs and composition of different group members. A variety of methods of presentation are used, including lectures, focused discussions, videotapes, handouts, sharing personal experiences and ways of coping (especially by the spouse cofacilitator), and optional homework assignments. A teaching manual for this workshop is available through the Mental Health Association of Southeastern Pennsylvania.

The National Alliance for the Mentally Ill has been sponsoring its own peer family educational program. The NAMI Family-to-Family Program "uses a unique combination of healing, consciousness-raising, and empowerment" (Burland, 1998, p. 33) to help families understand and come to terms with caring for and supporting a mentally ill relative. Courses are taught over a period of twelve weeks by a pair of leaders, usually family members certified as trained family education leaders. The Family-to-Family Program views mental illness in the family as a trauma that can engender isolation and helplessness. The program uses the technique of consciousness-raising to deflect blame from family members and help them heal from the trauma. The class concludes by encouraging participants to advocate and teaching them how to do so (Burland, 1998).

Other Ways of Healing

Up until now this chapter has discussed treatments that have been designed and recommended by professionals and their families. These approaches have been supported by clinical research and have been endorsed by consensus studies and family advocacy organizations. Nevertheless, there are other approaches that work for or are meaningful to clients.

Although intensive psychotherapy is generally not recommended for persons with schizophrenia, some clients with this and other major mental disorders seem to benefit from ego-supportive, structured, reality-based therapy. In Chapter 8 psychotherapeutic ap-

TABLE 12.6 ■ BEST PRACTICE   Spouse Coping Skills Workshop Syllabus

Week	Illness Topic	Coping Topic
1	Welcome and Introductions	Feelings: Identifying, Accepting, But Not Reacting
2	Overview of the Mental Illnesses: Definition of Common Terms	Regaining Respect and Empathy for Your Partner: What It's Like to Have Mental Illness
3	Bipolar Disorder and Cyclothymic Disorder: Video and Discussion	Coping with Bipolar Cycle
4	Major Depression and Dysthymic Disorder: Video and Discussion	Coping with Depression Fallout: Changing the Depressive Dance
5	Schizophrenia & Schizoaffective Disorder: Video and Discussion	Surviving Financially
6	Distinguishing Personality Traits, Personality Disorder, Symptoms, and Secondary Gains	Helping Children, Adolescents, and Adult Children Cope
7	Psychiatric Medications and Side Effects	Assessing the Dilemmas of Leaving or Staying: Tools for Decision Making
8	Asserting Your Role as a Partner in Treatment	Living with Mental Illness in a Partner/Ex-Partner

Source: Reprinted with permission from the Training, Education, and Consultation (T.E.C.) Family Center, Mental Health Association of Southeastern Pennsylvania, Philadelphia. Copyright © 1999.

proaches used with persons with major depression and dysthymia were discussed. Psychoeducational groups revolving around medication management are used for some clients with severe and persistent psychiatric disorders.

Because schizophrenia is characterized by cognitive deficits, cognitive approaches are promising means to intervene with clients with this disorder. One strategy, *cognitive rehabilitation,* aims to remedy deficits in information-processing skills such as vigilance, memory, and conceptual abilities (Penn & Mueser, 1996) that are not helped by medication (Storzbach & Corrigan, 1996). So far, interventions such as positive reinforcement, repeated practice, semantic encoding, and the introduction of an incompatible behavior have been found effective for treating deficits in attention and memory and for limiting hallucinations and delusions (Storzbach & Corrigan, 1996). Future treatment innovations and research should refine methods and indicate how generalizable such learning is.

Psychosocial rehabilitation is predicated on the idea that clients are to be actively involved in their own treatment and even the design of their rehabilitation protocols (Bachrach, 1992). The community support program, too, calls for the client's voice. At times, however, clients hear "a different drummer" from that heard by professionals and have their own ideas about what will help them recover. Accordingly, they may follow a specific diet, use homeopathic remedies, take certain vitamins, exercise, pray, or seek spiritual help or a healer. They may or may not follow these courses together with mainstream psychiatric treatment. Some, of course, choose to medicate themselves with alcohol and street drugs.

Young and Ensing (1999) conducted a qualitative study in which they inquired into the meaning of recovery from the perspective of persons with psychiatric disabilities. The following are statements from some of the consumers they interviewed:

> **I know that I will never recover fully. This illness will always be with me, and that I can arrest it and I can still recover but I'll have this disease for the rest of my life and I have to accept that.** (p. 223)

> **I now try to do things for myself. I go for walks and just do things for me. I know that sounds selfish, but that is what you have to do.** (p. 223)

> **It [exercising] builds my morale. It helps me to feel more confident about myself, [and] helps me want to do other things if I can manage my time properly. It helps me to be motivated, and have a desire to go ahead and achieve a better nature for myself [and gives me] a better outlook on life.** (pp. 226–227)

Another consumer (Fox, 1997) defined recovery as

> **the process of accepting my illness, along with finding a definite purpose and meaning to my life. Some of that purpose and meaning has come from my job, and some from being able to maintain a role as a wife, mother, and daughter in a family.** (p. 251)

From these statements it is clear that individuals with serious mental illness construct recovery differently and, accordingly, identify different ways in which they might heal. Whether they choose to take walks in the woods, garden, take care of their children, exercise, take vitamins, listen to music, or seek spiritual healing, these ways (and others) are *their* ways to assume control over *their* lives, experience pleasure, and maintain hope despite their illness. Professionals who construct and implement biopsychosocial interventions need to be mindful that their treatments are superimposed on individuals struggling with accepting their illnesses and seeking their own ways to be who they are.

Summary and Deconstruction

This chapter described a number of strategies social workers and other professionals use to help clients and families improve their lives when a family member has a severe mental illness. Although medication is prescribed by psychiatrists, social workers play a role in medication management through their observation of how clients use and are affected by medication. Atypical antipsychotic drugs treat negative as well as positive symptoms and have fewer deleterious side effects, thus enhancing clients' functioning and improving the quality of their lives; mood stabilizers can help individuals with bipolar and related disorders. Nevertheless, medication does not completely cure mental illness; nor does it entirely eliminate symptoms. It cannot help individuals with their interpersonal and problem-solving skills.

Social skills training helps clients improve their interpersonal relationships and coping skills. Cognitive and behavioral methods are used to help clients individually, in groups, or with their families. Clients enact role plays that simulate situations that they find difficult. Techniques such as modeling, behavioral rehearsal, and feedback are used. This chapter presented a case scenario that used a group format.

Although individuals with severe mental illness are constructed as "having" the disease, family members and others close to them experience the effects of the disease as well. Parents, who had other dreams for their children than those that were realized, are often the primary caregivers of their adult mentally ill children, even if they do not live in the same household. Likewise, siblings, spouses/partners, and children are affected by a family member's mental illness. Behavioral health professionals cannot expect families to continue to give care without receiving support for themselves.

The first generation of family interventions saw in the family a means to treat the identified client. A variety of family psychoeducational interventions were developed, including the one by Anderson et al. that was described in this chapter. Because these interventions were primarily with families of individuals with schizophrenia, in which there was high expressed emotion in the family, it is not clear how generalizable they are to other families. More important, they are not sufficiently family centered. Newer models focus on family *education,* rather than *psychoeducation.* These can be professionally run and/or run by family members. This chapter featured the Spouse Coping Skills Workshop of the T.E.C. Family Center, which is led by both a professional and a family member.

These are some of today's leading means of working with individuals and families in which there is severe mental illness. Although in-depth psychotherapy is generally not recommended for persons with schizophrenia, some clients with severe mental illness can be helped with psychotherapy and other means that have not been sufficiently studied by researchers. Meanwhile individuals, families, and family consumer organizations have come up with their own ways of healing. A need still exists to develop new client- and family-centered interventions that meet the needs of the heterogeneous individuals who are suffering from severe mental illness and its consequences for families.

DISCUSSION QUESTIONS

1. How do conventional antipsychotics affect symptoms? What symptoms do they ameliorate? Which remain unaffected?

2. What are the risks associated with conventional antipsychotic medication? Atypical antipsychotics?

3. Identify side effects and risks associated with mood stabilizing drugs.

4. What kinds of observations should a clinical social worker make with respect to clients on psychotropic medications?

5. Identify and discuss ethical issues associated with monitoring clients' psychotropic drug use.

6. What are special considerations that should be addressed in psychopharmacotherapy of women and older adults?

7. What is social skills training? What does it do that medication does not address?

8. Describe the therapeutic techniques used in social skills training.

9. Using the case descriptions that were provided in the social skills training section, conduct a social skills training session of your own in which the needs of clients other than Michael are highlighted. Evaluate how the group meeting went.

10. Develop a social skills training role play in the context of a family, rather than a group of clients. What are the advantages of social skills training with families compared with a group of clients? What are the disadvantages?

11. What are the special needs of families of persons with severe mental illness? Why are women particularly affected?

12. What is family psychoeducation? How does it differ from family education?

13. Explain how family psychoeducation helps both the client and the family.

14. Develop a mock psychoeducation program on one of the themes that were listed under Phase II. A group of students can be presenters; the rest can assume roles as family members. Invite the audience to ask questions. Incorporate a videotape available from your local Mental Health Association and set up a table on which literature is displayed.

R E F E R E N C E S

American Psychiatric Association (1994). *Diagnostic and statistical manual of mental disorders, (DSM-IV)* (4th ed.). Washington, DC: Author.

American Psychiatric Association (April 1997 Supplement). Practice guideline for the treatment of patients with schizophrenia. *American Journal of Psychiatry, 154*(4).

Anderson, C. M., Hogarty, G. E., & Reiss, D. J. (1980). Family treatment of adult schizophrenic patients: A psychoeducational approach. *Schizophrenia Bulletin, 6,* 490–505.

Anderson, C. M., Hogarty, G. E., & Reiss, D. J. (1981). The psychoeducational family treatment of schizophrenia. In M. J. Goldstein (Ed.), *New developments in interventions with families of schizophrenics* (pp. 79–94). San Francisco: Jossey-Bass.

Anderson, C. M., Reiss, D. J., & Hogarty, G. (1986). *Schizophrenia and the family.* New York: Guilford Press.

Andreasen, N. C. (1985). Positive vs. negative schizophrenia: A critical evaluation. *Schizophrenia Bulletin, 11,* 380–389.

Arvanitis, L. (1997). Quetiapine (Seroquel). *The Decade of the Brain, 8*(3), 9–11.

Bachrach, L. L. (1992). Psychosocial rehabilitation and psychiatry in the care of long-term patients. *American Journal of Psychiatry, 149,* 1455–1463.

Baldessarini, R. J., & Cole, J. O. (1988). Chemotherapy. In A. M. Nicholi, Jr. (Ed.), *The new Harvard guide to psychiatry* (pp. 481–533). Cambridge, MA: Belknap Press of Harvard University Press.

Bedell, J. (1994). Social skills training. In J. R. Bedell (Ed.), *Psychological assessment and treatment of persons with severe mental disorders* (pp. 95–119). Washington, DC: Taylor & Francis.

Brennan, J. W. (1995). A short-term psychoeducational multiple-family group for bipolar patients and their families. *Social Work, 40,* 737–743.

Burland, J. (1998). Family-to-family: A trauma-and-recovery model of family education. In H. P. Lefley (Ed.), *Families coping with mental illness: The cultural context* (pp. 33–41). San Francisco, CA: Jossey-Bass.

Cohen, D. (1988). Social work and psychotropic drug treatments. *Social Service Review, 62,* 576–599.

Conn, V., & Edwards, N. (1999). The portable medication record (PMR). *Psychiatric Rehabilitation Journal, 22*(3), 288–289.

Cowen, P. J. (1998). Psychopharmacology. In A. S. Bellack & M. Hersen (Eds.), *Comprehensive clinical psychology,* vol. 6, "Adults: Clinical formulation & treatment," ed. by P. Salkovskis (pp. 136–161). Amsterdam: Elsevier Science.

Dilk, M. N., & Bond, G. R. (1996). Meta-analytic evaluation of skills training research for persons with severe mental illness. *Journal of Consulting Clinical Psychology, 64,* 1337–1346.

Dixon, L. B., & Lehman, A. F. (1995). Family interventions for schizophrenia. *Schizophrenia Bulletin, 21*(4), 631–643.

Dixson, D. L. (1981). Manic depression: An overview. *Journal of Psychiatric Nursing in Mental Health Settings, 19,* 28–31.

Expert Consensus Panels (1999). Treatment of schizophrenia 1999. *The Journal of Clinical Psychiatry, 60,* Supplement 11.

Falloon, I. R. H. (1990). Behavioral family therapy with schizophrenic disorders. In M. I. Herz, S. J. Keith, & J. P. Docherty (Eds.), *Handbook of schizophrenia, Volume 4: Psychosocial treatment of schizophrenia* (pp. 135–151). Amsterdam: Elsevier.

Falloon, I. R. H., Boyd, J. L., McGill, C. W., Strang, J. S., & Moss, H. B. (1981). Family management training in the community care of schizophrenia. In M. J. Goldstein (Ed.), *New developments in intervention with families of schizophrenics* (pp. 61–77). San Francisco: Jossey-Bass.

Fox, L. (1997). A consumer perspective on the family agenda. *American Journal of Orthopsychiatry, 67*(2), 249–253.

Francell, C. G., Conn, V. S., & Gray, D. P. (1988). Families' perceptions of burden of relative care for chronic mentally ill relatives. *Hospital and Community Psychiatry, 39,* 1296–1300.

Frances, A. J., Kahn, D. A., Carpenter, D., Docherty, J. P., & Donovan, S. L. (1998). The expert consensus guidelines for treating depression in bipolar disorder. *Journal of Clinical Psychiatry, 59 Supplement,* 73–79.

Gantt, A. B., Goldstein, G., & Pinsky, S. (1989). Family understanding of psychiatric illness. *Community Mental Health Journal, 25,* 101–108.

Gerhart, U. C., & Brooks, A. D. (1983). The social work practitioner and antipsychotic medications. *Social Work, 28,* 454–460.

Goldstein, M. J., & Kopeikin, H. (1981). Short and long term effects of combining drug and family therapy. In M. J. Goldstein (Ed.), *New developments in intervention with families of schizophrenics* (pp. 5–25). San Francisco: Jossey-Bass.

Goldstein, M. J., & Miklowitz, D. J. (1995). The effectiveness of psychoeducational family therapy in the treatment of schizophrenic disorders. *Journal of Marital and Family Therapy, 21*(4), 361–376.

Gubman, G. D., & Tessier, R. C. (1987). The impact of mental illness on families: Concepts and priorities. *Journal of Family Issues, 8,* 226–245.

Hatfield, A. B. (1987a). Coping and adaptation: A conceptual framework for understanding families. In A. B. Hatfield & H. P. Lefley (Eds.), *Families of the mentally ill: Coping and adaptation* (pp. 60–84). New York: Guilford Press.

Hatfield, A. B. (1987b). Systems resistance to effective family coping. In A. T. Meyerson (Ed.), *Barriers to treating the chronic mentally ill* (pp. 51–62). San Francisco: Jossey-Bass.

Hogarty, G. E., et al. (1986). Family psychoeducation, social skills training, and maintenance chemotherapy in the aftercare treatment of schizophrenia: I. One-year effects of a controlled study on relapse and expressed emotion. *Archives of General Psychiatry, 43,* 633–642.

Hogarty, G. E., Anderson, C. M., Reiss, D. J., Kornblith, S. J., Greenwald, D. P., Ulrich, R. F., & Carter, M. (1991). Family psychoeducation, social skills training, and maintenance chemotherapy in the aftercare treatment of schizophrenia. II. Two-year effects of a controlled study on relapse and adjustment. *Archives of General Psychiatry, 48,* 340–347.

Hogarty, G. E., Reiss, D. J., & Anderson, C. M. (1990). Psychoeducational family management of schizophrenia. In M. I. Herz, S. J. Keith, & J. P. Docherty (Eds.), *Handbook of schizophrenia, Volume 4: Psychosocial treatment of schizophrenia* (pp. 153–166). Amsterdam: Elsevier.

Kane, J. M., & Lieberman, J. A. (1987). Maintenance pharmacology in schizophrenia. In H. Y. Meltzer (Ed.), *Psychopharmacology: The third generation of progress* (pp. 1103–1109). New York: Raven Press.

Kaplan, H. I., & Sadock, B. J. (1988). *Synopsis of psychiatry: Behavioral sciences/clinical psychiatry* (5th ed., chapt. 31). Baltimore, MD: Williams & Wilkins.

Kaplan, H. I., & Sadock, B. J. (1998). *Synopsis of psychiatry* (8th ed.). Baltimore, MD: Williams & Wilkins.

Keck, P. E., Jr., & McElroy, S. L. (1998). Pharmacological treatment of bipolar disorders. In P. E. Nathan & J. M. Gorman (Eds.), *A guide to treatments that work.* New York: Oxford University Press.

Lam, D. H. (1991). Psychosocial family intervention in schizophrenia: A review of empirical studies. *Psychological Medicine, 21,* 423–441.

Leff, J. P., Berkowitz, R., Shavit, N., Strachan, A., et al. (1990). A trial of a relatives' group for schizophrenia: Two-year follow-up. *British Journal of Psychiatry, 157,* 571–577.

Leff, J., Kuipers, L., Berkowitz, R., Eberlein-Fries, R., & Sturgeon, D. (1982). A controlled trial of social intervention in the families of schizophrenia patients. *British Journal of Psychiatry, 141,* 121–134.

Lefley, H. (1997). Prevention of schizophrenia: What does it mean? What's a family to do? *The Journal of the California Alliance for the Mentally Ill, 8*(3), 24–26.

Lehman, A. F., Steinwachs, D. M., and the coinvestigators of the PORT Project. (1998). At issue: Translating research into practice: The schizophrenia patient outcomes research team (PORT) treatment recommendations. *Schizophrenia Bulletin, 24*(1), 1–10.

Liberman, R. P. (1988). Social skills training. In R. P. Liberman (Ed.), *Psychiatric rehabilitation of chronic mental patients* (pp. 147–198). Washington, DC: American Psychiatric Press.

Liberman, R. P., et al. (1986). Training skills in the psychiatrically disabled: Learning coping and competence. *Schizophrenia Bulletin, 12,* 631–647.

Liberman, R. P., DeRisi, W. J., & Mueser, K. T. (1989). *Social skills training for psychiatric patients.* New York: Pergamon.

Mannion, E., Mueser, K., & Solomon, P. (1994). Designing psychoeducational services for spouses of persons with serious mental illness. *Community Mental Health Journal, 30*(2), 177–189.

Marder, S. R. (1997). Risperidone (Risperdal). *The Decade of the Brain, 8*(3), 5–6.

Marsh, D. T., Lefley, H. P., Evans-Rhodes, D., Ansell, V. I., et al. (1997). The family experience of mental illness: Evidence for resilience. *Psychiatric Rehabilitation Journal, 20*(2), 4–12.

Matorin, S., & De Chillo, N. (1984). Psychopharmacology: Guidelines for social workers. *Social Casework, 65,* 579–589.

McFarlane, W. R. (1990). Multiple family groups and the treatment of schizophrenia. In M. I. Herz, S. J. Keith, & J. P. Docherty (Eds.), *Handbook of schizophrenia, Volume 4: Psychosocial treatment of schizophrenia* (pp. 167–189). Amsterdam: Elsevier.

McFarlane, W. R. (1994). Multiple-family groups and psychoeducation in the treatment of schizophrenia. *New Directions in Mental Health Services, 62,* 13–22.

McFarlane, W. R., Link, B., Dushay, R., Marchal, J., et al. (1995). Multiple-family groups and psychoeducation in the treatment of schizophrenia. *Archives of General Psychiatry, 52,* 679–687.

Miller, L. (1991). Clinical strategies for the use of psychotropic drugs during pregnancy. *Psychiatric Medicine, 9,* 275–298.

Miller, L. J. (1996). Psychopharmacology during pregnancy. *Primary Care Update Ob/Gyn, 3*(3), 79–86.

Mogul, K. M. (1985). Psychological considerations in the use of psychotropic drugs with women patients. *Hospital and Community Psychiatry, 36,* 1080–1085.

Mueser, K. T., Drake, R. E., & Bond, G. R. (1997). Recent advances in psychiatric rehabilitation for patients with severe mental illness. *Harvard Review of Psychiatry, 5,* 123–137.

National Alliance for the Mentally Ill. (1997). *The Decade of the Brain, 8*(3).

National Alliance for the Mentally Ill. (1999). Fact sheet: New treatment options for bipolar disorder. *Advocate, 20*(5), 30–31.

Penn, D. L., & Mueser, K. T. (1996). Research update on the psychosocial treatment of schizophrenia. *American Journal of Psychiatry, 153*(5), 607–617.

Physicians Desk Reference (PDR). (1990). (44th ed.). Oradell, NJ: Medical Economics.

Prien, R. F. (1987). Long-term treatment of affective disorders. In H. Y. Meltzer (Ed.), *Psychopharmacology: The third generation of progress* (pp. 1051–1058). New York: Raven Press.

Prien, R. F., & Gelenberg, A. J. (1989). Alternatives to lithium for preventive treatment of bipolar disorder. *American Journal of Psychiatry, 146,* 840–848.

Rathus, S. A. (1973). A 30-item schedule for assessing assertive behavior. *Behavior Therapy, 4,* 398–406.

Reid, W. H. (1989). *The treatment of psychiatric disorders.* New York: Brunner/Mazel.

Riesser, G. G., & Schorske, B. J. (1994). Relationships between family caregivers and mental health professionals: The American experience. In H. P. Lefley & M. Wasow (Eds.), *Helping families cope with mental illness* (pp. 3–26). Langhorne, PA: Harwood Academic Publishers.

Rifkin, A., & Siris, S. (1987). Drug treatment of acute schizophrenia. In H. Y. Meltzer (Ed.), *Psychopharmacology: The third generation of progress* (pp. 1095–1101). New York: Raven Press.

Sands, R. G. (1984). Correlates of success and lack of success in deinstitutionalization. *Community Mental Health Journal, 20,* 223–235.

Sands, R. G. (1985). Bipolar disorder and social work practice. *Social Work in Health Care, 10,* 91–105.

Sheitman, B. B., Kinon, B. J., Ridgway, B. A., & Lieberman, J. A. (1998). Pharmacological treatments of schizophrenia. In P. E. Nathan & J. M. Gorman (Eds.), *A guide to treatments that work* (pp. 167–189). New York: Oxford University Press.

Simpson, G. M., Pi, E. H., & Sramek, J. J. (1986). An update on tardive dyskinesia. *Hospital and Community Psychiatry, 37,* 362–369.

Solomon, P. (1996). Moving from psychoeducation to family education for families of adults with serious mental illness. *Psychiatric Services, 47*(12), 1364–1370.

Storzbach, D. M., & Corrigan, P. W. (1996). Cognitive rehabilitation for schizophrenia. In P. W. Corrigan & S. C. Yudofsky (Eds.), *Cognitive rehabilitation for neuropsychiatric disorders* (pp. 299–328). Washington, DC: American Psychiatric Press.

Tarrier, N., Barrowclough, C., & Porceddu, K. (1988). The community management of schizophrenia: A controlled trial of a behavioral intervention with families to reduce relapse. *British Journal of Psychiatry, 153,* 532–542.

Terkelsen, K. G. (1987). The evolution of family responses to mental illness through time. In A. B. Hatfield & H. P. Lefley (Eds.), *Families of the mentally ill. Coping and adaptation* (pp. 151–166). New York: Guilford Press.

Thurer, S. L. (1983). Deinstitutionalization and women: Where the buck stops. *Hospital and Community Psychiatry, 34,* 1162–1163.

Torrey, E. F. (1988). *Surviving schizophrenia: A family manual* (rev. ed.). New York: Harper & Row.

Training and Education Family Center. (n.d.) Family education in mental illness. Philadelphia, PA: Author.

Wallace, C. J. (1986). Functional assessment in rehabilitation. *Schizophrenia Bulletin, 12,* 604–630.

Wallace, C. J., et al. (1980). A review and critique of social skills training with schizophrenic patients. *Schizophrenia Bulletin, 6,* 42–63.

Wasow, M. (1994). Professional and parental perspectives. In H. P. Lefley & M. Wasow (Eds.), *Helping families cope with mental illness* (pp. 27–38). Langhorne, PA: Harwood Academic Publishers.

Wittlin, B. J. (1988). Practical psychopharmacology. In R. P. Liberman (Ed.), *Psychiatric rehabilitation of chronic mental patients* (pp. 117–145). Washington, DC: American Psychiatric Press.

Young, S. L., & Ensing, D. S. (1999). Exploring recovery from the perspective of people with psychiatric disabilities. *Psychiatric Rehabilitation Journal, 22*(3), 219–231.

13 Clinical Practice with Clients Who Abuse Substances

DIANA M. DINITTO AND DEBORAH K. WEBB

"It's like I've got a shotgun in my mouth, with my finger on the trigger, and I like the taste of the gun metal." Actor Robert Downey, Jr. upon being sentenced to three years in prison after failure to submit to drug testing and a judge's denial of his request for another chance at drug rehabilitation.
—"Drug Test Relapse Puts Downey Away," *Austin American-Statesman,* August 6, 1999

Substance abuse and dependence are common problems. A 1992 study found that among adults in the United States (those age 18 and older), approximately 8.1 million (4.4 percent of the adult population) were alcoholics, and 5.6 million (3.0 percent of the adult population) were alcohol abusers (Grant et al., 1995). When drugs in addition to alcohol are considered, the National Comorbidity Survey indicates that 27 percent of U.S. citizens age 15 and older have had a substance abuse or dependence problem in their lifetime, and 11 percent in the last year (Kessler et al., 1994).

This chapter addresses social work practice with clients who have substance use disorders and those who have both mental and substance use disorders. The treatment of mental illnesses and substance use problems developed along separate lines, but in the past thirty years, clinicians have seen the need to treat these disorders simultaneously in individuals who present with both types of diagnoses.

We begin with an overview of commonly abused substances. The many etiologic theories of substance use disorders are considered as are some constructions of substance use disorders from both traditional and postmodern perspectives. We also discuss treatment approaches and adjunctive services for those with substance use disorders. We then address the prevalence of dual diagnoses and the ways these co-occurring problems have been treated, focusing particularly on psychosocial approaches. Finally, we consider the effects of managed care on services and the evidence of the effectiveness of chemical dependency and dual diagnoses treatment.

Substances of Abuse

Many substances are abused because of their psychoactive properties. These substances can be grouped into seven categories: (1) central nervous system (CNS) depressants, (2) CNS stimulants, (3) opioids or narcotics, (4) hallucinogens, (5) cannabis, (6) anabolic steroids, and (7) over-the-counter drugs. Table 13.1 describes chemicals that fall in the first six categories and that are included under the federal Controlled Substances Act of 1970 and its amendments. Many psychoactive drugs have legitimate medical uses, and most people who are prescribed them use them as directed. Others experiment with psychoactive substances (both prescribed drugs and drugs obtained on the streets) illegally. Because most people in these categories do not develop serious problems, we do not want to be alarmist about drug use, but many clients whom social workers and other practitioners see are well beyond the experimentation phase. Many of them are polysubstance users (they use more than one type of drug). The very brief review presented here is not meant to substitute for a more thorough introduction to psychoactive substances, as presented by authors such as Brick and Erickson (1998), Doweiko (1999), Hanson and Venturelli (1998), and Ray and Ksir (1999).

Depressants

Central nervous system (CNS) depressants include alcohol, barbiturates, methaqualone, benzodiazepines, and inhalants. CNS depressants are particularly dangerous drugs of abuse because consumption of high doses by individuals in general and withdrawal effects in those who are physically dependent can result in serious medical complications, including death. When combined, CNS depressants potentiate each other, resulting in a multiplier rather than additive effect. Deaths from CNS depressant use are usually due to suppression of respiratory and cardiovascular functions. Hanson and Venturelli (1998) suggest that individuals most likely to abuse these drugs are those trying to escape stressful problems, those who feel exhilaration when using these drugs after having developed tolerance to them, those who use these drugs to counteract negative effects of other abused drugs such as stimulants, and those who combine them with other depressants to get a faster "high" (pp. 173–174).

The CNS depressant alcohol is the most widely used and abused drug in the United States. Even underage drinkers often have little difficulty obtaining alcohol, and for those of all ages with little or no funds, alcohol is frequently shared on the streets. When beer, wine, and distilled spirits containing ethanol (ethyl alcohol) are not readily available, chronic alcoholics may misuse common products that contain alcohol, such as vanilla and other extracts and mouthwash. They may also resort to ingesting products containing various types of alcohol that are not meant for human consumption such as perfume, aftershave lotion, rubbing (isopropyl) alcohol, and "canned heat" (Sterno).

Barbiturates are used as anesthetics, anticonvulsants, sedatives (to reduce anxiety), and hypnotics (to induce sleep). The medical "uses for barbiturates today are limited, as for the most part newer, safer, and more effective drugs have replaced them" (Doweiko, 1999, p. 72), but these drugs continue to be abused.

One well-known depressant drug bought on the streets is methaqualone, also known as ludes, sopors, and quads. Like many other drugs, methaqualone was originally thought

TABLE 13.1 Controlled Substances, Uses and Effects, 1997

Drugs	Trade or Other Names	Usual Method of Administration	Possible Effects	Effects of Overdose	Withdrawal Syndrome
Narcotics					
Morphine	Duramorph, MS-Contin, Roxanol, Oramorph SR	Oral, smoked, injected	Euphoria, drowsiness, respiratory depression, constricted pupils, nausea	Slow and shallow breathing, clammy skin, convulsions, coma, possible death	Watery eyes, runny nose, yawning, loss of appetite, irritability, tremors, panic, chills and sweating, cramps, nausea
Codeine	Tylenol with Codeine, Empirin with Codeine, Robitussin A-C, Fiorinal with Codeine, APAP with Codeine	Oral, injected			
Heroin	Diacetylmorphine, Horse, Smack	Injected, sniffed, smoked			
Hydrocodone	Tussionex, Vicodin, Hycodan, Lorcet	Oral			
Hydromorphone	Dilaudid	Oral, injected			
Oxycodone	Percodan, Percocet, Tylox, Roxicet, Roxicodone	Oral			
Methadone and LAAM	Dolophine, Methadose, Levoalpha-acetymethadol, Levomethadyl acetate	Oral, injected			
Fentanyl and analogs	Innovar, Sublimaze, Alfenta, Sufenta, Duragesic	Injected, transdermal patch			
Other narcotics	Percodan, Percocet, Tylox, Opium, Darvon, Buprenorphine, Meperdine (Pethidine), Demerol, Talwin*	Oral, injected			
Depressants					
Chloral hydrate	Noctec, Somnos, Felsules	Oral	Slurred speech, disorientation, drunken behavior without odor of alcohol	Shallow respiration, clammy skin, dilated pupils, weak and rapid pulse, coma, possible death	Anxiety, insomnia, tremors, delirium, convulsions, possible death

	Trade or Other Names	Method of Administration	Possible Effects	Withdrawal Syndrome
Barbiturates	Phenobarbital, Tuinal, Amytal, Nembutal, Seconal, Fiorinal, Pentobarbital	Oral, injected		Apathy, long periods of sleep, irritability, depression, disorientation
Benzodiazepines	Ativan, Dalmane, Diazepam, Librium, Xanax, Serax, Tranxene, Valium, Verstran, Halcion, Paxipam, Restoril, Versed	Oral, injected		
Glutethimide	Doriden	Oral		
Other depressants	Equanil, Miltown, Noludar, Placidyl, Valmid, Methaqualone	Oral		
Stimulants				
Cocaine‡	Coke, Flake, Snow, Crack	Sniffed, smoked, injected	Increased alertness, excitation, euphoria, increased pulse rate and blood pressure, insomnia, loss of appetite	Agitation, increased body temperature, hallucinations, convulsions, possible death
Amphetamine/ Methamphetamine	Biphetamine, Desoxyn, Dexedrine, Obetrol, Ice	Oral, injected, smoked		
Methylphenidate	Ritalin	Oral, injected		
Other stimulants	Adipex, Didrex, Ionamin, Melfiat, Plegine, Captagon, Sanorex, Tenuate, Tepanil, Prelu-2, Preludin	Oral, injected		
Hallucinogens				
LSD	Acid, Microdot	Oral	Illusions and hallucinations, altered perception of time and distance	Longer, more intense "trip" episodes; psychosis; possible death
Mescaline and peyote	Mescal, Buttons, Cactus	Oral		Unknown
Amphetamine variants	2,5-DMA, STP, MDA, MDMA, Ecstasy, DOM, DOB	Oral, injected		
Phencyclidine and analogs	PCE, PCPy, TCP, PCP, Hog, Loveboat, Angel Dust	Oral, smoked		
Other hallucinogens	Bufotenine, Ibogaine, DMT, DET, Psilocybin, Psilocyn	Oral, injected, smoked, sniffed		

(continued)

TABLE 13.1 Continued

Drugs	Trade or Other Names	Usual Method of Administration	Possible Effects	Effects of Overdose	Withdrawal Syndrome
Cannabis					
Marijuana	Pot, Acapulco Gold, Grass, Reefer, Sinsemilla, Thai Sticks	Smoked, oral	Euphoria, relaxed inhibitions, increased appetite, disorientation	Fatigue, paranoia, possible psychosis	Occasional reports of insomnia, hyperactivity, and decreased appetite
Tetrahydrocannabinol	THC, Marinol	Smoked, oral			
Hashish and hashish oil	Hash, Hash oil	Smoked, oral			
Anabolic Steroids					
Testosterone (Cypionate, Enanthate)	Depo-Testosterone, Delatestryl	Injected	Virilization, acne, testicular atrophy, gynecomastia, aggressive behavior, edema	Unknown	Possible depression
Nandrolone (Decanoate, Phenpropionate)	Nortestosterone, Durabolin, Deca-Durabolin, Deca	Injected			
Oxymetholone	Anadrol-50	Oral			

*Not designated a narcotic under the CSA.

‡Designated a narcotic under the CSA.

Source: From *Drugs of Abuse*, 1997 Edition, by the Drug Enforcement Administration and National Guard, 1997, Washington, DC: Superintendent of Documents.

to have little potential for abuse, but this did not turn out to be the case. Methaqualone is no longer produced legally in the United States, although it continues to be manufactured or imported illegally (Doweiko, 1999, pp. 74–75; Hanson & Venturelli, 1998, p. 171).

One type of CNS depressant well-known in both general medical and mental health settings is the benzodiazepines. As discussed in Chapter 9, these anxiolytics are among the drugs used to treat anxiety disorders. The benzodiazepines include chlordiazepoxide and diazepam, better known by the respective trade names of Librium and Valium. More popular today in controlling anxiety are lorazepam (Ativan) and alprazolam (Xanax); another benzodiazepine called flurazepam (Dalmane) is often used to treat insomnia (Brick & Erickson, 1998, pp. 127–128). Benzodiazepines continue to be prescribed because of their beneficial properties, even though some people abuse them. Medical professionals have been criticized for being too quick to prescribe these drugs rather than considering the causes of the patients' problems and seeking other treatments when appropriate.

In the field of drug addiction, cross-tolerance and cross-addiction are also problems to be considered because tolerance to one drug in a class (such as depressants) may result in tolerance to another drug in the same class, and addicts may substitute another drug in the same class when their preferred drug is not available. Individuals recovering from dependence on CNS depressants must be alert to the possibility of relapse should they be prescribed drugs in this class for somatic complaints such as muscle strain.

Volatile substances, often called inhalants because they are sniffed or "huffed," are also included in the category of CNS depressants. Among these substances are plastic cement (used in making models), correction fluid, gasoline, brake fluid, nail polish remover, paint (especially in spray cans), nitrous oxide ("laughing gas"), which is found in cans of whipping cream, and many other household products. Their use may result in a wide range of physical problems, including kidney and liver damage, heart irregularities, respiratory depression, reduced production of blood cells, organic brain damage, and muscle damage, and some of these problems may cause death (cf. Doweiko, 1999, p. 192). Inhalants are most frequently used by youth because they are easily obtained (Ray & Ksir, 1999, p. 181).

Stimulants

Although caffeine is the most widely used stimulant, and nicotine, which has stimulant properties, causes more health problems than all other drugs, attention here is on amphetamines and cocaine. These drugs keep people alert by preventing drowsiness and sleep. They have abuse potential because of the feelings of increased energy and euphoria they produce, though these positive effects can turn to "anxiety, apprehension, or panic" (Hanson & Venturelli, 1998, pp. 354–355).

Amphetamines are synthetic drugs. Many long-distance truck drivers, musicians who work into the wee hours of the morning, and students studying for exams are aware of their ability to ward off sleep. Amphetamines were popular as diet pills because they suppress appetite, but newer drugs are a better choice for the treatment of obesity due to amphetamines' abuse potential (Brick & Erickson, 1998, pp. 84–85).

A popular type of amphetamine is methamphetamine, also known as *speed, crystal meth,* or *ice.* It is cheaply produced ("cooked") in illegal labs. Many unpleasant physical, mental, and behavioral effects can result from abuse of amphetamines, including repetitious behaviors, hallucinations, convulsions, and psychosis (Hanson & Venturelli, 1998, p. 259). Abusers often try to mitigate some of amphetamines' negative effects by using depressant drugs. Amphetamines can cause heart problems, and death may result from their use (Doweiko, 1999, p. 102).

Cocaine is a very popular stimulant drug. Despite previous debates, evidence demonstrates its potential for physical addiction (Brick & Erickson, 1998, p. 81; Ray & Ksir, 1999, pp. 142–143). As with amphetamines, cocaine use can result in psychosis and other serious problems, including death. Some people snort cocaine, and chronic users can destroy their nasal passages as a result. Some street names for cocaine are "nose candy" and "snow." Cocaine can also be smoked and taken intravenously. A smokable form is crack, or rock cocaine, which is purified. Crack can be purchased inexpensively on the street and has a very high potential for producing dependence (Ray & Ksir, 1999, pp. 31, 143). The euphoria (rush or high) from cocaine is said to be intense—like a terrific orgasm—and, thus, the popularity of the drug. However, a crash, or serious depression, including suicidal behavior, can occur when use is terminated or withdrawal ensues; these conditions warrant careful clinical attention (Doweiko, 1999, p. 121). Antidepressants may be used to mitigate the depression (Ray & Ksir, 1999, p. 146).

Narcotics

Opiates (opioids) or narcotics include heroin, codeine, and morphine, which are derived from the opium poppy. Since 1924 heroin has been classified in the United States as a drug with no medical value and a high potential for abuse. Codeine, morphine, and other drugs in this class continue to be prescribed for their analgesic (pain-relieving) qualities. Physicians are often reluctant to prescribe too much of narcotic drugs, fearing that patients will become addicted and find grounds for accusing doctors of malpractice. These factors can result in undermedicating patients for pain, even those with terminal illnesses.

Ray and Ksir (1999) note that for narcotic addicts, "withdrawal...is rarely life-threatening but most unpleasant" (p. 352). Table 13.1 notes these withdrawal effects. There is evidence of an extended withdrawal period following acute withdrawal from these drugs (Doweiko, 1999, pp. 151–152), which may contribute to difficulties in maintaining abstinence. Clonidine has been used to assist in shortening the withdrawal period from opiate drugs, but it can have serious side effects in some patients. Death from an opioid overdose is usually the result of respiratory depression (Brick & Erickson, 1998, p. 96).

Methadone is a synthetic narcotic used in treating heroin withdrawal and as a substitute drug in the long-term treatment of heroin addicts. Though methadone blocks much of the euphoria that results from heroin use, it is also addictive.

Hallucinogens

The key characteristic of hallucinogenic drugs is their ability to distort perception. These drugs include LSD (lysergic acid diethylamide), PCP (phencyclidine), often called "angel dust," psilocybin ("magic" mushrooms), mescaline, and peyote. LSD can produce adverse consequences, including panic reactions, psychosis, and flashbacks (Ray & Ksir, 1999, pp. 377–378). The well-publicized negative effects of PCP have included paranoid delusions, increased strength that can result in injury to others, and violent deaths (Doweiko, 1999, p. 181), although accounts of these effects may be exaggerated (Ray & Ksir, 1999, p. 39). The illegal "designer" drug MDMA or "ectasy" is an amphetamine variant that is classified as a hallucinogen.

Cannabis

Cannabis, or marijuana, is sometimes considered a hallucinogen, but it has substantially different effects than hallucinogens and other classes of drugs (Ray & Ksir, 1999, p. 401). The main psychoactive ingredient in cannabis is delta-9-tetrahydrocannabinol (THC). Marijuana is considered relatively benign by some and a source of problems by others. Like other drugs, whether someone tries the substance, likes the effects, continues to ingest the substance, and develops problems as a result depends on many factors such as the individual's motivations for drug use, state of well-being or distress at the time of drug use, expected effects from the drug, and the environment in which the drug is used.

In the laboratory, marijuana has been administered in doses high enough to produce withdrawal symptoms (indicating physical dependence), but this is hardly seen in patients in treatment (Brick & Erickson, 1998, p. 117; Ray & Ksir, 1999, pp. 417–418). Marijuana can, however, cause many negative effects such as short-term memory impairment; decreased strength, coordination, judgment, and ability to communicate; and distorted perceptions of time and distance. There is also evidence of anxiety, depression, and paranoia at high doses (Brick & Erickson, 1998, pp. 110–113). Evidence indicates that chronic use may result in lung damage, decreased testosterone levels and lower sperm counts in men, and increased infertility in women (Doweiko, 1999, p. 131). Some people believe that the THC content in marijuana purchased on the street has increased substantially (Brick & Erickson, 1998, p. 101), resulting in concern about the drug's negative effects. Amotivation (lack of motivation) may be observed in chronic marijuana users, but it is not clear whether marijuana causes amotivation, or if people with these characteristics are attracted to the drug (Doweiko, 1999, p. 133).

Anabolic Steroids

In our highly competitive society, it is not surprising that anabolic steroids have been added to the list of abused and controlled drugs. Anabolic steroids are abused in order to improve physical appearance, add muscle, and increase physical endurance. There are controversies about the physical and psychological effects of anabolic steroids, including whether "roid rage" (violent behavior) is a direct effect of their use, but these drugs have raised cause for concern (cf. Ray & Ksir, 1999, pp. 435–437).

Over-the-Counter Drugs

Over-the-counter drugs, which can be legally purchased without a prescription, can also be misused or abused. Among them are antihistamines that people buy to help them feel calm or to sleep; stimulants (containing caffeine) that help them stay alert; appetite suppressants to help them lose weight; cough and cold preparations containing alcohol or other drugs; and aspirin, acetaminophen, and ibuprofen to ease pain. Also of note are herbal preparations and dietary supplements that lack federal oversight. These products have become popular to increase energy, memory, sexual performance, and sleep and to induce other desired effects. It is no wonder that the seven classes of drugs discussed in this section appeal to a broad range of people throughout the United States and that they cause problems for many people, their families, and their communities.

Definitions of Psychoactive Drug Problems

Discussing drug disorders is difficult because there are many definitions of these problems. This section discusses definitional issues that are of particular relevance in the clinical treatment of substance abuse and dependence.

Much attention has been focused on definitions of alcohol abuse and alcoholism (the latter term is now frequently called *alcohol dependence*). Although Alcoholics Anonymous (AA), the world's largest self-help group, has no official definition, it states that "the explanation that seems to make sense to most AA members is that alcoholism is an illness, a *progressive* illness, which can never be cured but which, like some other illnesses, can be arrested" (Alcoholics Anonymous World Services, 1952, p. 4).

In the 1950s the American Medical Association accepted the illness or disease concept, and the World Health Organization (WHO) began to elaborate definitions of alcohol problems with the help of E. M. Jellinek. Jellinek (1960) believed that the disease concept could reduce the stigma associated with alcoholism in order to promote the humane treatment of alcoholics, but he conceptualized several types of alcoholism, only some of which he called diseases. (For a historical discussion of issues in defining alcoholism, cf. Davies, 1976.)

In 1958 Keller called alcoholism "a chronic behavioral disorder manifested by repeated drinking of alcoholic beverages in excess of the dietary and social uses of the community and to an extent that interferes with the drinker's health or his [her] social or economic functioning" (p. 2). Alcohol and drug dependence can certainly be thought of as habitual behaviors.

Definitions of alcohol and other drug problems have evolved in successive editions of the American Psychiatric Association's *Diagnostic and Statistical Manual of Mental Disorders (DSM)*. The current edition, the *DSM-IV*, contains three major sets of these diagnoses. One set of diagnosis is Substance-Induced Disorders, which includes the problems of intoxication and withdrawal from alcohol and other drugs. The second category is Substance-Induced Mental Disorders, which are found throughout the *DSM-IV*. They include hallucinogen persisting perception disorder (flashbacks) as well as the following disorders *if they result from substance use:* delirium, persisting dementia, persisting amnestic disorder, psychotic disorder, mood disorder, anxiety disorder, sexual dysfunction, and sleep disorder. The third set is Substance Use Disorders, which includes abuse and dependence. Abuse and dependence are both considered "maladaptive pattern[s] of substance use, leading to clinically significant impairment or distress" (American Psychiatric Association, 1994, pp. 181, 182). The general characteristics of substance dependence and abuse found

TABLE 13.2 Diagnostic Criteria for Substance Dependence

A maladaptive pattern of substance use, leading to clinically significant impairment or distress, as manifested by three (or more) of the following, occurring at any time in the same 12-month period:

(1) tolerance, as defined by either of the following:

   (a) a need for markedly increased amounts of the substance to achieve intoxication or desired effect

   (b) markedly diminished effect with continued use of the same amount of the substance

(2) withdrawal, as manifested by either of the following:

   (a) the characteristic withdrawal syndrome for the substance (refer to Criteria A and B of the criteria sets for Withdrawal from the specific substances)

   (b) the same (or a closely related) substance is taken to relieve or avoid withdrawal symptoms

(3) the substance is often taken in larger amounts or over a longer period than was intended

(4) there is a persistent desire or unsuccessful efforts to cut down or control substance use

(5) a great deal of time is spent in activities necessary to obtain the substance (e.g., visiting multiple doctors or driving long distances), use the substance (e.g., chain-smoking), or recover from its effects

(6) important social, occupational, or recreational activities are given up or reduced because of substance use

(7) the substance use is continued despite knowledge of having a persistent or recurrent physical or psychological problem that is likely to have been caused or exacerbated by the substance (e.g., current cocaine use despite recognition of cocaine-induced depression, or continued drinking despite recognition that an ulcer was made worse by alcohol consumption)

Source: Reprinted with permission from the Diagnostic and Statistical Manual of Mental Disorders, Fourth Edition. Copyright © 1994 American Psychiatric Association.

in the *DSM-IV* are reprinted in Tables 13.2 and 13.3, respectively. The *DSM-IV* also contains specific information on dependence and abuse for each type of drug. Dependence may be further classified as with or without physiological dependence and in early or sustained remission. Although abusers may become dependent, this is not necessarily the case; therefore, substance abuse and dependence are considered distinct diagnostic categories. The description of alcohol dependence in the *DSM-IV* is closely related to that of the alcohol dependence syndrome found in the World Health Organization's (1992) *International Classification of Diseases-10 (ICD-10)*.

Pattison, Sobell, and Sobell (1977) and Pattison and Kaufman (1982) offer an alternative to the two distinct diagnoses of abuse and dependence presented in the *DSM*. They suggest that alcohol problems can be thought of as occurring on a continuum, ranging from no problem to severe problems. There are other views of alcohol and drug problems. Fingarette (1985), for example, views alcoholism as a lifestyle in which drinking becomes a central

TABLE 13.3 Diagnostic Criteria for Substance Abuse

A. A maladaptive pattern of substance use leading to clinically significant impairment or distress, as manifested by one (or more) of the following, occurring within a 12-month period:

   (1) recurrent substance use resulting in a failure to fulfill major role obligations at work, school, or home (e.g., repeated absences or poor work performance related to substance use; substance-related absences, suspensions, or expulsions from school; neglect of children or household)
   (2) recurrent substance use in situations in which it is physically hazardous (e.g., driving an automobile or operating a machine when impaired by substance use)
   (3) recurrent substance-related legal problems (e.g., arrests for substance-related disorderly conduct)
   (4) continued substance use despite having persistent or recurrent social or interpersonal problems caused or exacerbated by the effects of the substance (e.g., arguments with spouse about consequences of intoxication, physical fights)

B. The symptoms have never met the criteria for Substance Dependence for this class of substance.

Source: Reprinted with permission from the Diagnostic and Statistical Manual of Mental Disorders, Fourth Edition. Copyright © 1994 American Psychiatric Association.

activity for individuals for a variety of reasons. According to this view, cessation of alcohol use is no different than giving up other activities that have become central in one's life.

For the postmodern, client-centered practitioner, a practical question remains: Is there a definition of substance abuse and dependence that clients can readily understand and appreciate? Kofoed and Keys (1988) suggest the following definition for use with clients based on Atkinson's (1985) work: "A loss of consistent control over substance use" (p. 1210). Another straightforward definition is the repeated use of substances that results in serious life problems, including family, social, psychological, job-related, and legal problems. An important role of the social worker is to help clients make a connection between their life problems and their use of alcohol or other drugs, a connection that is not always obvious to them. Although the definitions presented in this paragraph may seem simplistic, in a therapeutic context they can be useful.

Etiologic Theories of Substance Use Disorders

As with definitions, constructions of causes are multiple and complex. Here we summarize a variety of biological, psychological, and sociological explanatory models of substance use disorders.

Moral Model

The oldest explanations fall under the moral model in which alcoholism (and other drug problems) is seen as the result of personal weaknesses or shortcomings and occurs as a result of failure to exercise the will to end the problem. This model is reflected in the construction of drug possession as a crime and is particularly evident in the federal government's war on drugs. Evidence of the moral model is also seen in the welfare (public assistance) reform of the 1990s. Substance use disorders are no longer sufficient diagnoses for obtaining Supplemental Security Income payments, and individuals with drug convictions may be barred from participating in the Temporary Assistance for Needy Families and Food Stamp Programs, even though this support may be critical to them and their families (cf. DiNitto, 2000).

Biological Model

Among the many biological explanations of alcohol use disorders are that consumption of alcohol may result in the brain producing a morphine-like substance that triggers an addiction (Bloom, 1982) or that addiction may result from abnormalities in metabolizing sugar (Lundquist, 1971). Studies that suggest a genetic cause confirm that alcoholism occurs more frequently in some families than in others; alcoholism concordance rates are higher in identical twins than in fraternal twins; and adoptees whose biological parents were alcoholics are more likely to develop alcoholism (even if they are raised by nonalcoholic parents) than adoptees whose biological parents were not alcoholics (cf. Cloninger, Sigvardsson, & Bohman, 1996 and cf. Valentine, 1998 for an overview of these studies).

Researchers interested in genetics and biobehavioral functioning have studied differences between alcoholics and nonalcoholics in neurophysiological activity (such as brainwave activity) and biochemical activity (such as neurotransmitter levels) (cf. National Institute on Alcohol Abuse and Alcoholism [NIAAA], 1997). The Collaborative Study on the Genetics of Alcoholism (COGA), supported by NIAAA, provides evidence of the involvement of particular chromosomes in vulnerability to alcoholism (Reich, Edenberg, Goate et al., 1998). According to Dr. Enoch Gordis of NIAAA, in isolating the genes involved, we must also "determine whether they are specific for alcohol or define something more general, such as differences in temperament or personality that increase an individual's vulnerability to alcoholism" (NIAAA, 1995). The most widely discussed etiologic theories of substance dependence today fall under the biological model, perhaps because they hold the greatest promise for a cure.

Psychological Model

Among the psychological explanations are cognitive-behavioral, learning, and psychodynamic theories. They suggest that some people become dependent because substance use reduces tension or provides other positive reinforcement, such as the elimination of physiological pain or psychological distress from childhood or later experiences (for summaries of these theories cf. Valentine, 1998). Researchers have also expended efforts to determine whether certain personality characteristics or a particular personality profile characterizes alcoholics or other drug abusers. Alan Lang's research indicates that impulsivity, difficulty in delaying gratification, antisocial behavior, a tendency toward sensation seeking, nonconformity, social alienation, tolerance of deviance, and a high stress level may contribute to addiction (Nelson, 1983). No trait theory has, however, isolated the cause of substance use disorders.

Sociocultural Model

Sociocultural theories have also been used to study differences in the levels of substance abuse problems across cultures or among subgroups within a culture. Supracultural theories suggest that the degree of stress in a culture is positively related to its level of substance abuse problems, or that cultural norms that encourage, permit, or inhibit the use of alcohol and other drugs are related to the level of substance abuse problems (cf. Bacon, 1974; Bales, 1946).

Culture-specific theories attempt to explain why particular cultures differ in their rates of substance use problems. For example, despite their proximity and similarities, France has much higher levels of alcoholism than Italy. Perhaps this is because the French drink more distilled spirits in addition to wine and do more drinking apart from meals and apart from family than the Italians who disapprove more strongly of drunkenness (cf. Levin, 1990). Subcultural theories consider why rates of alcohol and drug problems vary among groups within the same culture with respect to factors such as age, gender, ethnicity, socioeconomic class, religion, and family background (Tarter & Schneider, 1976). For example, social norms and negative sanctions may contribute to lower levels of alcoholism among women compared to men.

A Postmodern Perspective

Most serious students of substance use disorders believe there is no simple or single explanation for these problems. For example, women may drink less than men as a result of social norms, but they also metabolize alcohol less efficiently than men (e.g., Frezza et. al., 1990), suggesting a biological explanation for their lower consumption. Cultural norms may also limit the amount of alcohol that many Asians consume, though after drinking, many Asians are said to have a discomforting "flushing response," a physiological reaction that may also produce aversion to alcohol (Murray & Stabenau, 1982). The interplay of biological, psychological, and sociocultural factors may be equally important in producing alcohol dependence. Such combinations of factors would constitute a postmodern model of substance use disorders in which various factors influence different individuals in certain locations at particular moments of history. This model situates substance abuse in diverse contexts, taking into account variables such as culture, gender, sexual orientation and age, as indicated later.

Although there is little to suggest that Native Americans metabolize alcohol differently than matched controls of other cultures, May (1994) notes that even among Native Americans, beliefs about inability to "hold their liquor" and of impaired alcohol metabolism persist. Some tribal groups do not drink, but alcoholism is a source of considerable health and social problems among the country's indigenous population. Authors generally suggest subcultural or structural explanations of Native Americans' problems with alcohol such as poverty and degradation. The alcohol problems of Native Americans are said to have originated with the introduction of alcohol by white settlers (MacAndrew & Edgerton, 1969), and the patterns of gulping alcohol and bingeing that persist among some Native Americans are thought to have developed from laws that made it illegal for them to possess alcohol (cf. Indian Health Service, 1977).

Among Native Americans, substance abuse is said to promote disharmony and disunity (Oetting, Beauvais, & Goldstein, 1982). The methods many Native Americans use to reestablish equilibrium are far different from those espoused by the medical establishment. For example, the hallucinogenic drug peyote, which is included in the Controlled Substances Act, has been used in religious ceremonies by the Native American Church without adverse consequences and is considered a treatment for alcoholism. As Karl Menninger (1974) wrote, "Peyote is not harmful to these people; it is beneficial, comforting, inspiring, and appears to be spiritually nourishing" (p. 699). Peyote is not used by the chemical dependency treatment establishment, but some programs incorporate traditional, Native American spiritual practices. One example is the "sweat lodge" in which participants congregate in a small, tentlike structure containing heated rocks, chant Native American songs, confess, and seek spiritual renewal ("VA Hospital Calls In...," 1991).

The alcoholism problems of African Americans have been traced back to the days when alcohol was used to appease slaves who toiled long hours in the fields and continues today in the practice of some segments of the African American population who drink heavily on weekends following a hard week's work (Harper, 1980). Abstinence among African Americans, particularly among women, likely derives from strong religious traditions and role expectations (Harper, 1980), and families often seek solace in their churches when substance use becomes a problem. Unfortunately, a culture of denial seems to prevent many African American church leaders from addressing alcohol and drug problems directly (McGee & Johnson, 1985). The chemical dependency problems of African Americans are compounded by the legal construction of drug problems. The criminal justice system not only incarcerates a disproportionate number of African Americans, it imposes harsher sentences for the possession of crack cocaine, a substance that is cheaply purchased, than it does for powdered cocaine, a substance which is more costly. Thus, blacks and others who are disproportionately poor often receive stiffer sentences for their drug crimes than whites, and their access to treatment is often through the criminal justice system.

Consistent with subcultural theories, Caetano (1988) writes that "alcohol problems do not appear in a contextual vacuum, but are linked to the status of Hispanics as an underprivileged ethnic minority in the U.S." (p. 356). The groups that comprise the Hispanic population differ in their alcohol use, but some suggest that many Hispanics see chemical dependency as a moral weakness rather than an illness (McQuade, 1989). Comas-Diaz (1986) writes that among Puerto Ricans, "folk beliefs encourage externalization, passivity and fatalism regarding the problem of drinking" with alcoholism sometimes thought to be caused by bad spirits, thus reinforcing denial (p. 3).

Many Hispanics place a high value on keeping problems within *la familia* (the family). Concepts such as assertiveness, detachment, and independence, typically used in chemical dependency programs, may be alien to Hispanics and can be seen as threatening to the family (cf. Aguilar, DiNitto, Franklin, & Lopez-Pilkinton, 1991). Hispanics may place reliance on God or divine intervention rather than professionals (McQuade, 1989) and seek assistance from the Catholic Church. Some may consult native folk healers (e.g., *curanderos* or *curanderas)* for help with alcohol and drug problems, practices that should not be summarily dismissed by treatment professionals. Acculturation is thought to be positively related to increased drinking among Hispanics (cf. Caetano & Kaskutas, 1995), also suggesting sociocultural influences on drinking.

Feminists have pointed to the lack of consideration of women's chemical dependency problems (cf. Davis & DiNitto, 1998; Van Den Bergh, 1991). Theories about chemical dependency generally emanate from research conducted on men. For instance,

McClelland and colleagues' (1972) *The Drinking Man* attributed some of the variance in men's drinking to their need to increase feelings of power. Speculation was that women's lower rates of alcoholism might be explained by their lack of interest in power. Only recently has gender been a factor in chemical dependency research. Wilsnack (1980) began considering explanations of women's alcohol problems related to sex role identification. This work has led to a contemporary hypothesis that individuals of either gender may use substances in an attempt to express the feelings of masculinity and femininity they feel they are lacking (Henderson & Boyd, 1992).

Researchers have discovered a common pathway for women into substance problems. Many women apparently begin their drinking or drug "careers" as a result of involvement with a partner who has alcohol or drug problems (Cuskey, Berger, & Densen-Gerber, 1981; Hser, Anglin, & Booth, 1987), a factor that warrants consideration in treatment. Also implicated is a high incidence of physical and sexual abuse among women who develop alcohol and drug problems (see, for example, Sheridan, 1995).

The women's movement increased awareness that women's treatment needs may be different from men's and may include the need for concrete services such as transportation and child care as well as all women's therapy and self-help groups. The self-help group Women for Sobriety (WFS) (Kirkpatrick, 1978) developed as a reaction to the incongruities that women might experience in Alcoholics Anonymous. For example, the first step of Alcoholics Anonymous says that "We admitted we were powerless over alcohol," while WFS's Thirteen Statements of Acceptance include "I am a competent woman." Kasl (1990) notes that because the Twelve Steps of AA "were formulated by a white, middle-class male in the 1930s, not surprisingly they work to break down an overinflated ego and put reliance on an all-powerful male God" (p. 30-31; also see Kasl, 1992). Kasl believes that women benefit from just the opposite—strengthening their sense of self and affirming their own inner wisdom. Some of those who take exception to such critiques see AA groups as a "narrative community" with members acting as storytellers who transform their lives by listening and sharing their "experience, strength, and hope" (Rappaport, 1993). A true appreciation of AA may require a new understanding from a rational service delivery model to a metaphorical, spiritual understanding (Davis, 1998). Powerlessness is reconceptualized like a Buddhist koan: "giving in is the greatest form of control" (Berg & Miller, 1992).

Alcohol and drugs may be used to assuage the homophobia that gay men, lesbians, and bisexuals have internalized growing up in a culture that negates their developmental experiences (Israelstam, 1986). As with intervention with other disenfranchised groups, substance abuse treatment for lesbians, gay men, and bisexuals should include affirmation of their rightful place in society. Self-help groups in which members share their identities as gay men, lesbians, or bisexuals reinforce pride in who one is and demonstrate that a clean and sober lifestyle can be maintained in a homophobic world.

As a rule, alcohol consumption remits with age, perhaps because alcohol is metabolized more slowly, causing older people to experience a greater effect from the ingestion of ethanol than they did in their younger years. Some alcoholics beat the odds of developing serious health problems such as cirrhosis and live long lives. Others do not develop alcohol or drug problems until later in life. Popular explanations for the late onset of alcohol problems in older people include bereavement, loneliness, and boredom, but research raises questions as to whether such problems precipitate increased consumption (cf. Vinton &

Wambach, 1998). Socialization programs have, however, been suggested as a strategy in the treatment of late onset alcohol problems.

Psychosocial Assessment and Treatment of Substance Use Disorders

Treatment for substance dependence is dominated by the disease or illness perspective and the philosophy of Alcoholics Anonymous. Cognitive and behavioral techniques are incorporated in these approaches. Treatment providers are also known to use a variety of other strategies in their efforts to find something that works for clients whose problems are more intractable.

Chemical dependency treatment is frequently described in terms of treatment modalities such as detoxification, inpatient treatment, halfway house services, outpatient services, and aftercare. Among the best practices in chemical dependency treatment is use of the *American Society of Addiction Medicine Patient Placement Criteria for the Treatment of Substance-Related Disorders.* The adult admission criteria, shown in Table 13.4, range from level 0.5 (early intervention) to level IV (medically managed, intensive inpatient treatment). The level of treatment recommended is suggested by the six dimensions in the left-hand column of the table, such as withdrawal potential and other biomedical complications, emotional and behavioral condition, treatment acceptance, relapse potential, and the individual's recovery environment. As the table suggests, treatment selection should be based on client needs. These needs change over time as clients progress or relapse.

Client Assessment

Alcohol and drug use has often been treated casually by psychiatrists, psychologists, counselors, and social workers. Every client presenting for mental health services deserves to be screened to determine whether his or her problems may be related to substance use or that of a family member (broadly defined). Depression, anxiety, spousal violence, child abuse, and many other problems often have roots in substance abuse.

Several easily administered instruments are available to screen clients for alcohol and drug problems in medical and mental health settings. Unfortunately, as a cost-saving measure, and perhaps because clinicians are uncomfortable discussing these problems, clients are often given screening forms to complete at intake before a clinician has seen them. Screening tools about sensitive topics such as alcohol and drug use work best when the client is properly prepared to complete them and when they are administered by a skilled clinician.

The briefest screening tool for alcohol problems is the CAGE questionnaire, which consists of the following four questions:*

1. Have you ever felt that you should cut down on drinking?
2. Have people annoyed you by criticizing your drinking?

*Questionnaire is from "Detecting alcoholism: The CAGE questionnaire," by J. A. Ewing, 1984, *JAMA, 252,* pp. 1905–1907. Copyright © 1984 by American Medical Association. Reprinted with permission.

TABLE 13.4 Adult Admission Criteria: Crosswalk of Levels 0.5 through IV

				Levels of Service			
Criteria Dimensions	Level 0.5 Early Intervention	OMT Opioid Maintenance Therapy	Level I Outpatient Services	Level II.1 Intensive Outpatient	Level II.5 Partial Hospitalization
DIMENSION 1: Alcohol Intoxication and/or Withdrawal Potential	No withdrawal risk	Patient is physiologically dependent on opiates and requires OMT to prevent withdrawal	I-D, Ambulatory detoxification without extended on-site monitoring Minimal risk of severe withdrawal	Minimal risk of severe withdrawal	II-D, Ambulatory detoxification with extended on-site monitoring Moderate risk of severe withdrawal
DIMENSION 2: Biomedical Conditions and Complications	None or very stable	None or manageable with outpatient medical monitoring	None or very stable	None or not a distraction from treatment and manageable in Level II.1	None or not sufficient to distract from treatment and manageable in Level II.5
DIMENSION 3: Emotional/Behavioral Conditions and Complications	None or very stable	None or manageable in outpatient structured environment	None or very stable	Mild severity, with potential to distract from recovery; needs monitoring	Mild to moderate severity with potential to distract from recovery; needs stabilization
DIMENSION 4: Treatment Acceptance/Resistance	Willing to understand how current use may affect personal goals	Resistance high enough to require structured therapy to promote treatment progress but will not render outpatient treatment ineffective	Willing to cooperate but needs motivating and monitoring strategies	Resistance high enough to require structured program but not so high as to render outpatient treatment ineffective	Resistance high enough to require structured program but not so high as to render outpatient treatment ineffective

(continued)

Criteria Dimensions				
DIMENSION 5: Relapse/Continued Use Potential	Needs understanding of, or skills to change, current use patterns	High risk of relapse or continued use without OMT and structured therapy to promote treatment progress	Able to maintain abstinence or control use and pursue recovery goals with minimal support	Intensification of addiction symptoms, despite active participation in Level I, and high likelihood of relapse or continued use without close monitoring and support
				Intensification of addiction symptoms, despite active participation in Level II.1; high likelihood of relapse or continued use without monitoring and support
DIMENSION 6: Recovery Environment	Social support system or significant others increase risk for personal conflict about alcohol/drug use	Supportive recovery environment and/or patient has skills to cope with outpatient treatment	Supportive recovery environment and/or patient has skills to cope	Environment unsupportive, but with structure and support, the patient can cope
				Environment is not supportive but, with structure and support, and relief from the home environment the patient can cope

Levels of Service

Criteria Dimensions	Level III.1 Clinically-Managed Low Intensity Residential Services	Level III.3 Clinically-Managed Medium Intensity Residential Services	Level III.5 Clinically-Managed Medium/High Intensity Residential Services	Level III.7 Medically-Monitored Intensive Inpatient Services	Level IV Medically-Managed Intensive Inpatient Services
DIMENSION 1: Alcohol Intoxication and/or Withdrawal Potential	No withdrawal risk	Level III-D, Clinically Managed Residential Detoxification Services No severe withdrawal risk, moderate withdrawal manageable in III.2-D	Minimal risk of severe withdrawal for Level III.3 and III.5. If withdrawal is present, meets Level II.2-D criteria	III.7-D, Medically-Monitored Inpatient Detoxification Services Severe withdrawal, but manageable in Level III.7-D	IV-D, Medically-Managed Inpatient Detoxification Services Severe withdrawal risk

TABLE 13.4 Continued

	Levels of Service				
Criteria Dimensions	Level III.1 Clinically-Managed Low Intensity Residential Services	Level III.3 Clinically-Managed Medium Intensity Residential Services	Level III.5 Clinically-Managed Medium/High Intensity Residential Services	Level III.7 Medically-Monitored Intensive Inpatient Services	Level IV Medically-Managed Intensive Inpatient Services
DIMENSION 2: Biomedical Conditions and Complications	None or stable	None or stable	None or stable; receiving concurrent medical monitoring	Patient requires medical monitoring but not intensive treatment	Patient requires 24-hour medical and nursing care
DIMENSION 3: Emotional/Behavioral Conditions and Complications	None or minimal; not distracting to recovery	Mild to moderate severity: needs structure to allow focus on recovery	Repeated inability to control impulses; personality disorder requires high structure to shape behavior	Moderate severity; patient needs 24-hour structured setting	Severe problems require 24-hour psychiatric care with concomitant addiction treatment
DIMENSION 4: Treatment Acceptance/ Resistance	Open to recovery, but needs structured environment to maintain therapeutic gains	Little awareness; patient needs interventions available only in Level III.3 to engage and keep in treatment	Marked difficulty with or opposition to treatment, with dangerous consequences if not engaged in treatment	Resistance high and impulse control poor, despite negative consequences; patient needs motivating strategies available only in 24-hour structured setting	Problems in this dimension do not qualify the patient for Level IV services
DIMENSION 5: Relapse/Continued Use Potential	Understands relapse but needs structure to maintain therapeutic gains	Little awareness; patient needs interventions available only in Level III.3 to prevent continued use	No recognition of skills needed to prevent continued use, with dangerous consequences	Unable to control use, with dangerous consequences, despite active participation in less intensive care	Problems in this dimension do not qualify the patient for Level IV services

DIMENSION 6: Recovery Environment	Environment is dangerous, but recovery achievable if Level III.1 structure is available	Environment is dangerous; patient needs 24-hour structure to learn to cope	Environment is dangerous; patient lacks skills to cope outside of a highly structured 24-hour setting	Environment dangerous for recovery; patient lacks skills to cope outside of highly structured 24-hour setting	Problems in this dimension do not qualify the patient for Level IV services

Source: American Society of Addiction Medicine, *Patient Placement Criteria for the Treatment of Substance-Related Disorders*, 2nd ed. (Chevy Chase, MD: American Society of Addiction Medicine, 1996), pp. 46–48 (1-800-844-8948). Reprinted by permission.

Note: This overview of the Adult Admission Criteria is an approximate summary to illustrate the principal concepts and structure of the criteria.

3. Have you ever felt guilty about your drinking?
4. Have you ever had a drink first thing in the morning to steady your nerves or get rid of a hangover (eye opener)?

A positive response to two or more questions indicates a drinking problem, and a positive response to one question indicates the need to further explore the possibility of a problem. Sciacca (1991) cautions that even if all answers are negative, further assessment is warranted if (a) the client's mode of responding is unusual; (b) information from other sources indicates a potential substance abuse problem; or (c) the professional believes the clinical picture is unclear.

Other widely used brief screening instruments are Selzer's (1971) Michigan Alcoholism Screening Test (MAST), the World Health Organization's Alcohol Use Disorders Identification Test (AUDIT) (Babor, de la Fuente, Saunders, & Grant, 1992), and Skinner's (1982) Drug Abuse Screening Test (DAST). All are face valid instruments; that is, the questions ask directly about alcohol and drug use and related problems. Because many clients are guarded in sharing this information (e.g., they may be facing criminal charges, risk losing custody of their children, or are otherwise defensive because of the stigma associated with alcohol and drug problems), clinicians often find it difficult to obtain accurate information. To address this problem, Miller's (1997) Substance Abuse Subtle Screening Inventory (SASSI) contains many unobtrusive (non–face valid items).

Screening may suggest a problem, but a formal diagnosis (often based on the *DSM-IV*), is necessary for managed care organizations and other insurers to authorize treatment. Information from collaterals and urine testing may also be necessary in establishing a substance use disorder. The social worker's skills at obtaining a social history, including an alcohol and drug history (see McNeece and DiNitto, 1998, pp. 82–90), is another important precursor to treatment planning. The Addiction Severity Index (ASI) (McLellan, Luborsky, Cacciola et al., 1985) is frequently used in chemical dependency treatment programs to assist in client assessment. The ASI is a structured interview used to determine the severity of clients' problems in seven domains: medical, employment, alcohol, drug, legal, family/social, and psychological. The ASI assesses both lifetime and current problems and can be administered to track client progress at follow-ups.

Brief Interventions

Treatment of problem drinking and alcohol abuse may be addressed through brief interventions, as brief as one session and usually not more than four (cf. Bien, Miller, & Tonigan, 1993; NIAAA, 1997). Rather than abstinence, which is usually the goal in chemical dependency treatment, brief interventions may be used to help individuals reduce their drinking. These interventions may be counseling, advice by a physician or other primary health care provider, medical check-ins, feedback on test results, the use of self-help manuals, and bibliotherapy (reading materials). Social workers might consider using these brief interventions in a variety of settings in which early-stage drinking problems can be identified.

Detoxification

Clients whose diagnosis is substance dependence may need detoxification services. Often this depends on the type of drug or drugs involved and the severity of withdrawal symptoms.

Many patients can be detoxified successfully in community facilities, though hospitals may be the choice in some cases, for example, when the patient experiences severe withdrawal symptoms or has other medical or mental problems that must also be addressed.

Some detoxification is done on an outpatient basis. Outpatient detoxification can be a cost-effective alternative to inpatient detoxification (Hayashida, Alterman, & McLellan, 1989), but it may not be a viable option if the person does not have a stable living environment. People with severe mental disorders who are also chemically dependent frequently fall into this category, another reason that inpatient detoxification may be preferable for them. Some programs (sometimes called social setting programs) assist those who do not exhibit significant withdrawal symptoms but need social support to help them terminate drug use. Detoxification is but the first step in recovery from chemical dependency. As the saying goes, "It is easier to get sober than it is to stay sober."

Missions and Shelters

People with mental illness, chemical dependency, and dual diagnoses often spend time in missions and shelters when they have nowhere else to go. Law enforcement officers may prefer to see people on the streets get to these facilities rather than arrest them for vagrancy or loitering. The informal communication network of street people also leads clients to these facilities when shelter is needed.

The Salvation Army (the "Sallie," as it is called) is the organization best known for providing shelter and meals to those with alcohol and drug problems. Alcoholics, drug users, and people with mental disorders are generally welcomed as long as they do not act out, but they are not usually permitted to remain at the shelter during the day. While there, participants are usually expected to attend religious services in the hope that they will be motivated to seek a different life. The stay in these facilities is often brief and is usually provided free or at minimal cost. Some residents remain for longer periods and may receive treatment provided by the Salvation Army or other community agencies; they may also work in the Salvation Army's thrift stores or in the community. Mission programs operate in a similar fashion.

Intensive Treatment

Traditional, intensive inpatient treatment (often referred to as Minnesota-model treatment) that used to be the mainstay of chemical dependency treatment is becoming rare in this era of managed care, but facilities such as Hazelden in Minnesota and the Betty Ford Center in California continue to offer it. The treatment modalities used in these programs include education, psychoeducation, group therapy, individual therapy, family education, family therapy, and an introduction to AA and other self-help programs. Nutritional counseling and other aspects of wellness may also be included. For those who can afford it through insurance or out of pocket, these programs provide an opportunity to focus on recovery away from the stressors found at home.

Although studies show that inpatient treatment is usually no more effective than outpatient treatment (NIAAA, 1987), it was not until the advent of managed care that intensive outpatient treatment came to be more widely used because it is less costly. These programs offer virtually the same services as inpatient programs, but they generally operate on evenings and weekends to accommodate clients' work or family schedules.

Residential Treatment

One form of residential care is the halfway house. Halfway house services may be used following detoxification or intensive inpatient treatment or in conjunction with outpatient treatment. Many residents have no other permanent housing, but halfway houses provide a therapeutic environment for recovery, not simply a place to stay. Halfway houses are also used as transitional facilities for people with chemical dependency problems who are being released on probation or parole. These facilities help residents make a successful return to the community.

Some halfway houses offer short-term stays and others have open-ended stays. Some have highly structured schedules with treatment as the main focus of daily activities. In other halfway houses, residents work at jobs in the community during the day and participate in treatment in the evenings. Most halfway houses require residents to attend AA or other self-help groups. Residents often pay a nominal fee and share responsibility for chores such as cooking. Program rules are usually clear, including no drinking or drug use (except for prescribed medications taken under supervision), no violence, and no sex in the house.

Whereas halfway houses originated to help people with alcohol problems, therapeutic communities (TCs) originated to assist those addicted to heroin or other illegal drugs. Reality therapy (Glasser, 1965) is often the basis for treatment. Group process and peer pressure, including confrontation, are used to address denial and help clients assume responsibility. Residents earn privileges as they progress in recovery. The recommended stay is often a year or two. Many TCs operate cottage industries in which residents work. Halfway house and TC staff are often individuals who have successfully worked their own recovery programs for a substantial period.

Domiciliaries are another type of residential care for people with alcohol and drug problems. The residents they serve have physical or mental impairments that preclude them from living independently. The Veterans' Administration operates domiciliaries and some communities have similar facilities.

Outpatient Services

Outpatient treatment, typically involving individual counseling and group therapy, has become the primary modality for treating people with substance use disorders. Education and counseling for family members are often provided, too, even when the member with the alcohol or drug problem refuses to participate. Family therapy and couples' or marital counseling may also be available.

Pharmacotherapy

Although many drugs are being tested, few have been approved for the treatment of alcohol and drug dependence following detoxification. Pharmacotherapies are intended to be used with counseling or other psychosocial services.

The best known long-term treatment for heroin addiction is methadone maintenance. Methadone maintenance provides addicts with a legal source of a drug substitute. Methadone, which is administered orally, reduces health risks, especially those associated with needle use. This is important in limiting exposure of addicts and their sex partners to the human immunodeficiency virus (HIV) and the various forms of hepatitis. It is also important because it eliminates the "rush" that users get from preparing drugs for injection (or other forms of administration) that reinforces drug use. Methadone maintenance curtails criminal activity, such as theft, pursued to obtain money to purchase heroin. Despite is effectiveness, methadone is addictive, and critics of this approach to addiction treatment consider it a poor substitute for a drug-free life (cf. Gerstein & Harwood, 1990). Though methadone may limit heroin use, addicts may turn to other drugs, such as cocaine and alcohol, to obtain their high. LAAM is another drug available to maintain heroin addicts. An increase in treatment choices may encourage more addicts to get help (cf. Strain, Stitzer, Liebson, & Bigelow, 1994).

Naltrexone (trade name ReVia) is also used to treat heroin addicts. Although it also blocks the high from using heroin, naltrexone is not a substitute for heroin; instead, it reverses the effects of opiate drugs. According to Landry (1995), naltrexone is most effective for opioid addicts "involved in meaningful relationships with nonaddicted partners, employed full-time or attending school, and living with family members" (p. ix).

Naltrexone also seems to be effective in treating alcoholics, though it is not clear why, since it supposedly blocks only the effects of opiate drugs. Speculation is that it works to block the pleasurable effects of alcohol as well, since reduced cravings and relapses have been reported. O'Malley et al. (1992) found that naltrexone coupled with supportive therapy produced the largest proportion of abstinent patients in their controlled study.

Disulfiram (better known by the trade name Antabuse) represents another way that drugs can help alcoholics, which is by deterring impulsive drinking. Antabuse interferes with the normal breakdown of alcohol in the system. If an individual taking Antabuse ingests alcohol, he or she becomes violently ill. Antabuse has produced only modest results, and it may be that motivation to remain sober is more important than taking Antabuse (NIAAA, 1987). Motivation may be the key to recovery from other drug addiction as well.

There is a great deal of interest in developing a drug to assist those recovering from cocaine dependence. A number of such drugs are in some stage of testing, but none has yet been approved for use.

Aftercare and Relapse Prevention

The use of alcohol or other drugs following a period of clean or sober time, known as a lapse or relapse, can be considered a natural event in the course of recovery from chemical dependency. Because relapse rates following treatment are high, the continuum of care for clients with substance dependence includes relapse prevention and aftercare services (cf. Gorski & Miller, 1986; Marlatt & Gordon, 1985).

Relapse prevention techniques are generally taught in inpatient and outpatient treatment programs, and most clients must continue to practice them to avoid relapse. Clients are taught to identify events, thoughts, or feelings (called cues or triggers) that precede their alcohol or drug use. These triggers may be fighting with a spouse, loneliness, depression, prolonged stress, being in the company of friends who use, or even driving by old drinking or using haunts. Clients may need encouragement to make new friends who are clean and sober, learn how to diffuse arguments or walk away from them, practice stress reduction techniques, avoid certain establishments, and attend AA or other meetings to reinforce sobriety. When relapse does occur, clients often think of themselves as failures and experience considerable guilt and remorse at "letting others down." Treatment providers generally help clients reframe relapse as a learning experience that they can utilize to avoid similar occurrences in the future.

Aftercare takes a variety of forms, such as attendance at group meetings, which some programs include as part of their treatment "package." Treatment personnel may make periodic telephone calls to former clients to check on their progress and to encourage them to follow their aftercare plan. Many clients have no formal aftercare program arranged through treatment programs. This is one reason why twelve-step and other self-help programs that offer regular meetings at no charge are essential to many people who wish to remain clean and sober. The twelve-step programs also serve an important function because they incorporate a spiritual component that many recovering individuals seek. A client's aftercare program lasts as long as she or he desires.

Adjunctive Services

Social workers generally espouse a holistic approach to treating clients. In addition to maintaining abstinence (or limiting alcohol use), clients often need help in other areas. They may have employment problems requiring referral to the state vocational rehabilitation agency, medical problems that require securing treatment when they have no health insurance, spiritual concerns that may be addressed through mainstream churches or other religious groups, or legal problems (civil or criminal) that may require assistance from a legal aid agency. Social workers need a broad knowledge of community resources because substance use disorders can disrupt all aspects of an individual's life.

Self-Help Groups

Our discussion has focused largely on the services that social workers and other chemical dependency professionals provide, but the best-known help for those dependent on alcohol and other drugs comes from the self-help movement, particularly Alcoholics Anonymous (AA). The fellowship of AA is based on a twelve-step program of recovery from alcoholism. Some AA groups are for women only, Spanish-speaking members, gay men or lesbians, or other groups. Other self-help groups include Narcotics Anonymous and Cocaine Anonymous. The twelve-step programs include references to God and a higher power, but rather than religious organizations, many people consider them spiritual programs.

For those seeking alternatives to the twelve-step programs, there are Rational Recovery (information is available on the Internet at http://www.rational.org/recovery) and Secular Organizations for Sobriety or Save Our Selves (http://www.secularhumansim.org/sos). Women for Sobriety (WFS) is another self-help alternative, but many women attend WFS in addition to AA (Kaskutas, 1994). Moderation Management is a self-help program for those who wish to cut down on their drinking rather than remain abstinent (Kishline, 1996).

Nontraditional and Alternative Treatments

One controversial treatment for alcoholism (cf. Pendery, Maltzman, & West, 1982) is controlled drinking in which clients are taught behavioral strategies such as monitoring their blood alcohol levels in order to avoid intoxication and practicing alternative responses to excessive drinking (cf., for example, Sobell & Sobell, 1973). Though controlled drinking treatment has been used with those who are alcohol dependent, most treatment providers consider it viable only for those with problems of alcohol abuse or misuse.

Acupuncture has been used in detoxification and following detoxification. Some individuals are quite enthusiastic about this adjunct to treatment (cf. Brumbaugh, 1993), and many chemical dependency counselors have been taught to administer it. Empirical evidence of acupuncture's effectiveness remains ambiguous, partly because of the difficulty in administering placebo acupuncture in controlled studies (cf. Avants, Margolin, & Chang, 1995)

There is also interest in stress reduction or relaxation techniques. Among them is alpha-theta brain-wave training (biofeedback) (cf. Peniston & Kulkosky, 1992). Its purpose is to increase alpha and theta brain-wave rhythms, because one theory is that those with chemical dependency problems are deficient in them. There is no strong evidence to suggest that the technique is particularly helpful in preventing drinking or drug use, but some clients may find it useful.

Providing positive rewards (incentives) rather than negative ones may promote better treatment outcomes. For example, evidence indicates that rewarding clients with take-home doses of methadone may deter their use of cocaine to get high (Stitzer, Iguchi, & Felch, 1992). Perhaps one of the most ingenious ideas is to provide tangible goods (such as household or recreational items) as an incentive for clients to refrain from alcohol or other drug use (Higgins, Budney, Bickel et al., 1994).

A different approach to abuse and addiction is harm reduction, which may be defined as attempts to reduce the negative consequences that result from substance use. Free taxi rides home for those who become intoxicated are one harm reduction technique. Sobriety checkpoints are another harm reduction technique that some people applaud and others see as a violation of civil liberties if there is no indication that a driver should be stopped.

Another controversial harm reduction approach is needle-exchange programs. In most places in the United States, these programs are illegal, though some communities do not interfere with their operation. Some programs operate in a fixed location; others use vans that enable them to reach various areas of the community and may cause less community controversy. Intravenous drug users generally turn in dirty needles and receive clean needles in return, no questions asked. The people who operate these services usually do not pressure addicts to stop using, but they are available to help them get medical attention or chemical dependency treatment if the user requests it. These programs are humanitarian efforts to prevent the spread of HIV and other serious diseases. Despite consistent evidence of their effectiveness in the United States and abroad, the U.S. government refuses to fund needle-exchange programs (cf. "Needle-exchange programmes...," 1998).

Alcohol and drug use depletes vitamins and other nutrients in the body, and individuals who abuse these substances may wish to use vitamin supplements (Balch & Balch, 1997). Individuals often take their own initiatives in addressing their alcohol and drug problems. A well-known saying in AA is "Never get too hungry, angry, lonely, or tired" (H.A.L.T.). Some alcoholics swear by eating at regular intervals because they believe that low blood sugar levels put them at risk of drinking. St. John's wort and other products being used to treat mental distress are undoubtedly being tried by those with alcohol and drug problems, too.

Dual Diagnoses

"I need a place where I can talk about all of my illnesses." (A client with dual diagnoses)

As discussed in earlier chapters, schizophrenia, schizoaffective disorder, bipolar disorder, and major depression are among the diagnoses considered severe mental illnesses. All these are classified as Axis I disorders in the *DSM-IV.* Substance abuse and dependence are also Axis I diagnoses. Individuals who have mental *and* substance use disorders are said to have dual, multiple, or co-occurring diagnoses.

Though substance use disorders may precipitate mental illness, and vice versa, the two types of illnesses may develop independently. In people who are truly dually diagnosed, mental illness such as moderate to severe depression is not "just a symptom" of substance abuse or dependence that will simply "go away" after the person gets sober and clean. Likewise, chemical abuse or dependence is not "just self-medicating" a mental illness and will not just "disappear" after the person is stabilized on psychotropic medications. In other words, in individuals with both Axis I mental and substance use disorders, each Axis I disorder is a primary disorder (Minkoff, 1990). As children begin alcohol and drug use at very early ages, before the ages at which particular mental illnesses would usually appear, it is difficult to know if mental illness would have developed without prior drug use. Thus, we have dropped the "chicken and egg" debates over which illness came first or is primary in favor of the current clinical convention of considering both Axis I mental and substance use disorders as primary.

Some of the Axis II diagnoses that commonly appear in conjunction with substance use disorders are borderline, antisocial, and dependent personality disorders (Ekleberry, 1996). Sciacca (1989, 1991) distinguishes two major combinations of mental illnesses and substance use disorders: The person who is mentally ill and chemically abusing or addicted (MICAA) has a severe Axis I mental disorder in addition to a substance use disorder, while the chemically abusing or addicted person with mental illness (CAMI) has no Axis I mental disorder but has a substance use disorder and an Axis II mental disorder. The following are examples of how these diagnoses may be recorded:

MICAA	Axis I:	295.30	Schizophrenia, Paranoid Type
		304.30	Cannabis Dependence
	Axis II:	V71.09	No Diagnosis
CAMI	Axis I:	304.20	Cocaine Dependence
	Axis II:	301.83	Borderline Personality Disorder

Such distinctions may be important in determining the course of a client's treatment. For example, Sciacca (1990) believes that the substance abuse problems of CAMI clients can be treated successfully in traditional chemical dependency programs because these individuals can better tolerate the confrontation that is often used in these programs. MICAA clients are more fragile and often need special services.

Many MICAA clients also have health problems, captured on Axis III of the *DSM-IV.* Diabetes and high blood pressure, for example, are common medical conditions that often require the use of medications—medications that may interact with psychotropic medications, alcohol, street drugs, and over-the-counter preparations, posing serious health risks. Social workers must consider clients' physical illnesses, including their symptoms, treatments, and medication side effects, in treatment planning and coordinate delivery of care with other service providers.

Consideration of *DSM-IV*, Axis IV stressors is also essential in understanding each client's unique needs and strengths. For example, if a client's life is devoid of primary relationships, the social worker may tell him or her about appropriate sources of peer support and look for ways to further enhance support in the natural environment.

Finally, Axis V, the Global Assessment of Functioning (GAF) scale, is useful in denoting an individual's functional ability over time. GAF scores of those with severe mental illnesses may fluctuate considerably or tend toward the lower end of the scale (indicating lower functioning) and can signal points at which intensive intervention is needed. GAF scores are also important because not everyone with an Axis I mental disorder functions poorly. For instance, some people have milder cases of schizophrenia than others, and some experience only one episode of this illness in their lifetime. Thus, the course of mental illnesses is variable, and with appropriate and timely intervention and ongoing follow-along, some individuals may be spared the *chronic* label.

People with multiple diagnoses are often described as presenting more serious life problems than persons with either a mental or substance use disorder. The thought of managing multiple illnesses may be overwhelming to them. A client seeking assistance may have difficulty with one or more illnesses at the same time because a flare-up of one illness may compromise progress made on other illnesses. Thus, a person with diabetes who has an episode of severe depression may start drinking alcohol again even though he or she risks a diabetic coma. Using the five *DSM-IV* axes, social workers can conceptualize each person's challenges and strengths in a more comprehensive way. It is not easy for people to cope with multiple illnesses, but it is possible.

How prevalent are dual diagnoses in the general population? In the NIMH Epidemiologic Catchment Area (ECA) Study, Regier et al. (1990) found that among those diagnosed with a lifetime mental disorder, 22.3 percent also had a diagnosis of alcohol dependence or abuse, and 14.7 percent had drug dependence or abuse (p. 2516). Those with a mental illness were more than twice as likely to develop an alcohol use disorder and more than four times as likely to develop a drug use disorder as those without a mental illness. The National Comorbidity Survey (NCS) identified higher rates of co-occurring illnesses than the ECA study: "41.0%–65.5% of respondents with a lifetime addictive disorder [including substance abuse] also have a lifetime history of at least one mental disorder, while 50.9% of those with one or more lifetime mental disorders also have a lifetime history of at least one addictive disorder" (Kessler et al., 1996, pp. 20–21). The high prevalence of comorbidity means that practitioners must be knowledgeable about both mental and substance use disorders.

Because the substance use disorders of clients with Axis II disorders can be addressed in traditional chemical dependency programs, the following discussion of dual diagnoses primarily concerns MICAA clients.

Recognizing Dual Diagnoses

Recognizing dual diagnoses is often difficult, especially in emergency situations, because substance-induced psychoses can look very similar to an acute exacerbation of a severe mental illness. When intoxicated clients with dual diagnoses whose history is not known to the treatment provider are admitted for care, their mental illness may not be recognized until detoxification occurs. The various subgroups or combinations of mental disorders and substance use disorders also complicate identification of clients' problems. A clinician may not realize that the paranoia being experienced by a client with schizophrenia is a result of marijuana use. Clients with depression are commonly drawn to depressant drugs, and service providers may find it difficult to identify the factors currently contributing to the depression.

Dual diagnoses may also be overlooked because individuals who think in very concrete terms tend to offer information only in response to specific questions and may not mention their alcohol or drug use unless specifically asked. They may not have insight into the deleterious effects of substance use on their precarious mental health, or they may want to present themselves in the "best possible light" when requesting services and fail to volunteer information about substance use. Like clients with a single diagnosis of substance use disorders, obtaining a clear clinical picture of clients with dual diagnoses may require detailed social histories, consultation with family and significant others, review of inpatient and outpatient records and court records, and urine toxicologies.

Another reason that substance use disorders are often overlooked is that even consumption of relatively small amounts of alcohol or other drugs (what many consider nonharmful, "social" use) can create imbalances in the fragile brain chemistry of those with mental disorders, resulting in serious problems such as psychotic episodes. For example, a caseworker was asked at a staffing whether a long-time client of hers, who had had multiple hospitalizations, drank or used drugs. The caseworker gave a strong negative response and offered a long list of observations about the client that did not indicate intoxication, abuse, or dependence. Subsequently, the client met with her mental health team and was asked what symptoms she noticed before admissions. Much to her caseworker's surprise, the client replied that every time she drank even one beer, the next thing she knew, she was in the hospital!

In another case, the professionals serving a young man who had three mental hospital stays in one year assumed it was noncompliance with medications that precipitated his admissions. None realized that before most episodes he had rapidly consumed up to a six-pack of beer. When the client himself recognized the association between his drinking and his psychotic episodes, he decided to quit drinking and was able to stay out of the hospital for years. These examples demonstrate the need to screen for substance use as well as abuse in clients with severe mental illness.

Until recently there has been no tool specifically developed to screen for substance use disorders in clients who have mental disorders. The Dartmouth Assessment of Lifestyle Inventory (DALI), designed to fill this gap, is an eighteen-item, interviewer-administered scale. The DALI focuses on alcohol, marijuana, and cocaine (the most widely abused substances) and is available on the Internet at: http://www.dartmouth.edu/dms/psychrc/dali.html (cf. also Rosenberg et al., 1998).

Dual Education for Clients

Many clients do not connect their alcohol or other drug use with exacerbation of their mental illness, perhaps because education about the dangers of substance use and abuse has not been routinely integrated into the treatment of people with psychiatric disorders. In mental health programs, strong emphasis is placed on compliance with psychotropic medications and potential side effects of these drugs. Equal emphasis should be placed on the adverse effects of using alcohol and nonprescribed drugs. Messages to consumers must be clear and consistent: use or abuse of alcohol or nonprescribed drugs can adversely affect mental stability. In addition, the interactions of nonprescribed and prescribed drugs can be harmful to one's physical health and even lethal. Professionals must continually differentiate between medications (drugs prescribed by their psychiatrist or primary health care physician and used as directed) and street drugs, over-the-counter drugs, alcohol, and improperly used prescription drugs (Bricker, 1988; Webb, 1997).

Clients may have difficulty connecting the temporal aspects of their drug use with the exacerbation of their mental health problems and vice versa (cf. Sciacca, 1987; Webb, 1997) because learning, judgment, and memory are generally impaired when they become mentally unstable. Attention to relapse cues and triggers can help them discover a repeated cycle of substance use before mental illness exacerbations occur (Schuckit, 1983) or a pattern in which increases in psychiatric symptoms (such as may occur when clients take their medication differently than prescribed, do not take it at all, or run out of medication) precede the use of nonprescribed, psychoactive drugs. Kofoed and Keys (1988) describe the use of a persuasion group with psychiatric inpatients to help them "acknowledge their drug addiction and to seek continued substance abuse treatment" (p. 1210; cf. also Osher & Kofoed, 1989, on engaging clients into treatment).

It is also useful to educate clients about the parallels or similarities between their two types of problems. In both conditions, for example, denial is common, there is a loss of control over behavior and emotions, and there is a need for treatment (cf. Bricker, 1989; Carey, 1989; Minkoff, 1989; Webb, 1997).

Best Practices in Dual Diagnoses Treatment

In many communities outpatient services for clients with mental illness and services for persons with chemical dependency are administered by two separate agencies, complicating the coordination of services for people with dual diagnoses. In other communities the same agency (typically a community mental health center) is responsible for mental health and chemical dependency treatment services, but these services are provided by separate programs or treatment teams. Despite these dual administrative structures, mental health and chemical dependency professionals have advanced beyond the once common practice of treating mental illness and substance use disorders separately.

Some chemical dependency programs offer help for mental illness by recruiting a mental health professional to provide additional services to clients who have dual disorders. Conversely, some psychiatric programs offer help with substance use disorders by having a chemical dependency counselor work with clients individually or in groups (cf. Hendrickson, 1988). Most providers now offer services that fall somewhere on a continuum between partially and fully integrated. By *integrated,* we mean that mental and substance use disorders are treated simultaneously and most optimally by treatment teams composed of dual diagnoses specialists. As service providers have come to see integrated treatment as an ideal approach for working with clients with dual diagnoses, they are seeking professional staff who are dual diagnoses specialists—those equally qualified in the delivery of mental health *and* chemical dependency services.

Integrated dual diagnoses programs (cf., DiNitto & Webb, 1998; Kofoed & Keys, 1988; Minkoff, 1989; Ridgely, Osher, & Talbott, 1987) usually present mental and substance use disorders as similar problems, and treatment focuses on the unique experiences of clients who have both problems (e.g., the cyclical nature and interplay of substance use and mental illness or making use of self-help programs designed for people with single diagnoses). Integrated programs provide clients a safe environment to discuss their dual problems without fear of being ostracized by other clients as might be the case when a client in a psychiatric program talks about "shooting" drugs, or when a client in a chemical dependency program discusses religious delusions.

Integrated treatment may take place in the context of other best practices in the treatment of people with severe and persistent mental illness such as supported housing, supported employment, and Assertive Community Treatment (ACT) Teams (Stein & Santos, 1998 and cf. Chapter 11). ACT teams can be modified into partially integrated dual diagnoses services by incorporating a licensed or certified chemical dependency specialist who takes the lead with mentally ill clients who have active alcohol or other drug problems. In addition, the team should be educated on how to serve those with chemical dependency. A fully integrated ACT team would be staffed by clinicians dually qualified to treat both illnesses at the same time. This optimal clinical situation lessens the burden dually diagnosed individuals may experience when they must deal with two treatment programs with different philosophies that answer to different funding sources with different service requirements.

Many chemical dependency practitioners are familiar with the process of changing addictive behaviors presented by Prochaska, DiClemente, and Norcross (1992). This process begins with *precontemplation* in which the individual lacks awareness of the problem and has no intention of changing. In the *contemplation* phase, awareness develops and the individual weighs the pros and cons of changing. During the *preparation* phase, the individual intends to make a change soon, and in the *action* phase, he or she successfully makes the change. During *maintenance,* the individual continues to change in order to prevent relapse. Practitioners help clients move from one phase to the next by using education, positive reinforcement, contracting, social support, and other therapeutic techniques. The literature on integrated treatment also emphasizes the stages through which clients progress in the therapeutic process. Minkoff (1989) describes four stages of treatment: (a) acute stabilization; (b) engagement to participate in treatment; (c) prolonged stabilization, including abstinence from substances and control of the symptoms of mental illness; and (d) rehabilitation. Osher and Kofoed (1989) refer to four similar phases of treatment: (a) engagement into treatment; (b) persuasion to stabilize over a long period of time; (c) active treatment; and (d) relapse prevention.

Dual diagnoses group therapy, psychoeducational groups, and dual twelve-step meetings are commonly used today. An example of these therapy groups is Good Chemistry groups, which are cofacilitated by a professional and an individual in dual recovery (Webb, 1997). The sessions combine fifteen minutes of didactic psychoeducation with forty-five minutes of structured group therapy. The psychoeducational component covers the signs and symptoms of mental and substance use disorders, how these illnesses overlap and interact, the dangers of mixing medications with alcohol and nonprescribed drugs (with particular emphasis on alcohol, marijuana, and cocaine), the use of AA and other twelve-step programs, AA's policy on medications (which supports the use of psychotropic medications when prescribed by a physician [cf. Alcoholics Anonymous World Services, 1984]), recognizing relapse cues and preparing solutions, asking for extra help when needed, and the importance of staying involved in treatment.

Good Chemistry groups are an alternative or supplement to twelve-step meetings like AA and NA that focus on a single diagnosis of problems with alcohol or drugs. Individuals with dual or multiple diagnoses and moderate to severe functional problems, thus, have the opportunity to address their illnesses simultaneously in a supportive, positive atmosphere, which lends structure and direction to their recovery. The groups offer hope and encourage clients to become more responsible for their own treatment plan and outcomes. Table 13.5 is an example of materials used in Good Chemistry groups.

Peer-led Dual Recovery Anonymous (DRA) meetings are growing in number throughout the United States and offer people with co-occurring illnesses support to work on both illnesses simultaneously (information on DRA can be found on the Internet at http://dualrecovery.org). This type of self-help meeting is an integral part of a full continuum of services for persons with dual disorders.

In order to encourage best practices for clients with dual diagnoses, a report of the Co-Occurring Mental and Substance Disorders Panel of the Clinical Standards and Workforce Competencies Project (1998), part of the Center for Mental Health Services' Managed Care Initiative, offers guidelines on service integration. For example,

- Integrated services should be provided "according to subtype of dual disorder and phase of treatment."
- Managed care programs should "reimburse *integrated* program models as distinct from 'single-diagnosis' programs, with higher rates as appropriate."
- Integrated services should be available "in the settings in which...[clients] receive treatment for their most serious disorder" (mental health or chemical dependency program).
- "'Integrated' peer support groups" should be available.

TABLE 13.5   Good Chemistry Mottos

1. I choose an alcohol and drug-free lifestyle for my own good physical and mental health.
2. I choose to take my prescribed medications for my own good mental health.
3. I will not enable myself or others to drink or drug.
4. I will point those having problems to appropriate helpers.
5. I believe in being a "Good Samaritan" by reaching out to and helping those in need.
6. I can make a positive difference in the lives of others when I value my own life and sobriety.
7. It is okay to discover and nurture the positive parts of myself so that I can continue to grow and be healthy.

Source: From Good Chemistry co-leader's manual, by D. K. Webb, 1997, Austin, TX: Author. Copyright © 1997 by Deborah K. Webb, Ph.D., LPC, LCDC. Reprinted with permission.

- "Primary caregivers and case managers…[should be] cross-trained and able to provide integrated treatment."
- "Managed care entities [should] require programs to demonstrate that there are sufficient dual diagnosis clinicians…to serve…dual diagnosed clients."

Treating Clients with Chemical Dependency and Dual Disorders in the Era of Managed Care

The Mental Health Parity Act of 1996, designed to improve access to mental health services (see Chapter 2), does not address services for substance use disorders. Some states go further in requiring parity for mental health services and some include chemical dependency services. Whether required to do so or not, many health insurers (including managed care plans) offer coverage for chemical dependency, though this coverage is often more limited than it is for mental health services. Insurers often carve out their behavioral health (mental health and chemical dependency) services, meaning that they contract with others to administer these services. Substance abuse services may be further carved out from mental health services, causing those in the chemical dependency field to worry that the services they provide will be a stepchild, not only to health services, but to mental health services as well. Carve-outs also raise questions about whether separate providers can serve clients in a holistic fashion.

A study of employer-provided health benefits by the Hay Group (1998) shows that from 1988 to 1989, the value of health care benefits for the treatment of substance use disorders declined from 0.7 percent to 0.2 percent of the plans' overall value. The Working Group of the ASAM Managed Care Initiative (1999) reports "a drastic reduction in frequency and duration of inpatient hospitalization [for people with substance use disorders], even for many patients who require this level of treatment intensity," with managed care plans authorizing inpatient treatment only in life-threatening cases). Detoxification may be the only inpatient service covered for those with chemical dependence (cf. Mechanic, Schlesinger, & McAlpine, 1995), despite knowledge that "detox" alone is generally ineffective in promoting recovery (cf., for example, Gerstein & Harwood, 1990). According to Shulman (1994), a patient may be required to fail at outpatient treatment before inpatient care is authorized.

After studying treatment services provided to more than 7,000 alcoholics and drug addicts, Miller and Hoffman (1995) concluded that many health care plans do not provide a continuum of care for these individuals; instead, most health care providers used an acute care model to treat chemical dependency—a problem that for many is chronic. Mechanic and colleagues (1995) conclude that "the probability of treatment for substance abuse is certainly no higher and may be significantly lower under prepaid care," including Medicaid capitated care arrangements (pp. 35–36).

As the following case illustrates, the American Society of Addiction Medicine is concerned that patients who are "more severely compromised," such as people with dual diagnoses, are also finding it difficult to obtain needed inpatient treatment.

A 28-year-old man with a history of polysubstance abuse was hospitalized at a private psychiatric hospital. His stay as an inpatient was initially limited to three days by his managed care company. While in the hospital, in addition to his polysubstance abuse including alcohol and cocaine, it was noted that there was a strong family history of bipolar illness and the patient reported both highs and lows while not on various substances. The diagnosis of bipolar disorder was, therefore, added to his substance abuse diagnosis. Following his three day inpatient stay, he was referred to an outpatient chemical dependency program for which his managed care company approved only six visits per year.

After showing up for his first visit, he dropped out of treatment and wound up at an emergency room some time later, stating: "I don't know what I will do with myself. I'm just totally lost. I need help." A call to the case reviewer led to a denial of further inpatient care since his insurance would cover only one hospital stay during the course of the year, and his relapse was blamed on the patient in the form of denial of further care and treatment. Since the hospital appreciated that this patient absolutely required extended inpatient treatment, it sought to transfer him to a state hospital; however, amid this confusion the patient suddenly bolted from the emergency room. He was found two days later frozen to death under a railroad bridge. (Working Group of the ASAM Managed Care Initiative, 1999)

Detoxification and other inpatient services for clients with dual diagnoses cost more than for clients with single diagnoses of chemical dependency. This is because individuals with co-occurring illnesses require more medical supervision and more expensive types of treatment, such as the "new-generation" psychotropic medications that have fewer side effects (see Chapters 8 and 12). The billing systems of many chemical dependency service providers, such as community detoxification centers, have not been set up to accept Medicaid, on which many clients with severe mental illness rely for their care. According to Schulman (1994), the treatment of clients with dual diagnoses should not be restricted to psychiatric hospitals because many clients with dual diagnoses can be treated in less expensive facilities, especially when their mental illness responds to psychotropic medication. Even if chemical dependency treatment programs want to accept more patients with dual diagnoses, they are hard pressed to do so because the funding streams for treating those with chemically dependency and those with mental disorders have not become integrated. Federal and state agencies that fund chemical dependency services may have restrictions against using the funds for services needed by clients with mental illness, and mental health funding agencies may prohibit use of their funds for services necessary for chemical dependency treatment (cf. National Advisory Council, 1998). Though chemical dependency and mental health funding agencies agree that integrated treatment is best for clients with dual diagnoses, turf issues make them reluctant to blend their funding to support it.

There are some positive aspects of managed care, such as greater emphasis on client and system outcomes, increased oversight of services and accountability, and input from clients, families, and other constituents in designing and evaluating services. The National Committee for Quality Assurance (NCQA) now requires facilities that it accredits to do studies of special populations, such as those with dual diagnoses. These clients may take longer to treat or need a greater number of services due to their multiple diagnoses. At the same time that awareness of the need for a continuum of integrated services for those with dual diagnoses has occurred, there is greater attention to utilization management, including justification for all services rendered. Clients with dual diagnoses may have fared worse under managed care if attention to the need for a continuum of integrated services for them had not emerged at the same time.

The Effectiveness of Treatment for Chemical Dependency and Dual Diagnoses

The question of whether chemical dependency treatment is effective has been asked many times. Despite high relapse rates, the literature shows that following treatment, many clients reduce their alcohol and drug use and criminal activity and become more productive, and that there are cost savings to society (cf. Gerstein & Harwood, 1990; Office of Applied Studies, 1998). As mentioned earlier in this chapter, other research findings indicate that outpatient treatment for alcoholism is generally as effective as inpatient treatment, that detoxification services alone usually do not produce long-lasting benefits, that longer stays in residential drug treatment often produce better outcomes than shorter stays, and that pharmacotherapies tend to work better when coupled with psychosocial treatments. The questions now being asked are not whether treatment works but how it can be made more effective.

Some alcoholism researchers have been particularly interested in whether clients can be better matched to alcoholism treatments to improve outcomes. To pursue this question, NIAAA conducted a large, multisite, multimillion dollar study utilizing three time-limited interventions: (1) twelve-step facilitation, which taught clients to participate in Alcoholics Anonymous and encouraged them to attend meetings; (2) motivational enhancement therapy designed to help clients engage in the process of change; and (3) cognitive-behavioral therapy, which focused on helping clients learn coping strategies instead of using alcohol to deal with problem situations (Project Match Study Group, 1997). On average, study participants reduced their drinking. But contrary to previous, smaller research studies, there were few "matches"; that is, the three treatments worked equally well, regardless of client characteristics such as gender, severity of alcohol involvement, readiness to change, social support, and other factors. The only robust match was that outpatient clients who had lower psychiatric severity drank on fewer days after twelve-step facilitation therapy than after cognitive-behavioral therapy.

It seems that at least among these three interventions, high-quality services can be expected to produce equally positive results almost without consideration of clients' individual characteristics. But one should not confuse this finding with the need for sensitivity to client characteristics such as gender, sexual orientation, and ethnicity. More information is needed on many questions, such as whether certain characteristics of chemical dependency professionals are associated with better client outcomes.

Because integrated dual diagnoses treatments are relatively new, studies on their effectiveness are limited. Most dual diagnoses researchers have studied treatment for male clients with schizophrenia in the context of mental health services, though inclusion of female clients and clients with mood disorders has increased. One group of pretest-posttest studies indicates that clients with dual diagnoses improve with treatment (Drake, Mueser, Clark, & Wallach, 1996; Mercer-McFadden, Drake, Brown, & Fox, 1997).

Among the small number of controlled dual diagnoses treatment studies (e.g., Burnam et al., 1995; Drake et al., 1998; Drake, Yovetich, Bebout, Harris, & McHugo, 1997; Jerrell and Ridgely, 1995; Webb & DiNitto, 1997), integrated treatments have produced either no better outcomes or modestly better outcomes than comparison services such as standard mental health care. There are several possible explanations for why clients with dual diagnoses did not make more impressive gains in integrated treatment. Studies often include clients who have various types of mental disorders and various types of substance abuse problems. More homogeneous study samples may help determine whether some treatments are more effective for clients with particular diagnoses. Few tools have been developed to measure alcohol and drug use and other outcomes for clients with dual diagnoses. The tools currently being used in the chemical dependency and mental health fields may not be sufficiently sensitive to measure changes among clients with dual diagnoses. Most treatment providers have become more sophisticated about dual disorders and have adopted some form of integrated treatment; therefore, even clients who did not receive treatment specifically defined as integrated may have benefited from increased awareness about the need to treat clients in a more integrated fashion (Mueser, Drake, & Miles, 1997). In both the single diagnosis and dual diagnoses fields, the key to improving the lives of clients seems to be in the availability of high-quality services provided by those who are interested in their care rather than in the different treatments tested.

Summary

Clinical social workers frequently see clients with substance use disorders and mental disorders in combination with substance use in the behavioral mental health field. Mental health practitioners and chemical dependency practitioners need a thorough grounding in both types of illnesses in order to serve their clients well. In fact, education in one field but not the other is quickly becoming an anachronism. The search for the causes of substance use and mental disorders continues as do efforts to identify treatment methods that will engage more clients and reduce the incidence of relapse. Practitioners are considering the array of treatments available, including those that have not been traditionally employed in treating mental and substance use disorders. A better policy response is also needed, including more focus on education, prevention, and treatment. A biopsychosocial framework for practice and a postmodern approach may help us to respond more fully to clients with substance use disorders and dual diagnoses.

DISCUSSION QUESTIONS

1. How do substance abuse and dependence interact with mental disorders?

2. What is a polysubstance user? Give examples of drugs that are used together. What are the risks of polysubstance use?

3. How does the *DSM-IV* classify problems related to substance abuse and dependence?

4. How are the various theories explaining substance abuse that were described in this chapter reflected in the methods of treatment used in the community?

5. Get copies of some of the screening and assessment tools that were mentioned in this chapter and use them to screen clients on your caseload. What did you learn about the individuals from using these instruments?

6. What kinds of services (if any) in your community are tailored especially for persons with dual diagnoses? If there are no specialized services, what existing resources are available to

this population? What kinds of services are needed in your community to serve persons with dual diagnoses? What can you do to help address this need?

7. Why are dual diagnoses underdiagnosed?

8. How is an intervention or program for persons with dual diagnoses different from a program for individuals with single disorders?

9. Escort a client you are working with to a support group for persons with a single diagnosis, and then to a support group for those with dual diagnoses, and observe the groups. How sensitive were the groups to participants with more than one problem?

REFERENCES

Aguilar, M., DiNitto, D. M., Franklin, C., & Lopez-Pilkinton, B. (1991). Mexican-American families: A psychoeducational approach for addressing chemical dependency and codependency. *Child and Adolescent Social Work Journal, 8*(4), 309–326.

Alcoholics Anonymous World Services. (1952). *Forty-four questions and answers about the AA program of recovery from alcoholism.* New York: Author.

Alcoholics Anonymous World Services. (1984). *The AA member—Medications and other drugs.* New York: Author.

American Psychiatric Association. (1994). *Diagnostic and statistical manual of mental disorders* (4th ed.). Washington, DC: Author.

Atkinson, R. M. (1985). Persuading alcoholic patients to seek treatment. *Comprehensive Therapy, 11,* 16–24.

Avants, S. K., Margolin, A., Chang, P., Kosten, T. R., & Birch, S. (1995). Acupuncture for the treatment of cocaine addiction: Investigation of a needle puncture control. *Journal of Substance Abuse Treatment, 12*(3), 195–205.

Babor, T. F., de la Fuente, J. R., Saunders, J., & Grant, M. (1992). AUDIT: *The Alcohol Use Disorders Identification Test, Guidelines for Use in Primary Health Care.* Geneva: World Health Organization.

Bacon, M. K. (1974). The dependency-conflict hypothesis and the frequency of drunkenness. *Quarterly Journal of Studies on Alcohol, 35,* 863–876.

Balch, J. F., & Balch, P. A. (1997). *Prescription for nutritional healing* (2nd ed.). Garden City Park, NY: Avery Publishing.

Bales, R. F. (1946). Cultural differences in rates of alcoholism. *Quarterly Journal of Studies on Alcoholism, 6,* 480–499.

Berg, I. K., & Miller, S. D. (1992). *Working with the problem drinker; a solution-focused approach.* New York: W. W. Norton.

Bien, T. H., Miller, W. R., & Tonigan, J. S. (1993). Brief interventions for alcohol problems: A review. *Addiction, 88,* 315–336.

Bloom, F. E. (1982). A summary of workshop discussions. In F. Bloom et al. (Eds.), *Beta-carbolines and tetrahydroisoquinolines* (pp. 401–410). New York: Alan R. Liss.

Brick, J., & Erickson, C. K. (1998). *Drugs, the brain, and behavior: The pharmacology of abuse and dependence.* New York: Haworth Medical Press.

Bricker, M. G. (1988). *STEMSS, Support Together for Emotional and Mental Serenity and Sobriety.* Milwaukee, WI: DePaul Belleview.

Bricker, M. G. (1989). *The twelve parallels between chemical dependency and mental illness.* Milwaukee, WI: DePaul Belleview.

Brumbaugh, A. G. (1993). Acupuncture: New perspectives in chemical dependency treatment. *Journal of Substance Abuse Treatment, 19,* 35–43.

Burnam, M. A., Morton, S. C., McGlynn, E. A., Petersen, L. P., Stecher, B. M., Hayes, C., & Vaccaro, J. V. (1995). An experimental evaluation of residential and nonresidential treatment of dually diagnosed homeless adults. *Journal of Addictive Diseases, 14,* 111–134.

Caetano, R. (1988). Responding to alcohol-related problems among Hispanics. *Contemporary Drug Problems, 15*(3), 335–363.

Caetano, R., & Kaskutas, L. A. (1995). Changes in drinking patterns among Whites, Blacks, and Hispanics, 1984–1992. *Journal of Studies on Alcohol, 56,* 558–565.

Carey, K. B. (1989). Emerging treatment guidelines for mentally ill chemical abusers. *Hospital and Community Psychiatry, 40*(4), 341–349.

Cloninger, C. R., Sigvardsson, S., & Bohman, M. (1996). Type I and Type II alcoholism: An update. *Alcohol Health & Research World, 20*(1), 18–23.

Comas-Diaz, L. (1986). Puerto Rican alcoholic women: Treatment considerations. *Alcoholism Treatment Quarterly, 3*(1), 47–57.

Co-Occurring Mental and Substance Disorders Panel, Clinical Standards and Workforce Competencies Project. (1998). *Co-occurring psychiatric and substance disorders in managed care systems: Stan-*

dards of care, practice guidelines, workforce competencies, and training curricula. Rockville, MD: Substance Abuse and Mental Health Services Administration, Center for Mental Health Services.

Cuskey, W. R., Berger, L. H., & Densen-Gerber, J. (1981). Issues in the treatment of female addiction: A review and critique of the literature. In E. Howell & M. Bayes (Eds.). Women and mental health (pp. 269–295). New York: Basic Books.

Davies, D. L. (1976). Definitional issues in alcoholism. In R. E. Tarter & A. A. Sugerman (Eds.), Alcoholism: Interdisciplinary approaches to an enduring problem (pp. 53–73). Reading, MA: Addison-Wesley.

Davis, D. R. (1998). Making meaning of Alcoholics Anonymous for social workers: Myths, metaphors, and realities. Social Work, 43(2), 169–182.

Davis, D., & DiNitto, D. M. (1998). Gender and drugs: Fact, fiction, and unanswered questions. In C. A. McNeece & D. M. DiNitto, Chemical dependency: A systems approach (2nd ed., pp. 406–442). Boston: Allyn and Bacon.

DiNitto, D. M. (2000). Social welfare: Politics and public policy (5th ed.). Boston: Allyn and Bacon.

DiNitto, D. M., & Webb, D. K. (1998). Compounding the problem: Substance abuse and other disabilities. In C. A. McNeece & D. M. DiNitto, Chemical dependency: A systems approach (2nd ed., pp. 347–390). Boston: Allyn and Bacon.

Doweiko, H. E. (1999). Concepts of chemical dependency (4th ed.). Pacific Grove, CA: Brooks/Cole.

Drake, R. E., McHugo, G. J., Clark, R. E., Teague, G. B., Xie, H., Miles, K., & Ackerson, T. H. (1998). Assertive community treatment for patients with co-occurring severe mental illness and substance use disorders. American Journal of Orthopsychiatry, 68(2), 201–215.

Drake, R. E., Mueser, K. T., Clark, R. E., & Wallach, M. A. (1996). The course, treatment, and outcome of substance disorder in persons with severe mental illness. American Journal of Orthopsychiatry, 66(1), 42–51.

Drake, R. E., Yovetich, N. A., Bebout, R. R., Harris, M., & McHugo, G. J. (1997). Integrated treatment for dually diagnosed homeless adults. Journal of Nervous and Mental Disease, 185, 298–305.

Ekleberry, S. C. (1996, March/April). Dual diagnosis: Addiction and Axis II personality disorders. The Counselor, pp. 7–13.

Fingarette, H. (1985, March/April). Alcoholism: Neither sin nor disease. The Center Magazine, pp. 56–63.

Frezza, M., di Padova, C., Pozzato, G., Terpin, M., Baraona, E., & Lieber, C. S. (1990). High blood alcohol levels in women: The role of decreased gastric alcohol dehydrogenase activity and first-pass metabolism. New England Journal of Medicine, 322(2), 95–99.

Gerstein, D. R., & Harwood, H. J. (Eds.). (1990). Treating drug problems (Vol. 1). Washington, DC: National Academy Press.

Glasser, W. (1965). Reality therapy. New York: Harper Colophon Books.

Gorski, T. T., & Miller, M. (1986). Staying sober: A guide for relapse prevention. Independence, MO: Independence Press.

Grant, B. F., Harford, T. C., Dawson, D. A., Chou, P., Dufour, M., & Pickering, R. (1995). Prevalence of DSM-IV alcohol abuse and dependence. Alcohol Health & Research World, 18(3), 243–248.

Hanson, G., & Venturelli, P. (1998). Drugs and society. Boston: Jones and Bartlett.

Harper, F. D. (1980). Etiology: Why do blacks drink? In F. D. Harper, Alcohol abuse and black America (pp. 27–37). Alexandria, VA: Douglass Publishers.

Hayashida, M., Alterman, A. I., McLellan, T., et al. (1989). Comparative effectiveness and costs of inpatient and outpatient detoxification of patients with mild-to-moderate alcohol withdrawal syndrome. New England Journal of Medicine, 320, 358–365.

Hay Group. (1998). Substance abuse benefit cost trends 1988–1998. Unpublished report commissioned by the American Society on Addiction Medicine. [Available on-line: http://www.asam.org].

Henderson, D., & Boyd, D. (1992). Masculinity, femininity, and addiction. In T. Mieczkowski (Ed.), Drugs, crime, and social policy: Research, issues and concerns (pp. 153–156). Boston: Allyn and Bacon.

Hendrickson, E. L. (1988). Treating the dually diagnosed (mental disorder/substance use) client. TIE-Lines, 5(4), 1–4.

Higgins, S. T., Budney, A. J., Bickel, W. K., et al. (1994). Incentives improve outcome in outpatient behavioral treatment of cocaine dependence. Archives of General Psychiatry, 51, 568–576.

Hser, Y., Anglin, M. D., & Booth, M. W. (1987). Sex differences in addicts careers. 3. Addiction. American Journal of Drug and Alcohol Abuse, 13(3), 231–251.

Indian Health Service. (1977). Alcoholism: A high priority health problem, a report of the Indian Health Service Task Force on alcoholism (Pub. No. [HSA] 77–1001). Washington, DC: Department of Health, Education, and Welfare.

Israelstam, S. (1986). Alcohol and drug problems of gay males and lesbians: Therapy, counseling and prevention issues. Journal of Drug Issues, 16(3), 443–461.

Jellinek, E. M. (1960). The disease concept of alcoholism. New Haven, CT: College and University Press.

Jerrell, J. M., & Ridgely, M. S. (1995). Comparative effectiveness of three approaches to serving people with severe mental illness and substance abuse disorders. Journal of Nervous and Mental Disease, 183, 566–576.

Kaskutas, L. A. (1994). What do women get out of self-help? Their reasons for attending Women for Sobriety and Alcoholics Anonymous. *Journal of Substance Abuse Treatment, 11*(3), 184–195.

Kasl, C. D. (1990, November–December). The Twelve Step controversy. *Ms. Magazine,* 30–31.

Kasl, C. D. (1992). *Many roads, one journey: Moving beyond the Twelve Steps.* New York: Harper Perennial.

Keller, M. (1958). Alcoholism: Nature and extent of the problem. In S. D. Bacon (Ed.), *Understanding alcoholism: Annals of the American Academy of Political and Social Science* (pp. 1–11). Philadelphia, PA: American Academy of Political and Social Science.

Kessler, R. C., McGonagle, K. A., Zhao, S., Nelson, C. B., Hughes, M., Eshleman, S., Wittchen, H., & Kendler, K. (1994). Lifetime and 12-month prevalence of *DSM-III-R* psychiatric disorders in the United States. *Archives of General Psychiatry, 51,* 8–19.

Kessler, R. C., Nelson, C. B., McGonagle, K. A., Edlund, M. J., Frank, R. G., & Leaf, P. J. (1996). The epidemiology of co-occurring addictive and mental disorders: Implications for prevention and service utilization. *American Journal of Orthopsychiatry, 66*(1), 17–31.

Kirkpatrick, J. (1978). *Turnabout: Help for a new life.* Garden City, NY: Doubleday.

Kishline, A. (1996). *Moderate drinking: The moderation management guide for people who want to reduce their drinking.* New York: Crown.

Kofoed, L., & Keys, A. (1988). Using group therapy to persuade dual-diagnosis patients to seek substance abuse treatment. *Hospital and Community Psychiatry, 39*(11), 1209–1211.

Landry, M. J. (1995). *Overview of Addiction Treatment Effectiveness.* Rockville, MD: Substance Abuse and Mental Health Services Administration. DHHS Pub. No. (SMA) 96–3081.

Levin, J. D. (1990). *Alcoholism: A bio-psycho-social approach.* New York: Hemisphere.

Lundquist, F. (1971). Influence of ethanol on carbohydrate metabolism. *Quarterly Journal of Studies on Alcohol, 32,* 1–12.

MacAndrew, C., & Edgerton, R. B. (1969). *Drunken comportment: A social explanation.* Chicago: Aldine.

Marlatt, G. A., & Gordon, J. R. (1985). *Relapse prevention: Maintenance strategies in the treatment of addictive behaviors.* New York: Guilford Press.

May, P. A. (1994). The epidemiology of alcohol use among American Indians: The mythical and real properties. *American Indian Culture and Research Journal, 18*(2), 121–143.

McClelland, D. C., Davis, W. N., Kalin, R., & Wanner, E. (1972). *The drinking man.* New York: The Free Press.

McGee, G., & Johnson, L. (1985). *Black, beautiful and recovering.* Center City, MN: Hazelden.

McLellan, A. T., Luborsky, L., Cacciola, J., et al. (1985). New data from the Addiction Severity Index: Reliability and validity in three centers. *Journal of Nervous and Mental Disease, 173*(7), 412–423.

McNeece, C. A., & DiNitto, D. M. (1998). *Chemical dependency: A systems approach* (2nd ed.). Boston: Allyn and Bacon.

McQuade, F. X. (1989, May/June). Treatment and recovery issues for the addicted Hispanic. *The Counselor,* 29–30.

Mechanic, D., Schlesinger, M., & McAlpine, D. D. (1995). Management of mental health and substance abuse services: State of the art and early results. *The Milbank Quarterly, 73*(1), 19–55.

Menninger, K. A. (1974). Discussion (following Robert L. Bergman, Navajo peyote use). *American Journal of Psychiatry, 128*(6), 699.

Mercer-McFadden, C., Drake, R. E., Brown, N. B., & Fox, R. S. (1997). The Community Support Program Demonstrations of Services for Young Adults with Severe Mental Illness and Substance Use Disorders, 1987–1991. *Psychiatric Rehabilitation Journal, 20*(3), 13–24.

Miller, G. A. (1997). *The Substance Abuse Subtle Screening Inventory Manual.* Bloomington, IN: The SASSI Institute.

Miller, N. S., & Hoffman, N. G. (1995). Addictions treatment outcomes. *Alcoholism Treatment Quarterly, 12*(2), 41–55.

Minkoff, K. (1989). An integrated treatment model for dual diagnosis of psychosis and addiction. *Hospital and Community Psychiatry, 40*(10), 1031–1036.

Minkoff, K. (1990, May). Dual Diagnosis Workshop. Austin, TX: Texas Department of Mental Health and Mental Retardation.

Mueser, K. T., Drake, R. E., & Miles, K. M. (1997). The course and treatment of substance use disorder in persons with severe mental illness. In L. S. Onken, J. D. Blaine, S. Gesner, & A. M. Horton (Eds.), *Treatment of drug-dependent individuals with comorbid mental disorders,* NIDA Research Monograph 172 (pp. 86–109). Rockville, MD: National Institute on Drug Abuse.

Murray, R. M., & Stabenau, J. R. (1982). Genetic factors in alcoholism predisposition. In E. M. Pattison & E. Kaufman (Eds.), *Encyclopedic handbook of alcoholism* (pp. 135–144). New York: Gardner Press.

National Advisory Council. (1998). *Action for mental health and substance-related disorders: Improving services for individuals at risk of, or with, co-occurring substance-related and mental health disorders.* Conference report and recommended strategy of the SAMHSA National Advisory Council. Rockville, MD: Substance Abuse and Mental Health Services Administration. DHHS Publication No. (SMA) 98–3254.

National Institute on Alcohol Abuse and Alcoholism. (1987). *Sixth special report to the U.S. Congress on alcohol and health.* Rockville, MD: U.S. Department of Health and Human Services.

National Institute on Alcohol Abuse and Alcoholism. (1995). Alcohol Alert: The Genetics of Alcoholism. [Available on-line: http://silk.nih.gov/silks/niaaa1/publication/aa18.htm].

National Institute on Alcohol Abuse and Alcoholism. (1997). *Ninth Special Report to the U.S. Congress on Alcohol and Health.* Rockville, MD: U.S. Department of Health and Human Services.

Needle-exchange programmes in the U.S.: Time to act now. (1998). *The Lancet, 351,* 75.

Nelson, B. (1983, January 18). The addictive personality: Common traits are found. *The New York Times,* pp. 11–15.

Oetting, E. R., Beauvais, F., & Goldstein, G. S. (1982). *Drug abuse among Native American youth: Summary of findings* (1975–1981).

Office of Applied Studies. (1998). *Service research outcomes study.* Rockville, MD: Substance Abuse and Mental Health Services Administration. DHHS Publication No. (SMA) 98–3177.

O'Malley, S. S., Jaffe, A. J., Chang, G., Schottenfeld, R. S., Meyer, R. E., & Rounsaville, B. (1992). Naltrexone and coping skills therapy for alcohol dependence: A controlled study. *Archives of General Psychiatry, 49,* 881–887.

Osher, F. C., & Kofoed, L. L. (1989). Treatment of patients with psychiatric and psychoactive substance abuse disorders. *Hospital and Community Psychiatry, 40*(10), 1025–1030.

Pattison, E. M., & Kaufman, E. (1982). The alcoholism syndrome: Definitions and models. In E. M. Pattison & E. Kaufman (Eds.), *Encyclopedic handbook of alcoholism* (pp. 3–30). New York: Gardner Press.

Pattison, E. M., Sobell, M. B., & Sobell, L. C. (1977). *Emerging concepts of alcohol dependence.* New York: Springer.

Pendery, M. L., Maltzman, I. M., & West, L. J. (1982). Controlled drinking by alcoholics? New findings and a reevaluation of a major affirmative study. *Science, 217,* 169–175.

Peniston, E. G., & Kulkosky, P. J. (1992). Alpha-theta EEG biofeedback training in alcoholism and post-traumatic stress disorder. *International Society for the Study of Subtle Energies and Energy Medicine, 2*(4), 5–7.

Prochaska, J. O., DiClemente, C. C., & Norcross, J. C. (1992). In search of how people change: Applications to addictive behaviors. *American Psychologist, 47*(9), 1102–1114.

Project Match Study Group. (1997). Matching alcoholism treatment to client heterogeneity: Project Match posttreatment drinking outcomes. *Journal of Studies on Alcohol, 58,* 7–29.

Rappaport, J. (1993). Narrative studies, personal stories, and identity transformation in the mutual help context. *Journal of Applied Behavioral Science, 29*(2), 239–256.

Ray, O., & Ksir, C. (1999). *Drugs, society, and human behavior* (8th ed.). Boston: WCB/McGraw-Hill.

Regier, D. A., Farmer, M. E., Rae, D. S., Locke, B. Z., Keith, S. J., Judd, L. L., & Goodwin, F. K. (1990). Comorbidity of mental disorders with alcohol and other drug abuse: Results from the Epidemiologic Catchment Area (ECA) Study. *JAMA, 264*(19), 2511–2518.

Reich, T., Edenberg, H. J., Goate, A., et al. (1998). Genome-wide search for genes affecting the risk for alcohol dependence. *American Journal of Medial Genetics, 81,* 207–215.

Ridgely, M. S., Osher, F. C., & Talbott, J. A. (1987). *Chronic mentally ill young adults with substance abuse problems: Treatment and training issues.* Baltimore, MD: University of Maryland School of Medicine.

Rosenberg, S. D., Drake, R. E., Wolford, G. L., et al. (1998). Dartmouth Assessment of Lifestyle Instrument (DALI): A substance use disorder screen for people with severe mental illness. *American Journal of Psychiatry, 155*(2), 232–238.

Schuckit, M. (1983). Alcoholism and other psychiatric disorders. *Hospital and Community Psychiatry, 34*(11), 1022–1026.

Sciacca, K. (1987, July). New initiatives in the treatment of the chronic patient with alcohol/substance abuse problems. *TIE-Lines, 4*(3), 5–6.

Sciacca, K. (1989, October). Workshop on the dually diagnosed. Big Spring, TX.

Sciacca, K. (1990, May). Dual Diagnosis Workshop. Austin, TX: Texas Department of Mental Health and Mental Retardation.

Sciacca, K. (1991). An integrated treatment approach for severely mentally ill individuals with substance disorders. In K. Minkoff & R. B. Drake (Eds.), *Dual diagnosis of major mental illness and substance disorder,* Social and Behavioral Sciences Series (No. 50, pp. 69–84). San Francisco: Jossey-Bass.

Selzer, M. (1971). The Michigan Alcoholism Screening Test: The quest for a new diagnostic instrument. *American Journal of Psychiatry, 127,* 1653–1658.

Sheridan, M. J. (1995). A proposed intergenerational model of substance abuse, family functioning, and abuse/neglect. *Child Abuse & Neglect, 19*(5), 519–530.

Shulman, G. D. (1994, May/June). Costs: Don't blame them all on providers. *Behavioral Health Management,* May-June, 63–65.

Skinner, H. A. (1982). The Drug Abuse Screening Test. *Addictive Behaviors, 7,* 363–371.

Sobell, M. B., & Sobell, L. C. (1973). Individualized behavior therapy for alcoholics. *Behavior Therapy, 4,* 49–72.

Stein, L. I., & Santos, A. B. (1998). *Assertive community treatment of persons with severe mental illness.* New York: W. W. Norton.

Stitzer, M. L., Iguchi, M. Y., & Felch, L. J. (1992). Contingent take-home incentive: Effects on drug use of methadone maintenance patients. *Journal of Consulting and Clinical Psychology, 60,* 927–934.

Strain, E. C., Stitzer, M. L., Liebson, I. A., & Bigelow, G. E. (1994). Comparison of buprenorphine and methadone in the treatment of opioid dependence. *American Journal of Psychiatry, 151,* 1025–1030.

Tarter, R. E., & Schneider, D. U. (1976). Models and theories of alcoholism. In R. E. Tarter and A. Arthur Sugerman (Eds.), *Alcoholism: Interdisciplinary approaches to an enduring problem* (pp. 75–106). Reading, MA: Addison-Wesley.

VA hospital calls in "medicine man" to help Indians beat alcoholism. (1991, August 25). *Austin American-Statesman,* p. D28.

Valentine, P. V. (1998). The etiology of addiction. In C. A. McNeece and D. M. DiNitto, *Chemical dependency: A systems approach* (2nd ed., pp. 23–35). Boston: Allyn and Bacon.

Van Den Bergh, N. (Ed.). (1991). *Feminist perspectives on addictions.* New York: Springer.

Vinton, L., & Wambach, K. G. (1998). Alcohol and drug use among the elderly. In C. A. McNeece and D. M. DiNitto, *Chemical dependency: A systems approach* (2nd ed., pp. 391–405). Boston: Allyn and Bacon.

Webb, D. K. (1997). *Good Chemistry co-leader's manual.* Austin, TX: Author.

Webb, D. K., & DiNitto, D. M. (1997). *Initial findings from the effectiveness of Good Chemistry with dually diagnosed consumers: An experimental study.* Austin, TX: Hogg Foundation for Mental Health.

Wilsnack, S. C. (1980). Femininity in a bottle. In C. C. Eddy and J. L. Ford (Eds.), *Alcoholism in women* (pp. 16–24). Dubuque, IA: Kendall/Hunt Publishers.

Working Group of the ASAM Managed Care Initiative. (1999). *The impact of managed care on addiction treatment.* Chevy Chase, MD: American Society of Addiction Medicine. Available at http://www.asam.org.

World Health Organization. (1992). *ICD-10 Classification of Mental and Behavioural Disorders, Clinical Descriptions and Diagnostic Guidelines.* Geneva: Author.

INDEX